The Collected Works of J. Krishnamurti

Volume VIII

1953-1955

What Are You Seeking?

COLLECTED WORKS VOLUME 8

Photo: J. Krishnamurti, ca 1955.

P.O Box 1560, Ojai, CA 93024

Website: www.kfa.org

Printed in the United States of America

ISBN 13: 9781934989418
ISBN: 193498941X

Contents

Preface

Jiddu Krishnamurti was born in 1895 of Brahmin parents in south India. At the age of fourteen he was proclaimed the coming World Teacher by Annie Besant, then president of the Theosophical Society, an international organization that emphasized the unity of world religions. Mrs. Besant adopted the boy and took him to England, where he was educated and prepared for his coming role. In 1911 a new worldwide organization was formed with Krishnamurti as its head, solely to prepare its members for his advent as World Teacher. In 1929, after many years of questioning himself and the destiny imposed upon him, Krishnamurti disbanded this organization, saying:

Truth is a pathless land, and you cannot approach it by any path whatsoever, by any religion, by any sect. Truth, being limitless, unconditioned, unapproachable by any path whatsoever, cannot be organized; nor should any organization be formed to lead or to coerce people along any particular path. My only concern is to set men absolutely, unconditionally free.

Until the end of his life at the age of ninety, Krishnamurti traveled the world speaking as a private person. The rejection of all spiritual and psychological authority, including his own, is a fundamental theme. A major concern is the social structure and how it conditions the individual. The emphasis in his talks and writings is on the psychological barriers that prevent clarity of perception. In the mirror of relationship, each of us can come to understand the content of his own consciousness, which is common to all humanity. We can do this, not analytically, but directly in a manner Krishnamurti describes at length. In observing this content we discover within ourselves the division of the observer and what is observed. He points out that this division, which prevents direct perception, is the root of human conflict.

His central vision did not waver after 1929, but Krishnamurti strove for the rest of his life to make his language even more simple and clear. There is a development in his exposition. From year to year he used new terms and new approaches to his subject, with different nuances.

Because his subject is all-embracing, the *Collected Works* are of compelling interest. Within his talks in any one year, Krishnamurti was not able to cover the whole range of his vision, but broad amplifications of particular themes are found throughout these volumes. In them he lays the foundations of many of the concepts he used in later years.

The *Collected Works* contain Krishnamurti's previously published talks, discussions, answers to specific questions, and writings for the years 1933 through 1967. They are an authentic record of his teachings, taken from transcripts of verbatim shorthand reports and tape recordings.

The Krishnamurti Foundation of America, a California charitable trust, has among its purposes the publication and distribution of Krishnamurti books, videocassettes, films and tape recordings. The production of the *Collected Works* is one of these activities.

India, 1953

First Talk in Madras

I think you must all be concerned with how to bring about a different world, a world in which we have a totally different set of values, a world in which man is not against man and in which wars have come to an end. We must have thought about these things, at least those who are serious and well-intentioned. Is there an answer to all these innumerable problems? The problems at different levels of which we are conscious, our activities and the various crises that occur, offer an opportunity to discover, for ourselves, the ways of our thinking. If we are earnest, perhaps we follow a particular leader, a particular system of philosophy or action, forming groups which are in conjunction with other groups. Seeing all this wide confusion, not only in this unfortunate country, but also throughout the world, what is our own individual response? Do we say someone else will solve these problems? We turn to the politicians, communists, or others; and if we are not at all inclined socially, we turn to religious gurus, Masters, or to the various systems of philosophy, and hope that by following them studiously and earnestly, we might be able to resolve or at least give a helping hand in this utter confusion and sadness of the world. Surely, we must have thought about all this. How are we to rebuild, if we are at all thoughtful? Will this mad confusion bring about a transformation, a revolution, not merely at one particular level, but a total revolution? I think that is really the problem.

If I may add, it is very important to listen rightly. Because most of us are confronted with problems, we want an answer; the answer is always applicable—and must be applicable—to the immediate issue, so we are answer-conscious. Please listen to what I am talking about as I feel very strongly that, if you can listen rightly, transformation will take place without the conscious effort of our conscious, everyday mind. But we do not know how to listen. We hear, but the hearing is only superficial. We have to listen without seeking an answer; we have merely to be confronted with the problem. There is no answer, there is only the problem. Please listen to what I am saying. Because, all of us have been trained from childhood to seek an answer; we put a question, wait and sit back, hoping that someone else is going to answer our question. If you will examine in your mind, you will see how conscious we are of this constant demand to find an answer. So we are never confronted with the problem itself. We do not know how to look at the problem even.

If you can establish a relationship between you and me, you are not expecting an answer from me with such an infantile, immature demand, but you and I together are going to look at the problem which is enormously complex. The problem must be understood. The man who is seeking an answer to any problem is shallow minded like a schoolboy who finds an answer at the end of the book—which indicates a great laziness and the fear of going wrong. We are all concerned that we do not make a mistake in the discovery of what is truth. So we go from continent to continent, leader to leader; we hear persons talking or giving lectures how to do things or what to do in this mad, chaotic confusion. One should be very alert to such people. They are really misleading because they have pet schemes—whether they are communists, socialists, capitalists, or any of the recent organizations with their leaders, with their Masters, with their gurus—because they have all the answers. A man who is seeking an answer will find an answer according to his demand; therefore, his answer will always be limited.

So let us, from the beginning of these talks, establish a right relationship between you and me. If you are seeking an answer, you should not be here because you will be utterly disappointed. But if you are willing to confront, to face, the problem, then together we can examine because the problem itself contains the answer. It requires an astonishing insight, a great deal of understanding, patience, to understand this complex problem of living.

What is the problem? Is the problem merely economic? That is what most of the world is pursuing at the present time. All the economic conditions give immediate effect to certain problems. That is the way of the politician and that is what most of us are satisfied with. The immediate remedy is reform. Is the problem intellectual, verbal, or is the problem a total revolution of one's own being at all levels of our existence—socially, morally, educationally, and religiously? Because, it is only when there is a total revolution that we can find out what is the truth, and it is the truth that will build and not those who labor in vain to build something which is traditional, which is of the immediate. Please listen to all this. There is a village next door. Those who are socially minded reform it and do something about it, which further increases the problems. So whatever reforms we bring about only increase and give more problems to man. We must be aware of this always. We want to stop war and yet we are doing everything to produce wars. So looking at all this vast confusion, we see the false leadership that exists. Later on, we shall go into whether there should be any leadership at all.

Surely, considering all this, is not a total revolution in man necessary? Not only a change of thought, change of ideas, change of morals, and so on, but a complete, unconscious revolution because a conscious revolution is still conditioned and limited. Because our training from childhood is limited and conditioned, we are either communists, or Hindus, Buddhists, Christians, and so on. Any conscious change by the upper levels of the mind—however desirous, however urgent, however cunning, inviting—will not solve the problem because our mind is conditioned, and a conditional mind concerned with this enormous problem can only have a conditional response. If you see that, you will never be caught up by any of the leaders. Politics is not going to solve our problems. No religious leaders, no hidden Masters, no secret societies—none of them is going to solve the problem. Because, they are all conscious effort by the limited mind seeking to answer the enormous problem, and such a mind can only give an answer—either traditional, reactionary, or something opposed to that tradition. So, if the conscious mind cannot give a total answer, a total comprehension to the problem, then what is one to do? Do you understand the problem? We will discuss this in the coming weeks.

Let us begin at the very beginning to see how to look at, how to grapple with a problem. If I, as a Hindu or a Catholic or a communist, am confronted with this problem of existence—not only at the level of the bread, but also at all the levels of my consciousness—my response will be according to my conditioning, and my conditioning will dictate my action with regard to that problem. Being a Hindu or a communist or what not, I will gather those people who will accept my particular response; because I am a strong personality or because of some kind of trick or dress or some woman or some kind of charm, I call, I gather people, and I build. My action as an Indian or as a Christian or as a communist must be conditioned, and that will create further confusion, further misery. So neither the capitalist nor the communist who is a reactionary essentially against something, nor a religious person who believes, nor the man who does not believe—none of these people will solve the problem because their approach is a conscious, deliberate approach which is conditioned. So at least some of us, even two or three, have to see and not accept what I am saying; namely, that a man who is conditioned can never approach this problem and resolve it and go beyond it, or transform it. All the politicians, all the builders, all the do-gooders who are collecting money for various schemes from the government and are putting up new buildings—they are all reformers with a conditioned mind, and their reforms only produce more sorrow, more misery.

So then, my problem is entirely different, is it not? There is only the problem. I am not responding because my response, my conscious response, will always be limited—such as becoming anti-Brahmin or some other stupid nonsense. So it behooves us, as human beings trying to understand this vast complex existence, to look at it without any conditioned response, to comprehend it. It is a most difficult thing to do, is it not? Because, I must look at all this without a background. You understand? Can I look at this problem without a background, without the background of Krishnamurti, or of a Catholic or communist, of the 'me' who has a vested interest in some property or in a society or in a system which offers a solution? Because we are not capable of looking at the problem without all this background, we jump into action which is a conditioned response; so we pile misery upon misery. So, until we understand the ways of conditioning—how the mind is caught in it and how to bring about liberation from this conditioning—whatever we do will create more misery. So is it not essential for those who are really serious—we must be really serious because the problems are appalling, complex, and serious—to consider the answer in a way of action, not what to do or whom to follow or what philosophy to accept or reject, but to understand this consciousness which is so conditioned, and in understanding to try and find out if there is a state of consciousness or a state of being in which there is no conditioning at all? That requires a great deal of investigation but not acceptance, a great deal of inquiry, talking it over.

To build, many are needed, many to understand the problem, and the understanding is not given by a leader, by a guru, or by a Master. These are all childish inquiries. Understanding comes when we know how to still the conscious mind, how a conscious mind, by facing the problem, becomes still. It is only when the mind is conscious, when the mind is utterly quiet without a background, without striving for its own vested interests, that there is a possibility of total revolution, and it is only in that state of total revolution that it is possible to build, and the builder will not be in vain.

So, if we know how to listen not only to what I am saying but to the problem itself—we can only listen rightly, deeply if we understand the conditioning of our own mind—the very understanding of our conditioning frees the mind. Be aware that you are a Hindu; you can never solve the problem as a Hindu, with all your systems of philosophy, because they are all manmade and therefore conditioned. So one can listen and look at the problem truly and in a revolutionary manner only when the mind is capable of not being anchored in any background. Memory is the anchoring of the mind to a condition. All knowledge becomes the vested interest of the mind in its use for its own importance, either for its own or identified with a particular group. So, the mind must be astonishingly free, free of the vested interest of the self and the anchorages of knowledge, free so as to look at the problem and thereby bring about a total revolution. It is this total revolution, in its activity, that will create a new world. Without that total revolution, all labor to build a new state, a new society, a new religion is in vain. Therefore it is very important for you and me to understand this revolution and bring it about in ourselves. We must begin small, unobtrusively, quietly because everything we begin is small. There must be no search for success, for membership, for show; such a search is the response of a conditioned mind eager to achieve a result, which is again seeking the answer to the problem. So, if we can during the coming weeks discuss patiently, not throwing ideas at each other, but going to the problem meticulously, wisely, intelligently, then you will see that without your making a concerted effort the revolution takes place. That revolution comes about because the truth is perceived, and it is that truth that liberates and not the conscious mind seeking an answer.

I have some questions and before I answer them or discuss them, perhaps it might be better if you can try to naturally ask what you think and not discuss it with me. Any problem you have, we will discuss on Monday morning at 7:30. But here, this evening, if something arises out of this talk, perhaps you would be good enough to ask, not to discuss and not to make long perorations; perhaps that would be worthwhile. If not, I have got questions.

You know, asking questions is very easy. The question arises, you put it down and ask, and there you are. Your response to the answer, if there is an answer, depends on whether you like it or not, whether it tallies with your knowledge, with your experience, or with your conditioning. You ask not to find out but, whether you agree or disagree, to confirm. So, merely asking questions has very little value. But what has value is to inquire, which requires an astonishing freedom on your side as well as on the other. If I rely on any authority or on my knowledge or my experience and so on to convince you, then it is mere propaganda; it is not an inquiry which will open the mind to truth.

So it is very important in asking your question how you regard the answer, if there is an answer. Because our minds are small, we look through particular gaps, avenues of thought—such as communist, socialist, religious, economist, or spiritualist. Through that avenue we want an answer. We think that by piling up answers, we come to the whole. The whole is not perceived or understood through the part. The whole can be understood only when the mind is capable of being the whole itself.

Questioner: Living as I do in the United States, appeals are made for financial help to various activities. Should one refuse to give any such help because they imply, according to what the lady says, conscious effort?

KRISHNAMURTI: I will discuss that question. But, watch your own mind in operation. Here is a problem: Living as I do in a world in which I must help—because there is starvation, there is war, and there are so many things demanding my charity, my generosity—should I withhold all these because they imply not only superficial reformation but more intrinsically, a conscious effort on my part to do something? What is your response? How is your mind operating? Because, it is your problem and not that lady's only. Should you support the division of a country, of a state, of immediate action in a village, such as giving medical aid, and doing innumerable other things as human beings living in daily contact with misery? What is your response? Do not answer me but watch the functioning of your mind. We have made this world consciously, deliberately, by our acquisitive discontent. We have separated peoples—India and Pakistan, America and Russia. We have broken up the world—you and I, and not some idiotic politicians—because that is what we want. We want to be separate; and meet a world in which all these things exist and where charity is necessary, where you have to act in order to stop some kind of misery. There is thus a conscious world produced by us consciously. Should we withhold all conscious action in order to understand the unconscious? Is it that until I understand and until there is a total revolution in me, I will not act? Is that possible? You do have your desire or ambitions and various forms of envious discontent. Is it not more important to stop those than not to give?

To understand this problem of conscious action, you are not going to do it in one talk. It requires a great deal of meditation to uncover, to go deep into the problem; and in the discovery and in the unfolding of that problem, you will solve the problem. I do not know if I am making myself clear. In uncovering a conscious problem, looking at it, investigating it, I shall come upon the unconscious revolution, and that is going to act, that is going to create. But in the meantime I cannot just sit and wait; I must use my intelligence—what to support and what not to support—which is totally and traditionally destructive. All that inquiry requires patience, intelligence, understanding, insight, does it not? That very insight, understanding, unfolding, is the problem of the unconscious.

You know, listening is very difficult because I have put to you a lot of ideas and you cannot absorb all of them; you remember at least one idea, so you have consciously excluded the comprehension of the whole. You are merely capturing one idea, living with it and examining it, hoping to understand the whole. The tree is not just the leaf. You cannot take home a leaf and understand the whole beauty of the tree. You have to look at the whole tree, and you cannot look at the whole tree if you are paying attention only to one part. That is why it is so enormously difficult to listen.

Questioner: Why is it that, in spite of your talks, no one has been transformed? If no one is transformed, what is the use of your talking to us?

KRISHNAMURTI: Do you think that by listening to a talk or to a number of talks you are going to be transformed? Do you know what it means to be transformed? If you knew, then you could judge. If you knew, would you be transformed? Please follow all this. A man who says "I know" is the most destructive human being because he really does not know. What does he know? So, when you are conscious you are transformed, when you are aware that you are transformed, you are not.

You must begin from the very beginning. To think that by listening to talks by someone, this extraordinary revolution is going to take place is purely infantile, is it not? Because, this revolution requires not just a day's, half an hour's, and one hour's casual listening, but a great deal of attention must be paid to the whole process of self-knowledge. Some of you are lawyers, some of you are doctors or businessmen or engineers. Could you tell me how to become an engineer in half an hour? Do not laugh at it. That is what we all want, a quick remedy. Transformation is something that cannot be caught by mere listening, by mere hearing of a few talks. If you know really how to listen—that is the beauty of listening—then you will see how your mind becomes astonishingly still, and in that stillness a revolution takes place, a total revolution. But we do not know how to listen. You may hear me year after year, unfortunately as most of you do, without any deviation from your daily habitual and stupid way of life. Then you say, "Why am I not changed and why is there no transformation in me?" We do not know how to look at the stars or the sun or the beauty of the sky. We have never listened except when we are told to listen. We look at things professionally as experts tell us. We never see a smile or tear. But to have that something which is not habitual and which is a constant revolution requires an enormous awareness, an awareness in which there is no choice, no judgment, but mere awareness without translation. If you can look, you can listen. In such a way, I assure you, there is transformation. Transformation implies complete revolution, total revolution. How can there be total revolution if you are anchored to any belief? If your mind is working in a system, if it is caught up in a particular philosophy, whether it is of Marx or of Shankara, or if your mind is caught in acquisitive discontent, how can it be transformed? But if you be aware of this acquisitive discontent without condemning it, without judging it, be merely aware of it, listen to it totally, then you will see an extraordinary thing happens. That is the truth of the transformation. The truth is not caught by the conscious mind. It must come to you darkly, unknowingly. Then such a mind is in a state of total revolution.

Questioner: Will it be correct to say, sir, that an unconditioned mind will have no problem?

KRISHNAMURTI: Sir, why speculate? That is one of our most extraordinary habits. After all, all our religious books are speculation, are they not? They may be experience for some people, but the moment you read them, they become speculations to you. Please listen to what I am saying. The gentleman wants to know if an unconditioned mind has no problem or can have no problems. Is that so? If I were to say yes or no, then where are you, of what value is it to you? Sir, all such questions indicate that you are not hungry. You look from the outside on the food inside and speculate about the food. But if you are hungry, you would be inside and you would not be asking questions about what it is. It would be like that if an unconditioned mind had no problem.

We think that by asking such a question our minds are active. We think we are intelligent, we are aware. Please, I am not personally answering that gentleman. Please do not think I am criticizing. I am talking about the problem of speculation. Is it not one of the characteristics of a lazy mind to speculate and think that it is active? Either you experience or you do not. Why speculate? Is not speculation itself a hindrance to direct understanding? You see, that opens up a vast problem of what it is to experience. I do not want to go into it now, but we can see how the mind prevents itself from discovering for itself. Speculation can never be true. A hypothesis is always a hypothesis. The mind has gone beyond it. As long as the mind is caught in a hypothesis, in a speculation, it is creating a barrier for itself. Such a state of mind is not an active mind. An active mind is a mind that is free from thought. For, all thinking is merely a verbalization of memory. A mind merely memorizing is not an active mind. An active mind is a mind that is free from all the process of thought. Please think it over, look into it, do not reject it; and you will see that when the mind is free from thought, how extraordinarily active it is. It is the mind that is always thinking that is a dull mind because thought is always springing from its own conditioning.

So what is important is how to listen to everything about one; then the mind becomes astonishingly sensitive. The mind is not sensitive if it is constantly judging, comparing, balancing. A sensitive mind is necessary to inquire and find out what truth is.

Questioner: What about the various systems of thought in India, which lead a man to liberation or moksha?

Krishnamurti: Do you think that any system can liberate you? The very idea that a system can liberate you is conditioning, is it not? Sir, surely this is an obvious question, is it not? Do you mean to say a man who has no system cannot free himself except through systems? Will any system, thought out consciously and laid out, bring liberation?

What is implied in a system? Conformity. Why do you conform? Because you want to gain liberation. As a man wants money, you want liberation. He must conform to certain rules in order to gain money; similarly, you say that in order to attain liberation, you must follow a system; then that system has engaged you or captured you. How can that system give you liberation? For centuries we have imitated, we have followed. Systems compete with each other, butcher each other, and liquidate each other. You say that one system is better than another. Can such immature thinking lead you to liberation? No revolution which is based on a system has produced happiness for man—the communist, the French, or any other revolution merely following a particular system of thought. Sir, to find reality, God, the mind must be free and not anchored to a system. If you are led through a system to discover it, then what you discover is not true. How can you be led to discover? It is a contradiction if I lead you to discover something; you have to discover for yourself. Because I have discovered, how can you be led to it? That is not liberation. That is conformity born of fear.

That is why I say that total revolution is necessary, not the superseding of one system by another, by the very latest system. That requires enormous freedom, freedom from fear, freedom from desire to be successful. If you search your heart and mind, you will see that we all want success; every leader—communist or religious—wants a great many followers. To discover what truth is, the mind must be fearless, the mind must be free from all imitation, and that requires a great deal of understanding.

December 5, 1953

Second Talk in Madras

As I was saying yesterday, what is important is the understanding of the problem and not the search for the solution of the problem. I think it is very important to understand this fundamentally, not superficially, but to see the whole implication involved in such an idea when our whole mind is geared or trained or conditioned to think in terms of seeking a solution. Because, the revolution is not so much in trying to find out a new answer, a new solution, but rather in the capacity to look at the problem without a particular background to which we are accustomed. If we are communists, we look at the problem with the particular conditioning, with the particular training, with the particular system or ideas of Marxism; and all our vested interests or the backgrounds of our approach are from that point. Similarly, if you are a capitalist or a religious person, your background dictates the solution to the problem. Problems always occur. There is no solution at all for the problem which is manifest in the world in the present time. If you observe the various activities, the various ideologies that are in conflict with each other, this is the process which is going on.

The revolution of which I have been talking does not lie in a new solution or in a new system of philosophy but rather in a complete freedom to approach the problem anew. Our problems are not only the materialistic welfare of each individual, the welfare state, and so on, but also the psychological well-being of man because that ultimately shapes the physical well-being of man, which again is fairly obvious to those who have given thought at all to this whole problem. So how is one to liberate oneself from the background? What is this background? You understand that there is this problem, the problem of material welfare for every human being—whether they are communists, capitalists, or people with vested interests—for the well-being of every people in the world, whether in the East or in the West. In our approach to the material problem, the problem of material welfare, the emphasis of our whole attention on material things will produce various new problems which are involved in it. Until we fundamentally alter our approach to the material problem, we will use the material as a psychological means to self-aggrandizement.

I hesitate here because most of us think that the psychological problem is irrelevant to the material problem. We are anxious to bring about material welfare and so say, "Let us organize, let us act, let us do something immediately, or plan to bring about material welfare," totally forgetting the whole psychological structure of the human being. So if we emphasize one at the expense of the other, we distort man's conduct towards life. What we are dealing with is a difficult problem, a very complex problem which needs attention, and most of us do not give attention. We hear very casually certain ideas and respond to those ideas depending upon our prejudices, our bias, and our conditioning. It is very difficult in a group like this to discuss problems deeply, with attention because if you do not follow carefully and if you miss certain points, the whole thing becomes a distortion.

As I said yesterday, it is important to know how to listen. Though I repeat it often, listening is the problem. If I can listen to this whole problem of man's existence, material welfare, psychological well-being, creativeness, creative reality, ultimate reality, and so on; if I can listen to this whole structure of man's endeavor or of man's struggle without interpreting it, without translating it in terms to suit me or my desires; if I can see this vast picture without immediately taking a particular route and traveling on that—which means not having an immediate urge for a result—then it is possible to look at this whole picture and comprehend it totally. It is this totality of understanding that is important and not a particular part of the picture. Do please see that. What is important is to see the whole structure and not the part, not one particular culture or one particular aspect of our whole existence. Because, if we take one part, discuss it, act upon it, it will produce problems which will be in constant conflict with all the other structures of the human being.

So what is important is not education, not peace, not the immediate social action, not the problem of war or peace or starvation, but the approach to these problems, totally, as a whole. That requires enormous insight. As most of us are politicians in one form or another, we want an immediate action, immediate response, immediate results. So our whole outlook, our whole approach to this problem is perverted. There is starvation of which we know very well. We need not discuss it. There are various organizations dealing with it, and in the very solution of that particular problem, we are introducing various other problems, such as the liquidation of man. Because certain leaders, certain dominant, urgent, strong personalities say that this should be done, they organize and liquidate others who do not fit in, or they create confusion in order to bring about a certain state when a group of people can control it, and so on. There is the multiplication of problems one after another because we never approach this whole human existence as a totality. If we can, during these talks, merely approach this problem totally without seeking an answer, we shall have done a great deal because then we shall act totally and not partially.

We know we have many problems of sex, of love, of reality, of God; what is after death; the whole implication of action and ideation; the problem of deterioration; the problem of not being able to create; the problem of not knowing what is creation, which is God, which is truth. Seeing all these problems, how is it that we approach it? In understanding how we approach it, the problem will be dissolved. Please listen to this. There is this whole complex problem of existence, and each leader, each specialist, each person who has had any thought or any experience translates these problems and gives a system and says, "Do these things and you will resolve them." The religious specialist, the economist, the psychologist, and so on—each is giving us a system to be followed, to be practiced, to be lived out; and we, in our ignorance, in our stupidity, follow them because we want a result. Whereas, if we can look at the problem totally, then the problem will have an entirely different meaning.

So how is one to look at the problem totally? That is the problem—not the problem of life or death or God or starvation, but how can you and I look at this vast problem totally and not partially? That is the problem. Because, after all, a great artist is one who sees the whole and not the part. He paints or writes poems or creates a marvel because he sees the whole and then works out the details. What is it that is preventing deeply, fundamentally, the perception of the whole, of the total problem? Why is it that you cannot and I cannot see the whole picture? If we can answer that, not merely verbally, but see the truth of it, then our approach to the problem will be entirely different. So our inquiry then is not how to answer this vast problem of existence, with all its cruelties, with its joys, with its ups and downs, with its loneliness, imitation, shades and brightness, but how to approach that problem totally and to see what is preventing us from approaching it entirely, completely, and wholly. So that is our inquiry—and that is the only inquiry—because small men, narrow men, men seeking answers will translate the problem according to their limitations.

So our inquiry then is not the solution of the problem but what it is that prevents each one of us from looking at the problem totally. Is it not fundamentally the 'self', the 'me', the 'I' which is the background? After all, what is preventing me and you from looking at the problem totally and therefore approaching it from a wholly different point of view? Is it not the 'me', the mind which is the state of 'me'? So without understanding the process of the mind—the total process of the mind, the psychological process, the conscious as well as the unconscious—merely to approach this vast complex problem by a mind which does not understand itself creates more problems, more miseries, more destruction. So what is important is not the problem but the understanding of the mind which is creating the problem. The mind, conscious as well as unconscious, is always creating a background, is always creating tradition from which it is acting. The background of tradition is the habit, the practice, the memory, the conclusion, the idea, and from that idea, conclusion, memory, tradition, practice. This is how the mind is acting. Realizing this, people say, "Let us control the mind, let us shape the mind to a particular action, and if it does not yield, we will wash the brain in order to conform." I hope you are following all this.

The mind acts from an anchorage, from a fixed point which is elastic, but always there is a center from which it acts. It is always tethered to a point, the point being the 'me'. The 'me' is the idea. The idea translated is the state, or identified with the state or God. So the mind which is tethered, which is anchored, which has a background, which has a tradition, which is the memory—such a mind can never approach the problem totally. How can I, anchored in my aggressive discontent or acquisitive discontent—for all discontent with us is acquisitive—how can such a mind look at this whole problem of life? When it does, it looks at it from the point of view of acquisitive discontent and translates this vast problem of existence in terms of what I want, consciously or unconsciously. So the inquiry then is how to free the mind from the 'me', from the background; and until we do that completely and totally, we shall have misery after misery, vast destruction, savage brutality, and every form of coercion and compulsion. This is what is happening in the world at present.

How is the 'I', which is the 'me', which is the whole process of our thinking, to come to an end? You see the problem? We think the 'I', the 'me', comes to an end when we identify ourselves with the state; the state then becomes all-important. Does the 'I' disappear because I put the state in front of me as the most important? No—only I have substituted another ideation, another tradition. So until each one of us, through the understanding of the whole process of relationship, as from a mirror, discovers oneself or one's activities and one's thought, and is aware of this whole process of the 'me'—which is self-knowledge—our struggle to merely reform, which reaches only the surface, has very little meaning. On the contrary, it only creates more mischief.

So the inquiry then is the understanding of the 'me', the 'self', the mind. To understand something requires no judgment. To understand the working of the mind, conscious as well as unconscious, demands no comparison. You must take it as it is and begin as it is. But it is very difficult to begin as it is because we are always comparing with something else. We have been fed on ideology, on ideals which are merely a substitution of *what should be* for the reality of *what is*. So to understand the mind, the workings of the mind have to be watched in relationship. Do they not? Going into the meaning and dwelling with it in the mind has very little significance. Then you can deceive yourself most extraordinarily. To watch constantly from day to day, from moment to moment, without drawing a conclusion or living in that conclusion, to watch in relationship without judgment, without comparison, but with constant awareness requires a great deal of persistency. Without doing that, all study of sacred books, all systems, have very little meaning; on the contrary, they are harmful to the mind which is stuffing itself with other people's ideas.

So only a man who has understood the way of the mind can know what is reality, what is God, whatever the name by which you call it.

The mere repetition of the word *God* or *love,* the practicing of rituals, have very little meaning; they only deviate the mind. But if you and I study this whole problem of the mind, inquire into the seat of the 'I', then you will see that in that inquiry comes the stillness of the mind, which is not induced, which is not disciplined, but which comes into being spontaneously, naturally, freely; and in that stillness, the totality is seen, and that totality will resolve the problem. It is that totality that will build, and not those who labor in vain not knowing the totality.

Perhaps, as I suggested yesterday, out of this talk there are questions you might ask me, if you are willing, but not discuss them because we shall have a discussion tomorrow. But if you are inclined after hearing this talk, there might be questions. If not, I have some questions written down.

Questioner: What is the function of a true educator?

KRISHNAMURTI: Now, you have asked a question, and you are waiting for an answer because you can then dispute with the answer like a clever lawyer, the pros and cons. That is what I am not going to do. That is infantile, immature. But you and I are going to find out, to discover, the functions of a true educator. You are not going to be told, "It is this," for you just to agree or to disagree. But you and I will investigate, will discover together that which will be truth, and it is the truth that matters. Please listen to this because these problems are very important nowadays because the world is going to greater sorrows, greater misery, and those who are listening have the responsibility. You have taken the trouble to come here. Therefore, you should listen to find out the truth of the matter and not indulge in mere speculative opinion, or answer, or judgment of another. What is important is that you should find out what the truth of the matter is. Then you are the liberator of man and not an imitator.

What is the true function of an educator? What is education? Why are we educated? Are we educated at all? Because you pass a few examinations, have a job, competing, struggling, brutalizing ambition, is that education? What is an educator? Is he one who prepares the student for a job, merely for a job, for technical achievement in order to earn a livelihood? That is all we know at present. There are vast schools, universities where you prepare the youth, boy or girl, to have a job, to have technical knowledge so that he or she can have a livelihood. Is that alone the function of a true educator? There must be something more than that because it is too mechanical. So you say that the educator must be an example. You agree with that? You will have to follow the truth of the matter, to go into it. When you go into it, you will see the truth of it, namely, no example is necessary. Put aside your conclusions or conditioning, and inquire. You say a teacher should be an example. What do you mean by that? An example, a hero, so that the boy or the girl imitates him? After all, there are many examples—Christ, Buddha, Gandhiji, and if you go to the other extreme, Lenin, Stalin, and God knows what not, and the various saints, heroes.

What is the implication of an example? If the functioning of a teacher is that he is to be an example, then is he not consciously or unconsciously imposing a pattern on the boy, on the student? Does conformity to a pattern, however noble, however well thought out, planned out, free the individual from fear? Because, after all, you are educating a student to face life, to understand life, not to meet it as a communist or capitalist or some other stupid conditioned individual. You are helping him to meet life. To meet life, there must be no fear, and that is a very rare thing. To be without fear implies no example, no hero. If there is no hero, no example, will the student go astray? That is the fear of the older people, is it not? So they say, "Because he will go astray, there must be an example. He must be compelled consciously or unconsciously." So we create a mediocre human being who has no initiative but who is a conforming entity, a machine, who is afraid to think out, to live, to find out. Does not an example imply the engendering of fear in the understanding by the student through himself of his own problems, and also in the attempt of the educator to help him to understand them? If the educator himself becomes the guide, the example, the hero, then is he not instilling fear in the boy, in the student? So surely the educator of the right kind is not an example, nor does he inspire a student, because inspiration implies dependence.

Please listen. You may virtually be bored with it because you think you are past the age for education. What has age got to do with education? Education is a whole process of life and not just at the college age only. So if we are to create a different world—which your sons or your daughters may create, but not you because you have made a mess of it—to bring about a new world we must create a different kind of intelligence which is not fearful. A student who is afraid because he has the example of saints, heroes, innumerable patterns of established thought, of tradition, cannot create a new world; he will create the same ugly world, mischievous and misery-creating world. So the true function of a teacher is not to be an inspirer, is not to be an example, but to awaken the intelligence in the child—which does not mean he becomes the awakener. If the teacher becomes the awakener, the student will immediately make him into a guru because he will depend upon the awakener; thus, the student allows himself to become dull because he has someone on whom to rely and who is going to awaken him.

So the teacher is not an awakener, the teacher is not an inspirer, not a guide, not a hero, not an example. The true function of a teacher is entirely different, namely, to help to educate the student to see all these problems. The student cannot see these problems if there is fear—economic, social, or religious fear. He is not a true teacher who is always comparing the student with somebody else, with his elder brother or with the brightest boy in the class, because that very comparison destroys the person with whom the comparison is made. Please follow all this. Such a teacher does not exist in any of the schools at present. So we have to educate the educator, and that is your responsibility because the state is not going to do that. The state is only concerned with conformity, with producing mass results.

Is not the true educator the parent, the mother, and the society about him—not a specialized entity who had a particular way? So it is your responsibility, is it not, to counteract it at home if there is no proper teacher, to see that there is the awakening of the intelligence in the child without fear, without comparison, to look at life, to understand all the conditioning influences so that he, as an intelligent human being without fear, without competition, without comparing, can create a new world in which there will be no wars, no appalling social miseries; or he can create a world of his own worse than ours; it is up to him. So the true function of a teacher is to create an atmosphere, an environment in which the student will grow to fruition without fear.

Sirs, ladies, you have heard this. It would be very interesting to find out your response. You will say, "This is not practical, this is utopian and only rishis can do it. We need to have jobs to earn our livelihood. What is to happen to me in my old age if my sons do not support me?" If this is your response, you have not understood the truth of the matter. If you have understood the truth of this question, it will act in spite of your cunning mind. It is very important to see the truth of it.

Questioner: Do you work on the conscious of your listeners or on their unconscious?

Krishnamurti: What is a conscious mind and what is an unconscious mind? Again, please find out, do not depend upon my answer or my definition. For that you can look in a dictionary. So let us find out, let us discover the truth of the matter.

What is the conscious mind? It is the everyday mind, is it not?—everyday mind of the lawyer, everyday mind of the general, the policeman, the specialist; everyday mind of the acquisitive intent; the mind that is discontented and wants to find contentment; the mind that is escaping from the problem; the mind that practices rituals, stupidly pursuing something other than facing *what is;* the mind that is gregarious; the mind that is committed to a certain conclusion; the mind that is traditional, copying; the mind that is following a particular pattern of action. It is the conscious mind that judges, evaluates, compares, seeking its own ambitious results. That is the conscious mind of everyday activity, is it not? That mind, seeking security, may place that security on an extraordinary level, but still it is the conscious mind, whether in the bank, or in nirvana, or in *moksha,* where you will. That is the conscious mind.

What is the unconscious? Do we know that there is the unconscious except that you might have read about it. If you are a psychologist, you might be slightly interested in it. Are we aware that there is a whole process of the unconscious deep down, hidden, very difficult to get at? Are we aware of it? I am afraid we are not because all our conscious effort is directed to the upper levels, and there we remain. Our ambitions, our social activities, our discontents, our jealousies, envies, comparing and judging—there we are. Do we know anything of the unconscious, do we really know anything about it except perhaps in a dream on a still night? The battles, the conflicts, are they between the unconscious and the conscious or only between the various conscious desires? Do you understand all this, please? When you ask a question of that kind, you must know what is the conscious as well as what is the unconscious. Is the revolution, the total revolution, to take place at the conscious level or at a level which is not controllable by the conscious? The mind can control the conscious. If it can also control the unconscious with a view to bring about a revolution, then it is no revolution; that is merely a conditioning of the unconscious.

Can a conscious mind delve into the unconscious? Can it see what the unconscious is? Let us consider collective tradition; you call yourselves Hindus, Muslims, Christians, or what you will—which is the conditioning of the unconscious, of which you are not conscious. You are calling yourself a Hindu, and to call yourself a Hindu, centuries of conditioning of the deeper layers of consciousness have been going on. Is it not so? To call yourself a Christian, it has taken centuries of social, economic, and religious influences. For centuries, until now, you say consciously, "I am a Christian or a Hindu or a Muslim." Now you hear that statement and you say that it is so. But you, as a conscious mind, have not discovered it, have not penetrated the process and the causes of that conditioning. Are you getting tired of this? This requires thought, and probably you are not used to this attentive talk for an hour and therefore you are not listening any more; you are just hearing words which have very little meaning now. It is very important to understand this question because a great many things are involved in it. I wish you could follow it, follow it not as I describe it, not my description, but follow the workings of your own mind; otherwise, it is merely my description which you are trying to follow. If you are interested, if you are attentive, if you are truly listening, then you will follow the things operating in your own mind; you will discover for yourself the whole process of consciousness.

We know what the conscious is; we know we live, move, function from day to day, keep going on without knowing, like a machine which is running down the hill or up the hill. When this is pointed out to you, the conscious mind then begins to watch itself. But there are hidden layers of the unconscious, which control the conscious because the deeper layers are much more vital and much more active than the so-called superficial mind. Is not the so-called unconscious mind the residue of all the struggles, pursuits, of all humanity, which expresses itself outwardly as in the Hindu, with its big tradition of custom and culture? You understand? Let us take, for instance, "culture." Everybody is talking about it nowadays—the Eastern culture, the Indian culture, the Western culture. Some say that we must have a pure Indian culture and that we must build buildings for that work. What does culture mean? Please follow this. Do not say yes or no, but inquire. Is there such a thing as Indian culture or European culture? There may be an expression of that culture, which is Indian or European. That feeling, that ecstasy, that appreciation of beauty may translate itself in a particular manner in India, in the East; the West may translate and express it in an entirely different way. But the content, the depth of feeling, is common, is it not? It is not Indian or English—which is simply stupid—though the expression may be Indian or English. So if one wants to understand the whole process of culture, one must go into the unconscious and not into the conscious. Culture may be something not traditional at all; it must be something totally creative and not imitative. Because culture, the so-called culture, has now become traditional, we are not creative.

So in the inquiry after what is culture, you have to go deeper and deeper, have you not? It is important to find out what is the unconscious. Do not read books. They will only describe what is the unconscious. But their description will prevent you from discovering it. But if you begin to inquire into it intelligently, not judging, not saying, "This is it" or "That is not it," but watching the whole process of the mind—which is meditation then you will see that there is very little difference between the unconscious and the conscious. The conscious is merely an expression, the outward action of the unconscious. There is no gap. It is one process, the deeper process controlling the outer, shaping, guiding it. The conflict is between the various desires in that consciousness.

The questioner wants to know if I am speaking to the conscious or the unconscious. Obviously in talking, in using words you may remember the words, and your acknowledging these words is a conscious process. Sirs, are you following all this? I find that some of you seem to be a little bit sleepy. I am not awakening you. I am not interested. If you want, you can have your sleep. That is for you. I am not your awakener. But together we can find the truth of this matter. It is the truth that will liberate. If you are awake, you can let it come to you. So what is happening is not that I am talking to the conscious or to the unconscious, but the truth is being uncovered which lies beyond the conscious and the unconscious, which means bringing about an extraordinary stillness of the mind.

Do not make your minds still. Do not close your eyes and become silent. Truth cannot be found by the conscious or the unconscious. Only when the mind is conscious, we know of both the conscious and the unconscious with all its workings, noises, strivings. When all that comes to an end, there is stillness. This stillness is not the product of the consciousness at all. It is only the stillness that is creative, that is eternal. In that stillness, that which is everlasting can be found, that comes into being. But for that silence to be, the whole process of consciousness must be understood—the workings of it and not the explanations of it. That is why these meetings will be worthwhile if you can pay attention and if you can listen rightly so that we can both be in that state of stillness in which truth can be. But that is not easy because you have the job, your wife, your husband, all the traditions, all the nauseating smells of life. They must be understood and quietened. That requires awareness of all things, of the trees, of the books, of the women, of the smiles, of your daily mischievous actions, pujas, appetites, passions. Of all these one must be aware, and to be aware is not to condemn, but to look at and to observe them without judgment. Then only it is possible to have self-knowledge which is not taught in books, which you cannot learn by attending one or two talks. It comes into being when you watch and understand all your feelings and thoughts, from moment to moment, every day. The totality of that understanding will resolve the problems of your life.

December 6, 1953

Third Talk in Madras

You may remember what we were discussing last week. We were considering how to approach the problem. As long as we are looking for an answer to the problem, a solution, the problem is of no importance in itself. If we are merely searching a way out of the problem, which most of us do, then the problem becomes insignificant. If we can approach the problem without a desire to find an answer, then, as we stated, we will find that the problem itself becomes all-important; and then it is a matter of how one approaches the problem, and not the search for an answer.

Now, I would like to discuss this evening the same thing, what we were saying last week, only differently, to approach it differently. But before I go into that, is not communication difficult? I have something to say, and you listen with your conclusions and your own biases or your own particular experiences. You listen from a conclusion and so you are not listening to it at all. Please pay, if you don't mind, a little attention to what I am saying. What I want to say is not so complicated. If you can listen, not with a conclusion, but trying to find out what I am trying to convey, then perhaps communication may be made easier. Most of us are told what to think, but we do not know how to think. Our minds are so conditioned and so full of what to think, that any statement of another—contradictory, silly, or wise—is translated through the screen of our conclusion. So we are not listening or understanding what the other fellow is saying at all. Is it possible to listen without a conclusion, purely to listen as you would listen to music?

What I want to discuss this evening is the problem of a mind approaching this vast complex problem of existence. The existence is not only the acquiring of a job or maintaining a job but the whole field of the psychological existence with which most of us are almost unfamiliar. We have been told by some that there is continuity and by others that there is no continuity, but we have never found out for ourselves. The problem of existence is this vast complex of wars, class, caste, division—the perpetual battle of man against man in competition. We have the desire to find out what is truth, what is God, what is mortality, if there is continuity after death. We have not found the reality of any of these things. But we believe what we are told from our childhood, or from out of our fear or for our security, we invent or grasp at some hope.

Now there is this enormous, psychological, unconscious or semiconscious complexity which we call life. How does the mind approach the problem? Can a mind which is constantly thinking in terms of 'becoming', acquiring, understand this complex state when the mind is only thinking in terms of acquiring or is being driven with acquisitive discontent? Do you understand? There is this problem. How do you approach the problem? Do you approach it in thinking of the problem in terms of the 'more', in terms of 'becoming', or in terms of 'being'? This is not a philosophical question. Do not translate immediately into terms of becoming, being, as a philosophical thesis.

Our minds are accustomed to think in terms of 'becoming'—becoming more rich, having a better job, having greater virtue, becoming more beautiful, in terms of the 'more', more time to develop, to become greater, wiser, more in knowledge—which we call discontent. That is our state of mind. The 'more' implies the whole process of time, "I must have tomorrow to learn more, to become wise; I must have more time to understand." So this is our approach, is it not? When we arc confronted with this problem, we are thinking of the 'more', in terms of time. We never begin to understand it as 'being'.

The fact is that there is this complexity, and we think of changing the fact in terms of time and not in terms of 'being'. This is what is mediocrity. I am not using that word comparatively, that is, in terms of one who is cleverer, more brilliant, a greater genius, greater capacity to create. I am not using that word comparatively, in terms of greater and lesser. But if you are going to translate that word in terms of the 'more' and the 'less', more clever, more genius or less, you are going to be misled by your own conclusions, which is not in my mind. I want to discuss this with you, for I feel this is one of the problems we are confronted with. A mediocre mind is middling, ordinary, average. I am not now talking of the mind which wants to be the 'more', which wants to be more clever, which wants to come out of level, which is not creative and therefore struggling to be creative, writing poems, writing sentences. I am talking of a mind which is mediocre. Now immediately, the mind—if you observe your own minds in operation—wants a definition of "What is mediocre?" Having a definition, you will think out according to that definition; either you are accepting it, or rejecting it. Is not the mind mediocre when it seeks a definition according to which it shall think? Please follow this.

As I have said last week, it is important to bring about a revolution, not an economic or particular revolution or a revolution at a particular level of our being or existence—a total revolution, a complete, whole, integrated revolution—and that is only possible if our whole thinking process undergoes a real revolution, not a mere substitution of one thought, of one belief, of one idea, by another. So if you are concerned, you will see the importance of a total revolution. The communist or the socialist revolutions are really no revolutions at all. Merely following a particular action or system of thought laid down according to Marx or according to Shankara is not revolution. A total revolution is necessary because the problems are enormous, and to understand problems we have to understand the mind because the mind will translate the problems according to its mediocrity, according to its wisdom, according to its knowledge. So, there must be a total revolution in the contents of the mind, which is thought.

So we have to inquire what is mediocrity—not the definition, not how to make the mind which is mediocre, whatever it is, into something else. We have actually to discover for ourselves what is mediocrity, not how to become less or more mediocre because in the problem of mediocrity, you will find this issue of discontent, and the pacification of discontent arises. In that, you will find a constant endeavor to become, to be something. Is a mind which is not trying to become something, mediocre, stagnant? All these problems arise when you enter into this question of what is mediocre. That seems to me to be one of our major difficulties in life.

Out of the inquiry into mediocrity arises the question, What is creativeness? A man who paints a picture, writes poems, gives a lecture, or uses his power as a means to compel others, in order to become self-important—is that creativeness? Or is creativeness something totally different, not comparable but totally different? If we can go into that question of mediocrity, all these problems will be dealt with. But before we can go into it, we must clear our minds, must we not, of all comparative thinking. I mean by comparative thinking a mind which is constantly comparing itself with somebody, with an idea, with becoming. For instance, especially in this country where caste or class is terrible, our mind is so shaped and so deliberately cultivated as to maintain these strata. We think always in terms of becoming less or more, or, despising them all, destroying what we consider to be the more intelligent in order to bring about equality. I hope you are following all this.

Your mind will say, "What is the practicality of all these? What is the use of all these in our daily life?" I will tell you. There is no use at all because your daily life is now not revolutionary, not creative, but dull, heavy, routine; and you cannot solve the problems with your minds as they are now. The moment your mind's thinking process changes, you will be able to deal with the problem. So when you ask about the practicality of what I am saying, then that very question will show that you are not thinking in terms of revolution but only how to bring about superficial adjustment.

Let us look into this question of what is mediocrity. Please follow this. Do not ask for a definition because you have it in a dictionary, you can go home and look into it. But how can you and I be aware of what mediocrity is? What do we mean by mediocrity? Please do not hold to anything I may say verbally in order to explain what is mediocrity because then you will use it as a conclusion, as a definition, and you will compare what I have said with what someone else has said, and choose the definition you prefer. Now, that process of mind which chooses a definition and compares it with another and in that comparison says, "This is applicable to me, this appeals to me"—is not that process a mediocre process? Do you understand what I am talking about?

If I am to inquire into what is mediocrity, I must be aware how my mind is operating, not how to become less mediocre. The demand of the mind, in wanting to change the mediocre mind into something intelligent, wise, clever, sets about inquiring and trying to find out the definition; and having found a suitable definition which appeals to the mind, it begins to carry that out. Is it not a mediocre mind that is doing this? I hope you are observing your own minds in operation, not merely listening to my words. My words are merely indicating the operation of the mind, the mind which is yours. So you are watching your own mind in operation and not following what I am saying.

When a mind compares because, either for reasons of fear or for security or for greater economic certainty, it wants to 'become', is not such a mind mediocre, which means a mind that is afraid? As long as there is fear, there must be comparison, there must be the process of becoming, imitation, conformity. So is not mediocrity a state of mind which, being discontented, finds easy pacification of that discontent? We think discontent is wrong, don't we? At least we are told not to be discontented, are we not? Is not the pacification of discontent an indication of mediocrity? I am not defining mediocrity, but watching how the mediocre mind works. Does not the mediocre mind seek comfort when there is a burning flame of discontent? That is what most of us want, to find contentment. Because I am discontented, I want to find some resting place somewhere where I can be at peace. So what is happening? My mind soon finds a way to be pacified, to be quiet, to be undisturbed—which we call tranquillity of the mind. My mind becomes slowly dull, and I am exhausted because I have not really understood the whole process of discontent. A mind being discontented sometimes becomes very clever, drives, is aggressive; such a mind also is a mediocre mind because it is trying to transform *what is* into something else.

So, is not a mediocre mind a mind that is constantly trying to become, not only in this world of acquisitiveness, but also in the so-called spiritual world, the whole hierarchical principle? "You know, and I do not know; you are the guru, you lead me to safety"—this total process of the mind indicates a mediocre mind. The 'becoming', away from *what is*—"I am little, small; I am ignorant; I am this, and I want to become that, the most supreme one, the God or the commissar or the cabinet minister"—is not this everlasting 'becoming', wanting more, not only physiologically or psychologically, but also spiritually, the cause of all discontent? Is not this whole process an indication of mediocrity? Now, do you realize that it is so, not merely verbally but actually? Do you see it as a fact, a defenseless fact? The mind that clings to God, Buddha, Shankara, Aristotle, Gandhiji, or X, Y, or Z—is not that also a mediocre mind because it is incapable of discovering what is truth for itself? Therefore, it must realize the fact. Now, when you are confronted with that fact, what is the operation of your mind? How does your mind work when you are confronted with this fact? If you are aware of the fact, you will also see that your mind immediately asks, "How am I to transform the fact?" Does it not? "I realize my mind is mediocre from all you have stated now; what am I to do?"—that very question shows that you have not understood the problem. When you are confronted with this fact of mediocrity and you say, "What am I to do?"—you are again caught in mediocrity because you are concerned with changing it. You are not aware of the fact and the truth of it. The very desire to change your mediocre mind into something bigger is preventing you from being creative—not the creativeness of writing poems, however clever, however marvelous. That creativeness which is timeless, which is of no class, no group, no religion, which is truth, which is God, whatever name you give it, that creativeness is not caught by a mediocre mind, a mind which says, "I must be creative, I must get at it, I must know more." But the creativeness comes into being when the mind is face to face with the fact and is still.

The fact of mediocrity and the mind confronted with that fact, and having no desire to alter the fact, form the state of being in which mediocrity melts away. But this requires a great alertness of mind. You cannot be alert when there is fear. No. Fear makes us dull, unintelligent. A person who is afraid may be very clever, may occupy the highest position in the land, may know all the scriptures, may climb the social ladder or the hierarchical ladder of what is called spirituality, which is only illusory; but his is only a dark mind capable of inventing mischief and illusion. Until we resolve that center of fear—not, How are we to resolve it?—we cannot be creative. Being aware of fear without any desire to resolve it, to overcome it, to run away from it, that very discovery of the fact and remaining with the fact is the dissolution of fear.

The gentleman asks, "Living in a country like this, with a neighbor who is aggressive, who wants to destroy, what is to be my action?" Now, sirs, let us go into the matter, not what to do, but how to think of the problem, how to approach the problem. What to do, what action should take place—you will find it out if your minds are clear. India has been unfortunately divided into Pakistan and India. It has been divided through many causes—by the politicians' greed to have immediate power, and by the politicians of other countries to bring about a disunited India and to divide and rule, which has been going on for centuries. It is not just an event happening out of context. It has been a growth. How are you to meet it? How do you meet it? You meet it by armament, and so you prolong the problem don't you? You are armed and I am armed, and by mutual terror we hope to have peace; that is what the world is doing, and that is the result of centuries of wrong thinking, is it not?

See how the world is divided. You think India is a separate sovereign country, so is England a separate sovereign country, and so on—different sovereign countries with different flags, different ministers, different laws, different economic barriers. We have been maintaining all this out of our greed, out of our fear, and you say, "How am I to act, and what am I to do as an individual?" Is that not the problem? Now, can you stop this division? The politicians want to divide because then only they can have more power. Are you not having the same, next door, the Andhras and the Tamils? Not so brutally, not so very antagonistically, but the same issue is at stake, is it not? You will have out of this division other problems; and when these problems arise, you say, "What am I to do?" So all that one can do is to think entirely and totally differently, as a human being—not as a Tamilian, Telugu, Indian, Christian, or a communist, but as an integrated human being concerned with the problem.

There is only the problem and not the answer to the problem. The moment you put the question, "What am I to do?" have you not already entered into a system of thought which is going to divide you? Then you have one system and I have another system. Please see the importance of this. There is only the man, not the Englishman, the Russian, the German, or the Hindu. As long as there are a few of us who are thinking in those terms and creating a new process of thinking about these matters, others will come in and rather bring about greater misery and destruction. This answer does not satisfy you because you want an immediate answer to a problem created through centuries by our deliberate desire to have a better position than the neighbor, to be more clever, to cultivate a brain, to exploit others—which the Brahmin has unfortunately become now. After creating the mischief, you say, "How am I to deal with it?" You cannot deal with it because it is going on from moment to moment. All that you can do is to have a total perception of that problem, and that perception will bring about a revolution, but you do not like to have this.

Before I answer any of these questions written to me, perhaps you will like to ask questions from the talk which I have just now given.

Questioner: Can a mediocre mind, as it is, realize self-realization?

KRISHNAMURTI: Sirs, it all depends. This is a question and answer meeting and not a discussion. If you want to discuss, please come on Monday morning, Tuesday morning, or Wednesday morning when we can discuss this problem. So let me explain what the question means. Because, if you understand the question, you will find the answer in the question itself, you do not have to ask me.

Can a mediocre mind realize God? Is that not it, sir? You may use the word *self-realization,* whatever that may mean. Can the mind be liberated, can it find truth, God, can it? Sir, please do listen. Can a mediocre mind, a small mind, a disturbed mind, a mind that is petty, broken up, that is average, find reality? Reality is something totally unknown. It is something to be from moment to moment. It is not a thing fixed there for me to get. If it is fixed there for me to get, it is an invention of the mind. We create God in our image, don't we? All the books, all the temples are filled with the works of our hands—the word, the image, or the symbol—which the mind considers very important because it is afraid to discover for itself. Can such a mind find truth or self-realization, whatever the word *self-realization* may mean? Can a small mind which is only thinking in terms of getting more, thinking in terms of time—that is, "I will do something tomorrow," "I will get something next life"—can such a mind understand that which is timeless, which is beyond the chronological and psychological demand of desire? Obviously not.

Sirs, God is not something that you acquire, as you acquire a suit or get a virtue. It is something incomparable, timeless, unimaginable, not nameable, you cannot come to it. It must come to you. It can only come to you when your mind is no longer seeking. Because you are seeking now in order to acquire, in order to become comfortable, in order to become something, because you are thinking in terms of time, in terms of growth, in terms of achieving results, you can never know what reality is. Such a mind is a mediocre mind. It can invent phrases, it can talk about God, it can talk about truth. But such a mind has no experience of reality. It cannot. It is only when the mind is no longer comparing, no longer acquiring—to such a mind that is still, reality comes into being, and that reality is not continuous, it is from moment to moment. That which was, is not, and that which is, shall not be. Sirs, these are not just words. When you really go into the problem of all that I have been saying, you yourself will find out what it is to be creative. You yourself will have the mind that is no longer comparing, acquiring, a mind that has come into a state of 'being', and into that 'being' reality comes. That reality is never the same. Therefore the mind cannot write, talk, describe about the reality. That reality has no appeal. You cannot say it appeals to me. Therefore it is really a vain foolish talk.

Only when the mind no longer is seeking, no longer demanding, no longer searching, wanting, becoming, only then the mind is still, and that stillness is not constant, that stillness varies from moment to moment. A mind that only knows continuity is not a still mind. All this requires a great deal of patience, awareness, and self-knowledge. That self-knowledge is not of some self you have heard of in books, in which you have been conditioned, brought up, but it is of the self of every day, the self that is finding, seeking, wanting, being acquisitive, discontented, corrupting, greedy, and vain, inventing the hierarchy in order to assert itself in more power. That is the mind that has to be understood. That can be understood from moment to moment, as you walk, as you talk. You will find when you talk to your servant, watching the language you use, how your mind is conditioned, crippled by tradition; such a mind can never find reality. There must be a total revolution in our thinking for that which is timeless to be.

December 12, 1953

Fourth Talk in Madras

Almost all of us are concerned with the problem of change. We see things in confusion. Every problem, every change, seems to produce more problems, more complex suffering, every kind of disturbance. As we think about the problem and in the process of changing from *what is* to *what should be*, we create other problems, do we not? I do not know if you have thought about it. Every one must have noticed that in the process of changing oneself, one creates problems not only in one's daily life but also politically, socially, in every direction. The very revolution brings other problems and yet we want to change to a state or into a stage in which no other problems will be created. That is what we all want, don't we? Please let us think this out together because it requires a little bit of attention, insight into what we are discussing.

I am not out to show you, or to twist your thinking to a particular pattern. But we are concerned with the problem of change and we see the necessity of it. For instance, most of us when we are young are very dissatisfied, we are discontented, we search, we grope after, we seek various avenues of knowledge, information, guidance, go to some guru, some Master to help us out of our discontent, out of our inquiry, to give us knowledge, information, and insight into things. The moment we have found someone who can give us knowledge, a way to act, a way to live, our dissatisfaction comes to an end, and we pursue that particular pattern of thought for years and years. That is the case with most of us, is it not? When you look back to your youth, that is what happens to most of us. I see the inequality in this world of the rich and the poor, the man who knows so much and the man who knows so little; there is the appalling misery, war, strife; and I am discontented with all that in my youth and I begin to inquire; then I join the Socialist party, the communist party, or become a very devout religious person. The moment I have joined, hoping that joining will bring about change, the discontent is gone. I want change according to a certain pattern of thought, according to a certain course of action. Then the discontent is only in following that course. That is the case with most of us, is it not? When we have become crystallized, heavy in that which we have accepted, we have destroyed our discontent. Then we need sanction; then we need authority to pry us from our set course of action. So we go to an authority as a final means of producing a change in ourselves.

This is really a very important question which I am not twisting to my particular way of thinking or looking or inquiring, but this is what is happening. There is a tremendous revolution in thousands and millions. Certain people have an idea what a change should be, how a change should be brought about, how a society should be built. So they assume powers of providence, and they mold, shape, and control the people because they say that people must change, and for that, they must be held in a certain pattern of action, and otherwise there will be no corporate action. So everybody, including the dull, heavy, insensitive person, is concerned with this problem of change. You may not change; you may have your corners of seclusion, safe gardens where nothing can penetrate; your whole mind may be enclosed by ideas, systems. But even in those minds there must be the germ of anxiety, the worry of change, because everything is changing. To what? We do not know to what, but we should like to change to what is the real which will not create more problems, more anxieties, more sorrow. After all, we are human beings. We have a certain sense of responsibility, and there is such a thing called love which may be smothered, destroyed; but there it is. We see misery, poverty, wars, the powerful and the weak; and that love must act and somehow find a way.

Are we not all greatly concerned with this problem of change? How easily we are satisfied when there is discontent which we think is so wrong! Give a man or a boy who is a communist, who is a socialist, who feels violently, strongly, about this problem, a good job, a safe position; let him marry and have children; there he is finished; he becomes a capitalist like ourselves because he wants his change to be continued in a particular direction. When we do change, it is the change in a particular cast, in a particular direction, towards a certain direction. So is it not a problem with each one of us, this question of change? Change to what? We want a change, and in the process of changing we have problems, and the very changing produces such catastrophes! So the mind hesitates. So what has one to do? Please let us think over this together, not that you are listening and I am giving a talk—which is quite stupid. But let us, you and I together, find out the truth of this—not my truth or your truth, because truth is not personal—how to think about this problem, but not what to change into. Every religion, every group, every society, every philosophy says, "You are this, change to that," and in the process of changing, there is conflict within and without. The conflict is not an indication of intelligence, it dulls the mind. One becomes insensitive, dull, weary, as most of us are—especially the older people, who have struggled, battled, disciplined, controlled in order to change, to achieve the result.

So just listen to this problem of change, not to my approach to the problem because I have shown I have no approach, not in terms of conclusion or how to bring about a change or in terms of what to change to. Just listen to the problem of complete revolution which will not produce other problems. Look at what is happening in the world. There are India and Pakistan, essentially one country but now two countries; therefore, more trouble, more wars, more destruction, more competition to fight with each other. Similarly, in Europe, everywhere there is a breaking up, there is a disintegration. Every leader, every political dogmatist, every religious tyrannist says his way is the way you must change. So if we can, even for this evening, put away all such thoughts and inquire into what to change into, then perhaps we shall have an understanding which is not merely the product of effort, of striving. First of all, the inquiry must be, must it not: From what intention do you want to change, and what authority do you need to change; what compulsion, what motive do you need in order to bring about a change? That is a very important question, is it not? Because on that depends whether you will change or not change. If my whole structure, if my thought is built on acquisitiveness, which is the case with most of us, on a sense of discontent which demands the 'more'—"you have, I have not, and I must have" indicates our discontent is acquisitive—then that discontent carries the mind.

Is change possible without any form of compulsion? Please follow all this. I am thinking aloud, I am not giving a talk to you. It is a problem of how to change the people who are in power, position, authority, who believe in such absurd nonsense. How to change them, how to change you and me? Must I not inquire why I want a change? What is the drive? What is the motive and towards what? Most of us change, do we not, when we are assured that which we are going to change into is satisfactory, is comfortable, is worthwhile. You follow? I will change if I am assured by an authority, by a man who knows, by a guru, by a system, by somebody who has written a book, that doing these things will produce that. Do you understand? You listen to me, why? Is it not primarily that somehow I will tell you something which will help you to change, to acquire, to be more happy, to be something else? Is that change? If I were able to guarantee, or if I were stupid enough to guarantee, that if you change you will have happiness, *moksha,* and whatever it is, then you will struggle violently to acquire that. But is that change? That is, when you know, when you are conscious, when you deliberately move towards the known, is that change? You understand? Is there a change in me when I move from a known to another known? The other known is always to be guaranteed, to be made satisfactory; it must be certain almost in getting to be successful. Is that the motive for most of us to change?

A change is possible only from the known to the unknown, not from the known to the known. Do please think this over with me. In the change from the known to the known, there is authority, there is the hierarchical outlook of life—"You know, I do not know. Therefore, I worship you, I create a system, I go after a guru, I follow you because you are giving me what I want to know, you are giving me a certainty of conduct which will produce the result, the success and the result." Success is the known. I know what it is to be successful. That is what I want. So we proceed from the known to the known in which authority must exist—the authority of sanction, the authority of the leader, the guru, the hierarchy, the one who knows and the other who does not know—and the one who knows must guarantee me the success, the success in my endeavor, in change, so that I will be happy, I will have what I want. Is that not the motive for most of us to change? Do please observe your own thinking, and you will see the ways of your own life and conduct. So we set up a society, build a structure in which there is this whole principle of authority—the authority of the one who knows, who is going to help me to that state in which I shall also know; I shall have the supreme satisfaction of achieving, arriving—and this is called change. I am not twisting it to my particular thinking; this is just what is happening in our daily life. When you look at it, is that change? Change, revolution, is something from the known to the unknown in which there is no authority, in which there may be total failure. But if you are assured that you will achieve, you will succeed, you will be happy, you will have everlasting life, then there is no problem. Then you pursue the well-known course of action, which is, yourself being always at the center of things.

So is it not a problem, in thinking this out, whether time brings about a process of change? Do you understand? I am greedy, envious; I look to time, tomorrow, day after tomorrow, next month, next year, as a means of destroying my greed, overcoming my violence, my passion. Does time produce change, revolution? Is not the psychological demand for time a process of being certain? After all, time, the psychological process of achieving the end through time—is that not the invention of the mind for its own convenience in order not to change but to continue in the same pattern of action, only calling it by a different name? Look, I am violent. I have the ideal of nonviolence, which is so much talked of in India—they have other ideals in other countries, unfortunately. I am violent and nonviolence is over there; to arrive there, I must have a gap of time; I am going to arrive there. That is the state, the ideal state. I think that is the state in which I will be happy, a perfect state in which there is no violence, and to achieve that, that distance, to travel from here to there, I need time. This process of traveling from here to there is called progress towards a state of nonviolence. Is that state of nonviolence, nonviolence at all? You follow? Or is it merely an idea away from *what is?* You understand, sirs?

I am violent. How is that violence to be changed? That is the problem, not into what, but the complete transformation in *what is.* If I am only concerned with the complete transformation in *what is,* then *what should be* is not. Therefore time is no concern. This is not a philosophical problem of time. If I am concerned with revolution, a complete total transformation, I must not think in terms of time—time being merely the invention of the mind. Therefore, a mind wishing to change can never change, can only modify *what is* as in a continuity. Is all this too difficult? I wonder if you are understanding what I am talking about. First of all, it is a difficult problem. You only know change in terms of time, in terms of the known, in terms of compulsion, in terms of social environment, squeeze. That is all we know. In these terms we think and are compelled to change fast. But we do not know the spontaneous change in which the consciousness of the effort to change is not—because when a conscious mind says, "I am going to change," that requires effort, and when the mind makes a conscious effort to change, that implies time. Please follow all this, and if you follow it, listen to it carefully and you will find how astonishing is the change that takes place without your making an effort.

So when a conscious mind makes up its mind to change, it must have time, and time implies the continuity of the same in a modified form. It is never a revolution. It is not what has been, but it is a continuity of what has been. When there is a conscious, deliberate act to acquire virtue through meditation, through practice, it implies time, does it not? Time is the very nature of the self, the 'me' that is going to acquire, to be. The man who says, "I must forget myself in virtue, and therefore I am going to practice virtue," takes the cloak of virtue as the 'self'; it is only the self, the 'me', which is clothed in virtue. Therefore, the 'me' is the cause of disturbance, is the cause of destruction, is the cause of misery. When the conscious mind uses authority, sanction, as the means to bring about a change, it must establish a whole hierarchical outlook of life in which there is no love. When you follow your guru who knows, you have no love; you have only fear which is covered over by the words *devotion, service, sacrifice,* because at the bottom of it, you want to be sure, you want to arrive; you do not want to suffer, you do not want to discover, to find out—which means uncertainty, inquiry. So, a man who is concerned with this problem of change is confronted with all this. It is only the most stupid or the cleverest politicians who say that they know and who take the role of providence.

So our problem is the change to the unknown, not to the known, and that is the only revolution, the change which comes about when the unknown comes into being in my mind. Please follow this. When the unknown comes into being, the unknown cannot be with the 'me' when the 'me' is pursuing consciously some end. Until that unknown, that truth, comes into being—which only can build—all labor is vain. So, for that unknown to come into being, the mind must cast away all knowledge of the thing which it has learned in its self-protection; the mind must be completely, totally, empty to receive the unknown; the mind itself must be in a state of the unknown. Then from that unknown we shall build, and then that which we build is everlasting. But without that, they who labor to build, labor in vain, which only creates more misery and more chaos in the world.

There are many questions sent in. I shall try to answer them. I will not give the answers, but we shall investigate the problems together and find the truth of the problem. The truth is not yours or mine; it is not what appeals to you or what appeals to me. Truth is not appealing, it does not depend upon your temperament. It can only be when you have no temperament. I have no temperament when I have no opinion, judgment, comparison. Truth is only when I am not and you are not. Therefore, it has not anything to do with your satisfaction or with mine; it has nothing to do with whether it appeals to you or not. It is there. Only the wise, experienced man who suffers, the man who loves, will know it.

Questioner: Sir, what kick exactly do you get out of these talks and discussions? Obviously you would not go on for more than 20 years if you do not enjoy them. Or, is it only by force of habit?

Krishnamurti: This is a natural question to put, is it not? Because, the questioner only knows or is aware that generally a speaker gets a kick out of it, some kind of personal benefit. Or is it merely old age? Or, whether one is young or old, is it the habit? That is all he is accustomed to, so he puts the question.

What is the truth of this? Am I speaking out of habit? What do you mean by habit force of habit? Because I have talked for 20 years, am I going to talk for 20 more years until I die? Is the understanding of anything habitual? The use of the words is habitual, but the contents of the words vary according to the perception of truth from moment to moment. If a speaker gets a kick out of it, then he is exploiting you. That is what most of us are used to. The speaker is then using you as a means of fulfillment, and surely it would destroy that which is real. As we are concerned to find the truth and *what is* from moment to moment, in it there can be no continuity; all habit, all certainty, all desire for fulfillment, all personal aggrandizement must have come to an end, must it not? Otherwise, it is another way of exploiting, another way of deluding people, and with that surely we are not concerned.

There are many questions or several questions about gurus—"Should I follow my own mind or my guru?" "You awaken in us the desire to discover the truth and so you are indispensable to us." So, similarly, "True realization is essentially an individual matter. Are not philosophies, systems, gurus, masters, helpful in lighting the spark within us and therefore necessary?"

This is really a very persistent question with most of us. We want an awakener, we want an inspirer, we want a guide, we want somebody to tell us how to behave, we want someone to tell us what love is, what to love. In ourselves we are empty, in ourselves we are confused, uncertain, miserable. So we go round begging to be helped, to be inspired, to be guided, to be awakened. Please follow this. It is your problem and not mine, and because it is your problem you should face it, understand it, not repeat it year after year until you die confused, utterly lost. You say an inspirer is indispensable, or a guru is a necessity. For what? Is a guru necessary for you to be led to what you call truth, what you call the real, to God, to self-realization? Do you understand? You want to be led. Several things are implied in this. First, that which is truth is never an abode or a fixed thing to understand; it has not a fixed spot in time so that you can carefully be guided, led, shown. If you are guided or helped, and if it be shown to you, then it is not truth; it is only an invention of the mind, which you want because that will give you satisfaction, certainty, and that will make you happy. So do follow this.

Truth is not a fixed point in time. Only if it is a fixed point, the mind can understand it. What the mind can understand is the creation of the mind, and so it has nothing whatever to do with reality, with God, or what you will. You cannot be led to reality because it is a living thing, because it is never the same from day to day, from moment to moment. Because you want permanency, a state of continuity, you seek a guru who will lead you to what you want. But what you want is not what is truth, and you cannot be led to discover truth. Do you understand? The process of leading you to discover truth is not discovery. You cannot be led to discover it; it must be discovered by you. No one can lead you to discover it. It is a contradiction. So I must be allowed to discover truth. Do please see this.

In India, it is one of our curses that you must have an awakener, a guru, a Master, someone who will help us, who will guide us to find the truth, and in that desire to find truth, you build up a hierarchy of authority. The building of authority and the hierarchy destroys love because then you discard everybody, you trample on everybody in your desire to get there. You talk of brotherhood, you found societies of brotherhood, and yet you maintain the hierarchy, the caste system. So you are not seeking reality. If you are really seeking reality, you will not stretch your hand out for it because reality must come to you. You cannot invite it, you cannot go after it because it is there every second if you know how to look at it. What you want is not truth, you want comfort, you want safety, you want success, you want self-fulfillment which is 'me'-fulfillment, in God, in truth, which is 'me' ever continuous, everlasting. That is all you are interested in. You want safety, spiritual safety as well as economic safety, and as you know very well there is no economic safety, you are after the permanency in spirituality, that permanent state you call truth. That is why you have leaders, religious organizations, philosophies, gurus, always guaranteeing safety, permanency for your comfort.

One who guarantees and one who seeks guarantee are, both of them, caught in illusion. They are not seeking reality. Once and for all, if you really understand this, you will put away your gurus, for light is not in a guru or through a guru—it is in yourself. But no one can lead you to find it because you will have to find it for yourself. When you say you are seeking truth, it is superstition and vanity; and those people exploit you through your superstition, through your vanity. Surely, to find truth you must be stripped, you must be completely naked of all desire, alone, not depending, unsheltered. Then only truth comes. Only then, it is possible to create a new world, a world in which there will be no problems. Because, there is action then not from fear, not from the desire to be certain, but from reality which is the unknown.

The questioner asks, "Should I follow my mind or my guru?" Your guru is made or born or chosen from your mind, from your temperament, from your like or dislike, from what appeals to you; your mind creates the guru. So you are following your own mind and there is no guru. You are following your desires, and your desire is to be safe, comfortable, to have certainty for great success. You are not successful in this world, fortunately for you; therefore, you want, unfortunately, success in the next world. A man who is seeking success will never find reality. Sirs, the mind must be understood, the ways of your thoughts must be fathomed, delved into. Then you will know the operations, the workings of your mind, how the mind, in its desire to be safe, projects everything—every illusion, every master, every guru. So the mind is the only guru which you have, but that guru is not going to help you; that guru is not going to lead you; that guru is only going to deceive you, to bring more confusion and more misery. You have to understand that mind which creates illusion. Just listen, do not say, "I have heard what Shankara says or what others say." Comparative thinking is not thinking. So when you know the ways of your mind, the mind becomes still, voluntarily and easily, without discipline, without compulsion; then only that reality will come into being. Then that reality will build a new world, not the mind, not your gurus, because that reality is love.

December 13, 1953

Fifth Talk in Madras

You may remember last week we were trying to discuss the problem of change. It seems to me that is one of the most fundamental issues that is confronting the present world at the present moment because we do not know what to change to. Because we do not know, all the professional religious people turn to the Vedas, or quote authorities, or follow a particular philosophical system of thought, hoping actually, if you observe, to divert in a particular direct action. The leaders themselves, like the followers, are very confused. They may profess that they are following a philosophy, that they know what they are talking about. But if you closely observe, you will see that fundamentally they are very confused. Is it not right that those of us who are really earnest should inquire into this problem of what is change and towards what? I discussed that last week. But I think, if we can go into it from a different point of view, then perhaps we shall be able to understand the deeper significance of the idea, of the words *to change.* Perhaps if we are able to inquire into what is religion, then we shall be able perhaps to understand what it is to change. But without understanding the whole significance of religion, mere outward reformation is most unrealistic, as it has been shown to us by all recent revolutions and reforms. Let us, if we can, seriously inquire into what is religion, and perhaps in understanding it, not at the verbal level, but as we go into it, as we actually experience the significance of that word, then perhaps we shall be able to understand the meaning of the words *to change* and to bring about a revolution which, as we are discussing for the last two or three weeks, is essential.

Things go on as they are, and those people who are well-established in position, in the religious or in the social order, or who have the means of power in their hands, obviously do not want a revolution; they want the things as they are to continue in a modified form. But if we are really serious in our intention to inquire into what is religion, obviously we must approach it without any vested interest. You know what is meant by vested interest, the vested interest in an organization? It means all the profits which accrue from it in the name of something, the personal benefits which soon become the personal racket of the leader though he uses it in the name of peace, Master, philosophy, or any particular political ideology. So really to inquire into the significance of what is religion, is it not necessary to begin not with what God is but with what the mind is that thinks of God? You understand? A mind that thinks of God, or believes in God and practices various forms of discipline and rituals, will never know God or truth because the mind that believes projects that which is most satisfactory to itself. That is a psychological fact. So a mind that believes in God or in truth or in something is obviously incapable of real inquiry because such a mind has a vested interest in that belief. From that belief it acquires security, hope, satisfaction, a sense of moral and physical well-being. So such a mind can never find it, it will deceive itself and others. It can never find what is real because psychologically it has committed itself to a certain pattern of action. Yet, most people who are religious—so-called religious—are steeped in beliefs, in rituals, in dogmas; and this is because they find this world to be very troublesome, to be very, very painful. All relationship leads to conflict. In the ordinary daily life there is no mystery. So the mind must have a mystery, something supernatural—either the worship of the state according to Marx or somebody, or the worship of an image made by the hand or by the mind in some dogma. The dogma then becomes mysterious, as it is placed by the mind and treated by the mind as mystery, and it cannot be touched because it is too mysterious for the mind to understand, but still, it is an invention of the mind, of the psychological urgency.

I hope you are following all this. I am not describing anything but the mind of each one of us, the mind that is caught in routine, in the daily boredom of existence. There is no mystery in our personal relationship, in sex, in nature. We have explored all that, but we want mystery, we want something beyond, further than what the mind can invent, than what the mind can project. But that very projection of the mystery is the process of the mind. So the mind gets caught in that mystery which is a dogma—whether dogma of the state, dogma of a Catholic, dogma or the belief of a Hindu, or the Master living somewhere beyond, mysteriously behind a hill. So the mind must have a mystery to worship, created either by the hand or by the mind, which has an idea round it. Round that idea, that image, grows a vested interest of property, power, position, and authority. So knowing all these—which is an everyday fact—it is only the knave and the thoughtless that fall into the trap by jobs, by personal vanity, and by personal ambition.

So, can a mind find that reality? After all, religion implies that search for reality, and can a mind which is steeped in all forms of superstitious personal ambitions and which believes in dogmas, ever find that reality? Please do listen. If you are to build a new world, it must be built on quite a different foundation, not on your or my personal ambition clothed in the name of the Master, in the name of the state or in the name of an ideology. It must be built totally differently because, otherwise, we shall have to go on from war to war at different levels, not only physical war, but also psychological, inner war with each other in order to bring about a radical revolution. In all that, must not there be a freeing of the mind freeing of your mind and my mind and the minds of every one, of all of us who are capable, who are earnest, who listen and see the urgency? Is it not important to strip ourselves totally from all these dogmas, rituals, and superstitious nonsense, and begin to find out how to inquire? This means really that each one of us must, in our daily life, strip ourselves away from the past, from the tradition, from the usual routine of ritual, the things on which we have been brought up. After all, they are essentially based, are they not, on our desire to be secure psychologically and physiologically. We want to be safe, and the mind cannot tolerate a moment when it is not safe, when it is uncertain. So the mind must have something to cling to, and the more mysterious, dark, fearful, unimaginable it is, the more and more it clings to that. So is it not necessary in order to build a new house that the house should be built on truth, on reality, with the perfume of the eternal? Must it not be built, not on dogmas, but on the understanding of the whole process of the mind that is trying to build, that is destroying and at the same time building, that is deteriorating and bringing something into being?

So the problem is not a new philosophy, a new system, a new economic order. We see divisions, armies, political or physical power do not create a new world. To think in those terms is quite out of order. The mind is a total being, and on the understanding of the mind we must build. So, can we not strip ourselves away from all those dogmas, and face what actuality is?—which is, we are ambitious, we are envious, we are seeking personal security, personal immortality. That is all we are concerned with. You may clothe it in all kinds of sweet, high-sounding words; but, in essence, all we want is physical security, psychological well-being. The physical well-being is destroyed by the psychological demand. So the psychological demand is far greater, far more urgent, far more significant than the mere physical demand for security.

So, is it not possible for the mind to understand this problem of envy?—because our society is based on that, on acquisitive discontent. Is it not possible for the mind to free itself from it? That requires enormous persistent inquiry, to free the mind from the 'more', from the demand for the 'more' so that the mind does not project, does not demand. When the mind does not project, it is active and yet still; it is only in that stillness reality can come into being, and it is only such a mind that can build a new world. Please follow this. Do not be deceived by your leaders—political, religious, or social. Do not be caught in organizations; they will not lead you to truth because they eventually become personal rackets. So a man who is really seeking the truth must be free from all organizations, the so-called spiritual organizations. Then when he is free of these outward compulsions which he has created, then he can begin to strip his mind of those ambitions, those personal antagonisms, envies. That is quite an enormous problem in itself, I assure you.

How is one to free the mind from acquisitiveness? For us acquisitiveness means to have more clothes, to have more houses, larger bank accounts, but that is not mere acquisitiveness, that is an expression of something much deeper. Until we understand the deeper impulses, the deeper compulsion, mere reformation in regard to our possessions—how much we should have and what we should not have—will have no result because the approach is totally wrong. But for the mind to be free from the demand for the more, from the demand to be acquisitive, is extraordinarily difficult because until the mind is simple, innocent, it cannot know what truth is, and innocence can never exist and come into being when there is this acquiring instinct of the mind. Please follow all this and listen to all this. Do not say that this is not practical.

The mind has to be free from the beginning and not at the end because there is no freedom at the end if there is no freedom at the beginning. You cannot go from slavery to freedom, from compulsion to freedom. So religion is surely a state of mind in which the 'me', the 'I', is absent, and into that absence of the 'I' comes reality. But that 'I' is not something mysterious; that 'I' is made up of our jealousies, ambitions, envies, desire for power, position, and intrigues. If one can really think about it, one can dissolve it without constant battle within oneself. So those who would really build a new house cannot build that new house, and their effort will be in vain unless they understand this problem of revolution, the inner revolution. The outward revolution will not affect the inner; it may find a different substitution. This inward revolution is not to be learned from another. You are not going to get this by joining a party. It can be brought about only by constant working, inquiry, and searching. Only then is the mind capable of that freedom in which there is silence, in which there is no movement, but in which there is a stillness and wholeness; the mind is then no longer seeking and therefore still, no longer wanting and therefore completely free from all discontent. Only into such a mind can reality come into being, and it is only that reality that can build a new house.

Would you like to ask, before I answer these written questions, anything that arises out of this talk?

Questioner: In a private conversation you said that the party system, single or multiple, is not democratic. Will you please go into this a little.

KRISHNAMURTI: Let us consider the question and not wait for an answer. You understand? Let us together find out, rather than you wait for me to answer and then you contradict or accept. Most of us are concerned, in political or any other action, with ideas first, aren't we? A political party is formed on an idea, on a system; and another party is formed either in opposition to it or totally different but still based on an idea, on a system, on a philosophy, on a vested interest either in philosophy or in property. So the parties are not concerned with people. They are concerned with a system that will help the people, a system based on an idea, on some philosophy which is essentially a conditioned reaction. You are a communist, I am a socialist or a capitalist; you have a system, I have a system, the communist has a system, which is going to help the people if they, meaning "I and my group," are put into power. So, we—I, my group, your group—have thought out what to do according to certain systems. My group is the outcome of my conditioned reactions, and yours also is similar. So neither of us is concerned with the people, I assure you. We are concerned with systems and how to carry out those systems because the systems offer the means, either personal or utopian. You understand all this? I say, my party says, "We know what is good, and if I get into power I will be ruthless totally, and then I will liquidate all the parties except me and mine because we know we have the approval of providence who is going to tell us what is going to happen, and you are going to fit into that plan."

So long as we have systems, we are not concerned with the people. That is an obvious fact, is it not? If you are really concerned with the people—that is, you and I, a poor man—you would not have systems, but you would all be doing, acting, thinking what is good for the whole, and not on an idea. Surely, neither a single nor a multiple party system is democratic, because neither of them is concerned with the people and their well-being. They want the people and their well-being according to a certain pattern of action. If every one of us, you and I and others, is concerned not with ideas but how to live rightly, how to find out the true relationship between each other—between you and me and between different parts of humanity—that does not require any system of thoughts, utopian or religious. That requires search and inquiry, not based on an idea and how to carry out that idea, but into how to live together. That requires a total revolution again. So none of us inquires sufficiently deeply into these matters because we think that by carrying out the idea immediately we shall have a result, and with results we are concerned; and we are not concerned whether the results multiply more miseries, more problems. So to bring about a revolution in our political thinking also, surely there must not be any action based on an idea or philosophy at the totalitarian, religious, or political behest, but a quite different approach to the problem, which is not based on an idea but on an inquiry into the ways and means of living together directly.

Questioner: How can there be any kind of education without some form of discipline, imposed either externally or from within?

KRISHNAMURTI: What is the function of education? Are we educated? Why do you send your children to school? Please think, and let us think together. Again, there must be a revolution in our approach to the problem.

What is the function of education? Is it not to help the student, the boy or the girl, to face life intelligently, being without fear? My mind is clouded with fear when there is competition. There is fear when I do not know how to meet this whole complex problem of living. There is fear when I am ambitious. A man who is happy is never ambitious, and it is only people who are ambitious that are unhappy. So is it not the function of education to help the student to grow without fear so that he can face life intelligently, not according to your intelligence or my intelligence, not according to your particular religious idiosyncrasies or political or economic condition, so that he can grow fully, integrally, as a whole human being?

The questioner asks then, "How is it possible to bring up a child, youth, or student without some form of discipline?" What is the purpose of discipline, even for the old or for the young? Why do we discipline ourselves, imposed by another or self-imposed? Why do we discipline children? What is the function of discipline in a school? You are parents, fortunately or unfortunately, and you should know. In life what place has discipline? Is not discipline the cultivation of resistance? Discipline implies resistance, and that resistance brings about fear, does it not? Look, you have a large class of students, 40 or 60. How can you keep order in such a large group? You cannot. Therefore you resort to discipline. You are not interested in education. All that you are interested in is that you wish to give them some information so that they will pass the examination and get jobs in which only the parents are interested. The parents are not interested in education, and, to most of us, education ceases after we pass an examination. Probably none of us ever touches a book. If you do not, you stop thinking also. You just have burned yourself out and are just living automatically. So, if we are to understand what is the function of education, is it not important to find out how we can bring a student, a youth, up—without compelling, without coercing, without persuading him, without disciplining him—so that he can function as a total human being. That requires surely a very small school, a small class with teachers who are capable of understanding this whole process of how to bring about this intelligence without compulsion, without everlasting competition of marks and examination, all this process of burning oneself up in these beastly examinations.

Sirs, you believe in souls, you believe in individual progress, you believe in all the rest of it, and yet you are doing the very opposite of that, are you not? So, there must be a total revolution in our education. A boy or student not only has technical knowledge which will help him to acquire a job but there must be also something different, a human being, an integrated human being—and not a human being with constant battle within himself—so that he can be a creative human being. You cannot be creative if you are competitive. There can be no reality if you are afraid, and in everything that we are doing—in our education, in our political action, in following the various gurus and in all the rest of it—there is fear, there is no creativeness, there is no happiness but an inward anxiety. How can such people create a new world and a new being? So the question of discipline implies so much, and a teacher, an educator, who does not understand this will naturally resort to discipline because it is the easiest way to control a large group. As the governments are only interested in mass education, the education that you know prevents revolution, does it not? You are all very educated, are you not? You know how to read, write, and read the morning paper. You will never revolt because you always see so many sides that you never see what is true. Therefore, to bring about the right education which demands a revolution on the part of the parent, on the part of the teacher, there must be an understanding of this whole problem of what is an integrated human being—not a definition, but the inquiry, the constant searching out of this integrated whole. Such a search obviously begins with being free from fear, psychological depths of fear, conscious and unconscious fears. The freeing of the mind from fear is meditation.

Questioner: India has won home rule by practicing the ideal of nonviolence. How then can you be against ideals?

KRISHNAMURTI: Do you really believe that you won freedom by practicing nonviolence? Historical events brought about the weakness of the ruling people, and so they had to withdraw. Hitler and the previous wars weakened Europe. After you have won your so-called freedom by your so-called nonviolence, has there not been violence, Muslim against Hindu? It is said that six million people have been either displaced or murdered. I suppose you do not call that violence.

The problem of ideals is entirely different. Ideals are fictitious, they are not realities, they are the projection of the mind. Please follow this carefully because there also we must have a fundamental revolution in order to create a different world, not this hypocritical, constant, idealistic world with such appalling cruelties. You have the ideal of brotherhood, the ideal of nonviolence, the ideal of love, the ideal of being kind. Why? Because, obviously you are not kind, is it not? Otherwise you will not have ideals. Obviously you are violent, fearful, hating. So you have all these marvelous ideals, and you think that by following these ideals, you will acquire love, you will be nonviolent, you will have brotherhood. Surely, by following an ideal, you are avoiding *what is,* are you not? "I hate, or I am violent; I am practicing nonviolence; it is my ideal." How stupid it is! Why can't I deal with *what is,* and not with *what should be*? You understand, sirs? Can a mind strip itself of these ideals? You put that question to yourself and see what your response is. How fearful you are the moment you put the question to yourself because you think ideals are keeping you within bounds, without overspilling. You say, "What shall I do if I have no ideals?" You are doing nothing, and you will do nothing if you have ideals. If you have no ideals then there will be no projection of the mind to escape from realities, and you will tackle *what is*—greed, envy—actually as it is; then there is the possibility of freeing the mind from the ideal. Sir, we have the ideal of brotherhood preached and not practiced, and yet, we have had no stoppage of war. So why not be away from all our ideals, all our examples, and be very realistic?—which is to understand *what is*. As it is, I am envious, I am ambitious, I am cruel, violent; and how can that be levered out? We think ideals are levers by which *what is* is shaped, moved, and so we are always having a conflict between *what is* and *what should be*. That is our problem, is it not?

I am greedy, I am envious and ambitious; and I should not be so. I am therefore struggling, there is a battle going on within me. This creates hypocrisy between 'what I am' and 'what I should be'. Cannot I strip myself of 'what I should be'? 'What I should be' is an invention of the mind and an escape from the fact, from what I am. That is the standard according to which I am trying to live, and the standard has no authority at all because, psychologically, it is an escape. The fact, *what is,* is one thing, and *what should be* is totally different, and we are fed on *what should be*. The more ideals you have, the more wonderful, the more noble you consider yourself to be. But if you are really facing *what is,* then there is the possibility of dissolving, going beyond. But none of us wants to because we find profit in ambition, we find vested interest in envy. So we have ideals, and we are everlastingly practicing ideals but never facing *what is.* It requires a tremendous revolution, does it not, to break away from this illusion of ideals on which we have been fed and on which the whole world is feeding, and to realize *what is* and be simply with that—to know that you are envious, that you are angry or violent, not to deceive yourself, and not to create this conflict between *what is* and *what should be*. Then you can put your whole energy in understanding *what is,* without escaping into *what should be* which is utopian, which is nothing and never achieved. It is like a man practicing virtue month after month, taking each virtue and meditating upon it. Virtue is something, sirs, which cannot be practiced. If you practice it, it is no longer virtue. For virtue is something unconscious and not to be cultivated by the mind; if it is, it is merely another coat, another color behind the 'me', the 'I'.

Please listen to what I am saying, and let it penetrate beyond your conscious mind so that there will be revolution, so that you and I can create a new world. It is not possible for one man to create a new world. This world is ours, yours and mine. We must build it together. To build it together, we must be very realistic, not phony, not idealistic, but to see things as they are and to go beyond them. To go beyond them requires a great deal of perception, insight into *what is.* Instead of spending our time, our energy, our thoughts, and our days in the understanding of *what is,* we are losing, wasting, destroying ourselves with ideals. You will listen to all this, and you will be temporarily assured to see the truth of what I am saying, or rather, not the truth, but the logical verbal conclusions; and you will go away and talk tomorrow of ideals. Leave that to the leaders, to the gurus, to those who have a vested interest in philosophies—which means really in property. Let us be simple, you and I, innocent with *what is* and not with *what should be*. The innocence of seeing *what is* and the beauty of that innocence brings about freedom from *what is.*

Questioner: I am full of hate. Please teach me how to love.

Krishnamurti: Why do you laugh? Is it not a very sad question? See that question. The questioner is quite conscious of what he is, which most of us are not. Those of you who laugh are unconscious of yourself. You also hate, you are full of envy, bitterness, and everlasting discontent. But the questioner, happily or unfortunately for him, is aware, and he says, "Teach me how to love."

Can love be taught? Can you go to school and learn how to love? Can you be taught wisdom, though there are schools for wisdom? Please listen. Is wisdom to be learned? Is love to be learned? Can you go to another and learn what love is? Does not that very question bring tears to your eyes? I am not being emotional and hypnotizing you into a state of emotionality. You see how you are, sirs, empty in yourselves and therefore everlastingly searching for wisdom, love, kindliness, and understanding. You go from school to school, from people to people to be taught because in yourselves you are empty and you want to fill that emptiness by words without much meaning.

Love cannot be taught to you, nor wisdom. Wisdom comes into being when the mind is free from experience. Please listen to what I am saying. When the mind is free from experience, there is wisdom. But as long as there is the mind that is seeking experience, there must be the experiencer who is seeking it; such a mind can never be wise. Similarly, a heart which is seeking to fill itself with love only will fill it with words without much meaning; it will be just empty words without meaning or conclusion. But one hates; that is the reality. One is miserable; that is *what is*. One is envious, ambitious; and that is the fact. How do you approach the fact? If I know I hate, it is very important to know how to approach it; if I know how to approach, then there is the possibility of its dissolution. But if I do not know, then there is merely the suppression of that fact, which introduces another fact. So what is important is to understand the fact, and you cannot understand the fact if you condemn or judge the fact. You would understand your child only when you do not condemn him; you have to study him, which means you must never condemn, never judge, never identify the child with yourself. If you similarly look at hate, ambition, there must be awareness without choice, without judgment; and that is extremely arduous because all our conditioning is to judge, condemn, to throw out in order to get some other factor. So what we are doing everlastingly is finding a substitution to *what is*.

Only when there is freedom from hate, freedom from ambition and envy, then you will know what love is. Then also you will know what wisdom is, for perhaps, love is wisdom. You cannot learn from another what love is, so also you cannot learn what wisdom is. No school, no book, no Master can teach you. It comes into being when you know all the secret recesses of your heart, and that can only happen when the mind is very still.

December 19, 1953

Sixth Talk in Madras

For the past few weeks we have been considering the problem of change. It seems to me one of the most difficult things in bringing about this change is the cessation of effort. Because, for us, change implies effort, does it not? We associate effort with change. To us, if we desire to bring about a change outwardly or inwardly, effort is implied, the action of the will. Is it possible to change at all radically, deeply, fundamentally, without effort? Or, is there a radical revolution only when there is the cessation of effort? I would like to discuss this problem with you because it must have struck you, when you observe yourself and things about you, how from childhood we are taught that we must make an effort to change. That is all we know, and we have never inquired into the possibility of a change radically without effort. It seems to me that this point is very important. Kindly listen, not with any preconceived idea of what I am going to tell you this evening, not with a prejudiced, experienced mind.

For most of us, change implies effort. I am this, and to become that I must make an effort. In a school, when we grow up, and almost up to when we are dying, this process of constant effort is inculcated into us; we are conditioned with that idea, and that is all we know. We say there must be right effort, right endeavor, constant practice, constant control, discipline, shaping the mind by words, by explanations, by constant directive, and this continual effort is what we know, and with that we live. When we look into the process of effort more deeply, we see that it is not only effort that is involved. There is this whole problem of power, gaining power not only in ourselves but over nature and also over others. We see man—not the man here, you and I, but man generally—increasing his power over nature, flight, underwater, calculating the distance between the various stars, the astonishing brain of the man that can invent the atomic bomb and the super-nuclear bombs, the astonishing brain that has produced all these things. All that implies not only the learning of a technique and the perfection of a technique but also the constant application of the mind to find, to discover—the enormous persistency of curiosity. In that is implied the problem of power—power over water, power over nature, power over others, to shape the lives of others, to change circumstances; all these always imply effort, but not for the man who really invents, who really sees something and is creative. So we are concerned with enlarging our power, power over others especially, by every crooked means or by the so-called idealistic means, which are also crooked, in order to achieve a position, prestige. All that implies power—power to change the economic conditions of man, power of idea, power of word, power of personality—to drive, to make people change. All that we know. With that we are much too familiar. Does that radically bring about a change in ourselves? That is the problem, is it not?

Until we can bring about a fundamental revolution at the core of our being, the mere conquering of outward circumstances may lead to various forms of convenience, but in the process there is a greater, more destructive element brought into being. So it seems to me that unless we can radically, deep at the root bring about a radical change, superficial changes, however vital, necessary, and immediate, only cause further misery, further damage, further mischief. Every reform brings further misery, further problems. Again, with all that we are quite familiar. When we apply that process of power to ourselves, we see that we want power over ourselves, which intoxicates us through asceticism or the extreme form of asceticism, the opposite of money, luxury, position, power, prestige, and all the rest of it. We use virtue, love, the action of the will as a means of conquering ourselves, our idiosyncrasies, and we think we are changing. But essentially when we go down to deeper layers, there it is still the same. When we are considering revolution, change, surely we are not concerned only with superficial changes which are necessary, but with the deeper issue which is the revolution, total revolution, the integrated revolution of our whole being. Can that change be brought about by effort, or must there be a cessation of all effort?

What does effort mean? With most of us, effort implies the action of the will, does it not? I hope you are following all this because if you do not listen wisely, you will miss totally what I am going to say. If you listen wisely, you will directly experience what I am talking. Total revolution must be wholly unconscious, not voluntary, not brought about by any action of the will. Will is still the desire, still the 'me', the self, at whatever level you may place that will. The will of action is still the desire, and therefore it is still the 'me', and when I suppress myself in order to be good, in order to achieve, in order to become more noble, it is still desire, it is still the action of the will trying to transform itself, to put on a different clothing, it is still the will of the 'me' trying to achieve a result.

Please, if I may request, listen not merely to the verbal effect but also to the deeper significance of the words. Most of us do not listen at all. You are listening to my words, to my ideas, to what I am going to say, through your own interpretations, through your own experience; that is not listening, that is like looking through a dark glass; therefore, you see nothing as it is. Similarly, we listen with a conclusion, with the previous knowledge, experience which is always translating what is being said; therefore, you are really not listening. The problem of listening is extraordinarily difficult because consciously or unconsciously, we do not want to listen because there is the fear of something happening, some new idea taking place unconsciously which will produce revolution. So, we only hear words without much significance. But if we can listen wisely—which is to listen without translation, without interpretation—then perhaps what I have said and what I will be presently saying will have a deeper significance.

It is very important to bring about a radical change, a revolution first, obviously, in ourselves—which is, in action, in relationship—which will produce a revolution in outward valuations. But the necessary and absolute revolution, a total and complete revolution, is not at all possible through the action of the will because will is essentially a process of desire, and the action of the will is conditioned. That word *conditioning* implies limited. I will change according to my conditioning, however wide, narrow, limited that conditioning may be. So my will to change is limited according to my conditioning, according to my desire, and the change produced by the will of action is limited and therefore never radical. If we are concerned and if we have given thought to this problem at all, the change must be radical, not superficial, because the problems which we have at present are so great that they need to be tackled radically, not superficially, not as a Hindu, as a Catholic, communist, Theosophist, or something or other. They must be approached totally differently, and because we are not doing it, we are creating more problems and not less. So we are concerned not only with the reduction of the problems, with the resolution of the problems, but also with the radical transformation of man's attitude, values, and process of thinking. We must obviously find a way in which change comes into being without volition. You understand the problem? Please follow this because if you do not understand this, what will come after will have very little meaning.

We only know conscious effort, the conscious acquiring of a technique in order to produce a change. That is all we know. The conscious, active drive to change is born out of desire, and that desire is everlastingly conditioned; and if I change voluntarily or involuntarily from that basis, from that function, from whatever idea—however noble or ignoble, however brotherly or the opposite—it is bound to produce more problems. We know this, we are aware of it. But, have we given serious thought to it at all? So, seeing that, how is it possible to bring about revolution basically, radically, without introducing the action of the will? You see the problem? I want to change, and my whole education, social environment, influence in which I have been educated, is acquisitiveness; our social structure and the religious upbringing are based on acquisition. Now, I see that, and I want to change, but not superficially, not through any action of will. Because will is still the result of acquisition, and therefore when the will says, "I will bring about action," that action will produce a change, but that change will still be the acquisitiveness.

How am I to produce, to bring about a radical transformation without the action of the will? That is an important question to put to yourselves. I see that every action produced by the will is limited, and therefore productive of greater misery and greater problems.

Yet there must be a radical change. Is the radical change possible without the action of will? Let us put the problem differently.

We use function to acquire status. I use office as a means of psychological power. I am an official, a teacher, an engineer—which are all function—and I use that function as a means of acquiring position, prestige, power—which is status. Most of us use, practically all of us use, function to acquire status, which is power. So there is conflict between the various functions because each one of us is seeking through function a psychological result. I hope you are following all this. So, in society, we are creating conflict, confusion, and competition psychologically, using the function to acquire position. There must be function because otherwise we cannot live; the problem then is how not to acquire through function, status. So, we devise various means to control man, to limit him to function and not exude his desire towards status, position, which brings about calamity between each other. So, through various forms of social sanctions, religious edicts, the status, which is the power, is held, controlled—which again is the same problem, only that is inaction. So when we are concerned with the problem of radical revolution, have we not to understand all these problems, all these issues and whether there is a possibility of change without the action of will? I say change is possible without the action of will. That is the only change, none other is change, none other is revolution. But to understand that, it requires a great deal of insight, a great deal of meditation—not the meditation of shutting eyes, gazing at a picture or image, or an imaginary phrase, but the meditation that reveals this whole process of effort.

That is, if you are really listening now to what I am saying, you will be meditating; you are meditating because through that listening, that watchful observation of what I am saying and watching your own mind in operation, you see how in everything you do there is the effort to change—which is the 'will of action'—and as you listen very quietly, you see that the 'will of action' comes to an end. Therefore, with that very ending of the will to act, is the beginning of radical transformation. Please listen.

The action of will is the 'me', and whatever clothes, whatever change, whatever hopes, failures, sorrows the 'me' has, the 'me' wants, it is still within the field of the 'me'. So, in that, there is no revolution, and the 'me' is the action of the will. When the 'me' says, "I must not be ambitious. I must not be envious," the will that says, "I must not," wants to be something else, negatively or positively. Therefore, it is still the 'me'. If you have really understood it—that is, if you are listening to it—you will see that the will of action comes to an end, and with that ending there is a radical transformation; then you are no longer concerned with the 'me' changing. For instance, I am envious, and I act upon envy in order to change it, to change *what is*. But if there is an understanding of that, there is the cessation of the will of action, then there is only the fact that I am envious. If there is no obstruction, no resistance, no judgment, no condemnation, which are all the process of will, then that fact has no longer any significance, that fact does no longer affect the whole process of your thinking. So there is the cutting away, at the root, of the problem of acquisitiveness, which no superficial, economic, communist, or any other kind of revolution can bring about.

So, really, this understanding demands a great deal of attention, self-knowledge—self-knowledge being the observation of what you are in your relationship from moment to moment. Mere observation, not trying to change *what is*, is to see yourself in your relationship with your wife, your servant, your boss;

is to see in a mirror what it is and not to bring the will of action upon it. Then you will find that a change comes into being unconsciously which is the radical revolution, which is not brought about by the conscious mind, and I assure you that the greatest miracle is to see and the thing ceasing to have any effect. So the mind becomes innocent, free; and it is only in such a free, innocent mind that reality can come into being. No search under the will of action can make the mind tranquil; the mind is tranquil only when it has understood the whole process of the will, the action of the will to be. The will to change comes to an end not through any form of compulsion but only when the mind really understands. When it is understood, there is an astonishing change, a revolution which is transcendental, which is not of the mind. It is only that revolution that can build a new house, and without that revolution, they labor in vain that build, they are mischief-makers, they produce sorrow, they multiply problems. Therefore, it is very important for you and me to understand this whole problem of effort.

Perhaps you would like to ask questions out of this talk. If not, I have some written questions.

Questioner: How can a cessation of effort be brought about?

KRISHNAMURTI: That is what I have been talking about.

Questioner: You advocate a small school for educating the young. But even in a small school several teachers are necessary, one for each subject. How can such a school be maintained in these days?

KRISHNAMURTI: So, what is the function of a teacher? Is it merely to impart to the student a subject, a specialized knowledge, which means therefore, you must have innumerable teachers, one for each subject, for English, mathematics, geography, history, physics, and all the rest of it. That is, if each teacher imparts only his specialized knowledge, naturally you must have many teachers for a small school. If the teacher is merely a specialized entity, then he is not an educator because he is only concerned with his subject and knows nothing else, and therefore you must have many specialized human beings to teach the children. But even the teacher who has his own special knowledge—knowledge of his own subject—if he is intelligent, can teach other subjects too, can he not?

Sirs, our difficulty in the modern world is we want immediate results, immediate success. We do not think in long terms, we think in short terms. We want our sons and daughters to pass the examination in order to get a job; that is all that we are concerned with. So we create an educational structure where this specialist exists. But if we look at the long term—that is, see the implication of educating children—then the teacher is not only the giver of information on his subject but he must also be an intelligent, fearless human being. So the problem is not the multiplication of many teachers to teach but teachers themselves having the capacity, intelligence, so that they can partake in different subjects. After all, this is not very difficult; if you are sufficiently intelligent, you can teach not only mathematics but also history. But neither the teacher nor the parent nor the society is intelligent. We do not really love our children. If we did, we would take care of so many things—of their diet, of the kind of teachers, the kind of school—and we would all be concerned with the larger problem. What is the point of education if the educated need be in arms, become lawyers or policemen—which are ways of destruction. They are the people who perpetuate wars.

So we educate children to die. So that problem must be tackled, but not just verbally, and it is not for me just to say how to do it, how to run a school with a few teachers. It is your problem as a parent, and unfortunately you are not interested in it. So the teacher, the low-paid entity who is kicked around, who is the least intelligent, has the greatest responsibility in any society. You have heard all this before, but you have never acted upon it because you are really not interested in your children, nor are you really interested in the whole problem of the freedom of the child. So, until you take the responsibility as a parent and see these things are worked out, no government is going to work them out for you. The government can only condition the children and make them more and more efficient either to run the industries or to join the army. So, the question is not how to have fewer teachers in a small school, but how to bring about in our relationship an intelligence which is not limited, which is not afraid, but which is really revolutionary, which is creative.

Questioner: Does not the mind need verbal preparation before direct perception is possible?

KRISHNAMURTI: What is the mind? Please follow this. Listen to find out whether the mind can ever perceive directly anything true. The questioner wants to know whether the mind must not be prepared verbally to understand the words in order to perceive what is true. That is, does not the mind need verbal preparation before direct perception is possible?

Is perception, direct perception, made by the mind, the mind as it is? We have to find out what is the mind. The mind is memory, is it not, the memory of all that you have learned from childhood and all the experiences of the conditioning, of the beliefs, dogmas, fears, hopes, longings. That is, the mind is thought, is it not? Without thought, there is no mind, and thought is based on the past—the past being memory, the past being time, the past being experience. To express all that experience, all that memory, you need words to communicate. So word, memory, experience, time, is mind, which is, essentially, thinking—thinking based on memory, the memory of pain and pleasure, the memory of a mind that is ambitious, that seeks power, position, prestige, uses others. That is the mind we have. Now you say that I must perceive with that mind, and you ask if I must not be verbally prepared to see what is true.

What do we mean by preparation verbally?—learning new words, learning the significance of conditioning, a definition, a conclusion, learning new authorities instead of old authorities, the tradition? Some kind of verbal preparation is necessary, is it not?—not the conclusions, not a definition, but to know the meaning of words. Otherwise, you and I could not communicate. I want to tell you something; you want to tell me something; I translate what you are saying in terms of my conditioning, of my conclusion, of my tradition; then there is no possibility of communicating, you with me or I with you. But if I am prepared to put away all my conclusions and listen to the words which you are using, then I do not merely stick to the words but go behind and see the whole content beyond; such an insight requires consideration, it needs alertness, watchfulness. So a mind that is merely caught in thought, in words, in memory, can never perceive what is true; it is not still. The mind that is made still through your absurd meditations, compulsions, resistance, is not a still mind; it is a dead mind. But the mind that is really still is astonishingly active, alive, potent—not towards anything in particular. It is only such a mind which is verbally free—free from experience, from knowledge. Such a mind can perceive what is true, such a mind has direct perception which is beyond time.

The mind can only be silent when it has understood the process of time and that requires watchfulness, does it not? Must not such a mind be free, not *from* anything, but be free? We only know freedom from something. A mind that is free from something is not a free mind; such freedom, the freedom from something, is only a reaction, and it is not freedom. A mind that is seeking freedom is never free. But the mind is free when it understands the fact, as it is, without translating, without condemning, without judging; and being free, such a mind is an innocent mind, though it lived 100 days, 100 years, having all the experiences. It is innocent because it is free, not from anything, but in itself. It is only such a mind that can perceive that which is true, which is beyond time.

Questioner: What is meant by the love of God which is advocated by many books and teachers?

Krishnamurti: I wonder what would happen if you had no books, no teachers. Would you be ignorant? Is there freedom from ignorance if you have the capacity to quote, to compare? Surely, mind which is thought ceases to function when it is caught in a conclusion, it is not active when it is held in a definition.

You want to know what the love of God is, as advocated by books and teachers. Now, suppose you do not have any advocate, would you want to know what love is?—not the love of God because, for us, love of God is the hate of man. Sir, you laugh. But that is a fact. If you really love God and love man, you would not have all these absurd religions, all the innumerable rituals, temples. That is not love of God. Because you do not know what love is, you worship God. You put flowers, you sacrifice, you worship an engraved image, made by the hand or by the mind, and you call that love of God. That is not love, that is fear. Praying for success in this world and the world next is a sign of mediocrity. But the love of God is the love of man; the beginning is the love of man; because we do not know that, we turn to some mysterious thing called God and try to find out what that love is. You will never find it because you do not love your neighbor, you do not know what love is, you do not love your children. Surely love must begin nearer and not far, and the difficulty with most of us is that we are too intellectual, too verbal, too conditioned in our thinking, which we call intellectual.

We have cultivated the brain; we have never thought of the heart; we have filled our minds with words, and we try to fill our heart with the word of love. So, surely, to understand what love is—which is not merely the love of man to man or woman or child, but beyond all this—we must begin with that which is near, must we not? If I do not understand myself, my mind, how can I understand that which is far more complex, more extraordinary, more mysterious? We seek the mysterious and give it all kinds of significance. If we can understand the mystery of ourselves, then we will find that it leads to one of the most astonishing mysteries in life, to the greatest mystery which is God, which is truth. But that truth, that God, is not of the mind. It comes into being when I understand myself, when there is no hate, when there is no fear. It is only when there is the cessation of hate, and not the transformation of hate into love, that there is a possibility of the mind being free from hate and fear; then only it is possible to know what that love is which is not merely sensual love of the senses. But that action implies self-knowledge and meditation.

Meditation of the heart is the beginning of wisdom. But to meditate, one requires essentially to understand the meditator—which is you, the thinker. Therefore it is essential to have self-knowledge, to know yourself in all your talks, in all your motives, in all your words, in your relationship, to know what you are from moment to moment. That is meditation, that is the beginning of meditation. Without that, do what you will—concentrate, go beyond, do all kinds of tricks—they are not meditation, they are escapes from reality, they lead to illusion. So, the beginning of meditation is self-knowledge, which is wisdom.

December 20, 1953

Seventh Talk in Madras

I think most of us must be very concerned in a world that is divided between the Catholics and the communists, the capitalists and the socialists, a world divided as Orient or Occident. In a divided world like this, the grave concern for those who are thoughtful must be "What to do and what is the right action?" It is not so much what to do but how to think about the whole problem.

It seems to me important to inquire into what to do because that question "What to do?" obviously springs from the desire to follow a certain course of action. The implication of what to do is, is it not, "Tell me the way, show me the way to act in a confused world of this kind where the Christian, the Hindu, the Buddhist, the Muslim, the communist, each has an idea, an ideology, utopia, belief, a dogma." Each one of us belongs to one or the other of these. We think that if we follow our particular system, we can shape the world, bring about clarity, a sense of well-being, individually as well as collectively. So, the following of a particular system, the action that springs from that system is what most of us are concerned with. So we ask, "What has an individual to do?" Now, is that the problem: What to do? Please have patience and let us think out this problem together because what I may suggest may be entirely different, and if you do not follow sufficiently, attentively, closely, you might miss it, and you will ask questions that will be irrelevant to the point.

Instead of thinking "What to do?" must there not first be the feeling of 'ourness', "It is our world, not the Christian, not the Hindu, Buddhist, or the communist, but it is our world, yours and mine"? You follow? We have not that feeling. We are Hindus and we want the Hindu world, or we are Muslims and want the Muslim world, or the communists the communist world, or the Christian the Christian world—each desiring to make a world according to his *ism*. But no one thinks of it as "It is our world, something that you and I can build together, and that it is your responsibility as well as mine to build it." The feeling "it is ours" is as you would have when you enter your house—a feeling of care, of love of the earth and the things thereof, the extraordinary feeling that you have when something belongs to you and you nourish it, you care for it, you want to protect it, guide it, help it. You have none of these feelings. You have only ideas, systems, philosophies, and according to those, you want the world to live, to be, to exist. You have not the feeling that it is our world, that you and I are building it together, not as Christians, or Hindus, or communists, or socialists, but as two human beings.

That is a very complex problem, developing each other's intelligence to meet the problem. All that is totally denied when we say, "What am I to do?" The feeling that it is our world is an extraordinary feeling; it is not a sentimental or emotional feeling but a true feeling, a feeling that you have about a tree that is in your garden, a pet, a dog, a cat, a human being. When you consider something as yours, think of the extraordinary care you bestow on it! Without cultivating that extraordinary feeling that it is ours—our world, our earth, our rice field, mango tree, the richness of the earth—we turn to ideas, systems, and thereby hope to build a different world. What is important nowadays is not the technological issue of how to run the world; that is very simple because we have got all the machinery, all the science, the information, the know-how of what to do with things. But as long as the world is divided—Christian, Hindu, communist, socialist, the Orient, the Occident—we shall never solve this problem. So it seems to me that the most important thing is not what to do but to bring about this feeling that it is our world, our earth, our garden. From that extraordinary, vital feeling we can discuss what to do; then I do not think that question, "What to do?" will ever arise.

So I would like this evening to discuss the problem, "What is it that prevents this extraordinarily rich feeling, rich mind, this rich freedom, the abundancy of it when we feel it is our world?" There is only one culture; the forms may vary, the expressions may vary, but there is only one feeling which creates the thing though it may be expressed in different ways, Orient or Occident. But without the feeling, that astonishing sense of this world as yours and mine to build together, we shall not succeed in creating a different world in which, though there may be inequality, the psychological distinction of status is gone. That is what I want to discuss, if we can, this evening.

The problem is this: What is it that prevents this rich feeling that this world is ours, that it is happy to live in a world which is so abundant, on earth that is so productive and that does not belong to some greedy, avaricious capitalists or lawyers or is not under the power of some commissars? What is it that prevents this thing? That is what we ought to go into and see if we cannot, not temporarily, but radically, cut away that impediment.

One of the most difficult things in all our culture, either of the Orient or of the Occident, is the psychological attitude towards life. We are all followers. We follow, and therefore, we create a world of hierarchy. Though you are all followers of various forms of hierarchy, please listen to what I am saying. Do not just brush it aside and say, "It is one of his pet aversions, pet complexes, conditioning." We are not discussing inequality, because the world is unequal, not equal. You have more brains than I have. You are totally different from me in many ways. You have gifts which I have not. You appreciate beauty, music, and the things of refinement, and I do not. Below me, there are still people unequal and who have no such gifts, capacity, intelligence as I have. So there is inequality; it is a fact which you and I must accept and not brush aside. You may develop your capacity to an astonishing extent; I may have very little, and I do not know what to do with it. It is no good trying to bring about equality in that, but we can approach the inequality quite differently. Inequality ceases when there is no comparison, when I do not compare myself with you or with another.

We have to accept the inequality as a fact, but it is much more important to break down the hierarchical attitude towards life—the high and the low, the Master, the guru, the worship of authority, either of Shankara or any one of the leaders—to cut down this sense of acceptance, following. Following is all we know, is it not?— "Tell me what to do and I will try to do it." You have innumerable examples of saints, saviors; and you imitate them, try to follow them. In the very attitude of following, you have set up authority. This hierarchical attitude towards life, this authoritarian justification, evaluation, is one of the most fundamental causes of all division in this world, and until we really tackle that problem, not accept it, but understand it, see the significance of it, go into it profoundly in ourselves, psychologically, inwardly, we shall not be the creators of a new world. This world will not be our world, yours and mine; it will be somebody else's world according to somebody else's ideas, systems. What we are talking about is of radical revolution and not mere substitution of authority.

So, as long as there is authority, the psychological authority of superior and inferior, the one who knows and the one who does not know, the one who does not know follows the other in order to be safe, to be secure. That is why we follow. All our systems of authority are based upon following psychologically, spiritually, and inwardly. I am talking not of an engineer who knows how to build; he is merely an engineer and I treat him as an engineer, as a function; psychologically, I do not follow him. But the moment I create the psychological, inward, authoritarian value, build a hierarchy of ideas, of people, we shall not create a new world; it will be a most destructive world, as before, with wars and divisions; it will not be our world—yours and mine. So it is your problem, our problem, to discuss this, to find out the truth of it and break it down entirely, totally, in ourselves and to eradicate it. Why do we follow a guru, a Master, one who is going to lead us to truth? We follow for the obvious reason that he will help us to get through—getting through is the method—and that which he will give or point out and to which he will guide is safety, happiness, security, and certainty. That is all we are concerned with. We call that certainty, that happiness, that goal as God, truth, or some other name. But in essence, fundamentally, what we want is the sense of being secure psychologically, inwardly certain; and wanting that, we follow. So we create authoritarian values, the Master, the disciple; and we believe we are gradually achieving Masterhood. But behind the desire, the urge, is this immense craving for certainty. It is a psychological fact that when you follow, you seek certainty, success, like when you follow your boss in a factory or in a school. You know very well why you are doing it. You may totally disagree with him, but you want to be economically or psychologically secure. So the following creates a hierarchy in our thinking—socially, mentally, and emotionally. We create it. Watch the way you talk to your servants and the way you approach your boss, spiritual or otherwise, with clasped hands or garlands. But with the servant you have a special language, with a kick. You talk of brotherhood. It is all phony because you psychologically want to be sure that you will come ultimately to be a master, to have reached the level which the others have not, in which you are well-entrenched, certain, assured. So you create a world of authority. All religions are based on that, are they not? All societies which preach brotherhood follow Masters. They are essentially authoritarian.

Now, those who are concerned have this problem—not how to live without authority but why does the mind create an authority, and can the mind drop authority? Please follow this a little bit closely. I follow authority. My guru, my law, whatever it is, is my authority. I have the hierarchical outlook: "You are nearer the Master; I am going to follow you, the priest, the bishop" who has not only economic division but also spiritual division. I see the whole absurdity of authority and that to follow authority is not spiritual; I see it is gross, material, materialistic, though clothed under the spiritual words of *brotherhood, love,* and all that nonsense. I want to break away from it; I break away from it when I see the impossibility of intelligence working while following authority, so I drop following authority. Then, through action, I want to prove to myself that I have dropped it; I leave the society, or I say to myself that I must not follow anybody, that I must not follow any spiritual leader, though economically I may have to follow someone a little bit painfully; there are going to be no more spiritual leaders for me because it is all nonsense. It is very important to understand this.

To follow another—a guru, a tradition, an ideal—is the most destructive thing you can possibly do because you are then destroying, by comparing, your own intelligence, your own freedom, and the discovery of what is real. When you compare yourself with another, you want to become like him, to have power, position, prestige, patronage like him. You have this constant urge to become better and better, in which there is no end. So, you really do not understand what you are. Ideals also create hierarchy—the one who is nearer and the other who is not nearer. So if I am at all serious, if I am at all earnest in my endeavor, I understand this whole process of living. I drop the following of another. But, I want to prove to myself that I have dropped. That is what we are concerned with. I follow, then I drop following; then I want to be sure that I have dropped following—my action is going to show it, I will no longer do rituals because that is tradition, that is based on hierarchy, imitation. The very process of authoritarian judgment, of valuation, is imitation, copying, comparing. To prove to myself that I have dropped the authoritarian evaluation, I am going to find out through action if I have dropped it or not; I am going to give up rituals, I am going to give up Masters, to drop being a member of a particular sect of society because, through action, I am going to prove to myself that I have dropped it. That is it. You follow? To me, action is proof that I am sincere in what I believe, is it not?

I believe hierarchy to be the most stupid way of acceptance, of hierarchical judgment, values, following; and I wish to prove it to myself, and I think that I must do certain things, and I do those things—which shows that I am an honest person in my thought, in my outlook because I have shown it through my action. I may have lost my job because of this, but I feel I am very honest because I am following what I think to be true. But if you go behind that action through which you want to see whether you have dropped the hierarchical principle or not, you will find that, through action, you are seeking certainty, that you are doing the right thing. You understand? I followed in order to be certain, in order to be assured that I was doing the right thing, not making a mess of my life. That is why I follow another. Now I see the absurdity of it and drop following, but through action, I want to be assured that I am doing the right thing by not following. So I have not changed at all. Only I have changed my coat. I used to follow but I do not follow now, yet the inner 'me' is still the same because I want to be sure that I will thrive in not following. Therefore, though I have discarded authority, I have created another form of authority. So what we are concerned with is the action that proves that I am honest, and the honesty is the sign of certainty. You see how the mind deceives itself.

I have followed, I have given up certain things which the spiritual bosses demanded, I have dropped following. Now, I want to prove to myself that I am not following by doing certain things—behind which is the fact that I still want to be sure of the sense that I am doing the right thing. You understand, sirs, what I am talking about? You have followed, and you see that the very nature of following is criminal, unspiritual, disintegrating and will lead you to nowhere. So you say to yourself, "I had better listen to that man; he has reputation, etc., so I had better be quite sure that I drop that, and through action, prove to myself that I am not following." So you are concerned with action that will show that you are honest, and being honest is to be certain. You understand?

You follow to be certain, you give up to be certain. So you have not changed at all. You have played a trick. The mind has played a trick upon you. The mind creates illusion when it seeks to be certain. But it is only a radical revolution of the mind which is going to create a new world and not an illusion.

You have followed, you have created illusion, a hierarchy. If you follow another, you cannot like to be yourself. If you follow another, there is no self-knowledge. If you follow another, however noble, wise, you will not know the workings of your own mind, and without knowing, without self-knowledge, there is no wisdom. So, if there is a desire to be certain, the mind creates an illusion. Now what we are concerned with is the power to create illusion from which there is action. If there is to be a fundamental, deep revolution, this power of creating illusion must stop, which means really that the desire to be certain—the psychological demand for safety, for assurance, for encouragement—must come to an end.

So, if you say that you are following and then dropping it, and through that your mind is still craving to be certain, what are you to do? It is the mind that wants to prove to itself, through action, that it is doing the right thing. That is all we know, is it not? That is all our life. Action will prove that I am honest, that I am respectful, that I am this. But the proof of your action is born of this illusion, the escape of the mind which wants to be certain.

If you have followed so far, the next thing that is important is not to prove to yourself that you have dropped the ugly, authoritarian evaluation or to find out whether you are following but to find out if you have radically cut at the root of the problem—which is that the mind, as long as it follows its own ideals, its own demands to be certain, its own cravings, will create illusion, and the cutting away of the power to create this illusion is what we are concerned with. You might say, "What has all this long, complicated talk to do with action? I want to know what to do and you tell me all this rigmarole." But without this rigmarole, your action will lead to mess, confusion, as it is doing now. So, what is important is to see the fallacy of following and to cut it, to drop following, and not to want to prove to yourself through action that you are not following. When we want action to convince us, we want action to spring from the known; we have no action springing from the unknown. It is the action that is springing from the unknown that is the liberating, creative action, not the action that is born from the known saying, "I have given up, and I am going to show that to myself." You can be sincere and yet be caught in illusion. You can prove to yourself that you are doing the right thing, but the doing of the right thing will be the outcome of an illusion.

So action born from freedom, freedom from all authority, is creative. We can build together, and then you and I can say we have no spiritual authority, and we can build this world which is yours and mine. You are not my spiritual leader. You may know a little about mathematics, build houses, bridges, by stresses and strains, but you are not my authority spiritually, I am not following you. Therefore, you and I are discovering together how to build this world because it is our world. It is only the mind that is free from all authority that can do this. Because we have been wrongly educated, because we have been conditioned so heavily in authority, we think that freedom will come at the end. So what is important is to understand the process of the mind—the ways of its thought, how it creates illusions, but not what are illusions—and to understand that there is the creation of illusion as long as the mind wants certainty. This certainty creates the follower and the leader; and the moment you have that relationship of the follower and a leader, you will create a world in which there will be no sense of yours and mine, of our world. There will not be that feeling. There will be the commissars, warmongers, the capitalists, exploiters—spiritual or otherwise. If you want to understand all this process, you have to go into this problem of action.

Perhaps you will ask questions from this talk. If not, I have got some questions written down.

Questioner: A vast number of people are inclined to think that another is more intelligent than themselves, and therefore they follow.

KRISHNAMURTI: Sirs, what is intelligence? Does intelligence consist in comparison? If you follow this for a minute, you will see. When a teacher in a school compares one boy with another, is he making him intelligent by comparison, or is he destroying him by comparing him with the cleverer boy? You understand, sirs? Are you not destroying by comparing one boy with another boy, one human being with another human being? When you compare yourself with another, the master with the disciple, by all these ugly horrors, are you not destroying yourself? Is that destruction intelligence? So, what is intelligence? Intelligence is that state when you are not comparing. In understanding what you are, you do not really compare yourself with somebody else. But in a school imparting the so-called education in which all of us have been brought up and in which we have all been conditioned, we are always comparing. Therefore we are destroying that thing by the way we talk. When you compare your sons—the elder with the younger—and you want the younger to work, to imitate, to copy, to struggle, to push up, to be as good as the elder, it means really that the younger is not important at all; you have an idea what the elder is, and you are pushing the younger into that. You call that education, you call that intelligence!

So to have this radical revolution, there must be no comparison. Surely, we are human beings, sirs. You are as good as I am. We are human beings, suffering, struggling, and understanding. You are not my Master, I am not your follower. To create a new world we must think of all this totally differently. I can only think totally differently when I do not compare. I am what I am. I want to understand what I am. I may be the greatest idiot; I want to understand what I am because out of this idiocy something marvelous would come, but if I smothered it, I remain an idiot for the rest of my life.

So, sirs, if there is to be radical revolution there must be radical thinking, and thinking does not come by mere action. Action is not the proof of the integrity of thought. The integrity comes when you understand what you are, whatever you are. You cannot understand what you are if you are comparing, judging, beating about. To look at things as they are is the greatest thing, and therefore a free mind will not create any illusion.

Questioner: Is not the idea of one world a utopia?

KRISHNAMURTI: I did not say anything about one world. I talked of the world that is ours. That is not utopia. You can make it into a utopia, an ideal which you are practicing, all the nonsense which are escapes from the actual fact that it is our world. You and I are living in the world, but we do not know how to live in it together. I say it is only possible to make that world ours when we have not a leader and a follower.

Questioner: If we give up authority, what is it we are living for? In giving up authority, is there another form of security?

KRISHNAMURTI: That is just what I have been talking about all this evening. A mind that follows security and the demand for security creates hierarchy in the authority, which is the poison of our present society. That is very clear. It is not giving up that matters but the desire to be certain. I want to be certain that I am living rightly according to the Bhagavad-Gita, according to the Master, according to Stalin, according to somebody else. I want to live rightly and so I ask you, ask the Masters behind the hills, ask the gurus round the corner. So the moment I want to be certain, secure, I have created an authority, and that is the greatest illusion which the mind can create because it destroys freedom and therefore creativeness.

Sirs, how many of you are really free from imitation? You all know the Bhagavad-Gita by heart. You do not know anything about yourself, or if you know about yourself, it is from Shankara. Sirs, you live and you all aspire to a noble life—which is, copying, imitating, and repeating; and that is what you call a noble life. But you never discover for yourself what you are, you never discover truth. You may say you are a great soul, atma, as stated by Shankara or Buddha—that is all nonsense because that is repetition that is false. Even though Shankara or Buddha said it, you have to find the truth through everyday discovery, from moment to moment.

Questioner: What is spontaneous action?

KRISHNAMURTI: This is not the moment for that. We are discussing this spontaneous mind in which there is no authority, in which there is no sense of security. I will not answer that question now.

Questioner: If everybody thinks of his individual liberty, then where is the question of feeling 'ourness'?

KRISHNAMURTI: Are you individually free? You are conditioned, you are not a free individual. But to understand your conditioning, to understand it fully, requires a great deal of work, does it not? Freedom is not a thing that you can easily buy. You do not know what it means. When you talk of freedom, you think you must be free according to me or according to the pattern or according to the idea. All that is not freedom. Freedom means something entirely different. It means being free in itself. There is such a state of being free in itself and not from something. That is what I have been talking about, being free, not free of authority, of the hierarchy; because, you have cut at the root of authority, and that is going to produce action. The cutting is going to produce action, and there is not the action that is going to prove that you have cut it. If you really understand what you are, then you will not want prestige, power, position, and patronage; you will not think of your individual liberty; you are free.

Questioner: May we know if you yourself have experienced that state of freedom?

KRISHNAMURTI: Sirs, why do you want to know? Please do listen. Do not laugh. I am not giving a clever, smart answer. You see how the mind works very cleverly. This is a meeting in which no discussion is possible. Discussions are over. Tomorrow will be the last day of the talks. The gentleman wants to know if I have experienced directly that freedom. Please see the importance of that question and the implications of that question. Is it setting up of authority when I say, "Find out for yourself"? When I say there is, is that setting up of authority? If you followed it, it would be authority. But I am cutting at the very root of authority by saying, "Find out for yourself. Do not follow another." Why do we ask such questions?

The gentleman says that you should not follow what I say. What have I said that you should follow? I have pointed out to you, if you have followed the talk, the workings of your minds, the operations of deception, how the mind thinks it has given up when it actually has not given up, how the mind creates illusion. I have not told you what to do. Therefore you are not following. I am showing the ways of your own mind. I have several times said to you to follow nobody, including myself. To follow anybody, including myself, is the most destructive, deteriorating factor in life. But do not misapply.

It is very interesting to find why this gentleman said, "We are not going to follow," and why the other asked, "Do you know that freedom?"

Questioner: The gentleman who says, "Give up authority," clings to authority.

Krishnamurti: I am afraid you have not followed at all what I have been talking about. I said to you at the beginning of the talk that the mind creates authority and accepts it or rejects it, and the very rejecting of it and the seeking of proof is another form of authority. There is only one process, one way of looking at it, the dropping of it but not being convinced that you have dropped it. I went into the problem of how the mind works, and this really demands attention. It is really a process of meditation, not the attention of enforced thought, but the attention that comes when you are really interested in something which is of vital importance.

This question is a vitally important question because it is confronting the whole world, the commissar and the worker, the Pope and the layman. The whole problem is there. Do not brush it aside. That is what we are tackling, and to understand it you must follow it. There must be meditation. This is very important, not to be accepted or rejected, but which requires extraordinary insight, and that insight can only come when you understand the working of your mind, why the mind creates authority and accepts it or rejects it, and how the very rejecting of it is another form of authority. That is what we have been discussing. It is very important to see this thing as a whole and not because you belong to some society or because you have some power over somebody else. It is a complex problem that necessitates your thinking very deeply about it, and you cannot think deeply if you are attached to any authority.

December 26, 1953

Eighth Talk in Madras

For the last four weeks we have been discussing what, I think, is a very important problem, which is, the way of total revolution—not the method, not the system, not how to bring it about, but the necessity of such a state. There is a vast difference between the two: the method or how to bring about such total revolution in oneself, and seeing the importance and the necessity of total revolution. The way, the system, the method, will not bring it about because the method implies practice, repetition, routine, thereby bringing about a mediocre mind. But if one can see that it is essential to have total revolution in oneself—not at any one particular level of our consciousness, not the economic or social or environmental, but a total psychological revolution—if one can see the importance of it, the necessity of it, the urgency of it, then it will not be a conscious revolution but an unconscious, involuntary revolution. That is what we have been discussing through different angles, from different points of view.

I would like this evening, if I can, to discuss how is it possible to bring about a fresh mind, a new mind, a mind that is not condemned by the past, a mind that is not merely the outcome of a time process—how to bring about, how to have a mind unburdened, a mind totally innocent. That is necessary because all the leaders—economic, social, religious—have totally failed; because, we still have wars, appalling miseries in the world, starvation, social divisions, growing unemployment, overpopulation, and so on. Each of us who is at all serious has tried to solve these problems according to his knowledge, according to his experience, according to his system, according to the communist, socialist, capitalist, Catholic, or Hindu ideal; and we have not solved them. The problem is not that we have not fully, completely, practiced the ideals of Hinduism or Catholicism or capitalism or communism intelligently or continuously. Because, the ideals and the practicing of ideals make the mind incapable of meeting the fresh challenge, and the practicing is only a constant repetition, the dulling of the mind, making the mind mediocre, small, petty, and bringing about the pursuit of the ideal. So what matters is not the ideal nor a better system, nor the search for a better system, a better philosophy, a better leader; the very following of authority is destructive, is disintegrating.

Is it not necessary to have a fresh mind, not an open mind, but a totally new mind to meet all these problems? Is it possible? I do not know if you have asked this question of yourselves. We have always asked how to meet the problem, what methods we should adopt, what ideals we should practice, the way, but we never said to ourselves that we must have a new mind, a totally innocent mind that can meet the problems, a fresh mind uncluttered, a mind that can see the problem without any bias. So when we inquire into that, should we not go into that question of what is experience because it is the experience that is dulling the mind? That is, does experience, as we know it, help to meet this extraordinarily complex problem of living? If I may suggest, it is important to know how to listen. You are listening obviously from experience; you have conclusions, you have had innumerable experiences, various trials, sorrows, afflictions, and with that background you are listening, you are listening with a conclusion. Is that listening at all? If I listen to what you are saying—which may perhaps be new, different—with a mind already entrenched in a particular ideology, in a particular experience, in a specific knowledge, can such a mind listen? That may be one of our difficulties because I feel that if we can listen rightly, we shall be able to break down the whole process of the mind that is entrenched in a particular point of view. So there is an art of listening, and I think it is very important, especially when we are dealing with the problems that confront each one of us.

Various leaders—economic, social, spiritual, and so on—have not solved our problems, and no leader will ever solve our problems—no guru, no Master—because the problems are created by each one of us. The only person that could solve the problem is none other than each one of us, as there are no leaders any more. It may be that each one of us will become a leader to himself, and to bring about the leadership in oneself or to oneself as understanding, liberation, I think it is very important to inquire into this whole question of experience—that is, what our mind is. The mind is the result of experience not only of these few years but the experience of centuries of man, man throughout the world, not just here. There is this process of experience going on all the time. After all, life is experience, living is experience; there is the impact of life all the time going on whether you are conscious or unconscious of it. When you walk down the street, when you meet a person, when you read, listen to music, when you see the stars, the shades of the evening, when you talk, when you cry, when there is the anguish to find out—all that implies, does it not, experience, the impact of various reactions of the mind to those impacts. That is experience, and the experience is the outcome of our conditioning, is it not? That is fairly simple. I experience according to my background. The background is either the conscious or the unconscious, the residue of all thoughts, of all experiences, of all knowledge. After all, that is my mind, that is your mind. It is the storehouse of experience and that experience does not react to any new stimuli, any new challenge, but translates the new challenge, the new demand, according to its conditioning, according to its background. So, the new challenge, the new demand, the new problem only strengthens the background; it does not liberate the background. I think that is fairly clear, is it not?

There is a challenge, there is a problem. I, who am a communist or some kind of "ist" or belonging to something, meet that problem according to my conditioning, the way I have thought, the way I have lived, the way I have been educated. So instead of the problem or the challenge liberating my mind, I translate the problem, the challenge, according to my education, according to my conditioning, according to my ideology, according to my belief, dogma. So, in the process of translation, my background, my conditioning is strengthened. It is not weakened. So, my mind is all the time gathering, strengthening in its own conditioning, in its own background, in its own limitation, in its own pettiness, narrowness, and in its own beliefs, and there is never liberation from experience. I think it is very important to understand this because we generally say, "Life will teach us." The more experience you have, the more you think you are wise; the more you read, the more you search, the more you inquire, practice, the more you think you are achieving.

If you really go much deeper and look at it, you will find there is always this entity that is accumulating, that is gathering. This entity is already conditioned, and so it is always translating, living, using every experience, every new challenge, every new problem in terms of the old, and therefore strengthening itself-so strengthening is the process of time. After all, that is what we mean by time, is it not, not the time by the clock, but the time process of thought—I was, I am, and I shall be. That is the whole psychological process of time, and in that time we are gathering experience, and our mind is the experience. Now, with that mind we approach all life's problems. I hope I am making myself clear. Because that is the only mind you and I have, not a higher mind or a lower mind. Because, the higher mind is still a thought process. The higher mind has been invented by thought, and thought is the result of time, experience; and therefore the higher self is still within the field of the mind. Therefore, it is incapable of meeting the problem. Though you may look to it, pray for it, long for it, the higher self, the thing that you are looking to as the higher entity is still within the field of time, which is the process of thought. When you look at the self, the mind, to solve the problem, you are still creating illusion of time and there is no solution. So if that is clear, if you are really paying attention, you will see that all experience only conditions the thought process.

So, can a mind which is experiencing, which is caught in experience, a mind which is bound, held in tradition, in knowledge, can such a mind be a fresh mind? Obviously not. Is it possible, not how is it possible, to have a fresh, uncontaminated, and innocent mind and yet have experience? You cannot live without experience; living is the process of experiencing; without experience life is not possible; there is experience or death. Is it possible to have a fresh mind though it is experiencing? Please follow. This is an important question because the revolution of which I have been talking implies that, and implies having a mind which, though it is experiencing, is not contaminated by experience and therefore is capable of meeting the problem afresh.

Am I talking Greek? I feel there is no contact of what I am saying with what you are thinking.

Look, sirs, we have problems at different levels of our existence—not the problem of bread and butter or the problem of war. There is this whole problem of living—inequality, brutality, death, war, sorrow, hatred, acquisitiveness, the sense of antagonism. There is this whole existence implying all that. Now, we have always to approach this problem of living with a conditioned mind—as a Hindu, as a Theosophist, as a Catholic, as a Buddhist, as a communist, and so on. So we are translating the problem according to our conditioning, and we are acting according to that translation; such action only strengthens our conditioning, and therefore there is no liberation. So, should not one ask oneself whether it is possible to have an uncontaminated mind, a fresh mind, a mind which is innocent, though it is living with its innumerable experiences?

What makes the mind contaminated? That is the problem. What makes the mind dull, stupid, routine, bound to routine, bound to habit, tradition? What makes the mind decay, grow old? If the mind can remain fresh, not decaying, not deteriorating, then experience cannot contaminate it, though we have to live, though there is experience.

What is the thing or the way or the process that makes the mind corrupt? Let us think out this problem together. Do not listen to me to tell you what it is. If you are waiting in the hope that I will discuss it presently, if you are waiting merely for me to tell you, you become a mere automaton waiting to be told what to do. That is the very state of mind which is the deteriorating factor—to be told what to do, what to think. Our education is, is it not, "What to do and what to think." All our religions tell us what to do and what to think. But there is not the release, the creative power of inquiry. So, please do not wait for me to tell you. Let us find out together.

What is this thing that makes the mind dull, that makes the mind all-deteriorating? One of the major factors is effort—this constant struggle to become, the struggle to do the right thing, to be successful, the struggle to understand, the struggle and the practicing of virtue, the following of an idea or ideal. Because of this everlasting struggle of the mind, the mind has never a moment of tranquillity or rest. You watch your own mind; it is never, even for a moment, quiet, quiet by itself. A mind that is enforced or disciplined to be quiet is a dead mind. There is this constant struggle of the lawyer trying to become a judge, and the clerk trying to become the boss, the pupil trying to become the master; there is this constant struggle to become, and there is never a moment of being. Such a mind, both conscious and unconscious, is like a machine that is running all the time ceaselessly. The consciousness is everlastingly in movement, everlastingly pushing, pushing, struggling, and struggling to acquire, struggling to change, struggling to understand, struggling to fulfill, and when not fulfilling, feeling thwarted, agonized, held, finding resistance, hindrance, blockages, and having ambitions, successes. That is our life. How can the mind that is everlastingly struggling be a fresh mind? The problem is not how such a mind can become a fresh mind; such a mind can never become a fresh mind. But if such a mind ceases its activity of everlasting struggle to be, then there is a possibility of the conditioned state ceasing and the mind being a fresh mind.

After all, the thing that we call the 'me', the 'I', is the entity that is gathering experience. Is that the entity that is everlastingly struggling? Please follow this, sirs. If you really listen, you will see an extraordinary thing that will take place in front of truth; there is a disintegration of the 'I', and therefore there is the possibility of a fresh mind, a mind that is really experiencing what is true, and therefore the mind itself is the truth.

What is, after all, the 'I', the 'me'? That is the center of the struggle, that is the center of ambition, this everlasting becoming—I was, I am, and I shall be—and that is the center, that is the deteriorating factor that makes the mind corrupt, that makes the mind dull, heavy, stupid, mediocre. Just see the fact that the struggle is the central factor of deterioration, the struggle of the 'me' becoming something, and therefore never a moment of real tranquillity, real stillness of the mind. A still mind can experience and yet be uncontaminated. But a mind that is acquiring, pushing, struggling, gathering, in itself experiencing—such a mind is a deteriorating factor. Simply see the thing as it is—not as I am describing, but actually what is taking place in your own mind.

We have had discussions for the last four weeks, every morning at 7:30 AM. But this is not a meeting of that kind. We are together here trying to inquire into the process of the mind. There are innumerable problems still, which I have not touched. But if one can understand the major root, the major factor that is destroying our minds, that is corrupting our minds, that is making our minds dull, mediocre, then one will see that it is only the still mind, the mind that is not becoming, the mind which is still, that can experience without gathering. The factor of gathering anything is deteriorating; it is that factor of gathering, accumulating, that must be understood, that must be seen, and not how to put away that factor. The moment you understand that accumulation, gathering, is the destructive factor, the mind will cease to gather; really the mind then is capable of being still and experiencing, but the experiencing is no longer the gathering process of memory which will be used for further experiencing.

A mind that is understanding, that sees the truth of becoming, of being, that sees the truth of gathering—such a mind is a still mind, and a still mind can experience without corrupting itself. Then the still mind can know, go deeper into the extraordinary state which no conscious mind or disciplined mind or a mind that is gathering can ever touch. Truth or God is not to be gathered—it is only from moment to moment. A mind that is continually becoming, that only knows the continuity of becoming, can never know the truth.

I think instead of your asking me questions as you did yesterday about the things I have talked about just now, it may be better that I answer these questions that have been given to me. But really I am not answering them, as there is no answer.

Questioner: What is a tender mind?

KRISHNAMURTI: Sirs, as I said, I am not answering questions from the audience this evening. I am only answering questions that have been given to me written down. As I was saying, I am not answering questions because there is no answer and there are only problems. You understand? Sirs, there are only problems and no answers. If I can understand the problem completely, totally, understand the inward nature of the problem, I need not seek the answer. It is easy to ask questions, but it is extremely difficult to uncover the problem and to go to the root of the problem, to understand it. So I am not answering. What we are doing is exploring the problem together, and in the exploration of that problem, you will see the truth of the problem, and the truth of the problem will free the mind from the problem. But if you wait for an answer, like a schoolboy, then you will miss what we have been talking about.

Questioner: I have listened to you for a long time. My mind has grown dull, weary, with endless repetition of a few basic statements. Is there any hope of my liberation?

KRISHNAMURTI: The questioner says that he has listened for a long time, his mind has become dull, weary by the few basic statements made by me. The problem is, has he listened at all? Please do listen, sirs. This is not a matter of laughter. This is not a political meeting, or a meeting of amusement or entertainment, and after 20 or 40 minutes you need distraction, and therefore you laugh.

The problem is, has he listened? If he has listened for a lifetime, naturally he has grown weary because he has been listening, has he not, according to his background, according to his fixations, his formulations, his experiences. He is not listening. That is why, sirs, to listen properly is an astonishing thing. If I know how to listen to one truth, one thing that is truth, that one thing is going to be the liberating factor. A mind becomes dull through routine and is so eager to gather, to accumulate. You have to just listen sweetly without any argumentation. When in front of a magnificent scenery, in front of a lovely thing, if your mind is chattering or comparing itself with another, do you ever see the magnificent thing? Because your mind is occupied with comparison, you do not see. So, if you can just listen without comparing, that very listening will tell you whether the thing that is being spoken is true or false. The truth of that will bring to the mind a freedom from innumerable burdens, effortlessly. You are not listening; your mind is either already dull or already gone away somewhere else.

Sirs, it is a great art just to listen not only to another but to oneself, to all the promptings, to all the unconscious demands, motives, pursuits, desires, and to be aware of them choicelessly. That very awareness without choice will show you the truth of that motive, and the truth of this is the creative factor, the liberating factor.

Questioner: Is it not better to have a contented mind than a still mind? In that case, do not the problems themselves cease to exist?

KRISHNAMURTI: What is the problem, to have a contented mind or a still mind? Is it not a problem that your mind is not contented, is not still, is disturbed, is confused? Being confused, you say, "I must have a contented mind or a still mind." So you are pursuing again a contented mind or gathering or saying, "How is my mind to be still?" Sirs, contentment is something which comes into being when I understand *what* is. What is important is not to have a contented mind but to understand the things as they are, not as you like them to be, to understand *what is.* Sirs, look! I am envious, and my mind is struggling not to be envious, and I think that by becoming nonenvious, I shall have a contented mind. But instead of pursuing the ideal which is utterly illusive, which is not existent, if I understood the whole content of envy, that which is in actuality, in reality, the thing as it is—"I am envious"—then with that understanding comes the contentment of the mind. To understand the thing as it is requires an extraordinary awareness in which there is no comparison, no judgment, no condemnation—to look at it as it is, not as you would like it to be, not as something different which you wish it to be. That requires extraordinary insight, and out of that insight the mind becomes quiet, which you may call contentment. A mind that is contented is a shallow mind. It is like the mind of a cow.

A still mind is entirely different from a contented mind. A still mind is acutely active. But that activity is not the activity of getting, conquering, making, gathering, and progressing. That is not active. That is death, decay, deterioration. The mind is still, with the understanding of *what is,* the thing I am and not what I think I am, the thing that I am—envious, jealous, anxious, fearful, struggling, afraid of what my neighbors say, afraid of my uncertainty, afraid of my job. To understand myself as I am requires a choiceless awareness in which there is no condemnation, but watching without any deflection, without any destruction. Seeing the thing as it is brings about the breaking down of a mediocre mind, and it is only that mind that really understands, that is capable of receiving that which is eternal.

Questioner: What we have learned about meditation from our sacred books, from our spiritual leaders, seems to be essentially different from what you term as meditation. Will you kindly go into this.

KRISHNAMURTI: Sirs, let us see what is meditation because this is a very important problem and, if I know how to meditate, then the problem of existence will be understood. Can I learn meditation from another, from the sacred book or from the teacher or from the school which teaches you to meditate? Please listen.

What is the problem involved in meditation? There is only the becomer; there is, in meditation, the thinker with the thought. Please watch your own minds through the description of my words. Do not follow my words but watch your own mind in operation, in listening to what I am saying. The problem of meditation is the meditator. But the meditator has many thoughts. The thoughts and the meditator are pursuing the 'becoming'. That is, I am meditating in order to find God, in order to understand, in order to cultivate virtue, in order to acquire tranquillity, in order to put away something from me, hoping in that state to be in a position where there is only 'being'. So when we inquire into the question of meditation, the problem is the meditator and the 'becoming'. What we know in meditation is the thinker and the thought, is it not? That is all we know—the thinker trying to change his thoughts, trying to push his thoughts higher up, climbing, climbing. The maker of the effort is the thinker, the 'I', molding, shaping, controlling, guiding, aspiring, suppressing thought. That is what you call meditation. You have the image of a Master, a picture of a guru, or some image made by the hand or the mind, and you concentrate. So there is a concentrator with the thing that is concentrated upon. In this, there is a division between the thinker and the thought. Now, is there actually such a division? We have created the division, the thinker and the thought. But is there actually the thinker apart from thought? If you take away thoughts, is there a thinker? Sirs, if you have no thoughts, is there a thinker?

The thoughts have created the thinker because thoughts are transcendent, and so we say the thinker is permanent. So thoughts seeking permanency have created a thinker. Then the thinker dominates thoughts and shapes thoughts in order to reach something else which is obviously not truth. Thoughts have created a thinker, whether the thinker is *paramatma* or a supreme being, whatever it is. Thoughts have created it, and without thoughts there is no thinker. So seeing the truth of that, there is no longer the controlling of thoughts, there is no entity shaping, pushing thoughts into all directions or in one particular direction—there is only thinking. If I say that and if that is understood, there is already a tremendous revolution, is there not, because there is no longer the thinker to actually experience, to actually see the truth of that, namely, that there is no thinker. To see the truth of that is the beginning of meditation. Without seeing that, your merely going to all classes of gurus, all the experiments of going to high and low, are all tricks of the mind. They are not meditation. They will lead nowhere, they are all illusion. Until you have understood this primary thing that the thought creates the thinker and without the thought there is no thinker, and until you experience that—not verbally but really reality will not come into being. Reality comes into being after a great deal of meditation—the meditation being the thinking out, watching, observing, not letting the mind play tricks, seeing the trick which the mind plays and has played upon us for centuries, that the thinker is completely different from thought, something divine, something extraordinary, totally out of time. As long as there is the thinker apart from thought, do what you will, your meditation is an illusion which will lead you to nowhere; it is the most destructive factor.

So meditation is not merely sitting still, controlling your mind. Meditation is something entirely different. Without self-knowledge there is no meditation—self being how the mind works and not the self of Shankara or Buddha—but the self is your mind, and you have to understand how it operates, how it works. Without understanding that, you do not know how to meditate, and all meditation and the labors of discipline are in vain, and they have no meaning. So, when you come to that point when there are only thoughts, then quite a different issue arises. Then what is the significance of thought, what is the significance of thinking? You understand, sirs? Thinking before had a significance because it created the thinker; then the thinker came into being, and he lived, functioned, experienced, acquired, or rejected. But when through self-knowledge—not the reading of books about self-knowledge, but the observation of self-knowledge in your relationship, in your talks, in your looks, smiles, watching everything you know how the self works; there is the beginning of meditation, and as you go into it, you must invariably come to the point when you will see the thinker and the thought are one and not separate. Then when you come to that state, what is the significance of thinking? That is merely a reaction to any response, to any stimuli, and if it is merely the stimulation that makes you think, then the mind is God. When there is no stimulation, when there is no asking, looking, then the mind is still. If there are only thoughts, then you see the significance of thoughts. From there, the mind is still.

The still mind is not a disciplined mind. There is no discipliner, one who controls and says, "I am still." That still mind has no experiencer because the moment there is the experiencer, he is experiencing, gathering; he is different from the experience. Yet, if you observe, all of us want to continue experiencing—"I want to experience truth," "I want to experience God." You will never experience God, never the truth, as long as there is the experiencer who is separate from thought. So there is only thinking—thinking without the thinker. Therefore, the mind is no longer concerned with what to think or with what is right thinking. It is only thinking and seeing the significance of thought. Therefore, there is no continuity of thinking. So the mind is still. That still mind is not experiencing because the experiencer has ceased. There is only the state of being in which there is no experiencer. Therefore, in that silence, in that stillness, the mind is nonrecognizing. I am using all these words, and if you have gone so far, you will immediately know what I am talking about.

The still mind is the creative mind. That which is creative is not of time, it is something beyond time. It is of no nationality, no race, no individuality. It is timeless, it is something eternal. If the mind can perceive that which is eternal in itself, the stillness, then the mind itself is the eternal. But all these will remain as so many words if you do not understand the beginning which is self-knowledge. That self-knowledge is to be found in our daily life from moment to moment, and without that, if you go and sit at the feet of any Master, or any guru, you are just wasting time. Self-knowledge is the beginning of wisdom. That which is creative—the creativeness of God, of truth—does not come into being, cannot come into being, when the mind is seeking. The mind must cease to seek, and then only reality can come into being.

December 27, 1953

India, 1954

First Talk to Students at Rajghat School, Banaras

I suppose most of you understand English, although it does not matter if you do not, as your teachers and your elders understand it. Perhaps you would ask them afterwards to explain what I have been talking about; make a point of asking them, won't you? Because, what we are going to discuss for the next three or four weeks is very important; we are going to discuss what is education and what are its implications, not just passing examinations, but the whole implication of being educated. So, as we are going to talk about that every day, if you do not understand what I am saying now, please ask your teachers to explain it carefully. Also, after I have talked, perhaps you would ask questions. These talks are meant primarily for students, and if the older people want to ask questions, they should only ask questions that will help the students to understand, that will explain further the problem. To ask questions about their own personal problems will not help the students.

Don't you ask yourself why you are being educated? Do you know why you are being educated, and what that education means? As we know, education is to go to school, to learn how to read and write, to pass examinations, and to play a few games; and after you leave school, you go to college, there again to study very, very hard for a few months or a few years, pass an examination and then get a job; and then you forget all about what you have learned. Is that not what we call education? Do you understand what I am talking about? Isn't that what we all do?

If you are girls, you pass a few examinations, B.A. or M.A., marry, and become cooks or something else, and then have children; and all the education that you have had for a number of years is useless. You know how to speak English, you are a little more clever, a little more tidy, a little more clean, that is all, is it not? And the boys get a technical job or become clerks or get some kind of government job, and that finishes it, does it not?

You see, what we call "living" is to get a job, to have children, to raise a family, and to be able to read newspapers or magazines, to discuss, to argue cleverly about something or other. That is what we call education, is it not? Have you noticed your own parents, your own elder people? They have passed examinations, they have got jobs, and they know how to read and write. Is that all that education means to us?

Education is something much more, is it not? It is to help you, not only to get a job in the world, but also to meet the world, is it not? You know what the world is. In the world there is competition. You know what competition means—each man out for himself, struggling to get the best, pushing the others aside. In the world there are wars, there are class divisions and the fight between them. In the world every man is trying to get a better job, to keep on rising; if you are a clerk, you try to get a little higher, and so fight all the time. Have you not noticed it? If you have a car, you want a bigger car. So, there is that constant fight going on, not only within ourselves, but with all our neighbors. then, there is a war which kills, which destroys people, like the last war, when millions were killed, wounded, or maimed.

Our life is all this political struggle. And also, life is religion, is it not? What we call religion is rituals, going to temples, putting on something like the sacred thread, mumbling some words, or following some guru. Life is also, is it not, the fear of dying, fear of living, fear of what people say and do not say, fear of not knowing where one is going, fear of losing a job, fear of opinion. So, life is something extraordinarily complex, is it not? You know what that word complex means? It is very intricate, it is not something simple, which you just follow; it is very, very difficult, a great many things are involved.

So, education is, is it not, to enable you to meet all these problems. You have to be educated so as to meet all these problems rightly. That is what education is—not merely to pass a few examinations in some silly subjects in which you are not at all interested. Proper education is to help the student to meet this life so that he understands it and won't succumb, won't be crushed under it as most of us are. People, ideas, public opinion, country, climate, food—all that is constantly pushing you in a particular direction in which society wants you to go. Your education must enable you to understand this pressure, not to yield to it, but to understand it and to break through it, so that you, as an individual, as a human being, are capable of a great deal of initiative, and not merely traditional thinking. That is real education.

You know that, for most of us, education consists in learning what to think. Your society tells you, your parents tell you, your neighbors tell you, your books tell you, your teachers tell you what to think. The machinery of "what to think" we call education, and that education only makes you mechanical, dull, stupid, uncreative. But if you knew how to think, not what to think, then you would not be mechanical, traditional, but live human beings; you would be great revolutionaries—not in the stupid sense of murdering people to get a better job or to push through a certain idea, but the revolution of knowing how to think rightly. That is very important. But, when we are at school, we never find out about all these things. The teachers themselves do not know. They only teach you how to read or what to read, and correct your English or mathematics. That is all their concern, and at the end of five or ten years, you are pushed out into this life about which you know nothing. Nobody has talked to you about it; or, if they have talked, they push you in certain directions—either to be a socialist, a communist, a congressite or some other—but they never teach you or help you to understand and how to think out all these problems, not just at one moment during a certain number of years, but all the time—which is education, is it not? After all, in a school of this kind that is what we must do, help you not merely to pass some stupid examinations, but to be able to meet life when you go out of this place, so that you are intelligent human beings, not mechanical, not Hindus or Muslims or communists or some such thing.

It is very important how you are educated, how you think. Most of the teachers do not know how to think; they merely get a job and settle down. They have families, they have worries, they have fathers and mothers who say, "You must follow certain rituals, you must do this, you must do that"; they have their own problems, their own difficulties. They leave all those at home, come to school and teach a few lessons, but they do not know how to think, and we do not know how to think. In a school of this kind, surely, it is very important for you, for the teachers, for all of us who are living here, to consider all the problems of life, to discuss, to find out, to investigate, to inquire, so that our minds become so very alert that we do not just follow somebody. You understand what I am talking about? Is not all that education? Education is not just until the age of 21 but until you die. Life is like a river, it is never still, it is always moving, always alive and rich. When we think we have understood a part of a river and hold to that part, it is only dead water, is it not? Because, the river goes by. To watch all the movement of the river, all the things that are happening on the river, to understand, to be faced with it—that is life, and we all have to prepare for it.

So, education really is not merely passing a few examinations but being able to think of all these problems so that your mind is not mechanical, traditional, so that your mind is creative, so that you do not merely fit into society but break it, create anew out of it—not a new thing according to the socialist, the communist, or the congressite, but a completely new thing—which is real revolution. And, after all, that is the meaning of education, is it not, so that you grow in freedom, so that you can create a new world. The old people have not created a beautiful world; they have made a mess of the world. Is it not the function of education, of the educator, to see that you grow in freedom so that you can understand life, so that you can change things and not just grow dull, weary, and die, as most people do?

So I feel, and most of us do feel who are serious about these things, that a place like this should provide an atmosphere in which you are given every opportunity to grow, uninfluenced, unconditioned, untaught, so that when you go out of here you can meet life intelligently, without fear. Otherwise, this place has no value; it will be like any rotten school, perhaps a little better because it happens to be in a beautiful place, people are a little kinder, they do not beat you, though they may coerce you in other ways. We should create a school where the student is not pressed, is not enclosed, is not squeezed by our ideas, by our stupidity, by our fears, so that as he grows, he will understand his own affairs, he will be able to meet life intelligently. You know what all this requires—not only an intelligent student, a student who is alive, but also an educator, the right kind of educator. But the right kind of educators and the right kind of students are not born; we must struggle, discuss, push until the thing comes about. You know, to grow a beautiful rose you require a great deal of care, don't you? To write a poem you must have the feeling, you must have the words to put it in. All that requires care, considerable watching. So, is it not very important that this should be such a place? If it is not such a place, it is nobody's fault but your own and the teachers'. Do not say, "The teachers do not do this. It is the teachers' fault if they do not create this place." Nobody else is going to create it; others are not going to create it. You and I and the teachers must do it. That is real revolution—to have the feeling that it is our school, which you and I and the teachers and all of us are building together.

So, it is very important, is it not, to understand what we mean by education—not ideals of education; such ideals are all nonsense. We must begin as we are, understand things as we are, and out of that, build. You do not have a ready-made garden or school; you take the soil as it is, you till it, manure it, water it, and so create something out of nothing. As there is nothing, you will have to create, to build together.

Is it not very important for each one of us to know how to think rightly, not what to think, not what the books say, but how to think? That is what I would like to discuss with you for the next three or four weeks, namely, how to think, so that you and I at the end of it will have our minds very clear; and with that clarity, with that thinking, with that capacity, we can then go out and meet life.

May I ask you the question, "What do you want to do when you leave the school and when you have been to college?" Do you know what you want to do? Don't you want jobs, is it not your primary concern to get a job?

You have all become dumb. It is the first day and you are a bit shy. It will be all right in a couple of days. Please do not keep your shyness too long, we shall only be here for a few weeks.

Questioner: What is intelligence?

Krishnamurti: What do you think is intelligence? Not what the dictionary says, not what your teacher or your books have said—leave all that aside and think and try to find out what is intelligence. Not what Buddha, Shankara, Shakespeare, Tennyson, Spencer, or somebody else has said, but what do you think is intelligence? Do you see that the moment you are asked not to think along those lines, you are stunned? Take a man who read Shankara or the communist philosophy or some other authority; he will tell you what intelligence is right off because he will quote somebody. But if you are asked not to quote, not to repeat what somebody else thinks, not merely to read in a dictionary what intelligence is, you are lost, are you not?

What do you think is intelligence? It is a very complex problem, is it not? It is very difficult in a few words to say what intelligence is. So let us begin to find out. The person who is afraid of public opinion, afraid of the teacher, afraid of what people say, afraid of losing his job, afraid of not passing an examination, is not an intelligent person; the mind that is afraid is not an intelligent mind, is it? What do you say? Is that very difficult? If I am afraid of my parents, that they may scold me, that they may do this and that, am I intelligent? I behave, I act, I think according to them because I am afraid to think freely, to act independently. So, fear prevents me, does it not, from being what I am. I am always copying, I am always following, trying to do things which other people want me to do because I am afraid. So, a mind which is imitative, which is copying because it is afraid, is not an intelligent mind, is it? What do you say?

Is it not the function of education to help the student to understand these fears, to show how you are frightened of your teacher, of your parents? So that you may not say, "As I am frightened, I will do what I like"—which is equally stupid. Education should help us to understand these fears and to be free from them. It is very, very difficult. It requires a great deal of digging, understanding, going into it. You know what "to thaw" means? You know it freezes when the weather is very cold, and when the sunshine comes out, it begins to melt.

This morning, we all feel frozen because we do not know each other. You are a little nervous because you may want to ask about something which you are ashamed of, or you may ask something which the teachers say you should not have asked, or you may be frightened of your fellow students. All that is preventing you from thawing, from feeling natural, spontaneous, easy, so that you can ask questions. I am sure you have got lots of questions bubbling inside, but you dare not ask because you are a bit apprehensive the first morning. Perhaps tomorrow the sun will have thawed us, and we shall be able to ask each other questions.

January 4, 1954

Second Talk to Students at Rajghat School, Banaras

I would like to talk this morning on a topic which may be rather difficult, but we will try and make it as simple and direct as possible. You know most of us have some kind of fear, have we not? Do you know your particular fear? You may be afraid of your teacher, of your guardian, of your parents, of the older people, or of a snake or a buffalo or of what somebody says or of death, and so on. Each one has fear, but for young people, the fears are fairly simple. As we grow older the fears become more complex, more difficult, more subtle. I want to fulfill myself in a particular direction. You know what "fulfillment" means? I want to become a great writer. I feel if I could write, my life would be happy. So, I want to write. But anything may happen to me, I may get paralyzed for the rest of my life, and that becomes my fear. So, as we grow older, various forms of fear come into being—fears of being left alone, not having a friend, losing property, having no position, and various other types of fear. But we won't go now into the very difficult and subtle types of fear because they require much more thought.

It is very important that we—you young people and I—should consider this question of fear because society and the older people think fear is necessary to keep you in right behavior. If you are afraid of your teacher or of your parents, they can control you better, can they not? They can say, "Do this and do not do that," and you will jolly well have to obey them. So fear is used as a moral pressure. The teachers use fear, say, in a large class, as a means of controlling the students. Is it not so? Society says fear is necessary. Otherwise, the citizens, the people, will just burst out and do things wildly. Fear has thus become a necessity for the control of man.

You know, fear is also used to civilize man. Religions throughout the world have used fear as a means of controlling man, have they not? They say that if you do not do certain things in this life, you will pay for it in the next. Though all religions preach love, though they preach brotherhood, though they talk about the unity of man, they all subtly or very brutally, grossly, maintain this sense of fear.

If you have a large number of students in one class, how can the teacher control you? He cannot. He has to invent ways and means of controlling you. So, he says, "Compete. Become like that other boy who is much cleverer that you." So, you struggle, you are afraid; your fear is generally used as a means of controlling you. Do you understand? Is it not very important that education should eradicate fear, should help the students to get rid of fear, because fear corrupts the mind? I think it is very important in a school of this kind that every form of fear should be understood and dispelled, got rid of. Otherwise, if you have any kind of fear, it twists your mind, and you can never be intelligent. Fear is like a dark cloud, and when you have fear, it is like walking in sunshine with a dark cloud in your mind, always frightened.

So, is not the function of true education to help you to understand fear and be free of it? For instance, suppose you go off without telling your housemaster or teacher, and you come back and invent stories, saying that you have been with some people, while you have been to a cinema—it means that really you are frightened, does it not? You may think that if you are not frightened of the teacher, you will do what you like, and the teachers think the same. But to understand fear implies a great deal more than doing exactly what you want to do. You know, there are natural reactions of the body, are there not? When you see a snake, you jump. That is not fear because that is the natural reaction of the body. In front of danger, the body reacts, it jumps. When you see a precipice, you do not just walk blindly along. That is not fear. When you see danger, a car coming very fast, you get out of the way. It is not an indication of fear. Those are the body's responses to protect itself against danger; such reactions are not fear.

Fear comes in, does it not, when you want to do something and you are prevented from doing it. That is one type of fear. You want to go to a cinema, you would like to go out of Banaras for the day, and the teacher says, "No, there are regulations." And you do not like these regulations, you want to go. So you go an some excuse. The teacher finds out that you have gone, and you are afraid of punishment. So, fear comes in when there is a feeling that you are going to be punished. But if the teacher talks over quietly why you should not go to town, explains to you the dangers, eating food which is not clean, and so on, you understand. Even if he has not the time to explain to you and go into the whole problem of why you should not go, you also can think, your intelligence can be awakened to find out why you should not go. Then, there is no problem, you do not go. If you want to go, you talk it over and find out.

To do just what you like in order to show that you are free from fear is not intelligence. Courage is not the opposite of fear. You know, in the battlefields they are very courageous. For various reasons they take drinks or do all kinds of things to feel courageous, but that is not freedom from fear.

Should not education help the student to be free from fear of every kind?—which means from now on to understand all the problems of life, problems of sex, problems of death, of public opinion, of authority. We are going to discuss all these things so that when you leave this place, though there are fears in the world, though you have your own ambitions, your own desires, you will understand them, and so be free from fear. Because, you know, fear is very dangerous. All people are afraid of something or other. Most people do not want to make a mistake, do not want to go wrong, especially when they are young. So they think that if they could follow somebody, if they could listen to somebody, they would be told what to do, and by doing that, they would achieve an end, a purpose.

Most of us are very conservative. You know what that word means, you know what it is "to conserve"?—to hold, to guard. Most of us want to remain respectable, and so we want to do the right thing, we want to follow the right conduct—which you will see, if you go into it very deeply, is an indication of fear. Why not make a mistake? Why not find out? But the man who is afraid is always thinking, "I must do the right thing, I must look respectable, I must not let the public know what I really am." Such a man is fundamentally, basically, afraid. A man who is ambitious is really a frightened person, and a man who is frightened has no love, has no sympathy. He is like a person imprisoned behind a wall. It is very important, while we are young, to understand this thing, to understand fear. It is fear that makes me obey, but if we can talk it over, reason together, discuss and think together, then I may understand and do what I am asked. But to compel me, to force me to do a thing which I do not understand because I am frightened of you, is wrong education, is it not?

So, I feel it is very important in a place like this that both the educator and the educated should understand this problem. Creativity, to be creative—do you know what it means? To write a poem is partly creative, to paint a picture, to look at a tree, to love the tree, the river, the birds, the people, the earth, to have the feeling that the earth is ours—that is partly creative. But that feeling is destroyed when you have fear, when you say, "This is mine—my country, my class, my group, my philosophy, my religion." When you have that kind of feeling, you are not creative because it is the instinct of fear that is dictating this feeling of "mine," "my country." After all, the earth is not yours or mine—it is ours. And if we can think in those terms, we will create quite a different world—not an American world or a Russian world or an Indian world, but it will be our world, yours and mine, the rich man's and the poor man's. But the difficulty is, when there is fear we cannot create. A person who is afraid can never find truth or God. Behind all our worship, all our images, all our rituals, there is fear, and therefore your gods are not gods, they are stones.

So, it is very important while we are young to understand this thing, and you can only understand it when you know that you are afraid, when you can look at your own fears. But that requires a great deal of insight, which we won't discuss now. Because it is a much deeper problem which the older people can discuss—so we will discuss that with the teachers. But it is the function of the educator to help the educated to understand fear. It is for the teachers to help you to understand your fears and not to suppress them, not to hold them down, so that when you leave this place, your mind is very clear, sharp, unspoiled by fear. As I was saying yesterday, the old people have not created a beautiful world; they are full of darkness, fear, corruption, competition; they have not created a good world. If you, going out of this place, can really be free from fear of every kind or understand how to meet fear in yourself and in others, then perhaps you will create quite a different world, not a world of the communist, or of the congressite, and so on, but a totally different world; truly that is the function of education.

Questioner: What is sorrow?

KRISHNAMURTI: A boy of ten asks what is sorrow! Do you know anything of sorrow? Do not bother who is asking. But a little boy asking what is sorrow is a sad thing, is it not, it is a very terrible thing. Why should he know sorrow? It is the old people, unfortunately, who know sorrow. But do you know what sorrow means? When you see a beggar and a rich man going by, when you see death, a body being burned, when you see a dead bird, when you see somebody crying, when you see degradation, poverty, people quarreling, hitting each other verbally and physically, all that is sorrow, is it not? When your father or mother dies, you are left alone, and you have sorrow. But here we grow with death. You understand what I am saying, that we grow with death? We are never happy human beings. You see a dead body being carried to the river, and if you are with your parents, they say, "Do not look, death is terrible." So it begins. When you see a beggar—even as a little boy you cannot help seeing a beggar—with torn clothes, disease, wounds on his body, you feel so sorry for that man, but your parents or the older people take you away without explaining. It is a calamity, a social misery that there are such people. The parents are responsible because they do not explain all these things; they want to protect you, hide you from all that. They do not want to make you a revolutionary—which does not mean becoming a silly communist; a revolutionary is someone very, very different. They do not explain to you all these things. They are frightened, and they want to protect you.

Sorrow is something that has to be understood, tears have to be understood. There is no need for understanding when you are happy. When you smile, that does not need an explanation! But you see we are brought up, here as well as outside, unfortunately, without knowing how to think, how to observe, how to watch, and so we increase sorrow and multiply our trouble. But if, in our education, our teachers can point out these things, discuss, talk them over, then we may not be just the ordinary, everyday, stupid fathers or mothers or politicians or clerks but real human beings who are truly revolutionary and out to create a new world. Then perhaps we can understand, change, and put away sorrow.

Questioner: What is the definition of the good world?

Krishnamurti: You know, as I said yesterday, this meeting is primarily meant for students who want to find out, who want to discuss. The older people, if they are interested to help the students, would do well not to ask questions about their own personal problems. Probably children are not interested in the definition of the "good world."

Now, why does the mind ask such a question? "What is the definition of a good world?" The statement is clear; you can look it up in a dictionary and there you will find a definition. We think that by finding a definition we have understood the problem. That is how we are trained; we think we understand when we have a definition. But definition is not understanding; on the contrary, it is the most destructive way of thinking. Why do you want to know the definition of the good world? Because you cannot think out the problem, you go to somebody—to Shankara, to Buddha, to me, or to someone else—and say, "Please tell me the meaning of the good world." If you can think it out, go into it, understand it, then perhaps you will have real enlightenment.

What do we mean by "good world"? It is really very important to go into this. The word has a meaning, has it not, it has a reference. A word like *God* or *love* or *sacrifice,* or a word like *India* has great significance. Because you think you believe in God, the word *God* has a meaning to you; nervously you react to that word; psychologically you respond to it. If you do not believe in God, that word is nonsense to you. If I have been trained in atheism or communism, in which I do not believe in God, then I react differently. Similarly, to you, *good world* might mean something, but to me it might have no meaning.

What do you mean by "good world"? There is no good world. The fact is the world is rotten because there are wars, there are divisions of people—the higher and the lower, the authority, the prime minister and the poor cook, the big politician and the starving man, the king who has got everything and the other fellow who has nothing. It is a rotten world. We are caught by the words *good* and *world.* We have to understand what that word *good* implies, and we have to create a world which is good.

It is no good being carried away by words. We are always taught from childhood what to think, but never how to think. There is a science called semantics; in Greek, it means the meaning of words. There is a whole science of words being developed now. Words affect us mentally as well as physically, and it is very important to understand them and not be affected by them. The moment the word *communism* is used, a capitalist goes into a shiver about it. Similarly, a man who has property is scared of the word *revolution;* if you talk about revolution, he will throw you out. If you say to those who follow a guru, "Don't follow another, it is silly to follow," they also get scared and want to throw you out. This constant fear of words is due to lack of understanding. After all, education is the understanding of words and the understanding of communication through words.

There is no such thing as a "good world." We must take things as they are and not idealize; we must not have ideals as to what the world should be. All ideals—the ideal school, the ideal country, the ideal headmaster, the ideal of nonviolence—are nonsense, they are ridiculous, they are all illusions. What is real is actually *what is.* If I can understand the actual thing as it is—the poverty, the degradation, the squalor, the ambition, the greediness, the corruption, fears—then I can deal with it, I can break it down. But if I say, "I should be this or that," then I wander off into illusion. This country has been fed for centuries on ideals which are all illusion. You have been fed on nonviolence when you are really violent. Why not understand violence, and not talk of nonviolence? If you have understanding of *what is,* there would be a real revolution.

Questioner: Can you tell me how to get rid of fear?

KRISHNAMURTI: You want to know how to get rid of fear? Do you know what you are afraid of? Go slowly with me. Fear is something which exists in relation to something else, it does not exist by itself. It exists in relation to a snake, to what my parents or teacher might say, to death; it is in connection with something. Do you understand? Fear is not a thing by itself, it exists in contact, in relation, in touch with something else. Are you conscious, aware that you are afraid in relation to something else? Are you not afraid of your parents, are you not afraid of your teachers? I hope not, but probably you are. Are you not afraid that you may not pass your examinations? Are you not afraid that people may not think of you nicely and decently and say what a great man you are? Don't you know your own fears? I am trying to show how you have fear, and you have lost interest already.

So, first you must know what you are afraid of. I will explain to you very slowly. Then you must know also, the mind must know why it is afraid. Is fear something apart from the mind? Does not the mind itself create fear, either because it remembers the past or it projects itself into the future? You had better pester your teachers until they explain to you all these things. You spend an hour every day over mathematics or geography, but you do not spend even two minutes over the most important problems of life. Should you not spend much more time with your teachers over this—how to be free from fear—instead of merely discussing mathematics or reading a textbook? You have asked this question, how to get rid of fear, but your mind is not capable of following it. The older people perhaps can. So, we are going to discuss this later with the teachers.

A school based on fear of any kind is a rotten school, it should not exist. It requires a great deal of intelligence on the part of the teachers and of the boys to understand this problem. Fear corrupts, and to be free from fear, one has to understand how the mind creates fear. There is no such thing as fear except what the mind itself creates. The mind wants shelter, the mind wants security, the mind has various forms of self-protective ambition; and as long as all that exists, you will have fear. It is very important to understand ambition, to understand authority; both are indications of this fear which is so destructive.

Questioner: It is true, as you said, that fear corrupts the mined, especially with old people. It is also true that corrupt minds, especially of the older people, create fear. The problem appears to be how to eliminate such minds.

KRISHNAMURTI: You have understood the question? The gentleman says, "Should we not eliminate the older minds which are corrupted by fear?" This means what? Destroy the older people, put them into concentration camps? All minds, whether old or young, are corrupted by fear, either imposed from outside or self-created. It is not a question of getting rid of somebody. That is what they are doing all over the world—if I do not agree with you, you liquidate me, you put me in a concentration camp. That is not going to solve the problem. What is going to solve the problem is the right kind of education which will help me to understand the problem of fear—how fear comes into being, how it comes from the past and is also created in the present and projected into the future.

Sirs, do think about this; this is far more important than all your examinations, your textbooks, your degrees; B.A. or M.A. after your name means absolutely nothing, though it may get you a job. The problem is not how to liquidate the old people or the young people with corrupt minds. What is wanted now is an inward revolution, a mind capable of thinking of all these problems differently and creating a new world.

January 5, 1954

Third Talk to Students at Rajghat School, Banaras

You know we were discussing yesterday, if you remember, the question of fear. Most of us are afraid of something or other, and if we can eliminate fear, get rid of it, perhaps we can create a different world altogether. It seems to me to be very important to understand this, especially while we are young. The older we grow, the more difficult it is to withstand the impacts of fear because circumstances are much too strong for most of us. I really want to communicate, to tell you something of this; I feel it is very important because fear corrupts our minds, and when we are afraid, there is no love.

In this world there is no love. We talk about love, we talk about brotherhood, we talk about kindliness, about life being one, but those are just words; they have no meaning, they are a lot of words bamboozling, deceiving people. In fact, love does not exist. How can there be love when you see the appalling poverty, the miseries, the very, very powerful people and the poor people?

I think one of the causes of there being no love is fear. If you are afraid of your teacher, of your parents, of what people say, and so on, how can you love? Yet without love, life has no meaning, it becomes very dry, dull, weary; without love you do not really see the flowers, the trees, the birds, and the sunlight on the water, you do not really live, you do not enjoy life. By "enjoyment" I do not mean going to cinemas or having a good job or having a car—those are external things. The real inward joy of living, the feeling of internal richness, whether you are materially poor or rich, that feeling of the earth being ours to be made more beautiful, that longing to bring about a different status in our relationships with each other—these are the important things. But if there is fear, you cannot have these. They come only when there is love in our being. Love is not a thing that you cultivate, it is not a thing you practice. Day after day you may say, "I must love, I must be kind, I must be gentle." Love does not come out of that; it comes like the sunlight in the morning, without your actually knowing it; it comes only when there is no fear. Please listen to this carefully because when we are young, if we can understand this and have the feeling of it, then nothing can destroy us.

You may be poor, you may have no capacity, you may not look well or beautiful, but the thing that makes life rich, really rich, is this quality of love, stripped of all fear.

So, in an educational place like this, surely the first concern, not only of the teachers, but of you and all the members of the Foundation, is to eliminate the real causes of fear. While you are here, it is necessary to explain to each one of you the causes of fear, just as mathematics, geography, or history is explained to you. The teachers may still be afraid, the Foundation members may still be afraid, but for you, it is important that all these things are explained because then you will create a new world, a new education.

I think one of the causes of fear is comparison. You know what "comparison" is? To compare you with somebody else, to compare you with a clever boy, or to compare you with a dull boy, to compare you with Gandhiji or Buddha or Christ—if you are communist, it won't be Buddha or Christ, it will be Stalin or Lenin—to compare you with somebody else is the beginning of fear. I will show you why; we will go into it, and you will see the importance of not fearing. Our whole society is based on comparison, is it not? We think comparison is necessary for growth. I compare myself with another politician and say, "Well, I must beat him, I must be better than him." When a teacher compares you with another boy who is perhaps a little cleverer, what is happening to you? Have you noticed what happens to you when you are compared with someone else? The teacher says to you, "Be as clever as that other boy." To make you as clever, as strenuous, as studious as the other boy or girl, he gives you grades, he gives you marks, and so you keep on struggling, competing; you are envious of the other boy. So, comparison breeds envy, jealousy; and jealousy is the beginning of fear. When you are compared with another boy, you, as an individual boy or girl, are not important, but the other is important. When you compare yourself with somebody else, the somebody else is more important than you. Is it not so? You as an individual with your capacities, with your tendencies, with your difficulties, with your problems, with your being, are not important, but somebody else is important, and so you, as a being, are pushed aside and you are left struggling to become like somebody else. In that struggle is born envy, fear. Watch yourself in class when the teacher compares you with another, gives you different marks, different grades; you are destroyed, your own capacities, your own innate being, get suppressed. You hear about "soul" and "freedom" and all the rest of it, but those are just words because when you are compared with somebody else, you are being destroyed. You may be dull or stupid, but you are as important as that other boy or girl whom the teacher or the parent considers intelligent.

So, should not a school, an educational center of this kind, eliminate comparison altogether because you are important and not somebody else? Then your teacher has to be much more watchful of each individual, has he not? The difficulty is that the parents are not interested in all this; they want you to pass an examination, to get a job, and that is all they are interested in. So, what do they do? At home, they compare you with your elder brother or nephew or niece and say, "Be as clever as that." That is not love. When there is comparison, there is no love. You know when there are many children, the mother, if she really loves her children, does not compare. Each is as important as the other. Is it not so? Unless the mother is stupid, callous, unintelligent, she does not pick out one boy of the family and say, "He is my favorite and you must all be like him." The real mother, with love in her being, does not compare. The cripple, the stupid, is as important as the clever. In the same way, here we must not have an ideal and say we are going to work towards it; we must eliminate all this competitive comparison.

The teacher has to study each boy and find out his capacities, in what way he is making progress, in what way he is studying. Perhaps you should not use that word *progress* at all. The difficulty is how to help each boy or girl to be studious, to learn. We learn now through comparison, through competition, through grades; we are forced, are we not? If you are lazy in the class, what happens? You are pointed out as being lazy and the other boy as active. The teacher says, "Why don't you be like him?" and you are given lower marks than the other boy or girl, so you struggle and struggle and struggle to learn mathematics, and what happens? Your brain, your being, is all the time being twisted because you are not interested in mathematics. But you may be interested in something else through which you can learn mathematics.

So, to eliminate fear is extremely difficult; it must he done radically, right from the beginning, from childhood, from the kindergarten, from the smallest age, until you leave this place. It is our job, it is not an "ideal." It must be done every day, and we must work it out as we are doing now because, you see, in this so-called civilized world, competition leads to ruthlessness. Do you understand what that word means? It means brutality, disregard of another, not thinking of another. Because you are ambitious, competitive, you are aggressive, you want to get more and more, but like you, everybody else also thinks he has a right to get more, and so he struggles. Our society is built on this—on envy, on jealousy, on ambition in the name of the country, in the name of the people, and all the rest of it—but you are the center. This competition leads ultimately to war, to the destruction of people, to greater misery. Seeing all this throughout the world, is it not right that a few of us who are really interested in this kind of education should sit down and work out a way of teaching, of living, of educating, in which there is no comparison, in which there is no sense of somebody being more important than you? You are as important as anyone else, but the teacher has not found out how to awaken your interest. If the teacher can find a way to arouse your interest, then you will be as good as the others.

So, I think it is very important, while we are young, to understand this business of comparison. We think we learn by comparison, but really we do not. The real inventor, the really creative person is not comparing, he is just acting, living; he does not say "I must be as good as Edison or Rama"; he works, he lives.

When you write a poem, if you compare your work with somebody else's, what happens to your poem? If you compare yourself with Keats, with Shelley, or any other great poet, then you cease to write at all. You should write because you have something to say. You may put it badly, what you write may not have the right rhythm, your words may not be rich, easy, flowing, but you have something to say. What you say—no matter how stupid it is—is as important for you as what has been said by Keats or Shelley or Shakespeare. But if you compare, you cannot write.

Have you ever painted? Do you ever paint? When you paint a tree, the tree tells you something. The tree gives you its significance. The beauty of it, the quietness, the movement, the shades, the depth, the shape, the flutter of a leaf all tell you something—and you paint; you do not merely copy a leaf, but you express the feeling of the tree. But in expressing it, if your mind compares your work with one of the great painters, then you cease to paint, don't you? I see you have not done any of these things. It is too bad! What you miss in life! Probably you are very good at mathematics or science—which are also necessary, but if you miss all the rest, mathematics and passing a few examinations have no meaning at all. You become such dull human beings.

What is important is to understand what fear is and to eliminate fear. One of the causes of fear is envy, and envy is comparison. A society based on comparison, envy, is bound to create misery for itself and for others. You know, a contented person is not one who has achieved a result but one who understands things as they are and goes beyond them. But to understand things as they are, it is no good if your mind is always comparing, judging, weighing. Such a mind can never understand things. To put it very simply, if you are compared with somebody else, you are not important, are you? In that comparison, there is no love, is there? Our society, our schools, our education, our big people—they have no love. So, all our society, all our culture is going to pieces; everything is deteriorating. That is why it is very important that at this place, here at Rajghat, that the teacher, the Foundation members, and the students create this new feeling.

Questioner: What are manners?

Krishnamurti: Did you listen to what I was saying previous to your question, or were you so concerned with your question that you did not listen to what I was saying?

You want to know what manners are. Manners are born of respect. If I respect you, I am kind, I am gentle. Respect and manners go together, don't they?—manners being conduct, conduct being behavior, behavior being action. That is, when a boy or girl or an elder person comes, I get up—not because he is an old man, not because he is a governor, not because he is somebody from whom I can get something, but because I have the feeling of respect for people whether they are poor or rich. Manners are conduct, behavior, and it is necessary, is it not, to have manners, to be polite, not artificially—which means superficially—but to have good feeling for others. Having that good feeling for others, you become respectful, you have good manners, you talk quietly, you consider others. That is necessary, is it not, because when there are lots of people living together, if everyone was thoughtless, we should have a chaotic society. So manners, if they are the outcome, the natural outflow of deep respect and understanding and love, have a meaning, a significance; they are a beauty on this earth.

Unfortunately, we learn superficial manners. Watch the way you talk to the servant and the way you talk to the headmaster. To the one, you are tremendously respectful; to somebody who, you think, has got something to give you, you almost go on your knees. But to the coolie or to the poor beggar, you are indifferent, you do not care. But real consideration is when you have respect both for the poor man or the poor woman as well as the rich man. If in yourself you are rich, then you have affection, you have kindliness for another—it does not matter whether he is a governor or a coolie.

Have you ever smelled a flower? The flower is not concerned whether the passerby is a rich man or a poor man. It has perfume, it has beauty, and gives it; it has no concern whether you are a boy or a governor or a cook. It is just a flower, and within itself is the beauty, the perfume.

If we have that sense of inward beauty, inward respect, inward love, inward feeling of being sensitive, then from that come nice, good, happy manners without compulsion. But without that, we are quite superficial; it is like putting on a coat—it looks very nice, but it is very shallow, empty.

Questioner: What is true love?

Krishnamurti: Again, the same business! We want a definition, we want words.

How can you love if there is fear? You see how easily we are satisfied with words. If I tell you what is true love, it will have no meaning for you. Is it not very important to find out if we love at all, not what is true love? Do we love a flower, a dog, husband, wife, child? Do we love the earth? Without knowing that, we talk about true love. The love we thus talk about may be phony love; it is unreal, it is an illusion.

How can I love if I have fear in me? I assure you it is one of the most difficult things to be free from fear. It is not easy. Without understanding the whole process of fear, the implications of fear—not only the conscious fears but the subtler fears that are hidden deep down—without understanding all that, it is no good asking what true love is. Then you can look it up in a dictionary and find out what "true" means and what "love" means. You see, the difficulty is, we have always been educated in what to think, but we do not know how to think; and the greatest difficulty is to break away from "what to think" and to enter into the stream of "how to think." To break away from "what to think," we must know, we must be conscious, we must be aware that our whole education, our cultural upbringing is "what to think." You read the Bhagavad-Gita or Shakespeare or Buddha or some other teacher or revolutionary leader, and you know what to think. They tell you exactly "what to think," and you think according to that pattern. That is not thinking at all; it is like a machine repeating, a gramophone playing over and over again. To know that and to stop it is the beginning of "how to think."

Questioner: Is it right to copy something?

Krishnamurti: Let us go step by step. When I use English, I am copying English, am I not? When you speak Hindi, you are copying the words, you are learning the words, you are repeating the words, and so it is a form of imitation. When I put on this kurta, this pajama, it is a certain form of copying. When I write, when I repeat a song, when I read, when I learn mathematics, there is a certain imitation, is there not? So, there is copying, imitation, at a certain level. But at a certain other level of our life, there need not be just imitation. There are all kinds of issues, problems. Let us go into them slowly.

We copy tradition, tradition is copying. When you do puja, when you put on sacred thread, that is also imitation. When you do puja or some of these things, do you say to yourself, "Why should I do it?" You never question it. You merely accept it because your parents do it, society does it; and you just thereby become an imitative machine. You never say, "Why should I do any puja? What is the meaning of it? Has it any meaning?" If it has any meaning, you have to find it out, and you are not to be told by somebody else that it has such and such a meaning. You have to find out, and to find out, you must be unprejudiced, you must not be against it or for it. That requires a great deal of intelligence, that requires fearlessness.

Most old people have some guru or other round the corner. Why should you have a guru merely because the old people have one? This means you have to find out why they have one. They have one because they are afraid, they want to arrive in heaven safely. Neither they nor you know if there is a heaven. Their heaven is what they imagine it to be. So, you need a great deal of skepticism—not doubt—to find out, and not to be smothered by the older people and by their ideas of what is true, what is real, what is right and wrong.

Inevitably, there must be a certain amount of imitation, like any song, or mathematics, and so on. But the moment that imitation is carried over into psychological feeling, it becomes destructive. Do you know what that word *psychological* means? It means the self, the ego, the subtler feelings, the inward nature. When imitation begins there, then there is no creativeness. This is a very complex problem because imitation means action according to a pattern. Imitation, copying, means the acceptance of action according to memory. Experience is inevitably imitation because all experience is dictated by the past, and the past is imitation.

The difficulty is to see whether imitation is inevitable and to be free inwardly of all imitation. That requires a great deal of thinking—that is real meditation. If the mind can free itself from all projected images and thoughts which are imitative, then only is there a possibility of reality, God, or truth coming into being. A mind that is imitative can never find what is real.

Questioner: How can we avoid laziness?

Krishnamurti: Let us find out together how to avoid laziness. Because it is your question, I am not just going to answer it. You and I are going to find out together.

You may be lazy because you are eating the wrong kind of food, or you may be lazy because you have inherited from your parents a lethargic body, or your liver is not working properly, or you have not enough calcium, which means milk. Your laziness may be an escape from the things which you are afraid of. You become lazy because you do not want to go to school, you do not want to study because you are not interested in study. But you are not lazy if you go and play a game, you are not too lazy to quarrel with somebody. Your laziness may be due to lack of the right kind of food, or an inherited tendency from the parents, or an escape. Do you understand what I mean by "escape"? You want to escape from what you do not want to do; therefore, you become lazy. You do not want to study because you are not interested in studies, studying is a bore, and the teacher is not very good, he is also a bore. So you say, "All right," and you become lazy.

So, the teacher and you have to find out if you have the right food; perhaps with right food you will become active. Your teacher has to find out what you are really interested in—mathematics, geography, or building something. Then, in doing that, you will become active. All these factors have to be gone into. The teacher must not say, "You are a very lazy boy, you will be punished, you will get lower marks."

Questioner: But for fear, we would have no respect for our parents. How can you say fear is destructive?

Krishnamurti: Do you respect your parents out of love or out of fear? I am saying, "How can one have respect if there is fear?" Such respect is not respect at all; it is an apprehension, a fear. But if you have love, you will respect, whether it is your father or the governor or a poor coolie. Is that not simple? Respect born of fear is destructive, false, and has no meaning.

Questioner: Why do we feel a sense of fear when we do not succeed?

Krishnamurti: Why do you want to succeed? You do something, and in itself it is beautiful, it is sufficient. Why do you want to have the feeling that you have succeeded? You have pride, and then you say, "I must not have pride." Then you try to cultivate humility—which is all absurd. But if you say, "I am doing it because I love to do it," then there is no problem.

Questioner: What are the qualifications of an ideal student?

KRISHNAMURTI: I hope there is no ideal student. Look what you have asked! You want an ideal student; you picture his image, his ways of behavior, his ways of conduct, and you want to imitate him. You do not say, "Here I am. I want to find out about myself. I want to find out how to live, but not according to a picture." You see, the moment you have an ideal, you become false; you say, "How wrongly I have been brought up!" The ideal becomes much more important than what you are.

What is important is what you are, not what the ideal is, not the ideal student or is qualifications. You are important, not an ideal. In understanding yourself, you will find out how false these ideals are. Ideals are the inventions of the mind which runs away from what the thing actually is. What is important is not an ideal but to understand *what is.* There is a beggar. What is the good of talking to him about an ideal? You have to understand him, to help him directly. The ideals of a perfect society are all fictitious and unreal, and it is the old people's game to talk about these ideals. *What is* is the actual, and it has to be faced and understood.

January 6, 1954

Fourth Talk to Students at Rajghat School, Banaras

Don't you think it is very important that while you are at school, you should not feel any anxiety, any sense of uncertainty, but should have a great deal of that feeling of being secure? You know what it is to feel secure? There are different kinds of security, of the feeling that you are safe. While you are very young, you have the security of relying on older people, the feeling that somebody is looking after you and giving you the right food, the right clothing, the right atmosphere; you have the feeling that you are being cared for, looked after—which is essential, which is absolutely necessary while one is very young. As you grow older and go out of the school into the college and so on into life, that security, that feeling that you are physically safe, physically being looked after, goes into another field. You want to feel inwardly, spiritually, psychologically safe; you want to have somebody to help you, to guide you, to look after you, whom you call a guru or guide; or you have some belief or ideal because you want something to rely on.

The problem of seeking psychological security, safety, is very, very complex, and we won't deal with that now. I think that while you are at school you ought to have physical and emotional and mental stability, the mental and physical feeling that you are being looked after, that you are being cared for, that your future is being carefully nurtured, carefully watched over, so that while you are very young, while you are at school, there is no sense of anxiety, no sense of fear. That is essential because to have anxiety, fear, apprehension, wondering what is going to happen to you, is very bad, is very detrimental to your thinking; in that state, there can be no intelligence. It is only when you feel you have teachers who are really looking after you, caring for you physically, mentally, and emotionally, who are helping you to find out what you want to do in life—not forcing their opinions or their ways of conduct—that you feel you can grow, that you can live. That is only possible when you are at a school with the proper environment, with the right kind of teachers.

One of the things that prevents the sense of being secure is comparison. When you are compared with somebody else in your studies or in your games or in your looks, you have a sense of anxiety, a sense of fear, a sense of uncertainty. So, as we were discussing yesterday with some of the teachers, it is very important to eliminate in our school this sense of comparison, this giving grades or marks, and ultimately the fear of examintion.

You are afraid of your examinations, are you not? That means what? There is that threat before you all the time that you might fail, that you are not doing as well as you should, so that during all the years that you live in the school, there is this dark cloud of examinations hanging over you. We were discussing yesterday with some of the teachers whether it is possible not to have examinations at all but to watch over you every day, month after month, to see that you are learning naturally and happily and easily, to find out what you are interested in and to encourage that interest so that when you leave the school, you go out with a great deal of intelligence, not just merely with the capacity to pass an examination. After all, if you have studied or you have been encouraged to study what you are interested in because you like to do it, in which there is no fear—if you have studied all the time, not just the last two or three months when you have to spurt and read for many hours to pass examinations—and if you are watched over all the time and cared for, then when the examination comes, you can easily pass it.

You study better when there is freedom, when there is happiness, when there is some interest. You all know that when you are playing games, when you are doing dramatics, when you are going out for walks, when you are looking at the river, when there is general happiness, good health, then you learn much more easily. But when there is the fear of comparison, of grades, of examinations, you do not study or learn so well, but unfortunately, most of your teachers indulge in that old-fashioned theory. Given the right atmosphere of enjoyment, of no fear, of not being compelled to do something, so that he is happy and enjoying life in that state, a student studies much better. But the difficulty is, you see, neither the teachers nor the students think in these terms at all. The teacher is concerned only that you should pass examinations and go to the next class, and your parents want you to get a class ahead. Neither of them is interested that you should leave the school as an intelligent human being without fear.

The teachers and the parents are used to the idea of pushing a boy and girl through examinations because they are afraid that if they are not compelled, if they have no competition, no grades, they will not study. To them, it is a comparatively new thing to bring up and educate boys and girls without comparing, without compulsion, without threat, without instilling fear.

What do you students really think will happen if you have no examinations, no grades? If you were not being compared with somebody else, what would happen to your studies? Do you think that you would study less?

Questioner: Of course.

KRISHNAMURTI: I do not think so. It is surprising that, even though you are young, you have already accepted the old theory! It is a tragedy. Look, you are young and you think compulsion is necessary to make you study. But if you are given the right atmosphere, if you are encouraged and looked after, you will surely study well—it does not matter if you pass examinations or not.

They have experimented with all this in other countries. Here, we have not thought about all these things, and so you as a student say, "I must be compelled, compared, forced; otherwise, I won't study." So, you have already accepted the pattern of the old. You know what the word pattern means? It means the idea, the tradition of the older people. You have not thought it out. Look! While you are young, it is the time of revolution, of thinking out all these problems, not just accepting what the old people say. But the old people insist on your following the tradition because they do not want you to be a disturbing factor, and you accept that.

So, the difficulty is going to be because the teachers and you are both thinking that compulsion of some kind, appreciation of some kind, coercion, comparison, grades, examinations, are necessary. It is going to he very difficult to remove all that and to find ways and means so that you study naturally, easily, and happily. You think it is not possible. But we have never tried it. This way—the way of examinations, appreciation, comparison, compulsion—has not produced any great, creative human beings. The people already produced have no initiative; they just become automatic—clerks, governors, or bookkeepers, with very small, meager, dull minds. Do you see this? You are not listening to all this because you think it is impossible. But we have got to try it. Otherwise, you will be living in an atmosphere of fear, of threat, and no one can live happily in such an atmosphere. It is going to be very difficult when one has been used to this traditional way of thinking, living, studying, to completely change, push that aside and find a way to study which you really can enjoy. That can be done only if we all agree, all the students and all the teachers, that there should be no fear, and that it is essential for all of us to feel a sense of emotional, mental, physical security while we are young. Such security does not exist when there are all these threats. The difficulty is that none of us is concerned with many of the deeper problems of life. The teachers are only concerned to help you to pass examinations, to make you study, but they are not concerned with your whole being. Do you understand what I mean? The way you think, the way you feel, your outlook, traditions, the kind of person you are as a whole—the conscious and the unconscious—nobody is concerned with all that.

Surely, the function of education is to be concerned with the whole of your being. You are not just a student to he pushed through certain examinations. You have your affections, your fears. Just watch your emotions, what you want to do, your sex life. Here, in the school, all that the teachers are concerned with is to make you study some subject in which you are not even slightly interested and to pass in it, and then they think you have been thereby educated. To be educated implies, does it not, to understand the whole, the total process, your total being. To understand that, there must be, on your part as well as on the teachers' part, a feeling that you can trust each other, that there is affection, that there is a sense of security and not fear. Look! This is not something impossible, something utopian, or a mere ideal. It is not impossible. If all of us put our heads together, we can work this out. It must be worked out in school; if not, the school will be a total failure, like every other school. So, you have to understand that one can really study much better, more easily, in an atmosphere in which there is no fear, in which you are not compelled, forced, compared, driven, in the old system, in the old ways. But of that, we must be completely sure. That is what we are working out here in the afternoon with the teachers. We talk over all these problems to see that you go out of this school not as a machine but as a human being with your whole being active, intelligent, so that you properly face all the difficulties of life instead of merely reacting to them according to some tradition.

Questioner: Why do we hate the poor?

KRISHNAMURTI: Do you hate the poor? Do you hate the poor woman who is carrying the heavy basket on her head, walking all the way from Saraimohana to Banaras? Do you hate her with her torn clothes, dirty? Or, do you feel a sense of shame that you are well clothed, clean, well-fed, when you see another with almost nothing and working day in and day out, year after year'? Which is it that you feel? An inward sensation, a sense of, "I have got everything, that woman has nothing," or, a feeling of hatred for the other? Perhaps we are using the wrong word *hate.* It may be really that you are ashamed of yourself, and being ashamed, you push away that which disturbs you.

Questioner: Is there any difference between cleverness and intelligence?

KRISHNAMURTI: Don't you think that there is a vast difference? You might be very clever in your particular subject, be able to pass in it, argue out, argue with another boy. But you might be afraid—afraid of what your father may say, what your neighbor, your sister, or somebody else says. You may be very clever and yet have fear, and if you have fear, you have no intelligence. Your cleverness is not really intelligence. Most of us who are in schools become more and more clever and cunning as we grow older because that is how we are trained, to outdo somebody else in business or in the black market, to be so ambitious that we get ahead of others, push others aside. But intelligence is something quite different: it is a state in which your whole being, your whole mind and your emotions are integrated, are one. This integrated human being is an intelligent human being, not merely a clever person.

Questioner: Does love depend on beauty and attraction?

KRISHNAMURTI: Perhaps. You know it is very easy to ask questions, but it is very difficult to think out the problems that those questions involve. To really think them out, not wait for an answer from me, to really think out step by step what is involved, to go into it, is much more important than to wait for an answer from me. These questions indicate, do they not, that we are used to being told what to think, what to do, and not how to think or do anything. We have not thought out these problems, we do not know how to think.

While we are young, it is important to know how to think, not just repeat some professor's book; we have to find out for ourselves the truth, the meaning, the implications of any problem. That is why it is very important, while we are here in the school, that all these things, all these problems, should be talked over, discussed, so that our minds do not remain small, petty, trivial.

Questioner: How can we remove the sense of anxiety?

KRISHNAMURTI: If you had no examinations, would you have the anxiety with regard to them? Think it out quietly and you will see. Suppose we are going out on a walk, and we are talking about this problem. Would you have any sense of anxiety if, in a couple of months, you had an examination? Would you have anxiety if, at the end of your examination, B.A. or whatever it is, you had to fight for a job? Would you? You are anxious because you have to have a job. In a society where there is keen competition, where everybody is seeking, fighting, you as a student are being trained from childhood in an atmosphere of anxiety, are you not? You have the first form to pass, then the second form to pass, and so on and on. So, you become a part of the whole social structure, don't you? That is not what we are going to do in this school. We are going to create an atmosphere in which you are not anxious, in which you have no examinations, in which you are not compared with somebody else—even if it involves the breaking of the school. Because, you are important as a human being. If there were such an atmosphere, then examinations would not be all-important, you could study freely, nor would it be difficult for you to pass the university examinations because if you had been intelligent during all the years you spent in school and college, you would be able to work hard for four or five months before the examination, and pass. After passing the final examination, when you go out into the world, you will want a job. But the job you take won't frighten you; your parents, your society won't frighten you; you will do something, even beg; you will not be anxious.

At present, your life is full of anxiety because from the very beginning of your childhood you have been caught in this framework of competition. All of us want success, and we are constantly told, "Look at that man, he has made a great success." But as long as you are seeking success, there must be anxiety. But if you are doing something because you love to do it and not because you want to be successful, then there is no anxiety. As long as you want success, as long as you want to climb the social ladder, there is anxiety. But if you are doing what you love to do—it does not matter whether it is merely mending a wheel or putting a cog together or painting or being an administrator—and not because you want position or success, then there is no anxiety.

Questioner: Why do we fight in this world?

KRISHNAMURTI: Why do we fight? You want something and I want the same thing, so we fight for it. You are clever, I am not clever, and we fight about it. You are more beautiful than I am, and I feel I must also be beautiful, and so we squabble. You are ambitious and I am ambitious, you want a particular job and I want the same job, and so it goes on and on, does it not? There is no end to squabbling as long as we want something. It is very difficult. As long as we want something, we are going to quarrel. As long as you say India is the most beautiful, the greatest, the most perfect, the most civilized country in the world, then you are going to have quarrels. We start in a small way—you want a shawl and you fight for it. That same thing goes on in life in different ways and in different walks.

Questioner: When a teacher or some other superior compels us to do a thing which we do not want to do, what are we to do?

KRISHNAMURTI: What do you generally do? You are frightened and you do what you are told, don't you? Suppose you are not frightened, and you ask the superior, the teacher, to explain to you what it is all about, what will happen? Suppose you say—not impudently, not disrespectfully— "I do not understand why you are asking me to do this, which I do not want to do; please explain why you want this to be done." Then, what will happen? What would generally happen is that the teacher or superior would be impatient. He would say, "I have no time to explain, go and do it." Also, the superior or your teacher might feel he has no reason; he just says, "Go and do it"; he has not thought it out. When you quietly, respectfully ask him, "Please tell me," then you make the teacher, the superior, think out the problem with you. Do you understand? Then, if you see the reason, if you see that he is right, that there is sense in what he says, then you will naturally do it; in that, there is no compulsion. But to do something that the superior says because you are frightened of him does not mean a thing. You do it only because you are frightened, and you would go on doing it even if he were not there.

Questioner: As puja is a form of imitation, why do we do it?

KRISHNAMURTI: Do you do puja? Why do you do it? Because your parents have done it. You have not thought it out, you do not know the meaning of all that. You do it because your father or mother or great-aunt does it. We are all like that. When somebody does something, I copy, hoping to derive some benefit from it. So, I do puja because everybody does puja. It is a form of imitation. There is no originality about it. There is no consideration of it. I just do it, hoping that some good will come out of it.

Now, you can see for yourselves that if you repeat a thing over and over again, your mind becomes dull. That is an obvious fact, like in mathematics wherein if you repeat over and over again, it has no meaning. Similarly, a ritual repeated over and over again makes your mind dull. A dull mind feels safe. It says, "I have no problems, God is looking after me, I am doing puja, everything is perfect," but it is still a dull mind. A dull mind has no problems. Puja, the repetition of a mantra, or any words which are constantly being repeated, make the mind dull. This is what most of us want; most of us want to be dull so as not to have any disturbance. Whether it is beneficial or not is a different problem. You know that by repeating you can make your mind very quiet—not in the living sense, but in the dead sense—and that mind then says, "I have solved my problem." But a dead mind, a dull mind, cannot be free of its problems. It is only an active mind, a mind that is not caught in imitation, not caught in any fear, that can look at a problem and go beyond it and be free of it.

You are quoting somebody else because you have not thought out the problem. You read Shakespeare or Milton or Dickens or somebody else, and you quote a phrase out of it and say, "I must know the meaning of it." But if, as you were reading, you thought things out, if as you went along, you used your mind, then you would never quote. Quoting is the most stupid form of learning.

Questioner: No risk, no gain; no fear, no conscience; no conscience, no growth. What is progress?

KRISHNAMURTI: What is progress? There is a bullock cart and there is a jet plane. In this there is progress. The jet plane does 1300 to 1500 miles an hour, and the bullock cart does two miles an hour. There is progress in this. Is there progress in any other direction? Man has progressed scientifically—he knows the distance between stars and the earth, he knows how to break the atom, he knows how to fly an airplane, go down in a submarine, he knows how to measure the speed of the earth. There is progress all along that line. Is there progress in any other direction? Is there any lessening of wars? Are people more kind, more thoughtful, more beautiful? So, where is progress? There is progress in one direction, but there is no progress in the other.

You say risk will bring about progress. We make statements without seeing all the implications. We then read some phrases, and students imitate, copy those phrases, put them up on the wall and repeat them.

Questioner: What is happiness and how can it be obtained?

KRISHNAMURTI: You obtain happiness as a byproduct. If you look for happiness, you are not going to get it. But if you are doing something which you think is nice, good, then happiness comes as a side result. But if you seek happiness, it will always elude you, it will never come near you. Say, for instance, you are doing something which you really love to do—painting, studying, going on a walk, looking at the sunshine, the shadows, something of which you feel, "How nice to do it." In the doing of it you have happiness. But if you do it because you want to be happy, you will never be happy.

January 7, 1954

Fifth Talk to Students at Rajghat School, Banaras

For several days we have been talking about fear and the various causes that bring about fear. I think one of the most difficult things, which most of us do not seem to apprehend, is the problem of habit. You know, most of us think that when we are young, we should cultivate good habits as opposed to bad habits, and we are told all the time what bad habits are and what good habits are; we are always told of habits that are worthwhile cultivating, and the habits which we should resist or put away. When we are told that, what happens? We have so-called bad habits, and we want to have good habits. So, there is a struggle going on between what we have and what we should have. What we have are supposed to be bad habits, and we think we should cultivate good habits. So, there is a conflict, a struggle, a constant push towards good habits, towards changing from bad habits into good habits.

Now, what do you think is important? Good habits? If you cultivate good habits, what happens? Is your mind any more alert, any more pliable, any more sensitive? After all, habits imply, do they not, a continuous state in which the mind is no longer disturbed. If I have good habits, my mind need not be bothered about them, and I can think about other things. So, we say, we should have good habits. But, in the process of cultivating good habits, does not the mind become dull? If you have so-called good habits and let your mind function, move along these rails called good habits, your mind is not pliable, is it? It is fixed. So, what is important is not good habits or bad habits but to be thoughtful, and to be thoughtful is much more difficult. The moment you are thoughtful, alert, aware, then it is no longer a matter of cultivating good habits. The thoughtful mind is sensitive and therefore capable of adjustment; whereas, a mind that is functioning in habit is not sensitive, is not pliable, is not thoughtful. One of the difficulties of a mind that is mediocre, small, petty, is that it functions in habit, and once the mind is caught in habit, it is extremely difficult to free itself from it. So, what is important is not cultivation of habits, good or bad, but to be thoughtful—not along a particular direction, but all round. Because, habit is thoughtlessness in a particular direction.

I hope you are following all this. Perhaps it may be a little difficult; if it is, do please ask your teachers, and when they talk next time of cultivating good habits, discuss with them , not to catch them in argument, but to understand what they mean by good habits.

Even good habits are also thoughtless. A mind that is caught in habit is not capable of quick adjustment, quick thought, or alertness. To be thoughtful, not merely superficially, but inwardly, is far more important than the cultivation of good habits. The mind is a living thing, but it is bound, held, hedged about, controlled, shaped, pushed by various forms of habit. Belief, tradition, is habit. My father believes in something, and he insists that I also believe. He does not put it that way, but he creates an environment, an atmosphere, in which I have got to follow. He does puja, which is a habit, and I naturally imitate him and thus cultivate the same habit.

Your mind is always trying to live in habit so that it won't be disturbed, so that it has not got to think anew or afresh, to look at problems differently. So, the mind likes to live in a half-awakened state, and habits come in very useful, like tradition, because you do not have to think, you do not have to be sensitive. Tradition says something and you follow—such as the tradition of putting something on your forehead, the tradition of wearing turbans, the tradition of growing beards. When you accept and follow a tradition, you are not disturbed; your mind is dull, and likes to be dull. That is our education. We learn mathematics, geography, or science in order to get a job and settle down in that job for the rest of our life. You are a Christian or a Hindu or a Muslim or whatever you call yourself, and in that you function like a machine without any disturbance. You have disturbances, but you explain them away by your habitual thinking, so that your mind is never thoughtful, never alert, never questioning, never uncertain, always half asleep—put to sleep by tradition, by habits, by customs. That is why, if you notice, when you are in a school, you just disappear in the mass of people. You are just like anybody else. You are educated, you are a B.Sc. or an M.A. You have children, a husband, a car, or you have no car and want a car. Thus you function, thus you live and gradually die and are burned on the ghats. That is your life, is it not? You are trained to be thoughtless, not to revolt, not to question. Any little occasional quiver of anxiety you may have is soon explained away. This you consider to be a process of education.

Surely, it is very important, is it not, that while you are at this school, you try and experiment with all this so that when the time comes for you to leave this place, you do so, not with a mind that is functioning in habits, in tradition, in fear, but with a mind that is thoughtful. This thoughtfulness is not to be along any particular direction, communist, congress, or socialist thoughtfulness; the moment it is labeled, it is no longer thoughtfulness. The moment you belong to something, to some society, to some group, to some political party, you have ceased to think, for you think only in habit, and that is not thoughtfulness. The chief concern of a school of this kind must be to create an atmosphere in which there is no fear, in which students are not compelled or coerced or compared with one another—so that there is freedom. This does not mean that the students are free to do what they want to do, but they have the freedom to grow, to understand, to think, to live, so that the mind never functions in habit, so that the mind becomes very active—not with the activity of gossip, not with the activity of mere reading, but with the activity of inquiry, of finding out, of searching for what is real, for what is true. Then the mind becomes an astonishing thing, a creative thing.

Surely, that is the function of education, is it not?—not to give you good or bad habits, not to let your mind live in tradition, but to help you to break away from all habits and traditions so that your mind is free from the very beginning to the very end, very active, alive, seeing things anew. You know, when you watch the river of a morning or of an evening, after you have watched for about a week, you lose all appreciation of its beauty because you are used to it. Your mind becomes habituated to it, your mind is no longer sensitive to the green fields and the moving trees; you see them and you pass them by. You are no longer sensitive, no longer thoughtful. You see those poor women go by, day after day, and you do not even know that they wear torn clothes and carry so much weight. You do not even notice them because you are used to them. Getting used to something is to grow insensitive to it. This process is destructive, as such a mind is a dull mind, a stupid mind. So, the function of education is to help the mind to be sensitive, thoughtful, so that it does not function in habit or tradition, so that it does not get used to anything, so that it is always fresh, alive. That requires a great deal of insight, a great deal of understanding.

Questioner: Why do we get angry?

KRISHNAMURTI: It may be for many reasons. It may be due to ill-health, to not having slept properly, to not having the right kind of food. It may be purely a physical reaction, a nervous reaction, or it may be much deeper. Because you feel frustrated, you feel caught, held, bound, and you have no outlet, you let off steam, you get angry. Anger is not just a matter of control. The moment you control, you have created a habit. You know, the so-called meditation of most people is the cultivation of habit; when they are meditating, they are cultivating a mind which will not be disturbed, which will function in habit, but such a mind will never find what is truth, what is God. If you merely control anger, the process is to cultivate a habit. Perhaps you do not understand what I am saying. Perhaps if the older people understand, they could explain this carefully to the children, not haphazardly, not impatiently, but explain the whole process of control, that it makes for habit and so makes the mind dull. They could explain why there is anger, not only the physical reasons, but also the psychological reasons; how the mind, which is sensitive, makes itself dull, insensible, through fear, through various forms of desires and fulfillments; and how such a mind can only think in terms of habit, control, suppression.

A mind that is very alert, watchful, may lose its temper, but that is not important. What is important is to watch the mind, to see that it does not function in habit, that it does not become insensitive, dull, weary, and ready to die.

Questioner: Stray thoughts prevent me from concentration, and without concentration, I cannot read.

KRISHNAMURTI: You do not read, not because of stray thoughts, but because you are not interested in what you are reading. You read a detective story or a novel; at that time your thoughts do not stray, do they? If you are interested in what you are reading, it gives you enjoyment; then you are not disturbed by any thought, are you? On the contrary, it is very difficult to let the book go. Do you read detective stories? Do you read novels? No? Then what do you read? What you are told to read in class? Naturally, you are not interested in those things, you are forcing yourself to read them. When you force yourself to read, your mind goes off—which is wrong education. But if you, from childhood, are given an opportunity to find out what you are interested in, then you will have natural, easy concentration without any effort to concentrate. But unfortunately, for the older students this has not been possible because they have been brought up in the old style, forced to read and to study. When your mind wanders, the problem arises: How can I control my thoughts? You cannot. Do not control your thoughts but find out what you are interested in. You have to pass your examinations, unfortunately. That is what is expected of you. But if you really want to understand the ways of your mind, the mind has to find out what it is interested in, vitally, for the rest of its life and not for ten days or for a few years. For such a mind, when it has found what it is interested in, there will be no problem of concentration; it naturally becomes concentrated.

Questioner: What is the outcome of meditation?

Krishnamurti: The outcome generally is what you want your meditation to be. You understand? If I meditate on peace, I will get peace. But it will not be real peace; it will be something which my mind has created. If I am a Christian, I meditate in a Christian way, and my mind will create a picture. If I am a Hindu devotee and I meditate, my mind will create an image, and I will see it as a living image. My mind projects whatever it desires, and sees the thing as living, but it is self-delusion. The mind deceives itself. If I am a Hindu, I believe in innumerable things, and my beliefs control my thinking, don't they? Suppose I am a devotee and I sit down and meditate on Krishna, what happens? I create an image of Krishna, don't I? My mind, brought up in Hinduism, has a picture of Krishna, and on that picture I meditate, and that meditation is the process of my conditioned thinking. So, it is no longer meditation, it is just a continuous, habitual form of thinking. I might see Krishna dancing, but it will still be the result of my tradition. So long as I have this tradition, the real thing cannot be perceived. So, my mind must free itself from tradition. That is real meditation.

Meditation is the process of the mind freeing itself from all conditioning, either of the Hindu or the Christian or the Muslim or the Buddhist or the communist. Then, when the mind is free, reality can come into being. Otherwise, meditation is merely self-deception.

Questioner: Why do we feel sorry for the beggar when he comes to us, and why do we feel angry when he leaves us?

Krishnamurti: I am not sure whether you are putting the latter part of the question rightly. Perhaps you have a different meaning when you say you hate it when they leave. Do you get angry merely because he leaves the place, or because he leaves the place with a curse because you do not give? I go to you as a beggar, and you give me something, and in the giving, you feel happy, you feel that you are somebody because you have given. For the majority of us, there is vanity in giving, is there not? Suppose you do not give, what happens? The beggar curses you and goes away. He gets angry, and in return you also get angry. Perhaps you do not want to be disturbed, and so you get angry.

I really do not understand this question. Is this what you are trying to say? You feel kindly when you see a person, a beggar, because your sympathies are aroused, and you feel it is good to have this natural sympathy, but at the same time, you feel disturbed because of his poverty and your being well off; you do not like to be disturbed, and so you get agitated. Is this what you mean? There are several things taking place—the natural outgoing sympathy to give something; the feeling of anxiety; the feeling of anger, of irritation that you cannot do anything, that society is rotten and you cannot help; your own natural fears that you might catch his disease. I do not see what you mean when you say you get angry when the beggar goes away.

Questioner: The habit of getting angry and the habit of getting vindictive—are they different psychological processes, or are they the same, but varying in degree?

KRISHNAMURTI: Anger may be immediate, but it passes and is forgotten. I think vindictiveness implies the storing up, the remembering of a hurt, the feeling that you have been frustrated, that you have been blocked, hindered. You store that up, and eventually you are going to take it out on that person, you are going to be violent. I think there is a difference. Anger may he immediate and forgotten, but vindictiveness implies the actual building up of anger, of annoyance, of the desire to hit back. If you are in a powerful position, and you say harsh things to me, I cannot get angry because I may lose my job. So, I store it up, I bear all your insults, and when an occasion arises, I hit back.

Questioner: How can I find God?

KRISHNAMURTI: A little girl asks how she can find God. Probably she wants to ask something else, and she has forgotten it already.

In answer to the question, we are talking to the little girl and also to the old people. The teachers will kindly listen and tell the girl in Hindi, as the question is important to her.

Have you ever watched a leaf dancing in the sun, a solitary leaf? Have you watched the moonlight on the water and did you see the other night the new moon? Did you notice the birds flying? Have you deep love for your parents? I am not talking of fear, of anxiety, or of obedience, but of the feeling, the great sympathy you have when you see a beggar, or when you see a bird die, or when you see a body burned. If you can see all these things and have great sympathy and understanding—understanding for the rich who go in big cars blowing dust everywhere, and understanding for the poor beggar and the poor *ekka* horse which is almost a walking skeleton, knowing all that, having the feeling of it not merely in words but inwardly, the feeling that this world is ours, yours and mine, not the rich man's nor the communist's, to be made beautiful—if you feel all this, then behind it there is something much deeper. But to understand that which is much deeper and beyond the mind, the mind has to be free, quiet, and the mind cannot be quiet without understanding all this. So, you have to begin near, instead of trying to find what God is.

Questioner: How can we remove our defects forever?

KRISHNAMURTI: You see how the mind wants to be secure. It does not want to be disturbed. It wants forever and forever to be completely safe, and a mind that wants to be completely safe, to get over all difficulties forever and forever, is going to find a way. It will go to a guru, it will have a belief, it will have something on which to rely and cling; and so, the mind becomes dull, dead, weary. The moment you say, "I want to get over all my difficulties forever," you will get over them, but your whole being, your mind, will be dead.

We do not want to have difficulties, we do not want to think, we do not want to find out, to inquire. I wait for somebody to tell me what to do. Because I do not want to be disturbed, I go to somebody who I think is a great man or a great lady or a saint, and I do what he tells me to do, like a monkey, like a gramophone which is repeating. In doing so, I may have no difficulties superficially because I am mesmerized. But I have difficulties in the unconscious, deep down inside me, and these are going to burst out eventually, though I hope they will never burst out. You see, the mind wants to have a shelter, a refuge, something to which it can cling—a belief, a Master, a guru, a philosophy, a conclusion, an activity, a political dogma, a religious tenet. It wants to go to that and hold on to it when it is disturbed. But the mind must be disturbed. It is only through disturbance, through watching, through inquiry, that the mind understands the problem.

The lady asks, "Can a disturbed mind understand?" A mind that is disturbed and is seeking an escape from the disturbance will never understand. But a mind that is disturbed and knows it is disturbed and begins to inquire patiently into the cause of disturbance without condemning, without translating the causes—such a mind will understand. But a mind which says, "I am disturbed, I don't want to be disturbed, and so I am going to meditate on nondisturbance," is a phony mind, a silly mind.

Questioner: What is internal beauty?

Krishnamurti: Do you know what is external beauty? When you see a beautiful building or a beautiful tree, a beautiful leaf, a lovely painting, a nice person, what happens to you? You say, "It is beautiful." What do you mean by "beautiful"? There must be something beautiful in you to see the beauty outside, must there not? You understand? Please tell that boy. The teacher who is responsible, his housemaster, will please listen to this and take the trouble to tell these boys and girls what we have been discussing, This is far more important than the usual classes.

Please listen. One boy wants to know how to be free forever from all trouble. The other boy wants to know what is internal beauty and when I ask if you know what external beauty is, you all laugh. But if you know that which is beautiful, if you have a feeling for beauty, then you have sympathy, you have sensitivity, an appreciation of what you see—a magnificent mountain or a marvelous view. To have the appreciation of beauty, there must be something in you to appreciate, and that may be inward beauty. When you see goodness, kindness, when you see something lovely outside you, you must have it inside you as well. When you see the lovely curve of the railway bridge across the Ganges, there must also be something in you which sees the beauty of a curve. Most of us do not see beauty outside or inside because we have not got it in ourselves; inside, we are dull, empty, heavy, and so we do not see the beauty in anything, we do not hear the noise of the train going over the bridge, which has its own beauty. When you get used to anything, it loses its meaning for you.

January 8, 1954

Sixth Talk to Students at Rajghat School, Banaras

We have been talking about fear, and I think if we can go more deeply into it, perhaps we shall awaken to initiative. Do you know what that word *initiative* means? To initiate means to begin. I will explain further as I go along.

Don't you think that in old countries like India—because of various things like climate, overpopulation, and poverty—tradition and authority control thinking? Have you not noticed in yourself how you want to obey your teacher, obey your parents or your guardians, to follow an ideal, follow a guru? The spirit of obedience, the following, the being told what to do—that creates an authority, does it not? You know what "authority" is? It implies someone to whom you look up, someone whom you want to obey, to follow. Because you yourself are afraid, because you yourself are uncertain, you create an authority. And by the creation of authority, you not only follow but you want others to follow; you take a delight in following and in forcing others to follow.

I do not know if you have noticed in yourself that behind this desire to obey, to follow, to imitate, to comply with somebody else's wishes, is fear—fear of not doing the right thing, fear of going wrong. So, authority gradually kills any kind of initiative—which is, to know how to do something easily, spontaneously, freely, out of yourself. Most of us lack that because the sense of creativity is being destroyed in us. For instance, you may initiate some mischief of your own, you may tear up, destroy, create some mischief, but that feeling of doing something for yourself, out of yourself, without being asked, without being told what to do, that spirit of initiative is lost because you are always surrounded by authority, by the older generation who seem to think they know what they are about—although they do not—and who control you. So gradually, the sense of doing things because you love to do them goes out of yourself and is destroyed. Have you ever walked down the road and picked up a stone that is in the way, picked up a piece of paper or torn rag, or planted a tree which you will care for? When you have not been told to do these things, you do them yourself, naturally; that is the beginning of initiative. When you see something to be mended, you mend it; when you see something that has to be done, without being told what to do, you do it, either in the kitchen or in the garden or in the house or on the road. Your mind gradually becomes free from fear, from authority, so you begin to do things yourself. I think it is very important to do that in life; otherwise, you become mere gramophones, playing over and over again the same tune, and so you lose all sense of freedom.

But the older generation, the past generation, because of their nervous desires, their fears, their apprehensions of insecurity, want to protect you, they want to guide you, they want to hold you in fear, and through fear they gradually destroy in you the freedom to do things, to make mistakes, to find out, so that you begin to lose this extraordinary thing called initiative. Please ask your teachers about all this. You see how very few of us have that freedom—freedom not merely to do things but freedom out of which we want to do things. When you see somebody carrying a great weight, you want to help him, don't you? When you see the dishes being washed, you want to do it yourself sometimes. You want to wash your own clothes, you want to do things out of freedom. Do you know what that means? If one goes into it very deeply, you will find an extraordinary creativity coming into being.

Truth is not something very far away, to be sought after, to be struggled and searched for. If you have freedom from the very beginning, from childhood, you will find as you mature and grow that there is initiative to do things spontaneously, easily, naturally, without being told what to do. It is creative to write a poem, to be unafraid, to look at the stars, to let your mind wonder, to look at the beauty of the earth and the astonishing things that the earth holds. To feel all this is really an extraordinary activity, and you cannot feel it without that freedom, without that sense of initiative in which there is no authority, in which you do not obey merely because you are told what to do but do things naturally, freely, easily, happily. As you go into it, you will see that you begin to take a tremendous interest in everything, in the way you walk, in the way you talk, in the way you look at people, in the feelings you have—because all these things matter very much. If you have cultivated intelligence, this sense of freedom, all the time while at school, then a few months of intense study will be sufficient for you to pass your examinations. But now, what you are doing is to be concerned all the time with studies, with books, and you do not know what is happening all around you.

Have you watched those village women carrying weights on their heads—cow-dung cakes, wood, hay, or fodder? How extraordinarily beautiful is their walk! Have you watched the so-called well-to-do people? Do you notice how heavy they grow and how dull, because they do not look at anything? They are concerned only with their petty worries and their desires and with how to control their fears and their appetites, so they live in fear, and living in fear, they have to follow somebody, to obey, so that they create authority—the authority at one level of the policeman, of the lawyer, of the government, and also the spiritual authority of books, of leaders, of gurus—so that, in themselves, they lose the beauty of living, of suffering, of understanding.

That is why it is very important that while you are at this school, you should understand all these things. Go out one day and plant a tree and look after it all the time you are here. Find out what kind of tree to plant, what kind of manure to give it, and look after it. Then you will see something happening to you; you are close to the earth and not merely close to books. You will not be interested in books after you get a job; after you pass your examination you will never look at another book. But there are trees, numerous flowers, living animals all around. If you do not have sensitivity to all these, you lose initiative and your minds become very small, petty, trivial, jealous, envious. It is very important while you are at this school to consider all these things, so that your minds become awakened to them.

You know, scientists say that we are only functioning 15 percent. Our capacity to think is only 15 percent; probably, if we learned to function 50 percent we would do much more mischief. But without cultivating sensitivity, understanding, affection, kindliness, even with the 15 percent capacity we do a great deal of damage and mischief, and with 50 percent capacity but no kindliness, we would do monstrous things.

If you understand all this, there comes a feeling of freedom from fear. How can you understand if you just listen to these talks and forget them? Do not listen to them that way. Listen so that you can live without fear, without following somebody; listen to be free, not when you are old, but now.

To be free requires a great deal of intelligence. You cannot be free if you are a stupid person. Therefore, it is very important to awaken your intelligence while you are very young, and that intelligence cannot be when you are frightened, when you are following, when you want somebody to obey you or when you yourself obey somebody. All this requires a great deal of thinking over, and that is real education. The education that most of us now get is only superficial.

Questioner: How can we create a happy world when there is suffering?

KRISHNAMURTI: You did not listen to what was being said. You were occupied with your question. While I was talking, your mind was wondering how you were going to ask your question, how you were going to put it into words, so your mind was occupied with what you were going to ask, and you did not really listen. There was no pause, no gap, between when I stopped and your question. You immediately jumped into it—which means, really, you did not listen, you did not see the importance of what I was saying, you were not paying attention. It is really important to know how to listen to people—to the old man or to your sister or to your brother or to the man who goes by—which means really that your mind is quiet, so that a new idea, a new feeling, a new perception can penetrate. What I was saying is really very complex, very difficult. You did not let that penetrate, enter your mind, because your mind was occupied with, "I must ask a question. How shall I put it?" Or, you were looking out of the window—it is nice to look out because the trees are beautiful—but then you saw somebody come in, and your mind became agitated like those leaves on the tree. So, please, as I suggested, write out your questions, and when I finish talking, wait a minute and then read your question. Then your mind will follow what I am saying, so that you begin to really listen. I think if we know how to listen, we will learn much more than all the time struggling to pay attention.

Someone asked, "What is a beautiful world, and how can one create it when there is so much suffering?" Let us think together why it is that most of us want to do something. We think that activity, doing something, is more important than understanding what the problem is, what it is all about. You see a beggar, and your instinct is to give him something. But what generally happens is that, after giving, you forget all about it. You do not understand, you do not inquire into the whole question of poverty, here and everywhere in the world. You know there are poor people, and you also know that there is inward poverty. You may have a great deal of money, you may live in a luxurious house, but inwardly you may be as poor as a beggar. If you realize this, you are afraid, and so you begin to read books, to acquire knowledge. It is like a man who covers himself with jewels and lives in a palace and thinks that he is rich.

You learn to read or quote a great many spiritual teachers and the Bhagavad-Gita. You may want to do good, but you do not stop at that. You want to help the whole world and put an end to the misery in the world. So you join groups, you join a society, or you form an institution. You become a secretary, you pay dues, and you gradually get lost in some organization. Actually, you do very little good in the world.

To do good really, you must understand yourself as you are, in the very process of doing good. Any action you do should help you to understand yourself, to go into yourself. Then in the transformation of yourself, in the changing of yourself, there is a possibility of bringing about a different world. Merely to do good or to join a society for doing good, seems to be superficial. But if, in the very action of doing good, you begin to understand the complications of life, then out of that there can be a change, there can be a world in which suffering will not exist.

Questioner: Why is stealing considered to be bad?

KRISHNAMURTI: Why do you think stealing is bad? You have a watch and I take it away from you. Do you think that is right? I take away something from you which belongs to you, which your father has given to you, or which you have got by some other means. I take it away from you without telling you, without your knowing it. Is that a good action? It may be that you have got the watch because of your greed. But I am equally greedy, equally acquisitive, so I take it away from you. This is called stealing. Obviously it is not right, is it? You see, there are some boys and girls who steal as a habit. Older people do that too; though they have money, though they have things which they really need, the desire to steal overcomes them. That is a disease. It is a kind of mental perversion, an aberration, a mental twist. Without understanding that twist, the older people generally punish or hurt you and say that you must not steal, that it is very bad, and that you may be put in prison. They frighten you, and so the twist becomes more twisted, hidden, darker. But if there was an explanation, if the parent or the teacher took the trouble to explain and not condemn, not threaten, then perhaps that twist might disappear. One of the difficulties is that the teachers and the parents have no time, they have no patience; they have so many other children; they want a result, a quick result, and so, they threaten and hope that the boy will stop stealing. But it does not generally happen that way. The boy goes on quietly stealing.

I think, in a school of this kind, the teachers should explain all these things to you. You spend an hour in a class reading mathematics or geography. Why not spend ten minutes out of that time in discussing these problems? As you begin to talk them over, the teachers as well as the students become intelligent. I am not saying that the teachers are not intelligent, but they become more intelligent.

Questioner: What is a soul?

Krishnamurti: You think you have a soul, don't you? How do you know? You see, that is one of your difficulties. You accept things from your parents, and you repeat them again and again, and you say, "Yes, I have got a soul."

What is a soul? Let us go into it slowly, step by step, and you will see something. In Banaras, which is a city of the dead, so many people die. You have also seen a dead bird. The leaf on a tree, which is green, lovely, dancing, tender, withers and is blown away. Seeing all this, man says, "Everything goes, everything disappears, nothing is permanent." Black hair becomes gray; early in life you can walk ten miles or more, but later on, you can walk only two or three miles. A tree which has lived for two or three hundred years is struck by lightning and disappears. There are trees in California which are three to five thousand years old, yet they too will die. Everything disappears; very few things are permanent.

Seeing this extraordinary state of impermanence, man says, "There must be something permanent, something which does not die, which is not corrupted by time." And he begins to invent things that have permanency, creating out of his own mind God, the soul, atma, paramatma, and so on. He himself sees that he is impermanent, so he longs for something which is permanent, which will never die, which no thief can take away. So his mind speculates, and in his fear he invents, he imagines. He says there is a soul which cannot be destroyed. He says, "My body may go, I may die, I may be eaten away by worms; but there is something in me which is imperishable." He states that, and then he worships that invention; he builds theories round it, he writes books and quarrels about it, but he never finds out for himself if there is really anything permanent. He never says, "I know everything is impermanent. I too will die. I too will grow old, and disease and decay will take place. But I want to find out if there is something beyond. So let me not invent, let me not say there is a soul or there is atma or there is this and that. But let me find out, let me inquire." If only I make up my mind to find out, to inquire, then through that inquiry, through understanding my fears, my greed, through knowing myself, I may go deeper and deeper and find out something which is beyond mere words.

You say there is character, and that character may be the soul. But what are you? You have certain tendencies, have you not, certain idiosyncracies, certain ways, certain desires; all that is in you. You say, "I am all that, but if I die, what happens to me? There must be something which goes on and on." But do not accept anything unless you have searched out, unless you have gone into it yourself. Unfortunately your mind is engaged, and you are not awakening the mind so that it can go into this problem. When you accept, when you believe, you have stopped inquiring. So, to really inquire requires a mind which is very wide awake. Such a mind is not possible if you are following an authority or if there is fear. If you merely accept, you will never find out.

Questioner: What is joy?

KRISHNAMURTI: A little boy asks, "What is joy?" I wonder why he asks! Either he does not know what joy is—which would be really very sad—or he knows what joy is and wants to find out more about it. The boy won't understand what I am going to say because unfortunately I cannot speak Hindi, but will those who are responsible for that boy please explain carefully and help him to understand his question.

The boy wants to know what joy is. When you see a flower, you have a feeling, have you not? When you see a sunset, when you see a nice person, when you see a beautiful painting, when you walk freely up a mountain and look from the top of the mountain into the valley and see the various shades, the sunshine, the houses, when you see somebody smile, have you not a feeling which you call joy? But the moment you say, "I am joyous, I feel joy," the thing is gone. Do you follow? The moment you say, "I am happy," you are no longer happy.

You see, we live in the past; we are already dying all the time; death is always with us. Duration is always our shadow because we are always living in the past moment. That is why we say, "I have known joy, and it has gone, and I want to get it back." So the problem is to be conscious, without the "experiencing" which is becoming the past. I am pursuing much too difficult a question. Sorry!

When you enjoy something, when you write a poem or read a book, when you dance or do something else, just leave it at that; do not say, "I must have more of it." Because that will become greed, and therefore it is no longer a joy. Just be happy in the moment. If there is sunshine, enjoy it, do not say, "I must have more." If there are clouds, let them be; they also have their beauty. Do not say, "I wish I had a more beautiful day." What makes you miserable is the demand for more.

You listen to all this and wisely shake your heads, but it does not penetrate, does not go down deep. When you really stop demanding the 'more', when you are no longer acquisitive, joy will come without your seeking.

Questioner: What is pathos?

KRISHNAMURTI: The boy wants to know what is pathos. I wonder why he is asking such a question. Probably somebody else has put it, through him. I wish the older people would not do that; they are really corrupting the young mind. Boys are not interested in all this, the feeling of sorrow, the feeling of being pathetic, hopeless. I am sure the boy does not feel these things. The boy has his own problems. He wants to know why a bird flies, why there is light on the water, why his teachers or his parents are cruel to him, why he is not liked, why he must study, why he should obey some stupid old man. Those are his problems, not pathos. He only wants to know what God is because it is so much talked of. Do encourage them to ask questions about their own problems.

If you only want to know the meaning of pathos, look it up in a dictionary, and you will find the meaning; you do not need any explanation or definition from me. Our minds are so easily satisfied with definitions, and we think we have understood. Such a mind is very shallow.

Questioner: How can one listen to somebody?

KRISHNAMURTI: You listen to somebody if you are interested. If you really want to know how to listen to somebody, you will find out. You are listening now, aren't you? I want to know how to listen. I ask you and I listen to you because you may tell me something, and from that I will learn, I will know how to listen. There is in that very action, in that very question, an indication of how to listen.

You ask me how to listen. Now, are you listening to what I am saying? Have you ever listened to a bird? Can you listen—not with a great strain, not with great effort, but just listen easily, happily, with interest—so that your whole attention is there?

We do not listen that way, we are only eager to get something out of somebody. When you read, when you talk, you want to get something out of it. So, you never listen easily, happily. And when you do listen, you translate it into what is suitable to you, or you translate it according to what you have already read, thus getting more and more complicated, never listening peacefully, easily, quietly. Have you ever watched the moon for any length of time?—just watched it, or seen the waters go by, watched them without all the paraphernalia of sitting down and struggling to watch? If you do listen that way, you will hear much more, you will understand much more of what is being said. Even if you have to listen to your mathematics or geography or history, just listen; you will learn much more. And you will also find out if your teacher is teaching you properly, or if he is merely becoming a gramophone record, repeating the same thing over and over again. Listening is a great art which very few of us know.

January 11, 1954

Seventh Talk to Students at Rajghat School, Banaras

Have you ever sat still? You try it sometime and see if you can sit very quietly, not for any purpose, but just to see if you can sit quietly. The older you grow, the more nervous, fidgety, agitated, you become. Have you noticed how old people keep jogging their legs? Even little ones do it, all the time. It indicates, does it not, a nervousness, a tension. We think this nervousness, this tension, can be dispelled by various forms of discipline. You know what that word means? Your teachers talk to you about discipline. The religious books talk to you about self-imposed discipline. Our life is a process of continuous discipline, control, suppression. We are held, blocked, restrained, so that we never know a moment in which there is a freedom, a spontaneity. We are controlled, self-enclosed. Ask your teachers. Ask what these words mean.

Did you, as I suggested yesterday, spend ten minutes of your classtime discussing these things? Did some of the teachers talk to you about all these things before the class began? Why don't you insist on it? Why don't you make the teachers talk to you about this? The teachers and the grown-up people are all anxious to get on with their classes, with their jobs. They never have time to look around. But if you insist, every morning, that you spend ten minutes of your classtime talking about more important things, you will learn a great deal.

As I was saying, we never know a moment of real freedom, and we think that freedom comes through constant discipline, training, control. I do not think discipline leads to freedom. Discipline leads only to more and more self-enclosed minds. I know I am saying something which probably you have not heard before.

You have always heard that you must have discipline to have freedom. But if you inquire, if you look into that word, into the meaning and significance of that word, you will find that discipline means resistance against something, the building of a wall and the enclosing of yourself behind that wall of ideas. That is foolish because the more you become disciplined, the more you control, suppress, restrain, the more your mind becomes narrow, small. Have you not noticed that those people who are very disciplined have no freedom? They have no spontaneous feelings, no width of understanding. The difficulty with most of us is that we want freedom, and we think discipline will lead us to it, and yet, on the other hand we cannot do just what we want; to do exactly what we please is not freedom because we still have to live with others, we have to adjust, we have to fit in with things as they are.

As well as this superficial desire to do just what we like, is there not also a deeper want, an urge to do something creative, out of ourselves? But we really are not able, freely, spontaneously, to do what we want; there is contradiction, a conflict, between what we want to do and what we should do. Gradually, what we want to do begins to give way, to disappear, and the other thing remains—what we should do, the ideal that others want us to do, what the teachers, the parents, the other boys or girls want us to do. Deep down within me there is a feeling, there is an urge, there is a demand to do something creative, just really out of myself. But to find out what that action out of myself is, requires a great deal of understanding. It is not just doing what I like. Each one, in his self-imposed prison, does what he likes, but that is a superficial action.

To find out and do something which you feel deeply, inwardly, spontaneously, easily, is very difficult because we are suppressed. Have you noticed how people say, "Do this and do not do that"? Are they not always telling you that? So, gradually you get into the habit of doing things without much thought; so you become automatic, like a machine that functions, but without much vitality, without energy, without a great deal of thought, insight, love, affection, sensitivity. So, you have difficulty in finding something that you love to do. Also, your education does not help you to discover what you really, deeply, inwardly want to do because your teachers and your parents find it so much easier to impose through education, through control, something that you should do. What they consider to be your duty, your dharma, your responsibility, is forced on you, and gradually the things of beauty, the things that you yourself feel you could do if given an opportunity, are destroyed. So with most of us, there is inwardly a conflict going on all the time between the thing that I want to do deeply—in which I am interested and which demands a great deal of understanding, a continual putting aside of things which are worthless—and what I should do, what society demands, what the teachers have told me, what tradition has said. So, there is conflict between the two, and we think that freedom comes through controlling one thing against the other, through disciplining ourselves to a particular pattern of thought.

In a school of this kind, is it not very important to understand the question of discipline? We must have order when there are three hundred or one hundred or even ten boys and girls. But to bring order among many is very difficult because every boy and girl wants to do something of their own. The students here are well-fed, young, full of vitality and pep, and they want to burst out; the teachers want to hold them, to keep them in order, to make them study, to regularize their life.

Now is it not very important for the educator and also for you to find out what discipline means, what it implies? Certainly we must have order, but order requires explanation, intelligence, understanding, not suppression and saying, "Do this and do not do that. If you do not do that, you will get lower marks, you will be reported to the principal, to your guardian, to your parents." Suppression does not bring order; really it brings chaos, it really produces a revolt, an ugly mind. Whereas, if we take trouble, if we have the patience to explain the importance of having order, then there will be order. For instance, if you do not all turn up for a meal at the right time, think what a lot of trouble you will give to the cook. Your food will get cold, it will be bad for you to eat cold food. You will become more and more inconsiderate—that is really the problem. If you are considerate, if you are thoughtful—both the old and the young—then you will have order. Unfortunately, the old people are not considerate either; they are concerned about themselves, about their problems, their difficulties, their jobs.

In this school, right from the beginning, we have to understand intelligently what discipline is. Discipline comes naturally out of consideration. Discipline is not resistance; it is really adjustment, is it not? When you consider somebody, you adjust, and that adjustment is natural because it is born out of thought, care, affection. Whereas, if you merely say, "You must be very punctual for a meal; otherwise, you will have no meal and will be punished," there is no understanding, no consideration. Suppose a boy does not get up early in the morning, the housemaster disciplines him and says, "You must get up early; otherwise, you will be punished," or he persuades the boy through love. But these are all forms of fear, of inconsideration. The teacher has to find out why the boy is lazy. It may be that the boy wants to attract the teacher, or probably he has had no love at home and therefore wants protection, or he is not getting the right food or enough rest or enough exercise. Without going into all this, the problem of discipline is very trivial.

So, what is important is not discipline, control, or suppression but the awakening of that understanding which will regard all these problems intelligently, without fear. That is very difficult because there are very few teachers in the world who understand all these things. Surely, it is the job of the Rajghat School and the Foundation to see that this thing is done so that when the students leave this place, they are real human beings with consideration, with intelligence, who can look at everything without fear, who will not function thoughtlessly, but who will understand and be able to fit even into a society which is rotten. All these questions should be thought over every day, not by mere lectures given by the teachers, but by discussion between the teachers and the students so that when the students leave this place and enter life, they are prepared to face it in such a way that life becomes something happy and not a constant battle and misery.

Questioner: It is said that science has produced benefit as well as misery. Is science really beneficial to man?

Krishnamurti: Before I answer that question, I should like to know if you listened to what I have just been saying? The question came right on top of what I was saying. There was no gap, no interval. I am not criticizing you; I am not saying you are right or wrong. But is it not important to find out what the other man is saying? You really were not listening to what I was saying because your question was going on in your mind. You know, I have said this half a dozen times so far, and yet you go on doing it. Does it not show a lack of consideration? If you were really interested in what was being said, you would have listened. It requires thought because we are dealing with difficult subjects, and so if you want to listen, you cannot just jump into questions. May I suggest that tomorrow you write out your questions? Take the trouble to put them down on a piece of paper. Then when I have spoken, wait a few minutes or seconds and then ask. This will help you to see how your own mind is working. What I am saying is not very complicated. I am putting into words the operation of your own mind. If you want to understand, if you want to see how your mind works—and that is the only way we can look at life—it is very important to understand what is being said.

You say science has brought great benefits to man and also great misery and destruction. Is it on the whole beneficial or destructive? What do you think? Communication has improved. You can send letters to America in a couple of days. You can have the latest news from all over the world tomorrow morning or this evening. Extraordinary miracles are going on in surgical operations. At the same time, there are warships and submarines which are most destructive. The latest submarines can go round the world indefinitely under water, never coming to the top, run by atomic power. There are airplanes with bombs that can destroy thousands of human beings in a few seconds. Is it science that is wrong, or the human beings that use science? I am a Hindu or a Muslim or a Christian, so I have a particular idea which I think is more important than anybody else's idea, and I am very nationalistic. You know what that means? I feel I want to dominate, I want to control not only individuals but also groups of people. So, I use destructive means, I use science. It is me that is misusing science, not that science in itself is wrong. Jet planes are not wrong in themselves, but it is how America or Russia or England uses them. Is this not so?

Can human beings change? Can they cease to be Hindus, Muslims? There is a division between India and Pakistan, between Russia and America, England and Germany, France and other countries. Can we be human beings without being Frenchmen or Indians so that we can live together? Can we have a government which looks after all of us, not India or America only, but all of us together as human beings?

When human beings misuse science, we blame science. But it is you and I, the Russian and the American, the Frenchmen and the German, who are responsible for all this. That is why, in a school of this kind, there should be no feeling of nationality, no feeling of class, no feeling that you are a Brahmin and I am an Untouchable. We are all human beings, whether we live in Banaras or New York or California or Moscow. It is our world. This world is ours, yours and mine, not the Russians' or the Englishmen's, not the Indians' or the Pakistanis'; it is ours. And with that feeling, science *will* become an extraordinary thing, but without that feeling we are going to destroy each other.

Questioner: You say old people are fidgety and bite their nails. Have you not marked younger people also doing these things? Then how is it that the poor old people who have many difficulties are pointedly mentioned as if they are fit for nothing?

KRISHNAMURTI: Why do I point out the ugly habits of the older and not point out the ugly points of the young?

Now, you know, young people are great imitators, are they not? They are like monkeys, imitating. They see somebody doing something and they immediately do it. Have you not noticed that children want to dress alike? In some countries, children put on uniforms, and a boy or girl who does not put on a uniform feels out of place, feels something is wrong with him. The imitative process is strong in young people, and when they watch older people, they begin to copy. The old people as well as the young people are not aware of what they are doing, and so the circle goes on increasing. The old people put on a sacred thread, and the young people also put on a sacred thread. Some older person puts on a turban, and the young men also put on turbans. I was not criticizing the older generation. It is not my business, and it would be impudent on my part to do so. But what is important is for you to watch, to be aware of yourself, to be aware of your actions—such as, when you bite your finger nails, when you scratch, or when you pick your nose—then you will stop doing them. You have to be conscious of all the things that are happening in you and outside of you so that you do not become an imitative machine.

Questioner: How can we suppress the inner conflicts?

KRISHNAMURTI: We have conflicts. Why do we want to suppress them? Do listen carefully. I am not trying to argue with you but trying to find out, trying to understand the problem. So, I am not taking your side or my side.

We have conflicts, have we not? And if we can understand them, then there will be no suppression. We suppress when we do not understand. The older person suppresses the child because the older person has no time, or he has got other things to do. So he says, "do not" or "do," which are both forms of suppression. But if the older person took time, had patience and explained, went into the question with the child, then there would be no problem of suppression. In the same way you can look at your conflicts without fear, without saying, "This is right, this is wrong; I must suppress, I must not suppress." If you see a strange animal, it is no good throwing a stone at it. You have to look at it. You have to see what kind of animal it is. In the same way, if you can look at your feelings and your conflicts without throwing bricks at them, without condemning them, then you will begin to understand.

Right education from the very beginning should eliminate this inner conflict. It is faulty education that makes us have these inward struggles, inward battles, inward conflicts. Do not suppress but try to look at the conflict, try to understand it. You cannot understand it if you want to push it aside, if you want to run away. You have to put it, as it were, on a table, and look, and then out of that watching, comes understanding.

Questioner: What is real simplicity?

KRISHNAMURTI: What is simplicity? What is love? What is truth? What is a good world, and so on? I have explained every day, and I shall explain again, how our minds want a definition, and how by having a definition we think we understand.

The same question could be put differently. Let us discuss what is simplicity, and then find out what is real simplicity. The meaning of the two words, *real* and *simplicity,* you can find in the dictionary. But, to understand what simplicity is requires a great deal of thinking, a great deal of inquiry. Perhaps the lady meant that, I do not know. So, she wants to talk about it, she wants to inquire, to find out what is simplicity—not real or false simplicity, but simplicity.

What is simplicity? Is there real simplicity as distinct from false simplicity? Surely there is only simplicity—not false or true. Now, what is simplicity? Does it consist in having a few clothes, just one or two saris, dhotis, or kurtas, living in mud houses, putting on a loincloth and talking all the time about simplicity? Is that simplicity? Please find out. Do not say yes or no. A man who has a great deal—power, position, clothes, houses—can also be very simple, can't he? More clothes, more of the outward appearances do not indicate that a man is not simple. Simplicity is something entirely different. Obviously, it must begin from within and not from without. You understand? For instance, I may have very few clothes, only a loincloth, I may live in a mud hut, I may live as a sannyasi; but inwardly, if I have conflicts, if I have fears, if I have gods, puja, rituals, mantras, is that simplicity? I may put on ashes, I may go to temples, but inwardly, I may be extraordinarily complex, ambitious. I may want to be the governor, or I may want to reach *moksha*—which are both the same thing, for in each case there is the seeking for security. But you call the man who seeks *moksha* a religious person, and the man who wants to become governor a worldly person.

Though outwardly very, very simple, sleeping a couple of hours, washing his own clothes, living a hermit's life, a man may be inwardly a very complex person, he may be very ambitious; and so he will discipline himself, force himself, struggle with himself to achieve perfection, the ideal. Such a person is not a simple person. Simplicity comes when you are really inwardly simple, when you have no struggles, when you do not want to be anybody, when you do not want *moksha,* when you have no ideals, when you are not craving for anything. Being simple implies to be nobody, here in this world or in the next world. When there is that feeling, whether you live in a palace or have only a few clothes is of very little importance.

We have a tradition of simplicity on which people live and which they exploit. The tradition is that you must have few clothes, you must get up very early in the morning, you must do some meditation, you must go around trying to improve the world, you must not think about yourself. But inwardly you are thinking about yourself from morning until night because you want to be the most perfect human being. And so, you have ideals of violence and nonviolence, you have ideals of peace. Inwardly you have battling feelings, you struggle, and outwardly you are a very simple person. This is not simplicity. Simplicity comes when there is a feeling of not wanting anything—which is arduous, which requires a great deal of intelligence. Real education is the education of simplicity, not the tradition of having few things.

Now that I have answered this question, I want to know whether the lady has understood and how it will operate in her daily life. Is she now going to say, "I do not care very much whether I have ten saris or a great many things; first of all, I must be very simple inside"?

What are you going to do? Can you leave the outside and say, "It does not matter. I must begin from within"? It is all one process, is it not? If I understand the full significance of simplicity, the thing comes into being. I do not have to struggle to be simple. To struggle to be simple is not to be simple. But if I see the truth that the outward and the inward are one process, one thing, then I am simple; then I do not have to struggle to be simple; that very struggle brings complexity.

Questioner: Why do we exist, and what is our mission in life?

KRISHNAMURTI: You exist because your father and mother have produced you, and you are the result of centuries of man, not only of India but of man all over the world, are you not? You are the result of the whole of India, of the whole of the world. You are not born of any extraordinary uniqueness; you have all the background of tradition, you are a Hindu or a Muslim. You are the product of the climate, the food, the social and cultural environments, the economic pressures. You are the result of innumerable centuries, the result of time, of conflicts, of pain, of joy, of affection. Each one of you, when you say you have a soul, when you say you are a pure Brahmin, is merely following the tradition, the idea, the culture, the heritage of India, the heritage of centuries of India.

You ask what is your mission in life. First you must understand your background. If you do not understand the tradition, the culture, the heritage, if you do not understand the whole picture, then you will merely take an idea, a twist, out of the background and call that your mission. Suppose you are a Hindu and you have been brought up in that culture. Then, out of Hinduism, you pick up an idea, a feeling, and make that into your mission, don't you? Do you think differently, totally differently, from any other Hindu? To find out what the innate, potential being or urge is, one must be free of all these outward pressures, outward conditions. If I want to get at the root of the thing, I must remove all the weeds—which means, I must cease to be a Hindu or a Muslim, and there must be no fear, there must be no ambition, no acquisitiveness. Then I can go much deeper and see what the real potential thing is. But without removing all this, I cannot assume something potential. That only leads to illusion and is a philosophical speculation.

Questioner: How can this come into being?

KRISHNAMURTI: First, the dust of centuries must be removed, and that is not very easy. It requires a great deal of insight. You have to be deeply interested in it. The removal of the conditioning—the dust of tradition, of superstition, of cultural influences—requires the understanding of oneself, not learning from a book or from a teacher. That is meditation.

When the mind has cleansed itself of all the past, then you can talk of the potential being. You asked that question. Now go on with it, keep on operating on it until you find whether there is a real, original, incorruptible thing. Do not say, "Yes, there must be," or "There is no such thing." Keep on working at it, but not to find out, because you can never find out, with a mind that is corrupt, something which is not corrupted. Can the mind cleanse itself? It can. And if the mind can purify itself, then you can see, then you can find out. That purgation of the mind is meditation.

Questioner: Why do we weep in sorrow, and why do we laugh in happiness?

KRISHNAMURTI: Do you know what sorrow is? I am sorrowful when my brother or sister or father or mother dies. I have sorrow when I lose somebody whom I love. That acts on my nervous system, does it not? I cry, there are tears, I weep. I laugh when I feel very happy. It is the same reaction, the laughter being the nervous reaction.

Sorrow and happiness—are they different? When you hurt yourself, when the pain is very bad, you cry, don't you? You have tears in your eyes. The pain is so strong that it brings tears. That is one kind of sorrow—pain, physical pain. But there is also the pain when you lose somebody, when death comes and takes away the person whom you like. That gives you a shock, that gives you a sense of loneliness, a sense of separation, a sense of being left alone. That shock, the reaction of it, brings tears. You laugh when you see a smile. When you feel joyous, you dance, you laugh, you smile. These are the obvious reasons for laughter and tears.

We are human beings. We want to have constant happiness; we do not want to suffer; we do not want to have tears in our eyes; we always want smiles on our lips, and so the trouble begins. We want to discard sorrow and have happiness, and so we are in constant struggle, constant battle. But happiness is not something that you get. It comes when you are not seeking. If you seek happiness for itself, it will never come. But if you do something which you feel is right, which you feel is true, which you really love to do, in the very doing of it comes happiness.

January 12, 1954

Eighth Talk to Students at Rajghat School, Banaras

We have heard people say that without ambition we cannot do anything. In our schools, in our social life, in our relationships with each other, in anything we do in life, we feel that ambition is necessary to achieve a certain end, either personal or collective or social or for the nation. You know what that word ambition means? To achieve an end, to have the drive, the personal drive; the feeling that without struggling, without competing, without pushing, you cannot get anything done in this world. Please watch yourself and those about you, and you will see how ambitious people are. The clerk wants to become the manager, the manager wants to become the boss, the minister wants to be the prime minister, the lieutenant wants to become the general. So each one has his ambition. We also encourage this feeling in schools. We encourage students to compete, to be better than somebody else.

All our so-called progress is based on ambition. If you draw, you must draw much better than anybody else; if you make an image, it must be better than that made by anybody else; there is this constant struggle. What happens in this process is that you become very cruel. Because you want to achieve an end, you become cruel, ruthless, thoughtless, in your group, in your class, in your nation.

Ambition is really a form of power, the desire for power over myself and over others, the power to do something better than anybody else. In ambition, there is a sense of comparison, and therefore, the ambitious man is never really a creative man, is never a happy man; in himself he is discontented. And yet, we think that without ambition we should be nothing, we should have no progress.

Is there a different way of doing things, a different way of living, acting, building, inventing without ambition, without this struggle of competition in which there is cruelty and which ultimately ends in war? I think there is a different way. But that way means doing something contrary to all the established customs of thought. When we are seeking a result, the important thing to us is the result, not the thing we do, in itself. Can we understand and love the thing which we are doing without caring for what it will produce what it will get us, or what name or what reputation we shall have?

Success is the invention of a society which is greedy, which is acquisitive. Can we, each one of us, as we are growing, find out what we really love to do—whether it is mending a shoe, becoming a cobbler, or building a bridge, or being a capable and efficient administrator? Can we have the love of the thing in itself without caring for what it will give us or what it will do in the world? If we can understand that spirit, that feeling, then, I think, action will not create misery as it does at the present time; then we shall not be in conflict with one another. But it is very difficult to find out what you really love to do because you have so many contradictory urges. When you see an engine going very fast, you want to be an engine-driver. When you are young, there is an extraordinary beauty in the engine; I do not know if you have watched it. But later on that stage passes, and you want to become an orator, a speaker, a writer, or an engineer, and that too passes. Gradually, because of our rotten education, you are forced into a particular channel, into a particular groove. So you become a clerk or a lawyer or a mischief-monger, and in that job you live, you compete, you are ambitious, you struggle.

Is it not the function of education while you are very young, particularly in a school of this kind, to help to bring about such intelligence in each one of you that you will have a job which is congenial to you and which you love and want to do, and that you will not do a job which you hate or with which you are bored but which you have to do because you are already married, or because you have the responsibility of your parents, or because your parents say that you must be a lawyer when you really want to be a painter? Is it not very important, while you are young, for the teacher to understand this problem of ambition and to prevent it by talking it over with each one of you, by explaining, by going into the whole problem of competition? This will help you to find out what you really want to do.

Now we think in terms of doing something which will give us a personal benefit or a benefit to society or to the nation. We grow to maturity without maturing inwardly, without knowing what we want to do, but being forced to do something in which our heart is not. So, we live in misery. But society—that is, your parents, your guardians, your friends, and everybody about you—says what a marvelous person you are because you are a success.

We are ambitious. Ambition is not only in the outer world, but also in the inner world, in the world of the psyche, the spirit. There also we want to be a success, we want to achieve the greatest ideals. This constant struggle to become something is very destructive, it disintegrates, it destroys. Can't you understand this urge to "become" and concern yourself only with being whatever you are, and then, from there, move on? If I am jealous, can I know I am jealous or envious, and not try to become nonenvious? Jealousy is self-enclosing. If I know I am jealous and watch it and let it be, then I will see that out of that something extraordinary comes.

The "becomer," whether in the outer world or in the spiritual world, is a machine, he will never know what real joy is. One will know joy only when one sees what one is and lets that complexity, that beauty, that ugliness, that corruption, act without attempting to become something else. To do this is very difficult because the mind is always wanting to be something. You want to become philosophers or become great writers, you want to become an M.A. But you see, such ambition is never a creative thing. In that ambition there is no initiative because you are only concerned with success. You worship the god of success instead of understanding the ambition itself. However poor you may be, however empty, however dull, if you can see the thing as it is, then that will begin to transform itself. But a mind occupied in "becoming" something never understands the "being." It is the understanding of what one is, the *being* of what one is, that brings an extraordinary elation, a release of creative thought, creative life.

All this is probably a bit difficult for the average student. As I said yesterday, you should discuss this with your teachers. Did you ask your teachers? Did you take ten minutes of your classtime for this? What happened to you, and what happened to the teacher? Could you tell me? Could you understand, through the teacher, what was said?

This morning, we are talking about something which is entirely different from the usual traditional approach to life. All the religious books, all our education, all our social, cultural approaches are to achieve, to become something. But that has not created a happy world, it has brought enormous misery. Hitler, Stalin, Roosevelt are all the result of that, so also are your particular leaders, past and present.

Ambition is the activity of an unhappy person, not of a happy person. But to live, to act, to think, to create, without ambition, is extremely difficult. Without understanding ambition, there cannot be creativity. An ambitious person is never a creative, joyous person; he is always tortured. But a man who feels the love of anything, the being of anything, is really creative; such a person is a revolutionary. A person who is a communist, a socialist, a congressman, or an imperialist cannot be revolutionary. The creative human being is inwardly very rich, and out of that richness, he acts and has his being.

Ask your teachers the implications of all that I have said, and find out if one can live without ambition.

We live now with ambition. That is our daily bread. But that bread poisons us, produces in us all kinds of misery, mentally and physically, so that the moment we are thwarted and prevented from carrying out our ambition, we fall ill. But a man who has the inward feeling of doing the thing which he loves without thinking of an end, without thinking of a result—that man has no frustrations, he has no hindrances, he is the real creator.

Questioner: Why do we feel shy?

Krishnamurti: It is good to be a little shy, is it not? A boy or a girl who is just pushing everyone without reservation, without a sense of hesitation, is not as tender and sensitive as a shy person. A little shyness is good because that indicates sensitivity. But to be very shy implies also self-consciousness, does it not? What does the word *self-conscious* mean? To be conscious of oneself, to be conscious of one's person, to be conscious of one's own dignity. Such a person is shy in the wrong way because he is the center of comparison. He is the center from which he looks out. When a boy is always comparing himself with somebody, he becomes self-conscious, he is conscious of himself.

Most young people are self-conscious; as they grow to adulthood, they feel a little awkward, a little shy and sensitive. I think one has to have throughout life that sensitivity, that sense of being tender, being slightly timid, because that implies great sensitivity. This is denied when I say, "I belong to this class; I have position, authority; I am somebody." When you think you are somebody, you have lost all sensitivity, all tenderness, and the beauty of being timid goes out of life. You know, one must be hesitant, timid, to inquire, to find out. If you can be hesitant in approach, very sensitive, then you will find out the whole complication, the beauty, the struggle of life. But without that feeling of hesitancy, a timidity which is not tinged with fear, you will never see the delicate things of life, you will never see the trees and their shades or the bird sitting quietly on a telegraph post.

Questioner: How can human beings progress when there is no ambition?

Krishnamurti: Do you think inventions are the result of ambition? Do you think the inventor, the scientist who really thinks out a problem, or the true research worker has ambition? Do you think the man who invented the jet plane, the jet engine, was ambitious? He invents; then the ambitious people come along and use the invention for their purpose—

to make money, to make wars, to make an end for themselves.

Have you done anything through ambition? You may have moved from here to there. You may get a better job, or a better position; you may become the principal or the governor or the collector. But is that really living, is that progress? There is the bullock cart and there is the jet plane; that is generally called progress. There has really been a tremendous progress from the bullock cart to the jet plane, from the post chaise to teletype and instantaneous communication. Our idea of progress is always in one particular direction, and we do not take into account all the implications of ambition. Suppose an oil well is discovered here. Then, what do you think will happen? There will be all the machinery of exploitation. It is not that there should not be an oil field in Banaras, but the idea of progress is to use that oil and produce more and more, without understanding the whole complex problem of ambition.

Take a very simple example. A missionary in the South Seas regularly held Sunday classes and read the Bible to his parishioners. When he read the Bible stories, they listened very attentively. After some time, he thought how good it would be if they all knew how to read. So he went to America to collect money. He came back and taught them how to read and write. But, to his great disappointment, he found that they were reading comic magazines, not the Bible.

So, real progress is in what is happening to your mind. Are you making progress there, or are you just gramophone records, repeating over and over again the same old comic, tragic, or stupid stories?

Questioner: Why are people born in the world?

KRISHNAMURTI: For various reasons—sex, passion, the desire to have children. It is a very simple reason. You look at a tree or a bush that flowers. Nature wants to keep on breeding its own species, does it not? You understand? The mango tree has flowers; the flower is pollinated and becomes the fruit. There is a stone in the mango and that stone you throw away; it falls in fertile soil and grows into a tree which produces many more mangoes. There is a continuity in this process, is there not? So in human beings also there is continuity in the species. But the mangoes do not fight among themselves; tigers do not kill each other; only we human beings destroy each other; we are the only species that kill each other, and the capacity to kill is, by us, called progress. Is this progress?

Questioner: Some say, "Mystery, thy name is woman."

KRISHNAMURTI: Is this a conundrum or a puzzle that you are asking me? Do you know what a conundrum is? It is a puzzling question which you have to think over and work out. Why do you bother about all this? You see, first we read something in a book and then we try to work it out. Some say, "Mystery, thy name is woman." What does that mean? Women are not such mysterious organisms, are they? The real mystery is not that. But we are satisfied with superficial mysteries, we like a conjurer, a dark room, mysterious people. We look for mysteries. But, there are no mysteries. What we think are mysteries are all inventions of the mind.

If you can understand the workings of the mind and go beyond them, there is the real mystery. But very few of us go beyond and reach that mystery. You are all satisfied with the superficial mysteries of a detective story or of a shrine. If one can understand the workings of one's own mind and go beyond that, then one will find extraordinary things.

Questioner: How do we dream?

KRISHNAMURTI: Do you have dreams? What kind of dreams do you have? If you go to bed with a full stomach, you have some kind of dream. There are various other kinds of dreams.

What do you think dreams are? A dream is a very complex thing. Even while you are awake, while you are wandering along a street or sitting quietly, you may be dreaming because your mind is thinking of various things. You may be sitting here, but you think you are in your home, and you imagine what your mother is doing, or what your father is doing, or what your younger brother is doing. That is a kind of dream, is it not? Though you are sitting quietly, your mind is off, imagining, speculating, wandering.

Similarly, when you are asleep, your mind goes off, imagining, wandering, speculating. Then there are dreams born out of your deep unconscious. And there are dreams which foretell, which give you a warning, which give you hints. It is possible for human beings to have no dreams at all but to sleep very profoundly, and in the deep profundity, to discover something which no conscious or unconscious mind can ever discover, an intimation of something which no mind can ever conjure up.

The mind is such an extraordinary thing. You spend eighteen or twenty years learning the same subjects and passing several examinations, but you do not spend an hour or even ten minutes to understand this extraordinary thing called the mind. Without understanding the mind, passing examinations, getting jobs, or your becoming a minister has very little meaning. It is the mind that creates illusions, and if you do not understand the maker of illusions, your life has little meaning.

Do you understand all the things that I am talking about? The difficulty is, I am speaking in English. But I doubt very much whether you would understand even if I spoke in Hindi. You would understand the words, but not the meaning, the implications that lie behind the words. You have to find out the implications by asking your teachers or your parents.

What I have said is a question of your whole existence. It is not enough to find out for a day or two; you have to find out the implications as you live, throughout life. But you cannot live, you cannot find out if you are merely driven by ambition, by fear. To find out, there must be a sensitivity, a freedom in the psyche, and all that is denied if you do not understand the workings of your mind.

Questioner: How should we think out any problem?

KRISHNAMURTI: That is quite an intelligent question—how should we think out a problem? Most people want an answer to a problem. But that boy wants to know how to think out a problem—which is quite different. He is not looking for an answer; at least I hope not.

There is no answer at all to a problem, and so it is foolish to seek an answer. But if I know how to think out a problem, then the answer is the very thinking out of the problem. Look, sirs. You have a mathematical problem. You do not know the answer, but the answer is at the end of the book, so you keep turning to the end of the book to find the answer. But life is not like that. Nobody is going to give you the answer. If anybody thinks he can give you the answer, he is stupid. But if you know how to think out a problem, how to look at it, how to approach it, the very thinking, the very looking at it, is the solution.

You want to know how to think out a problem. The first thing, obviously, is not to be afraid of the problem. You understand? Because, if you are afraid, you won't look, you will run away from it. The second thing is not to condemn it, not to say how terrible, how awful, how miserable it is. Then, not to compare that problem with any other problem, or have a comparative value when you approach the problem. All this is a bit difficult. When you approach a problem, if you have already got a definite judgment, an answer to that problem, you do not understand the problem. So, to understand the problem, there must be no comparison, no fear, no judgment; those are the essential things which will help you to understand the problem. There are really no problems except those which are created by comparison, fear, and judgment.

Please discuss all this with your teachers and among yourselves. Let these ideas, let these words, go through your mind so that you are familiar with all these issues. Then, you will be able to face the problems of life.

January 13, 1954

Ninth Talk to Students at Rajghat School, Banaras

We have been discussing for several days the question of fear. We shall now consider what I think is one of our greatest difficulties—how to prevent the mind from becoming imitative.

We see there are obvious imitations: copying, learning a thing, eating in a certain way, putting on certain clothes, learning to ride a bicycle or a motor car, learning a technique, and so on. These are the superficial , the obvious imitations which are necessary, which are useful and essential. But, through which merely functions in the groove of imitation.

Perhaps I am going to talk of something that is difficult. If you find it difficult, talk it over with your teacher. Ask them questions because it is very important to free the mind from crystallizing, from becoming dull, from merely functioning as a machine without much creative release.

It is very important to understand how the mind both creates for itself tradition and has tradition imposed upon it—through social, environmental pressures, by conditioning, patterns, barriers. The way of imitation is what we have to think about, and not how to free the mind or how the mind can free itself from its own imitative process.

For most of us, experience becomes a tradition. Do you understand what I mean by "experience"? You see a tree; the seeing, the perception creates an experience, does it not? You see a car; the very seeing is the experiencing, and the experience creates a tradition. Your mind is bound by tradition, tradition being memory, and the older the people, the older the race, the more oppressive are the traditions. The mind lives in tradition, functions in tradition, acts in tradition. The mind becomes an imitative mind because it is experiencing all the time—seeing a bird, seeing a man, seeing a woman, having pain, seeing death and disease, seeing an airplane, a bullock cart, a donkey with a huge bundle on its back, an overloaded camel, or one bull charging at another. All these are experiences. And when the mind is stirred up, it creates, out of every experience, a tradition, a memory; and so the mind becomes a factor of imitation.

The problem is to be really free from imitation, from the accumulation of tradition, because without that freedom there is no creativity.

Practically everybody in the world has so little freedom to live, to create, to be. I do not mean having children or writing a few poems, but the creative release of the mind in freedom from tradition, freedom from the experience which makes for tradition, freedom from memory. This is, as I said, rather difficult, but you should listen to all this as you would listen to music, as you would see the beauty of the river and the lovely trees that are old and heavy and full of shade. You should see all this as you see the beautiful pictures in a museum, the lovely statues of the Greeks and of the Egyptians. Similarly, you should listen to all this, and if you are at all serious, at all inquiring, you have to come to this freedom because an imitative mind, a traditional mind, can never be creative.

You function in tradition because you are afraid of what people say, of what the neighbors or your parents or your guardians or your priests say. You are afraid. So you act in the old way of thinking. You are a Brahmin or something else, and you keep on being the same until you die, moving in the same circle, in the same pattern, in the same framework. That is not freedom. The mind is not then free from thought which is born of experience, of tradition, of memory; it is anchored in the past, and therefore it cannot be free.

We talk a great deal about freedom of thought. There are books written about how thought must be free. But thought can never be free. The mind is experiencing all the time, consciously or unconsciously, whether you are looking out of the window, or whether you have closed your eyes, or whether you are sleeping; it is experiencing various influences, the pressure of people, of climate, of food. Various beliefs and thoughts keep impinging on the mind; the mind keeps on accumulating, and from that accumulation, from that tradition, from the innumerable memories, it acts. To expect such a mind to be free is like telling a man who is dying to be free. A dying man can never be free, he can never see anything new because of his memories. Memory is the result of yesterday, and to see anything new, to create anything totally new, that which is anchored to the past, that which is the past, must come to an end; then only can there be freedom to think.

Of course, you must have freedom to think, but tradition, governments, party politics—these do not allow you to think. They want you to think in a particular direction, and that thinking is a limited thing, and to break away from it and to think differently is still limited. Say, for instance, I am a Muslim, and I break away from the Muslim habits, traditions, habits of thought, and become a Christian or a communist. Such a breaking away is still thinking; it is still the process of imitation, the process of experience, the process of memory; and to think in the new pattern of the communist instead of the old pattern of the Muslim is still limited thinking.

So, our question is: Can the mind be free—not free from experience, but free to experience and not accumulate? To be free from experience is not possible; you might as well be dead. But can the mind, in the very experiencing, cease to create tradition? Suppose you see a nice, new, polished bicycle with chromium handles; you see the beauty of the design, you see t he polish, and you are attracted; you want it, and you get it. The very getting of a cycle is an experience to you, and that experience is stamped in your mind, and you say, "It is mine." You polish it for a few days or weeks and then forget about it. But it has created in your mind an experience which becomes a tradition, and that tradition holds your mind; then from that you want a car, and if you have a car, you want an airplane—if you are rich enough to buy one—and so on and on, all within the field of imitation. This movement from wanting a cycle to wanting a jet plane is still in the same pattern, but this is not freedom.

Freedom comes when the mind experiences without creating tradition. Do not say, "How is that possible?" "How can I do it?" When you ask such a question, you have already created the pattern. The "how" means the pattern. The "how" implies the way of getting toward that pattern, and in the very process of copying the method, the mind has created tradition and has been caught in it. So, there is no "how" to freedom, there is no way to freedom. But if you merely observe, see and are conscious of the way the mind experiences and creates tradition and is caught in it, if you are just aware of it and realize the process, then out of that realization comes something entirely different, a freedom which is not tethered to experience.

This is important to understand because in schools, in our education, all we are taught is the cultivation of memory, the learning of formulas; the mind is trained only in the process of imitation. When you read history, when you learn science, physics, philosophy, or psychology, the teacher is merely functioning in imitation; you learn from him, and you also imitate. So, from childhood until you die, this process of imitation, this cultivation of memory goes on. You are just living in a groove of imitation, of tradition. That is all you know, that is your culture, and so there are very few creative human beings. To drop all that, to see whether memory is essential or whether it is a detriment, a hindrance—that is the function of education. But we begin at the wrong end; we first cultivate memory and then say, "How am I to get to the other?" But if the other is emphasized or talked about, seen, investigated, felt—which is real education—then the learning of some technique for some particular job becomes immaterial, though necessary.

Is not the function of education primarily to free the mind from its own experiences so that there can be creative life, that creativeness which we call God or truth?

Questioner: Why do we hate anybody, and from where does this feeling of hatred come?

KRISHNAMURTI: Why does one hate? Do you hate anybody? Or, is it merely an academic question, just it casual question? Do you dislike anybody? I am sure you do. First of all, you dislike some persons because they have done some harm to you, they have insulted you, they have called you names, or they have taken away your toy, or you do not like their face, or they do not smile nicely, or they are crude, vulgar, heavy. So, your natural reaction is to say, "Do not come near me." That is just a natural reaction, is it not? There is nothing wrong in this.

To condemn anything is the most stupid form of action. You must not condemn hatred but examine how dislike, hatred, comes into being. If you say, "To hate is wrong, it is stupid," then it is only your condemnation that is stupid. But if you begin to question how dislike comes into being, like a flower in sunshine, then you can do something. But if you merely condemn it and push it aside, it is still there.

You dislike for many, many reasons. It may be because of a personal reason—because you have been hurt, you have been called names, or something has been taken away from you, or you have been humiliated, or you feel jealous, envious of another, and you hate the other. You may dislike somebody who is nice, clean, good-looking, because you are not like that; you want to be like that, but you are not. You have asked how hatred comes into being. I am trying to show you how it comes into being. You plant a tender tree; another boy comes along and pulls it out, and you dislike that boy because something which you love, which you care for, has been destroyed.

Our life, from childhood up to old age, is a constant process of envy, jealousy, hatred, and frustration, a sense of loneliness, of ugliness. But if the teacher, the parent, the educator—instead of saying hatred is right or wrong, or how to get over it, which is all a stupid way of dealing with it—takes the trouble to explain how the hatred arises and so brings about intelligence and clarity in the student, then the student will see for himself how hatred comes into being; then he will see the conflict within himself, and realize that this struggling and fighting will lead nowhere.

Questioner: How can we be free from indignation?

Krishnamurti: What do you mean by indignation? You mean when a man beats a heavily laden donkey, you feel angry? You say you feel righteously angry when some big man beats a little boy. Is there such a thing as righteous indignation?

You asked a question, and I am not at all sure you are interested in finding out what it means. Most of us get angry for various reasons, and we try to find out after getting angry how to get over it. But what is important is to know the way of anger, how it comes into being and to stop it before the poisoning takes place. You understand what I am saying? How anger arises is our problem, not how to be free from anger, do you understand? I feel jealous because you have something which I have not got; your wife is more beautiful than mine, and I feel jealous; I struggle, then I feel most ugly to myself, I feel bitter with myself, and then I say, "I must not be angry, I must conquer anger. How am I to do it?" As I do not know how to prevent it, how to prevent the arising of jealousy, how to put an end to the feeling before it arises, I go to some guru. But the problem is still there.

Is it possible to understand how jealousy arises so that the feeling does not arise? You know, it is much better to eat the right food and be healthy rather than to eat wrong food, fall ill, and then go to the doctor. We eat wrong food all the time; then we take pills or go to the doctor. But if we took the right food, we would never need to go to the doctor.

So what I am saying is: Let us find out how to eat right food, how to look at all this, so that these problems do not arise. Surely education is this, the prevention of the problem rather than finding a cure for it.

Questioner: Does constant suffering destroy man's sensitivity and intelligence?

Krishnamurti: What do you think? A mind that is constantly occupied with something, with puja, with following somebody, with a theory, with a philosophy, with its own sorrow, with its own beauty, with its own suffering, with its own failures and successes—surely such a mind becomes insensitive. You know, if your mind, if your attention, is fixed on something all the time, you have no occasion to look around. Can such a mind be sensitive?

"To be sensitive" implies to be looking all around—seeing beauty, ugliness, death, sorrow, pain, joy. So, a mind that is suffering obviously becomes insensitive because suffering is its occupation; the mind uses suffering as a means for its own protection. My son dies, or my husband dies, and I am left alone; I have no companion, and I feel my life has been blotted out. So I keep on suffering, and my mind now is not concerned with freedom from suffering, but I make suffering into another means of my existence. You understand? The mind uses suffering as it uses joy to enrich itself because the mind thinks that without being occupied, it is poor, it is empty, dull. This very occupation of the mind creates its own destruction. Sorrow is not a thing to be occupied with, any more than joy. The mind must understand why there is sorrow and not keep on merely being occupied with sorrow. The mind wants security, whether it is in suffering or in joy. So sorrow becomes the way of security. This is not a harsh thing I am saying, for if you think about it, if you look into it, you will see how the mind plays a trick on itself. It is only the unoccupied mind that is intelligent, that is sensitive.

It is no use asking how the mind can be unoccupied. In the very "how" the mind is playing a trick on itself.

Questioner: How can one differentiate between memory which is essential and memory which is detrimental?

KRISHNAMURTI: The mind creates tradition, memory, through experience. Can the mind be free from storing up, though it is experiencing? You understand the difference? What is required is not the cultivation of memory but the freedom from the accumulative process of the mind.

You hurt me, which is an experience, and I store up that hurt, and that becomes my tradition, and from that tradition I look at you, I react. That is the everyday process of my mind and your mind. Now, is it possible that, though you hurt me, the accumulative process does not take place? The two processes are entirely different.

If you say harsh words to me, it hurts me, but if that hurt is not given importance, it does not become the background from which I act, so it is possible to meet you afresh. That is real education, in the deep sense of the word. Because, then, though I see the conditioning effects of experience, the mind is not conditioned.

Questioner: But why does the mind accumulate?

KRISHNAMURTI: Why do you think it accumulates? Listen to this carefully. Do you know the answer? Are you waiting for me to answer so that you can say yes? If you do not wait for an answer from me, then asking yourself that very question, "Why does the mind accumulate?" brings about a creativity in you. You have asked it because you do not know the answer. But if you are actually confronted with the problem, your mind becomes alert and has to find an answer. The asking of that question, therefore, awakens, releases your own initiative, your creativity, the capacity to discover, to have a totally different outlook.

The problem is: Why does the mind accumulate? Please look at the problem. Probably some religious book or some teacher or some psychologist has told you why the mind accumulates. Whether it has been said by Ramanuja or by Shankara or by Jesus, it is what other people have said, it is not your own discovery. Do you understand? You have to discover. For you to discover, what other people have said must be put aside, must it not? So, you have to put aside all that you have been told about it, all that you have read about it. Then, you can find out why the mind accumulates.

To begin very simply, why do you accumulate clothes? For convenience, is it not? Apart from the necessity, which is convenience, you also feel the gratification that goes with having many clothes, the feeling that you have a cupboard full of clothes, the feeling from which you get a sense of well-being, a sense of security. First there is a necessity, which is convenience; from convenience it becomes a psychological elation, and from that feeling, the cupboard of clothes gives you the sense of "I have got something, I am somebody." The cupboard is your security. So, the mind gathers knowledge, information, reads a great deal, talks a great deal, knows a great deal. So knowledge, this gradual storing up in the cupboard of your mind, becomes your security. Is it not so? So, the mind accumulates because it wants to feel safe.

Don't you feel very proud that you know lots of things? You know history, science, mathematics. You know how to drive a car. Does not the capacity to do something give you security and satisfaction? That is why the mind accumulates. When you cultivate the virtue of being good or kind or loving or generous, the cultivation is the process of accumulation, and in that accumulation which you call virtue, you feel very secure. Your mind is all the time gathering in order to be secure, to be safe. It has various cupboards. It has always a cupboard in which it can feel completely safe. But such a mind is an imitative mind, an uncreative mind. If you watch the mind in operation and understand the process of accumulation, then your mind will cease to collect. You will have memory because it is necessary, but you will not use it to feel secure, to feel that you are somebody.

There are memories which are necessary. It is stupid to say, "I have built bridges for 35 years, and now, I must forget how to build a bridge." I am talking of the process of accumulation of the mind from which tradition, the background, is built, from which thought arises. Such thought is never free. It is only when the mind has no accumulation, and there is no thinking from accumulation, that it can be creative.

Questioner: Why does a man leave society and become a sannyasi?

KRISHNAMURTI: You know, life is complicated, and so one wants a simple life. The more cultured, the more beautiful, the more watchful, the more alert one is, the greater is one's demand for a simple life. I am not talking of the phony sannyasi who merely puts on colored robes and has a beard but of the real sannyasi who sees the complexity of life and puts it aside. Unfortunately, most sannyasis begin at the wrong end. Simplicity is at the other end. The two ends must meet, but you cannot begin from the outer. The feeling of simplicity arises, comes into being, when the mind is free of accumulation.

Generally, a sannyasi who leaves the world says, "The world is too stupid, too complicated; there are too many things to worry about—the family, the children, and the jobs that they will get or will not get, and so on." So, he says, "I won't have anything to do with all this," and he withdraws from the so-called worldly life. He puts on a saffron cloth and says, "I have renounced the world." But he is still a human being with all his sexual and other appetites, with all his prejudices, with all his illusions. So, his mere renouncing of the world is nothing.

How easily we are deceived! We think we leave the "worldly life" by merely putting on a saffron cloth, which is the easiest thing to do. But simplicity comes only in understanding the complex process of desire, of belief, of pain, of sorrow, of envy, of accumulation. One may have much of worldly possessions or little; one may have children or no children. Simplicity does not lie in possessing little. The understanding of inward beauty brings simplicity, inward richness. And without that inward richness, the mere giving up of some possessions or putting on of a yellow robe means nothing.

Do not be deceived by saffron or yellow robes. Do not worship the mere outward show of renunciation, which has no meaning. What has meaning can never be had, can never be learned, from another. You can find it yourself when you are really simple—when you have not the ashes of outward renunciation but the inward freedom from all conflicts, suppressions, ambitions, imitations. Such a person is really a creative human being who will really help the world—not a sannyasi who sits, caught in his own dreams, on the bank of a river.

January 14, 1954

Tenth Talk to Students at Rajghat School, Banaras

I do not know if you have found that fear is a very strange thing. Most of us have fear of some kind or another, and it lurks behind so many forms, it hides behind so many virtues. Without really understanding the cause of fear, the root of fear, all feeling for beauty merely becomes imitative. Without understanding the deeper layers of fear, there is very little significance in the appreciation of beauty. For most of us, the appreciation of beauty is tinged with envy, and so is the desire for beauty. You know what envy is—to be envious of somebody, to be envious of another's capacity, his position, his prestige, the way he looks, the way he walks? For most of us, envy is the basis of our actions; remove envy and we feel we are lost. All our effort is towards success, and in that there is envy; behind that envy there is fear. Fear is the drive, the motive, the spirit, which moves us. Without really understanding the significance of fear and envy, we are only social and moral imitators.

So, I think it is very important to understand this thing we call envy. If you watch your own mind in operation, your own activities, you will find that there is hardly any moment which is not towards something, towards the 'more', towards the greater, towards the desire for wider experience. The moment there is comparison, there must be envy. When I want more, not only of the mundane things, of the worldly things, but also of love, of beauty, of inward richness, the very movement towards the 'more', towards the end, towards the thing which you are going to get, has envy behind it.

After all, beauty is something not tinged with envy, beauty is something which *is*, in itself. You do not become more beautiful or more good—which are all the movements of envy—but you have to understand *what is*, which does not mean you are satisfied with things as they are. The moment you enter into satisfaction and dissatisfaction, there is envy. You can understand the thing as it is, yourself as you are, only when you do not compare, because in comparison, there is also envy. To understand *what is* seems to me to be the real creative beauty of life, and not merely getting somewhere in virtue or in respectability or in power or in position. But all our education, all our thinking, is instinctively towards the 'more', which we call progress.

It is, I think, very important to understand this while we are young, while we are not caught in the web of responsibility, of family, of jobs, of position, of activity, of undertakings done blindly and foolishly. Is it not the function of education to free the mind from the comparative? You understand what I mean by that? You see, our education, our social life, our religious aspirations, are all based on this urge for the 'more'—more spiritual life, more happiness, more money, more knowledge, greater virtue—a perfect ideal towards which I go and you go. We are brought up in that atmosphere, and so we never discover *what is*, what we actually are.

We are always trying to become something else. We are always trying to become noble, to become a hero, an example, an ideal; and if we really go behind this urge to become, we shall find there is envy, and that behind that envy there is fear, the fear of what one is. So we begin to cover up what we are with all these outward and inward movements which we call progress, which we call 'becoming'. It is very difficult for the mind not to think in terms of becoming, of moving towards the greater, the wider, the more extensive activities, and that movement is based on fear and envy. But there is a totally different movement which is real creativity and real understanding, namely, the movement of the understanding of *what is,* what you actually are. In that movement, you do not change *what is* but you understand *what is.*

We are accustomed to think in terms of getting somewhere, of achieving, of succeeding, of changing this into that—of changing violence into nonviolence, which is an ideal. I am inwardly poor, and I want to find those inner riches which are incorruptible. That is the movement we know; in that movement we are brought up, we are nurtured, we are conditioned. In that movement, if you observe, there is envy, there is fear, the fear of not being what one wants to be. The urge to become has created this society, this culture, these religions. Our culture is based on envy. Our religion, as we practice it, as we think of it, as we know it, is the worship of success in a distant future. So, this movement is based on envy, acquisitiveness, and fear.

Is it not the function of education to break up that movement and to bring about a totally different activity which is the understanding of *what is,* as one actually is? In this activity, there is no fear, there is no envy, no desire to become something. This activity is the initiative of the thing as it is.

The movement of envy leads to utter discontent and disintegration. Let me put it very simply. I am aggressive, violent, and I am told from childhood that I must change that, that I must become nonviolent, nonaggressive, that I must have love. All this is a movement towards changing *what is,* and that movement is based on envy, on fear, because I want to change 'what I am' into something else. But if I see the truth of that movement which is envy and in which there is fear, then I can see 'what I am'. When I see I am aggressive, I do not change 'what I am', but I watch the movement of aggression. In that watching, there is no fear, there is no compulsion. The very watching of 'what I am' brings about a totally different activity. That is surely the function of education; that is creation.

Creative activity requires a great deal of perception, insight, and understanding because it does not emphasize the self-centered activity of the mind. At present, all our activities emphasize self-centeredness, from which spring our social and economic difficulties and miseries. All of us can observe these two movements in ourselves. In the observation of the two, there is the dropping away of all activity based on fear and envy, and there is only the other activity which is creative, in which there is initiative and beauty.

Questioner: What is experience?

KRISHNAMURTI: When you watch yourself, is it not an experience? When you put on a kurta, is that not an experience? When you watch the boat going down the river, is that not an experience? When you cry, when you laugh, when you are jealous, when you want to possess something and want to push others aside, is it not an experience? Living is experience. But, we want to keep experiences which are pleasant and avoid experiences which are unpleasant. That is not life. Choosing between the pleasant and the unpleasant is not living. Life is everything from the dark clouds to the marvelous sunset; life is the whole thing which you can watch—the song fields and the barren of birds the green earth, the fears, the laughter, the struggles, death. But, we generally view life differently; we say, "This is life, that is not life," "This is beautiful, that is not beautiful," "I am going to hold to the beautiful and push away the ugly," "I am unhappy, I want happiness." When we begin to choose, there is death.

If you really think about all this, you will see that when the mind chooses between that which is pleasant and that which is unpleasant, and holds on to one and discards the other, then deterioration takes place, then death comes in. But to see this whole process in movement, to be aware of it totally without any choice, stirs the mind and frees it from its self-enclosing activities of choice. A mind that is free from choice is wise, intelligent, capable of infinite depth.

Listen to all this. These are not mere words to be heard and then put aside. Experiences of various kinds are impinging all the time on our minds, and our minds now are only capable of choice, choosing one experience and holding on to it and discarding another experience. When a mind retains an experience, from that experience it creates a tradition, and that tradition becomes choice and action. A mind that is merely caught in choice can never find out what truth is. So, it is only the mind that sees the whole movement of darkness and of light that is highly sensitive, intelligent. Only then can that which we call God come to be.

You have been listening for some clays to all that has been said. Are you aware of what is taking place in you, how your mind thinks, how your mind watches things and people around? Are you watching more, seeing more, feeling more? Are you aware of all this? Do you understand what I am talking about? Are you aware of what is going on within yourself, in your mind, in your feelings? Do you ever watch the trees, the river? Do you see how you are looking at the river? What are the thoughts that come into your mind as you watch that river?

If you are not aware of all that is going on in your mind when you see something, then you will never know the operations of your mind, the workings of your mind, and without knowing that, you are not educated. You may have a few alphabets after your name, but that is not education. To be educated, you have to find out if your mind functions in tradition, if it is caught in the usual habitual routine. Do you do things because your parents want you to do them? Do you put on a sacred thread merely because that is the custom? Do you go to the temple to do puja because you have been told to, or because you have been meditating, or because you like it? Surely, all this indicates the operation of your mind, does it not? And without knowing that, how can you be educated?

The brain is an astounding thing if you watch it. There must be millions and millions of cells in it, and it must be a very complex mechanism. It must be most complex and concentrated because when I ask you a question, when I look at things, the mind goes through such a lot to produce an answer. You understand what I am talking about? If I ask you where you live, how quickly your mind operates! See the astounding rapidity of memory! If you are asked a question which you do not know, again look at what the mind goes through.

We are so rich in ourselves, but without knowing that richness, without knowing all its beauty, its complexity, we want every other richness—the richness of position, of office, of travel, of comfort, of knowledge—but these are all trivial riches compared to this thing. To know how the mind works and to go beyond it seems to me to be real education.

It has just been said that when we are confronted with something complex, when there is a problem, our mind becomes blank. Does your mind become blank? Do you understand what I am asking you? Look, your mind is ceaselessly active, it is in constant movement. When you open your eyes, you have various impressions, and the mind is receiving all these impressions—the light, the pictures, the windows, the green leaves, the movement of the animals and people. When you close your eyes, there is the inward movement of thought. So, the mind is constantly active; there is never a moment when it is still. That is the mind, not only at the superficial level, but also deep down. You know, after all, the Ganga is not just the surface water on which you see the ripples and the beauty of the sunshine; there is also the great depth of it, about 60 feet of water below the surface. The mind is not just the superficial expression of annoyance, of pleasure, of desires, of joy and frustration, but deep down, there is the whole mind, and all that is in movement all the time—asking questions, doubting, being frustrated, longing. When that movement is confronted with something which does not answer, it is shocked into paralysis for a second or two, and then it begins to act.

Have you not noticed when you see a beautiful thing, a beautiful mountain, a lovely river, a beautiful smile, how your mind becomes quiet? It is too much for the mind; for a second it is still, and then it begins to function. That is the case with most of us. Seeing that, is it possible for the mind to be still the whole way, not just at one level? Can your mind be totally still all the time, not through the shock of beauty or pain, not with any purpose—because the moment you have purpose, there is fear and envy behind it—but be totally still, deep down and also on the surface? You can only find out, you cannot answer yes or no.

There is real freedom when the mind right through knows its activities, its shades, its lights, its movements, its deliberations, its elations. The very knowing by the mind of all its movements from deep down to the top, the very seeing of it all, is the stilling of the mind. All this has to be very intelligently thought out, watched for, unearthed, so that you know the whole thing that is the mind, so that you are aware of the whole process; then only is the mind really still.

Questioner: What is jealousy?

Krishnamurti: Don't you know what jealousy is? When you have a toy and the other person has a bigger toy, don't you want that bigger toy? When you have a small bicycle and you see a big beautiful bicycle, don't you want that? That is jealousy. On that jealousy, people live, exploit, multiply.

Please, will the teacher who is responsible for that boy's education explain this to him. Please take the time and the trouble to point out what jealousy is—if you understand what jealousy is yourself.

Jealousy begins in a small way and then one gets drawn into a stream of action, clothed under so many names. We all know jealousy. That little boy wants to know what jealousy is. Do not say it is wrong or right, do not condemn it. Do not tell him it is not desirable to be jealous, that jealousy is ugly, evil. What is evil is your condemnation of it, not jealousy itself. Please explain to him the whole business of jealousy, how it arises, how our society is based on jealousy, how our instincts are based on it, how it shapes all our actions. You do not condemn a map, you do not say the road should not go that way. You do not say that the villages should be here and not there; the villages are there. Similarly you must look at jealousy and not try to push it aside, not try to transform it, not try to make it idealistic.

Jealousy is jealousy. You cannot make it into something else. But if you can look at it, understand it, then it gets transformed; you do not have to do a thing about it. If you can explain this deeply to every boy and girl, we shall produce quite a different generation.

Questioner: Why do we want to show off and to assure ourselves that we are something?

KRISHNAMURTI: Why do you want to assure yourself that you are something? Why do I want to be sure that I am something?

You know, the maharajah wants to show that he is something. He shows off his cars, his titles, his position, his riches. The professor, the pundit, assures himself that he is somebody through his knowledge. You also want to show that you are somebody in your class with your friends. It is the same thing, on a small scale or a big scale. Why do we do that? Please listen to what I am saying.

If you are inwardly rich, there is no need to show off because that in itself is beautiful. Because inwardly we fear we have nothing, we put on lots of airs. The sannyasi does it, the prime ministers and the rich men do it. Strip them of their power, their money, their position—they are dull, stupid, empty. So, a person who wants to show off, who wants to be assured that he is somebody, or who tells himself that he is somebody, is really very empty. You know, it is like a drum; you keep on beating it to make a noise, and the noise is the showing off, the assurance that you are somebody. But the drum in itself has no noise, it has to be beaten to produce the noise; in itself it is empty. In yourself you are empty, dull, uncreative; and because you are nothing, you want to assure yourself that you are somebody. That is the movement of envy. But if you say, "Yes, I am empty, I am poor," and from there begin not to change but to understand it, to go into it, to delve deeply into it, then you will find riches that are incorruptible. In that movement, there is no assurance that you are somebody, because you are nobody. The man who is really nobody, who is nothing in himself, is the only truly happy man.

Questioner: You have been talking all these days with the idea of bringing about a change in our lives. If you want us to think differently, how is it different from the attitude we have been having so far, to be something which we are not today?

KRISHNAMURTI: The question needs to be made simpler. Your question is: You want us to change and in what way is that different from our own desire to change in the old pattern?

Do I want you to change? If you change because I want you to change, then that change is the movement of envy, of fear, of reward and punishment. That is, you are this, and you want to change into that because you are being persuaded by me to change into that—which is the movement of jealousy, of fear, of envy. If I realize what I am, just realize without any desire to change, without any desire to condemn, if I can just be that, just see that, then from that there is a totally different action. But to bring about that totally different action, the other movement—the movement of envy, of fear, of condemnation, of comparison—must cease. Is that clear?

Questioner: At present, we are not thinking in the way that you are thinking. You are talking to us with a view to making us see your way of thinking. Is that not so? Is that not a change that you would like us to bring about in ourselves? There is only a subtle difference between the two. We are not thinking in the way you are thinking because we do not take life in the way you are taking it.

KRISHNAMURTI: The way we generally think is the way in which we have been brought up—in that pattern, in that groove, in that framework. Now, when you realize your thinking is conditioned, is there not a breaking up of that conditioning? When I realize that I am thinking in terms of Communism or Catholicism or Hinduism, is there not a breaking away from that? That is all I am talking about. There is a breaking away, which is quite a different movement from habitual thinking—in which there is no change.

When we talk of change, we mean we must change from this to that. When we change from this to that, "that" is already the known; therefore, it is not change. When I change from greed to nongreed, the nongreed is my formulation, is my idea. Therefore, I already know the state of nongreed. Therefore, when I say I must change greed into nongreed, the movement is still within the field of the known, from one known to another known. Therefore, it is not change at all. Do you see that?

Please listen, all of you. It is not that gentleman alone who is asking the question, but all of us are involved in this. When we talk about change, about revolution, changing from this to that, "that" is the state we already know; therefore, it is not change. When I change from Hinduism to Catholicism, I know what Catholicism is. It is a thing I want. I do not like this and I like that. That which I like is already what I know. Therefore, it is the same thing only in a different form.

What I am talking about is not change but the cessation of the desire to change, which does not mean I am content with *what is*. There must be the cessation of the desire to change from the known to what I think is the unknown, but which is really the known. If that movement ceases, then there is a totally different activity.

January 15, 1954

Eleventh Talk to Students at Rajghat School, Banaras

I think we ought to talk about something of which some of us may be aware, namely, the peculiar desire for power over others and over oneself, which most of us have.

I think that power is one of the deeper desires, behind which really lies that fear which comes from a sense of loneliness, a sense of frustration. What I am saying may be difficult, but please listen. If one can understand this and go beyond, then there is a different kind of state, in which love is. If one has not that love, life becomes dull, weary, empty, and shallow.

I think it is important to understand this thing that we call power—not electric power or steam power, not the capacity to do something efficiently, which are all necessary. I am talking of something which is of greater significance and of much deeper value, and without understanding which, efficiency, the capacity for doing things, becomes a means of creating greater misery, greater suffering for man.

Most of us desire some kind of power; it may be over the son or the wife or the husband, or it may be over a group of people, or it may be in the name of an ideal or in the name of a country. This desire to have power over others is always operating—even over a servant, to order him about, to get angry with him, to push him around. Does not this desire for power spring from a sense of loneliness? Have you ever felt lonely? You know what it is to be alone, to have no friends, to be completely alone, to be an isolated being? To have no friend, no sense of anyone on whom you can rely or whom you can trust, is to be in a state of complete self-isolation. Probably you have not felt it. Most of you avoid it, run away from it. You are only awakened to it in a great crisis, in death; but you run away from it. Without understanding this emptiness, mere control through power leads to every form of frustration.

Probably, it is very difficult to understand all this while one is young, but one should talk a great deal about it because when one grows older, one begins to have power over others and over oneself. The sannyasi wants to have power over himself, and so he controls himself through asceticism; that gives him a sense of power, a sense of domination over himself and over his desires. His wanting only a few things for himself creates in him an extraordinary sense of power, a power which is self-centered. And you also demand power over others, and in that you feel a great sense of release, of happiness, of delight. You feel capable of dominating several thousands of people, through ideas, through political power, through words. Fear lies behind all this urge for power.

After all, when you compare yourself with somebody, with an idea, with a person, with an example, does not the desire for power lie behind that comparison? I have no power, no position, no capacity, but if I can imitate a hero, copy him, I shall become powerful, I shall be somebody. So, the very desire to be somebody, the copying, the imitation, the comparison, gives me a sense of power.

I think it is very important, while we are young, to understand this thing because that is what almost everyone is seeking in the world. The clerk wants power over his under-clerk, and the boss has innumerable employees over whom he has power. The ministers have power to give position or to give prestige, and they have the means of controlling others. The whole structure of society is based on this, and we think we can use power as a means of changing people's lives. The very possession of power is a great delight. The man in power says, "I am doing this for the sake of my country, I am doing this for the sake of an ideal." When he says this, he is conscious that he is in a position of authority and that he is controlling people.

While you are being educated, while you are at school or college, this thing has to be understood. You have to see if you can live in this world without dominating people, without controlling people, without shaping their minds. Because, after all, each one of us is as important as the politician, the wielder of power; each one of us wants to grow in freedom so that we can be what we are, so that we can understand what we are and, from that, act, so that we are not imposed upon by society or by our teachers or by our parents or by any other person who is trying to dominate and shape our particular lives. It is very difficult to withstand all this because each one of us wants power. The teacher wants to become the principal because the principal has power over so many people and has more money.

When you are controlled by another through money, through position, through status, the feeling that you are an individual, a human being, a single unit, is completely denied, destroyed. Whereas, it seems to me, it is very important in a school of this kind, that we should create a feeling that this is our school, yours and mine, in the sense that you, as a student, are as important as the teacher or the principal. This feeling of 'ourness' does not exist anywhere in the world—the feeling that this is our earth,yours and mine, not the Russians' or the Americans' or the Englishmen's or the Africans'; the feeling that it is our world, not a communist world or a socialist world or a capitalist world; the feeling that it is our earth in which you and I and others can live and be free to find out the whole significance of living.

The significance of living and the understanding of it are denied if we are seeking power in any form. The mother has power over the little child and wants him to grow in a certain way. The father says, "This is what he should be," and pushes him into a pattern. But, education is surely the freeing of the mind to function in freedom without any twist, without any corruption through power, through comparison. We should create such a school; you and I must create it. Otherwise, you will go out of this school and college just like any other human being, dull, with your brain stuffed with superficial information; you will not have any clear initiative of your own but be a machine that is driven by circumstances, by society, by the politician, because each one of you wants power, like the politician.

So, even though you may not understand for the time being what I am saying, talk to your teachers, make them explain all this to you, that it is our earth where all human beings can live, understand, exercise their capacities, without destroying anyone. The moment we want to use our capacity to gain power, position, prestige, we destroy. So, we ought to talk about how to create a school here where each one of us, the student, the teacher, the members of the Foundation, all create this place together—with you as a student looking after the trees and the roads, feeling and caring for the things that are of the earth, not because it is your school, but because it is our earth.

I think this is the only spirit that is going to save the world, not clever scientific inventions, but the sense that you and I are creating together, in a world which is ours. But that is very difficult to come by because, now, everything is "mine" and not "yours," the "mine" being divided into many classes, many holdings, many functions, many nationalities. That feeling of 'ourness' does not exist in this world, but without that feeling, we will have no peace in the world. Therefore, it is very important that you, while you are young, should understand this and have this feeling so that when you go out of this place, you can create a new world and a new generation.

Questioner: Why does one feel sad when someone dies whom one knew, whom one loved?

KRISHNAMURTI: You feel sad when any friend or near relation of yours dies. Do you feel sad for the person who is dead or for yourself? The other person is gone, and you are left to face life. With that person you felt somewhat secure, somewhat happy; you felt a companionship, a friendship. That person is gone, and you are left with your insecurity, are you not? You are constantly aware of your loneliness. You are aware that you have been stripped of companionship. There was a person with whom you could talk and express yourself as you were. When that person is gone, you feel very sad; out of your loneliness, out of your sense of not having anyone to whom you can turn, you feel very sad, but you do not feel sad for that person. You feel sad for yourself. And feeling sad, you create all kinds of theories, all kinds of beliefs.

It is very important, is it not, to understand this process of dependence. Why does one depend on another? For certain things I depend on the milkman, on the postman, on the man who drives the engine, on the bank, or on the policeman; but my dependence on these is entirely different from the dependence based on fear and on the inward demand for comfort. As I do not know how to live, I am confused, I am lonely, I want someone to help me; I want someone to guide me, someone on whom I can rely, a master, a book, or an idea. When that dependence is taken away from me, I feel lost, and this sense of loss creates suffering.

Is it not important, while we are at school, to understand this problem of dependence so that we may grow without depending on anyone, inwardly? That requires a great deal of intelligence, a great deal of inquiry. Surely, it is the function of education to help to free the mind from any sense of fear, which makes for dependence. Being dependent, we say, "How can I be free from dependence?" But if one understood the process, the ways of dependence, then there would be no problem of how to be free from it. The very understanding frees the mind from dependence.

Questioner: What is a star?

KRISHNAMURTI: I am sorry I cannot give you a scientific explanation. You can find out what a star is from any scientific book or from your science teacher.

Have you looked at a star? What do you feel when you look at a star? When you look at the sky of an evening and see the many thousands and millions of stars and planets, what do you feel? Do you just look and move away? Most of us do that. We are talking with somebody and we say, "Look at the stars and the moon, what a beautiful night!" and go on with our talk. But, if you are alone or with people who are not always chattering or talking but who want to look at things, then when you look at the stars, what do you feel? Do you feel small in this vast universe, or do you feel that it is part of you, the whole thing—the stars, the moon, the trees, and the river? Have you the time to look and find out your own feeling?

How difficult it is to look at anything beautiful without the mind interfering, without the mind with its memories saying, "This is not such a good night as the other night," "It is not as beautiful as it was last year," "It is too cold, I cannot look." The mind never looks without words, without comparison. It is only when you can look without comparison, or without words, that the stars and the earth and the trees and the moon and the light on the water have an extraordinary significance. In that, there is great beauty. To look without comparison, one has to understand the mind because it is the mind that looks, it is the mind that interprets what it sees, giving it a name. The very naming of a thing by the mind becomes the way of pushing it away.

So, when you look at a star or at a bird or at a tree, find out what is happening to you as you look, and that will reveal a great deal about yourself.

Questioner: Man has made great progress in the material world Why is it we do not see progress in other directions?

KRISHNAMURTI: It is fairly clear why we make progress in the material world, especially in the new world where there is a great deal of energy, a great release of intellectual capacity. When you are colonizing a new world, you have to invent, you have to struggle. Man has made progress from the bow and arrow to the atom bomb, from the bullock cart to the jet plane that travels about 1600 miles an hour; that is generally called progress. But is there progress in any other direction, inwardly? Have you, as an individual, progressed inwardly? Have you found anything for yourself?

We know what other people have said, what other people have found. But, have we found anything for ourselves? Are we more charitable, more kind? Are our minds more expansive and alert, inwardly? Have we put away fear? Without these things, to make progress in the world is to destroy ourselves.

Questioner: What is God?

KRISHNAMURTI: You know how for the villager, the peasant, God is that little image before which he puts some flowers. Primitive people call thunder their God, and others worship trees and nature. At one time, man worshipped the apple tree and the olive tree in Europe. There are people in India even now who worship trees.

Go into any temple, and there you will see an image covered with oil and garlands and jewels; you call that your God, and you put flowers and do puja before it. You may go further and create an image in your mind, an idea that is born of your own tradition, out of your background; and that, you call your God. The man who threw the atom bomb thought that God was by his side. Every warlord, from Hitler and Kitchener to any little general, invokes God. Is that image or that idea really God? Or, is God something unimaginable, not measurable by our minds?

God is something totally unfathomable by us and comes into being only when our minds are quiet, when our minds are not projecting, struggling. When the mind is still, then perhaps we shall know what God is.

So, it is very important, while we are young, not to be caught by the word God, not to accept what we are told God is. There are many eager to tell us what God is. But, we must examine what they tell. And there are many people who say there is no God either. We must not be caught by what they say but examine it equally carefully. Neither the believer nor the nonbeliever will ever find God. It is only when the mind is free of belief and nonbelief, when the mind is still, that there is a possibility of finding God.

We are never told of these things. From childhood, you are told there is God, and you repeat it. When you go to some guru, he will tell you, "There is God. Do this and do that. Repeat this mantra, do that puja, practice such and such a discipline, and you will find God." You may do all this, but what you find will not be God. It will only be your own projection, the projection of what you want.

All this is difficult and requires a great deal of thought and inquiry. That is why, when you are in a school of this kind, you should grow in freedom so that your mind may find out for itself, may discover; then the mind becomes creative, astonishingly alert.

Questioner: Why does a human being suffer though he does his best with whatever capacity he has?

Krishnamurti: Whatever capacity I may possess, why do I feel sad when I cannot fulfill, when I am not successful in carrying out my intention? When you are doing something to the best of your capacity, why do you feel sad? Is it not simple, this question?

We are not satisfied with just doing what we love to do. We want what we do to be a success. To us, the doing is not important, but the success, the result, what the doing will bring. When our action is not successful, when it does not bring about what we want, we feel sorrow-laden. The drive behind our action is our desire for success, our desire for power, for recognition, for position, for status. We want somebody to tell us how marvelously we have done. All this means, really, we never know how to love a thing and do it just for itself, not for what it will bring. We do everything with an eye on success, on the future, on tomorrow, and when tomorrow does not come we feel miserable; this is because we never do anything for the love of the thing itself.

There are many here who are teachers and others who are professors or big business people or officials. Why are you in those professions? Not because you love what you do, but because there is nothing else for you to do. So, whatever you do, you want it to be successful. You want to ride on the wave of success, and so you are always competing, struggling, destroying the capacities of the mind thereby.

Questioner: How can we live a life without experience and memory?

KRISHNAMURTI: You want to know how to get rid of memory. That is, you want to find a method, a system. But the system, the method, only gives you further experience; it only cultivates memory, does it not? When I know how to do a thing, it becomes a habit. If I know how to read and write, the "how" then becomes a part of my memory, and with that memory I write and recognize every word, every syllable.

What I said the other day was about something entirely different. I said that life is a process of experience and memory. The very living is experience, and experience creates tradition, memory; with that tradition, memory, and habit, we live. So, there is never anything new. Is it not possible to live with experience which does not corrupt, which does not merely become a memory through which we look at life? We discussed this very carefully. But one has to go into it over and over again from so many different viewpoints to get the whole meaning of it.

Questioner: Does history prove the existence of God?

KRISHNAMURTI: Is it a matter of proof? History may or may not prove that there is or is not God. Millions say there is God, and millions say equally emphatically there is no God. Each side quotes authority, history, scientific proof.

The mind is frightened, it wants something to rely on, something on which it can depend. The mind wants something permanent to which it can cling. With this desire for permanence it seeks authority, negatively or positively. When it seeks authority in those who say there is no God, it repeats and says, "There is no God." It is perfectly satisfied in that belief. And there are those who, seeking permanency, say that there is God. So, the mind clings to that and seeks to prove through history, through books, through other people's experiences that there is God. But that is not reality, that is not God.

The mind must be free from the very beginning to find out what God is. And the mind is not free when it is seeking security, when it is seeking permanency, when it is caught in fear.

January 18, 1954

Twelfth Talk to Students at Rajghat School, Banaras

From childhood, we are brought up to condemn some things or some persons, and to praise others. Have you not heard grown-up people say, "You are a naughty boy"? They think that by doing that, they have solved the problem. But to understand something requires much insight, a great sense, not of tolerance—tolerance is merely an invention of the mind to justify its activities or other people's activities—but of understanding, a great width and depth of mind.

I would like to talk, this morning, of something which may be rather difficult, but I think it is worthwhile to understand it. Very few of us enjoy anything. We have very little joy in seeing the sunset or the full moon or a beautiful person or a lovely tree or a bird in flight or a dance. We do not really enjoy anything. We look at it, we are superficially amused or excited by it, we have a sensation which we call joy. But enjoyment is something far deeper, which must be understood and gone into.

When we are young, we enjoy and take delight in things—in games, in clothes, in reading a book or writing a poem or painting a picture, or in pushing each other about. But as we grow older, this enjoyment becomes a pain, a travail, a struggle. While we are young, we enjoy food, but as we grow older we start eating food that is heavily laden with condiments, spices, and then we lose all taste, delicacy, and refinement of taste. When young, we enjoy watching animals, insects, birds. As we grow older, although we still want to enjoy things, the best has gone out of us; we prefer other kinds of sensations—passion, lust, power, position. These are all the normal things of life, though they are superficial; they are not to be condemned, not to be justified, but to be understood and given their right place. If you condemn them as being worthless, as being sensational, stupid, or unspiritual, you destroy the whole process of living. It is like saying, "My right arm is ugly, I am going to chop it off." We are made up of all these things. We have to understand everything, not condemn, not justify.

As we grow older, the things of life lose their meaning; our minds become dull, insensitive, and so, we try to enjoy, we try to force ourselves to look at pictures, to look at trees, to look at little children playing. We read some sacred book or other and try to find its meaning, its depth, its significance. But, it is all an effort, a travail, something to struggle with.

I think it is very important to understand this thing called joy, the enjoyment of things. When you see something very beautiful, you want to possess it, you want to hold onto it, you want to call it your own—"It is my tree, my bird, my house, my husband, my wife." We want to hold it, and in that very process of holding, the thing that you once enjoyed is gone because in the very holding there is dependence, there is fear, there is exclusion, and so the thing that gave joy, a sense of inward beauty, is lost, and life becomes enclosed. You consider the thing as belonging to you, so gradually enjoyment becomes something which you can possess, which you must have. You enjoy doing a ritual, doing puja, or being somebody in the world; you are content with living on the surface, seeking one sensation, one enjoyment, after another. That is our life, is it not? You get tired of one god, and you want to find another god. You change your guru if he does not satisfy you, and then you ask him, "Please lead me somewhere." Behind all this, there is the search to find joy. You live at a superficial level and think you can get enjoyment from it.

To know real joy, one must go much deeper. Joy is not mere sensation. It requires extraordinary refinement of the mind, but not the refinement of the self that gathers more and more to itself. Such a self, such a person, can never understand this state of joy in which the enjoyer is not. One has to under stand this extraordinary thing; otherwise, life becomes very small, petty, superficial—being born, learning a few things, suffering, bearing children, having responsibilities, earning money, having a little intellectual amusement, and then to die. That is our life. There is very little refinement in clothes, in manners, in the things that we eat. So gradually, the mind becomes very dull.

It matters very much what you eat, but you just like to eat tasty things, you like to stuff yourself with a lot of unnecessary foods because it tastes good. Do please listen to all this. It matters very much the way you talk, the way you walk, the way you look at people. Search your mind, be aware, watch your gestures, watch the meaning of your speech. If you are really very alert, the mind becomes very sensitive, refined, simple. Without that simplicity and refinement, life is very superficial. But the refinement of the self is like being enclosed behind a beautiful wall with a great many decorations and pictures. That refinement of the self is still not enjoyment because in it there is pain, there is always the fear of losing and hope of gaining. But if the mind can go beyond the refinement of the self, the 'me', then there is quite a different process at work; in that, there is no experiencer.

All this may be rather difficult, but it does not matter. Just listen to it. When you grow older these words may have a meaning, a significance; they may mean something to you later when life is pressing on you, when life is difficult and full of shadows and struggle. So, listen to it as you would listen to music which you do not quite understand—just listen.

We may move from one refinement to another, from one subtlety to another, from one enjoyment to another, but at the center of it all there is the 'me'—the 'me' that is enjoying, that wants more happiness, the 'me' that searches, looks for, longs for happiness, the 'me' that struggles, the 'me' that becomes more and more "refined," but never likes to come to an end. It is only when the 'me' in all subtle forms comes to an end that there is a state of bliss which cannot be sought after, an ecstasy, a real joy, without pain, without corruption. Now, all our joy, all our happiness, is corruption; behind it there is pain, behind it there is fear.

When the mind goes beyond the thought of the 'me', the experiencer, the observer, the thinker, then there is a possibility of a happiness which is incorruptible. That happiness cannot be made permanent, in the sense in which we use that word. But, our mind is seeking permanent happiness, something that will last, that will continue. That very desire for continuity is corruption. But when the mind is free from the 'me', there is a happiness, from moment to moment, which comes without your seeking, in which there is no gathering, no storing up, no putting by of happiness. It is not something which you can hold on to. A mind that says, "I was happy yesterday and I am not happy now, but I will be happy tomorrow"—such a mind is a comparing mind, and in that mind there is fear. It is always copying and discarding, gaining and losing; therefore, it is not really a happy mind.

If we can understand the process of life without condemning, without saying it is right or wrong, then, I think, there comes a creative happiness which is not "yours" or "mine." That creative happiness is like sunshine. If you want to keep the sunshine to yourself, it is no longer the clear, warm, life-giving sun. Similarly, if you want happiness because you are suffering, or because you have lost somebody, or because you have not been successful, then that is merely a reaction. But if we can go beyond, then there is a happiness that is not of the mind.

It is very important from childhood to have good taste, to be exposed to beauty, to good music, to good literature, so that the mind becomes very sensitive, not gross, not heavy. It requires a great deal of subtlety to understand the real depths of life, and that is why it matters very much, while we are young, how we are educated, what we eat, what clothes we put on, what kind of house we live in. I assure you that the appreciation and love of beauty matters very much, and that without it the real thing can never be found. But we go through school, through life, brutalized, disciplined, and we call that education, we call that living.

It is very important, while we are at this school, to look at the river, the green fields, and the trees; to have good food, but not food that is too tasty, that is too hot; not to eat too much; to enjoy games without competition; not to try to win for the college, but to play for the sake of the game. From there you will find, if you are really observing, that the mind becomes very alert, watchful, recollected; and so as you grow, you are bound to enjoy things right through life. But merely to remain at the superficial level of enjoyment and not to know the real depth of human capacity, is like living in a dirty street and trying to keep it clean. It always gets dirty, it will always be spoiled, it will always be corrupt. But if one can, through the right kind of education, know how to think and to go beyond all thought, then, in that, there is extraordinary peace, a bliss which the superficial mind, living in its own superficial happiness, can never find.

You have heard what I have said about food and clothes and cleanliness. Try to find out for yourself something more beyond it. See if you can restrain yourself from eating food which is too hot or too tasty. After all, it is only while you are young that you can be revolutionaries, not when you are sixty or seventy. Perhaps a few of us may be, but the vast majority are not revolutionaries. As you grow older, you crystallize. It is only when you are young that there is the possibility of revolution, of revolt, of discontent.

To have that revolt, there must be discontent all through life. There is nothing wrong with revolt. What is wrong is to find an avenue which will satisfy you, which will quiet the discontent.

Questioner: When I read something, my mind wanders. How am I to concentrate?

KRISHNAMURTI: Do you know what concentration is? Do you know that you are concentrating when you are watching a dance which you really like? Last night we saw a dance. When you watched it, did you know that you were concentrated? When you are watching something in which you are interested—two bulls fighting or a bird in flight or two boats with full sail going on the river against the current—are you conscious that you are concentrated?

When your mind is not attracted to something, when you are forcing yourself to listen to music which you really do not enjoy, then you are conscious of making an effort to listen. This forcing you call concentration. But if you listen with real delight because you are really enjoying the music, then your whole mind, your whole being is in it. You are not saying, "Well, I must concentrate." You are already there with the dancer, you are almost dancing yourself. But you see, we never look at, or listen to, or read anything that way, we are never interested in anything so completely. We are only partially interested. One part of the mind says, "I do not want to read that beastly book, it is boring," and the other part says, "I must read it because I have to study for my examination." When one part says that you must read, the other part, which knows the book is terribly boring, wanders off. So you have a struggle, and you say, "I must begin to concentrate."

You do not have to learn to concentrate. Please listen to this. Do not force yourself to concentrate but be interested, love the thing that you are doing for itself. When you paint, paint for itself; when you look at a dance, enjoy it, look at it, see the beauty of it so that your mind is not broken up into different parts, so that the mind is a whole thing, a complete thing, so that there is no fractional looking with a mind that is broken up into different parts and which says "I must look."

What is important is not concentration but the love of the thing. The very love of the thing for itself brings an astonishing energy, an energy which is attention; without that, your learning, your looking, has no meaning, and you merely pass examinations or become glorified clerks.

Questioner: Is it true that the lunar eclipse affects our life? If it does, why is it so?

KRISHNAMURTI: If you are a lunatic, if you are a little touched in the head, it may affect you. But I do not see otherwise how it can.

This question opens up the problem of superstition. You live in a society, among religious people, who say, "The lunar eclipse affects the mind." They have got all kinds of theories, and you are brought up on them. You see how all these pilgrims, thousands of them, gather and bathe at the Sangam and in the Ganga. When thousands of people think about something, there is an atmosphere created, is there not? In that atmosphere, in that activity, the child watches and is impressed. When you are young, the mind is sensitive like a photo plate that absorbs. That is why the kind of atmosphere you live in is very important. But we do not pay attention to all this. We live in this chaotic, dark, miserable world in a superficial way. You hear old people say, "The lunar eclipse affects your life," and you accept. You do not question, you do not think for yourself.

To think simply is very difficult because the mind is not simple, the mind invents, it creates every kind of illusion, mystery, and it gets caught in that. To have a simple mind is really to understand the complexity of life. You cannot merely deny the complexity of life and say, "I have a simple mind." A simple mind is not a thing to be cultivated; it comes into being when you understand the complexity of existence.

Questioner: What is the goal of our life?

KRISHNAMURTI: What is the significance of life? What is the purpose of life?

Why do you ask such a question? You ask this question when, in you, there is chaos, and about you there is confusion, uncertainty. Being uncertain, you want something to be certain. You want a certain purpose in life, a definite goal, because in yourself you are uncertain. You are miserable, confused; you do not know what to do. Out of that confusion, out of that misery, out of that struggle, out of those fears, you say, "What is the purpose of life?" You want something permanent that you can struggle after, and the very struggle for a goal creates its own false clarity, which is only another form of confusion.

What is important is not what is the goal of life but to understand the confusion in which one is, the misery, the tears, and all the other things. We do not understand the confusion but only want to get rid of it. The real thing is here, not there. A man who is concerned does not ask what is the purpose of life. He is concerned with the clearing up of the confusion, of the sorrow in which he is caught. When that is cleared, he does not ask a question like this. You do not ask, "What is the purpose of sunshine?" "What is the purpose of beauty?" "What is the purpose of living?" It is only when life becomes a misery, a constant battle, and when you want to escape from that misery, from that battle, that you say, "Tell me what is the aim of life." Then you go after various people, migrate from one teacher to another, trying to find out what is the purpose of life. They will tell you, though they are equally foolish. You can only choose a guru who is as confused as you are, and from him you will get what you want.

If you can understand the confusion, the struggle, the misery, the deep longings that you have, then in that very understanding, you will find something about which you do not have to ask another.

Questioner: Why do we cry?

KRISHNAMURTI: You know, there are tears of joy and tears of pain. The tears of joy are very rare. When you love someone, tears come to your eyes. But that is a very rare thing. It does not happen to us because we do not love. As we grow older, we become more and more serious. We know at least the seriousness of frustration, the seriousness of hopeless misery in life—the depths of which have not been seen, enjoyed, known. Most of us have shed tears—the little child and the old person. We know what those tears mean—the tears of pain, of losing something, of losing a person, of not having success, of not being happily married. We know all those things. But to understand and go beyond all that, to go beyond every thought, requires a great deal of insight.

Questioner: How can we deal with the unconscious?

KRISHNAMURTI: This question has been put, not by a grown-up person, but by a child. A child does not know anything about the unconscious. All that he knows is playing a game, learning subjects, bullying people around him, feeling hunger and fear, and so on.

You are a child and you cannot watch much while you are young. But even if you watch a little, you will find that there are various things going on under the superficial ripples of your mind. Have you ever watched the river? You know, there is an astonishing life going on below the river, in the deeper depths. A Frenchman went down to a great depth underwater and found astonishing life, fishes that you have never seen, colors that are utterly unimaginable, darkness that is incredible, silence that is impenetrable. But we know only the tiny ripples that ruffle the water, only the currents on the surface of the river. But if we go deeper—there are artificial ways of going deep down—then you can see the number of fishes, the variety of life, the strange happenings below the water.

In the same way, to see below the surface of the mind, below the ripples in it and all its activities, you must be capable of going deep down into the mind. It is important to know that the mind is not just the little layer of superficial activity, that you are not merely studying to pass examinations, not merely following some tradition in the matter of how you dress, doing puja, or anything else.

To go below the superficial activities, you must have a mind that can understand how to go deep. I think that is one of the functions of education, not to be merely occupied with the surface, whether it is beautiful or ugly, but to be able to go deep, like the diver with his diving dress, so that in the depths you can freely breathe, so that you can find out in those depths all the intricacies of life, the limitations, the fluctuations, the varieties of thoughts—because, in oneself, one is all that—and then go beyond all that, transcend all that.

You cannot go very deep if you do not know the surface of your mind. To know the surface, one has to watch; the mind has to watch the way one dresses, puts on clothes, puts on a sacred thread, does puja, and understand why. Then, you can go deep. But to go deep, you must have a very simple mind. That is why a mind that is held in conclusions, in condemnation, in comparison, can never go beyond its own superficial activities.

Questioner: How should we observe things?

KRISHNAMURTI: What matters is not how you should observe but how you actually observe.

You do not know how to observe. Many people will tell you how; just to accept that would be silly. You have to find out how you actually look at things. Have you ever noticed how you look at things? How do you look at a tree? Do you look at it fully, or do you immediately give the tree a name, look at it casually, and wander away? When you give it a name, your mind has already wandered away. If you look at a parrot, do you observe the red beak, the claws, the curious way it flies? Just watch, and as you watch, you observe and learn to see. The moment you say that bird is a parrot, your mind has already been distracted from observation.

We never look at anything freely, completely, because we do not observe it without comparing. We say, "That bird is not as beautiful as the other bird," "That tree is not as tall or as magnificent as the other tree"; we also give it a name. The process of comparison is going on all the time. Only that mind which really looks can look without this process. That is how a thing has to be observed. When you hear it said that you should look without comparison, without naming, then you will struggle to look that way. But do not try to look that way. Just see how you look at a beautiful object, how you compare, how you judge. Just watch how your mind is always wandering, never fully looking. To look, the mind must be quiet, not wander, not be distracted.

January 19, 1954

Thirteenth Talk to Students at Rajghat School, Banaras

One of the greatest difficulties that we have is to find out what makes for mediocrity. You know what that word means? A mediocre mind really means a mind that is impaired, that is not free, that is caught in fear, in a problem; it is a mind that merely revolves round its own self-interest, round its own success and failure, its own immediate solutions of the sorrows that inevitably come to a petty mind. It is one of the most difficult things, is it not, for a mind that is mediocre to break away from its own habits of thought, from its own pattern of action, and be free to live, to move about, to act. Most of our minds are very small, are very petty. Look at your own mind and you will see what it is occupied with—such small things as passing an examination, your own success, what people think of you, how you are afraid of somebody. You want a job, and when you have that job, you want to have a better one, and so on. If you search your mind, you will find it is all the time occupied with this kind of small, trivial, self-interested activity. Being thus occupied, it creates problems, does it not? It tries to solve those problems according to its own pettiness but cannot do so, and merely increases them. It seems to me that the function of education is to break down this way of thinking.

The mediocre mind, the mind that is caught in one of the narrow streets of Banaras and lives there, may read, it may pass examinations, it may be socially very active, but it still lives in the narrow little street of its own making. I think it is very important for all of us, the old and the young, to see that as the mind is so small, whatever effort it makes, whatever struggles it may go through, whatever hopes or fears or longings it may have, they are still small, they are still petty. It is very difficult for most of us to realize that the gurus, the Masters, the societies, the religions which the petty mind forms, are still petty. It is very difficult to break this pattern of thinking.

Is it not very important while we are young to have teachers, educators, who are not mediocre? Because, if the educators are dull, weary, are thinking of little things and are caught in their own pettiness, naturally they cannot help to bring about an atmosphere in which the student can be free and break through the pattern which society has imposed upon people.

I think it is very important to be able to know that one is mediocre because most of us do not admit we are mediocre; we all think that we have something extraordinary lurking behind, somewhere. But we have to know that we are mediocre, to realize that mediocrity further creates pettiness, and yet not act against it. Any action against mediocrity is itself born of mediocrity; to try to break down mediocrity is still petty, trivial.

Don't you understand all this? Unfortunately, I am speaking only in English, but I hope your teachers will help you to understand. In explaining this to you, their own triviality will break down. The very explanation will awaken them to their own pettiness, smallness. A small mind cannot love, is not generous, quarrels over trivial things. What is needed in India and elsewhere in the world is not clever people, not people with degrees or big positions, but people—ordinary people like you and me—who have broken down the triviality of their mind.

Triviality is essentially the thought of oneself. That is what makes the mind trivial—the constant occupation about its own success, with one's own ideals, about one's own desires to become perfect. Because the 'me', the self, however much it may expand, is still very small. So, the mind that is occupied is a petty mind; the mind that is constantly thinking about something, worried about its examinations, worried as to whether it will get a job, what its father and mother or teachers or gurus or neighbors or society thinks, is a petty mind. The occupation with these ideas only makes for respectability, and the respectable mind, the mediocre mind, is not a happy mind.

Please listen to all this. You all want to be respectable, don't you?—to do the right thing, to be well-thought of by somebody, by your father or by your neighbor or by your society—and this creates fear; such a mind can never think of anything new. What is needed in this deteriorating world is a mind that is creative, not merely inventing or having some other capacity. That creativeness comes only when there is no fear, when the mind is not occupied with its own problems. All this requires an atmosphere in which the student is really free—free not to do whatever he likes, but free to question, to investigate, to find out, to reason, and to go beyond the reason. The student requires a freedom in which he can find out what he really loves to do in life so that he is not forced to do a particular thing which he loathes, which he does not like.

A mediocre mind never revolts; it submits to government, to parental authority; it puts up with anything. I am afraid in a country like this, where there is overpopulation, where livelihood is very, very difficult, these pressures make us obey, make us submit, and gradually the spirit of revolt, the spirit of discontent, is destroyed. A school of this kind should educate the student to have that tremendous discontent right through life, which cannot be truly satisfied. The discontent begins to find out, becomes really intelligent, if it does not find a channel of satisfaction, of gratification.

So education is a very complex thing, it is not just going through some classes and passing examinations and getting a job. Education is a life process, a constant uncovering of the whole significance of life, and the teachers are not prepared for it. That is why they must be educated, in order to educate the children. You go through these examinations, get jobs, and then what happens to you? You get married, you have children, you are worried, you have little money, and you are swallowed up in this whole mass of the average mind. That is what happens. All those who have passed the gates of any university just disappear; they do not revolt and create a new society, a new way of thinking, they do not break down the old pattern. Instead, they just become the average, mediocre mind. I think really the function of the school at Rajghat is to break down this mediocrity so that you can be a different person when you leave here, a creative human being who will bring about a new world. You see, that requires on the part of the teachers, on the part of the elders, on the part of the parents, a great deal of understanding, a great deal of affection. If a school of this kind cannot do that, it has no business to exist. It is very important that all of us—the students, the teachers, the parents, everyone who comes here—should understand this and create conditions in which the petty mind, the small, mediocre mind, is transformed so that it can live and be in that creative spirit without fear. To do so, we must have great affection and understanding.

Questioner: Why do we boys and girls feel shy of each other?

Krishnamurti: Why do you feel shy? Have you ever seen two sparrows, male and female sparrows, two birds on the windowsill, chattering away? They are different, are they not? The male has a black chest and the female has not. One is rather timid; the other is more aggressive, it attacks. Have you not noticed it? Obviously a boy and a girl are not the same physically. Girls have a different body, their nerves are different. Perhaps a girl is sensitive, shy, and a boy is more rough. Physically a girl is differently constructed from a boy. There is a whole problem behind that, the problem of sex, which is nature's way of creating babies. Nobody tells us of these things and all the implications. We are allowed to grow up wild, ignorant in this thing, and that is why we feel shy.

Also the Indian society keeps the male, the female, and the little children apart. The old people have a great many ideas of what is right and what is wrong—that the woman must be kept in the house, the woman is inferior, someone to he looked down upon, to be used, made into a cook, someone to have children. Naturally if you are a girl, you grow up in fear, in apprehension, in nervousness, anxiety, so that you are not a creative human being at all but just a dull, hard-working woman. You have no amusements, you do not paint, you do not think, you may have passed some examinations, but they do not mean a thing to you. You become an ordinary woman like the rest, and the boy exactly the same.

Education at present is the most destructive way of dealing with human beings. We are not helped to understand life, to love life, to see the enormous beauty, the richness of existence, to know of death and also the living thing of life. We are not shown all that. All that we are told is "do" and "don't." Brutally or aggressively you are beaten, scolded, bullied, so naturally when you are young, and when you grow up, you are shy. The whole problem is never understood because behind it there is fear. Is it not the function of the educator to explain, to show all this so that, while a student, you understand the difficulties, the subtleties? You can understand the difficulties, the subtleties, the immense problems involved in all these things, only when there is no fear.

Questioner: Is it right that fame comes after death?

Krishnamurti: Do you think that the villager who dies will have fame afterwards?

Questioner: A great man, after he dies, becomes famous and is honored.

Krishnamurti: What is a great man? Let us find out the truth of that question. Is he one who seeks fame? Is he one who would give himself tremendous importance? Is he one who identifies himself with a country and becomes a leader? If he does this, he has fame while he is living. That is what we all want; we all want the same thing, to be great people. You want to lead the procession, you want to be the governor, you want to be the great ideal, the great person who is going to reform India. Since you want that, maybe you will lead the procession. But is that greatness? Does greatness consist in being publicized, in having your name appear in the papers, having authority over people, making people obey because you have a strong will or personality or some kink in the mind? Surely, greatness is something totally different.

Greatness is anonymity, to be anonymous is the greatest thing. Great cathedrals, great sculpture, all the great things of life, must be anonymous. Like truth, they do not belong to any particular person. Truth does not belong to you or to me, it is totally impersonal and anonymous. If you say you have got truth, then you are not anonymous, you are making yourself more important than truth. But an anonymous person may never be great because he does not want to be great—great in the sense of the world, or even inwardly, because he is nobody. He has no followers, he has no shrine, he does not puff himself up. But most of us, unfortunately, like to puff ourselves up, we want to be great, we want to be known, we want to have success. Success leads to fame, but that is an empty thing, is it not? It is like ashes. Every politician is known, for it is his business to be known; therefore, he is not truly great. Greatness is to be unknown, inwardly and outwardly to be as nothing, and that requires great penetration, great understanding, great affection.

Questioner: If we respect anyone, there is fear. Then why do we respect?

Krishnamurti: It is fairly simple. If you respect out of fear, you want something from that person, don't you? Therefore you do not respect him at all. All that you want is to get something out of him. So, you bow down very low, touch his feet, and put a garland round his neck. That is not respect; respect is something entirely different. To respect another requires affection, not fear. When you respect somebody from whom you are hoping to get something, then you will despise people who are below you, you will have contempt for others. A man who has contempt for another can never be free from fear, can he?

Is it not possible to have affection in oneself which naturally expresses itself as respect for every person, regardless of whether one gets something or not? Watch the way you treat the coolie, the laborer, the servant of your hostel, and the way you treat your housemaster or the principal or a member of the Foundation—the scale going up and up—and you will see the manner of your behavior. You do not get up when the coolie comes in, but when your teacher comes in, you jump up, and the teacher demands that you jump up because he thinks that you must show respect to him. But he does not insist that you should treat the servant with equal respect and talk to him gently and kindly.

Is it not important to know all this while you are young so that you do not become slaves to authority, so that you have real affection and respect for people, which you show to the servant as well as to the man whom you think to be more important? But as long as there is fear and no affection, you are bound to have contempt for the one, and so-called respect for the other.

Questioner: Why does the elder brother beat the younger sister, and the younger sister beat the younger brother?

Krishnamurti: That is a very good question. Have you ever watched a chicken and seen how the more powerful pecks the weaker, and the weaker chicken pecks the still weaker one? But you do not watch anything, though there is life all about you. You do not look, you do not observe—neither your teachers nor yourselves. That is how life is. Among the animals, the stronger destroys the weaker. And that is what we also do in human society. The strong man pushes out his chest and beats everybody, and the weaker one gets angry with the still weaker.

You ask why we do this. For the very simple reason that we want to do it. If we are beaten by a big man, we want to take it out on the little man. You know the desire to hurt is very strong in us. We want to hurt people. There is a pleasure in hurting people, in saying cruel things about people, ugly things, belittling them. We never speak of people with kindliness. We never speak of their goodness but always talk with a sneer. That is what has to be understood—not why the elder sister beats the younger sister, and so on. The elder sister is probably beaten by the father or mother, therefore she has to take it out on somebody. She beats the younger and the younger takes it out on the little ones.

To understand cruelty, to understand animosity and not create it is very difficult for most people. We never think of all these things. In our schools these acts of cruelty are never pointed out because the teacher does not see them himself. He has his own problems, he has to get through the class and push the students through some examinations. Please do watch all the things that are taking place about you—how the chickens fight each other, how the strong bulldog dominates everything else. You will find that the same spirit of domination, anger, hatred, and animosity is in each one of us. To dispel this, we have only to be aware of it, and not to consider it as wrong or right.

Questioner: What is freedom?

KRISHNAMURTI: I wonder if you really want to know what freedom is! Do any of us know what is freedom? All that we know is that we are made to do things, we are compelled by circumstances or through our own fears to do things, and we want to break away from them. The breaking away from restraint, from compulsion, from fear, or anything else is what we call freedom. Please listen.

The breaking away from restraint, the breaking away from a hindrance, the breaking away from some form of compulsion, is not freedom. Freedom is something in itself, not away from something. Please understand this. The man put in a prison for some cause wants to break away and be free. He only thinks in terms of breaking away. If I am envious, I feel that if I can only break away from envy, I will be free. But the overcoming of envy is not freedom; the breaking away, the suppressing, is merely another expression of the same thing. The love of something for itself is freedom. There is freedom when you paint because you love to paint, not because it gives you fame or gives you a position. In the school, when you love to paint, that very love is freedom, and that needs an astonishing understanding of all the ways of the mind. Surely it is very simple to do something for itself and not for what it brings you, either as a punishment or as a reward. Just to love the thing for itself is the beginning of freedom.

Do you spend ten minutes of your class period talking of all these things? Or do you plunge immediately into geography, mathematics, English, and all the rest of it? What happens? Why don't you do this for ten minutes every day, instead of wasting your time on some stupid stuff which does not really interest you but which has to be done? Why don't you spend some time with your teacher in class talking about these matters? This would help you in your life—though it might not help you to become great or successful or famous. If you talk about these matters every day for ten minutes, intelligently, fearlessly, then it will help you all through life because it will make you think and not merely repeat things like parrots. So, please ask your teachers to talk to you about these matters. Then you will find both the educator and yourself becoming more intelligent.

Questioner: Can nature get rid of nature's dependence? If dependence is equivalent to fear, can we ever get rid of nature's dependence?

KRISHNAMURTI: When we are very young, as babies, we are dependent; we depend on the mother for milk; we need to be protected, to be watched, to be cared for. That is inevitable for the child and for every bird, every animal. All the puppies in this place are guarded by the mother. That is a natural thing. But as we grow, if we depend on somebody for happiness, for comfort, for guidance, for security, then out of that dependence comes fear. Dependence makes us dull, insensitive, fearful. We do depend on the railway, on the post office, but that is not dependence; that is a function in which both of us are partaking. But the dependence of which I am talking is inward, inside. It is that inward dependence that creates fear, that clouds our mind, making it dull, heavy, insensitive.

We depend because in ourselves we are so empty, in ourselves there is nothing, not a seed that is flowering. But we do not know anything about these things, and it is the function of education, is it not, to show all the implications of human existence, outwardly and inwardly. Our living is not just what appears outwardly; that is very superficial. A great many deeper things are hidden in us. To understand all that, to unravel it and go beyond, is the function of education, is it not?

January 20, 1954

Fourteenth Talk to Students at Rajghat School, Banaras

A lovely morning! Did you notice the blue sky? How extremely limpid it is, clear, very quiet! Did you notice the river this morning? There was no ruffle on it, and the sun early in the morning, how peaceful it was! You know, that is the kind of thing that we all want—and not only the people who live on the riverside—this extraordinary peace. When we have it, we do not know that we have it. That is the strange part of it. Those fishermen living in that village, they also do not know. They have all that beauty, that quietness, that sense of being alone with nature, but they are not satisfied because they are hungry. They have to struggle for life, so in spite of this extraordinary beauty and quietness, there is a constant battle going on. They want more money, their children are ill, their wives, their husbands, or mothers are dying, and so, in spite of this tranquillity, there is a great deal of disturbance. It is so with most of us, too.

When we are young, we are not concerned with peace, with tranquillity, with beauty; we only want to enjoy ourselves, to have a good time, to play about. Then as we grow older, we want so many things; we want to be happy, we want to have virtue, we want children, we compete with each other for a better job, we want to have a position where there is more power, and so on. But underneath all that, we want to be left alone, we do not want to be disturbed; we want our thoughts to run in easy grooves, and so we set up habits of easy thought, easy existence, have a comfortable job and there stagnate. So most of us, as we grow older, want to be left alone, we do not want to be disturbed, and this state of nondisturbance is what we call peace. For most of us, that is peace—having a clear sky. But in this apparently clear sky there are a great many things going on, a great disturbance in the atmosphere, which we do not see. What we see is very superficial, is just on the surface. The kind of tranquillity we want is a superficial calm, an easy existence, and that we call peace. But peace is not so easy to come by. We can only understand peace when we understand the great disturbance, the discontent in which each one of us is caught, when the mind is free from easy thought, easy grooves of patterns of action, when we are really disturbed—which we all avoid.

We do not want to be disturbed; we want things to remain as they are. If you are in a comfortable position, if you own a good house or car, you do not want to be disturbed; you want to let things remain. But there is disturbance going on all the time, around you and in you. There is social disturbance—so you become a reactionary, a conservative, you want to let things remain, you are constantly avoiding any form of change and are always going back to the good old days when things were as they were. While we are young, we are disturbed, we question, we are curious, we want to know. As we grow older, we want not to be disturbed, we do not want to find out the answers. Our religion is merely a solace to us, it gives us peace, gives us tranquillity, gives us the hope, "We shall be better off next life." We accept things as they are. When we talk about peace it is a state, for most of us, in which there is no disturbance of any kind. We imagine, we meditate on that peace as a state in which there is no kind of disturbance, no kind of revolution, no kind of deep radical change. So, our minds become very dull, lethargic, dead; what we call peace is death.

But I think there is another kind of peace; a peace that is much more difficult to understand, a peace which is not a reaction, not just an opposite of conflict. Do you understand what I am talking about?—that peace in which there is no conflict. Now we only know the opposites, the dual process—I was happy yesterday and I am unhappy today, and I would like to get back to that happiness tomorrow. We keep these opposites going on, working, struggling, and when we have a moment which we call happiness as opposed to unhappiness, we want to remain in that state. Remaining in that state is what we call peace, happiness, constant security. That is all we know, and we are always asking, "How am I to get back to that state in which I was happy, in which I was secure?" But I do not think that is peace.

Peace is not something which is an opposite to conflict. It is not the outcome of struggle, of pain, of suffering, of unhappiness. If it is, then it is not peace—it is just the opposite reaction to what is. This is a bit difficult, so please ask your teachers about it because it is very important to understand this. Peace is like freedom. Freedom is the love of a thing for itself, it is not just the opposite of slavery. The love of something is not for what it will bring you—position, prestige, money, fame, notoriety, or what you will. It is something in itself, without a reward, without being afraid of punishment or failure, or hoping for success. So, also, is this thing called peace not the opposite of conflict, disturbance, revolution.

To understand this peace which is not an opposite, we must understand the conflicts of the mind. Being disturbed, the mind wants peace, it wants to be left alone, not to be disturbed. So, it creates a haven, a belief, a refuge, which it calls "peace." But that is not peace; it is only a reaction, a movement away from "this" to "that." But life does not leave you alone. Life is very disturbed—life being the poor people, the rich people, the camel that suffers with so much weight on its back, the politicians, the revolutions, the wars, the quarrels, the bitterness, the unhappiness, the joy, and the dark shadows. The whole of that life is very disturbed, and since we do not understand it, we want to run away; we sit on the banks of the river, close our eyes and think about something which we call peace. That is merely an escape, a reaction, an opposite to the state of disturbance. But, if we can understand all these disturbances of living—the joy, the unhappiness, the struggles, the jealousies, the envies—if we can understand all that, not run away from it, just look at *what is* without condemning, just understand *what is,* then out of that there will be the peace which is not an opposite. In that peace there is great depth, a totally different activity which is creativeness, which is God, which is truth. But one cannot come to it or understand it if one does not understand the disturbances. In understanding these disturbances, these discontents, these constant inquiries, perplexities, anxieties, the mind becomes very clear. Peace is not something apart from the mind, but it comes when I understand all the difficulties. To understand the difficulties, I must not condemn them, I must not compare one difficulty with another. I must not say, "I suffer much more! You suffer less." Suffering is suffering—you do not suffer more and I less, or I more and you less. If we can know suffering without comparison, we shall understand it. Out of that understanding, the mind becomes very simple, very clear, very innocent, and it is this innocence that is peace. The mind that goes through experience, understands the experience, and does not store it up, is innocent and it knows peace.

It is rather complex for a young student to understand all this, but you should know about all these things because you will be going out of this place into a world where there is frightful competition, where everyone is out for himself—for his own family, his own country, his own God. If we do not understand this process, we will be caught in it, we will be driven along by society, by circumstances. It is very important, while we are young, to be educated—or to educate ourselves—so clearly, so simply, that we can understand the battle of life. But the difficulty is that we spend our days in things that do not really matter. Have you noticed how you spend your day as a student? Mostly in the classroom, a few hours of play, go to bed exhausted, wake up, and then begin again. You never spend an hour or even ten minutes a day talking about these things that really do matter. Neither the educator nor those who are being educated spend any of their time going into these matters, finding out the truth of them and discovering how to improve life. That is far more important than passing an examination. Thousands pass examinations all over the world, but they do not mature. Life is a process of learning all the time, understanding continuously. There is no end to understanding; you cannot say, "I have finished my examinations, I will throw away my books, I am ready for life." But this is what we generally do. We never pick up the books again after we have passed the examinations.

If we can read rightly, then the books have much to tell. But there is something far deeper than books; that is ourselves. If we know how to read the thing that we are in ourselves, there is immeasurable richness. Then you do not have to read a single book. It is all there, in ourselves. But it requires a much greater capacity than reading a book. None of you is helped in reading the thing that you are, you never spend time every day in coming to it and understanding it; you are bored with it. You are tired when the real things are mentioned. Most of us do not want to be disturbed; outwardly we have jobs, we have occupations, we are teachers, and so on; we carry on, and the beauty of life passes by.

Questioner: How can we progress in this world?

Krishnamurti: Does progress in this world consist mainly in being somebody socially or climbing the ladder of success? Why do we want to progress in this world? Why do we want to become more clever, more learned, more powerful? More money, a bigger house, means to us progress; that is why we all want more. We all want to keep on climbing, don't we, not only in this world but spiritually, inwardly. We have to see the truth of this thing, that this so-called progress, outward or inward, does not bring tranquillity and peace but only leads to wars, to destruction, to greater misery. We do not understand ourselves, the ways of our own existence, and so we are enamored of this progress—the progress of the airplane, the very latest car, the astonishing things the inventors are producing. These things have their own uses, but unless we change ourselves, we use these things in a manner which causes destruction and misery.

Questioner: At every meeting, you tell us to have a discussion with the teachers for at least ten minutes in the morning, but many of our teachers do not come to the meetings. So what are we to do in order to have a discussion?

Krishnamurti: If most of them do not come to the meetings, ask the others who do come. When you attend the class, you must have a teacher there. Why don't you ask him? Why don't you say, "Please, before we start our classes, let us talk about what was said at the morning meeting." But, I think the question is a little more difficult. Because, the teachers, when you ask them to discuss with you before the classes begin, get rather annoyed, don't they? They do not want to be questioned about these matters because they do not quite understand. They do not want to feel that they do not understand. They are teachers, you know, they are superior people, and you are only the students. So they want to keep you in your place. You, being impudent, want to catch them out. So it works both ways, does it not?

I think it is important for the teachers as well as for the students to listen to these talks and to discuss them together. What I am talking about is life; this is not just a fancy, a belief, a religion, a sect. This is life, and if the teachers do not understand it, then naturally they cannot help the students to understand. If the students want to discuss with them, why should they get angry or annoyed or disturbed? If they begin to think, they also will see the problems; then they will find a way of talking about them. But unfortunately, most of our teachers are not interested in all this. They have their own problems, they have their jobs, they are well-established, and they want you to leave them alone. The young mind, the mind of the student, wants to know, to find out, to inquire, to disturb the teacher. That is why you, the older people, should pay attention to what is being said because, in your hands, a new generation can come into being. If you are not interested in all these things, you are going to produce a generation as cursed as your own. You are really producing a curse on the land if you insist on educating your children according to your own pattern. The pattern of the older generation is nothing to be proud of. It is really important that the older people, the teachers, should inquire into all this.

Questioner: What is self-confidence and how does it come into being in man?

KRISHNAMURTI: Sir, you dig a hole in the garden, manure it, water it, and then put a plant in and watch it grow. You feel that you can at least do something, don't you? So you dig another hole, plant another tree, and that gives you a sense that you can do things, that gives you a confidence, as when you pass examinations one after the other. The capacity to do anything, to plant, to drive a car, to write a book, to pass examinations, gives you a sense of confidence, does it not? When you write a poem without effort, often you say, "By Jove! I can do it very easily." It gives you a sense of confidence. But, what happens? That confidence becomes a way of self-importance, "I can do things." So, when you use your capacity, you begin to have self-importance. That is, if I am able to speak well on a platform, which may be my sole capacity, I use the platform for my importance, as a means of expanding myself. Or I may be able to perform some dance, and that gives me enormous self-importance because I show myself off. So, I use capacity as a means of giving strength to my subtle, inward forms of selfishness.

What is important is to have the capacity to do things without the strengthening of the self. You understand? When you write a poem, when you plant a tree, do not say, "I have written a poem, I have planted a tree." It requires a great deal of intelligence to see that and to stop using capacity—however great or little it may be—for self-expansion, for making oneself important.

Questioner: As a boy grows, he becomes curious about sex. Why is it so?

KRISHNAMURTI: It is a natural thing. Are you not curious about how trees grow? Have you not seen that the cows have calves? Everything is curious. How a little plant grows, becomes a tree, and produces fruit—is that not astonishing? Please listen carefully. We do not use this interest to find out in every direction. You understand? You never inquire why a tree grows, why a bird flies. You never see the beauty of the bird and the shades of the tree. You never dig in the garden, and you never plant a tree, a bush; you never smell a flower, you never breathe the air with enjoyment; you never create anything with your own hands. Because you are not interested in all these things creatively, you become interested in one thing which you call sex, but if you are interested in all these things, then that also is a part of your life, that also is a natural thing. It is nature's way of producing babies, there is nothing wrong about it, but that should not become our occupation; our mind should not be completely concentrated on that, as most of our minds are.

When we are young, if we have not taken interest in the flowers, in the rivers, in the fish, in creating something with our hands, then that thing, sex, becomes more important. If we can be creatively interested in everything—in painting, in music, to play an instrument, to write a poem, to play games, to eat right food, to put on the right clothes, to see the sky of an evening and early morning, see the beauty of the trees, our mind taking in all that, creatively enjoying, seeing the beauty of it all, which is, after all, education—then sex is not an ugly problem. But because we have not been encouraged to look at all these things creatively, this thing sex becomes a nightmare.

I do hope the elder people are listening. After all, that is education—to help the students to plant trees and care for them, to let them make things with their hands, milk the cows, go for walks—not always everlastingly playing games. To look at the trees, the birds, the skies, to widen the mind creatively, extensively—that is education, not the passing of some stupid and silly examinations.

Questioner: When we see girls we try to show ourselves off. Why is it?

KRISHNAMURTI: I have answered that question. We are attracted to what we call the opposite sex, the opposite person, the girl; that is a normal thing, not to be ashamed of, not to be condemned. When you see a tree, are you not attracted by the tree? When you see a lovely bird—that kingfisher, blue and marvelous in flight—are you not delighted by it? Perhaps you are not because you never look. Last night, there was thunder, lightning, rain. You never looked, did you? You never felt the rain on your face. To see everybody running for shelter, to see how the roads are washed clean and how the leaves are brighter—this also is an attraction.

Unfortunately, we are all girls or boys or grown-ups, insensitive to everything in life except to that one thing, and that becomes an enormous problem afterwards in our life, a problem with which we struggle. We have to be sensitive to everything about us, to those wretched bullocks that are drawing the heavy carts day after day—how thin they are, and how tired the drivers look!—the poor villagers, the disease, the empty stomachs. To be aware of all this is part of education. If you are sensitive to all these things, then you will not want to show off.

Beauty is something only sensitive minds and hearts can find. Mere attraction, mere sensation, though it may be pleasurable at the beginning, does not completely satisfy, so there is pain in it. But if the mind can look at all the things of life, all the depths and heights and qualities of it, if the mind can be sensitive to them, then the attraction of boy and girl has its right place, but without the other, this becomes a very shallow petty affair.

Questioner: How can we create the feeling of the necessity of manual work?

KRISHNAMURTI: How can we feel that manual work is important? Sir, when you have to do things yourself, the question does not arise. The question arises when somebody else sweeps the floor instead of you. When you have your own physical work to do, day after day, you do not put that question. The villager digging, plowing, does not say, "How can I make manual labor important?" He has to do it. But we are thankful that we have not got to do manual labor. We, the upper middle class, have withdrawn from all manual labor because we have a little money; and we have the tradition of centuries that the educated men, the Brahmins, the upper class people, have nothing to do with the squalid affair of manual labor. If you live in America, you have to do everything yourself—wash the floors, do the laundry, cook, wash dishes—because there are no servants. There, only the very, very rich can afford servants. They are not called servants, they are called helpers, and they are treated like human beings. But, in this country you have overpopulation and there are thousands for one job. If you have a little money, you employ somebody to do the dirty job, and you gradually withdraw from doing anything with your hands. If you see that, and if you see the importance of doing something with your hands, then you will naturally do it. The mentality of the so-called educated people, whether they are clerks or high officials, is the same—mediocre, petty, small.

Those people who refuse to touch the earth, to tend the flowers, do not know what they miss. If you really dig into the garden and plant, see things grow, milk a cow, look after chickens, then something happens to you, there is an astonishing richness in it. Those who have no touch with the earth miss a great deal. Try to have a garden of your own, plant a tree of your own, do it, organize it; then you will see what will happen to you inwardly. It gives you a sense of release, beauty, the love of the earth, of the little worms inside the earth. But unfortunately, we do not know that feeling, nor do we know the feeling of sitting still and actually looking at something. We know none of these inward riches, and not knowing, we acquire superficial, transient riches.

Questioner: What is the sun?

KRISHNAMURTI: Have you asked your teacher? The sun is, according to scientists, a ball of fire, and it gives you heat, light, strength, everything. Why don't you ask your teachers about it?

Questioner: How can one be satisfied with what one is?

KRISHNAMURTI: The thing is very simple if you listen to what I am saying. Please listen carefully. Dissatisfaction comes when there is comparison. When you see somebody else having more and you having less, and you compare yourself with that other person, then dissatisfaction comes, but if you do not compare, then there is no problem. But not to compare requires a great deal of interest and understanding because all our education, all our training is based on comparison: "That boy is not as good as you," "You are not so clever as that boy," and so on. Then you struggle, and the other boy struggles also. So we keep up this game of constant comparison and struggle. But if you love the thing which you are doing, you do it because you love it, and not because somebody else is doing it better than you, or you are doing it better than somebody else. When you make no comparison of any kind, then the thing that you are doing, that itself, begins to produce its own depths, its own heights.

Questioner: Why can't we see the sun?

KRISHNAMURTI: Because it is too bright. You cannot look at an electric lamp if it is a powerful lamp. The eyes are too sensitive.

January 21, 1954

Fifteenth Talk to Students at Rajghat School, Banaras

You know, one of the strange things of life is what we call religion. You may have wealth, success; you may be very famous, well-known, or you may have failures, sorrows, a great many frustrations, but at the end of it all, death awaits all of us. Whether we live to be 100 or 10 or whatever it is, there is always death. Seeing all this, seeing our own littleness and sorrows, we want to find something beyond ourselves. Because, after all, one very soon gets tired of oneself, of one's success, one's vanities, the things that one does, of the family, the money, the position. When people get tired of these things, they feel they have been deceived. Then, in order to forget themselves, they try to identify themselves with something greater. That is, they like to think that there is something greater, and they say, "Perhaps if I could think about that, live in that, meditate upon that, have an image, a picture, an idol of that, then I could forget myself in it.

When man tries to go beyond himself, beyond his struggles, beyond his sorrows, beyond all the things that perish round him, beyond all the things that live and die, he begins to search, to invent, to speculate. Actually, he does not really search, he does not really want to find out, but he hopes there is something which he calls God, and he clings to the belief in that which his own mind has created, thus trying to escape from all these troubles. So, he begins to speculate, he begins to have theories of what God is, he writes books about it. The more clever, the more cunning, the more subtle you are, the more ideas you have about God, and around that you will build a great many philosophies, systems of thought. From that grows the thought that you must have beliefs in order to attain reality, you must do certain practices, you must give up the world, you must do this, and you must not do that in order to get there, in order to forget the troubles, the sorrows, and the death that await all of us. So, we have a religion which demands that we shall believe. Society demands likewise. Because that is what each one of us wants—to believe in something much greater than ourselves, since we ourselves are very small.

All our conflicts, all our ambitions, are very small, very petty. So, we want to identify ourselves with something. If it is not God, it is the state—the state being the whole of India or the whole world—the government, the people who rule, the society. If it is not that, it is utopia, something very far away, a marvelous society that we are going to build; in the building of it you destroy many people, but that does not really matter to you. If you do not believe in any of these, you believe in having a good time and forget yourself in material things. Such a person is called materialistic, and the man who forgets himself in the spiritual world is called spiritual. Both of them have the same intention—one to forget himself in cinemas and the other in books, in rituals, in sitting on the banks of the river meditating, in renunciation—not to have any burden, to lose oneself in some kind of action, to lose oneself in the worship of something.

So, there is the desire to lose oneself because one feels very small. The self may not be small to you when you are young. But, as you grow older, you will see how little substance there is in it, how little value it has; it is like a shadow, with few qualities, full of struggles, pains, sorrows, and that is all. So, one soon gets bored with it and pursues something else in order to forget oneself. That is what all of us are doing. The rich want to forget themselves in night clubs, in amusements, in cars, in traveling. The clever ones want to forget themselves, so they begin to invent, to have extraordinary beliefs. The stupid ones want to forget themselves, and so they follow people, they have gurus who tell them what to do. The ambitious ones also want to forget themselves in doing something. So, all of us, as we mature, as we grow older, want to forget ourselves, and so we try to find something greater with which to be identified.

When we try to forget ourselves through something, through the state, through God, through a belief, through a guru, through action, then it creates illusions, it creates a false thing. When I forget myself through an idea, then the idea becomes important because I am forgetting myself through it. The ideal, being an invention of the mind, can also create illusions. So, I multiply illusions. These illusions, superstitions, beliefs, are what we call religion, and many books have been written about it—not how to dispel illusion, but how to arrange illusion in order to philosophize. But that is not religion, surely. Religion is not beliefs and dogmas, rituals and puja, putting on a sacred thread, muttering some words, however ancient they are. All those methods are a way of escaping from yourself through some kind of illusion. The escape which we call religion is not religion. Religion is something totally different, and the mystery of it is to find that which is not the mere invention of the mind.

So, we have to find out what is real religion, the true religion which is not merely an invention of the mind; it does not matter whether that invention is of Shankara or of anybody else, all such invention is still just a theory.

Religion is a state of being which each one of us must find. That state of being cannot be understood, it cannot come into being if we do not know how the mind creates illusions through its various subtle desires. As I said the other day, the mind is not just a superficial activity. Ganga is not just what we see on the surface, Ganga is the whole river from the beginning to the end, from where it starts till it goes to the sea, and it would be foolish to think that Ganga is just the water on the top. Similarly, we are very, very complex entities, and the inventions, the ideas, the theories, the superstitions, the rituals, the repetitions, the mantras— those are all just on the top. We have to go through and push all that aside—all of it, not just one or two ideas, not one or two beliefs or rituals that we do not like. That is very arduous, very difficult, because most of us are afraid—afraid of what society, friends, parents will say. But if one truly wants to find out what is reality, God, one must go beyond all that, push all that aside. You can only push it aside if you understand and so go beyond.

So, religion is something entirely different from the beliefs in which we have been brought up. But, you see, very few of us are free from fear, and it is fear that prevents the discovery of what is God. When we have fear, we become very insensitive. After all, when we look at a tree or a beautiful cloud or a beggar or a woman in tears, or when we see something beautiful, the love of that thing, the love of it for its own sake, is the beginning of real religion. But we do not live that way, we live in order to get something. I love my country because it is my country,, this love of my country is a very subtle form of loving myself. But if you can love a tree, an animal, a human being—not for what they will give you but just to love, without asking a thing in return—that is the beginning of religion. You can know that love only when there is no fear. When the mind is no longer afraid, then it can go beyond its own imaginations, its own projections, its own ideas.

So, religion is something which is not an invention of the mind. It is a state of being in which the mind is not inventing—as it does now, because it functions in fear, in desire, in success, in ambition, in various forms of activities. Only when the mind has understood the whole working of itself is there then a possibility of it being quiet, being very still. That stillness is not the peace of death; that stillness is very active, very alert, very watchful, intensive, passive. Then alone, one can find out; then alone that which we call God, truth, or whatever name you like, comes into being. But one cannot go after it. One has to understand the trees, the love of the trees, the love of the beautiful; one has to understand sorrow, joy, and all the struggles of human existence. Then one can go beyond all that; then the mind is really a cessation of the self, the 'me'. Only then can that which we all worship, that which we are all seeking or trying to find, come into being.

Questioner: What is emotion? Is it good or bad since human beings have it?

KRISHNAMURTI: Don't you know what emotions are? When somebody punches you, you cry; when somebody dies, you cry. When you see something beautiful, you laugh. It is a form of sensation; it is not right or wrong.

You see, we always like to think in terms of good or bad—"this is right," "this is wrong," "this is bad," "this is good"—and we think we have solved the whole problem of existence by calling everything good or bad. We want to suppress an emotion in order not to feel because that emotion creates pain, so we say it is bad. But if it is a pleasurable emotion, we do not want to suppress it, we want to keep it, have more and more of it.

So, emotion is a thing to be understood, to be watched over, to be cared for, so that you will understand it, so that you will not say it is good or bad. It is the instinct, or rather the conditioning of the mind, which makes us call anything good or bad, as though you have really understood the little child if you call him good or call him naughty. If you want to understand the child, you study him, you watch him when he is playing, when he is crying, when he is sleeping; you do not condemn him. But you see, condemning something or somebody or some quality is so easy. You say, "that is bad," and there it ends, but to understand the thing requires a great deal of care, patience, attention; that means watchfulness.

Questioner: What is a giant? Why are we afraid of it?

Krishnamurti: You know, fairy tales are good to read because they contain a lot of things very instructive. As there is always a reward, a boon, you ask for something, but after asking, you are always punished. You know, there is a fairy, a good angel or the good judge or the good something from whom you ask something, in all fairy stories. It gives you something, but there is always a snag behind it. Similarly, in fairy tales, there is a giant.

Questioner: When we are on the stage and acting, why is it that we cannot act freely?

Krishnamurti: Do you act freely and easily all the time? When you are with older people, with people who are criticizing you, with people who are watching, do you act freely? No. We are shy, are we not? We put on airs. We become self-conscious. On the stage, you are confronted with a lot of people, and you are shy.

Acting is all right while you are young and are playing with all this. But most of us, as we grow older, begin to act; in our daily life we are posing. We think we are somebody and must live up to that part, and so we are always putting on a mask. Have you not noticed it? You think you are a great saint, a great idealist, and you put on that mask, which is a pose. It is really one of our great misfortunes that we are always taught to become something. The "becoming something" is posing, pretending. But if you do not become anything, if you are really simple just as you are, there is no posing, there is no pretending, you are just what you are, and from there, you can go really far.

Questioner: Why do the birds fly away when they see us?

Krishnamurti: Why do you run away when you see a big cow or when you meet a stranger? It is the same thing.

Questioner: What is conflict, and how does it arise in our mind?

Krishnamurti: You want to be the captain of a cricket team, but there is somebody else better than you. You do not like that. So, you have a conflict, have you not? You want to get something and you cannot, and so there is conflict. If you can get what you want, then the difficulty is to keep it, so you struggle again, or you want more of it. So, there is always a conflict going on because you are always wanting something. If you are a clerk, you want to become a manager; if you have a cycle, you want a motorcar, and so on and on. If you are miserable, you want to be happy.

So, what you want is not important, but what you are is important. The understanding of what you are, going into it, seeing all the implications of what you are—that frees you from conflict.

Questioner: What is interest?

KRISHNAMURTI: When you have a toy, you are very interested in the working of that toy, are you not? Your whole mind is there, you do not think about anything else. When you are interested in something, in a toy, in a play, in a dance, in an idea, you are completely absorbed in that. That is interest.

Most of us have very little interest in life; as we grow older, we are not interested in anything really. So, we have trouble in preventing the mind from wandering away. So, we learn discipline, control, concentration. In a school of this kind, what we should find out—each one of us, the teachers and the students—is what we are interested in, the thing which we love, and that creates no conflict in life afterwards. That is our vocation, that is what we want to do. If you are an artist and your parents and society want you to become a clerk, then you are forced to become a clerk, and all the rest of your life you are struggling, struggling. Really, you have never been able to do what you want to do.

Education is a way of helping each student to find out what he wants, which is quite a difficult thing because we want so many things at different times. Education of the right kind can help you to find out , amongst all the various interests, what really gives you interest, that which you love, that which is one of the requisites, one of the necessities of life.

Questioner: Why do we fear death?

KRISHNAMURTI: You have asked that question, "Why do we fear death," but do you know what death is? You see the green leaf, it has lived all the summer, danced in the wind, absorbed the sunlight; the rains have washed it clean; and the winter comes, it withers and dies. The bird on the wing is a beautiful thing and it too withers and dies. You see human bodies being carried to the river to be burned. So, you know what death is. Why are you afraid of it? Because, you are living like the leaf, like the bird—but then a disease or something else happens to you, and you are finished. So you say, "I want to live, I want to enjoy, I want to have this thing called life to go on in me." So the fear of death is the fear of coming to an end, is it not?—not playing cricket, not enjoying the sunlight, not seeing the river again, not putting on your old clothes, not reading books, not meeting your friends constantly; all that comes to an end. So, you are frightened of death.

Being frightened of death, knowing that death is inevitable, we try to find out how to go beyond death; we have various theories. But, if we know how to end, there is no fear; if we know how to die each day, then there is no fear. We do not know how to die because we are always gathering, gathering, gathering. We always think in terms of tomorrow—"I am this and I will be that." We are never complete in a day, we do not live as though there is only one day to be lived. We are always living in the tomorrow or in the yesterday. If somebody told you that you were going to die at the end of the day, what would you do? Would you not live richly for that day? We do not live the rich fullness of a day. We do not worship the day; we are always thinking of what we will be tomorrow—the cricket game that we are going to finish tomorrow, the examination that we are going to take in six months, what we are going to do tomorrow, how we are going to enjoy our food, what kind of clothes we are going to buy, and so on—always tomorrow or yesterday, and so we are never living, we are always really dying in the wrong sense.

If we live one day and finish with it and begin another day as if it were something new, fresh, then there is no fear of death. To die each day to all the things that we have acquired, to all knowledge, to all the memories, to all the struggles, not to carry them over to the next day—in that there is beauty; even though there is an ending, there is a renewal.

Questioner: When we see new things, why do we like having them?

KRISHNAMURTI: New clothes, new toys, new bicycles, new pictures, new books, new pencils—you see something new and you want it. It is the same thing with the young and with the old. We all want to possess, we all want to acquire, and the shops are full of things we want to possess. We are never content with what we have or what we are. If I am stupid, I want to become clever. The man who is becoming clever is really a stupid person. Please think about it and you will see how true it is. Because, a stupid person can never become clever, he will always remain stupid, but if he understands, if he is aware that he is stupid, then that very awareness of his stupidity is the beginning of intelligence. But, we never think in those ways. You say, "I am stupid, or I am told I am stupid. I must become clever like my brother or like that boy over there!" So, you start to acquire, to possess. But if you see you are stupid, if you know you are stupid, then you can begin; then that very awareness that you are stupid does something.

If I know I am blind, then I know what to do. I will walk very carefully, I will have a stick, move very quietly, very gently. But if I do not know I am blind, I will go all over the place. We do not acknowledge that we are stupid. I may be a little stupid, but I am trying to become very clever. Wisdom lies in understanding *what is.*

Questioner: What is love?

KRISHNAMURTI: You have listened to me for three weeks. I have talked every morning for five days a week, and then you ask me, "What is love?" I have talked to you of love in different ways—of truth, of the mind, of fears. You ask, "What is love?" It is very sad, is it not, because you do not know how careless you are when you ask that question. What matters is not what love is but that you do know your own state, what you are. Do you mean to say that by asking another, a man knows what love is? The man who says, "I want to know what love is," in order to have it, will never have loved. If you know that you have no love, then love will come to you. But to know it, you must know what you are, you must not try to become something which you are not.

Do think about all these things. Do not spend your days merely studying, reading some books, playing games, but think about all these things. We are trying to arrange for some of the teachers to talk to you every day, to have an assembly at which all the teachers talk from time to time about all these matters. You may be bored with the teachers and with what they say. What they say may have some importance or no importance. But you have to listen to find out, have you not? If what they say is true or false or absurd or silly, you have to listen to find out, and to listen, you have to pay attention. So, do not accept anything they say. Find out.

To be critical is very important because it is the only way you will find out. You merely accept or listen with a bored air because you are tired; if you are bored, you can never find out. If you pay attention to everything that the teacher tells you, what everybody tells you including myself—not just accept, but understand, find out—then, that sharpens your mind and quickens your heart. Then, when you have finished with school, when you go to college, you have a mind which can deal with the complexities of life.

Questioner: How can we shake off nation and provincial feelings?

KRISHNAMURTI: First understand if you have got them, how you have created them. It is no good saying, "I must shake them off." Why have you got them? Because your parents, society, your neighbors, your teachers, your newspapers, your books, have all set up nationalism, provincialism, for various complicated and subtle reasons—to control you, to shape you, to make you do things they think you ought to do. A general will say nationalism is important because then he can use you, through nationalism, to fight, to kill. There are various reasons why you have these feelings of nationalism, of provincialism, and also, you like them. You like to say, "I am a Hindu, I am a Brahmin, I belong to this little part of India." And the political parties, the priests, the clever ones, use you to get what they want.

If you understand this, then there will be no problem, it will drop away; then you will laugh at the whole thing. If you do not understand, it will be very difficult to put away this stupid nationalism and provincialism.

Questioner: Why is there danger?

KRISHNAMURTI: Is there not danger when you go near the precipice? Is there not a danger of getting drowned when you do not know how to swim? Is there not danger when you meet a snake?

Danger means fear of something, does it not? It is a natural thing to be aware of danger, that is a habit, protection, a natural physical resistance. Otherwise, if you have no sense of danger, you might kill yourself any moment when a car dashes by; if you are not aware of the danger that might destroy you, then you will be killed.

So , this kind of awareness of danger is a form of self-protection, a response which is natural, but what is abnormal is when we want to protect ourselves inwardly; then all the mischief, all the misery, begins.

Questioner: Are you happy or not?

KRISHNAMURTI: I never thought about it. I have never thought, "Am I happy or not?"

Happiness is not something of which you are conscious, you cannot ask yourself, "Am I happy?" The moment you ask that question, you are unhappy. Happiness is something that comes not because you are seeking it but because you are doing something which really interests you. You are doing something because you love it; in the very doing of it, there is something which is called happiness, but if you are conscious that you are happy, it is already gone. The moment you say, "I am happy," has not happiness already gone?

You understand what I am talking about? Please ask your teachers to explain all these things, and if they do not understand and do not explain it, you search it out. Do not accept anything. Do not be brow-beaten, do not be bullied by the older people. Find out, inquire, search, and never be satisfied. Then, you will find out what it is to be happy.

January 22, 1954

First Talk at Banaras Hindu University

I think it is very important to find out for ourselves what the function of education is. There have been so many statements, so many books, so many philosophies and systems that have been invented or thought of by so many people, as to what the purpose of education is, what we live for. Apparently, every system so far has failed, including the very latest, because they have produced in the world neither peace among human beings nor deep cultural advance—the cultivation of the mind and the full development of the mind. Is it necessary to have this system?

It seems to me it is very important for each one of us to find out what the function of education is, especially in a university—why we are educated, and at what level our education is. When you look around the world, you find education has failed because it has not stopped wars, nor has it brought peace to the world, nor has it brought about any kind of human understanding. On the contrary, our problems have been increased, there are more devastating wars and greater misery. So, is it not important for each of us to find out what the whole intention of being educated is? Great authorities tell us what education is or what it is not or what it should be, but such authorities, like all specialists, do not give the true meaning of education. They have a particular point of view, and therefore it is not a total point of view. Therefore, it seems to me, it is very important to put aside all the authority of specialists, of educationalists, and to find out for ourselves what the meaning of education is, why we are educated, and at what level this education is to take place. Is education to take place only at the technological level—that is, to have a job, to pass through various examinations in order to have a job—or is education a total process, not merely at the bread and butter level and the organization level of that kind?

Is it not important for each one of us to find out what this education implies, the total education of man? If we can find out, not as a group of people, but as individuals, what this education implies, what the principles of this total education of man are, then we can create a different world. We see that so far, no form of revolution has produced peace in the world—even the communist revolution has not brought about great benefit to man—nor has any organized religion brought peace to man. Organized religions may give an illusory peace to the mind, but real peace between man and man has not been produced. So, is it not very important for each one of us to find out how to improve this state of affairs?

We may pass examinations, we may have various kinds of jobs, but in an overpopulated country like India where there are so many linguistic and religious divisions, there is always a threatening of wars, there is no security, everything about us is disintegrating. In order to solve this problem, is it not important to inquire—not superficially, not argumentatively, not by putting one nation against another or one idea against another—and to find out, each one of us, the truth of the matter? Surely, truth is entirely different from information, from knowledge. Neither battles nor the latest atomic destructive weapons nor the totalitarian systems of thought, either political or religious, have solved anything. So we, you and I, cannot rely on any system or any opinion but must really try to find out for ourselves what the whole purpose of being educated is. After all, that is what we are concerned with.

Does education cease when you pass an examination and have a job? Is it not a continual process at all the different levels and processes of our consciousness, of our being, throughout life? That requires not mere assertion of information but real understanding. Every religion, every school teacher, every political system, tells us what to do, what to think, what to hope for. But is it not now very important that each one of us should think out these problems for ourselves and be a light to ourselves? That is the real need of the present time—how to be a light to ourselves, how to be free from all the authoritative, hierarchical attitude to life so that each one of us is a light to himself. To be that, it is very important to find out how to be, how to let the light come into being.

So, is it not the function of education to help man to bring about a total revolution? Most of us are concerned with partial revolution, economic or social. But the revolution of which I am talking is a total revolution of man at all the levels of his consciousness, of his life, of his being. But, that requires a great deal of understanding. It is not the result of any theory or any system of thought. On the contrary, no system of thought can produce a revolution; it can only produce a particular effect, which is not a revolution. But the revolution which is essential at the present time can only come into being when there is a total apprehension of the way in which man's mind works—not according to any particular religion or any particular philosophy like Marxism or any system like the capitalist system—that is, when there is the understanding of ourselves as a total process. It seems to me, that is the only revolution that can bring about lasting peace.

Surely, such a thing implies, does it not, the unconditioning of the mind because we are all conditioned by the climate, by the culture, by the religion, by the political or economic system, by the society in which we live. Our minds are shaped from the very beginning until we die, and so we meet the problems of life either as a Hindu or as a Christian or as a communist or something else. Life is full of complications, it is moving all the time. Yet the way of our living is determined by a conditioned mind, and the conditioned mind translates the problems of life according to its own limitations. So is it not important, if we would solve this problem, to find out how to uncondition the mind so that the meeting of the problem becomes much more important than the mere solution of the problems?

Most of us seek an answer to a problem. But, what is more important is how to meet the problem. If I know how to meet a problem, then I need not seek an answer. It is because I do not know how to meet the problem—economic, social, religious, sexual—that I am confronted with, that my mind immediately seeks an answer, a way to resolve it. But if I know, if I am capable of meeting the problem, then I do not seek an answer. I shall meet and resolve it, or I shall know what to do with it. But as long as I do not know nor have the capacity to find out, I go to another, to a guru, to a system, to a philosophy. All the gurus, all the teachers of philosophy, have completely failed because they make us into automatons, they tell us what to do. In the very process of following them in what we do, we create more problems.

So, is it not very important to find out how to think—but not what to do—and how to free the mind from all conditioning? A conditioned mind will translate the problems, will give significance to them, according to its conditioning, and the problems, when met with a limited mind, are only increased. It is therefore important to inquire if it is at all possible to free the mind from its own self-created limitations so as to be able to meet the complications, the problems of living. I think the real issue is not whether you are a communist or a socialist or what not, but to be able to meet the very, very complex problems of living, totally anew, with a new mind, with a mind that is not burdened, a mind that has no conclusions.

Is it possible to have a new mind, a fresh mind, a clear mind, a mind which is not polluted so as to meet this very living problem of existence? I say it is possible. Most of us think that it is impossible to free the mind of conditioning. We only think that the mind can be conditioned better, in a better pattern, into a better mold of action, but we have never asked ourselves if the mind can totally uncondition itself. I do not know if you have ever thought about this because most of us are thinking of how to improve, how to modify, how to change—the change, the modification, and the improvement being a better condition, a better social relationship, a modified capitalism, a change in our attitude. But we never ask ourselves if it is possible for the mind to be totally free from all conditioning so that it can meet life fully—life being not only the earning of a livelihood but the problem of war and peace, the problems of reality, of God, of death. Can all this, the whole process, be understood by a mind which is conditioned? Or is it not the function of education, from the very beginning until we pass out of the university, to help us understand the conditioning influences and to know how to improve them so that we are human beings in total revolution all the time?

It is very important to find out how the mind works. After all, education is to understand how the mind works and not merely to pass some examinations which will give us a job. It is the working of the mind that is creating mischief; that is what is producing wars. Though we have scientific knowledge sufficient to help man to live sanely with health and with all the things that he needs, such living is almost impossible because the mind of man, which is conditioned as a Christian, a Hindu, an Indian, a Pakistani, a communist, a socialist, a believer and a non-believer, is preventing it. So is it not important for each of us to understand the mind, not according to Shankara or Buddha or Marx but according to ourselves, to see how our mind works? If we can understand, that will be the greatest revolution, and from there, a new series of actions can take place.

So, how is one to understand the mind? What does that word *understanding* mean? Is it merely the verbal understanding, is it merely superficial or is it the understanding that comes when, through the observation of the activities of the mind, there is awareness, knowledge, there is no judgment, there is no comparison, but an observation in which there is the cessation of the movement of the mind? You understand?

There is this problem of problems, the problem of war. There is the problem of hate, the problem of love, or whether there is reality, whether there is God. How is one to understand these problems? We can only understand them if we can approach them with a free, quiet mind—not a mind that has a conclusion, not a mind that says, "I know how to deal with the problem," but a mind that is capable of suspending all judgment, all comparison. You see, the difficulty is, is it not, our minds have been trained to function along a certain line. We know there is the conscious and the unconscious mind, and most of our activity is at the conscious level; we do not know the unconscious process of our mind. We have to earn a livelihood, or we do puja, or we imitate—all with the superficial mind. Is it not very important to understand the unconscious mind because that is the directive? To understand the unconscious mind requires that the conscious mind shall be still, and this is only possible when, through self-knowledge, through understanding the mind in relationship in daily life, I discover the process of my mind, being aware of the words I use, my habits, the way I talk, the customs, the rituals, those which I can see only in relationship with another.

So, to understand the mind, I have to discover the total process of myself. It is that discovery in relationship with another—which is, after all, society—that brings about a total revolution in me, and it is that revolution that can meet these constant conflicts of life, these troublesome and extraordinary problems of existence.

Perhaps, some of you would like to ask questions. There are no answers. There is only the problem, and if we are looking for an answer, we shall never understand the problem. If my mind is concerned with the solution of a problem, then I am not investigating the problem, I am only concerned with how to find out, how to resolve it.

You ask a question hoping I will give an answer. To me, there is only the problem, no answer. I will show you why. If I can understand the problem, I do not have to seek an answer. But the understanding of the problem requires an astonishing intelligence which is denied when I am concerned with an answer. If I can meet, for example, the problem of death, if I can understand the whole implication of it, the problem ceases to exist, but I can understand it only when there is no fear.

Questioner: A gentleman asks how far do you agree with Shankara who says, "Eliminate the mind completely"?

KRISHNAMURTI: Not having read Shankara, I cannot answer. But I think it is very important to find out for ourselves and not repeat Shankara or Buddha. The difficulty with most of us is that we have read, we know what other people have said, but we do not know at all what we ourselves think. Truth is not something given to you through a book, through a teacher; you must find it out for yourself. Truth is not the ultimate truth but the simple truth of living, the truth of how to solve any problem—which cannot be solved by merely having a revolution on that level.

So, it is very important to find out for ourselves how to think. You cannot think if your mind is burdened with authority, with other beliefs. The truth of the Buddha or of the Christ or of Shankara is not your truth. Truth does not belong to any of us. It must be found. It can only be found when I understand the total process of my mind. For the mind is the result of time, and so long as I am thinking in terms of time, I cannot find truth. So, if you compare what I say with what Shankara or Buddha has said, you will never find the truth of the matter. But you will find the truth of the matter if you can pursue your own mind in operation; that alone is the liberating factor—not an economic or social revolution.

Questioner: Is there such a thing as an absolute truth, timeless, measureless, and permanent?

KRISHNAMURTI: Is not truth something that is to be found from moment to moment—not a thing which is continuous, absolute, permanent? Those very words *absolute, permanent, continuous* imply time, and that which is of time cannot be true. That which is true is only from moment to moment, and it cannot be continuous. What is continuous is memory, and memory can project anything, any kind of illusion. But to find what is true, mind must be free from the process of time, from memory, from the experiencer and the experienced. To find out what is truth, the mind must be from moment to moment, without continuity.

Questioner: You have said that truth is beyond knowledge. Is the knowledge of an unconditioned mind truth or falsehood?

KRISHNAMURTI: I do not understand the question. One of our difficulties is that we want to go into abstractions immediately. We want to know what truth is, we want to know what God is, but we do not know how to live without acquisitiveness. Instead of understanding that, we want to discuss what truth is, but a man who is acquisitive can never find out what truth is. But if I can begin to understand the whole process of acquisition, the demand for the 'more', then perhaps, I shall understand what reality is.

Questioner: "To think for oneself is to think like others." Is that so?

KRISHNAMURTI: Is that not life? Is our thinking now so very different from others? To think for oneself is to think like anybody else because we are all patterned after one type or another of belief or disbelief, so we do not think individually, creatively; we all think alike. You think like a communist, if you are a communist; if you are a Hindu, you think like a Hindu. To think freely, you have to be aware of thinking alike, to understand all the implications of thinking alike, why you think alike, why you are conditioned. Obviously, to think freely, completely, revolutionarily, means great danger, does it not? You may lose your job.

To think freely is to be unconditioned. But we are all conditioned in our own peculiar limited ways. So, if I know I am conditioned as a Hindu, and if I free myself from that conditioning, then only is it possible for me to be entirely revolutionary, to be not like "this" or like "that." But first I must know that I am conditioned, which very few of us are willing to admit. To know one is conditioned, and to set about freeing the mind from that conditioning, requires a great deal of insight, persistence, constant watchfulness—a watchfulness in which there is no judgment, no comparison. Then you will find the mind becomes very quiet, very still. Then only is it possible for the mind to know what truth is, what freedom is.

Questioner: Man lives in poverty and fear. The gods of such a society are bread and security. What else can earnest men offer?

KRISHNAMURTI: To bring about a revolution in which bread and security are given to all, is that revolution? Is revolution merely at the economic level? You understand?

We see there is poverty, hunger, every kind of economic misery. Earnest men want to see the necessity for change now. At what level is this change to be brought about? On the economic level only? Or is it necessary to have a total revolution in man's thinking? If such a total revolution is possible—I say it is possible—that is the only way of solving our problems.

There can be real revolution only when you understand the total process of your being—which is, your thinking, the ways of your living—and cease to be a Hindu or a Christian. When you are a total human being, only then will the economic problem be solved, and not otherwise.

Questioner: What is personality? How can it be built?

KRISHNAMURTI: You talk about personality as though it were something like building a house. The very desire to build a personality brings about self-enclosure. We are talking of something totally different from building a personality—coat, tie, trousers, and clever talk, all that. We are talking of something entirely different, not of self-improvement, but of the cessation of the self—the self as a Hindu, the self as a professor, the self as a political or religious leader, the self that says, "I must save the country," the self that says, "I know the voice of God." It is that self that must totally cease in order that the world may live.

Questioner: Agreeing that the mind is to be unconditioned, how is one to achieve it?

KRISHNAMURTI: If you agree that the mind must be unconditioned, how are you to achieve an unconditional mind?

I think most of us see the importance of the mind which is not conditioned. But actually most of us feel that the mind can be made better, with a better state of conditioning. That is one of the great fallacies. The problem is not how your mind and my mind are to be unconditioned but how the conditioning of the mind takes place.

The conditioning of the mind takes place through education, does it not, through tradition, through family, through society, through religion, through belief. But behind tradition, belief, experience, there is a desire; there is a mind that is constantly acquiring, possessing, dominated by desire; it is that which conditions. Then, you will say, "How am I to stop desire?" You cannot. But, if you understand the process of desire, then there is a possibility of desire coming to an end.

These problems are much too complex to be discussed casually. You see again what is happening. We want to deal with abstractions. We do not see the importance of living from moment to moment without authority, without fear, without the desire to find out that one is acting rightly.

To find for oneself from moment to moment the way of living—the way you treat your servants, the way you talk to your superiors, the way you think and feel—it is there that the truth lies, not somewhere behind the Himalayas. But you see, we are not interested in all that. We are interested in discussing Shankara and other deep philosophies; that is an escape. But if I know the workings of my mind, the ways of my heart, then there is a possibility of bringing about a total revolution, and it is that revolution that can bring peace and security to the world.

January 10, 1954

Second Talk at Banaras Hindu University

It seems to me that without understanding the way our minds work, one cannot understand and resolve the very complex problems of living. This understanding cannot come through book knowledge. The mind is, in itself, quite a complex problem. In the very process of understanding one's own mind, the crisis which each one of us faces in life can perhaps be understood and gone beyond.

I do not know if you have heard it said that the cultural influence of the West is destroying the so-called culture of the East. We accept one part of the Western culture—science and militarism and nationalism—and yet retain our own so-called culture. Though we have only taken a part of the Western culture, a section or a layer of it, this is gradually destroying, poisoning, the other layers of our being. This can be seen when we look at the incongruity of our modern existence in India. I think it is very important to see how we are talking of India as taking on the Western culture, without totally understanding what we are doing. We are not adopting entirely the Western culture but retaining our own and merely adding to it. The addition is the destructive quality, not the total adoption of the Western culture.

Our own minds are being destroyed by the adoption of certain Western attitudes without understanding their attitude and their way of life. So there is a mixture of the Western and the Eastern in our minds. It seems to me that it is very important to understand the process of our own minds if we are not to be poisoned by an outside culture. Very few of us have really gone into the philosophies, the systems, the ideas of others, but we have merely adopted or imitated some of them.

We do not know the workings of our own mind—the mind as it is, not as it should be or as we would like it to be. The mind is the only instrument we have, the instrument with which we think, we act, in which we have our being. If we do not understand that mind in operation as it is functioning in each one of us, any problem that we are confronted with will become more complex and more destructive. So it seems to me, to understand one's mind is the first essential function of all education.

What is our mind, yours and mine?—not according to Shankara or Buddha or someone else. If you do not follow my description of the mind, but actually, while listening to me, observe your own mind in operation, then perhaps it would be profitable and worthwhile to go into the whole question of thought.

What is our mind? It is the result, is it not, of climate, of centuries of tradition, the so-called culture, the social and economic influences, the environment, the ideas, the dogmas that society imprints on the mind through religion, through so-called knowledge and superficial information. Please observe your own mind, and not merely follow the description that I am giving, because the description has very little significance. If we can watch the operations of our mind, then perhaps we shall be able to deal with the problems of life as they concern us.

The mind is divided into the conscious and the unconscious. If we do not like to use these two words, we might use the terms, superficial and hidden—the superficial parts of the mind and the deeper layers of the mind. The whole of the conscious as well as the unconscious, the superficial as well as the hidden, the total process of our thinking—only part of which we are conscious of, and the rest, which is the major part, we are not conscious of—is what we call consciousness. This consciousness is time, is the result of centuries of man's endeavor.

We are made to believe in certain ideas from childhood, we are conditioned by dogmas, by beliefs, by theories. Each one of us is conditioned by various influences, and from that conditioning, from those limited and unconscious influences, our thoughts spring and take the form of a communist, a Hindu, a Muslim, or a scientist. Thought obviously springs from the background of memory, of tradition, and it is with this background of both the conscious as well as the unconscious, the superficial as well as the deeper layers of the mind, that we meet life. Life is always in movement, never static. But, our minds are static, our minds are conditioned, held, tethered to dogma, to belief, to experience, to knowledge. With this tethered mind, with this mind that is so conditioned, so heavily held, we meet life, which is in constant movement. Life, with its many complex and swiftly changing problems, is never still, and it requires a fresh approach every day, every minute. So, when we meet this life, there is a constant struggle between the mind that is conditioned and static, and life that is in constant movement. That is what is happening, is it not?

There is not only a conflict between life and the conditioned mind, but such a mind, meeting life, creates more problems. We acquire superficial knowledge, new ways of conquering nature, science. But the mind that has acquired knowledge still remains in the conditioned state, bound to articular form of belief.

So, our problem is not how to meet life, but how can the mind, with all its conditioning, with its dogmas, beliefs, free itself? It is only the free mind that can meet life, not the mind that is tethered to any system, to any belief, to any particular knowledge. So, is it not important, if we would not create more problems, if we would put an end to misery, sorrow, to understand the workings of our own minds? The understanding does not come into being by following anybody, it does not come through authority, it does not come through imitation or through any form of compulsion. But it comes into being when one is actually aware how one's own mind is working.

Each one of us can observe our motives, our activities, our purposes, can understand them and solve this problem of existence without creating more misery, more wars, more confusion. To understand the workings of the mind is the most essential thing. After all, relationship is the mirror in which the mind can be seen in operation—the way I talk to the servant, the way I create a self-importance. There, I can observe the operation of my mind and see the extraordinary intricacies of motives—for instance, when I do puja, the innumerable rituals, the absurdity of following somebody who offers you a heavenly reward. In the process of our relationship, we can observe the mind, and if we can observe it without any sense of judgment, without any sense of condemnation and comparison, then that observation begins to free the mind from the thing to which it is tethered.

If you will experiment with this, you will see that your mind is tethered to a particular dogma, to a particular tradition. In that very observation, in that very awareness of the particular dogma or tradition to which the mind is bound—mere awareness without condemnation, without judgment, without wanting to be free—you will see that the mind begins, without making an effort, to free itself.

Freedom comes without compulsion, without resistance, without struggle. Take, for instance, the superficial example of your doing puja, a ritual, as a Hindu or a Muslim or a Christian, whatever you are. You do it out of tradition; there is no thought behind it. Even if you think about it, the very thought about this puja is conditioned because you do it as a Hindu or a Christian. When you think about the puja or the Mass, your thought is conditioned either to accept or reject; you cannot think about it afresh, anew, because your whole background or whole tradition, conscious as well as unconscious, the superficial and the deeper layers, is held in Hinduism or Christianity, and when you do think about it, there is no clarity but only a reaction which provokes another form of complication, another problem.

I do not know if you have observed all this in yourself. If you have observed, how is one to be free from a ritual? I am taking that as a superficial example without an analytical process. I do not know if this is too complex or too difficult. When a particular issue is analyzed, the analysis is bound to be still conditioned because the thinker is conditioned. His analysis is conditioned, and therefore whatever he does will produce problems more complex than the problem which he is trying to resolve. After all, in our thinking, there is the thinker and the thought, the observer and the observed. Now, when you do puja, the observer, the thinker, is always analyzing what is wrong, what is right, but the analyzer, the observer, the thinker, is conditioned in himself. So, his analysis, his observations, his experiences, are conditioned, are limited, biased. I think until we see this really very important point, mere self-introspection and analysis—whether psychoanalysis or the analysis which intellectually and theoretically you perform on yourself—are utterly useless.

Is there a thinker, an observer, an analyzer, different from the observation, the analysis? Is there a thinker without the thought? If there is no thinking, there is no thinker. If the thinker were not a part of the mind, part of the consciousness, then that thinker must be free from all conditioning in his analysis and understanding. But if one observes, there is no thinker without thinking. When I am thinking, I am analyzing, I am observing, the 'I' is still the result of thought which is conditioned. I, as a Hindu or communist, observe. The thought which produces the 'I' is the result of a communist background or the result of a Hindu or Christian belief. So, the thinker is always conditioned as long as there is thought because thought has produced the thinker, and thought is conditioned, limited by bias.

Your thoughts continually arise. If you want to go into them deeply, the question arises whether thought can ever come to an end—which is not a forgetfulness but which is really a very deep problem of meditation. As long as there is the meditator, meditation is illusion because the meditator is the result of thought, the result of a mind that is conditioned and shaped by the whole process of living with its fears, apprehensions, ambitions, desires, longing for happiness, longing to be able to live with success, without fear or favor, and so on. All that creates the thinker. We give a quality of permanency to the thinker, who we think is above all passing, transient experience. But the thinker is the result of thought. There is no thinker if there is no thinking. So, there is only thought which is the reaction to a form of experience, and that experience is the result of our conditioning. So, thought can never resolve our problems.

Our problem is freedom from the conditioning which produces limited thought. This is the whole process of meditation, not the stereotyped, traditional, illusory form of meditation, but the meditation that comes into being when we understand the whole process of our thinking, all the worries of our complex living. And in that there is no thinker, but only the uncovering of that, and therefore the ending of that.

At the time of such meditation, the mind is still. This quality of stillness is not just acquired through some stupid determined effort to be quiet.

The mind has to understand the whole significance of the thought process, and how it creates the thinker, and understand the whole process about the stillness of the mind. It is in this stillness of the mind that the problems are resolved, and not multiplied by the stupidity of the thinker who is conditioned.

I think, really, you must go into this problem, as most serious people must, because the crises are much too many and the problems that are pressing on us are much too intense.

Surely, it is the function of education, not how to meet life, but how to free the mind from all its conditioning, from all its traditional values so that the free mind can meet, and therefore resolve, the innumerable problems that arise daily. Only then is it possible to realize what we call God, truth. It is truth alone that resolves the problems.

Questioner: Is it wrong to be full of desires and passions?

Krishnamurti: Which is more important, to understand our desires and passions or to condemn them? The moment you use the words *wrong* or *right*, the implication is condemnation, is it not? If you are really interested, please follow this to the end. You are trained from childhood to condemn because the older people do so; they have no time, no interest, and condemnation is the easiest way of resolving any problem.

The question is: Is it wrong to have desires and passions? The first thing to see is that any form of condemnation puts an end to every thought or thinking, to every form of investigation and inquiry. A mind which functions in do's and don'ts is the most stupid mind. Unfortunately, most of us are educated with stupidity; when we can get over that, we can begin to inquire into the whole problem of desire, not if it is right or wrong, but to understand it. Because, if we understand something, then it is no longer a problem to us. If I know how to run a motor, an engine, it is no problem to me; I do not say it is wrong or right, I know how to work it. If I do not know, I do not condemn the motor. The same is the case with desires. It is no use getting confused or frightened, encouraging or condemning them. If I can understand the workings of desire, then the desire is no problem. It is only the fearful attitude towards desire that creates the problem.

Where is this 'I'? What is desire? Please listen without any condemnation or justification. Desire has to be understood. In the very understanding of it, desire becomes something else, not a thing to be frightened of, to repress.

What is desire? I see a beautiful car, highly polished, new, of the latest model, full of power. There is perception, then there is contact, then sensation and desire. Desire is as simple as that—perception, contact, sensation, and desire. Then with that desire comes the urge to acquire and the identification process—which is, "I desire that car." Then the whole problem arises whether I should or should not desire, the desire being conditioned or questioned by my background. If you are brought up in America, you are psychologically persuaded, all the time, to possess a car. So your desire to have a car is not a problem. But if your tendency is towards asceticism, towards renunciation, to turn to God, then the problem arises.

Then there is the desire for various forms of beauty, of sensation, for various things for which the mind craves, such as comfort security, a demand for permanency. We all want permanency—permanency in relationship, permanency in security, in continuity. Then we think there is a permanent God, there is permanent truth, and so on. Such an abstraction becomes theoretical, valueless, academic.

If you can understand this process of desire, which is very complex, very subtle, then there is a possibility of the mind seeing all the significance of desire, all the implications, and going beyond it. But we do not understand the significance of all this, but merely say, "This is a right desire," "That is a wrong desire," and "The cultivation of right desire is essential." If we adopt such an attitude towards desire, then the mind becomes merely an automatic, thoughtless, insensitive mechanism. Therefore, it cannot meet this whole complex problem of living.

Questioner: I am afraid of death. What is death, and how can I cease to be afraid of it?

KRISHNAMURTI: It is very easy to ask a question. There is no yes or no answer to life, but our minds demand yes or no because our minds have been trained in what to think, not how to understand, how to see things. When we say, "What is death, and how can I not be afraid of it?" we want formulas, we want definitions, but we never know how to think about the problem.

Let us see if we can think out the problem together. What is death? Ceasing to be, is it not, coming to an end. We know that there is an ending; we see that every day all around us. But I do not want to die, the 'I' being the process—"I am thinking, I am experiencing, my knowledge, the things which I have cultivated, the things against which I have resisted, my character, my capacities." I do not want all that to end, I want to go on, I have not yet finished it, I do not want to come to an end. Yet, there is an ending; obviously, every organism that is functioning must come to an end. But my mind won't accept that. So, I begin to invent a creed, a continuity; I want to accept this because I have complete theories, complete conditioning—which is, I continue, there is reincarnation.

We are not disputing whether there is continuity or not, whether there is rebirth or not. That is not the problem. The problem is that even though you have such beliefs, you are still afraid because, after all, there is no certainty, there is always uncertainty. There is always this hankering after an assurance. So, the mind, knowing the ending, begins to have fear, longs to live as long as possible, seeks for more and more palliatives. The mind also believes in continuity after death.

What is continuity? Does not continuity imply time, not mere chronological time by a watch, but time as a psychological process? I want to live. Because I think it is a continual process without any ending, my mind is always adding, gathering to itself in the hope of continuity. The mind thinks in terms of time, and if it can have continuity in time, then it is not afraid.

What is immortality? The continuity of the 'me' is what we call immortality—the 'me' at a higher level, the atma, or whatever you call it. You hope that the 'me' will continue. The 'me' is still within the field of thought, is it not? The 'me', however superior you may think it to be, is the product of thought, and that is conditioned, is born of time. Sirs, do not merely follow the logic of what I say but see the full significance of it. Really, immortality is not of time, and therefore not of the mind, not a thing born out of my longings, my demands, my fears, my urges.

One sees that life has an ending, a sudden ending; what lived yesterday may not live today, and what lives today may not live tomorrow. Life has certainly an ending. It is a fact, but we won't admit it. You are different from yesterday. Various things, various contacts, reactions, compulsions, resistances, influences, change "what was" or put an end to it. A man who is really creative must have an ending, and he accepts it. But we won't accept it because our minds are so accustomed to the process of accumulation. We say, "I have learned this today, I learned that yesterday." We think only in terms of time, in terms of continuity. If we do not think in terms of continuity, there will be an ending, there will be dying, and we would see things as they are, clearly, simply, directly.

We do not admit the fact of ending because our minds seek, in continuity, security—in the family, in property, in our profession, in any job we do. Therefore, we are afraid. It is only a mind that is free from the acquisitive pursuit of security, free from the desire to continue, from the process of continuity, that will know what immortality is, but the mind that is seeking personal immortality, the 'me' wanting to continue, will never know what immortality is; such a mind will never know the significance of fear and death, and go beyond.

Questioner: "Thinking does not solve the problem, it is its product." Is this not a piece of thinking, or is this different from the thinking which you impugn?

Krishnamurti: When one sees the limitations of reason, one goes beyond reason. But one must know how to think, how to reason. But if you do not know how to reason, how to think, you can never go beyond it. Most of us do not know what thinking is; we only know what to think, which is entirely different. But to know the extraordinary complexity of the mind, which cannot be learned from another, to find out for yourself how the mind works, you have really to observe. What you learn of psychology or philosophy in a college or in a lecture hall is not a living thing, it is a dead thing. But if you observe your own thoughts and actions in daily living—when you talk to a servant or to your wife or child, when you react to beauty—if you see your motives in action, then, out of that observation, you will know the various barriers of your mind, how the mind deceives itself, how the mind twists, in the way it reasons. Seeing all that, you go beyond all thought, beyond reason, and there is freedom.

This is not a thing to be casually interested in or casually repeated. Some of you who have heard me may say, "Poor fellow! He does not know what he is talking about. How can thinking come to an end? If there were no thinking, how could there be the questions that the mind puts in order to understand the whole complex problem of thought?"

It is very important to find out how we think. Unfortunately, most of our educationists teach you what to think, and you merely repeat it. If you can repeat either in Sanskrit or in English or in any other language, you think you are marvelously learned. But to rind out, to discover, the ways in which your mind works, and to speak of what you have discovered, without repeating what another has said, is a tremendous thing; that is the indication of initiative; that is the beginning of creative living.

Unfortunately, in India, we are clerks from the high to the low; we have been trained in what to think. That is why we are never revolutionary in the deep creative sense. We are merely gramophone records, playing the same tune; therefore, there is never true discovery.

Questioner: What is the significance of life?

KRISHNAMURTI: The significance of life is living. Do we really live, is life worth living when there is fear, when our whole life is trained in imitation, in copying? In following authority, is there living? Are you living when you follow somebody, even if he is the greatest saint or the greatest politician or the greatest scholar?

If you observe your own ways, you will see that you do nothing but follow somebody or another. This process of following is what we call "living," and then at the end of it you say, "What is the significance of life?" To you, life has significance now; the significance can come only when you put away all this authority. It is very difficult to put away authority.

What is freedom from authority? You can break a law. That is not the freedom from authority. But there is freedom in understanding the whole process, how the mind creates authority, how each one of us is confused and therefore wants to be assured that he is living the right kind of life. Because we want to be told what to do, we are exploited by gurus, spiritual as well as scientific. We do not know the significance of life as long as we are copying, imitating, following.

How can one know the significance of life when all that one is seeking is success? That is our life; we want success, we want to be completely secure inwardly and outwardly, we want somebody to tell us that we are doing right, that we are following the right path leading to salvation, to *moksha,* and so on. All our life is following a tradition, the tradition of yesterday or of thousands of years, and we make every experience into an authority to help us to achieve a result. So, we do not know the significance of life. All that we know is fear—fear of what somebody says, fear of dying, fear of not getting what we want, fear of committing wrong, fear of doing good. Our minds are so confused, caught in theory, that we cannot describe what significance life has to us.

Life is something extraordinary. When the questioner asks, "What is the significance of life?" he wants a definition. All that he will know is the definition, mere words, and not the deeper significance, the extraordinary richness, the sensitivity to beauty, the immensity of living.

Questioner: How can peace be established in the world? We and the whole world are trying to be in a peaceful atmosphere, but the dangers of another world war are approaching towards us.

KRISHNAMURTI: We want to live in peace. Do you? Don't you compete with your neighbor? Don't you want a job as much as your neighbor? Don't you hate? Don't you call yourself an Indian with all the patriotic nonsense of conflicts? How can you have peace when you are doing the opposite thing, the thing which is contrary to peace? As long as you call yourself a Hindu, a Muslim, a Christian, or a communist, you will never have peace in the world.

Peace is in the layman. As long as one is following one party, political or otherwise, opposed to another party, as long as politics is merely a division of power, obviously you will have no peace in the world. Politicians are not concerned with people, they are concerned with power, and as long as the party system exists, there cannot be any peace. This does not mean that there must be only one party. Parties really are not concerned with people at all; they are concerned with ideas of how to give people food, and therefore there is little action in the matter of actually giving food.

So, as long as we are pursuing the path of war, as long as we have armies, police, and lawyers, we will have wars. We are talking all the time about nonviolence, and yet we support armies. On the one hand we are prepared in ourselves, through our present-day education, to hate one another, and on the other hand we want peace. In ourselves, we are in contradiction, each one of us—the nation, the group, the race. There can be peace in the world only when that contradiction in each one of us is dissolved. What is essential is for each one of us to think out for oneself, to inquire, to search out. Repetition of slogans or the carrying of flags are of little use.

We want to be nationalistic, we want to have our flag. Because the individual, through identifying with the greater, gets a satisfaction, gets a sense of security. That is what is being done in India, America, Russia, and elsewhere. In schools and universities, our education is nothing but the cultivation of this hatred and aggressive acquisitiveness. So, we are preparing for complete and utter destruction.

Peace is surely something which is not a reaction to a particular system or society, to a particular organization, to ideas or action. Peace is something entirely different. It comes into being, surely, when the whole total process of man is understood, which is the understanding of myself. This self-knowledge cannot be had from a book, cannot be learned from another. When there is love in your heart, and when you observe and understand yourself every moment of your life, truth comes into being, and out of that truth comes peace.

January 17, 1954

Third Talk at Banaras Hindu University

The problem of knowledge and specialization, it seems to me, is very important. Let us consider it and see if the mind which is trained in specialization and in knowledge can be free to investigate and to discover whether there is nothing more beyond what it has known, to investigate where knowledge is leading us and the significance of specialization.

There are many avenues of knowledge, and more and more information on a vast scale is becoming available to us. Where is it all leading us to? What is the function of knowledge? We see knowledge is essential at a certain level, in our conscious and unconscious living, in our existence. Can such knowledge be a hindrance to further investigation of man's realization of the total significance of existence? For instance, I may know how to build a bridge: will that knowledge bring about a radical change in my ways of thinking? It may produce a superficial change or adjustment but in this present crisis in the world, which is necessary: a mere superficial adjustment or a radical revolution? It seems to me that revolution born of any particular pattern of action is not revolution at all, and that if we are to bring about a new generation with a new way of thinking, we must find out what the function of knowledge is.

What is knowledge?—not the dictionary meaning, or a definition. Is it not the cultivation of memory along a particular line? Is it not the development of the faculty of gathering information to be utilized towards a particular end? Without knowledge, obviously, modern existence is almost impossible. Can knowledge, which is the cultivation of memory, the gathering of information, and the using of that information for special purposes—for surgery, for wars, for uncovering new scientific facts, and so on—be a hindrance to the total understanding of human society?

As I said, knowledge may be useful at one particular level. But if we do not understand the total process of human existence, will not that knowledge be a hindrance to human peace? For example, we have scientific information enough to create food for the whole of mankind and to give them shelter. Why is it that that scientific knowledge is not used? Is that not a problem to most of us? Is not that very knowledge preventing the consideration of human understanding and peace?

What is preventing the stoppage of war, of feeding man, clothing him, giving him shelter? It is surely not knowledge, it is something entirely different. It is nationalism and vested interests in various forms—capitalistic or communistic or of a particular religious group—which are preventing the coming together of man. Unless there is a radical change in our ways of thinking, knowledge is used, is it not, for the further destruction of man. What are the universities of learning doing, the academic as well as the spiritual? Are they producing, bringing about, a fundamental revolution in our hearts and minds? It seems to me, that is the fundamental issue, and not the constant accumulation of further information and knowledge.

Can a total revolution take place through knowledge which is, after all, the continual development of the mind through memory? I may know various facts, I may know the distances between the various planets, I may know how to run jet planes, but will that knowledge, will that information, bring about a radical change in my thinking? If it cannot, what will it bring about? Is it not a problem for most of us?

We want peace in this world; we want to put an end to envy which arises in human individuals in their search for power; we want to put an end to wars. How is this to be done? Will mere accumulation of knowledge put an end to wars, or must there be a radical revolution in our thinking? Will thinking produce that revolution? I do not know if you have considered any of these points, but it seems to me, a revolution based on a particular pattern of thought is not a revolution at all. After all, thinking is the response to a particular condition, the response to a challenge according to a particular background. I respond to a challenge according to my conditioning, to my training, to my upbringing as a Christian or a Hindu or a Muslim or whatever I am. How is that background, that conditioning, that peculiar pattern of action to cease, and a new way of thinking to be born? Is this not a problem to most of us? Because, there cannot be a radical revolution unless the breaking of all the background takes place, of the pattern of our constant thinking along a particular line.

Will knowledge, the accumulation of information about facts, bring about the breaking of my conditioning? Yet, this is what we are doing; we are constantly accumulating information, knowledge, training our memory. All this is important at one particular level. We may search out information about the whole consciousness of man, about the psychological process of uncovering oneself—mostly intellectual, mostly verbal—through specialization. But, will that bring about a radical change? It seems to me that mere information, knowledge, will not bring about a radical change. There must be a totally different factor, and that is the understanding of the process of consciousness, of the mind that is constantly accumulating, gathering information.

Why are we gathering information, knowledge? It is for the purpose of security, which is essential at one level of our being. Some people think that knowledge is a means of discovery. Do we discover through knowledge? Does not knowledge impede discovery? How can the mind find this out if the whole mind is trained to merely gather information, knowledge? Must not the mind examine this question free from any anchorage, from any belief, from any knowledge? The mind, having information, having knowledge, must be free of it in order to find out; otherwise, it cannot find out.

After all, there is a conflict in all of us between the conscious and the unconscious, between the superficial ways of thinking and the hidden processes of motives, desires, anxieties, and fears. We are gathering information, knowledge, at the superficial level, without fundamentally altering the deeper levels of our consciousness. The most important thing in the present crisis is that the revolution should take place at the unconscious level, and not merely at the conscious level. Revolution at the unconscious level is not possible if the conscious mind is merely cultivating memory. Is not the problem, with all of us, how to bring about this revolution deep in ourselves?

After all, the individual is the man; the whole world is not different from you and me, and it is the individual that brings about the radical transformation. History shows how a few individuals, different from others in their way of living, have wrought a change in society. Unless we individually transform ourselves deeply, fundamentally, I do not see any possibility of having peace and tranquillity in this world.

How is the individual—that is, you and I—to change radically at the deep, unconscious level? Is it brought about by the practice of a particular ideal or a particular virtue? Is not the cultivation of a particular virtue merely the strengthening of that consciousness which is pursuing the accumulative process of memory, the strengthening of the self, of the ego? Is not the practice of a particular idea or an ideology still a strengthening of the self, the 'me', with the inevitable conflict within and without which is the fundamental cause of wars?

Can there be a revolution in the 'me' through the action of will? I do not know if you have exercised will in order to bring about a change. You must have noticed that the action of will is still at the conscious level and not at the unconscious level, and mere alteration or exercise of will at the conscious level does not produce a revolution, an alteration, a radical change in our ways of thinking. So, is it not important to find out, for each one of us, how the mind works, not according to any particular philosophy, but actually observing the ways of our mind in action, the ways of our life, so that through the understanding of the superficial mind, it may be possible to go beneath the surface and understand the whole mind?

Unless we bring about an integration between the thinker and the thought, mere thinking, reason, philosophy, accumulation of knowledge, will be used by the thinker as a means of self-aggrandizement, either of the individual or of a group, or for the propagation of a particular ideology. So is it important, for those who are really serious about these matters, to find out how the total integration of man can take place. Obviously, it cannot be through any form of compulsion or persuasion or through disciplinary processes, or through any action of will, because they are all, if one really looks at it, on the surface level.

So, our problem then is, how is this total transformation of our being to come about? We have tried through authority, through compulsion, through conformity, through imitation. If we understand the truth of compulsion, the truth of discipline, the truth of imitation or conformity, then the superficial mind becomes free from these compulsory imitative processes, and so the superficial mind becomes quiet. Then, the total, unconscious processes can project themselves into the conscious, and in their projection, there is a possibility of uncovering them, understanding them and being free.

Whenever there is understanding of any deep facts of life, the mind is invariably still, not making an effort to understand. It is only when the mind is entirely still that there is a possibility of an understanding which brings about a radical revolution in our life.

Questioner: I have to study a boring book. I don't find any interest in it, yet I cannot but study it. How am I to create an interest in it?

KRISHNAMURTI: How can you create interest, sir, if you are not interested in something? How falsely we think about life! Your parents send you to a university, to a college. They never inquire, nor do the teachers and professors, about your true vocation, your true interests. Because of political, economic, and social conditions, you are pushed into a particular groove, you are forced to become a mathematician when you are really interested in painting, and so you say, "How am I to be interested in mathematics?"

In a country where there is overpopulation, innumerable economic, social, and religious conditionings, it is almost impossible to break away and do what one really wants to do. But, to find out what one wants to do, to discover the capacity of each one, is extremely difficult. That requires a total revolution in our educational process, does it not? Because most of us here are trained to be alike, we are not able to do anything for which we have the capacity or the inclination, and so most of us become low-paid clerks.

Interest in a book is not possible because you have not found your own true vocation. I think it is far more important to live creatively than to pass examinations, than to have a few degrees. I think it is much better to starve, if necessary, doing what one wants to do, than being compelled to do what one loathes. Because, when one does under compulsion what one loathes, then one destroys the mind; life then becomes a rotten, ugly thing—like the life which most of us are leading.

Questioner: What is your opinion on concentration, on Sushumna and the chakras, and on Om? These are mentioned in books regarded by us as most authoritative, although perhaps not read by yourself. The tantras contain an enormous amount of information on individual mantras, individual pranayama, yantras, etc., as a means of realization. All this is practically forgotten in modern India, but is known to a few gurus who remain hidden. What is your esteemed opinion about this?

KRISHNAMURTI: Concentration? Fixing the mind in a particular puja, on an idea, giving full attention to it?

If there is any form of compulsion, any form of effort in concentration, is that concentration? Is it concentration when there is any form of exercising the will in order to concentrate? In that process of doing the puja on which you concentrate, there is the entity that concentrates, that says, "I must concentrate." So, there is a dual process, is there not? Perhaps, this is a little out of the way, and I hope you don't mind my discussing this, my going into this question, because it seems to me we have a wrong formulation of what is concentration. If I concentrate on reading a book which I find boring but through which I think I am going to get a result or success, is that concentration? In that, is there not a dual process in operation, the concentrator and the thing upon which he concentrates? In this dual process, is there not a conflict between the concentrator and the thing upon which he concentrates? If there is any form of effort to push away other forms, to control the mind so that it will concentrate on one particular idea or a series of ideas, is that concentration or something entirely different?

In the usual concentration which we know, one part of the mind concentrates on another part which is an idea, which is a symbol—an angel, and so on. In that process, various other parts of the mind come and interfere, and so there is constant conflict going on, the straying of the mind, as it is called. Is it possible not to create this conflict but to be totally attentive, to be completely one with the thing that you are meditating upon and so really understand?

It is important to find out and to understand the meditator himself, not the thing upon which he meditates or concentrates, but the meditator himself, because this whole question is concerned with the meditator, not the thing upon which he meditates. If one goes really deeply into the question, we only know that the meditator is meditating upon something, and in his attempt to meditate there is a constant conflict, constant control, constant battle going on between the meditator and the thing upon which he meditates. When there is the understanding of the ways of the meditator, not only at the conscious level, but also at the deeper levels of consciousness, it is then possible to find out the truth. Truth cannot be found when there is a separation of the mind and then the control of the one party over the other. It can be found only when the mind is utterly still, not through any form of compulsion, discipline; and the mind cannot be still as long as there is the meditator as a separate entity, who is always seeking, searching, gathering, denying.

Really, this question, being very complicated and subtle, should be discussed very carefully and not answered or passed off in a few minutes. There is no answer, but only the problem. The answer lies in understanding what the problem is, but most of us, unfortunately, want to find the answer yes or no, and we listen with that attitude. But if we can put away that attitude and merely concern ourselves with the problem, then there is real concentration without any effort.

There are so many methods of concentration advocated by others, but they are all bound to lead nowhere.

We have to understand the whole process of the entity who concentrates. Meditation is the understanding of the meditator. Only in such meditation is it possible for the mind to go beyond itself and not be caught in the illusion of its own projection.

Questioner: The burning question of our time is war. You suggested that war can be avoided if individuals are integrated in themselves. Is this integration of the individual possible? As far as I know, there is no such individual. Even the best institutions like the League of Nations and the U.N. have been rendered ineffective by the egotistic self-interest of individuals or groups.

KRISHNAMURTI: The question is: Is integration possible?

What do we mean by integration? Integration between the various processes of our thinking, of our doing, of our consciousness; integration between hatred and love, between envy and generosity, between the various cleavages, between the various components in our total makeup—is that what we mean by integration? Or, is integration something entirely different?

Now, we think in terms of changing hate into love. Is that possible? If I hate, which is important—that I should love, or that I should understand hatred? Is it not important for me to understand the whole process of hate, not the ideal of love? If I am envious, what is important is not to be free from envy, not to have the ideal of love or of generosity and so on, but to understand the whole process of envy. The understanding of *what is* is more important than *what should be*. If I am stupid, it is very important to understand that I am stupid, to know that I am stupid, not try to arrive at cleverness. The moment I understand the whole problem of how stupidity comes into being, then naturally, there will be intelligence.

So, is integration to be brought about by the dual process involved in our thinking, or does integration come into being only when *what is* is understood, without any concern for *what should be*? Integration takes place only when I understand what I actually am not what I am according to Shankara, Buddha, or any modern psychologist or a communist. That actuality I can find out only in my relationship in daily existence, the way I talk to people, the way I treat people, my ideas as they arise.

Life is, after all, a mirror in which I can see myself in operation. But we cannot see what is actually taking place because we want to be something totally different from what we are. I think integration is possible only when I see what I actually am, without the blinding process of an ideology or an ideal. Then it is possible to bring about a radical change in what I am, in *what is*.

Questioner: How do these illuminating talks fulfill and help your purpose? The world has been listening for a long time to the gospel of revolt, the cult of attaining to supreme truth or destroying the self and thereby achieving the highest and the sublimest. But, what is the reaction, is it creative or recreative?

KRISHNAMURTI: What do you mean by fulfilling? You ask whether these talks help you to fulfill. Do you think there is such a thing as fulfillment? It is only when you are thwarted that you want to fulfill. It is only when you want to become a judge or somebody that there is the fear of not fulfilling. But if you do not want to become anything, then there is no problem of fulfillment.

All of us want to become something, either in this world or in the next world, inwardly or outwardly, and our purpose is well defined because our desires are always compelling us towards a particular end which we call fulfillment. If we do not understand these desires, then when they are thwarted there is conflict, misery, pain, and so an everlasting search for fulfillment. But, when one begins to understand the ways of desire, the innumerable urges, conscious as well as unconscious, there is no question of fulfilling. It is the self, the 'me', that is always craving to fulfill, either as the "great people of this land" or to fulfill inwardly—to become something, to attain liberation, *moksha,* or what you will. But if we understand the implications of desire—that is, the implication of the self, of the 'me'—then there is no question of fulfilling.

Questioner: Does not the emphasis on quieting the mind reduce creativity?

KRISHNAMURTI: What is creativity and what is understanding?

To understand creativity, there must be no fear. Is it not so? After all, most of our minds are imitative. We are ridden by authority, we have innumerable fears, conscious as well as unconscious. A mind so elaborate, so small, so petty, so conditioned—can such a mind be creative? It can only be creative in the deeper sense of the word—not in the sense of writing a couple of poems or painting some pictures—when you understand the whole process of fear. To understand fear, must you not search into the workings of your mind, must you not be watchful of the ways the mind imitates, why it copies authority? Only then is it possible for the mind to be creative.

Is the mind creative or is creativeness something entirely different? After all, what is the mind? Mind is the result of time, time being a process. Mind is the result of the past, the past being the culture, the tradition, the experience, the various economic and other unconscious influences; all that is the mind. Can the mind, which is the result of time, be creative? Is not creativeness something out of time, beyond time, and therefore beyond the mind? There is no "Indian creativeness" or "European creativeness." Culture is not Indian or European, Occidental or Oriental, although the expression of it may be.

That creative something, that creative reality, that truth, God, what you will, is surely beyond time.

The mind that is the result of time cannot conceive or experience the unknown, so the mind has to free itself from the known, from knowledge, from its various experiences, traditions; then only is it capable of receiving the unknown. It is the unknown that is creative, not the mind that knows how to create.

Questioner: When there is conflict between the heart and the mind, which should be followed?

KRISHNAMURTI: Is conflict necessary? Is this not the question: What to follow, the mind or the heart?

First, let us understand if conflict is necessary. When conflict arises, then the question comes into being, "Which should I follow, this or that?" Why do we have conflicts? Will conflict produce understanding?

Perhaps you think I am not answering your question. All that you want to know is what you should follow. It is a very superficial demand, and you are satisfied if you are merely told what to do. Unfortunately, as most of us are today, we know only what to think, not how to think; therefore, the problem becomes very superficial. If we want to think out a question of this kind, we must put aside "what to think" and inquire into "how to think." If we know how to think, the problem is not. But if you say, "I must follow this," or "I must not follow that," or "Which shall I choose?" then the problem arises.

If you once really go into it clearly, deeply, the problem "what to do" is a choice, is it not? Will choice clarify or put an end to conflict? Is there not another way of acting, not between the two, but which is the understanding of the demands of the mind and the demands of the heart without saying which should be done. Between them all, I must not follow one or the other but understand each demand without comparison. Then only is it possible to free the mind from choice and therefore conflict.

All this requires a mind that is really attentive not only to what I am saying, but also to its own processes, and, understand them. But very few of us want to do that. Very few of us are serious. We are serious about something superficial diversion or excitement. But to really go into the whole problem of existence, of the ways of thought, requires not an hour's attention at a particular meeting but requires the understanding of the mind all the time as it lives and acts. For that, few of us are willing. In that, there is no risk, you do not get a good job, you do not become famous, you do not become successful. As long as we want to become famous, successful, powerful, popular, we create misery and conflict, which brings about war.

January 24, 1954

First Talk in Bombay

I would like this evening to discuss the problem of change. It is really quite a complex problem, and I do not know if you have thought about it. If you have, you must have seen how extraordinarily difficult it is to bring about a change in oneself. We see the necessity of change, of a certain adjustment to life, of a radical revolution in oneself at certain moments—not along any particular pattern of thought or compulsion. Observing the various complications of existence, one feels the immense desire of bringing about a revolution in oneself. You must have thought about it—at least those of you who are serious—how this change is to be brought about, how it will affect the relationship that one has with another or with society, and whether this revolution will affect society. It is really, if you go into it, a very, very complex problem involving a great many issues, not only on the superficial level of our thinking, but also deeply at the unconscious level.

But before I go into it, I would like to say that, as I begin to explore the problem, you should kindly listen without resistance; then perhaps, if you are listening attentively and without any resistance, it may be possible to find yourself in that state of total revolution in yourself. After all, that is the purpose of my talking—not to convince you of any particular form of change, not to say that you must change according to a certain pattern; that is not at all change; that is merely adjustment, conformity to a particular pattern of action which is not change; that is not revolution. If you listen without any resistance, then I am sure you will be in a state of revolution in yourself, not because of any compulsion from me, but naturally. So I would suggest, if I may, that you should listen without resistance. Most of us do not listen at all. We listen with an intention, with a motive, with a purpose which indicates an effort. Through effort one never understands anything.

Please see the importance of this. If you have to understand something, you must listen without effort, without compulsion, without any form of resistance, bias, opinion, or judgment. This is quite a difficult thing in itself, and we do not know how to listen. The problem is not how to bring about a change; if one can listen rightly without any form of resistance, the change will come about without a conscious act. I do not think a radical change can come about through any conscious action, through any motivation, through any form of compulsion, through any motive.

I will go on to explain how this change comes into being without motivation. But to understand that, one must have an attentive attitude of listening, without any barrier, without any restriction, without any resistance. The moment you hear the word *revolt, change,* or *revolution,* that word has a definite meaning to you, either according to the dictionary or according to the communists or according to the socialists, or if you are a religious person, according to your own particular pattern of thought. These patterns of thought are constantly interfering with what you are listening to. So the difficulty is going to be, not the understanding of the problem itself, but how we approach the problem, how we listen to the problem. This is really very important to understand before we can go into any problem.

To bring about understanding requires no resistance to what you hear, but the following of the current of thought that one is listening to. One cannot follow if one is merely resisting, translating, putting against it barriers of one's own ideas. If we can listen without resistance, we can think out together, then together we will find the mind in a state of change, which comes into being without any form of persuasion, reason, or logical conclusion.

I think that, for most of us who are aware of world events and the things that are happening in this country, some kind of revolution is necessary; some kind of a change of attitude, of thought, a revolution in one's sense of values is essential. It is obvious that there must be a change to bring about peace, to have sufficient food for all the world, to bring about human understanding. To cultivate the total development of man, some kind of a vital, total change is necessary. Now, how is this change to be brought about, and what does this change imply? Is there change when the mind, thought, is merely conforming to the pattern of a particular culture—the Indian, the Christian, the Buddhist—or to the communist pattern of thought and action? Can conformity at any level of our existence bring about change? Obviously, if one conforms to a pattern, either imposed or developed by oneself, it is no longer change because the pattern, the end, is the result of our conditioning. If I, as a Hindu or a communist or a Christian, change according to the plan on which I have been brought up, according to an idea, according to a particular mode of thinking, surely that is not change because I am merely conforming to a conditioned reaction. And when I change myself according to the pattern of a fear, of a defense, of a tradition, obviously that is not change; that is not revolution, that is not a radical revolt from *what is.*

So, in inquiring into the question of change, must I not inquire how my mind functions? Must I not be aware of the total process of my thought? Because, if there is any form of fear and that fear makes me change, it is not change; the fear projects a pattern and according to the pattern I change; it is merely conformity to a particular pattern projected by fear. If I wish to bring about change, must I not inquire into the many, many layers of my being, both of the conscious as well as of the unconscious? Must I not inquire into the superficial reactions of my thoughts and motives, the deep underlying currents from which all thought, all action, springs? If I wish to change, can I have a pattern according to which I change? Though I repeat this, please pay attention to what I am saying; otherwise, you will miss what is coming.

I see the necessity of change in myself and in society. Society is my relationship with another, and in that relationship which I call society, there must be change, there must be total uprooting and complete revolution of thought. As I see the importance of it, my question is, "How is this to be done?" Is it a matter of intellectual reasoning, having a knowledge of history and translating that history, or having information of various social affairs, reformations? Will all this knowledge bring about revolution, the total change of me, in my thinking, in my attitude, in my activities, in my thoughts? So must I not inquire, if I am serious about this matter of change? Must I not inquire into my motivation for change, the urge to change? Does the urge to change bring about a radical change? The urge may be merely a reaction to my conditioning, to my background, to the various social, economic, or cultural impressions. Can change be brought about through any form of compulsion?

Or is there a change which is not of time? Let me put it this way: We know change in terms of time, time being the compulsion of various forms of society, of culture, of relationship, of fears, of the desire to gain or to avoid punishment. These are all in the field of time, are they not? They are functions, they are the results, they are the activities of a mind which is the product of time. After all, the mind is the result of time—chronological time, centuries of cultivation of tradition, of education, of compulsion, of fear. So the mind is of time. Can the mind which is the result of time bring about a total revolution which is not of time? If we change within the field of time—which is, if I change because my society demands it, or because I see the necessity through any form of compulsion, or because I gain something, or because of fear, which are all surely the result of the calculation of a mind that is thinking in terms of time, today and tomorrow—there cannot be a total revolution; that is fairly obvious, is it not? When the mind thinks in terms of time, in relationship to change, is there change? Or is there merely a continuity, an adjustment to a particular pattern, and therefore no change at all?

So, the problem is: Is there change, is there revolution which is out of time? And is that not the only revolution, which is not the product of the mind, of thought? After all, thought is the reaction of memory—memory being experience, knowledge, the storing up of innumerable reactions, of experiences—that is the mind; with that background the mind reacts, and that reaction is thought. So thought is of time. So as long as I am changing in time—that is, according to any pattern, communist, socialist, capitalist, Catholic, Hindu, Buddhist, or what you will—it is still within the field of time. When change is according to a pattern, however expansive that pattern may be, it is still within time and therefore there is really no change, no revolution. Please listen to this and understand. Do not reject it, do not say, "It is all nonsense, it does not lead us anywhere," but just listen to it though you may not be used to the idea. Perhaps it is the first time you are hearing this. Do not reject it because if you will really go into it, you will see the extraordinary thing in it.

Change comes into being when there is no fear, when there is neither the experiencer nor the experience; it is only then that there is the revolution which is beyond time. But that cannot be as long as I am trying to change the 'I', as long as I am trying to change *what is* into something else. I am the result of all the social and the spiritual compulsions, persuasions, and all the conditioning based on acquisitiveness; my thinking is based on that. To be free from that conditioning, from that acquisitiveness, I say to myself, "I must not be acquisitive; I must practice non-acquisitiveness." But such action is still within the field of time, it is still the activity of the mind. Just see that. Don't say, "How am I to get to that state when I am non-acquisitive?" That is not important. It is not important to be non-acquisitive. What is important is to understand that the mind which is trying to get away from one state to another is still functioning within the field of time, and therefore there is no revolution, there is no change. If you can really understand this, then the seed of that radical revolution has already been planted, and that will operate; you have not a thing to do.

There is difficulty in the way of that seed of real timeless revolution operating because we are not listening, because we are opposing, because we are only concerned with immediate results. We see we need to change, but immediately we want to know how to change, what is the method; that is all that we are concerned with. The method implies continuity of the activity of the mind, and it can only produce an action which is still according to a pattern and therefore of time and producing suffering.

Can there be an action which is not of time, which is not of the mind, which is not conditioned by thought, which is merely the experience of knowledge? These are all of time. Therefore such activity can never produce a revolution, a total revolution in the human development of ourselves. So the problem is: Is there a revolution, is there a change which is not in the field of time? Can there be a change without the mind interfering? I see the importance of change. Everything changes, every relationship changes, every day is a new day. If I can understand the new day, if I am dead to the old yesterday completely, to all the things I have learned, acquired, experienced, understood, then there is a revolution in that which is coming, there is change. But dying to yesterday is not an activity of the mind. Mind cannot die by a determination, by evolution, by an act of will. If the mind sees the truth of the statement that through an action of will or by a determined conclusion or through a compulsion, the mind cannot bring about a change, and that what is then brought about is only a continuity, only a modified result, but not a radical revolution, and if the mind is silent only for a few seconds to hear the truth of that statement, then you will find an extraordinary thing happening in spite of yourself, in spite of the mind; then there is transformation inwardly without the interference of the mind, the mind being that thought which is conditioned. That is an extraordinary state of the mind when there is no experiencer, no experience. From that, there is a total revolution. That total revolution is the only thing that will bring peace in the world. All national adjustments, all economic reformations of one group dominating another and liquidating all other groups, will fail; they all will bring greater miseries, wars. What will bring peace, understanding, love in the world, is not reason—reason being based on a conditioned reaction—but only the mind which understands itself totally and is capable of being in that state which is everlastingly, timelessly new. That is not an impossibility, it is nothing idealistic or dreamy or mystic. If you can pursue the thing truly, you will find that it is there, you can experience it directly, but that requires a great deal of meditation and hard research and understanding.

So, what is important is the understanding of the mind, and not how to bring about the change in oneself and so a change in the world. The very process of understanding the problem of change brings about a change in spite of yourself. That is why it is very important to listen to these talks, not to be persuaded by what I say but simply to listen to the truth of what is being said. It is the truth that brings revolution, not the cunning mind, not the calculating mind. Because, truth is not of time, not of India, Europe, Russia, or America; it does not belong to any group, to any religion, to any guru, to any follower. If there is a guru, if there is a follower, if there is a nationality, truth will not be there. Truth comes into being only when the mind has understood and is still; then only that reality can come into being.

There are several questions. I think, before I answer them, it is important to find out whether you are listening with a view to getting an answer, or whether you are listening entirely to the problem. These are two different states. It is easy to ask questions like a schoolboy who pops up a question hoping, waiting, listening for an answer, and thinking that the answer is going to solve all his problems, and that all that he has to do is just to follow the answer or to refute the answer and discuss like a cunning debating student. It remains at that level only when we are looking for an answer, listening for an answer. But when we are concerned with the problem and not with the answer, then the whole attitude is entirely different. The one comes from an immature schoolboy, it is the result of thoughtless education. The other requires mature inquiry.

So it depends upon you, how you are listening, whether with an attitude of trying to find an answer, and if there is no answer, being disappointed and saying, "He never answers questions." I do not intend to give an answer because life has no answer, yes or no. Life is much too immense, much too vast; everything goes into it like into the sea. It is like a big river that flows all the way into the sea, carrying with it the good, the bad, the evil, the beautiful, the ugly. The whole of that is the ocean, not just the superficial activities, the ripples. To inquire into a problem with no resistance, with no barriers, with no prejudices is very difficult. We have to inquire into the problem to really understand the deeper issues of the problem. So there are only problems and no answers. I think that if we can really understand, if we can really feel it out, that life as a problem is not a thing to be concluded, that it is not a refuge where you are everlastingly safe, then our whole attitude, activities, thoughts will be entirely different. Then, we shall receive everything and at the same time be as nothing.

Questioner: In India today one meets absence of beauty and destruction of form on all fronts—political, social, psychological, and cultural. How do you account for this, and in what manner can this total social disintegration be met?

Krishnamurti: Why is there disintegration, not only in this unfortunate, overcrowded, miserable, starving land, but also all over the world? Why is there such disintegration? Don't find an answer, wait. Don't give immediate reasons because your reasons will be according to your background, according to your conditioning—communist, Hindu, capitalist, Christian, or what you will. Please listen. When you are asked a question, "Why is there disintegration?" your response is according to your background, according to your knowledge, according to your experience, is it not? That very reaction is the cause of disintegration. We will go step by step into it, and you will see the truth of it. Why is there disintegration? Why does the mind become small, petty? Why are we only concerned with our little selves? Why do we identify ourselves with a bigger self—which is still petty? Because I am petty, I identify myself with something which is greater, but my mind is still petty. I may identify myself with God, truth, or nation, but my mind is still petty. However much the mind may identify itself with something greater, the very identifying process is still petty.

Sirs, why are we caught in this pettiness, in this deterioration? Are you aware that your mind is deteriorating? Or do you say, "My mind is not deteriorating, it is functioning beautifully without any effort like a perfect machine, without any resistance, without any fear, without thinking of tomorrow"? Obviously, only very, very few of us can say that. If you can understand why the mind deteriorates, then you can understand why culture, social values, the various forms of expressive beauty are all disintegrating.

Why is the mind deteriorating? That is the problem, not "Why is there disintegration in India on all fronts?" Why is your mind disintegrating? If one or two of us can really understand this, one or two of us can change the world. Because most of us are not interested in this, we are not able to bring about a complete revolution. So it is only the few that can really understand that will bring about a tremendous revolution in the world.

Why is your mind deteriorating? You say that, culturally, we are disintegrating. What is culture? Is it merely an expression, the imitation of a form conceived by the human mind? At present, in India, the mind is completely held, tethered, bound, by so-called culture, by tradition, by fear, by a lack of joy, by the fear of not having a future, by lack of security, or by the lack of a job. Is that the reason why the mind, being so completely conditioned, so completely held, has no initiative, no creative impulse? Is it because the mind is imitative, conforming, copying, that it is disintegrating and therefore not intensely active, creative?

How can a mind be creative when there is fear? So is that not the problem: Is it possible for the mind, your mind, the average mind, the mind that is troubled, the mind that is caught in family ties, caught in joy, in the routine of an office with an ugly boss, the mind that is caught in tradition, in richness, can such a mind be creative? If the mind can free itself from its conditioning, it is obviously creative. If the mind sees the truth that every form of imitation is destructive to itself, then obviously it will put all imitation aside. But we do not see the truth of that. Therefore, the slow process of disintegration goes on and on and on.

Can a mind be free from fear? That is the central issue because fear is disintegration. When you frighten a boy, he complies, but in the very imitation, in the very compulsion, you are destroying the mind. Can the mind be free from fear? Fear is not in just one particular form—the fear of being punished, the fear of losing a job, of being a loser. But the mind has fear in all its relationships. Can the mind be free from fear, wherever it be, in the office or in the family, wherever it functions? Don't say, "No." If I know I am afraid in my relationships in various directions, the very knowledge, the very awareness that there is fear, will bring about a transformation. But that transformation is not possible if you want to change that fear into something else, say love, because then love is another form of fear. Please see this, sirs. If I am aware that I am frightened of you and if I have no wish to change that fear into something else, if I just know that I am afraid of you and I remain in that state, then fear begins to transform itself into something totally different from that which the mind wants.

Sirs, let us put the problem in another way. The problem exists because of resistance, and if there is no resistance, there is no problem. But to understand resistance requires astounding insight, not mere determination, not an action of will which says, "I am not going to have any resistance." The very statement, "I am not going to have any resistance" is another form of resistance. But if you understand the depth, the quality, the various forms of resistance within the mind—which are extraordinarily difficult to uncover—then you will find that the problem of fear does not come into being. Therefore the mind is dying every day, it is not accumulating. And this dying to the day means dying to knowledge, dying to experience, dying to all the things that one has accumulated, one has valued, cherished. Then only is there a possibility of a new mind, of a creative mind coming into being.

As long as you are a Hindu, a communist, Buddhist, or what you will, you cannot have a new mind. As long as your mind is caught in fear and therefore is doing a particular routine or ritual, it is not a new mind. As long as you are doing your puja, your various forms of compulsion, which are the projections of fear, the mind cannot be a new mind. By just listening to this and saying, "I must have a new mind," you cannot have a new mind. A new mind cannot come into being by desire, by compulsion. It comes only by itself when the mind has understood the whole capacity, activities, the depth of itself.

It is important to understand the truth of change. Mind cannot put away fear because mind itself is fear, and that is all you know of the mind—fear of what people will say, fear of death, fear of losing, fear of being punished, fear of not gaining, fear of not fulfilling. So the mind, as your mind is now, is itself fear. And when such a mind wishes to change, it is still within the field of fear; that is an obvious psychological fact. So the mind invents a superior self, the atma that is going to alter, but it is still within the field of fear because it is the invention of the mind. It does not matter what Buddha, Shankara, or anyone else has said. It is still within the field of thought and when the mind wishes to change within the field of thought, within the field of time, it is not change, it is still a form of the continuance of fear.

A man who is pursuing an ideal can never know a new mind, and that is the curse on this land. We are all idealists wanting to conform to nonviolence, to this or to that. We are all imitators. That is why we have never a fresh mind, a mind which is completely, totally new, which is yours, not Shankara's, not of Marx, not of somebody else. That total newness, that complete state of mind, can only come into being when there is no experiencer and no experience; that state is there only when you can die totally to each day, to everything that you have gathered psychologically. Then only is there a possibility of a complete regeneration. That is not an impossibility, that is not a rhetorical statement. It is possible if you think it out, go into it deeply; that is why it is important to know, to listen to what is truth. But you cannot listen to what is truth when your mind is not silent. If your mind is continually asking, demanding, begging, wanting this or that, putting this away and gathering that, such a mind is not a quiet mind.

Just be quiet, be still. Look at the trees, the birds, the sky, the beauty, the rich qualities of human existence. Just watch silently and be aware. Into that silence comes that something which is not measurable, which is not of time.

February 7, 1954

Second Talk in Bombay

As we were saying last Sunday, the right kind of revolution, a radical transformation, can only take place, not at the physical level but, fundamentally, at the level of the spirit, and I would like this evening to go into that matter still further.

The true revolution is the religious revolution, not the merely economic or social. A fundamental revolution can only take place when man is truly religious, for every other kind of revolution or change is merely a continuity in a modified form of what has been. I say it is very important to understand what I mean by religious revolution. Unless there is a transformation at the fundamental level of our thinking, of our being, any superficial changes, persuasions, compulsions, or adjustments to environment are no transformation at all. Such transformation can only lead to greater mischief, to greater sorrow. So the revolution must be at the level which we call religious, and I would like to discuss that.

Before I go into that, it seems to me it is very important to know how to listen because we do not listen. We hear the words, we know their general meaning, and we are merely satisfied with the meaning of those words. But listening is quite a different thing. I think if we know how to listen, that very listening will produce that fundamental revolution. Listening is not an effort because effort implies continuity of purpose, a continuity of memory in a particular direction, and memory is directive, it is not creative. Listening, if we know how to listen, is really creative because, in that, there is no memory involved at all. But most of us listen with an attitude of resistance. If I say something you do not like or if I say something which you like, you immediately judge, you reject what you do not like and accept what you like, but that is not listening. Listening is a process in which the mind is really quiet, not interpreting what it is hearing, not translating, but actually following without any kind of effort, because effort destroys. If you knew how to listen, then the full significance of what is being said, the truth of it or the falseness of it, would come into being; but if you oppose one suggestion by another suggestion, one idea by another idea, you will never find the truth or the falseness of a statement. I think it is very important to understand what I am saying now—which is, to find out the truth of what is being said, the truth or the falsehood of what is being said. You must listen and not merely oppose it by an opinion or by a memory or an experience which you had. What we are trying to do in these talks is not to convince you of anything, not to persuade you to a particular activity or action, because that is merely propaganda and that has no value at all. What we are trying to do, you and I together, is to bring about that radical revolution, not at any particular level of our existence but in the process of total development of man. And so it is very important, it seems to me, to know how to listen. I am not suggesting any particular course of action, I am not offering any particular pattern or thought or philosophy. Revolution according to a pattern is not revolution. To know what you are changed into is not change at all, but to change fundamentally into something which is not known, the 'unknown', is revolution. And I want to discuss that, if I can, this evening, fairly simply. It is a very complex problem, but I think if we can quietly follow without any opposition or resistance in ourselves to what is being said, in order to find out the truth or falsehood of what is being said, then the truth or the falsehood will produce its own action.

For most of us, religion is dogma, belief, whether it is the communist, the Christian, or the Hindu religion. The dogma, the tradition, the rituals, the hopes, the everlasting struggle to become something, the ideal—the ideal man, the ideal love, the ideal state—and the pursuit of that ideal is what we call religion. But surely that is not religion. Religion is not conformity, religion is not the pursuit of continual thought. Religion is something totally different. That is why it is very important to understand that word, not according to you or to me, but to understand the meaning of that word, the significance and full implication in its totality. Mind can create any form of illusion, and that illusion can be the ideal, the God; and the worshiping of that illusion is not religion. The illusion, the projection of the mind that most of us worship in any form, at any level, is born out of hope, out of desire, out of longing, and that desire can create an image, and the imitation, the pursuit, the becoming of that ideal is still within the continuity of the mind. The mind cannot produce revolution, the radical change. What can produce the radical revolution, the total revolution in man's thinking is the cessation of the continuity of the mind as thought.

Please listen. Don't compare what I am saying to what you have learned or what you have read either from a sacred book or from any other book. Don't compare. If you compare, then you are not listening to what is being said. What is important is to listen to what is being said. When you compare, you never find the truth or the falseness of what is said because your mind then is occupied with comparison and not with the understanding of *what is*. So the inventions of the mind, whether purely physical, scientific, or abstract, the inventions of its own projections, its own ideas which it calls God, truth, love, the imitation of them, the pursuit of them, are all the continuance of the mind.

We know what envy is, and we have an idea that to be really religious is to be in a state of non-envy. Obviously, an envious man is not a religious man any more than the ambitious man, either on the physical level or the psychological level. Now, hearing that envy is not religious, and finding that envy is a series of struggles, pains, and that it brings about suffering, the mind says, "I must not be envious." This is the 'becoming' which is the continuity of the state of being envious, as we call it. The ideal, the pursuit of the ideal which we call "to become non-envious," are all still envy.

We are now talking of the cessation of 'becoming', in which alone there can be that revolution which is the real religious revolution. I think it is important to understand this. Our whole education, culture, influence, and conditioning is a 'becoming'. That is an obvious fact, is it not? I am poor, I want to become rich. I am envious or violent or angry, I must become peaceful, I must become non-ambitious—that is, I must become something. So our whole social, economic, religious conditioning and culture is to become, is the process of becoming. That is a fact, is it not? Watch the operation of your own minds, and you will see it is an obvious fact. The 'becoming' is the continuity of the 'me', of the idea, a constant process, and that process can never produce a revolution. A revolution, a change, a radical transformation takes place when the 'becoming' has ended—that is, not when I become non-envious, but when there is no envy.

Let us take the ideal of nonviolence. You say, "I will become nonviolent." You say that you will practice the ideal of nonviolence. That is, you are going to become nonviolent. You are violent, but through a process of thought, of practice, of discipline, you are going to become nonviolent. The continuity from violence to nonviolence is not a revolution; it is merely a process of becoming, and so there is no radical transformation at all. The mind that is constantly becoming, pursuing, being persuaded, being conditioned, can never become nonviolent; in that mind, there can never be a fundamental revolution. It is only when the mind sees that this is the process of becoming in time, and that the cessation of 'becoming' is the 'being', that there can be 'being'; in that 'being' alone, there can be a radical revolution.

Now, if you will listen, you will see that as long as the mind—which is the center of all 'becoming' because the mind is the result of time, and time is continual—is pursuing an ideal and becoming something, there can be no change. There can be revolution, a radical revolution, a total revolution in the development of man, only when the 'becoming' comes to an end—not when the mind becomes a perfect mind; the mind can never become a perfect mind, the mind can never be free, not becoming, because freedom implies the cessation of the continuity of what has been. So when you really see the truth of that, there is the silence of the mind, not that the mind becomes a silent mind; silence can never be achieved, mind can never become silent. But when the mind sees that 'becoming' is the process of struggle, is the process of effort, and that effort can never produce peace because what has been will be in continuity, in time, there is no 'becoming'. Only with the ending of 'becoming' is there silence of the mind.

Please follow this. When there is silence, in that silence there is no 'becoming'. You cannot become silent. If you make an effort to become silent, it is merely the continuity of an activity which you call silence now but which you called pain previously. So the understanding of 'becoming' is the beginning of silence, and that silence is the state of being, the total understanding of man's process, and that 'being' is the revolution, the total transformation of one's being, and then only is there a possibility of that which is timeless to come into being. Only such people are really revolutionary because they are not thinking in terms of economic, social, or temporary adjustments.

I think it is very important to understand this because most of us, especially in this country, are cursed with the pursuit of the ideal. We all want to become the ideal person, the perfect being, and so we practice discipline, the everlasting struggle to become something, and so we never 'are' at any moment. We always are 'becoming', we never 'are'; the moment is never full, it is always tomorrow that is full, and so we miss the full movement of life. If you observe your own mind, you will see that we never are still for a minute, but we are always trying to be still. The trying is what we know, the 'becoming' is what we know.

We know the ideal of silence, our mind is constantly pursuing that ideal, struggling, disciplining, controlling, shaping in order to have that silence in which the real can take place; and the real can never take place in that silence because that silence is a 'becoming'. It is only when the mind understands the total process of becoming, of pursuing, of trying to shape itself into something else, that there can be the cessation of 'becoming'; then alone there can be revolution. Only then is the mind truly religious. The religious man is not the man who becomes a sannyasi, not the man who becomes, who pursues virtues, or who tries to become an ideal man. The religious man is the man who has stopped becoming; therefore, to him there is only one day, there is only one moment—not the moment of yesterday or of tomorrow. Such a man is the real revolutionary, for he is of reality.

It is important not merely to listen to what is being said but to go away from here as a human being that is totally transformed—not with new ideas, not with a new outlook, not with new values, not with the putting away of tradition. Those are all childish things. They are all activities of immaturity. What is important is for the mind to have no space in it except of the state of 'being'.

Our minds are continuously being shaped by ourselves, by circumstances. We are pushed about, conditioned as the Hindu, as the Catholic, as the Christian, or as the communist. So long as we are in that state, we cannot produce a new world. It is only the man who has no other religion than the religion of 'being'—the state of being has no space, it has no corners in which the mind can become something—that will produce a new world.

You and I will have to produce a new world—not the new world according to the communists or the Catholics or the capitalists—a new world that is totally different, that is a free world, that is free in 'being' and not in 'becoming'. The man who 'becomes' is never free; he is always struggling, striving to become, and such a man is never a free man. Please follow this. Please listen to this. You will see that if you really listen, there is freedom from 'becoming'. It is only when there is freedom from 'becoming' that a man is really happy; he is the happy man, happy in that fundamental spirit that creates the new world.

As I was saying, the importance in asking a question is not to find the answer but to understand the problem, because there is only the problem and not the answer. To ask a question is easy, but to go into the problem is extremely difficult because once you know what the problem is, the very seeing of the problem is the understanding of the problem. The moment I can state the problem very clearly, simply, the answer is there; I do not have to look beyond. But most of us do not know what the problem is. We are confused about the problem, and so naturally we look, in our confusion, for answers, and that will only produce further confusion.

Please understand once and for all that there are no answers to life. Life is a living thing, not an ending thing, life is the problem. If I can understand the whole total process of the problem, then it is a living thing, not a thing from which to run away, to escape from, to be frightened about. So what is important is not the answer but to state the problem clearly and simply and to see the full implications of the problem; then the mind becomes acutely sharp. But, when a mind is seeking an answer, it is a dull mind, a stupid mind. If the mind sees the whole problem, the subtlety, the implications, the significance, the variations of the problem, the extension of the problem, the mind itself becomes the problem. The mind that is the problem itself does not seek an answer. When the mind is the problem, the mind itself becomes quiet, and the moment the mind is quiet, there is no problem. So what is important is not to inquire for an answer but to take the journey into the problem.

Questioner: In India today man faces a growing totalitarianism. Political leaders cloak their authority in smugness, virtue, and good intentions. On the one hand, there is this growing authority, on the other hand, there is a creeping servility, corruption, and disintegration. How is man to meet this debacle except by fighting authority on all fronts? What is your way of meeting this totalitarian challenge?

KRISHNAMURTI: Is there my way and your way? Or is there only the truth that will meet the challenge? You understand, sirs? There is not your way and my way of meeting the challenge; such a way is an ugly thing. There is only the right way of meeting it. The moment you talk of your way and my way, you are not stating the problem at all; you are only creating another authority which is myself. You see the question?

If you can put it entirely differently, the problem is: Why do we follow? That is the problem, not the politician using authority or the religious man using authority; they cover their authority, cloak it under sweet sounding words. People will always do that for their own interests, they will cloak their ambition by calling it the "love of India," the "love of peace," the "love of God"; being ambitious, they will use patriotism or the name of peace to serve their own interests. There will be always people of that nature, but that is not the problem.

The problem is: Why do you follow? You understand, sirs? Why do you follow—not a particular leader, a particular guru, a particular idea, a particular experience, or a particular ideal—but why do you follow at all? If we can understand that problem, this problem will be answered immediately. It is no problem at all. We are not discussing whether you should follow or not follow, we are not seeing whether it is good to follow or bad to follow. Whether it is immoral to follow, that is not the problem for the moment. The problem is: Why do I follow? Why do you follow? You may reject outward authority, you may have no outward guru, the example, but you have your own ideal, you have your own experience, or your own accumulated knowledge which you follow. I am questioning the whole total process of following, not the substitution of one authority for another or of one guru for another—those are all childish activities. But if we can inquire into the question, into the problem: Why do we follow? then perhaps we shall understand the problem of authority.

When you are asked why you follow, you do not know the reason why you follow. The reason is fairly obvious. You follow for some satisfaction, for some motive, for some gain, for an end in view. But this whole instinctual response to follow somebody, to follow an ideal, to follow an experience which you have had ten years ago and which you want now, and therefore follow and strive after in order to get that richness—this total process of following is the problem. The moment you follow, you have a guru, you create the authority. But if there is cessation of following, there is no authority, there is no guru; then you are a light to yourself. Please put yourself this question: "Why do I follow?" You are unaware that you are following, and that is of real importance. You are totally unaware—not only superficially, but at the deeper layers of your consciousness—that you follow. But if you say, "I follow because of this motive, because of this desire, with this end in view, because I am frightened, because I am this and I am that," then you are not finding why you follow; you are only giving reasons, logical conclusions. But do you know, are you aware that in following a political leader, a guru, or a book—sacred or profane, the Gita, the Upanishads, the Bible, or Marx's—you are only following words? Our whole process of life, deeply as well as superficially, is one of following. Following is imitation; we all know that. How can such a mind which only knows and functions in the field of following, imitation, creating authority, face and understand and break down authority? Following is destructive, following destroys. Can you see the truth or falseness of that, the truth or the falseness of the statement that following of any kind at any level is totally destructive, is disintegrating? Either you see the truth of it and accept it or you reject it. But you cannot reject or accept it if you don't know that you are following. If you are not following somebody, then either you are following your own desire or you externalize those desires and follow the politician or the guru or the book.

So, as long as there is the following of your own motives, your own desires, you must have authority. And following is destructive, is a disintegrating process—we know so well in India where we have nothing else but leaders and followers. Don't you follow? You are not a free people. You may have a new government, a brown bureaucracy, but you are not a free people because freedom implies "not following." Sir, when you really think about and understand all this, in that only there is freedom, there is total revolution; then only can a new world be created. But, if you follow you are destroying yourself. When you follow your guru, you are destroying both yourself and the guru. Please listen to this, find out the truth of it. Don't say I disagree or agree—which is an immature way of thinking. If you do not know that you are following, then you have no authority to give an opinion. If you do not know why you follow, if you do not know the whole process of it, then you cannot decide whether to follow or not to follow. But if you understand the idea of following, then you will not create the duality of not following, then there will be no struggle to follow or not to follow.

Our mind, which is so accustomed to follow, to imitate, can only react by not following, by not imitating. So, it sets up the problem of duality: "I have followed so far; now I must not follow." But that is not the answer. When you say, "I must not follow," that itself produces its own authority. Then you become the authority or the person who says you must not follow. But, if you understand the significance, the total meaning—of which most of us are totally unaware—then there is the cessation of following. Then there is creativity, and that is what is needed—not the putting away of one authority and taking up of another authority, more pleasant or less pleasant. But you have to see that all following is destructive, is a process of disintegration; you have to be aware of it choicelessly so that there is no duality. Awareness is a process in which there is no duality. Awareness is a state in which there is no choice, but there is seeing *what is* and not trying to change *what is* into something else. Only in such awareness is there a possibility of freedom, and only in that freedom can there be creativity.

Questioner: I have heard you every time you speak in Bombay. When I hear you, I feel great clarity and understanding; when you go, I get caught back into the innumerable habits of action and thought. Is it not necessary for me, once and for all, either to understand you or to give up hearing you?

KRISHNAMURTI: Sir, what is important is to know how to listen not only to me but to everything in life—to the song of birds, to the roar of the restless sea, to the voice of a bird, to everything about you. Because we do not know how to listen, we keep on hearing, and hearing dulls the mind. If you keep on coming to these talks year after year and merely hear but not listen, then your mind becomes dull. Your coming here becomes another ritual, a yearly performance. That is what has happened to most of us. We have become dull through repetition of ideas, hearing the same thing over and over and over again, performing the same stupid, vain ritual, pursuing the same ideals or substituting other ideals. This constant struggle within and without, primarily within, this battle 'to become', is making us dull. But if you know how to listen to one talk, really, how to listen to one idea, then you will see your mind becoming astonishingly alert, sharp, clear, subtle. Then you can listen to the talks over and over again, and you will see that each talk has meaning in it afresh every time, that it has significance, that there is a richness all of which you would miss when you merely hear.

Sir, you do not know how to see the beauty of a tree or of a person. Though you pass by every day, the beauty is there. You never look at the stars, the skies. You never hear the child's cry. You never listen to those things, your mind is too occupied—God knows with what—with its own anxieties, with its own 'becomings', with its own fears. Through this screen of fear, anxiety, hope, frustration, you hear and decide what it is that I am saying. There is nothing, literally nothing at all, which you cannot understand. I am not putting through new ideas, I am not giving directions for you to follow, because that would create merely another authority. You must forsake all authority to listen properly. If you listen after forsaking all authority, all following, then the truth or the falseness thereof comes into being. But a mind which is occupied can never listen. Most of our minds are occupied with love, with hate, with anxieties, with envy, with trying to be good. An occupied mind is a petty mind.

If you listen, your mind becomes a fresh mind, a clear mind, an unspotted mind; such a mind cannot be bought, nor can it come into being through any authority, through any following. So one must understand what one hears, and find out the truth of the matter by observing one's own mind. Truth is not something away from the mind. It is away now because the mind is so confused. A man who seeks answers seeks truth out of confusion, and so his answer of truth will also be confused.

Questioner: In moments of great anguish and despair, I surrender without effort to Him, without knowing Him. That dispels my despair; otherwise, I would be destroyed. What is this surrender, and is this a wrong process?

KRISHNAMURTI: A mind that deliberately surrenders itself to something unknown is adopting a wrong process, like a man who deliberately cultivates love, humility, when he has no love, no humility. When I am violent, if I am trying to become nonviolent, I am still violent. If I am practicing humility, is it humility? It is only respectability, it is not humility. You see the truth of this, sirs? Don't smile and say how clever the statement is. It is not clever. A man who is deliberately persuading himself into being good, who is surrendering himself to something which he calls God, or to Him, does so deliberately, voluntarily, through an action of will. Such a surrender is not surrender; it is self-forgetfulness, it is a replacement, a substitute, an escape; it is like mesmerizing oneself, like taking a drug, or like repeating words without meaning.

I think there is a surrender which is not deliberate, which is totally unasked, undemanded. When the mind demands something, it is not surrender. When the mind demands peace, when it says, "I love God, and I pursue the love of God," it is not love. All the deliberate activities of the mind are the continuance of the mind, and that which has continuity is in time. It is only in the cessation of time that there can be the being of reality. The mind cannot surrender. All that the mind can do is to be still, but that stillness cannot come into being if there is despair or if there is hope. If you understand the process of despair, if the mind sees the whole significance of despair, you will see the truth of it. There is bound to be despair when you want something and when you cannot get what you want—it may be a car, it may be a woman, it may be God; they are all of the same quality. The moment you want something, the very wanting is the beginning of despair. Despair means frustration. You would be satisfied if you would get what you want, and because you cannot get what you want, you say, "I must surrender to God." If you got what you wanted, you would be perfectly satisfied; only that satisfaction comes to an end soon, and you seek another thing. So you change the object of your satisfaction constantly; this brings with it its own reward, its own pains, its own sufferings, its own pleasure.

If you understand that desire of any kind brings with it frustration, despair, and so the dual conflict of hope, if you really see the fact of that, if without saying, "How am I to be in that state?" you just see that desire makes for pain, then the very seeing of it is the silencing of desire. Being aware choicelessly, purely, simply, that the mind is noisy, that the mind is in constant movement, in constant struggle, that very awareness brings about the ending of that noise choicelessly. Awareness is the important thing, not the dispelling of despair, not the silence. Pure intelligence is that state of mind in which there is awareness, in which there is no choice, in which the mind is silent. In that state of silence there is 'being' only; then that reality, that astounding creativity without time, comes into being.

February 10, 1954

Third Talk in Bombay

I would like to continue with what we were talking about last Wednesday, namely, the problem of change. It is quite an important issue which deserves to be really deeply considered, for change seems to produce more confusion, more travail, and more sorrow, as can be observed by us from day to day. I would like to discuss this evening whether it is possible to change, to bring about a radical breaking up of the center rather than merely indulging in peripheral or superficial changes. Is it possible to change at the center without the action of will, without cultivating a background, and without strengthening the background in the process of change? Is change—a breaking up, a revolution, a complete transformation—possible without the cultivation of memory? Generally, in the process of changing, we are always breeding memory—"I was this yesterday, and I shall be that tomorrow." This "I shall be" is the cultivation of memory, and therefore there is no fundamental, radical change at the center.

I hope you will have the patience to listen to this. Communication is anyhow very difficult because words have definite meaning; consciously, we accept certain definitions and try to translate what we hear according to those definitions. But if we begin to define every word or merely define certain words as a reference and leave it at that, communication will be at the conscious level. It seems to me that what we are discussing is not merely to be understood at the conscious level, but also to be absolved—if I may use that word—unconsciously, deep down, without the formulations of any definition. It is far more important to listen with the depth of one's whole being, than merely indulge in superficial explanations. If we can listen with totality of being, that very listening is an act of meditation.

The meditation that we do consciously is no meditation at all; it is merely the projection of the conscious mind, memory. You have to listen with the totality of your being, without any effort, without any struggle, and with the intention to understand, to explore, to discover, really to find out the truth or falseness of what I am saying. To discover is to be in a state of mind in which the struggle, the constant conflict to find out, must cease. It seems to me that such an act of living is meditation. To find out the truth of something—not according to what you wish, what you like or dislike, or according to the particular tradition in which you have been brought up—the mind must be capable of not only understanding the superficial sound that it hears, the vibrations of sound, but also entering much deeper through that sound.

It is a very difficult problem to listen with the totality of one's whole being—that is, when the mind not only hears the words but is capable of going beyond the words. The mere judgment of a conscious mind is not the discovery or the understanding of truth. The conscious mind can never find that which is real. All that it can do is to choose, judge, weigh, compare—comparison, judgment, or identification is not the uncovering of truth. That is why it is very important to know how to listen. When you read a book, you might translate what you read according to your particular tendency, according to your knowledge or idiosyncrasy, and so miss the whole content of what the author wants to convey; you might also listen similarly. But to understand, to discover, you have to listen without the resistance of the conscious mind which wants to debate, discuss, analyze. Debating, discussing, analyzing is a hindrance when we are dealing with matters which require not mere verbal definition and superficial understanding but understanding at a much deeper, more fundamental level. Such understanding, the understanding of truth, depends upon how one listens.

What we are concerned with is the necessity of change. We see that a fundamental revolution is necessary. I am using that word *revolution* not in the political sense. In the political sense, if there is revolution, it is no longer a "revolution," it is merely a modified continuity. But I am talking of fundamental transformation which alone can be called change. Is it possible to bring about such a radical change by the action of will—which is what we are used to? Will is the continuity of a decision based on memory, on knowledge, or experience; will is the reaction of a conditioned mind, the mind that lives in tradition, in experience, in knowledge; and knowing decides, creates the pattern according to which it shall change. Therefore, can a change, through an action of will, be a radical change? When I know in what direction I am changing, and also the implications which are in the change based on my experience—my experience being the reaction of my conditioning—can such a change be radical?

I wish to change because I see the importance and the necessity of change not only in myself but in society; I see the imperative necessity of it, logically and inwardly, because society as it is and myself as I am only produce a further mess, further chaos, further misery; that is an obvious fact, whether you accept it or not. As we are conditioned, any action from the conditioned mind is only productive of further confusion because if I am confused, any action out of that confusion is still further confusion. We are confused, whether we like it or not; whether we admit it or not, it is a fact. Whether you call yourself a communist, a socialist, a Christian, a Hindu, or a Buddhist, your mind, if you observe, is in a state of contradiction, is in a state of confusion. When you have a certain belief, a certain dogma, you hold to that dogma, to that belief. It is obviously, psychologically, an indication of confusion because that belief acts as a security away from yourself; that security is your projection, the projection born out of confusion.

A mind that seeks to understand the fundamental necessity of change must ceaselessly ask itself, "Is it possible to change without the action of will?" You understand, sir, the difficulty of the question? That is, my will is born out of my past, out of knowledge, out of the experiences that I have gathered. The gathering is the result of my conditioning. The conditioning is the culture in which I have been brought up, the religion, the social values, and so on. Out of that background is born the will to be, to change, to continue. This is a psychological fact. When you observe the action of will, you will find that the will cannot bring about a radical change. If it cannot, what else will bring about a radical transformation? What will break up the center of this constant accumulation of memory, of experience, of knowledge, from which there is action? This is an important question to ask yourself and to find the truth of. It is not enough if you merely listen to what I say because that is your problem. You have really to go into it.

The will is the 'I', the process of the 'me'; as it cannot bring about a radical transformation, the mind projects the idea of God and says, "God has the power to change," "There is the grace of God," and so on. That is, when the mind sees that it cannot bring about a radical change in itself through its own power, through its own action, through its own volition, the mind projects and identifies itself with something which will bring about the transformation. But that projection is still the action of will, the action of the 'me' that wishes to change, and as it sees that it cannot change through its own activities, it identifies itself with an idea, or with a so-called reality which it has created—relating to a Buddha, a Christ, or anyone it likes—and hopes that, through that, there will be a transformation. But that projection, the activities of that projection, and the response of that projection are still part of the action of will, so there is no radical transformation at the center.

Surely the problem now is: What can bring about the breaking up of that center? Is it grace, is it God, is it an idea? Is it something totally different, which is not the projection or the activity of the mind? That change which is the breaking up of the center, of the 'me', of the self, cannot be brought about by the action of the self, by will. The 'myself' which changes is the result of pain, of pleasure, of experience, of memories; and when it says, "I must change to something," that something is the projection of 'myself', the projection being the Master, the guru, the savior, and so on. Through the savior, through the guru, which is the projection of myself, I hope to bring about a change.

If you deny all that and say that circumstances or the control of nature would be the only possibility of change, then your mind is controlled by the so-called education on the communist lines or the Catholic lines or the Hindu lines. This process controls the mind, shapes the mind, and the shaping of the mind cannot bring about that radical transformation at the center.

Do you understand the problem? I want to change. I see the impossibility of change through action of will. I see that there can be no change through the projection of the past into the future, through the known projecting itself into the future as the unknown which is, however, the known. I see also how the mind can be shaped by circumstances. By the way I am brought up from childhood, my mind can be so completely conditioned that it functions like a machine, that it believes or does not believe. I also see that this is not change. In order to bring about a completely new world, a new state, a new being, to understand that this world is not a Catholic or a Hindu world but it is "our" world—to feel that is to understand the richness of it—there must be radical transformation at the center, in which there is no longer the 'me' or 'mine', my India, my religion, my experience. It is there that the radical change has to take place. How is that to take place?

Now, please listen. Is that the right question: "How can it take place?" Is there a method, a system? A system, a method, implies the continuity of memory, cultivation of memory, and therefore no radical change at all. When I ask myself how can this center be broken up, and when I seek a method, the very method, the very system produces the result which the system gives. But that is not change; I am only following the system, cultivating the memory of that system; instead of the system, the method which I had cultivated in the past, now I cultivate a new method, a new system, so the very "how" is the denial of the radical change. Please observe your own mind. When this problem of radical transformation is posed, the moment you hear it mentioned, your immediate response is, "Tell me what to do." The telling you of what to do is not change at all. You want to arrive at the stage of security or certainty through a method, and the very desire for certainty is no change. If you understood all this, you would not say at the end of the talk, "You have not told us what to do, you are too vague."

There is only the problem and not the answer. If you know the depth of the problem, the answer is at the depth. The problem itself will reveal the answer, but as long as you are looking for the answer at the depth, you are dealing with the superficiality of the problem. There is the problem of change, of radical transformation of the center. This change cannot be brought about through any volition, through an act of will, through practice, through a system of meditation. The very process of meditation, as you practice it, is the cultivating of a certain idea, a certain discipline, and so it only strengthens the self, the center, and any form of projection from the background, or the experience of that projection as reality, is still the strengthening of the center. When you have this problem, when you really are confronted with this problem, you will see that your mind becomes completely still. It is only when you are trying to change, to bring about a superficial change, that the mind becomes agitated, works, strives, struggles. But when you see the full significance of the fundamental revolution, transformation, then the mind, in front of this enormous complex problem, is still. If you are listening rightly and if you have understood the problem profoundly, then you will see your mind is still. The problem itself makes the mind still. When the mind is still in front of this problem, then there is transformation at the center.

This whole process of understanding the problem is meditation. This meditation is not the sitting down and grappling with the problem, but understanding as you go for a walk, when you look at the stars, at the sea, and the shadows of a tree, when you see a smile. It is a total process, for the problem involves the total understanding of man's development. Then only the mind is still, without any movement or projection of the mind, a wish, a hope. Silence is not a word, it is a state of being. A mind that is trying to become can never understand that state of being. You cannot become still, do what you will—practice, discipline, control, subjugate. All such action leads only to results. Silence is not a result, it is a state of being from moment to moment. So when the mind understands the problem of radical transformation, from moment to moment, then there is silence which is not the silence of accumulation, which is not the silence of memory, but a state of being; it is out of time, it is timeless. If there is such silence, you will see that there is a radical transformation of the center.

If you have listened rightly, you will find the seed of transformation has taken root. But if you are merely verbally resisting, then you will have only resistance and not truth. Unfortunately most of us are left with the ashes of resistance and not with reality. We are not educated from childhood to listen, to find out, to understand; we are never confronted with the problem, we are always given answers—what should be, the example, the hero, the saint—for you to copy, to imitate. So we are never shown the implications of the problem—such showing is real education. As we have not been educated in the subtleties of problems, in the understanding of problems, we become confused when we are thrown against a problem, and we want to find an answer. There is no answer to life. Life is a living thing from moment to moment, and a man who is seeking an answer to life is creating a little pool of mediocrity. So the question is not to find the answer but to understand the problem; the problem holds the truth, and not the answer.

Questioner: The awareness you speak of must mean the stripping away of the many facets of personality; in India, this search for self-knowledge has led inevitably to the destruction of personality, and the sapping away of all initiative and drive which are the driving forces of personality. That is why we see in India a refusal to fight social evil. Will not then your teachings only lead to further lethargy of the spirit?

KRISHNAMURTI: Are you individuals who have personalities? Will the understanding and the awakening of awareness with all its implications deprive you of that personality? Are you an individual, or are you a mass of conditions? When you are a Hindu, a Christian, a Buddhist, a communist, are you an individual? When you belong to some society or group, are you an individual? And are you an individual because you have a little property, a name, a few qualities and tendencies?

Sir, what is individuality? It is something which must be totally unique. But we are not unique. When you call yourself a Hindu, a Muslim, a communist, you are just repeating, it is merely the tradition. You are conditioned by your society, by your culture; according to that conditioning you experience, and the experience is the memory, is knowledge; the knowledge does not constitute individuality, it is only the reaction of the condition. When you become aware of this total process of conditioning, experiencing, accumulating knowledge, and that it does not constitute individuality but is the destruction of all creative being, when you are aware of all this, then you will not be a Christian, a Buddhist, a Hindu, a communist, or what you will; you will be in a total state of revolt. But as long as you are accepting, as long as your mind is conditioned as a Hindu, a Catholic, a communist, you are not an individual, you are only a cog in the machine.

Look at your own mind and the operations of that mind. Are you an individual in the sense of creating a unique state of mind in which there is freedom, the freedom of being? How can you have individuality, personality, when culture, religion, throughout the world are based on imitation, copying? When you are pursuing the ideal, when you are Gandhi-ites or some other "ites," how can you be an individual? Are you aware of the total process of fear which makes you imitate, which makes you follow, which makes you accept the authority of an ideal, of a guru, of a savior, of a priest? It is that fear that makes you comply, conform, imitate; it is that fear that destroys the real creative mind. It is that fear that seeks a result, security, a state of being in which there is no fear, and therefore it projects. And you follow that projection as your savior, as your guide, as your ideal. So your fear is compelling you to conform. And as long as there is fear, you cannot possibly be an individual, you cannot have a creative mind.

It is very important to understand fear, especially in a country that is overpopulated, that is deep in tradition—whether modern or scientific or ancient. As long as there is fear, there can be no creativity, and it is only the creative mind that is the real, that is unique. Awareness in which there is no choice does not destroy that creative reality.

Your mind from childhood is conditioned, it is educated from childhood in fear, it is subjugated, it is compelled, pursued, compared, various values are imprinted upon it; how can such a mind be a free mind? All that it knows is fear. Therefore it everlastingly struggles to do good and to avoid evil. The very doing good is to overcome fear; it is not freedom from fear but the overcoming of fear; therefore, there is still fear. How can such a mind be creative, be happy?

The mind that is free from fear is the creative mind; such a mind, through awareness, through self-knowledge, cannot lose that reality. The mind can be free only through self-knowledge—not the self-knowledge of the specialist, not the self-knowledge of Ramanuja or Buddha or the Christ; such "self-knowledge" is not self-knowledge. To know yourself according to somebody, Marx or Buddha or what you will—that is not knowing yourself. You can physically know yourself only if you are aware of yourself, aware of your actions, thoughts, feelings, words. But you cannot be aware of the total process, see the fullness of that awareness, if you compare, if you choose, if you say, "This is good, that is bad." So, self-knowledge through awareness does not destroy, does not sap away initiative. You have no initiative. You just follow some powerful personality, somebody who you think is a leader. So long as you follow anybody, any authority, any book, you are not creative. You are following because of fear, and the understanding of fear is the beginning of creativity.

It is very difficult to understand fear. I am not talking of the cultivation of the opposite. The mind which is cultivating the opposite is still caught in fear. The awareness of which I have been talking is a choiceless state in which you can see things as they are and not as you wish them to be, in which you can know exactly what you are, without any choice, and that awareness is intelligence. The man who is constantly choosing is not an intelligent man. A man is truly intelligent when there is no choice, for choice is the outcome of his background, and a free mind is not a mind of choice. Choice will exist as long as there is fear, choice will exist as long as you have any kind of authority at different levels of your consciousness. Therefore, to follow another is destructive. But to be completely aware is to be the light yourself.

Questioner: What is the true value of equality? Is equality a fact or an idea?

KRISHNAMURTI: To the idealist, it is an idea, to the man who observes, it is a fact. There is inequality—you are much cleverer than I am; you have greater capacities; you love and I don't; you paint, you create, you think, and I am merely an imitator; you have riches, and I have poverty of being. There is inequality existing—that is a fact, whether you like it or not. There is also inequality of function, but unfortunately we have brought inequality of function into the inequality of status. We do not treat function as function, but use function to achieve power, position, prestige—which becomes status. And we are more interested in status than in function, so we continue with inequality.

There is not only the psychological inequality but also the obvious outward inequality. These are all facts. By no amount of legislation can one wipe out this inequality. But I think, if one can understand that there must be freedom psychologically from all authoritarian outlook, then equality has quite a different meaning. If one can wipe away the psychological inequality which one creates in oneself through status, through capacity, through ideas, through desire, through ambition, if there is a wiping away of that psychological struggle to be something, then there is a possibility of having love. But as long as I am striving, psychologically using function to become somebody, as long as there is a becoming of the 'me', inequality of spirit will exist. Then there will always be a difference between me and the savior, there will always be a gap between one who knows and the one who does not know, and there will also be the struggle to come to that state. So as long as there is no freedom, all this 'becoming' will be used for the strengthening of the existing inequality, which is destructive.

Sir, how can a man who is ambitious know equality or know love? We are all ambitious, and we think it is an honorable state. From childhood we are trained to be ambitious, to succeed, to become somebody, and so inwardly we want inequality. Look at the way we treat people, how we respect some, and we despise others. If you look into yourself inwardly, you will find that this sense of inequality creates the Master, the guru, and you become the disciple, the follower, the imitator, the becomer. Inwardly, you establish inequality and dependence on another; therefore, there is no freedom. There is always this division between man and man because each one of us wants to be a success, to be somebody.

Only when you are inwardly as nothing because you are free, is there a possibility of your not using inequality for personal aggrandizement, and of bringing about order, peace. But to be as nothing is not a series of words; you have to be literally as nothing, inwardly; that can only be when the mind is not 'becoming'.

Questioner: How did you find God?

KRISHNAMURTI: How do you know, sir, I have found God? Sirs, don't laugh. It is a serious question.

Sir, is God to be known? Is God to be found? Please listen. Is God something which is lost and is to be found? Can you recognize that reality, that God? If you can recognize it, you have already experienced it; if you have already experienced it, it is not new. If you can experience God or truth, your experience is born out of the past; therefore, it is no longer truth; it is merely a projection of memory. The mind is the outcome of the past, of knowledge, of experience, of time; the mind can create God; it can say, "I know this is God," "I know I have experienced God," "I know the voice of God speaks to me." But that is all memory, that is the past reaction of your conditioning.

The mind can invent God and can experience God. The mind which is the result of the known can project itself forward and create all the images, all the visions, which is still within the field of the known. God cannot be known. It is totally unknown. It cannot be experienced. If you experience it, it is no longer God, truth. It is only when there is no experiencer, no experience, that reality can come into being. Only when the mind is in the state of the unknown, does the unknown come into being. Only when there is the wiping away of all experience, of all knowledge, is the mind truly still, and in that stillness which is immeasurable, that which has no name comes into being.

February 14, 1954

Fourth Talk in Bombay

We have been talking, the last three times we have met here, of the importance of a religious revolution. I mean by religion not dogma, not belief, not rituals. Nor does revolution consist of substituting one belief for another, but is a total revolution in our thinking, and this revolution is really the freedom from the known. I would like, if I can this evening, to go into this question because it seems to me that any activity from the known is not a change, not a radical transformation at all. It is merely a modified continuity of what has been known. Most of the political, economic, social revolutions or even the so-called scientific revolutions are always the continuity of the known.

I would like, if I can, to commune with you. I am using that word *commune* expressly, for it seems to me that it is not a matter of mere mental exchange of ideas, of trying to persuade one to a particular point of view, of trying to lay out a blueprint for action. To commune with each other is really quite a different thing because we must both be interested in the subject at that same time and at the same level. Communion is not possible if you are interested in something and I in something else, and we talk; then there is no communion—communion is only possible when both of us, you and I together, at the same time and at the same level, are interested not merely to listen to the verbal expression but also to commune with each other at a deeper level of consciousness over things that cannot merely be put into words. That means a great deal of insight, penetration. There is no communion possible if you are obstructing the significance by a series of screens, objections, ideals, or prejudices.

There is communion only when we both love, together at the same time, at the same level, and that love is not possible if we remain at the verbal expression or at the argumentative level. We have to use words to communicate. I think it is possible, if we are interested, if we love the thing we talk about, to go beyond the verbal expression and to commune with each other over things that are of vital importance; then that communion is neither yours nor mine, it is understanding; it is the perception of that which is real, true—which is not personal, of the group, of the nation, neither Western nor Eastern.

I think it is very important to know how to commune with each other, especially in matters that are of great significance and importance. There is no communion if we do not love the thing about which we are talking, if we do not give our whole mind and heart to the thing into which we are inquiring. Such love does not demand the effort of attention; it demands that state of easy, open loving, that attention which you pay when you are absorbed in something. We are now discussing a problem which, I think, is of great significance, so communion is essential. Such communion is not possible if each one obstructs the exchange, the discovery, with a series of objections, acceptances, denials, or resistances.

I would like to go into this question of freedom from the known because religion is not the continuance of the known. The known is the belief, is the discipline, is the practice, is a particular form of meditation invented by another as a means of attainment of a particular state, is the practice which one has invented for oneself, or is the practice of a particular system with the experience which that system brings and the continuance of that system as memory. The continuance of memory is the known, and it is only in the freedom from the continuity of the known that there can be communion. It seems to me that religion has always been, with most of us, the practice of the known—the known being the belief, the dogma, the hope, the fulfillment of an experience of a mind that has been brought up either in religion or in a state of denial of everything. The believer and the nonbeliever are both the continuance of memory, conditioned by the known.

The difficulty for most of us is the freedom from the known. The continuity of an experience, of an idea, of a belief, makes for mediocrity; it makes the mind live in a state of certainty. When the mind is certain in knowledge or in experience or in belief, when it feels secure, when it has taken refuge in any experience, in any dogma, or in any belief, such a mind is a mediocre mind, is a small mind. Because, through the desire to be secure, to be certain, it clings to every form of certainty invented by the mind, and such a mind can only function and live and move within the field of the known, and so the mind and the heart remain mediocre, small, petty. Our minds are conditioned by our beliefs, by our experiences, by our knowledge. With that mind we try to find what is real, what is God, something beyond and above human invention and illusion.

As long as there is the continuity of the known, there must be a mediocre mind, not a free mind. It is very important to understand this, not merely verbally or intellectually, because there is no such thing as intellectual understanding. But this requires a great deal of penetration and understanding of the operations of one's own mind because our whole structure of thinking is based on the known: "I have had an experience yesterday, and that experience is shaping me, is shaping my thought, my conduct, and my outlook." The experience may be not of yesterday but of a thousand years ago, which we call knowledge. So knowledge is a confusing factor in the search for reality. For most of us there is confusion; we are confused not in what we do not know but with the knowledge of the things we know; it is the knowledge that creates confusion. Is it not fairly obvious that most of us are confused? In spite of all that they may assert, are not most of the political leaders, religious leaders confused? Is there not confusion on the part of the follower of any leader, political or religious? Both the leader and the follower are confused. This confusion is due to choice because our knowledge is memory, and we shape our life and action according to that. But we are not willing to admit we are confused.

Life is a thing which is living, constantly moving; we recreate according to our memory and are not capable of adjusting to the immediate demands of life. So we approach reality which is living, which is a very complex process, with a mind that is already burdened with knowledge, with experience, with ideas. A mind is not free which is always meeting life with memory. It seems to me that religious revolution is the freeing of action from memory. Because, after all, the 'me', the ego, the self, is the accumulation of various experiences, of knowledge, of memory; the 'me' is nothing but background, the 'me' is of time; the self, the ego, is the result of various forms of accumulated knowledge, information; it is that bundle which we call 'I'. The 'I' is the many layers of memory; though the 'I' may be unconscious of the many layers, it is still part of the known. So when I seek, I am only seeking that which I know. That which I know is the projection from my past, and it is the freedom from the known that is the real revolution. That freedom cannot be brought about through any discipline.

I cannot be free through any discipline, through any practice, because I am a bundle of memory, experiences, knowledge; and if I practice a discipline to free my mind from the 'I', it is merely another continuance of memory. So there is no freedom from the 'me', the known, whether you are conscious or unconscious of it. That freedom can only come about when I understand, when there is the understanding of the whole process of the 'me'—not to direct the process because in the 'me', when it directs, there is the director and also the thing it directs, which are both the same. There is no observer different from the observed; there is only one entity, the experiencer and the experienced. As long as there is the experiencer, which is the 'me', experiencing something which he wants, it is still the known. So our difficulty is, is it not, that our mind is always moving from the known to the known. How is this movement to be stopped?

Creativity is the action of the unknown, not of the known. The unknown is truth, God, or what you like. The activity of that state, of that reality, is creative; it is the action without memory. That is why I feel it astonishingly, immensely important to find out not how to free the mind from the known but to be in that state when the mind is free from the known. The being of freedom from the known is the true religious revolution.

Our minds are so used to being told what to do. The religious books, the gurus, the saints, political leaders, and leaders of every other kind are telling us what to do—how to be free, how to be led to be free, what you should do, how you should discipline, practice virtues, and so on. Now, if you examine, if you look at it carefully, you will see that it is the practice of the known all the time; in that, there is no creativity at all. It is merely the continuity of the 'me' in a different form. That is all we know, that is our knowledge. The movement from that state to a state in which there is the freedom from the known cannot be brought about by any practice, by any discipline, by any thought process. I think that is the real thing to be understood. If one really understands it, the revolution, that extraordinary thing, is there. But as long as we think in terms of getting there, in terms of practice which will help us to get there, it is the continuance of the known which is in time.

When one really grasps, understands, the process of the movement of the mind from the known, and that any movement from that known cannot be in the state of the unknown—if one really understands, has the feeling, communes with that truth that any movement of the known will never lead to the unknown—then only is there the unknown. But our mind refuses to see that fact because our minds are so used to being told of various kinds of yoga, the following of certain ideologies, sacrifices, the building of virtues, the development of character, and so on.

You know all the movements of the known. But if you can really grasp the significance of this movement of the known and see the truth of it, then the other state of being, of the unknown, comes into being. That is why it is very important to understand the process of the mind—which is, after all, self-knowledge—to know, to see the mirror image of thought, of the activity of the mind, to just be aware of it without condemning it, without giving it a name. In that awareness without choice, you will see that the other comes into being. But a mind that is looking for the unknown, trying to experience the unknown, can never experience it. When the mind itself becomes the unknown, only then there is creativity, and that which is timeless comes into being.

Sir, what is the purpose of a question? Is the purpose to find an answer to the problem or to understand the problem? I have a problem, you have a problem; do we want to understand the problem, or do we seek an answer through the problem? Do we want a solution or to understand the intricacies, the complexities of the problem?

Most of us suffer; there is pain, anxiety, and most of us are concerned with how to get rid of it, how to do away with pain, with disturbance. So we all the time seek ways and means to overcome it, to put it away. The inward psychological suffering of the 'me' is always trying to find an answer, a way out. But if we could understand the maker of the problem, the 'me' that is everlastingly following, that is frustrated, that is feeling lonely, anxious, fearful, then in the very understanding of the problem and of the maker of that problem, there is the answer. But to understand the problem requires a mind that is not seeking a result, an answer. If you will observe your own mind, you will see what is happening. If you have a problem, you want someone to tell you what to do, so your emphasis is on the solution and not on the understanding of the problem.

In answering this question, we are concerned with the problem and not with the answer. If you go away disappointed because your question is not answered, it is your fault because there is no answer to life. Life has no answer. Life has only one thing, one problem—which is, living. The man who lives totally, completely, every minute without choice, neither accepting nor rejecting the thing as it is, such a man is not seeking an answer, he is not asking what the purpose of life is, nor is he seeking a way out of life. But that requires great insight into oneself. Without self-knowledge, merely to seek an answer has no meaning at all because the answer will be what is most satisfactory, what is gratifying. That is what most of us want; we want to be gratified, we want to find a safe place, a heaven where there will be no disturbance. But as long as we seek life will be disturbed.

Questioner: Truth, to you, appears to have no abode. Surely truth is one absolute. Do you not, by making it a matter of perception in the moment, reduce and limit it so that it loses its absolute nature?

Krishnamurti: How do we know it is absolute, final, timeless? How do you know? Is it a guess, a speculation, or have you read about it in books? Is truth something of time? Is it of the known, a projection of the known? Our difficulty is, is it not, that we want something permanent. Because we see life is transient, we want something fixed, permanent, absolute, changeless; because everything about us is changing, we project the absolute, the changeless, the permanent. When we are given the assurance of that permanency, of the absolute, we feel safe because we want that absolute, that permanency.

Is there anything permanent? The mind can invent the permanent, the idea of permanency, and take shelter in that permanency, but it is still an invention of the mind, a projection of the mind, a thing from the past, from its own knowledge of uncertainty, from the fear of its impermanency.

Is truth something to be remembered, to be recognized? If I can recognize truth, it is already the known. Recognizing implies the action of the known, does it not? Can the mind which is the product of time, the product of the past, the center of memory, can that mind know truth? Or does truth come into being when there is the freedom from the process of the known, when there is the cessation of the process of recognition? Then there is the truth which may be from moment to moment, which may have no quality, no time. But the mind experiences for a single second what is truth, then remembers and says, "I must have that again." The desire to have it again is the projection, is the continuity of memory, which prevents the next experience of truth. Sirs, that which is real is not to be gathered, to be held. The mind must be free from all sense of acquisitiveness. But the mind, which is the only instrument we have, is gathering, takes impressions. With that mind we create the unknown, we project into the future the things which we want.

For truth there is no path, there is no discipline; all the sacrifices of the mind are in vain—the rituals, the practices. There must be freedom not at the end but right from the beginning—freedom to inquire, to search, to find out, to discover about truth. Through discipline, there can be no freedom from fear. So our problem is not whether truth is absolute but how to be free from the acquisitive process of the mind, free from gathering. A man who has great experiences, great knowledge, is never free because his knowledge, his experience, prevents that freedom which is necessary for discovery. If one really understands this, then books, sacred or otherwise, have no significance, they are not shelters, they are no use to you as a way to reality. They are hindrances when they become a means to knowledge, when they are a shelter, when they are part of the acquisitive process. See how difficult it is for a mind that has an experience which it calls rich to be free from that experience because it is always wanting more, more, and more, and the demand for the 'more'—with which the mind is occupied—prevents the immediate experience of the real.

So the question is really: Will the mind ever be free from the experience of yesterday or from the immediate experience and leave the acquisitive memory behind? That is the truth. A mind is never free so long as it is acquisitive—not the acquisitiveness of things only, but the acquisitive pursuits of the mind that demands more, asks for more experience, or looks back to an experience that it had which it calls rich. Such a mind is in constant movement of experience, constantly gathering; such a mind can never experience or be in the state of the unknown—which is obviously a thing from moment to moment, which is not in time but from moment to moment, in which there is no action from one experience, one state, to another state; each state is a new, unknown thing, and that state cannot possibly be understood as long as there is an experiencer experiencing, gathering.

Questioner: I am a businessman. I have heard you, and I feel that I would like to do something for my employees. What am I to do?

KRISHNAMURTI: Sir, this is our world, is it not? It is our earth, not the businessman's earth or the poor man's earth. It is our earth. It is not a communist world nor the capitalist world, it is our world in which to live, to enjoy, to be happy. That is the first necessity, to have that feeling—which is not a sentiment but an actuality in which there is love, a feeling that it is "ours." Without that feeling, mere legislation or union wages or working for the state—which is another kind of boss—is of very little meaning; then we become merely employees either of the state or of a businessman. But when there is the feeling that this is "our earth," then there will be no employer and the employed, no feeling that the one is the boss and the other is the employee, but we have not that feeling of 'ourness'; each man is out for himself; each nation, each group, each party, each religion is out for itself. We are human beings living on this earth; it is our earth to be cherished, to be created, to be cared for. Without that feeling, we want to create a new world. So every kind of experiment is being made—sharing profits, compulsory work, union wages, legislation, compulsion—every form of coercion, persuasion, is used.

It seems to me that the primary thing is to have the feeling that we are all human beings, not businessmen, not employees. That is why it is important to have a religious revolution, not an economic revolution only. The revolution must begin at the center and not at the periphery. I know you will say that it is impossible, that it is a utopia, that this can never be worked out, and so on. But, sir, this is the most practical thing. You say it is impractical and silly, out of focus, because you are looking at it from a particular point of view, you are not concerned with the total development of man. The businessman asks, "What can I do?" If he has that feeling, he can do a hundred things; he can make the poor rich by sharing, he can make his employees share in the business, he can make the business a cooperative concern. There are so many ways. But without this extraordinary feeling that we are one humanity, that this is our earth, mere legislation and compulsion or persuasion will only lead to further destruction and further misery.

Questioner: Help us to understand this terrible fear of death that pursues every man and woman.

KRISHNAMURTI: Is fear to be got rid of through any reason, through any logical conclusion, through the assertion of any beliefs? Even if you are told that, after death, you are going to live your next life, would you be free of fear? It may pacify you, quiet you for the time being, but that sense of not knowing, not being certain, still pursues. So is fear to be put aside through belief, through reason? You know that you will die—which is the lot of everyone. Logically, you know everything ceases, and there is a peculiar continuity because you continue in your son, in your daughter, in your neighbor, and you are the continuity of your father and mother. Though you know logically there is death, are you free from fear?

Logically, intellectually, verbally, inwardly, can you be free from fear? Fear exists only in relationship, does it not? You are afraid of death, death being the unknown; you are afraid of your mind ceasing to be. Though you know you are going to cease, and you believe you will be resurrected or you will be reborn, will you ever be free from fear? So, how are you to be free from fear? Is there a way to be free from fear? If I tell you how to be free, will you be free? You may practice, you may say, "I know everything ends, and ending may be a new beginning, and in the ending there may be a creativity, or when I cease, the unknown comes into being." You may persuade yourself, you may reason, but will fear cease?

So fear is something not to be understood or to be put aside by the mind because the very mind is fear. It is the mind that creates fear, the idea of ceasing, the idea of coming to an end. It is the mind that says, "I have lived so long, I should not come to an end. I must experience more, I have not fulfilled." It is the mind that asks, "What is going to happen to me tomorrow?" The tomorrow is created by the mind. The tomorrow and the coming to an end of tomorrow are ideas which form the process of the mind. Fear therefore is created by the mind, and the mind cannot overcome fear, do what you will. If you see the truth of this—that the mind creates fear—then there is the ending of the process of thinking of the tomorrow.

Sir, as long as the mind operates as being in time or knowing this ending of time, there is fear. Fear is the process of the mind and the mind cannot free itself of its process; all that it can do is to be aware of the process that there is fear, and not try to overcome it or to do something about it, but to observe fear and not to act, for to act is still to create fear. So, only when the mind does not create tomorrow—which means the dying of today, the ending of the thought process now—only then is there no fear. When the mind sees this truth, then the mind is itself in a state of the unknown and is not the accumulation of all the many yesterdays. It is only when we die, from day to day, to all the things that we have gathered, then only is there such a thing as the ending of fear.

February 17, 1954

Fifth Talk in Bombay

It seems to me that if we could find for ourselves an ever-refreshing and refilling source of happiness or bliss, most of our problems would be solved. We are everlastingly searching after that source in all our relationships, in the things that we pursue with motive and sometimes without motive. The things that we accumulate as knowledge and the things of the heart and the mind are all surely an indication, are they not, that we want to find some inexhaustible source of bliss from which we can always live and be happy and create. But that fountain seems to elude us. We are always pursuing a phantom, and we never have the substance itself. I think, perhaps, if we could consider what we have been discussing the last few times we met here—namely, the problem of religious revolution—if we know how to bring about that revolution, it may give us that source, and bliss may come into being in our lives.

Is total revolution a matter of process? Is it a matter of how to get there? Total revolution is not a revolution through a process, through gradual adjustments, denials, resistance, and discipline. Total revolution is in the moment. Every other form of revolution or change, it seems to me, is a process of adjustment to a particular pattern, to an ideal, to a utopia, or what you will; it is a gradual process, and it seems to me, such a process, such a gradual approach, the so-called evolutionary method, is not religious—it may be scientific, but it is radically not a religious approach at all. It seems to me very important to understand this religious state, and be there, but not come to it. That is not possible, it seems to me, if we think in terms of time—as getting there, arriving, practicing a certain method, having a certain approach which will gradually reveal that astonishing, creative release of the timeless. It is a matter of dying each day to all the things that we know, all that we have experienced, all that we have learned. The important thing is the dying, but not how to die each day.

Before we proceed further, it is very important to find out how we listen. If you are an intellectual, if you have read a great many books, if you have acquired great knowledge, and if your brain and your mind are full, can you listen? Does not that very knowledge interfere with what is being said, with your discovery of truth? Your brain may be very sharp, intellectual, capable of progressive, rational examination, but will such a mind, the so-called intellectual mind, come to that state? That state surely can only be when the activity of the mind has ceased. So, is it not important for this so-called intellectual mind to put aside, if it can, all the things that it has learned, studied, read? I am sure that, otherwise, the intellectual mind will never find that which is real. The intellectual mind is capable of great deception because in the process of analysis, it discards, it puts away; there is always the fear of uncertainty and therefore it clings to some form of belief, as most intellectuals do.

Is it not important for those of us who are not too brainy to know how to listen? The average person who is struggling, who is miserable, feels lost; he does not know where to find comfort, where to find understanding, on whom to rely, because all the political and so-called religious leaders have led him nowhere; there is greater confusion, greater contradiction in his life. Being the average, so-called mediocre mind, he is everlastingly struggling to be something. Is it not very important for him to find out how to listen? The mediocre man, the average man, like any other mind, really wants to find a method of immediate action; he wants to know what to do because he is caught in circumstances, in life that has become a routine, a boredom, a self-revealing frustration. Is it not important for a mind which is always striving for an end, for a result, for something to get at, for something by which it will be guided, to know how to listen?—because what we hear is translated in terms of action. Not that action is not important. It seems to me that the happy man knows to live, and living is his action, but the unhappy man is everlastingly seeking a pattern of action.

As most of us are unhappy, struggling, trying to find some light or happiness, we are more concerned to listen in order to find a pattern of action, and so we are caught in this vain search for a pattern for action, and we lose the art of listening, listening not only to what is being said here but to everything about us—to the roar of the sea, to the song of birds, to children's voices, to the books that we read. We do not listen because our minds are too occupied, and our occupations are petty. Even the mind that is occupied or concerned with the search for God is petty because it is occupied. It is only the mind that is free, quiet and unoccupied, that has bliss, that has infinite space. To such a mind comes that which is eternal. A mind that is occupied with worries, with the salvation of mankind, with social reforms, with knowledge—such a mind can never listen because there is no space, no emptiness, in which a new thing, a new seed, can come into being. I think it is very important to have such a space in your mind, unoccupied, quiet, without striving, because only in those dark moments, the light is seen dimly, but you cannot see this when the mind is constantly occupied, pursuing, asking, begging.

There are those minds which listen, which are immature—the students. They also listen, do they not, in order to learn, in order to gather information according to which they are going to live; they want examples, similes; they want to be shown the way what to do, how to listen. Surely, all such minds—the student, the average, and the so-called intellectual person—are occupied, they have no space, no emptiness in which something real or something false can be discovered. Surely, a mind must have space in which a new seed can be born—the seed that comes not through striving, not through a process, not through the deliberate evolution of the imitator, not through any practice in order to arrive. The mind must have that small space in the mind, however else the mind is occupied, and that little space must be undisturbed, uncontaminated; in that space an eternal fountain of bliss can come into being. But, to create that space is not an act of volition; you cannot say, "How am I going to create it?" The moment you put the "how," then your mind is occupied.

If you see the importance, the sheer beauty, and the necessity of quietness, then that space is there; that space is the dying to everything that one has known, to all the memories, to all the experiences, to all the accumulations of knowledge, information. We do die, the body is undergoing a change, obviously; there is an ending to the noble, the ignoble. But the mind refuses to die to the things of yesterday. We carry over from day to day, and this carrying over is memory by which we give continuity to that. We hope that in this continuity of learning, acquiring, modifying, changing here and there, there will be a revolution, a radical transformation. That which can continue is never a religious transformation. It is only when thought comes to an end and has no continuity that there is a dying to the mind, and in that, a radical transformation can take place.

Just listen to this. Don't say, "How am I to get those things of which you say?" I am not saying anything, I am just describing the state of the mind, a machinery, an organism that is perpetually making a noise, that can never hear silence. Our thoughts are in constant motion, in constant movement, and thought is the continuity of yesterday—which is the process of time—and, in the process of time, there can never be a radical transformation; there can be only a change, an escape, a modification, but not that real religious revolution in which there is no process but there is 'being'. For instance, a man who is acquisitive, however much he may practice, control, discipline—which is the process of time—will never find a state in which that nonacquisitive state is. Freedom from acquisitiveness is not a process; it is a state which must happen, and the happening can only take place when there is dying because it is only when you come to an end that there is something new.

The mind refuses to come to an end because mind is the result of time, of centuries of compulsion, of conformity, of imitation; the mind only knows struggle, judgment, values based on that struggle, and it is trying to change by struggling, by saying, "I must change; there must be an action by me which will produce happiness." So we have economic, scientific, or social revolutions, but not the real religious revolution which is the only revolution. Religion is not the worshiping of idols, the performance of ritual, or the pursuit of the ideals of the mind. Surely religion is something entirely different from the repetition of what the ancient teachers have said in the Vedas or in the Upanishads—all that must go, it must all end in the fire of silence.

The difficulty is we never want to be uncertain, we are afraid of losing everything. So the mind, being uncertain, pursues certainty; thereby, it creates fear; out of fear comes imitation, the establishment of authority—political, religious, or of one's own volition—because the mind demands a state of continuity in which it is certain. And a mind that is seeking certainty never has space in which the real can come into being.

So it seems to me that those of you who are listening should be concerned not with 'how' but rather with 'being'—to be, to have some space in the mind in which there is no movement of thought—thought being the continuity of yesterday. Thought can never produce a new world. The intellect can never produce a new state. It is only when thought comes to an end, when I am dead to all the yesterdays, that there is a possibility of that religious revolution which is so necessary to create a new world. Every god must go for the real God to come. We have too many gods now in our mind, so the real God can never come into being. Just see the truth or falseness of it, just listen to the fact whether it is true or not. Just to know the fact in itself is liberation. To know that, there must be an ending of yesterday, one must die to the memories, to the enrichment of one's experiences, to the knowledge that one pursues in order to be certain; all that must come to an end, for they are all things made by the mind.

The mind is the result of time. You, as the self, as the 'me', as the ego, are a product of the mind. The character, the tendency, the various disciplines, the various controls and persuasions are all the result of time; they are the product of time. Mind is what nature, what the environment, has made it through culture, through fear, through imitation, through comparison, through so-called education; such a mind, do what it will—progress, struggle—can never bring about an action which is the outcome of bliss, which is the outcome of the revolt to find reality. Really, one has to see the simplicity of it—not the simplicity of the external, but the simplicity of being in that state—not to arrive, not to struggle to be something, but to be like a flower. It is in itself perfume, it is in itself beauty; there is no effort, no struggle.

The mind that struggles to have the timeless beauty of that perfume is incapable of knowing it. The mind that struggles can never know it; all its rituals, all its experiences, all its sacrifices, are in vain because the self is always there and the self is the center of all thinking. One must die to that thinking every day. The rebirth in tomorrow is the religious revolution.

Let us now consider the problem of isolation. When you have a problem, have you not isolated yourself? You have no communion because your mind is so concerned with the problem and with the solution of that problem that you shut yourself off from the real understanding of that problem. When the mind is occupied with the problem, the mind is isolating itself. Don't put your mind to work, but see what creates the problem. It is the mind. The mind in isolation, in that state of noncommunion, has a problem, and then we ask questions to find an answer which will unlock the problem. So we are looking for a key and not at the problem itself. A mind that is occupied with the problem can never look into the problem.

We have so many problems in life, not only economic, social, which are all surface problems, but the unconscious problems, the deep problems which control and shape the economic, the outer issues. They are the result, the fruit, of our confusion, of our inward struggle. The mere superficial alteration of the economic will not break down the inward entity which is shaping everything to suit itself.

So to really understand the problem, the mind must not be occupied with the problem. But most of us are so eager to solve the problem confronting us that we want an immediate answer; for us the answer is very important because we think that by having an answer, we have solved the problem. A mind that seeks the answer is a very superficial mind, it is really a mediocre mind.

We are all educated to find answers, to be told what to do, to copy, to practice what we are told to do. Surely life is a process of living from day to day, and living has no answer. There is only the problem and living is the problem. A mind that is merely seeking an answer to the problem will find an answer, but the problem will still remain and it will come in another form. So, if I know how to understand the problem, if I can know how to look at the problem, then the problem is resolved. Because I do not know how to look at the problem, I seek the answer. I cannot deal with the problem if I condemn it. That is the real basic thing that prevents us from understanding the problem. The problem is there so long as we judge, condemn, compare. Sir, when you do not condemn, when you do not judge or compare, is there a problem for the mind?

The mind that condemns, judges, analyzes, compares, creates the problem. Do not say, "How am I to act?" If you learn a method, the method becomes the master of your mind, and again there is the problem, but if you see the truth of the statement that to condemn, to judge, to compare creates the problem, then you will see that the problem itself has already full significance.

Questioner: I see how wrongly I have been educated. What am I to do? Can I reeducate myself or am I mutilated for life?

Krishnamurti: Sir, when the mind is diseased, when the brain is diseased, then education is impossible, is it not? But we are living human beings, and there is that quality, that intelligence which can be awakened, which can educate itself. There is no human entity who is so mutilated that he cannot bring regeneration to himself.

To understand how wrongly we have been educated is a very difficult thing to do. Before you say you must reeducate yourself, must you not know how you have been wrongly educated? Is it so easy to say that you have been wrongly educated? That is, you may be educated to a particular technological job, and you find that is not your way of life, but you are sticking there because of your responsibilities. To break that and to go to a new job, is that education? Or to learn a new language, to learn a new technique, is that education? Surely, to find out what is wrong education requires a great deal of perception, insight. It is not so easily to be asserted that most of us are wrongly educated.

Education from childhood has been the cultivation of fear, and that is all we know. We have ever been brought up with that. Through examination, through comparison with the clever boy, with what the father was, with the mother, with the uncle, we are made stupid through various forms of compulsion from parents, from teachers, from society; the cultivation of fear is there. As we go out of college, we fit into a wrong pattern of life and do what we are told to do. Fear produces the inevitable course of life, and as we grow, life becomes darker and more confused. That is your life, but parents do not understand that fear destroys and that fear does not come into being if there is no comparison from childhood, if there are no examinations but only records kept of each child.

All our education has been the cultivation of fear—religious, economic, social. Everything is based on fear. You want to be somebody; otherwise, you are nobody; therefore, you struggle, compete, destroy yourself. Only that man is "nobody," who is not afraid. Being nobody is true education. There is the sense of anonymity in the great things of creative life. Truth is anonymous, not yours or mine. There cannot be anonymity when the mind is frightened. So to uncover the ways of fear and to be free—not at the end of life but to be free from the very beginning so that I understand what fear is—that is real education. From childhood, the ways of fear are to be understood so that as one grows, one can meet fear, can meet all the problems of life, so that one's mind, though it always meets problems, is always fresh, new, so that there is no deteriorating factor such as the memory of yesterday.

Questioner: Has prayer no validity, or is true prayer the same as meditation?

Krishnamurti: Prayer and the thing that you call meditation are acts of volition. Are they not? We deliberately sit down to meditate, we take a certain posture, concentrate in order to understand. We pray because we suffer. Behind prayer and the ways of meditation that we know, there is an act of volition, an act of will. When you pray, obviously it is an act of will; you want, you beg, you ask; as a result of your confusion, misery, suffering, you ask someone to give you knowledge, comfort, and you do have comfort. The asker generally receives what he asks for, but what he receives may not be the truth, and generally it is not the truth. You cannot come to truth as a beggar. Truth must come to you; then only you see the truth, not by asking. But we are beggars, we everlastingly seek comfort, we seek some kind of state in which we will never be disturbed; we ask for that, and we will have the reward, but the reward is death, stagnation. Don't you know the people who demand peace? They have peace, but their peace is isolation, and they keep on repeating the same phrases which they memorize. The mind makes them quiet. It is like a stagnant pool with moss, the words are covered with the activities of the mind. The mind is made dull. Surely, that is not meditation.

Meditation is something totally different, is it not? Please follow what I am saying and see the truth of meditation. To meditate, there must be the understanding of the meditator; that is the first requirement—not how to meditate, because how to meditate only develops concentration, which is exclusion. You may be absorbed in your exclusion, but that is not meditation. Meditation is the process of self-knowledge which is the knowledge of the meditator—not the higher meditator who is meditating, not the higher self which is searching. To think about the higher self is not meditation. Meditation is to be aware of the activities of the mind—the mind as the meditator, how the mind divides itself as the meditator and the meditation, how the mind divides itself as the thinker and the thought, the thinker dominating thought, controlling thought, shaping thought. So in all of us, there is the thinker separate from the thought; the thinker has become the higher self, the nobler self, the atma, or what you will, but it is still the mind divided as the thinker and the thought. The mind, seeing thought in flux, impermanent, creates the thinker as the permanent, as the atma which is permanent, absolute, and endless. The moment the mind has created the higher self, the atma, that higher self is still of time, it is still within the field of memory, it is an invention of the mind, it is an illusion created by the mind for a purpose. That is a psychological fact, whether you like it or not; you may resist it, you may say that it is all modern nonsense, that what is said in the Upanishads, in the Gita, is contrary to what I am saying. But if you really examine closely and are not afraid and do not resist, you will see that there is only thinking which creates the thinker, not the thinker first and thinking afterwards.

You do not think you are nobody. Because your thoughts are conditioned, because you think as a Hindu, you consider yourself to be a separate mind, a separate state in which there is the thinker. As long as there is an experiencer experiencing, there can be no true meditation. But the discovery that the experiencer is the experience is meditation.

Can one discover for oneself—not according to what Shankara or Buddha has said—can one see the truth that the experiencer and the experience are one, that the thought and the thinker are integral? I can only discover it by the process of meditation—which is, to understand what is actually taking place, to observe the ways of my mind. That is not a trick, a thing to be learned, that the experiencer and the experience are one. You cannot glibly repeat it, it means nothing. But the moment I see through meditation the truth of that, then meditation begins; then meditation is no posture for an hour, but it is a state which continues throughout the day because the mind is in a state of awareness, not as the experiencer experiencing—therefore judging, weighing, clearing, evaluating—because, after all, every experience makes the experiencer, every thought makes the thinker, puts the thinker together.

Look what happens when you have an experience of any kind: your mind immediately registers it, remembers. The remembering of it is the creation of the experiencer because then the experiencer says I must have more of it or less of it. Watch your own minds and see how any experience creates the thinker, the rememberer, and then the thinker, the experiencer, says, "There must be more," and so it perpetuates itself. It is the process of time. The mind is everlastingly seeking an experience—a richer, wider, nobler, deeper, purer experience—and so it receives, and the very reception is the creation of the chains that bind humanity. Memory is the 'me', which is the experiencer. So when I as the experiencer, seek God, when I seek truth, which I shall know, from which I shall receive help, my mind moves from the known to the known, from time to time, and this process is what you call meditation. But it is an ugly practice, it is not meditation at all, it is merely the perpetuation of the self in a different way. There is no meditation in the deeper sense of the word, when there is an experiencer and the experience.

There must be the cessation of the experiencer and the experience, the things which the experiencer recollects, recognizes—which means there must be a state in which there is no recognition, which means dying to every experience as it comes and not creating the experiencer. If you really listen and see the truth or falseness of it, you will know what meditation is—not how one is to meditate, but to see the full significance of what meditation is.

After all, virtue is order. What you are, so you must be. Real virtue is a clean thing, but it is not an end in itself. What you put in the room is more important, not how clean your room is. So the cultivation of the mind or the building up of virtue is not important; that is not the emptying of the mind necessary to receive that which is eternal. The mind must be empty to receive that.

That which is measureless can only come into being, you cannot invite it, it will only come into being when the mind no longer demands, is no longer praying, asking, begging, when the mind is free, free from thought. The ending of thought is the way of meditation. There must be freedom from the known for the unknown to be. This is meditation, and this cannot come through any trick, through any practice. Practice, discipline, suppression, denial, sacrifice only strengthen the experiencer, they give him power to control himself, but that power destroys. So it is only when the mind has neither the experiencer nor the experience that there is that bliss which is, which cannot be sought, which comes into being when the mind is silent and free.

February 21, 1954

Sixth Talk in Bombay

I think if we can understand the problem of frustration, we shall have a mentality that is not merely intellectual but an integrated activity. Our religions, our social activities are based on frustration and sorrow. If we can go into this question of frustration, which is really the problem of duality, we may be able, for ourselves as individuals, to come onto this creativity, which is not a mere capacity or gift but a totally different action. If we can go into this question of what is duality and the conflict between *what is* and *what should be*, then perhaps we shall understand the mind that is without root, because most of our minds have roots.

The very existence of mind indicates, does it not, thought having root in the past. It is that root which creates duality. Is it possible not to give continuity to that root in the present or in the future? It is only a mind that is without root, that can be truly religious and therefore capable of radical transformation, for reality to come into being. I would like to go into that, which may be rather a difficult question, but if we can deal with it simply, not philosophically, then perhaps we may be able to see and understand it for ourselves. But the difficulty is going to be that most of us have read so much about this problem of duality; we know the problem according to some philosophy, according to some teacher, but we do not know it directly, without it being pointed out. If we can discuss the problem of duality, not intellectually or philosophically, but observe the activities of our own minds as I talk, then perhaps we will see the problem in a different manner. If you can listen not to my description but to the activities of your own minds as I begin to describe, as I begin to verbalize, then it will be a direct experience, which is far more vital and significant than merely discovering a dual process in all of us, which some philosopher or some religious teacher or some book has indicated. But the difficulty is going to be that those of you who listen have already come to a conclusion, or you have heard what I have said previously, and so your mind is full of the ashes of memory of what I have said; therefore, it will not be a fresh experience, something real, living. Those of you who are here for the first time will only be puzzled because I may be using words that have a different significance than yours. But knowing all the difficulties of the ashes of memory, of previous knowledge and experience, of coming here for the first time and listening to something so very philosophical and difficult and therefore brushing it aside, you have to listen with a freshness of mind. That freshness of mind cannot come into being if you do not observe your own process of thought as I begin to talk about this problem of frustration and duality.

I am not telling you anything, I am only stating facts. You and I can understand the fact, can look at it without any condemnation, without any judgment, can merely observe it and be aware of it entirely—not as the observer watching, but to see what is actually happening, to actually experience the process, how the mind creates duality and therefore brings into being frustration upon which our whole culture, religions, social activities are based. If we can understand this, then we shall find out what true freedom is.

The difficulty is that most of you treat these talks as lectures, as something to be listened to, something to be remembered, something in which you will have many experiences, thrills, emotional excitations. But that is not at all what is intended, at least from my part. What is important is to have this religious revolution, a radical, fundamental religious transformation, because all other changes have no meaning, all other revolutions merely end in further misery. If we can see the truth of that, the importance of a radical, religious revolution, and that it alone can bring about a radical change in our relationships towards all men, then these talks will be not merely an intellectual or an emotional excitement or amusement but something that will have significance in our daily life. So, we have to listen as though we are hearing it for the first time, we have to listen with a freshness, and that freshness cannot come into being if you do not watch your own minds as I begin to talk, as I go into the problem.

The problem is, is it not, one of struggle, conflict, the constant struggle of what I am and what I should be, the conflict between *what is* and *what might be*. The mind is everlastingly striving, struggling, accommodating, adjusting, disciplining, controlling according to *what should be*. That is all we know. This "should be" is more important to us than *what is*. We have these ideological patterns, and the mind is constantly adjusting itself to those patterns. The adjustment is the action of will through compulsion, through persuasion, and this brings about struggle, and the struggle produces frustration. This is not oversimplification. This is what actually happens with each one of us, "I am this, and in the future, I should be that." But the future, *what should be,* the ideal, is the projection of *what is,* it is a contradiction of *what is*. The mind sees, "I hate," and it says, "I should love," so the mind is everlastingly adjusting, forcing, disciplining itself into a state which it calls love. I never know love, but my mind pursues what it thinks is love—which is an idea, the opposite of what I am. The projection of an idea of what love is, is not love because it is a reaction of what I am, which is "I hate." In my struggle to capture that love, I am violent, and I have the idea of nonviolence, so I practice, I discipline, I control, I shape my life according to that background, according to that particular pattern, and that pattern I never fulfill. I can never be that because when I do reach it, the mind has already invented another pattern. So I keep on changing from one pattern to another. So my life is a series of frustration, sorrow, always striving for one thing after another. So my whole life is a series of struggles and unhappiness, and that is all I know.

What is important is not *what should be,* but *what is*. *What is,* what I know, is the fact. The other is not. If the mind can pursue totally *what is,* without creating the opposite, then I will find out what is love—not the love as the opposite of hate. But the problem involved in understanding what is hate requires awareness in which there is no condemnation. Because, the moment I condemn, I hate, I have already created the opposite. I hope I am making it very clear and simple. If we can see this thing, it is really an extraordinary release from all the frustrations that we have developed.

We are an unhappy people; our religion is unhappy, it is the product of unhappiness, of strife, of frustration; our gods and the very culture that we have is the result of this frustration. So, we have to understand not merely verbally, intellectually, but very deeply, the fact of what I am, the fact of *what is*. The fact is "I hate, I am violent"; that is all. But the mind does not want to accept that fact; therefore, it creates the opposite—that is, it condemns the fact and so creates the opposite. The very condemnation is the process of creating duality. Now, if I can be aware that my mind condemns, that through condemnation I create the opposite and therefore bring into being struggle, that very realization of the fact that condemnation creates the opposite in which there is conflict, that very awareness stops the whole process of condemnation—not through any compulsion but merely through the awareness of the fact. So I have only the fact that I hate, without any mental projection of the opposite.

You understand, sirs, what an extraordinary release it is when you have no opposite? Then you can deal with the fact. Then the thing that I have called hate, if I do not condemn it, is not hate. But I condemn hate and wish to transform it into love because my mind has its root in the past. The valuation is the judgment of the past, and with that background I approach hate and wish to transform that hate into what I call love; this brings about conflict, struggle, with all its disciplines, controls, and so-called meditations.

Now, can there be freedom from the past? Can there be freedom from thought projecting itself into the future? I hate; that hate is the result of the past, a reaction; then thought condemns it and projects it into the future as "I must love," so thought establishes a root in the present and in the future; thus thought is continuous, and in that continuity there is the struggle to continue in the form of the opposite. What I am trying to find out is whether the mind can ever be free totally and not have root. The moment mind has root, it must project, it must stretch out; the stretching out is the opposite, so thought is continuous, it never comes to an end; it is the continuity of my conditioning, of my background, to the future, and therefore there is never freedom. I am trying to find out if the mind can ever be in a state in which it is not establishing roots through experiences. Without being in that state, the mind is never free, it is always in conflict. Therefore, to a mind that has root, there is always frustration, and whatever be its activity—social, cultural, religious—still it is the outcome of frustration; therefore, it is not the real religious transformation in which there is the cessation of all projection of thought taking root in the mind.

Can the mind ever be without root? You do not know. All that you can do is to find out, to see if the mind can be without rootlike the sea, living, having its being without root, without establishing itself in a particular place, in a particular experience, in a particular thought. Sir, it is only the mind that is without root that can know what is real. Because, the moment the mind experiences and establishes that experience in memory, that memory becomes the root, the past; then that memory demands more and more experiences; therefore, there is constant frustration of the present. Frustration implies, does it not, the condemnation of the state of the mind as it is. The mind as it is, is full of tradition, time, memories, anger, jealousy. Can we understand that mind without condemnation—that is, without the creation of the opposite? The moment we condemn *what is,* we do not understand it. The very understanding of *what is* can only happen without condemnation; then only, there is freedom from *what is.*

To me, a mind which has no struggle of duality is the really religious mind—not the mind which is struggling to conquer anger, not the mind that is struggling to become nonviolent; such a mind is only living in the struggle of the opposite. It is only the truly religious mind that has not the conflict of the opposite; such a mind never knows frustration; such a mind does not struggle to become something—it is what it is. In understanding what it actually is, the mind is no longer putting roots in memory.

Please just listen to this; it does not matter whether it is false or true, but find out for yourself. A mind that has continuity in memory will always be frustrated, will always be struggling to be something. The 'becoming' is the taking root—in an idea, in a person, in an object. Once the mind has taken root, then the problem arises: How is it to free itself? The freeing of itself becomes then the opposite, and the struggle then is: How to free oneself? But if one sees, understands, is aware of the truth of how the mind is always taking root in every experience, in every reaction, then, in that awareness, there is no choice, there is no condemnation, therefore no creation of the opposite, and therefore there is no struggle. Then the mind has no root, but it is living; it has no continuity but is in a state of being in which time is not. I think, it is important to understand this, not merely verbally or intellectually, but actually to see how the mind is creating the struggle and the dual process.

The action of the mind that is without root is creative because that mind is no longer in a state of frustration, from which it paints, it writes, or seeks reality. Such a mind does not seek—seeking implies duality, seeking implies struggle, the stretching out of the past into the future, in thought, which establishes itself in the root of the future. If the mind can see that, be aware of it, then there is an astonishing release from all struggle, and therefore there is a happiness and bliss, and that happiness and that bliss are not the opposite of sorrow, misery, or frustration. These are not just words, they are direct states which the mind takes hold of and establishes itself in the experience. They are actually states which cannot be experienced by a mind that is struggling to become the opposite.

All this requires, does it not, awareness of the process of the mind. What I mean by awareness is the total process of existence—sorrow, pain, love, hate, feeling, the emotions, all of which is the mind. Is it not therefore important to see how your mind works, how it operates, how it projects, how it clings to the past, to tradition, to the innumerable experiences, and so prevents the experience of reality? To be aware of all that is not what the modern or the ancient teachers or the psychologists or the gurus say; what other people have said is merely information and has really no significance at all, but one has to discover for oneself this whole process of the mind. This discovery is not possible by the withdrawal to a dark corner of a mountain, but by living from day to day. You have also to see that what you had discovered may have already become the root from which you act—that is, you have to discover how the mind uses the very discovery as an experience from which it thinks, and therefore that experience becomes the hindrance and leads to frustration. To see all this is awareness. That awareness can only happen when there is no condemnation—which means, really, the breaking down of all conditioning of the mind so that the mind is in a state in which it is no longer establishing roots, and therefore it is a mind without anchor, and therefore there is real experience. It is only such a mind that can know and see that which is eternal.

Sirs, in answering these questions, watch your own minds creating duality—how the mind is expecting an answer. It poses a question out of its own frustration, out of its own sorrow, out of its own troubles and confusion. It puts a question and makes it a problem, and it waits for an answer. On receiving an answer, it says, "How am I to get there?" The "how" is the struggle—the struggle between the problem and the answer, between *what is* and *what should be*. The method is "how," the method is the struggle, and therefore, the method in its very nature produces frustration.

So it is the most stupid mind which says, "How am I to do this?" "How am I to get there?" "I am this, but I would like to be that, and so how?"

What is important is *what is* and not *what should be*. The understanding of *what is* demands cessation of condemnation, that is all. Don't say, "How am I not to condemn?" Then you will be back again in the same old process. But see the truth of the statement that condemnation produces struggle and therefore duality and therefore the struggle towards the opposite. Just see that, just realize that fact; then there is the revealing of *what is* which is the problem.

Questioner: I know loneliness, but you speak of a state of aloneness. Are they identical states?

KRISHNAMURTI: We know loneliness, don't we, the fear, the misery, the antagonism, the real fright of a mind that is aware of its own loneliness. We all know that. Don't we? That state of loneliness is not foreign to any one of us. You may have all the riches, all the pleasures, you may have great capacity and bliss, but within, there is always the lurking shadow of loneliness. The rich man, the poor man who is struggling, the man who is writing, creating, the worshiper—they all know this loneliness. When it is in that state, what does the mind do? The mind turns on the radio, picks up a book, runs away from *what is* into something which is not. Sirs, do follow what I am saying—not the words, but the application, the observation of your own loneliness.

When the mind is aware of its loneliness, it runs away, escapes. The escape, whether into religious contemplation or going to a cinema, is exactly the same; it is still an escape from *what is*. The man who escapes through drinking is no more immoral than the one who escapes by the worship of God; they are both the same, both are escaping. When you observe the fact that you are lonely, if there is no escape and therefore no struggle into the opposite, then generally, the mind tends to condemn it according to the frame of its knowledge, but if there is no condemnation, then the whole attitude of the mind towards the thing it has called lonely has undergone a complete change, has it not?

After all, loneliness is a state of self-isolation because the mind encloses itself and cuts itself away from every relationship, from everything. In that state, the mind knows loneliness, and if, without condemning it, the mind be aware and not create the escape, then surely that loneliness undergoes a transformation. The transformation might then be called "aloneness"—it does not matter what word you use. In that aloneness there is no fear. The mind that feels lonely because it has isolated itself through various activities is afraid of that loneliness. But if there is awareness in which there is no choice—which means no condemnation—then the mind is no longer lonely, but it is in a state of aloneness in which there is no corruption, in which there is no process of self-enclosure. One must be alone, there must be that aloneness, in that sense. Loneliness is a state of frustration, aloneness is not, and aloneness is not the opposite of loneliness.

Surely, sirs, we must be alone, alone from all influences, from all compulsions, from all demands, longings, hopes, so that the mind is no longer in the action of frustration. That aloneness is essential, it is a religious thing. But the mind cannot come to it without understanding the whole problem of loneliness. Most of us are lonely, all our activities are the activities of frustration. The happy man is not a lonely man. Happiness is alone, and the action of aloneness is entirely different from the activities of loneliness.

All this requires, does it not, awareness, a total awareness of one's whole being, conscious as well as the unconscious. As most of us only live on the superficial consciousness, on the surface level of our mind, the deep underground forces, loneliness, desperations, and hopes are always frustrating the superficial activity. So it is important to understand the total being of the mind, and that understanding is denied when there is awareness in which there is choice, condemnation.

Questioner: Surely, sir, in spite of all that you have said about following, you are aware that you are being continually followed. What is your action about it, as it is an evil, according to you?

KRISHNAMURTI: Sir, we know that we follow—we follow the political leader, the guru, or we follow a pattern, or an experience. Our whole culture, our education, is based on imitation, authority, following. I say all following is evil, including the following of me. Following is evil, destructive, and yet the mind follows, does it not? It follows the Buddha or Christ or some idea or a perfect utopia because the mind itself is in a state of uncertainty, but it wants certitude. Following is the demand for certitude. The mind, demanding certitude, is creating authority—political, religious, or the authority of oneself—and it copies; therefore, everlastingly it struggles. The follower never knows the freedom of not following. You can only be free when there is uncertainty, not when the mind is pursuing certainty.

A mind that is following is imitating, is creating authority, and therefore has fear. That is really the problem. We all know that we do follow, we accept some theories, some ideas, a utopia, or something else because deep down in the conscious, as well as in the unconscious, there is fear. A mind that has no fear does not create the opposite, it has no problem of following, it has no guru, it has no pattern, it is living.

The mind is in a state of fear—fear of death, fear of something—and to be free it does various activities which lead to frustration; then the problem arises: Can the mind be free from fear, not how to be free? "How to be free from fear" is a schoolboy question. From that question, all problems arise—struggle, the achieving of an end, and therefore the conflict of the opposites. Can the mind be free from fear?

What is fear? Fear only exists in relation to something. Fear is not an abstract thing by itself, it is in relation to something. I am afraid of public opinion, I am afraid of my boss, my wife, my husband; I am afraid of death; afraid of my loneliness; I am afraid that I shall not reach, I shall not know happiness in this life, I shall not know God, truth, and so on. So fear is always in relation to something.

What is that fear? I think that if we can understand the question of desire, the problem of desire, then we will understand and be free from fear. "I want to be something"—that is the root of all fear. When I want to be something, my wanting to be something and my not being that something create fear, not only in a narrow sense but in the widest sense. So, as long as there is the desire to be something, there must be fear.

The freedom from desire is not the mental projection of a state which my desire says I must be in. You have simply to see the fact of desire, just be aware of it—as you see your image in a mirror in which there is no distortion, in which you see your face as it is and not as you wish it to be. The reflection of your face in the mirror is very exact; if you can be aware of desire in that sense, without any condemnation, if you merely look at it, seeing all its facets, all its activities, then you will find that desire has quite a different significance.

The desire of the mind is entirely different from the desire in which there is no choice. What we are fighting is the desire of the mind—the desire to become something. That is why we follow, that is why we have gurus. All the sacred books lead you to confusion because you interpret them according to your desire, and therefore you see only the reflection of your own fears and anxieties; you never see the truth. So it is only the mind that is really in a state in which there is no desire that does not follow, that has no guru. Such a mind is totally empty of all movement; only then, the bliss of the real comes into being.

February 24, 1954

Seventh Talk in Bombay

I would like to discuss this evening rather a difficult problem, and I hope you will listen with consideration, not for the result, not at the end but from the beginning.

I feel that neither the reformer nor the radicalist has the real solution to the problem. Their actions are born out of confusion. Now, most of us are concerned with action; we must do something, we must change the social order radically. Our whole outlook, our whole valuation, is based, is it not, on the result. The reformer and the radicalist both promise us results. Both are sure of their results; they say they are not confused beings, and they are clear in their pattern of action and will.

Now, I would like to discuss a step which is not action at all. The action we know is born out of choice, out of determination. As we know, as we observe in the world, action is of various forms—acceptance of authority, liquidation, redistribution, decentralization, and so on. But I feel that there is an action which is not action at all nor is it reaction. We know the action of choice, of determination, of result, of a utopia, but such action is not true action because it leads to conflict, to struggle between man and man. So we have to find out a state from which action springs and which is not the reaction or the result of the action of a reformer or of a radicalist. It seems to me very important to find out whether we are confused or not, because the action which comes out of a confused state is not true action.

We all know that we are confused. If we were not confused, then our action would have been true action. But we are not certain. No human being, neither the capitalist nor the communist nor the socialist, is quite clear. But they all want to be clear and the very desire to be clear creates the action of uncertainty because basically they are all confused.

I think that it is an important thing to admit to oneself that one is confused. But one does not admit it. The reformist and the radicalist assert that they know and that they are clear, and therefore their action which is born out of confusion inevitably breeds destruction and uncertainty.

Now, most of us know that we are confused, not at one layer of consciousness, but right from the conscious to the unconscious layers, but we dare not admit it. If we really try to understand the question of action and if we go into it, not verbally, not intellectually, we would have to admit that we are confused, and it is the seeing of this confusion that itself produces an action which is not of the mind. We start all our actions on the assumption that we know. But we only *say* that we know. Beyond that, do we know anything? The reformist and the radicalist say that they know, and they drive others into the pattern of their action, which has really come out of confusion. Any action of a confused mind is bound to be a confused action.

I am confused and in that confused state of mind I persuade myself to accept a particular way; but basically, I am confused, and out of that confusion I try to create certainty which is essentially a confused certainty. But I give it a name and a pattern, and some people follow me. But the fact is that they and I are all confused. You and I are confused. Our political, social, and religious leaders, all are confused. If we can admit that, not merely intellectually or verbally, but actually, we will see that the result of all this action is bound to be confused.

Each one of us must see that we are confused basically. But it is very difficult for us to admit that we are confused. Now, if we are confused, can we say that we must act? If I am confused and if I see that I am confused, what would happen is that my confusion would bring about its own action which is uncertainty. I think it is very important to understand this because then action will take care of itself. For the moment, I am not concerned with action. I think that relationship must be established between you and me. I do not believe in the action of a reformist or of a radicalist; all that I am concerned with is confusion. Therefore there is humility, and there is no assertion.

Now, let us see what happens to a mind that knows that it is confused. It has no leader because to choose a leader out of confusion is an action of confusion. Obviously, to have a theory, to have a plan, to have a pattern of action born out of confusion is still confusion. Please don't say, "What are we to do then?" If you admit that you are confused, it means you know nothing. So it would be futile for you to follow any authority, any book, any leader, or any pattern of action with regard to what is good, what is bad, what is right, or what is wrong.

A man who is confused does not know what is right and what is wrong. He has no leader. He knows no authority, no book on which he can rely because his mind is fundamentally confused. He is not in a state in which he can read a book or follow an authority. I am not mesmerizing you to admit that you are confused. But you have to think for yourselves and see whether you are confused or not, and if so, whether your decision as regards what is right and wrong has any meaning.

Now, if the whole world is in a state of confusion, you are also confused because you are a part of that world. So if you are really aware that you are confused, then what action would be yours? Your action would be neither the action of a reformer nor that of a radicalist. So what do you do? When there is no choice, when there is no leader, no guide, no following of any authority—because you are aware that the very choosing out of confusion is still confusion—what do you do? What happens to your mind? A man who is confused and knows that he is confused does not know what to do because he is uncertain. But our social, political, and religious leaders think that if they tell us that they are confused, we might abandon them, and therefore nobody is prepared to admit that he is confused. But once we admit that we are confused, our whole pattern would be destroyed. The very confusion of our mind brings an action which is not a reaction of the mind but which is an action of uncertainty; therefore, there is no utopia, no leader, no teacher.

In a state of entire confusion you are trying to find out what is true. There are many others who are like you, who are in a state of confusion, and all of you come together. But all of you are in a state of confusion, in a state of uncertainty, and therefore there is little cooperation between you.

Now, the man who says that he knows is really not admitting that he is confused. But the man who admits that he is confused, and therefore is incapable of knowing anything, is a sincere man. When I say I do not know, in the deepest sense of the word, I admit that I am confused, and therefore there is a state of humility. I do not become humble, but there is a state of humility which itself is an action, and that action is real action. Because I see

I am confused, leaders have no significance at all; I will not follow anybody and my mind will be quiet. My mind will no longer be certain; it will be in a state of humility. That which is really humble is in a state of love. This love is not something which can be cultivated. Without this love, life has no meaning.

Now, most of us are concerned with problems and their solution. But we should always be concerned with the understanding and the resolution of the problem so as not to create more problems. Our solution of a problem only serves as a root to the problem in the future. You may find a solution of the problem which you have today, but that solution is such that it carries the problem over to tomorrow and gives rise to other problems tomorrow—that is, it is not a real solution at all.

Now you have got several problems. You have the problem of death, you have the problem of frustration. If you carry over the problem of frustration into tomorrow, you add strength to it. Please, do understand the significance of all this and the need not to give root to any of our problems in the future.

How can I, how can the mind, not give root to the problem in the tomorrow? Do you understand what I am saying? If you can really grasp this, you will see that there is no problem at all. Today, you have a problem because you have made it a problem for the last few days, and therefore your mind is never fresh; it is always living in the past which is really dead. But if we really understand and not give a root to our problems in the tomorrow, there would be no problem at all.

Questioner: I am addicted to drink. You say that discipline and self-control will not save me. Can you then tell me how I can be free from the vice of drinking?

Krishnamurti: Sir, there are many reasons why one drinks. There is frustration, the constant struggle in life, the struggle between husband and wife, family worries; and you want to escape from all this and therefore you drink. Now, the question is, how can you stop drinking? Will mere analysis—the analysis of frustration, the analysis of your worries—free you from the habit of drinking? When you know why you have a frustration, when you are aware of it, then that awareness itself, without choice, will act, and the habit will cease.

Please see the importance of what I am saying. You know the effects of drinking. Suppose you decide that, because you have seen the implications of drinking, you will drop the habit from tomorrow, then you will be creating a problem for tomorrow. Sometimes it also happens that to drop something you adopt a method, but that very method becomes your habit. So the mind is not really free from habit. Instead of one habit, it cultivates another habit. Even the routine of performing puja or reading sacred books is a habit. It may be said that it is a good or respectable habit, and some other habit might be said to be an evil habit. But, psychologically, both are habits. If you want to get rid of these habits, you have to go to the root of them. If you really understand that there is no method, no system by which you can drop the habit, then you will see the truth, and that truth will act upon you, you will not have to act upon the truth.

Most of us want to act upon the truth, but if we let truth alone to act upon us, then truth will bring about its own action.

Questioner: I am a Hindu, and you ask me to be free from Hinduism. Can I ever be free from Hinduism?

KRISHNAMURTI: This is a very complex question. We must go into it very carefully to understand it.

Now, you call yourself a Hindu. You have a certain background, there are certain traditions which you follow. You call yourself a Hindu, and therefore you want to follow the traditions of Hinduism. Now, if you want to find out the true implications of following, if you want to find out whether following is evil or not, you have to see whether it is really necessary to follow your experience, your traditions, and your culture. But in order to see this, you must be absolutely free.

Now, when you say that you are a Hindu, what do you mean by that? Can you say that you are a pure Hindu or a pure Aryan? There is no such person because we are a mixture of others' culture also. Most of us have the background of Hinduism with some Western conditioning. So we are neither this nor that. But the mind wants to have a root in something. The mind wants to be secure in something, and when it feels that it will be secure in Western culture, it gives up the Eastern culture, and vice versa. That is exactly what is happening in the case of all of us; really speaking, we are in a state of confusion. It is only when we are totally free from any culture that we shall be able to see clearly. But if we accept one culture, either the Western or the Eastern, then it acts as a poison.

If we want to see clearly and to find out the real truth, then there must be complete clearness of the mind, and that can only come when you do not belong to any society. The truth will act upon you only when your mind is absolutely free, and that freedom can only come when you do not belong to any community. That means, when the mind is fearless, when it has no background, no root anywhere, then only can you see what is the truth.

Questioner: Physically time has no dimension. But you speak of psychological time as different from chronological time. Can you tell me whether time is nonexistent or it has existence which is phenomenal?

KRISHNAMURTI: This is not a philosophical question, philosophical in the sense of theoretical or verbal. The question implies that time has a phenomenal existence. There is a tomorrow, and there was also a yesterday. So time is chronological. That is a fact. But there is a difference between psychological time and chronological time. There is a time which the mind establishes—the time as distance between me and what I shall be, me and the idea, me and death, me and the future, me as mortal and me who would become immortal. There is a wide gap between what I am and what I shall be. We cannot deny phenomenal time. But the time which the mind creates—has it reality? There is *what is.* I think I should be something else than what I am. There is the distance between what I am and what I shall be according to my desire—to become immortal and so on. In all that there are two things—*what is* and *what should be*. The moment I introduce the factor of desiring to change, I introduce time.

Suppose I am stupid. My being stupid is a fact. But the moment I say I must become clever, I condemn my stupidity and introduce the factor of time. But if I do not condemn the fact that I am stupid, then there is no sense of time. But the moment I decide to become clever, I introduce time. Now my mind is the result of time, and through the mind I am going to achieve what I want to achieve. So my mind is equivalent to time. But there is only one thing which is a fact, and that is what I am today.

Now let us put it the other way. The mind is the result of the thought of yesterday, of today, and what it will be tomorrow. Mind is the result of the thoughts, of the traditions, of the ideas, of centuries of man. The mind is the 'I'. The future is the unknown, and the mind which is the result of the known is trying to get the unknown. Mind can never be free from the past. But if you look into it very closely, if you can really go into it precisely, then the past is burned away. Then you will see the truth.

February 28, 1954

Eighth Talk in Bombay

This is the last talk of this series and there will be no more discussions.

Living has so many accidents, and the mind gets so many scars. As we grow older, the accumulation of accidents, experiences, the constant battle with life, leaves many scars on the mind. We only know suffering with very little joy, and problems increase; that seems to be the lot of most of us, whatever our capacities are—intellectual, scientific, or otherwise. We seem to burden our minds with all kinds of activity, our hearts wither away with the sense of frustration, fear, and the everlasting shadow of loneliness. Very few of us are happy, and we never know the feeling of being creative . Having been grooved, it is very difficult to heal the mind again so that it is once again fresh and unspotted. And in the search of this happiness, this feeling, we pursue so many things, we have so many desires, unfulfilled and fulfilled. And our society, our culture, our parents, our neighbors, husbands, wives are all the time impinging on the mind, shaping the mind, conditioning the mind so that we hardly are individuals, though we have a particular name, a special face. If we are lucky, we have a house and a little bank account and also a few capacities—that is what we call individuality. But beyond the name and the few little qualities and the little puddles which we call our minds, we are not individuals at all; we are conditioned entities with very little freedom.

We think we are free when we choose, but we are not, are we? Where there is choice, there is no freedom because that very choice springs from our conditioned state. We think we have a will of our own, and we exercise that will through choice. But, if you observe, you will see that will is the outcome of innumerable desires, of many forms of frustration, fears, and these frustrations, fears, desires are the outcome of our conditioning, of our background, so when we choose, we are never free. Choice in itself indicates the lack of freedom. A man who is really free has no choice; he is free not to do this or that but to be. As long as we have choice, we are really not free and we are not really individuals.

It is very important to understand this because most of us live with choice—choosing a virtue, a person, an action—and choice invariably leads to misery; there is no good choice and bad choice. Only the mind that is free from choice is capable of perceiving what is true. Truth does not come through choice. Truth does not come with analysis, with the capacity to choose between this and that, right and wrong; on the contrary, all choice is the outcome of our conditioning which is based on fear and acquisitiveness. We, you and I, call ourselves individuals, but we are really not individuals at all. It is only when we are free from the background, from our conditioning, that there is real individuality, and that requires a great deal of thought, inquiry.

Let us now talk about creativeness, which I think is essential in this world that is so confused, where the mind is ridden with so many systems, so many methods, where all the time the mind is seeking certitude through methods, through action, and therefore it is never free to be creative, to understand what that creative reality is. Unfortunately, most of us do not directly experience something true because we have read so much, listened to so many talks, accumulated so much knowledge, and having read, we compare. If we can listen not only to what I am saying but to everything in life, with a deep inward listening, then we will see that freedom comes in spite of all the accidents to the mind, in spite of all our frustrations, in spite of our stupid activity that leads us nowhere.

Is it possible for the mind that is gathering so much knowledge—that has had so many experiences of centuries, and wherein every accident leaves a residue which is called memory—to be free of all that so that it is rejuvenated, it is fresh? I think the real problem with all of us is to be reborn anew and not to give room to memory, to tomorrow.

I think it is very important to understand this because most of our lives are a series of continuities, broken off and begun again. Our daily life of routine, of earning a livelihood, of doing social activities, of going to political, religious, social meetings, is all the same, continuity in the same direction. There is never a breaking off because the mind is always afraid to live anew, not knowing a thing, because mind surely is always seeking the certitude of being something.

Our problem is we want to be something; every one of us, the saint as well as the sinner wants to be something, and so we cultivate memory, and so there is no ending, and so there is never real discovery—there are only accidents and the choice of accidents. That is our life. Through all this confusion, through this demand for action, there is always fear.

Can we free ourselves from the past and be reborn again with a freshness of mind? Can we live happily, not doing work with intellectual demand, but living fully each day, each minute, with the worship of that minute? If that can be done, life is very simple because a happy man has no problem. It is the unhappy man, the frustrated man, that seeks action to overcome his frustration.

Is it possible for each one of us to wipe away the past, to put an end to it, not through a gradual process, but to cut it off? We have to put this question to ourselves and leave it at that. If you say, "How am I to do it?" then you have already destroyed it because the "how" perpetuates the memory of yesterday.

I think it is really important to completely live each day so fully, so creatively, so richly that you have no tomorrow. After all, that is life, is it not? Love knows no tomorrow. Love is not of the mind. As we have only cultivated the mind, we do not know how to love, and the continuity which we give to memory precludes every form of love, and that is one of our difficulties.

We only know unhappiness, sorrow, and frustration, and from that there is action, which creates further misery, further suffering, so surely there must be freedom from the known for the unknown to be. The known is the mind and the ways of the mind. Mind can only reason, and reason is the outcome of memory, of the known. Reason cannot lead to the unknown, do what you will, whether you practice forgiveness, sacrifices, rituals, meditation. As long as the mind has its roots in the known, the unknown can never be.

So, our problem is really to free the mind from the known. The mind cannot free itself from the known because the mind itself is the known, it is the result of time. So what is the problem? You understand the question? My mind is the result of the known; my mind can only function in the known, and my problem is, how can the mind which is the result of time cease? How can thought come to an end?

Thinking is the result or the reaction of the known, of yesterday, of all the accumulations, of the wounds, of the accidents, of frustrations, fears. How can such thinking come to an end? The mind cannot bring it to an end. Mind cannot say, "I will put an end to thinking"; then thinking is separate from the entity which says, "I will put an end to it." The entity that desires an ending is the product of thought.

Please listen to the extraordinary mystery of something which the mind cannot fathom. There is the astonishing mystery of the unknown, and without letting that operate, our life has no meaning. You may be very clever, you may have the most astonishing mind, but without realization, without that unknown coming into being, life has no meaning. All that we can know is suffering and the dangers of frustrations. So, if we can see that the mind can never find the unknown; that without the unknown, life has no significance at all—life is a travail, life is sorrow, life is pain—and that the mind cannot do anything because any movement of the mind is the outcome of the known, is the movement of the known—if the mind realizes that—then the mind becomes quiet.

The realization that any movement of the mind is the outcome of the known is meditation. There must be meditation in life—not the orthodox, stupid meditation; that is no meditation at all, that is merely self-hypnosis—to be aware of this whole process of living, of choice, how choice does not bring freedom, how choice denies freedom because choice is the outcome of the background. The freeing of the mind from the background, the freeing of the mind from all conditioning is real freeing. The mind freeing itself from the desire to be something—that process is meditation. In that, there is the freeing of the mind from the known; then the mind becomes quiet. Now this quietness, this stillness of the mind, is not a thing which can be experienced or known without unconditioning the mind. It is not a thing to be sought after; if you do, that is merely another form of self-hypnotism, an illusion; it has no reality.

If the mind can free itself from its conditioning, from its desires, from all the disciplines, patterns, accidents, then there is freeing of the mind from the past. Out of that freedom, there comes silence, a quietness of the mind. That stillness cannot be made, but it happens when the mind is free. It is the stillness of great movement in which there is no meaning; in that stillness, there is no search for anything because it is not the outcome of any frustration, of any hope, of any desire. That which is in great movement, great speed, great action, is still. Then only, out of that stillness, does that mystery of creativity come into being, that truth which is not measurable by the mind, and without that, life can only mean more sorrow, more mischief, more frustration.

We are unhappy human beings, and we want to escape from that unhappiness into every kind of activity; we are lonely entities, and we want to fill that loneliness with knowledge, with action, with amusement, with scriptures, but that emptiness cannot be filled; it can only be resolved when the mind realizes that in itself it is lonely and does not try to cover it up or to run away. One must go through that loneliness in order to be still; then surely the creativity of truth comes into being.

This is not a matter of being continuously earnest. Anything that is continuous is merely a determined mind, a mind that says, "I will be." Therefore it perpetuates the memory of itself. But in moments of seriousness—which may last half an hour, that is enough—in that moment there is the awareness without choice, the awareness to see oneself as in a mirror without any distortion, the thing "as is." That very awareness of the fact brings about liberation, freedom. But when, in that mirror of awareness, you see yourself as you are, you condemn, you want to change the image, you want to reshape it, you want to give it a particular name, and therefore you give it a continuity. But, if you be simply aware of the image in that mirror of awareness, then you will see, in that awareness, there is an ending of everything that has been, and that awareness brings freedom, a quietness of the mind in which there is bliss.

What is important is not to give root to a problem. We have problems, they are there. Every accident is a problem, but not to give it a future, not to give it the minute in which it can take root, that is the problem—not that which we carry in our minds. The more the mind thinks of a problem, the more it gives soil in which the problem can take root. Do think, do watch, do listen to this, sirs.

The problem is not how to solve a problem but how not to give the problem that I have a continuity. It is the continuity that creates the problem, not the problem of yesterday. If I know, if I see the truth of that, then I will deal with the problem entirely differently; I will end the problem in myself as it arises, not giving it root—which is, not to enjoy, not to condemn, which means really to have that astonishing quality of humility.

A petty mind has always a problem; the little mind is always occupied, and this occupation goes on, day after day. The petty mind can never solve the problem because whatever it solves, however much it thinks about the problem, it is still petty, small, confused. All that the petty mind can do is not to give the problem a future. If the mind has a problem and does not give it a future, it is no longer petty because it is not occupied, it is the occupied mind that is small. It is like a river that receives everything, all the sewage of the town, passes the dead bodies through, the good and the bad; and because it is in constant movement, it is no longer a puddle, it is a living stream, everything is living in it, and it is not dead. So the mind that has a problem and is occupied can never understand its own problem; all that it can do is to put an end to its continuity and not to give the problem soil in the tomorrow of its memory.

All this may sound very difficult, but it is not, if you really observe how your mind likes to continue with a problem, day after day. Your mind is occupied with something—with what the neighbor says or what the book says or what the purpose of life is—everlastingly making its own grooves. An occupied mind is a small mind, and the small mind will always have problems.

Questioner: I feel that it is not enough for people to hear you. In order to understand what you are saying, people have to be nurtured and educated by a careful study and explanation of your teachings, and through books about your teachings, and by the organizations of study groups. Only then will people understand you better. Please tell me if I am right.

KRISHNAMURTI: In this question is involved, is it not, the mediator, the interpreter, the priest—"I understand, but the others do not understand." "I understand a little, and I must share that little"—which is entirely different. So let us inquire into this whole question.

Who creates the interpreter, the mediator? You. If you understand something directly, you don't need the interpreter, the mediator, the priest. But, if I do not understand, I look to somebody else to explain, and he will explain according to his conditioning, according to his aptitude. So, I create the interpreter, the mediator, the priest, the sub-teacher. I am lazy, I am not aware of myself—which is so simple; you don't have to read books about that, it is so clear. To be aware of yourself in all the things that you do, to watch yourself—not according to some pattern, that is not watching, but merely to watch yourself—talking at dinner, at table, in your office; just watching and seeing how you condemn, how you compare, how cruel you are—just to watch it all, to watch choicelessly—that does not need interpreters, mediators. Just to know what is happening to your mind, to know for yourself how your mind operates—not according to somebody else—that is not difficult; you don't need interpreters, mediators, for that. But you need interpreters, mediators, if you are frightened, if you don't know yourself and if therefore you look to somebody.

Sir, following is evil—all following is evil. There is no good following and bad following; whether you follow politically, religiously, or whether you follow your own experiences or ideals, all following is evil because it creates authority, it creates the follower. The mentality that says, "I do not know, but you know, so tell me, give me a safe seat in heaven" creates the mediators, interpreters, the priests, who are going to act and save us. The political leaders, priests, commissars, or the poor Catholic priests are all the same because the followers say, "We do not know."

Please listen though you may have heard this many times, listen as though for the first time. If you listen to this as though you were hearing this for the first time, it will have meaning, it will have depth. But if you say, "I have heard this hundreds and thousands of times because I have grown with you for the last twenty-five years, and I know what you are going to say," you are not experiencing directly the thing that is being said, and therefore your mere listening to the words has no meaning.

As long as the mind seeks certitude, you must have interpreters, and a mind that is seeking certitude is never free, it is always frightened; the very demand to be certain about something—an ideal, a relationship, a truth to be made certain—implies that you must have a mediator, somebody who is going to help you. But if what you have heard is truth to you—not according to somebody, but is really truth to you—then you will talk rightly, you will dance rightly, you will live, you will love, you will create; then you have not to create authority, then you have no following, then you don't belong to any society.

But the difficulty with most of us is that we are so uncertain and confused in ourselves that we want help, but the help we want is the help that a blind man can give to another blind man. But there is help which comes when I know that I am confused, uncertain, and remain in that state. To know I am uncertain, to know I am confused, to know that I do not know a thing-that very state is a state of humility, is it not, a profound sense of humility, which creates its own action. A man who is nothing—he does not intellectually say he is nothing, but knows it inwardly, he is aware that in the state of uncertainty he can be nothing—does not want an interpreter.

Please beware of interpreters, guard against interpreters. The interpreters can only give you certainty, they cannot give you freedom. Freedom comes only amidst the total awareness of the whole process of living.

Questioner: You say that one must die to be reborn, that in the ending there is beginning. But to us, all ending is suffering, whether it is ending of life or of a happy and rich experience. How then can I see the truth of the ending you talk about?

Krishnamurti: Sir, do you see the truth of what I am talking about? All that you see is the fact that that which has continuity, that which goes on through time, is always in sorrow. That is all you know, is it not, with an occasional rare moment of delight, a joy, but otherwise, all that you know is sorrow. Sorrow comes with all the innumerable aptitudes of the 'I' or the 'me', of the ego. You have to see, you have to realize that that which continues psychologically, inwardly, brings sorrow. Sir, don't you know that that which has an ending has always a freshness, a beginning? If I do not end my thoughts of today, complete them, finish them today, I carry those thoughts over to tomorrow, and in that, there is no freshness, no newness; the mind becomes dead. But if I simply see that fact, that is enough. The very perception, the very awareness of that fact without any choice, without any condemnation, is the ending in which there is a newness.

But we do not want the new, we do not want to be reborn. All that we want is to be made certain. After all, what we want is permanency, a continuity for us with the indications of the permanent—a permanent house, a permanent relationship, a permanent name, a permanent family, a continuity of activity, success—that is all we want. We do not want a revolution, we do not want to die each day to everything, we want to perpetuate memory; that is why we practice, we discipline, we resist, because the mind abhors a state of uncertainty. Sir, it is only the uncertain mind that can discover, not a certain mind. It is only the mind that knows that it is confused, and in that confusion, is quiet, that can discover. But the mind that is certain, that has continuity, that is a series of memories—everlasting—such a mind can never discover truth.

So it is only the mind that comes to an end each day, that can find truth each day. Truth is something to be discovered from moment to moment, truth has no continuity in terms of time. That which continues is in a state of permanency which the mind can recognize, so the mind which has continuity which has association which is the process of recognition, such a mind can never find what is real. It is only the mind that sees the fallacy of all this and therefore choicelessly comes to an end, that can be creative; only such a mind can receive the creativity of truth.

Questioner: What is the relationship between me and my mind?

KRISHNAMURTI: Now, sirs, let us go into this so that you and I directly experience what is being said. It is a process of meditation, and without meditation there is no wisdom. Wisdom comes into being through self-knowledge. When I know myself as I am—not according to what other teachers have said or what anybody else has said—when I know what I am from moment to moment, that is self-knowledge, and that self-knowledge can only come into being through meditation. Meditation is to be aware of all the conflicts in the mirror of my activities, of my relationships, of my states. So let us inquire into this question, the relationship between me and the mind.

Is the mind different from the 'me'? Am I different, is the observer, the thinker different from the thought? You understand, sirs?

I say, "I think." Is thinking different from the entity who says, "I am thinking"? We say that the two are separate, that the 'me' thinks it is different from the thought. We assume that the 'me' comes first; the ego, the self, is the thinker—that is the first, then the thought, the mind. So we have broken up the 'me' and the mind. But is that a fact? You may break it up, but in reality, is the 'me', the thinker, different from consciousness which says, which thinks, which exists? Can you remove the qualities of the diamond and say that what remains is the diamond? The 'me' has various qualities, various memories, various activities, hopes, fears, frustrations which are all of the mind, are they not? Remove all your qualities; then, is there 'you'? The mind is the 'me'. The mind thinks there is the higher self, the atma, paramatma, higher and higher; it is still what the mind projects; the mind has separated itself as the 'me' and the thought.

After all, what is the mind? The mind is surely the conscious as well as the unconscious. The sea is not just the surface of the water which you see in the sunshine, sparkling, living; it is the whole depth that makes the sea. Similarly, our mind is the whole content, whether we are conscious of it or not. The mind is so occupied, so taken up with activities, problems, that it never begins to question, to inquire, to find out, to fish in the unconscious. We know what is the unconscious; it is very simple. Our motives, our accumulated knowledge, the collection of experiences, fears, hopes, longings, frustrations—all that is our consciousness; the desire for God and the creation of gods—all that is consciousness. So to divide the 'me' and the mind has no reality.

Please see this, realize this. The whole of this consciousness is the 'me'—the me that has a job; the me that has a wife, a husband; the me that is ambitious, envious, acquisitive; the me that values; the me that has a tradition; the me that wants to find reality, God; the me that is petty, acquisitive—all that is the mind, all that is consciousness. That consciousness you may push far up and call it atma, paramatma, or whatever you like, but it is still a product of time, it is still consciousness. Now, with that consciousness, you want to find something which is beyond the mind itself, but you can never find that.

You may have occasional quietness when the whole consciousness right down to the bottom is still, and you may dream of something unimaginable, immeasurable, because in sleep your mind, your consciousness, may perchance occasionally be quiet. But when you are aware of all this process choicelessly, this pattern of consciousness is broken, and then you will see there is real stillness in the totality of your consciousness. That is something far beyond the measure of the mind. But to pursue what is beyond the measure of the mind has no meaning. What I say or what someone else says has no meaning. What has meaning is to be completely aware of this consciousness and of all its many layers. This awareness cannot be learned through any analysis; one knows the whole thing if one is observant.

To know the whole process of the mind—all its inclinations, motives, purposes, its talents, its demands, its fears, its frustrations, its success—to know all that is to be quiet and not let that act. Then only that something which is beyond the mind can come into being. That can only come when there is no invitation; that can only come when you are not seeking. Because our search is born out of frustration, the mind that seeks can never find. It is only the mind that understands the total process that can receive the blessings of the real.

March 3, 1954

United States, 1954

First Talk in New York City, New York

I think it is important that each one of us should not merely listen to the words that are being spoken but should actually experience the things we are talking about as we go along, and it seems to me that the words should convey their significance without resistance. Most of us listen to a talk and go away without directly experiencing what is being said, and it would be a great pity if you merely listened without experiencing. But, if we can really experience what is being said, then perhaps the essential change will come about which is so obviously necessary at the present time of crisis throughout the world.

I do not believe in ideas because ideas can be met with other ideas, and mere argumentation, refutation, or acceptance takes place. Merely to listen to ideas, to accumulate new forms of knowledge, or to acquire a particular technical capacity—all those things are really of no avail to meet life. What is necessary, it seems to me, is to be able to live in this mad, confused world with surety, with clarity and simplicity, meeting life as it arises without a thought of tomorrow. That is a very difficult thing to do because most of us live in ideas—ideas being knowledge, experience, or tradition. To us, ideas are very important, they guide our life, they shape our thinking and our future action, and so we never live a complete life, but are always overshadowed by the past. Surely, what is important is not a change which is merely a continuity of what has been in a different form but a total revolution in our thinking, which means letting go of the things that we have known and being in a state of the unknown.

It seems to me that most of us are utterly confused, and there are so many new ideas, so many influences, so many experiences, so many teachers, each telling us what we should do, what pattern of life, what philosophy, what teaching we should follow; or if these fail, we go back to the old, to the traditional. From among all these confusing and contradictory influences and ideas, we are forced to choose what we think is the truth and follow it, but in the very process of following what we consider to be the truth, there is also confusion. If we consider our lives closely and fairly seriously, we will see that we are confused. I think it is very important to start from there and not to seek clarity. A confused mind can never find clarity because whatever it finds will still be confused. I think it is very important to understand that.

After all, you and I are trying to find out what is true, and the discovery of that may bring about a revolution, a liberation in our thinking, in our being, but that discovery, that liberation cannot take place until we know what we actually are—not what we would like to be, but actually *what is.* And it is very difficult for most of us to accept *what* is, to see what we actually are. We would like to change what we are, and with that desire, with that impulse, we approach the state of what we are. So, we never see what we actually are.

I think that is the real basis of uncovering or discovering what is true—to know exactly what we are, to know actually what is, without any modification, without judging, without trying to alter or shape it. *What is* is not a permanent state, it is a constant movement because we are never the same from moment to moment, and to find out what is true, it is essential to see what we are from moment to moment.

So, it is important to see what we are, is it not? And if we look we will see that we are confused human beings. We are unhappy. We are caught in innumerable beliefs, experiences. We are always seeking some authority to point out the right direction, the right action that will lead us to some future hope, to some happiness, to some tranquillity. Being confused, the very search to find reality, to find truth, to find happiness, to find clarity, will only lead to further confusion. That is an obvious psychological fact, is it not? If my mind is confused, whatever action, whatever decision, whatever book, whatever teacher I may follow, or whatever discipline I may impose upon myself, will still be within the field of confusion. That is very difficult for most of us to accept. Being confused we think, "If I can only find the right teacher, the right method, the right discipline, if I can only understand, it will help me to evolve, to grow, to change, to transform." But a confused mind, whatever its action, must always be confused. Whatever decision it may take will still be within the field of confusion. As that state of confusion is the reality, the actual fact, I think we ought not merely to see it intellectually or verbally but to actually experience the state of confusion and proceed from there, observing the whole process of how the mind, being confused, seeks help.

After all, that is why most of you are here, is it not? Most of you are here to be told, to be encouraged, or to be confirmed in your own particular experiences. You want to be helped. Other teachers, other books, other philosophies may have failed, so you turn to a new person, but the mind that is seeking is still the confused mind, and a confused mind can never understand what is put in front of it. It will translate what it sees according to its idiosyncrasies, its particular pattern of thought, or its own experiences. Therefore it is incapable of seeing truly.

So, if I may suggest, it is very important to know how to listen. Our minds are incapable of listening as long as they are translating, justifying, condemning, accepting, or rejecting something. Surely, any such activity is not listening. If you observe your own mind—and I hope you will, during the talks that are to take place here—you will see how difficult it is to listen. Your knowledge, your experiences, your prejudices, your fears for the American way of life, your fear of communism, and so on—all that is preventing you from listening not only to what I am saying but to everything in life. What is important is that you should listen in the right way, not only to me, but to everything, because life is everything, and it is in constant movement. If you listen partially, with a particular prejudice or bias, if you listen as a capitalist, as a communist, as a socialist, as a member of any particular religion, or God knows what else, obviously you are only listening to what you want, and therefore there is no liberation, no understanding of the new, there is not the breaking away, the complete revolution which is so essential. Surely, it is only when the mind is in a state of the unknown that there can be the creativity of reality, but a mind that is caught continuously in the field of the known, it is not possible for such a mind to change itself, to bring about its own transformation and thereby find a new significance to life.

So, is it not important from the outset that as we are talking, we should know how to listen? I think the whole problem is solved if one knows how to listen not only to what is being said here but to all the hints, the unconscious urges, the influences, to the words of a friend, or your wife or husband, of the politician and the newspaper. If you know how to listen, then that very listening is a complete action in itself. I think it is important to understand this, if I may labor the point, because I am not giving out new ideas. Ideas are not at all important. One may have new ideas, or you may listen to something which you have not heard before, but what is important is how you listen not only to ideas, to something new, but to everything because if you know how to listen, that very act of listening is a liberation.

If you really experiment with what I am saying, you will discover the truth of it for yourself. A mind that is capable of listening without translation, without interposing its own particular ideas, experiences, knowledge, or desires, is surely a tranquil mind, a quiet mind. It is only when the mind is still that the new can take place, the new being the eternal, or whatever name you may like to give to it, which is not important. But, you see, most of us have innumerable ideas, desires, and longings, and so there is never a moment when the mind is really still.

So, it seems to me, what matters in all these talks—which are going to take place here this weekend and next weekend—is to know the art of listening, and you can be aware of that art only in observing your own reactions to what is being said, because you will have reactions, you are bound to have them. The mind must be aware of its reactions and yet be capable of going beyond those reactions so that they do not impede further discovery.

Being confused, most of us want to find a way out of that confusion. We turn to books, we turn to leaders, we seek political or religious authority, or the authority of a specialist of some kind to help us clarify our own thinking. Is that not what each one of us is trying to do? We want to find somebody who will help us out of our confusion, out of our frustrations, out of our misery and turmoil, so we seek authority. But is not that very authority the cause of our confusion? And is it not important to shed all authority? After all, the mind seeks authority in different forms in order to be sure. That is what we want: to find a refuge where we can be safe, where we shall not be disturbed, because for most of us thinking is a pain; every action brings its own confusion, its own misery. Knowing that, being aware of it, we seek authority in order to find shelter. It may not be the authority of a person, but it may be the authority of an idea.

Please follow all this; do not reject it. You may ask, is not the authority of a policeman, of the government, and so on, essential? But if we understand the whole significance of the creation of authority, how authority is bred in each one of us, then we shall understand the details of authority and be free of authority.

Now, the world is being broken up into several authorities, the left and the right, into various political pressure groups, all having the sanction of some book, of some teacher, of some idea. And is it possible for each one of us to find out how to be free from authority of every kind, not only external authority, but the inward authority of experience, of knowledge? Can we find out what is true, not through somebody but directly for ourselves, so that there are no teachers, no pupils? It seems to me that this is what is necessary not only now but at all times.

As long as the mind is seeking security of any kind, whether in a leader, in a particular way of life, in a particular nationality or group, or in any belief, such a mind can only create confusion in the world and more misery, which is being shown at the present time. So, it is important for each one of us to find out for ourselves *what is* by shedding all authority, which is extraordinarily difficult, and seeing *what is,* the very discovery of *what is,* will be the liberating process. But, you see, most of us are afraid to be naked, completely alone; one avoids standing by oneself to find out for oneself.

If that is not understood, I am afraid you will go away from these talks disillusioned and disappointed because what I am saying is not anything new, but what will be new is your discovery of what is being said. Isn't it important to bring about a different way of thinking? Isn't it important to find out for yourself how to live in this extraordinarily confusing, brutal, and aggressive world? And can anyone tell you how to live, or what pattern of action you should adopt, or which leader or group you should follow, or what belief you should hold? All such things seem so utterly infantile when you are confronted with an extraordinary crisis. This crisis has been brought about by the leaders, and it is we who have created the leaders—the leaders being the embodiment of some particular idea or belief, whether religious or economic.

So, is it not very important for each one of us to free the mind from all sense of authority?—which really means, if you go into it very deeply, from all sense of knowledge so that the mind is new, fresh, and can therefore function in a totally different way.

You see, we rely so much on knowledge. The man who writes a book about the mind or speaks about the mind, we accept. We call his thought by some name, and we accept it. We never investigate into the whole process of our own thinking and discover it for ourselves. That is why we have innumerable leaders, each asserting and dominating. And can one put away all that and find out for oneself? Because, you see, knowledge becomes a hindrance to understanding. When you want to build a bridge, for that you must obviously have knowledge, you must have a certain technical capacity. But can one have knowledge of a living thing—that is, the understanding of it beforehand? That which you call 'me', the self, is a living thing, and you cannot have previous knowledge about it. You may have experiences concerning it, or the information of what others have said about it, but when you approach yourself with previous knowledge, you never discover what you actually are. If you are religiously inclined, you say, "I am the eternal, I am a son of God," and so on, and if you are not, you assert that the self, the 'I', is merely the result of environmental nature.

So, we approach everything with knowledge, with conclusions which have already been made, and with these patterns of thought we go through life; therefore, knowledge becomes a hindrance in the discovery of truth. If I want to know the truth about myself, surely I must discover myself every minute as I am, not as I have been or as I should be. Please listen to this because more and more books are being written, more and more lectures are being given, everything—the radio, the television, the newspapers, the speeches, the politicians, the teachers—everything is conditioning you, shaping you to a certain pattern, and with this conditioning you are trying to find out what is true. Conditioning is knowledge, tradition; it is what has been, the past, both the past of yesterday and of a thousand years ago. That is our mind, and with that mind we try to find out what is true. Surely, to find out what is true there must be freedom from conditioning, the conditioning as an American or as a Russian, as a Catholic or a Protestant, as an artist or a poet; there must be freedom from the conditioning of a particular capacity because identification with capacity gives pride.

So, a mind that is to find out what is true must be free of knowledge. But if you observe, you will see how your mind is constantly gathering knowledge, storing it away; every experience becomes a further strengthening of knowledge. Our minds are never free to be still because they are too crowded with information. We know far too much, and really about nothing, and through this immense weight we are trying to be free. But you see, we are unconscious of all this, and if we are made conscious of it, we resist because we say that knowledge is essential to liberation. Surely, knowledge is an impediment, a hindrance to the discovery of what is true. Truth must be something that is living, it must be totally new each second, and how can a mind that has accumulated knowledge, information, ever find out what is the unknown? Call it God, truth, by whatever name you like, it is not to be sought after because if you seek it, you already know it, and knowing it is the denial of it.

Please listen to all this. All religions are based on the idea of knowing, experiencing, believing, and so from childhood we are conditioned to believe. We already know, and we worship that which we already know. We are always frightened of the unknown. The unknown may be death, the unknown may be tomorrow. A mind that is living with the known can never be in a state of revolution, it can never bring about that state when truth can come into it.

Our particular job, then, is not to seek God or truth because when we seek it, we have already destroyed it. What we seek is what we want, it is something gratifying, satisfying, which means, really, the projection of our own desires into the future. We project our own past into the tomorrow and worship the past in the tomorrow.

If you would really understand this, listen to it without making an effort to free the mind from the past; merely listen to it, see how the mind is the result of the past, not only the conscious mind, but also the unconscious mind, the mind which functions whether we are awake or asleep. The many layers of the unconscious, the hidden fears, the impulses, the motives, the hindrances—all that is the result of the past, as well as the conscious mind which is struggling with the immediate.

In listening to all this, if one makes an effort, it is still a result of the known. After all, most of us live through the action of will, do we not? To us, will is very important, that is, the will to be or to become. The will to become, to be, is the action of the known, is it not? Therefore the action of will can never find what is real. Just see the fact that all knowledge, all experience, only strengthens the will, the known, the 'me', the self, and that such a will, such a 'me' can never perceive clearly what is true, can never find God, however much it may try, because its God is the known. It is only when the mind is in a state of the unknown, when the mind itself is the unknown, only then is there a possibility of creativity, which is truth.

What we are talking about is not conformity to any particular pattern of thought, the acceptance of any particular belief, or the joining of any particular group, but a total revolution which can come about only when the mind is totally still. It comes when one understands the ways of the self. With self-knowledge alone comes true stillness of the mind. Without self-knowledge, stillness of the mind is merely a deception, a convenience, a thing put together by the mind for its own security, and in such a stillness the mind is not capable of perceiving, of realizing or receiving the unknown.

So, as we shall be discussing these things during the coming talks, what is important at all times is to know how to listen, and you cannot listen if there is an argumentation going on between you and me. If you belong to any society, to any group, to any religion, if you accept any belief, you are incapable of listening because your mind is already conditioned. A conditioned mind cannot listen; it is not free to listen. But if one can listen totally, then I think a fundamental change, a fundamental revolution will take place which is not brought about by an action of the 'me', and therefore it will be a true transformation. That is the only problem we have: How to bring about a complete change in ourselves, not mere adjustment to a particular society which is infantile. It is immature to desire to adjust oneself to a particular society because the society is created by environmental influences, by our own reactions and relationships, and merely to adjust oneself to a particular pattern of society is not freedom.

What is necessary, it seems to me, is this fundamental transformation that comes about through no volition, no authority, but only when we understand the total process of our own being. To know ourselves as we are, to see ourselves as clearly as we see our faces in the mirror, without any distortion, is the beginning of truth. That requires a great deal of awareness, an awareness in which there is no choice. The moment you choose, you are already acting according to your conditioning. But to know that you are acting according to your conditioning, and to see the truth of it, is already the beginning of that awareness in which there is no choice.

All this one can observe in oneself. You don't have to go to any philosopher, to any teacher, or belong to any group. Your various groups are limiting, confusing, contradicting each other, they create animosity though they talk of brotherhood. If one knows that truth cannot be found through any person, through any book, through any religion, that reality comes into being only when the mind is utterly still, that stillness can come only with self-knowledge, and that self-knowledge cannot be given to one by another but has to be discovered for oneself from moment to moment—then, surely, there comes a tranquillity of mind which is not death, a peace which is really creative, and it is only then that the eternal can come into being.

May 22, 1954

Second Talk in New York City, New York

As I was saying yesterday, I think it is important not merely to listen to what I am saying but rather to experience the thing that is being said because this is not an ordinary lecture from which you are going to learn something. If you merely listen in order to learn, I am afraid you will be disappointed, but if you listen in order to discover for yourself, then you will find astonishing results. Unfortunately, most of us are so conditioned, our thinking is so obstructed with unknown fears and anxieties, that we are incapable of really experiencing directly, and therefore we miss the deeper significance of what is being said. Words have a limited significance; they are only symbols, and I feel it is important to go beyond the symbol, but most of us worship symbols, and we are blocked; we are hindered by merely accepting certain verbal definitions and living within those definitions. So, may I again suggest that in listening to what is being said you relate it to yourself, directly experiencing it rather than merely following the description.

I feel that as long as the world is broken up into innumerable nationalities, as long as it is divided by many faiths, many beliefs and dogmas, there can be no peace at all. There can be peace only when all nationalism ceases, when all beliefs which divide man come to an end, and that can happen only when the mind is free from all conditioning, when the mind no longer thinks in terms of America or of Russia, when it no longer thinks as a communist, a socialist, or a capitalist, as a Catholic, a Protestant, or a Hindu. We can deal with the many problems that arise only when we approach them as human beings, that is, when we are not conditioned in any of these patterns which have been cultivated for generations, and it is very arduous, really difficult to break down the enclosures that the mind has built around itself. So, I would like to talk about it, go into the matter, and if you, on your part, will take the journey, not merely following what I am talking about, but seeing the actual state of your own mind as we go along, then I think listening to a talk of this kind will have significance. As I said yesterday, the very act of listening breaks down the barrier, the conditioning, because to listen implies no resistance. I am obviously not asking you to join anything, to believe anything, or to accept anything, but to investigate your own mind, the mind that is functioning daily, and also, perhaps, to look into the unconscious.

It is impossible to be aware of the total process of our being as long as we are not aware of our own conditioning, and if we are to survive in this mad, chaotic world, surely it is imperative that each one of us who is at all earnest and thoughtful should consider this problem of freeing the mind from its conditioning. This does not mean the cultivation of a better conditioning but freedom from all conditioning. Each one of us is conditioned by the climate, by the food we eat, and by other psychological influences. Those we know how to deal with. But of the deeper conditioning of the psyche, the inward, very few of us are aware, and it is that which dictates, controls, and shapes our actions.

If we are to have peace in the world, we can no longer belong to any particular nationality or religion because it is this very division of nationalities, of groups, of religious faiths, that is destroying us, and unless we are alert to this whole problem, it will bring still greater misery. Surely, if you are thoughtful, if you are alert to the problem, you will see that we have to begin by inquiring whether the mind can free itself from all conditioning. Those who are important people in the world, who have great wealth, who have position, prestige, will naturally not experiment with this at all because it is too dangerous. It is only the ordinary people, those who have no power, position, and who are struggling, trying to understand—it is they, perhaps, who will begin to experiment and find out for themselves.

As most of us are unconscious of our conditioning, is it not first of all essential to be aware of it? Each one of us is conditioned as a Christian, or as belonging to some other group with certain ideas, with certain beliefs and dogmas which are contrary to other beliefs, to other ideas and dogmas. Obviously, then, these very beliefs and dogmas create enmity between man and man, do they not? And, realizing that beliefs do create enmity and maintain this division between man and man, why do we cling to certain beliefs and try to have others join our particular group?

So, is it not important to ask ourselves whether it is possible for the mind to free itself from all conditioning? Is it possible not to belong to any group, to any religion?—which does not mean entering some other conditioned state, becoming an atheist, a communist, or something else. To be free from all conditioning is not to seek a better conditioning. I think that is the real crux of the matter because it is only when the mind is unconditioned that it can tackle the problem of living as a total process and not just on one sectionalized level of our existence.

Can you and I be aware of our conditioning? Is it possible to be free of it? And will any action of the will bring about that freedom? Do you understand the problem? I realize that I am conditioned as a Hindu, or what you will, and I see the effects of that conditioning in my relationship with others, which is really a relationship of resistance, creating its own problems. I realize that. And can 1, realizing it, break down that conditioning by an act of will, by saying to myself that I must not be conditioned, that I must think differently, that I must consider human beings as a whole, and so on? Can the conditioning be broken down through any action of the will? After all, what is it that we call the will? What is the will? Is it not the process of desire centered in the 'me' that wants to achieve a result?

Please, this is not a highbrow talk. If we can think simply about the matter, we shall find the right solution to the problem, but it is very difficult to think simply because within ourselves we are so complex. We have so many ideas, we have read so much, so many things have been told us, and amidst this complexity it is very difficult to think directly and simply, but that is what we are trying to do.

I see I am conditioned, and I want to know how to break it down because that conditioning prevents me from thinking clearly. It prevents a direct relationship with people. It creates resistance, and resistance creates its own problems. So, seeing the whole implication of the effects of conditioning, how is my mind to free itself from conditioning? Do you understand the problem? Is the entity that desires to free the mind from conditioning different from the mind itself? If it is different, then the problem of effort, the action of will, comes into being. Is the 'I', the thinker, the person who says, "I am conditioned and I must be free," the 'I' who makes an effort to be free, is that 'I', that will, that desire, different from the conditioned state? Please, this is not complicated. You are bound to ask yourself this question when you look at the problem. Am I who wish to free myself from conditioning, different from the conditioning, or are they both the same? If they are the same, which they are, then how is it possible for the mind to free itself from conditioning? Do you understand?

I realize I am conditioned as a Hindu, with all its implications—the superstitions, the information, the experiences of a Hindu. My mind is conditioned in that way. Let us take that as an example. Now, I see the importance of freeing the mind from conditioning. How is that to be done? Does freedom come through an action of will? If I say, "I must free myself from the conditioning of the past," then the 'I' who wishes to free himself from the past conditioning is different from it, but is that 'I' different from conditioning, or is it still a conditioned result? And if that 'I', which is the will, is not different, then in trying to break down conditioning, it is only finding a substitute for the previous conditioning.

Please, as I said, what is important is for you to listen and experiment. Perhaps this is something which you have not heard before; therefore, you are puzzled; there is a resistance, but if you can listen without any resistance, merely observing your own mind in action, then the very listening becomes an experiment. Your own mind is conditioned, and it is this conditioning that is really preventing peace, that is creating war, destruction, and misery. Unless you resolve your conditioning completely, there will be no real peace in the world; there will be the peace of politicians between two immense powers, which is terror. To have peace, the mind must be totally unconditioned. One must realize that, but not superficially, not as insurance for your security, or for your bank account. Peace is a state of mind; it is not the development of monstrous means of destroying each other and then maintaining peace through terror. I do not mean that. To have real peace in the world is to be able to live happily, creatively, without any sense of fear, without being secure in any thought, in any particular way of life. To have such peace, surely the mind must be totally free from all conditioning, either externally imposed or inwardly cultivated. And can your mind, which is conditioned—because all minds are conditioned—can such a mind free itself from its own effects, from its own desires, from its own conditioned state? So, the problem is: Is there a part of the mind which is not conditioned and which can take over, control, or destroy the conditioned mind? Or is the mind totally conditioned at all times and therefore cannot act upon itself? When it realizes that it cannot act upon itself, will not the mind then be utterly still, without movement towards its own conditioning?

For most of us this implies freedom from something. Freedom from something is resistance against something, and therefore it is not freedom. I am talking not of freedom from something but of being free. Being free is not becoming free, being peaceful is not becoming peaceful. There is no gradual process towards freedom, towards peace. Either you are peaceful or you are not peaceful, and what we are trying to find out is whether the mind which has been conditioned for centuries, generation upon generation, whether such a mind can free itself. Surely, it can be free only when there is no action of will, when it realizes that it is conditioned and does not make any effort to free itself from its own conditioning. When my mind knows that its way of thinking is Oriental, whatever that may mean, when it fully realizes that, will it then think along the Western line, which is another form of conditioning, or will it cease thinking in any particular pattern and therefore be free to think?

You see, I feel this is a very important point to understand; it is the crux of the matter because a conditioned mind can never find out what is true, a conditioned mind can never discover what God is. It can project its own images, its own dogmas, its own beliefs, and think it has found God, but that is still the action of a limited, conditioned mind. And if I see that, if I perceive it as a fact, will any action on my part be necessary? If I know I am blind, then I have quite a different approach to life, I develop a totally different perception. In the same way, when I know that I am conditioned, that my thinking is limited, and that a limited mind, whatever its experiences may be, however much knowledge it may acquire, is still limited—when I realize that, is any action on my part necessary to break down that limitation? Will not that limitation break down of itself when I know the mind is limited? Therefore, is there not an instantaneous freedom from conditioning? Most of us think that an analytical process will ultimately bring about the freedom of the mind because we are so used to thinking in terms of making effort. We say, "I must break down this conditioning, I must produce a result, I must do something." But the 'I' who is acting is itself conditioned, the 'I' is the conditioned mind, and therefore it cannot break down that conditioning.

Now, when the whole of me realizes that I cannot break down the conditioning, that whatever I do about it—discipline, worship, prayer, anything through which the 'me' makes an effort to break down any part of itself—is still limited, then does not the action of the 'me' come to an end? And the very ending of this effort is the cessation of conditioning.

Please, you experiment with this. If you have listened rightly, you will see that the mind cannot do a thing about its conditioning. It can explore, it can analyze, it can achieve certain results, but it is always limited. Whatever its projections, its hopes, its fulfillments, they are always the result of its own background and therefore limited, and when the mind realizes that, is there not an instantaneous cessation, without any compulsion, of this 'I' which is seeking, searching, hoping, gaining and thereby being frustrated? After all, that is meditation, which is really not through any action of will; it is the meditation of the mind, which is tranquillity. A mind that is merely caught in desires, in achieving a result, in knowing, in experiencing, can never be a still mind, and when a limited mind meditates, when it thinks of God, its God and its meditation are still petty. It seems to me that however much a mediocre mind may be expanded, however much it may know, it is still mediocre, small, petty, and therefore its problems will always remain petty, unsolvable.

So, what is important is to realize all this not merely through hearing what I am saying but through seeing it for yourself, experiencing directly for yourself that your mind is small, limited, and being limited, however much it may know, whatever experiences it may have, it is still limited, and therefore it can never find out what is true, what is real. Reality comes into being only when there is a total cessation of all conditioning, that is, when the mind is free—not from something, but being free—and therefore it is still.

I have some questions which I will try to answer—or rather, not answer, because there are no answers, there are only problems. Please, this is not a witty or a clever remark, but a true thing, because a mind that is seeking an answer to a problem will find an answer according to its own desires. Most of us have problems, and we are always groping for an answer. That is why there are churches, these lecture halls. All of us are trying to find somewhere an answer, and we may find it, but it will not be the real thing. What is true is the problem. If there is an understanding of the problem, there is the cessation of the problem, not an answer to the problem. Please, this is important to listen to. It is the petty mind, the shallow mind, that seeks an answer, that wants to know what happens when I die; it has innumerable questions, and all it is concerned with is the answer. But to understand the problem requires an alert mind, a mind that is not seeking a result, an escape, or trying to cover up its own emptiness. So, the solution of the problem is in the problem itself, only I must know how to approach the problem, and I cannot approach it rightly if I desire to solve it, if I wish to find an answer to it, because then my mind is concentrated on the answer and not on the problem. I think it is very important to understand this, which is really a revolution in our way of thinking. You see, we create the problem by our way of thinking and then try to resolve the problem through further thinking; we begin to question, we go to analysts, to priests, to God knows what else, trying to find an answer. So, we must know how to remain with the problem, to look at it without translating it according to our wishes, according to our belief, according to our tradition. It is our tradition, our belief, our dogma that has created the problem, and if we would understand the problem, we must be free from all these things and look at it directly.

Questioner: I have always tried to be sincere to my ideals, but you say they are destructive. What have you to offer in their stead?

Krishnamurti: There are several things involved in this problem: sincerity, ideals, and if there are no ideals, whether there is something to put in their place. Let us go into the problem slowly and look at it.

What do we mean by sincerity—to be sincere to something? If I have an ideal, I try to live according to that ideal, and if I live as much as I can, according to that ideal which I have set for myself, I am considered a sincere person. Now, the ideal is the creation of my mind in seeking its own security, is it not? Please follow this, don't resist it. You will go on with your ideals, you will go on with your particular pattern of action, unfortunately, so you don't have to resist what is being said, but you can at least listen to find out.

You have an ideal because it gives you comfort. It may be a difficult ideal for you to live up to, but the very struggle to live up to that ideal gives you satisfaction, it gives you a sense of conformity, a sense of well-being, a sense of respectability. In essence, the ideal gives you security, and that is why you project these ideals. If I am violent, I do not like that state of violence, so I project the ideal of nonviolence and pursue it. The ideal and the pursuance of that ideal give me security, a sense of well-being. I am being sincere to my own desire, I am being sincere to what I want, and such a man, who is pursuing what he wants, you call noble.

So, ideals are destructive because they are separative, they are the projection of our own desires, they bring about a conflict between what I am, which is the actuality, and what I should be. The ideal creates a duality between 'what I am' and 'what I should be', and this struggle between 'what I am' and 'what I should be' is called living according to the ideal. We are afraid not to struggle because, being conditioned to struggle everlastingly between good and bad, between the evil and the noble, we say, "If I do not struggle, what will happen?" If the ideal is taken away, we feel completely lost, and the questioner wants to know what can be placed in its stead.

To me, the idealist is one who is caught between *what is* and *what should be* and is therefore in a state of hypocrisy because *what should be* is not. Why should I turn my attention to *what should be?* I can only understand *what is.* If I am violent, can I not resolve my violence rather than try to become nonviolent? Instead of pursuing the ideal and thereby creating a conflict between *what is* and *what should be,* this conflict of the opposites which creates innumerable problems, can I not look at *what is?* Instead of projecting the opposite and creating the conflict, can I not look at what I actually am? But that is the very thing we avoid, is it not? Because most of us do not want to know what we actually are. Either we are ashamed of it and we condemn it, or we are afraid of it, or we want to change it into something else.

So, we never look at *what is,* and before we can change *what is,* must we not know its structure, what it is in actuality? And how can I know what it is when I am all the time concerned with trying to change it, to rearrange it, to run away from it? We are so afraid of being naked, empty, without a thing. We want to fill our emptiness with something. If I am lonely, I run away from that loneliness, I turn on the radio, read a book, go to church, pray, plunge into social activities, do anything to escape from it; but if I do not escape from it, I am afraid of it.

So, fear prevents us from understanding *what is,* fear makes us carry on various forms of activity which act as an escape from the reality of *what is.* Therefore, is it not important for each one of us to put away all ideals, since they have no meaning, and see what is actually taking place in us from moment to moment? And if we are aware of ourselves from moment to moment, choicelessly, without condemning, without judging, without yielding to that which we have considered before as fearful, ugly, bad, evil, will it then exist? Fear exists only when we are running away. The very process of running away is fear, and when, without running away, we can look at the thing that we have condemned before, the thing from which we have run away, the thing which we are struggling to change, when we can look at it without doing any of these things, will not the very thing from which we have been trying to escape, cease to exist?

If you really go into this question, you will see that when a mind is violent because it has the ideal of nonviolence, because it is escaping from the state in which it is, because it wants to alter that state, therefore it is resisting violence. This does not mean that the mind must yield to violence, but when the mind is free from all resistance with regard to violence, does the problem exist at all? Surely, the problem exists because the mind resists.

Please, as I said, this thing has to be thought over, or, which is much better, directly experienced, and then you will see that when the mind has no ideal, when it is not trying to become something, there is a state of being in which time is not. For time is the problem. Old age, the sense of frustration, the fear of not achieving, not becoming, not fulfilling—all that involves time, and that is all we know, in that state we live and function, we struggle. So, this conflict between *what is* and *what should be* is a never-ending process, and when the mind realizes that, then is there not a freedom of 'being' in which there is no 'becoming'? Therefore you don't need any ideal, and I think it is very important to understand this. Surely, this is the real revolution, not the process of creating the antithesis and then struggling with the antithesis to produce a synthesis. If you can think in these terms, not of 'becoming', but of 'being'—which is astonishingly difficult and subtle to understand—then you will find that the many problems which involve time completely cease. Therefore the mind is free to uncover and to find out what is the real, and the blessing of it.

May 23, 1954

Third Talk in New York City, New York

As I was saying yesterday and the day before, I do not think that ideas fundamentally change our activities, though they may modify them. Ideas play a certain superficial part, but they obviously do not affect the deeper motives, purposes, the things that we really want, they do not bring about a radical transformation or revolution in our attitude towards life. And so it seems to me that what is important is to understand the total process of our thinking, of our consciousness, and perhaps in that very understanding a change can take place, not according to any particular pattern of thought, or according to any desire, but a change from the known into the unknown.

When we are confronted, as we are, with an enormous crisis which is probably unprecedented in history, it seems to me that a transformation, a radical revolution is necessary, but not in the political or the economic sense because I do not think we can meet this crisis with ideas. A totally different process must be born in us in order to meet this crisis, and that birth cannot be brought about by the conscious mind.

I would like, if I can this evening, to discuss the problem of what it is that we are seeking, what it is that most of us are groping after in trying to find out how to meet this constant movement of life. Life actually has no resting place, though we try to enclose it by our own conditioned thinking, by our peculiar upbringing as Christians, as Catholics, as Protestants, as Hindus, or what you will.

It seems to me that it is very important to listen to this talk not in order to gather information, knowledge, or more ideas, or in order to refute what is said by cunning arguments, greater information and knowledge, but rather to investigate together the process of our own thinking. And as I am talking, if we can follow together the ways of our own mind, which is really self-knowledge, then perhaps that transformation, that radical change can come into being without volition. Any act of will is conditioned by our experience, by our education, by our social influences, and being conditioned, limited, it cannot bring about this change, however much it may try. And yet that is what we are used to—this constant effort, this constant struggle of ambition, of trying to change, or trying to bring about a reformation. But if we can approach this whole problem of living, this extraordinary crisis, without the action of will, then perhaps we shall be able to bring about a different understanding, a different set of values, values which are not based on nationalism or on any particular religion.

To understand this freedom from will, one must understand, follow the movements of one's own thinking, and that process is not to be learned from any book; it does not depend on any psychologist, but one has to discover it anew every day in one's relationship with life. And to discover it, there must surely be the understanding of how the mind is constantly seeking some form of security. That is what most of us want, is it not? We want to be secure in order to have peace. We want to be secure in order to be able to fulfill, to live our beliefs, our morality. The various efforts that we make to achieve, to fulfill, do they not all imply the fundamental demand of the mind to be safe, to have a security in which there will be no disturbance, an experience or a form of knowledge which will be permanent, unchanging? Some kind of permanency is what most of us want; that is what most people are seeking, is it not? There is this urge to find security, security in relationship, security in things, in property, in people, and if it is not found in people or in property, then we turn to ideals, self-projected urges, demands, and there take shelter, either in the idea of God, in a belief, in a dogma, or in virtue.

When you look into your own mind closely, you will find, I think, this constant demand to be secure. But does peace come with security? Or must one find peace first, which will then bring security? The effort to be something is a form of ambition because social ambition and so-called spiritual ambition are the same, and as long as there is this constant effort to be something, which brings about the importance of the self, surely there cannot be peace. And yet, if we observe the ways of our thinking, our searching, our beliefs, they all lead to this one constant demand to have some kind of permanence. And when that permanency is disturbed, as it is being disturbed all the time, we develop a resistance which creates innumerable problems.

So, is it not important to find out for ourselves if there is such a thing as permanency? The mind, the self, the 'me', is constantly demanding, seeking to establish permanency for itself through memory, through experience, through relationship, through the so-called search for reality. The constant urge of the mind is for permanency, and effort is made to maintain this permanency, and so we develop will. The will is essentially the 'me', the self, and whether it pursues virtue or denies virtue, or creates various forms of experience for itself, its constant struggle is for permanency, security. Identification with any form of thought, with any idea, or experience, will give this sense of security, of permanency, and that is why we identify ourselves with a nation, with a group of people, with a religion, with knowledge, or with an experience. This constant process of identification with something is all that we know; this constant battle is our life, and our whole culture, all our values are based on it.

Now, it seems to me that peace is not the result of this battle. A mind that is ambitious, a mind that is identified with any particular group, nation, class, belief, religion, or dogma, is incapable of having peace because it is seeking security and thereby emphasizing, strengthening the will of the 'me', of the self, which must naturally be an everlasting conflict.

So, if one is to see that not merely as an idea but actually, as one is listening, one must be aware of this process of the mind that is seeking. And what is it that we are seeking? Some kind of fulfillment, is it not? A fulfillment in which there will be some permanency. There is this constant urge to fulfill, to be, to achieve, and after achieving, to further achieve. And a mind which is constantly seeking, struggling, endeavoring to understand, to establish itself in some form of permanence, can such a mind be at peace at any time? And is it not essential that the mind should have complete tranquillity without effort so that that creative thing which we call God, or what you like, can come into being?

You see, what I mean is that all our life is a struggle, and through struggle will we find that thing which we call the real? After all, that is what we all want—a permanent state of bliss, of happiness, call it God, truth, or by whatever name you will. But that is a thing which cannot be imagined by the mind because the mind is the result of time, and any projection of time, of the mind, is still limited; it is the result of the past, and therefore there is nothing new in it; it is not the real, the creative.

Now, can all of that process—not only the conscious, but the unconscious struggle to be, to fulfill, the ambition which has actually created such havoc in the world—can that whole process come to an end so that the mind can be truly peaceful? It is only then that there is a possibility of true security.

You see, what is happening in the world is that each individual is identifying himself with a nation, with a group, with a religion, and so creating for himself an artificial permanency, a security as opposed to other nations, a group opposed to other groups, because each one of us wants to be identified with something greater, something nobler, something much more immense than the petty little 'me'. The state, the belief, the religion, offers an escape from the 'me', and through this escape we hope to find a permanent peace. But that permanency is the result of our desire to be secure in some form of identification, and therefore there is a constant battle going on between individuals, between groups, religions, and nations.

As I was saying yesterday, what is important in listening to what is being said is that you should not merely accept or reject but actually listen without any form of judgment—which is not to put oneself in a hypnotic state. To listen without judgment is to listen in order to find out, which means listening to the operation of one's own mind, to one's thoughts, so that the mind becomes astonishingly separate and apart. When the mind is still, not artificially made to be still, then you will find that there is a sense of total insecurity in which there is complete security because there is the absence of the 'me', of the self which is constantly battling. That is why it is so very important to have self-knowledge, to know for oneself the many thoughts, the many urges, the ambitions, the frustrations in which one is caught, and be aware of them.

When most of us are aware, our awareness consists in judging, condemning, choosing, accepting, or denying. That is not awareness, that is merely the action of will upon thought. But if you can observe, be aware without any choice, just see what is happening, then you will find that the whole process of the unconscious, which is hidden, dark, kept underground, will come to the surface through dreams, through hints, through various forms of spontaneous reaction, and as they arise they too can be observed without any sense of condemnation or justification, without acceptance or rejection. Then the mind is not merely an instrument of evaluation, of analysis, and such a mind, being no longer moved by the will of the 'me', of the self, with all its conditionings, demands, and pursuits, is really still. In that stillness, every thought, every response, every reaction, every movement of the self is turned away, and that, it seems to me, is important if we are to solve any of our problems in life.

The understanding of the 'me', the understanding of oneself, is not a thing that can be learned immediately, all at once. But to say, "I shall learn it gradually," is again wrong because it is not through the process of time that one understands. You see, we think understanding comes through accumulation, the accumulation of experience or knowledge. Does understanding come through knowledge, or does understanding come when the mind is no longer burdened by the past?

As I say, experiment, think as I am talking, directly experience what I am saying, and you will find out for yourself. You may have a problem, and the mind has gone into it, worried over it, but the moment the mind is still, not concerned, as it were, with the problem, then a feeling of understanding comes into being. In the same way, if one can understand the mind, if one can simply be aware of its movements when one is riding in a bus, when one is sitting at a table and talking, the way one talks, the way one gossips, the escapes, the worship, the prayers, then all those things reveal the depth of one's consciousness. Surely, to find that which is eternal, that which is beyond the futile projections of the mind, the mind must come to an end, not artificially, not through any discipline, but through awareness of the process of thinking. So, the mind itself, though capable of the highest reason, in its reason comes to an end, and then only is it possible to have that inward peace which alone can stop these monstrous wars and bring salvation to the world.

But the difficulty is that we say, "We are nobodies, we are just ordinary people. What can we do?" I think we all ought to be very thankful that we are people without any power, without any position, without any authority, because those who are in power, who have position or authority, do not want peace. They want political peace, which is entirely different. And I think it depends on us, who are very simple people, though we have a great many conflicts and miseries, though we are in travail—it is for us to start, as it were, in our own backyard to experiment with ourselves, to know the various activities of our mind so that each one of us becomes a center of real peace, not the phony peace which the armies and governments create between two wars.

Without that real peace there will be no security, there will be only fear. Fear is the very nature of the self, for it is the self that is being threatened in different ways continuously, especially in crises, and being frightened, we have no answer, we run away into various forms of escape, or turn to leaders, political or religious. This problem cannot be solved through any leader, through any dogma. No army, no nation, no idea is going to bring peace to the world. When each one of us understands oneself as a total process—not merely the economic problem or the mass problem, but the whole process of ourselves as individual people—in the understanding of that process there comes peace. It is only then that there can be security. But if we put security first, if we regard it as the most important thing in life, then there will be no peace; there will be only darkness and fear.

As I was saying yesterday, I shall be answering some questions, but may I again point out that what is important is to understand the problem, and not seek an answer to the question. If we seek an answer, it is an escape from the problem, but in understanding the problem itself, the problem ceases. So, there are only problems, not answers. It is the immature mind that seeks answers. If we know how to think, how to look at the problem—the problem of war, the problem of relationship, it does not matter what the problem is—if we can look at it and not try to dissolve it or find a solution for it, then we shall discover that the mind itself is the creator of the problem, but that requires a great deal of understanding, penetration, insight, and awareness. You see, most of us are crippled with ideas and explanations; we know so much, and that very knowledge is impeding a simple, direct understanding.

So, in discussing the problem, I am not answering it, but rather we are exploring it together. After all, that is the function of talking things over. You are not merely listening to a talk, but together we are trying to find out how to resolve the problem, and that requires a great deal of interest, attention.

Questioner: I gave my son the very best education, and yet he does not seem to be happy and cannot find his place in society. What is the cause of his failure?

Krishnamurti: Why should one fit into society? *[Laughter]* It is not just something to be laughed off. That is the wish of every parent—that his son or daughter should fit into society. Why? Why should the child fit into society? What is this marvelous society that we have? Please, this is not a mere superficial remark to be brushed off by laughing it away. In India they want their children to fit into society. Here it is the same. In Russia it is the same. Everywhere we want the present state to continue, and we want our children to fit into it.

What is this thing called society? Let us think about it simply, not in the grand economic or philosophical sense. What is this society? This society is the outcome of acquisitiveness, of ambition, greed, envy, of the individual's pursuit of his own fulfillment, and of his search, his everlasting search to find some permanency in this impermanent world. Of course, in this society there are also passing joys, various forms of amusement, and so on. That, crudely, in a few words, is our society, and we want our sons to fit into it and make a success. We worship success. Our education is a process of teaching children to conform, is it not? It conditions them to fit into a certain pattern, it teaches them certain techniques so they will have jobs. And there is a constant threat of war.

So, that is our society. And why do we educate our children? What is it all about? We never investigate. What is the purpose of education if our sons are ultimately going to be killed or kill others in a war?

Surely, it is important that we think of this whole thing totally anew, and not do patchwork reform here and there. Should we not try to solve our problems, not in terms of America or Russia or any other particular country, but as a whole? Should we not approach this problem of man's existence, not as Americans or as Englishmen, but in terms of human relationship? Until we do that, we shall have constant wars, there will be starvation in the world. There is starvation, perhaps not in America, but in Asia, and until that problem is solved, there will be no peace here. And you cannot solve it as an American or a Russian, as a communist or a capitalist; you can solve it only as a human being.

Please don't brush all this off as though you had heard it ten thousand times before. If you really understand this as a simple individual, then you will be solving the problem. But if you are merely concerned with trying to help your son to fulfill himself in a particular society, if you are merely concerned with a particular problem—which of course must be dealt with, but which cannot be dealt with unless you tackle the problem as a whole—then you will find no answer, and therefore you will have more complications, more misery.

So, we have to tackle really fundamentally the problem of what is education. Is it merely to teach a technique so that the young person will have a job? Or is it to create an atmosphere of true freedom, not to do what one likes, but freedom to cultivate that intelligence which will meet every experience, every conditioning influence—meet it, understand it, and go beyond it? That requires a great deal of perception, a great deal of insight and intelligence on the part of each one of us. But, you see, we are all so frightened because we want to be secure. The moment we seek security, the shadow of fear is cast, and in trying to overcome that fear we further condition ourselves, we condition our minds and create a society which is bound to limit our thinking. And the more efficient a society becomes, the more conditioned it is.

To really tackle the problem of what is true education, to understand the whole significance of education, why we are educated, what it is all about, is an immense thing, not just to be talked about for a few minutes. You may have read or be capable of reading many books, you may have great knowledge, an infinite variety of explanations, but surely that is not freedom. Freedom comes with the understanding of oneself, and it is only such freedom that can meet without fear every crisis, every influence that conditions, but that requires a great deal of penetration, meditation.

Questioner: How can I have peace of mind in this disturbed world?

Krishnamurti: Probably, if we want peace, it is of the kind that is a complete escape from the world, and to escape is something which most of us can successfully do. We escape through the radio, through dogma, through belief, through activity. To become completely absorbed in some form of activity gives us what we consider to be peace. Surely, that is not peace. You see, peace is not the opposite of disturbance. But if I can understand what causes disturbance and not seek peace, if I can understand what is the process that brings about disturbance in me, in my relationships, in my values and therefore in society—if I can understand the whole process of disturbance, then in freeing myself from that disturbance there is peace. But to seek peace without understanding the total process of myself, which is the cause of disturbance, merely becomes an illusion. That is why the people who meditate in order to be peaceful, who read, who do various practices, who take drugs in order to be peaceful, are really seeking sleep.

What brings about peace, real tranquillity and stillness of the mind, is to understand the total process of oneself—which is not to seek peace but to understand the 'me' that is causing the disturbance. This understanding of the 'me', of the self, with all its ambitions, its envies, greeds, acquisitiveness, violence—to understand all that is the way of meditation, is it not? It is the meditation in which there is no condemnation, no choice, but heightened awareness, an observation without any sense of identification.

You see, for most of us peace is a withdrawal, it means entering into a cave of darkness, or holding on to some belief, some dogma, in which we find security, but that is not peace. Peace comes only with the total understanding of oneself, which is self-knowledge, and that self-knowledge cannot be bought. You need no book, no church, no priest, no analyst. You can observe the process of yourself in the mirror of your relationship with your boss, with your family, with your society. If the mind is alert, watchful, without choice, then there is freedom from the limitation of the self, and therefore there is peace, which brings its own security.

May 24, 1954

Fourth Talk in New York City, New York

As I was saying last week, I think these talks will be utterly useless if we do not know how to listen. I see some people taking notes, which indicates, really, that they are not listening. These notes are taken, obviously, as pointers to be thought over, but it seems to me that if we can think together over our many problems while we are here listening, it will be much more worthwhile than merely taking notes or comparing what I say with what you have already read or heard. When your mind is occupied with taking notes or with comparing what you hear with something else, you are actually not listening, are you? You are not directly experiencing what is being said, and it seems to me very important that we should directly experience these things. To directly experience what is being said is not to compare it with what you know. If we know how to listen, then I think the very act of listening is a form of release. If the thing that is being said is true and one listens to it without any comparison, without taking notes, without opposition or resistance; then that very listening acts as a release; it is the beginning of freedom because it sets going a process of freeing the mind from the very things with which we are burdened.

So, instead of taking notes, or comparing what is being said with the books you have read, or labeling it as oriental and putting it out of your mind, may I suggest that you listen with alert passivity, which is quite a difficult art, and then perhaps these talks will be worthwhile. We are not discussing a philosophy or a system of ideas, but we are trying to find out and actually experience how to liberate the mind from its own pettiness because that, it seems to me, is the major problem of our life. Our thoughts, our activities, our knowledge, our religious beliefs, are very petty and very small. Ideas and beliefs may be vital in themselves, but we reduce them to the size of our minds, and because the mind—it does not matter whose it is—is the center of the 'me', of the 'I', the ego, the self, it is very little, very small and petty.

Being confronted with a series of crises, both racial and individual, religious and economic, I think it is very important that we should be able to meet these crises with a mind that is not limited, conditioned, already burdened with religious beliefs, with dogmas, with previous knowledge, and so on, for how can the vast problems involved be dealt with by a petty, small, narrow mind? And if we have thought about these things at all, is it not a problem with most of us how to free the mind from its own narrowness, from its own limitations? Surely, only with a free mind is it possible to attack these problems anew, to comprehend them in a totally different way, because every problem, though it may appear old, is always new. There is no old problem. It is only the mind which is old and which, in meeting the new problem, reduces the new in terms of the old.

So, is it possible to free the mind from its own pettiness, which means really, from the center of self-acquisitiveness, of self-improvement, from the urge to become something great, noble? Because all that indicates a process of the 'me', of the 'I', of the ego, does it not? And as long as that process goes on, it must surely create its own self-enclosing activity. And is it possible ever to be free from this self-enclosing activity?

I am not putting this as a question for you to play with but to actually find out about because it seems to me that this is the major issue in our life. We have reduced religion to mere ritual or belief, and our gods, our self-disciplines lead not to reality but only to respectability. Our gods have really no meaning at all, and religion has become merely a series of beliefs and rituals without significance. Their influence is conditioning, like any other organized influence, whether it be the communist, the Christian, or the Hindu. The influence of dogma, belief, ritual, is tyrannical, limiting because it conditions and therefore makes the mind small, petty. Being confronted by immense problems, we are meeting them with our conditioned minds, and so we make these vast problems stupid and petty, thereby increasing the problems.

So, is it not very important to find out, actually to understand and experience for oneself, how the mind can be free from all the influences which religion has imposed? Because religion which is organized obviously does not lead to reality. Reality can come into being only when the mind is free, when the mind is unconditioned. And is it possible not to belong to any religious group or organization, to any church, but to stand alone and find out what is true? Surely, religion as we know it is merely a process of make-believe. From childhood we are forced into a particular pattern of thought, and the mind believes for its own security, for its own safety, but religion is something totally different, is it not? It is a state in which reality can come into being—reality, truth, God, or what name you will. But when the mind is conditioned, shaped by belief, can it ever be free to receive that which is true? Is not religion that state of mind in which the known is not, so that the unknown can come into being? Because, after all, our gods are self-projected. We create our gods, we pursue ideals and beliefs because they give us satisfaction, comfort, solace. But surely none of these things free the mind to discover reality, and that is why it seems to me very important to strip ourselves of all these conditionings, not as an ultimate gesture, but right from the beginning, and to find out whether the mind can remain uncorrupted.

Similarly, we accumulate knowledge, hoping that the petty mind can be enlarged and its shallowness wiped away through more and more learning, information. But can knowledge free the mind from its pettiness? We have vast information, scientific and otherwise, about so many things, and yet our minds are petty. We are only using this knowledge for our petty purposes, and we are destroying each other. So, knowledge has become a hindrance instead of a liberating process.

Should we not be aware of all this, how we are influenced by the external environment, by impulses, reactions, by knowledge, and by so-called religion? And is it possible ever to free ourselves from these limitations and conditions, from these self-imposed compulsions, so that the mind remains uncorrupted and is therefore able to meet life anew from moment to moment? I think that it is possible if we can be aware of all these issues without reacting to them, without being entangled in them. You see, after all, a belief, a dogma, is a means of self-protection, is it not? If we had no dogma, no belief, we think we should be lost, so dogma, belief, acts as a means of protection against that loneliness, against fear. We multiply beliefs, dogmas, to assure ourselves of security. So, our search is not for reality, truth, but for a means to be satisfied, to feel secure. And isn't it important just to be aware of this fact without reacting against it? Isn't it important to see how the mind is constantly pursuing its own security through nationality, through belief, through dogma, through ritual, thereby making itself petty, narrow, small, and creating problems?

What is being said is a fact, it is not an invention, a psychological perversion; it is actually what is taking place within each one of us. We want leaders, we want someone to tell us what to do. Being afraid to stand alone, we turn to some form of shelter, refuge, so the mind is made petty, and its gods, its troubles, its disciplines are equally petty. If we really see that, there is a release, there is a liberation without making an effort.

I think this is the important thing, the only important thing: to find out how to free the mind from the self, whose activities are always narrow, limited, self-enclosing. The more we struggle against this limitation, the stronger the limitation, but if we see it, if we are aware of it, and if we know how to listen to what is being said, then that very listening will set each one of us free so that we can look at the problem anew, afresh—which is, to have a mind that is not corrupted.

The difficulty in all this is that we are afraid of the consequences of letting go, of not belonging to some organization, of not calling ourselves patriotic; we are afraid to stand alone, not to have any support. But to find that which is real, you must be alone, mustn't you? The world is obviously caught in illusion, in hatred, in fear, with all its various absurdities and brutalities; and surely, to find out what is true, one must shed all that, mustn't one?—which means really standing alone. But you cannot stand alone by volition, by an act of will. It is like seeing something false. When you see the false, there is that which is true. Seeing the false is not an act of volition, but it creates its own action. I think that is the really important thing because what is needed now is not more knowledge, not new beliefs, whether communist or any other kind, but individuals who are capable of understanding all this conflict, who can look at it with clarity, with a mind uncorrupted, so that they are a light unto themselves. You cannot be a light unto yourself if you are merely a part of the social mechanism, which has very little significance. I think the real revolution is not economic or political but a deep psychological revolution which makes you aware of the false as the false and thereby brings about that which is new, the real, the true.

I shall answer some questions, but before I begin to discuss them, I think it is important to find out what a problem is. A problem exists only when it has taken root in the mind. Once an issue takes root in the mind, it becomes a problem, and then the mind will have to solve the problem, but having its root in the conditioned mind, the problem becomes insoluble. And is it possible not to allow any issue to take root in the mind but to deal with it directly and immediately as it arises? But we cannot deal with it directly if we condemn it, if we are identified with it, if we in any way judge it, because our judgment, our condemnation, our comparison, is the outcome of our conditioning, and therefore it only strengthens the problem.

So, what is important is to look at a problem, an issue, without condemnation, without comparing it with something else, and that is very difficult because we are brought up from childhood to compare, to judge, to evaluate, and thereby we create a duality and hence conflict. And is it possible to look at the problem, whatever it be, without allowing it to take root in the mind by comparing, judging, condemning it, or by identifying oneself with the problem?

What I am saying is not very difficult if you will observe your own process of thinking. You see, you have a problem because it has already taken root, and to resolve it, you either find an answer for it, or you condemn it, you push it away and think about something else, escape from it, which only strengthens the problem. But if one can really look at it without any sense of condemnation, without any sense of identification, then surely the problem has quite a different significance, has it not?

So, problems exist only when they have taken root in the mind, and the mind which has absorbed the problem, in which the seed of the problem has already taken root, is incapable of solving it, however much it may struggle with the problem. To understand the problem, the mind must be really still, and the mind is still only when there is no sense of condemnation, identification, or comparison. And when the mind is still, will there then be a problem at all? The problem exists because we are confused, and confusion arises when we are seeking some form of solution to the problem, or when we are following a particular system, or are casting the shadow of some dogma or belief, or are caught in previous knowledge. But if we can understand the process of how the problem arises and therefore cease to condemn, compare, will there be a problem? Obviously you cannot answer because you have never tried any of these things. All that you have done is to condemn, to compare, or to identify yourself with the problem. And it is extraordinarily difficult to be free from that process because all our training is to compare, and we think that through comparison, we shall understand. Surely, understanding comes not through comparison, not through pursuing all kinds of activities, but only when the mind is very quiet, undisturbed.

You see, we are so afraid of a mind that is not occupied. A mind that is merely occupied is a petty mind, whether it is occupied with the highest knowledge, or with the daily activities of the kitchen, or the job. Such a mind is incapable of being free. Being occupied, when the problem arises we are incapable of dealing with it because we have not understood the whole process of our thinking, and so we turn to leaders, or we turn to books, we turn to knowledge, we turn to religion, which are the outcome of our own confusion and the confusion of our leaders.

So, in discussing these questions, there can obviously be no yes and no. There is no answer to life, there is only living, but we have made living into a problem. In our living there is no joy, there is not the real bliss that comes with aloneness, with that freedom in which alone reality can come into being.

Questioner: How can we achieve enduring peace within ourselves?

Krishnamurti: Do you think peace is a thing to be achieved, to be got as a result, as a reward? Or does peace come into being when we understand the various factors that bring about disturbance? It is like a man who is full of hatred wanting love. He may practice love, but it has no meaning. Whereas, if we understand the whole process of hatred and fear, then perhaps that which is love will be.

But, you see, our difficulty is that we want to find peace, though we are violent. We want to find love when we are creating antagonism, hatred. When there is fear in our hearts, without understanding fear, without understanding what that disturbance is, we run away from it in order to find peace, and so there is a duality in us.

The problem, then, is not how to attain peace but what is preventing us from understanding the causes that bring about disturbance, chaos, misery, struggle, pain, both in us and outside of us. Surely, if we can understand that, there will be peace, we don't have to seek it. If we seek peace, we are running away from *what is.* In the understanding of *what is,* the actual, there is peace.

Please, this is not a theory. If we really go into this problem of why the mind is disturbed and understand it, then without creating a schizophrenic action, a dual process, a conflict within ourselves, we shall find peace. Peace is not the result of discipline; peace of mind does not come about through any form of compulsion, through any practice, which only puts a limitation on the mind. A petty mind can have no peace. A petty mind practicing various forms of discipline, looking for peace, will never find it. It may find some kind of consolation, satisfaction, but that is not peace.

So, what is important is to understand why the mind is disturbed. What is this disturbance? Basically, fundamentally, does it not come about when there is this constant urge to be something, the desire for a result, the desire for self-improvement, the desire to achieve a certain noble action? As long as one is competitive, ambitious, there must be disturbance, there must be conflict. Without beginning near, we want to go far, but we can go far only when we begin very near. And beginning near is freedom from ambition, from wanting to be something, from the desire to be successful, to be recognized, to be famous—a dozen things which are all indications of the self, the 'me', the ego.

As long as the ego exists, there must be disturbance, and if the ego seeks peace, its peace is the result, the opposite of a disturbance, therefore it is not peace at all. If one realizes this, if one does not merely hear it but actually experiences it, then peace will come. But that requires a great deal of awareness, an awareness in which there is no choice because if you choose, then you are back again in the process of acquiring, attaining.

What is important, surely, is not to search for peace, not to pursue swamis, yogis, teachers in Oriental form, but to find out for ourselves how our own minds are working, how ambitious we are. You may not be personally ambitious, but you may be ambitious for a group, for the nation, for the party you belong to, or for an idea, or you may worship God, as you call it. Having failed in this world, you want to succeed in another world. So, as long as any movement of the self exists, there must be disturbance, there can be no peace.

Questioner: Will the practice of yoga help me spiritually and physically?

Krishnamurti: How eager we are to improve ourselves! Do you think self- improvement will bring you bliss or reality? You may derive from yoga certain benefits physically. But do you think self-improvement—that is, the 'me' becoming better, gaining more knowledge, more information, the self improving and becoming more virtuous—do you think that process will bring about the tranquillity of the mind? In that process there is not the abnegation or the disappearance of the self, but on the contrary, the self, the 'me', is becoming something better, and therefore it is always struggling, there is a battle going on both within and outside of itself. And do you think that will bring tranquillity to the mind? Do you think that is spiritual?

What do we mean by the word *spiritual?* It is something of the spirit, something which is not of time, something which is not manufactured by the mind, is it not? Surely, the real, that which is truly spiritual, is not a thing put together by the mind, and therefore it cannot be practiced by the mind. The mind is the result of many yesterdays, of innumerable experiences, of knowledge, influences; it is put together by time. And can the mind, which is the result of time, find that which is timeless, measureless? You may practice any amount of virtue, but surely that is not spiritual. When the mind, understanding the whole process of becoming, is totally free from every form of ambition—which means, really, when the mind is utterly still and is therefore not projecting itself into the future—only then is there that which may be called the spiritual. But as long as we are struggling to be spiritual, we are just being ordinarily petty, that is all, only we call it by a big name.

Questioner: I am attracted by your philosophy, but if I were to follow you, I should have to leave my church. What do you offer in exchange?

KRISHNAMURTI: Following another is evil. Please listen to this. To follow another is evil because it breeds authority, fear, imitativeness. And through following you will never find anything except that which you wish to find, which is your own gratification.

What I am saying is not a philosophy. What we are trying to do is really to discover through our own awareness the process of ourself. To discover what is true, we have to find out what is illusory and what is false. You cannot be led to discover. If you are led, there is no discovery. Discovery comes only when the mind is very quiet, not demanding, not asking, not begging, unafraid.

But we are afraid. That is why we worship leaders, that is why we have churches, priests, and the whole gamut of modern civilization. Being afraid, we want to escape from it, we want to find a refuge, and so we belong to something.

I am not asking you to leave your church or to belong to a church. To me, that is all immature activity, it doesn't mean anything. As nationalism separates man and causes wars, so religions, churches separate man and create antagonism. They do not lead to truth. Though everyone says there are many paths to truth, there is no path to truth. It is to the free mind—the mind that stands alone, uncorrupted, uninfluenced—it is only to such a mind that truth comes, which means, really, a mind that is unafraid.

So, there is nothing to be offered to one who leaves his particular cage and enters another. We are talking not of the different cages, the different churches and religious organizations, but of understanding oneself. The way of understanding is not merely to be free from a particular church, from a particular organization, nationality, or belief, but to be totally free, unafraid, and only such a mind can receive that which is ever timeless. And it seems to me that only such a mind can solve the present problem, not a mind that is becoming more religious, which means becoming more entrenched in a particular dogma, or following a particular system of thought. Such a mind is not a religious mind. The truly religious mind is a free mind, and being free, it is quiet, still; therefore, reality can come into being. It is that reality, which creates its own action, that will solve the problems of the world, not the mind that is burdened with knowledge, or the mind that has accumulated experience, because knowledge, experience, is the result of our particular conditioning.

When you realize all this, not merely intellectually, verbally, but when you actually experience it, then you will find that you do not have to belong to anything, that you are a total human being with complete self-knowledge; therefore, there is no disturbance, and hence there is that peace of mind in which reality can come into being.

May 28, 1954

Fifth Talk in New York City, New York

It seems to me that without self-knowledge most of our beliefs and activities have very little significance. And self-knowledge is not acquired from books; it is not a matter of learning from someone how to know about yourself, nor is it, I think, merely a process of gathering information about oneself. Most of us know only a positive way of thinking, which I feel is the lowest form of thinking. That is, merely to accumulate knowledge about oneself and live according to that knowledge only leads to a further strengthening of the ego, of the 'me', with all its complications. The highest form of thinking is negative, is it not? Surely, negative thinking is the highest form of thinking, and the discovery of how to think negatively can come about only through awareness of the responses of the self from moment to moment.

We all know what to think, that is, we have been brought up from childhood to judge what is right, what is wrong, to compare, and so on, which is a positive way of thinking. This positive way of thinking is the strengthening of experience, and the more we acquire it, the more we think we are learning, finding out about ourselves. That is, we think that the strengthening of the past will give us understanding.

Isn't that the way we think? The more we can study, the more we can analyze, the more we can store up experience and let that experience, that knowledge, guide our activity, the more secure, the more positive we are. That is the way we live, is it not? And that doesn't give any space to discover because our experience is always conditioning us, always telling us what to think, how to approach life, and so on. Therefore there is never a negative approach to the problems of our existence because the more experience we have, the more the mind is conditioned, is it not?

I may be saying something which perhaps you have not heard before, and if so, please don't discard it or listen to it merely to find out what you think about it because what you think about it will be according to your experience. To listen in order to discover the truth of what is being said and to listen in order to form an opinion about it are two different things, are they not? When I make a statement, what is important, surely, is not whether you can accept it or how you can use it but to find out whether in itself it is true or false, and to see the truth or the falseness of what is being said, one has to suspend all one's judgments, one's reactions, which is quite an arduous task. That is why the way you listen is very, very important. As I have said over and over again, these talks will be utterly useless if you are merely gathering ideas to be utilized or to be thought over later. But if, as we proceed, we can together find out the truth of what is being said, then perhaps this, and the past talks, and the last talk tomorrow may be of some significance.

As I was saying, we have been trained in what to think about God, about truth, we have been educated to be nationalistic, and so on. Our minds are shaped from childhood, influenced by ideas, and any experience we have must be related with those ideas, with those beliefs. Therefore, experience never frees the mind. Do please listen to this. Experience never frees the mind, and yet we are pursuing experience, greater, wider, more significant experience. And when we do have an experience totally unconnected with the past, we take that experience and hold it in memory, which prevents the further birth of new experience. That is, our minds are being constantly influenced, shaped by past experience, and so the mind can never renew itself, it can never be a totally new instrument. Our own past experiences are conditioning both the future and the immediate, the now, because we are thinking positively in terms of time—what I have been, what I am, what I shall be—and all further experience, all human knowledge, is based on this conditioning. So, knowledge in that sense becomes an impediment to creative understanding.

It seems to me that the highest form of thinking is negative. Negative thinking is not accumulation but the constant discovery of what is true in relationship, which means seeing myself as I actually am from moment to moment. This self-knowledge is not a process in which the mind is gathering information in order to act rightly or to avoid wrong action. And self-knowledge is essential because if I do not know the process of my own thinking, if I am unaware of my own reactions, of my background, of the unconscious responses, compulsions, urges, then whatever thought I may have is conditioned by my past, and hence there is no freedom. So, is it not important to find out what is, to be self-aware without the process of accumulation? Because the moment I accumulate in the understanding of myself, that accumulation is going to dictate how I shall understand the next discovery.

You see, we are concerned with how to improve ourselves, or how to improve society; therefore, change is merely a modified continuity, is it not? I gather, I learn, and I am using what I have learned to change, but what I have learned depends on my conditioning; my learning is always dictated by the past, so experience is never a liberating factor. If I see that, if I see the truth of it, then I can proceed to find out without accumulation.

Please, it seems to me that this is important to understand. Why does the mind accumulate knowledge, acquire virtue? Why does the mind constantly strive to become something, to perfect itself? Why? And in the process of acquisition, accumulation, is not the mind burdened? Surely, all accumulation in self-knowledge is a hindrance to the further discovery of the self, and it is this accumulation that is making us think positively. Now, is it possible to discover and not be acquisitive so that the discovery does not leave an experience which will condition further discovery?

I hope I am making myself clear because I think this is important. This is really the freedom from the self so that there is no accumulative entity, and therefore there is creative being. Accumulation is not creativeness. A mind which is constantly acquiring can obviously never be creative. It is only the free mind that is creative, and there can be no freedom if every experience is stored up because that which is accumulated becomes the center of the 'me', of the 'I', which thinks positively. Positive thinking is the result of accumulation.

Let me put it this way, and perhaps it will be more clear. In my relationship with another—if I am at all awareness—I discover my reactions, I watch my own status and how the previous experiences of discovery either condemn or justify what I have newly discovered in relationship. That new discovery is also stored up, and when next I am aware of my relationship with another and see my reactions, which is the process of self-knowledge, the past again dictates or translates in terms of the past what I have discovered.

Surely, what I am saying is not very complicated. It is simple enough if we look at it. You see, as long as I am accumulating, gathering, storing up, my mind is thinking in terms of what to do and how to do it, and therefore my mind can never be free because the whole process of my thinking is based on past accumulation, on past experience. So, thinking only prevents further discovery. What is thinking? It is the response of the past, verbalized and communicated, the past being the accumulations, the various influences, the conditionings of the mind. Thinking can never resolve the problem, thinking can never bring about a completely new state, a total transformation of our being, because thinking is the result of the past.

Now, is it possible for thought to come to an end? That is the problem. If thought can come to an end, then there is the cessation of all accumulation, and hence there is a possibility of the new. This is not as fantastic as it sounds, if you really go into the matter. When you think, surely your thinking is the result of the past, of your conditioning, of your belief, of your background, conscious or unconscious. According to your background you respond, and that response is called thinking, and through thinking you want to solve your problems. And the more you acquire, the more you accumulate experience, the greater you think will be your capacity to go into the problem and resolve it.

So, when you see that, then the inevitable question arises within yourself, which is: Can thought come to an end so that I can discover the truth of the problem and not translate it in terms of my experience or according to my background? Thinking is really a positive process and not a liberating process. We are brought up from childhood to know what to think; newspapers, magazines, everything around us tells us what to think. We are accustomed to gathering, to accumulating, which prevents us from actually understanding any particular problem totally and completely. We can understand a problem completely only when the mind is still, which is when there is no compulsion of any kind.

If you have really listened to this, you will not ask how thought is to come to an end, you will not say, "Tell me the method." The very asking of that question, the desire for a method, is another form of accumulation. But, if you see the truth that only with the ending of thought can the problem be resolved, if you see it without trying to utilize it, then you will discover the significance of the whole process of thinking. Thinking actually strengthens the 'me', the self—the self which is the maker of trouble, the maker of mischief, misery, whether it is identified with a nation, with a group, with a religion, or with an idea. Thinking is the outcome of the 'me', which has been accumulated for centuries, so thinking will not solve our problems; on the contrary, it will multiply them, bring greater misery. If we see the truth of that, if through self-knowledge we see the truth of how the mind works, the conscious as well as the unconscious, if we are aware of the total process, then that very awareness will bring about the cessation of thought, and therefore stillness of the mind.

You know, we all have many problems which we seem to multiply. The resolution of one problem produces other problems, so our minds are everlastingly caught in problems, and we are always seeking answers to these problems because fundamentally we want to use everything for our own benefit. If we hear something which is true, which we have caught the significance of, we immediately want to utilize it, we say, "How can I use it in order to improve myself, to arrive at a more advanced stage?" So, we are always increasing our problems. Whereas, if we are able to see what is true and leave it alone, not try to utilize it, then that very truth will operate, we don't have to do anything. As long as we are doing something about it, we shall create problems.

Please listen to this. The difficulty is to pay attention, to give our whole being to discover, to find out. And when we do find out what is true, we want to utilize it, either socially or to make ourselves happy, to be peaceful. Whereas, if we really give our whole attention, listen completely with our whole being, then that very perception of what is true, if we leave it alone, will begin to operate in spite of us.

Questioner: In this country we have always felt secure, but now our spiritual and physical well-being is threatened and fear is shaping our thinking. How can we overcome this fear?

KRISHNAMURTI: As long as you are pursuing security in any form, there must be fear. Please listen to this, follow it. As long as you as a nation, as a group, as an individual, want to be safe, secure in your belief, in an idea, in anything, you are inviting fear, your shadow is fear. As long as you remain an American, a Hindu, a Russian, a communist, a Catholic, a Protestant, or what you will, there must be fear.

You see, we know this; we are deeply aware of this fact, but superficially we create a system which we think will give us security—nationalities which are separative, religions which are mere bigotry, dividing man against man. So, as long as we remain isolated in our nationalism, in our belief, in our own security, there must be wars, there must be hatred, there must be antagonism, and therefore fear.

And do we ever directly experience what is fear? Please, listen to this question. Do we ever directly experience what is fear? Knowing that we are afraid, we run away from it, do we not? We try to overcome it, we justify or condemn it, which are ways of avoiding and not directly experiencing fear.

Do you understand what I am saying? You experience directly any form of pleasure, you don't let anything interfere with it, but any form of unpleasantness you try to avoid. Fear is unpleasant, so you are never in direct relationship with it, you never directly experience it. When there is fear, you try to overcome it, you try to find out what to do about it. Your mind is already occupied, not with the direct experience of fear, but with how to overcome it. Do you ever experience fear directly, without any interpretation, without avoidance, justification, or condemnation so that there is a direct relationship with fear, and you know totally that you are afraid? Are you ever in that state? Obviously not. Because, when one is directly experiencing fear, then is there fear? It is only when one is avoiding or running away that there is fear. As long as your mind is seeking security in any form, physical, emotional, or psychological, there must be fear. That is a fact, whether you like it or not. As long as you are only thinking of the American way of life, of improving your own standards, of having more money, more material welfare, while half the world has only one meal, or half a meal a day, there must be fear.

Now, if you know that you are afraid because of this desire to be secure, can you look at that fear and be with it completely? Experiment with what I am saying and you will see that the thing which we call fear is a process in which the mind gives a name to a particular quality, and that this very naming strengthens the quality.

Suppose I am jealous, envious, and I am aware of that feeling. My awareness of it is a process of naming and then recognizing that feeling through the name. So the naming of it strengthens that particular feeling. The process of recognition is a process of strengthening what is recognized. When I name fear, I have strengthened fear, and therefore I run away.

Observe for yourself the process of your own thinking. When you have fear, watch and you will see how you condemn it, how you want to run away from it. You want to shape it, you want to push it away, you want to do something about it, because it is unpleasant.

But when you have a pleasant thing, you are identified with it totally. Identification and avoidance is the process of naming, is it not? And when you give a term to a particular feeling, you strengthen that feeling.

Is it possible for the mind to be free from the desire to be secure, and therefore free from fear? The two go together, do they not? You cannot get rid of fear and yet seek security. The desire for security in any form —security in relationship with another, in any experience—can only breed fear, and after you have bred fear, you want to overcome it. You cannot overcome fear. All that you can do is to find out the whole process that brings about the state of fear, see the truth of it, and leave it alone. Then you don't have to overcome fear. The truth will operate. The fact that you are afraid and are not directly related to the fact—that is in itself the factor which, if you are conscious of it, is going to liberate the mind from fear.

Please, you are not learning anything from me. If you are learning, you are accumulating, and therefore you are not discovering. What I am saying is actually what is happening in each one of us. If you don't discover it, but merely learn it, then it has no meaning. But if, as you listen, you observe your own process of thinking, then you will discover it—then it is yours, not mine. Then you don't have to follow a single thing, you don't have to follow any person or idea because you are a light unto yourself. Then there is no fear of authority, and all the evils of following it are gone.

Questioner: Compulsive judgment and self-incrimination hold the mind in a firm grip. Since the compelling force is so strong, how is one to free oneself from these things? How are we to stay with an essential problem since our strength of endurance is undermined by fears?

Krishnamurti: You see, one of the difficulties is that we want to be free—free from fear, free from compulsive urges, free from our background, free from our conditioning. That is, we want to be free from suffering and hold on to pleasure. Please watch your own mind. You are not merely listening to me, you are observing the process of your own mind because I have nothing to say except to point out how your own mind is operating and destroying freedom.

As long as you want to be free, there is no freedom. But is it not possible to know all the compulsive forces, influences, to be aware of them and not try to be free from them? If you want to be free from them, you resist, and that very resistance creates problems. And if you observe these compulsive forces in yourself, with their strength and their fears, you will see how difficult it is simply to be aware of them without condemning, without choosing, without saying, "This is good, that is bad, this I am going to hold, that I am going to let go"—which is really not being aware. After all, each one of us is caught in various forms of compulsive force, and when this is pointed out to us, or when we casually or superficially become aware of it, we want to free ourselves of it, and this very desire to be free creates a resistance against it.

So, knowing that you have compulsive urges, what is important is to look at them, live with them, and understand them; and you can understand them only when you don't want to run away from them, when you don't justify, compare, or condemn them. If you see the compulsive force and just remain there without trying to free yourself from it, then you will find that the thing which you wanted to be free from has dropped away from you without your making an effort to be free.

Questioner: What to you is prayer and meditation?

Krishnamurti: It does not matter very much what they are to me, but let us find out what is the truth, the significance of prayer and meditation. If I tell you what to me is prayer and meditation, it will only be an opinion, and apparently many people are interested in gathering opinions, but here we are not concerned with opinions. We want to find out what is the truth of this matter and not look at it according to the opinion of the Catholics, the Protestants, the Buddhists, or the Hindus. That does not bring about liberation of the mind but only a superficial change, a modified continuity.

So, we are not concerned with opinion, whether Oriental or Occidental, but with trying to find out the implications of prayer and of the whole question of what is meditation.

Is meditation synonymous with prayer? Do you pray? Why do you pray? We are not concerned with how you should pray, or what is the best form of prayer, but with why you pray because that is the fact—so let us start with that.

Why do you pray? When there is clarity, when there is joy, bliss, or what you will, do you pray then? Surely, that very joy, that bliss, is a form of heightened intelligence or living. We pray only when we are confused, when we are in sorrow, when we want something. That is so, is it not? A mind that is very clear, free, untrammeled, without any problems—why should it pray? It is itself in a state of incorruptibility. It is when we do not know whom to follow, when we have the multiplication of problems, when we are in sorrow, when we are hopelessly lost, frustrated, unfulfilled—it is only then that we want someone to help us, and therefore we pray. We repeat certain sentences, we force the mind to be still because the very suffering compels us to be quiet.

The compulsion to prayer, then, is the desire to overcome fear or sorrow, and naturally there is a response. When you ask, you are given, and what you receive depends on the state of your mind, of your desire, of your misery. When you pray, you take a certain posture, repeat certain words, and thereby quiet the conscious mind; and when the conscious mind is quiet, the unconscious may produce an answer to your particular suffering, to your immediate problem; or the answer may come to the quiet conscious mind, not from within, but from outside yourself. But surely, that is not meditation. Meditation is emptying the mind of the known. After all, meditation is not concentration. You can concentrate on anything in which you are interested, which is an obvious fact. Being absorbed in a particular idea, in the repetition of a particular word or sentence, or in projecting an image, a symbol, a savior—surely, none of that is meditation. The projection comes from the background of your conditioning, and living in that image is not meditation. And yet this is what most of us call meditation, is it not? We want to know how to meditate. Books have been written about it, and when they talk about meditation, concentration, absorption, it implies resistance, discipline, which only strengthens the past, filling and narrowing the mind.

It seems to me that meditation is something totally different because concentration on an idea is an exclusive, acquisitive process which merely brings certain forms of satisfaction and gratification. Surely, meditation is the discovery of what is true from moment to moment. Please listen to this. As long as I am practicing a method, the method will produce a result, but the result is not what is true. It is a product of the mind in its desire to be safe, to be comforted; therefore, the mind is never empty, it is filled, occupied, and such a mind can never allow the unknown to come into being. You may practice meditation for years and be able to control your mind completely, but then what? What have you done? Your mind is still petty, small, conditioned by the past, filled with the known, and so the unknown can never come into being.

Meditation, then, is a process of freeing the mind through self-knowledge from all the things that it has accumulated—not just from one form of accumulation which is painful but from every form of accumulation, from everything that it has known, experienced so that not only the conscious mind but consciousness as a whole is totally empty, free. It is only then that the immeasurable, that which is not put together by the mind, which is not sought after, comes into being. But it cannot come into being if you invite it because your invitation is merely the desire for comfort, the desire to save yourself, the desire to avoid pain.

So, your mind is everlastingly struggling to become something or wanting greater experience through meditation. But true meditation is the understanding that comes through self-knowledge, and that understanding is not the outcome of accumulation. If there is any sense of the experiencer apart from the experience, then the mind is not empty. As long as the mind is seeking experience, there must be the experiencer; therefore, there is an urge, a compulsion to expand, to gather, to accumulate. When the mind sees the whole significance of thinking or experiencing, only then is there a possibility of emptying the mind so that the mind itself is the unknown, not the experiencer of the unknown.

May 29, 1954

Sixth Talk in New York City, New York

If I may repeat what I said the other day, these talks have very little significance if we do not directly experience what is being said, and that experience is immediate; it is not to be thought over or remembered and put into practice, because direct experience of what is true will have its own effect without the mind seeking to act upon it. That is why it is very important to listen not only to what is being said but to everything in life. When we hear another say something, when we read, when we hear the birds or the sound of the restless sea, it is important to listen because in the very act of listening there is a direct experience which is uncontaminated by any of our prejudices, our particular conditioning. It seems to me that most of us find it extremely arduous to listen because we have read so much and we justify or compare it with what we hear, or we try to remember what is being said in order to think it over. So the mind is restless and therefore not listening.

Most of us have many problems, and the solution to these problems lies not in searching for the solution but in listening to the actual content of the problem. We are all seeking happiness at different levels—we want permanency, security, someone to take us over to the other side, to a permanent state of bliss. We are searching for something, and that is our life, moving from one object of search to another. We are never satisfied. Consciously or unconsciously, we are always pursuing, searching, and the background of this search, if we go into the process, is really the urge to find some kind of satisfaction, some kind of permanency, happiness. We have made search as inevitable as breathing, living, and we say life has no meaning if we do not seek. So, we are everlastingly pursuing, looking for something at different levels.

As long as we are seeking, we must create authority, we must follow or have a following. And it seems to me that this is one of the most crucial points: Whether there is anyone—a savior, a Master, an enlightened one, it doesn't matter who it is—who can ever lead us to reality. Yet that is what each one of us is seeking, and we have accepted the search as inevitable. Without seeking, we say life has no meaning, but we never go behind that word to find out the whole significance of this urge to seek, to find. You have been told that if you seek you will find. But your search, if you go into the process of it, is the outcome of a desire to find some kind of security, some kind of hope, some kind of fulfillment, a bliss, a continuity in which there is no frustration. And as long as you are seeking, you must create authority—the authority that will take you over, that will lead you, give you comfort.

Is it not important to ask ourselves if there is anyone, any authority who can give us that truth which we think will be satisfactory? And we have never asked ourselves what is the state of the mind if all search ceases. Search implies a process of time, does it not? So, we use time as a means of understanding something which is beyond time. Search implies a continuity, and continuity means time, a series of experiences which we hope will lead us to truth, and if those experiences do not take us to that which we are seeking, then we turn to somebody else; we disregard the old and take on a new leader, a new teacher, a new savior.

So, what I am asking is not that we should deny search, because we are caught in it, but will seeking lead to reality?—reality being the unknown, that which is not the product of the mind, which is a state of creativeness, which is totally new from moment to moment, which is timeless, eternal, or whatever other word can be used to indicate that it is out of time.

I think it is important to ask ourselves this question. You may not find the answer. But if you are really persistent with the question, "Why do I seek?" and let that question reveal the content of your search, then perhaps there may be a moment, a second, when all search ceases. Because, search implies effort, does it not? Search implies choice—choice from among the various systems that will lead you, the various methods, practices, disciplines, saviors, Masters, gurus. You have to choose, and your choice invariably depends on your conditioning and your gratification. Therefore, your search is really dictated by your conscious or unconscious desire.

Please follow all this—not that I am trying to guide your thinking, but I am just pointing out what it is we are doing. At the moment of rest from this constant struggle, is there not the freedom from search? And so inevitably, when one examines this process of search, the question arises, does it not, whether anyone can lead us to what we call truth, reality, God, or whatever name you like to give it?

Do you understand the problem? We are used to being led, following a savior, a Master, having someone to tell us what to do. We follow what another says because he has fasted, practiced discipline, become an ascetic; we think he has arrived, found enlightenment, and so we go to him. All religions maintain that you must have someone who is enlightened, who knows the truth, and that in his presence, with the example of his way of life, you will find it. But is there anyone who can lead you to truth? To me, that whole process is destructive, it is uncreative, it will not lead to that which is timeless because the very process of seeking implies time. We use time to understand that which is beyond time. And can the mind which for centuries, generation after generation, has been caught in this process of seeking—can that mind not seek? That is, can the search for any kind of gratification come to an end?—which doesn't mean that you should be satisfied with *what is*.

You see, the difficulty in this is that when we have gone far in our questioning, in our inquiry, we come to an impasse, and then we stop, but the stopping is merely a compulsion. If we could find a way out, we would pursue it. So, can you who are listening be without a guide, without seeking, and therefore understand this whole process of time?

Even though one may not understand the full significance of what is being said, I think it is very important to listen to it. Because, after all, life isn't merely a series of conflicts, it isn't just a matter of earning a livelihood, of living comfortably in a sumptuous flat and enjoying worldly things. That isn't the whole content of life. That is only part of it, and if one is satisfied with the part, then inevitably there is confusion leading to misery and destruction.

Life is a total process, is it not? It must be lived at all levels, completely, and a mind that is satisfied with any one particular level of existence is inviting sorrow. In its very structure, by its very nature, the mind is always curious, wanting to know, wanting to find out whether there is something beyond this thing that we call living, beyond our struggles, our efforts, our miseries, our passing joys, sensations. But can I know what is beyond through mere curiosity, by reading what someone has said who has had experience of something beyond? Or can the mind experience what is beyond only when it is uncontaminated, totally alone, uninfluenced, and therefore no longer seeking? If you are listening, not to what I am saying, but to the process of your own mind, doesn't this question inevitably arise—the question as to whether this struggle to find reality, to discover something beyond the transient, has any meaning? If we cannot find satisfaction in one direction, don't we turn to something else? In the Orient they are starving, therefore, they turn to God. This is the process of existence in the Orient and in the Occident, it is not only limited to the oriental people.

Can there be the cessation of all search, and therefore the freedom from all compulsion, all authority—the authority created by religions, the authority which each one creates in his search, in his demand, in his hope? We all want to find a state in which there is no disturbance of any kind, a peace which is not put together by the mind, because what is put together can be undone by the mind. And it seems to me that as long as the mind is seeking, it must create authority, and when it is completely lost in fear, in imitation, it can no longer find what is true. Yet that is what is happening throughout the world. Through the tyranny of governments and the tyranny of religions, there is the conditioning of each child, each human being, to a particular form of thinking, however wide or however narrow, and this conditioning, whether here or in Russia, is obviously going to prevent any discovery of what is true. And is it possible for each one of us to find out what is true without seeking? Because search implies time, search implies gaining an end, search implies dissatisfaction, which is the motive of your search for gratification or happiness. All that implies time, the tomorrow, not only chronologically, but psychologically, inwardly.

And is it possible to experience, not in terms of time, but immediately, that state when the mind is no longer seeking? The immediacy is important, not how to arrive at that state when the mind is no longer seeking because then you introduce all the factors of struggle, of time. And I think it is important not only to listen to that question but actually to put it to yourself and leave it, not try to find the answer to it. According to the way you put it and the earnestness of your question, you will find the answer. For that which is measureless cannot be caught by a mind that is seeking, by a mind that is full of knowledge; it can come into being only when the mind is no longer pursuing or trying to become something. When the mind is completely inwardly empty, not demanding anything, only then is there that instantaneous perception of what is true.

In discussing some of these questions, we are not trying to solve the problem; we are together taking the journey of investigation. As long as we are limited by our own experience and knowledge, the problem can never be solved. And is it possible for the mind to look at the problem, not in terms of its own cognizance, but just to look at it, without any resistance? Surely, resistance is the problem. If there is no resistance there is no problem. But our whole life is a process of resistance; we are Christians or Hindus, communists or capitalists, and so on. We have built walls around ourselves, and it is these walls that create the problem, and then we look at the problem from within our particular wall. Don't ask, "How am I going to get out of the enclosure?" The moment you put that question, you have brought in another problem, and so we multiply problem after problem. We don't see the truth simply and clearly that resistance creates problems, and leave it there. Surely, what matters is to be aware of the resistance, not how to break down the resistance. And awareness is not something extraordinary, beyond. It begins very simply—by being aware of your talk, of your reactions, just seeing, watching all that without judgment or condemnation. It is very difficult to do this because all our conditioning for centuries is preventing awareness without choice. But be aware that you are choosing, that you are condemning, that you are comparing; just be aware of it without saying, "How am I not to compare?" because then you introduce another problem. The important thing is to be aware that you do compare, that you are always condemning, justifying, consciously or unconsciously—just be aware of that whole process. You will say, "Is that all?" You ask that question because you hope through awareness you will get somewhere. Therefore your awareness is not awareness but a process in which you are going to get something, which means that awareness is merely a coin which you are using. If you can simply be aware that you are using awareness as a coin to buy something, and proceed from there, then you will begin to discover the whole process of your own thinking, of your being, in the relationship of existence.

Questioner: You have said that nationalities, beliefs, dogmas are separative. Is the family also a separative force?

Krishnamurti: As long as there is any form of identification with the family, with a national group, with a dogma, with a belief, obviously it is separative. If I identify myself with India, with its past, with its religion, with its dogmas, with its nationality, I am obviously building a wall around myself through identification with what I think is greater than myself.

Surely, the question is not whether the family or the group is separative, but why the mind identifies itself with something and thereby creates division. Why do I identify myself with India? Because, if I do not identify myself with India, with America, with the Orient, or the Occident, or what you will, I am lost, I feel alone, deserted. This fear of being lonely, alone, compels me to identify myself with my family, with my property, with a house, with a belief. It is that that is bringing separation, not the family. If I do not identify myself with something, what am I? I am nobody. But if I say I am an Indian with oriental wisdom and all that nonsense—you know the whole business of it—then I am somebody. If I identify myself with America or with Russia, it gives me prestige, it makes me feel worthwhile, it gives me a sense of significance in life, because I do not want to be nobody, I do not want to be anonymous. I may bear a name, but the name must bring importance. I am unwilling to be really nobody, to have no identification of the 'me' with something which I call bigger: God, truth, country, family, or ideology.

It is this process of identification that is separative, destructive. Please listen to this. This is your problem because the world is being divided now into two dogmatic identifications which are increasing the separative force. We are human beings, not Indians or Americans or Russians, and is it possible to live without identifying, to be nobody in this world where everyone is struggling to be somebody? Surely it is possible. Your trying to be somebody is leading to misery, to wars, all of which implies the search for power, and when you seek power as an individual, as a group, or as a nation, you are bringing about your own destruction. This is a fact.

Can you and I remain in solitude inwardly, without seeking power, without identifying with anything?—which means, really, having no fear. You will find the answer for yourself if you go into the problem.

Questioner: Do you deny the value and integrity of saints in all ages, including Christ and Buddha?

KRISHNAMURTI: This raises a very interesting question. Why do you want saints? Why do you want heroes? Why do you want examples? And who is a saint? Because a church canonizes somebody, is he a saint? And what is your measure of a saint? Your measure will be according to your desires, hopes, and conditionings. But, you see, the mind wants somebody to cling to, something beyond itself. You want leaders, saints, examples to follow, to imitate, because in yourself you are poor, insufficient, so you say, "If I can follow somebody, I shall be enriched." You will never be enriched, you will be made the poorer because it is only when the mind, when our whole being is empty, not seeking, that the creativeness of reality comes into being.

You don't have to believe what I am saying. Your saints, your leaders have led you nowhere. You have only wars, misery, strife, a continuous battle within and without. But if you can see what you are—that you are inwardly poor, that you are caught in struggles, miseries—see it and not try to change it into something else, which only modifies it, if you can remain with *what is* without any desire to transform it, then there is transformation. But as long as the mind is trying to imitate, to adjust, to measure with its preconceived ideas who is a saint and who is not, then it is merely pursuing its own fulfillment, which is vanity.

Questioner: I am a young man without any religion. I do not consider any system of government as my authority. I lack ambition, and I do not have a job, nor can I keep one for very long because I am not ambitious. I create misery in my home because I am financially dependent on my parents, and they are not sufficiently well off to support me. How might we look at this problem?

KRISHNAMURTI: You are living in a society whose structure, morality, and ethics, though it may say the contrary, are based on acquisitiveness, on envy. Not to fit into that society implies either that you are totally free from ambition and are therefore not acquisitive, or that mentally there is something wrong, because to be without ambition is astonishingly difficult; I may not be ambitious in the worldly sense, but I may be seeking something else; I want to be happy, I want to fulfill myself in my children, in my activity, and so on. So, it is a very rare thing to find someone who is not ambitious, competing, striving.

But it is comparatively easy to be lazy. Please don't laugh at this or misinterpret what you have heard to suit your particular mode of thinking. If one is not ambitious even though one lives in a world that is full of ambition, where every individual, group, and nation is seeking power, position, prestige, then to find out why one is not ambitious is very important, is it not? It may be a disease; it may be a weakness of mind. Or you may have imposed upon yourself the condition that you must not be ambitious.

To understand the whole problem of ambition, of strife, and to find out what it really means to live in a competitive society without striving to be somebody is a very difficult thing to do because if we fail in this world, we want to succeed in the next world, we want to sit at the right hand of God. Not to seek any form of fulfillment requires great understanding, for each one of us is seeking fulfillment, and when we seek fulfillment, there is frustration. You may be aware of that frustration beforehand and therefore try to avoid all kinds of ambition, all desire to fulfill, but that only imprisons you in your own conclusion. Whereas, to understand the process of fulfillment, to go through it, to be aware that one's whole drive, urge, compulsion, is towards fulfillment, and that thereby there is frustration and sorrow, and to ask oneself if there is any such thing as fulfillment at all—surely, all that requires self-knowledge.

Questioner: If we could experience immortality, would there be fear of death?

KRISHNAMURTI: Is it possible for the mind, for you, to experience something which is not mortal, which is not created by the mind, which is not of time? Obviously, if we could experience that, there would be no fear of death. But is it possible? Is it possible for a mind which is afraid, which functions within the field of time—is it possible for such a mind to experience that which is beyond time? Perhaps if you did various tricks you might experience something, but it would still be within the field of time.

So, let us leave for the moment the question of what is the immortal because we do not know what it is. But we do know the fear of death, of old age and withering away; we are quite familiar with that, so let us take that and examine it, go into it, and not ask if we can be free of fear by experiencing immortality. Such a question has very little meaning.

We are afraid of death, which means we are afraid of coming to an end. All the things we have acquired, the experiences we have gathered, the knowledge, the relationships, the affections, the virtues we have cultivated—we are afraid of all that coming to an end. You may have a hope, a belief that there is a resurrection in the future, but fear is there because the future is uncertain. Though your religions, your priests, your hopes have said that there is a continuity in some form or other, there is still uncertainty. You do not want to die. That is a fact. So, is there the understanding of fear in relation to death?

Is it possible to die while living? Please listen. If I am not accumulating, if I am not living in the future, in tomorrow, if I am content in the rich worship of one moment, there is no continuity. Continuity implies time: I was, I am, and I shall be. As long as I am sure that I shall be, I am not afraid, but the 'shall be' is very uncertain, and so I seek immortality, a confirmation that I shall continue.

In continuity is there a transformation? Can anything that continues in time be in a state of complete revolution? Can a continuity have newness? And is it not important inwardly to die each day, not theoretically, but actually not to accumulate, not to let any experience take root, not to think of tomorrow psychologically?

As long as we think in terms of time, there must be fear of death. I have learned, but I have not found the ultimate, and before I die I must find it, or if I do not find it before I die, at least I hope I shall find it in the next life, and so on. All our thinking is based on time. Our thinking is the known, it is the outcome of the known, and the known is the process of time, and with that mind we are trying to find out what it is to be immortal, beyond time, which is a vain pursuit; it has no meaning except to philosophers, theorists, and speculators. If I want to find the truth, not tomorrow, but actually, directly, must not I—the 'me', the self that is always gathering, striving, and giving itself a continuity through memory—cease to continue? Is it not possible to die while living—not artificially to lose one's memory, which is amnesia, but actually to cease to accumulate through memory, and thereby cease to give continuance to the 'me'? Living in this world, which is of time, is it not possible for the mind to bring about, without any form of compulsion, a state in which the experiencer and the experience have no basis? As long as there is the experiencer, the observer, the thinker, there must be the fear of ending, and therefore of death. As long as I am seeking further experience, giving strength to my own continuity through the family, through property, through the nation, through ideas, through any form of identification, there must be the fear of coming to an end.

And so, if it is possible for the mind to know all this, to be fully aware of it and not merely say, "Yes, it is simple"—if the mind can be aware of the total process of consciousness, see the whole significance of continuity and of time, and the futility of this search through time to find that which is beyond time—if it can be aware of all that, then there may be a death which is really a creativity totally beyond time.

May 30, 1954

India, 1954

First Talk in Madras

I think it is very important, especially now in this unprecedented crisis throughout the world, to know how to listen, not only to a speaker, to the human voice, but also to the birds, to the sound of the sea, to everything about us. It seems to me that it has become extraordinarily urgent for each one of us to find out what is true and what is false, irrespective of the innumerable teachers here and in the West and of all the sacred and other books that have been and are being published. Surely one must be able to listen without being converted to any particular point of view, to any particular philosophy or ideology, and discover for oneself beyond the words, beyond the similes and intricate thoughts, exactly what is true behind all this verbiage.

First of all, do we ever listen to anything? Are we capable of listening? If you observe yourself you will see how difficult it is to listen because you have preconceived ideas, opinions, and judgments based on your own tradition, your own experience and cultural influences, and these constantly intervene. They are like screens between you and that which you are trying to hear, so there is no listening at all but merely a translation of what you hear in terms of your own conditioning.

Do observe, watch your own mind when you are listening to what is being said, and you will see this extraordinary process actually taking place. You are really not listening. You have already an opinion about what is going to be said; you have conclusions, formulations, certain definite ideas, and the knowledge of the experience you have gathered is corrupting your mind. So your mind is never quiet, never still, to find out what is true.

Is it not essential for a man who wants to find out for himself what is true to put aside all the things he has gathered, all the knowledge, the conclusions based on his own experience, so that the mind can perceive directly what is true without the screen of interpretation? Can you be told by another what is true? From childhood we have been taught not how to think but what to think, not how to listen but what to listen to. So we must now endeavor to find out how to listen, which means really how to think anew about all the problems of life, how to look at things very clearly without the prejudices of any race or culture, without the interpretation of our particular conditioning.

As I said, we are in an extraordinary crisis both historically and culturally. In a fortunate way there are no leaders any more because you can no longer trust any leader. You do follow leaders when you want to get something from them spiritually or politically, but if you are intelligently observant you will be aware that the process of leadership does not bring about a fundamental revolution. The revolution of a leader is merely the continuation of the old in a different form. To change one pattern into another pattern is no change at all, it is merely a modified continuity. To bring about an inward revolution, a revolution in the whole process of our thinking and in the ways of our behavior, demands on the part of each one of us a putting aside of all our preconceived ideas, a freeing of ourselves from every kind of thought pattern in order to find out what is true. That is the only thing you and I can have in common because what I am saying is neither Eastern nor Western; our problems are too colossal to be divided as Indian and British, Russian and American. These divisions are merely political and are absurd. Our problems are enormous and they cannot be solved from any political or sectarian point of view because they vitally concern us all as human beings, whether we live here or there.

Do you understand? To discover, first of all, what is our major problem, we cannot think in terms of the Orient or the Occident, we cannot think as Hindus, Muslims, or Christians. If we do, we create from the major problems innumerable secondary problems which have no significance at all. Please understand this one simple thing, listen to and see the truth of it. We cannot think in terms of the Hindu, the Christian, the Islamic or any other culture because the problem is much too vast to be dealt with according to a religious dogma or a particular pattern of philosophy. That is obvious, is it not? But can your mind put aside all that, actually and not merely verbally? Theoretically you will spin words about it in order to discuss, but actually you are caught in the web of your own traditions, your own conditioning; therefore, it is impossible to look at any problem comprehensively.

What is happening in the world at the present time, and perhaps has always happened? There are various political leaders each wanting to reform the world in a particular way, to push it to the left or to the right or to maintain neutrality. Innumerable religious leaders are saying that there is a God, a divine end for man, and that a particular path will lead to it. Then there are the economic gurus who offer an earthly utopia in the future if you will work hard for the party and conform to the authority of the book. The reformers, the historians, the politicians, the religious teachers, with their various patterns of thought, all point in different directions and say what is the right thing to do, and the greater the authority the more the followers.

Now, all that is happening in the world is a projection of our own confusion and misery, is it not? We want to have both physical security and inward peace, we want to be without conflict, sorrow, and pain, without the constant battle between the opposites, between *what is* and *what should be,* we want a haven from the ceaseless strife within ourselves. Seeing this whole process going on, don't you ask what it is all about? This may seem a very childish question, but you have never found the answer, have you? Nor can great philosophers answer it for you. What Shankara, Buddha, and others have said may be false, it may be utterly inadequate. To find the truth you must first understand the problem, which means that you must be capable of looking at it without any conditioning.

So, don't you ask yourself what this conflict and misery is all about? You strive, you add a degree to your name after passing an examination, you go to the office every day to earn a few rupees, and there is the endless struggle between the rich and the poor. What is it all about? Must you not find out for yourself and not rely on any person, on any book? It is not a question of capacity, it is a question of interest and drive. The moment you are really interested in this, you will find that you have the enthusiasm, the passion to find out, and therefore you are willing to examine anything that may help you to discover the truth. What is important, then, is not the solution of any problem but how we approach the problem, because practically all of us have lost the spirit of creative search, creative exploration, to discover what is true, which cannot exist if there is any form of acceptance.

Please listen to this, but do not merely accept what I say. I am telling you nothing, literally nothing, because wisdom cannot be conveyed through words. You have to discover it for yourself, and to discover it your mind must be free. But your mind is not free, is it? Your mind is obviously hedged about by every form of fear, tradition, hope, and anxiety. So, can your mind free itself from fear and tradition, from the accumulated knowledge of a thousand years? Can you put aside all the gurus, the religious teachers, whether ancient or modern, and look at these things for yourself? That is the real problem, is it not?

Civilizations and cultures do not bring about religion, they exist for religion; their proper function is to help man to find out what is true, what is God. But you cannot find truth, God, if you are not inwardly free. Freedom does not come about through the cultivation of any particular practice because the moment you practice, you are already caught in the "how." A man who meditates according to a system can never find out what is true, but when the mind becomes aware of the habit in which it is caught and sets about freeing itself from the practice, the thoughtlessness that is perpetually creating habit—such a mind is in meditation. It means really a complete inward revolution—which most of us are not willing to undergo because we want to be respectable. I do not mean the respectability of Mylapore,* that is absurd, but the respectability of feeling that we are progressing, advancing spiritually, that we are moral, safe. All this indicates absorption in oneself, does it not? However modified, refined, it is still self-concern.

So our problem, not only here, but throughout the world, is this: Can the mind free itself from the past, from all its accumulated knowledge—knowledge, not of the machine, not of technology, but the knowledge of what we should be, the theories, the dogmas, the beliefs—and with that freedom consider the whole issue of existence? And when the mind is free from dogma, belief, fear, will there be any problem? After all, what is the mind, the mind which you have? What is your response when you are asked that question? Please experiment with what I am saying, if only for the fun of it. What is your mind? When you are asked such a question, observe how your mind operates. Its instinctive response is to look for an answer, either what Shankara said or what the modern psychologists say, or what has been said by the scientists or by your favorite guru or newspaper. You are looking for an answer among the various records which you have collected, are you not? You do not observe your own process of thinking, and it is only in watching that process that you find out what the mind is, not by quoting somebody.

To find out what the mind is—is that not meditation? If the mind can understand the total process of its own existence, then perhaps it can go beyond itself and discover what is true. But reason and logic are not passionate, vital, and that is why, to understand and transcend itself, the mind must go beyond reason and logic. The mind that is passionate to find out what is true—only such a mind can come to know the whole process of reasoning, with its

*A suburb of Madras.

illusions and falseness, and so transcend itself. A mind that is logical, reasoning, traditional, fearful, may be enthusiastic in terms of a dogma, creed, or political formula; it may be keen to bring about a particular reform, but it can never be vitally free to find out what is true.

Do experiment with this because, after all, why are you listening to me? If you are listening to find out what is true, you will never find it. If you are listening to be told how to meditate, you will never know meditation. God is not to be found through words, through any book or philosophy, through any of the systems of meditation which you practice. That which is true can only be found from moment to moment, and the mind that has a continuity cannot find it. Our mind is the result of time, is it not? It is the outcome of many yesterdays and accumulation of both experience and knowledge. The mind as we know it has a continuity, which is memory, so it can only function in time, and with that continuity we approach the timeless, we try to find out what is true; therefore, what we find will be in terms of our own continuity, our own habit, our own conclusions. We cannot be free of continuity as long as we do not understand the whole process of the mind, of the 'I'. The mind is not separate from the 'I'. Whether it is high or low, whether you call it personality, soul, or atma, the 'I' is the self, the mind that is capable of thinking. Please listen to this. As long as your God, paramatma, and all the rest of it, is within the field of thought, it is still in time, and therefore it is not true. That is why it is very important to understand the whole process of the mind, not only of the superficial everyday mind, but also of the unconscious. What is true can only be found from moment to moment; it is not a continuity, but the mind which wants to discover it, being itself the product of time, can only function in the field of time; therefore, it is incapable of finding what is true.

To know the mind, the mind must know itself, for there is no 'I' apart from the mind. There are no qualities separate from the mind, just as the qualities of the diamond are not separate from the diamond itself. To understand the mind, you cannot interpret it according to somebody else's idea, but you must observe how your own total mind works. When you know the whole process of it—how it reasons, its desires, motives, ambitions, pursuits, its envy, greed, and fear then the mind can go beyond itself, and when it does, there is the discovery of something totally new. That quality of newness gives an extraordinary passion, a tremendous enthusiasm which brings about a deep inward revolution, and it is this inward revolution which alone can transform the world, not any political or economic system.

If you listen rightly to what is being said, that very listening is a process of revolution. I assure you of this fact—not that you must accept it, but you will find out for yourself, if you listen rightly, that there comes an astonishing revolution in your life because you will have discovered the truth, and the truth brings about its own creative enthusiasm, its own creative action from moment to moment. That discovery is the highest form of religion, it is that for which all civilizations exist and every individual strives, and without it we are going to create an appalling world; without it we are going to destroy each other with the hydrogen bomb, and if there are no wars, we will destroy each other through separative beliefs, through dogmas, through false gods such as nationalism, through religions that no longer have any meaning but are mere superstition.

So the problem is to free the mind to discover what is true because truth cannot be handed to you by another. You cannot read it in books, it is not contained in any theory, it is not born of speculation nor of experience or the translation of experience. Truth comes into being only when the mind is quiet, utterly still, not hedged about by fear, by hope, by dogmas, by any form of ritual or belief. Mind is still only when it is free, and there is freedom only when the total process of the mind is understood.

There are several questions to answer. What is the point of putting a question? Is it to solve the problem or to explore the problem? Do you see the difference? With which are you mostly concerned when you put the question? Are you not mostly concerned with the answer? And when I answer in one way, you can go to someone else for a different answer and then choose the answer according to your judgment, your evaluation, which depends on your conditioning, on your desires and hopes, so you are really wanting the question to be answered to suit your theories and prejudices. But if the question is put in order to explore the problem together and find out what is true, then our relationship is entirely different. Then there is no lecturer, no division of speaker and listener, no guru, *sishya,** and all that nonsense. Then you and I are two human beings confronted with a problem of which we are unafraid and into which we are inquiring to find out what is true, and such inquiry gives tremendous enthusiasm, does it not? Then the inquiry is neither yours nor mine, neither Hindu, Muslim, Christian nor Buddhist. There is only the mind that is inquiring to find out what is true.

Please, sirs, if you listen to all this very casually, it has very little significance, but if you listen to it with your whole being as though your life depended on it, then it will have a totally different meaning.

Questioner: Religious ascetics give up worldly things, political "sannyasis" dedicate themselves to work of various kinds for bettering society, while others are active in their own way to change conditions in the educational, social, and political fields. Similarly, the people associated with you, though not belonging to any organization, are apparently dedicated to your work. Is there any difference between all these persons?

KRISHNAMURTI: I hope there are none who are dedicated to my work, and that is very important to understand first. You cannot be dedicated to another's work. And what is my work? To publish a few books? Surely not. The inquiry to find out what is true is surely your own work, it is not mine. It is your life, your sorrow and misery that have to be understood, whether you live in a village, in Mylapore, in New York, London, or Moscow. If you understand your everyday life as an individual and bring about freedom in yourself, you will create a revolution in the collective will which is called civilization, but if you cannot bring about this fundamental revolution in yourself, which is your own work, then how can you be dedicated to someone else's work?

So what is it that we are trying to do? The political reformers, the sannyasis, those who belong to welfare societies, those who serve various Masters, who meditate, who quarrel and then try to be peaceful—what is it that they are all trying to do? Have you ever questioned it? Have you ever asked yourself what it all means? Religious, political, and social reform is all part of what is called civilization, is it not? And what is civilization? Surely it is the product of the action of collective will. That is fairly clear. Civilization comes into being through the action of collective will, and that civilization either rises and goes beyond the secular to discover what is ultimately true, or

*Disciple.

it declines and goes under. There can be a radical revolution in civilization only when there is a fundamental change in the action of collective will, and the action of collective will cannot change if the individual will does not undergo a transformation in itself. So you and I must discover what is true for ourselves, and we cannot discover what is true unless we free ourselves from the collective, which is tradition, the hopes, fears, superstitions, and anxieties with which the mind is burdened. But we do not want to do that; all that we want to do is to carry on in the traditional way, hoping by some miracle there will be a revolution that will bring us happiness and peace.

There are many social and political reformers, many yogis, swamis, and sannyasis all struggling in their different ways to bring about some kind of change, collective or individual. But change without an understanding of the total process of the mind can only lead to further misery. These reformers, political, social, and religious, will only cause more sorrow for man unless man understands the workings of his own mind. In the understanding of the total process of the mind, there is a radical, inward revolution, and from that inward revolution springs the action of true cooperation, which is not cooperation with a pattern, with authority, with somebody who "knows." When you know how to cooperate because there is this inward revolution, then you will also know when not to cooperate, which is really very important, perhaps more important. We now cooperate with any person who offers a reform, a change, which only perpetuates conflict and misery, but if we can know what it is to have the spirit of cooperation that comes into being with the understanding of the total process of the mind and in which there is freedom from the self, then there is a possibility of creating a new civilization, a totally different world in which there is no acquisitiveness, no envy, no comparison. This is not a theoretical utopia but the actual state of the mind that is constantly inquiring and pursuing that which is true and blessed.

December 5, 1954

Second Talk in Madras

I think it must have struck most of us that problems all over the world are on the increase. There is always patchwork reform, a mediocre struggle to solve our many problems, but we do not seem able to solve them in their entirety. And why is it that we human beings keep on suffering indefinitely without ever solving the problem of sorrow? We have explanations for it depending upon our reading, explanations which suit our particular conditioning. If we are Hindus, we look at the problem in one way; if we are Christians or communists, we look at it in another, and explanations seem to satisfy the majority of us. This satisfaction, it seems to me, is the fundamental cause of mediocrity—which does not mean that we should reject everything without thought. But the desire to be satisfied does breed a mediocre outlook, a narrow objective, the acceptance of superficial answers to our immense problems, and if we could deliberately and radically set aside the desire for satisfaction and go behind the verbal explanations, then I think we should be able to solve our many problems.

So, if I may ask, with what desire, with what intention are you listening to me? Are you listening merely for an answer, or to find out if you and I together can investigate some of the many problems that confront us and discover the truth for ourselves, irrespective of any authority, of any book or ideology? If we can so explore our human problems, then I think the narrow walls of mediocrity will be broken down, and the desire to accept things as they are with patchwork reform here and there will give way to a radical, inward revolution.

Though many of our problems are petty, superficial, if we are to solve them fundamentally, is it not very important to ask fundamental questions? In understanding the fundamental, the superficial will be solved; but if we ask questions merely with the desire to find the most satisfactory explanation, this satisfaction will not fundamentally alter our struggles, fears, and sorrows. Most of us just intellectually enjoy quoting a few phrases from Marx or the Bhagavad-Gita; we like to show our knowledge or offer reasons why we should support a certain form of society, or a certain religious or political movement, and that is why we never find a fundamental answer to our many problems.

Please, if I may point out, this is quite an important issue; you cannot just brush it aside and go on to something else; you must really ponder over it. In asking fundamental questions, will you not solve the so-called superficial, the immediate social problems? It all depends on how we ask, does it not? A petty mind can ask a fundamental question, but its answer will be very superficial because such a mind will not know how to penetrate, how to explore, inquire into the question, and it will accept an answer that is reasonable and logically satisfying. So, when we do ask fundamental questions—questions like what is God, what is death, what is this conflict, this contradiction within oneself?—is it not very important for each one of us to observe how easily we are satisfied by some explanation, whether psychological, sociological, or religious? And is it possible to explore a fundamental question without accepting or being satisfied with any superficial response?

Now, let us take the problem of self-contradiction and see whether we can explore it in this way, for if we can understand the contradiction within ourselves, then perhaps we shall be able to understand the contradiction in relationship, which is society.

What brings about self-contradiction, this dual morality, this conflict within oneself? Most of us, I am sure, are unaware of it. When we are aware of it, it is a torture, and then begins the process of trying to overcome the contradiction, of trying to find a synthesis in the conflict between thesis and antithesis. Can the mind think without contradiction, without this conflict of the opposites? Is it capable of thinking without an ideal? It is the ideal that brings about the contradiction, is it not? And yet all our philosophies, all our religions insist on ideals as a means of improvement, as a means of change. Can the mind cease to think in terms of *what should be,* which is the ideal, and be free to pursue *what is?* Can it give complete attention to *what is* and not be distracted by 'what should be', the ideal?

It is really very important to follow this to the end, actually experience it, and not merely consider it intellectually. Why is there in all of us this contradiction? Do you understand what I mean by contradiction? It is the inner conflict between *what is* and 'what should be', the ceaseless attempt to better oneself, the constant comparison of oneself with another. And can the mind function without comparison? Does understanding come about through comparison and condemnation?

Is it not very important for each one of us to understand these fundamental issues directly and not just accept what another says? It is our own lives we are concerned with, and if we do not understand the fundamental issues, merely to indulge in political or social reform has very little significance. What is needed, surely, is an integrated outlook, which does not come about through conflict, adjustment, or resistance but only when the mind understands the whole problem of self-contradiction.

Is it not also very important to find out for ourselves if there is such a thing as God? If we are able to find out what is God, truth, or what name you will, it may bring about a fundamental revolution in our inward lives which will then express itself outwardly, but surely that requires some freedom, and the mind is not free when it is burdened with knowledge. Therefore, the whole conception of experiencing reality through knowledge becomes utterly fallacious, does it not? Mere description of what God is, the belief of the knowledge you have acquired in reading various religious books, or the rejection of these things because you happen to be an atheist, a nonbeliever—is not all this an impediment to discovery? Must not the mind be free to explore, and is the mind free when it is burdened with knowledge, with the dogmas of belief or nonbelief? After all, what is it that we call religion? When you really come to think of it, it is nothing but a formulation of rituals and dogmatic beliefs, and whether the dogma is Christian or Hindu, Buddhist or communist, is of very little significance.

So merely to ask what God or truth is, is not the solution because different people will give you different answers, and you will choose the one which is most rational, most convenient or satisfactory, but that is not the discovery of God or truth. It requires extraordinary insight to put aside all authority, all knowledge, and discover for yourself what is true. Knowledge is useful only as a means of communication or as a means of action. Before you act you must first be capable of investigating, must you not? In action you need knowledge. But can a mind burdened with knowledge discover what is true? Or must it be free of knowledge so as to investigate, and use knowledge only after discovery? With most of us knowledge has become a hindrance because we think that by reading certain books, attending certain talks, and all the rest of the nonsense, we shall find out what is truth. To discover what is truth, the mind must be stripped naked, must it not? Surely that is the fundamental question one must ask and explore for oneself.

I feel that the present world crisis is not merely social or economic but much more fundamental. If you look within yourself and about you, you will see how little creative thinking there is, how little understanding. Most so-called thinking is not original, it is merely repetitive, what Shankara, Buddha, Christ, Marx, or somebody else has said. Actually to put aside all authority, all books, and try to find out for oneself what is true, requires a great deal of creative intelligence, does it not? Acceptance may merely be the reaction of a conditioned mind, so is it not important, not only to ask what is truth, what is God, but to explore the question directly for oneself? And to do that, must not the mind be free from all conditioning—Hindu, Buddhist, Christian, communist, or any other? This requires a tremendous inward revolution, rebellion against everything, does it not? It demands revolt, not for revolt's sake, but a revolt which sets the mind free to discover.

When we talk about revolt, we generally mean revolt according to a certain formula, do we not? We revolt in order to bring about adjustment to a chosen pattern of thought or to establish a particular type of society. What we call revolt is a process of resistance, suppression. Now, can the mind revolt without accepting any formula, the formula being a reaction, a conditioned response? Can it put all that aside and discover what is truth? It is only such revolt that brings about creative thinking, creative understanding, and that is what is essential now, not more leaders, spiritual or political. Each one of us must actually discover for himself what is truth, and we cannot find out what is truth unless we are in total rebellion. You listen to all this, you shake your heads in assent, but if you merely go home and carry on as before, it will have no meaning. You see, sirs, unless we accept the challenge of the new, we are already dead, and the mind cannot understand the new if it is not free, if it is burdened with a particular belief or formula.

So, can the mind be in total revolution and not merely accept and be satisfied with an economic revolution such as the communists offer? Can there be a total revolution in our thinking? It seems to me that our only salvation is to be a light unto ourselves. A ship which is anchored cannot go out to sea, and a mind which is tethered to any belief or ideology is incapable of discovering what is truth. One must become conscious, aware, that one's mind is entrenched in certain forms of security, not only physically, but much more psychologically, that is caught in phrases, in beliefs, in ideas, in various manifestations of fear. Acceptance of a belief may give us great satisfaction, a sense of security, and in that security there is a certain power, but such a mind obviously cannot find out what is truth. It may repeat what Shankara, Buddha, or other ancient teachers have said, but that is not individual, creative discovery.

Not to seek any form of psychological security, any form of gratification, requires investigation, constant watchfulness to see how the mind operates, and surely that is meditation, is it not? Meditation is not the practice of a formula or the repetition of certain words, which is all silly, immature. Without knowing the whole process of the mind, conscious as well as unconscious, any form of meditation is really a hindrance, an escape, a childish activity; it is a form of self-hypnosis. But to be aware of the process of thinking, to go into it carefully step by step with full consciousness and discover for oneself the ways of the self—that is meditation. It is only through self-knowledge that the mind can be free to discover what is truth, what is God, what is death, what is this thing that we call living.

Do you understand, sirs? Why do we suffer, why do we obey, why is there this conflict within ourselves and in society? After all, living for most of us is suffering, it is a constant battle or the boredom of a routine. And is that life? The desire for fulfillment with its frustrations, the battle of ambition with its fear and ruthlessness, this constant struggle within oneself and with one's neighbor, the agony of relationship—is this living? Or, have we created this appalling society because we do not understand what living is? So is it not important to find out the real significance of all these things? And can the mind find out? What is the mind, the mind that is capable of reason, logic? Reason and logic depend on memory, memory being conditioned by past experience, and can such a mind discover what is truth? Or, is the discovery of truth possible only when the mind understands the whole process of experience, of memory, of knowledge, reason and logic, and by going beyond itself brings about a stillness in which reality can be? But it is impossible for a mind that is everlastingly caught in the acquisition of knowledge and experience to discover what is truth.

All this raises an immense question: Whether you are really an individual, or merely a movement of the collective. Civilization, whether Hindu, Christian, or communist, is obviously the result of the collective will, and a mind which is absorbed in the collective can never find out what is truth. To be an individual, the mind must understand and be free of the collective, and only then is it capable of discovering the highest. This means really a total revolution because the collective is tradition, belief, knowledge, experience, and the authority of the book.

Unless we understand these problems fundamentally, mere reformation becomes further misery. Have you not noticed that politicians all over the world are trying to establish peace and yet preparing for war? Every problem they touch brings other problems, and so it is in our own lives. There is a multitude of problems, a multitude of sorrows, and never a moment of deep happiness, of quietness, of full rejoicing. Happiness and enduring peace cannot be brought about by any legislation, by any superficial reform. When the mind, being aware of itself and knowing its collective movement, is in total revolution against the collective and is therefore discovering its own incorruptibility—only then is it able to discover what is truth, and this discovery is the only solution to all our human problems.

Questioner: What is the true spirit of cooperation? If it is not born of a common work or a common interest, then how does it arise?

KRISHNAMURTI: Sirs, what is it that you call cooperation? You cooperate with authority, with those who you think have the right ideas, the right plan, do you not? Is that cooperation? When you accept and cooperate with any kind of authority, is that cooperation? When you drive on the left as the law requires, are you cooperating? Surely we must first find out what we mean by that word. If we understand what cooperation is, we shall also know when not to cooperate, and both are important, for to cooperate with another under certain circumstances may lead to destruction and misery.

To cooperate is to work together, is it not? But if there is a plan, a blueprint enforced by authority, that is not cooperation, it is merely compulsion. Working together through fear, through reward, through necessity, through enforcement, is obviously not cooperation. Then what is cooperation, and how does it come into being?

Now, is there a form of cooperation in which you and I are capable of working together without authority? We may build a house together, and for that a blueprint, the architect's plan is necessary, but what you do and what I do is not psychologically important to us. I may carry the bricks and you may put them in place, but our intention is to build the house together, and therefore there is no authority, no compulsion. We cooperate because we want to work together to produce something. Can you and I work together in that spirit? Surely this is not a Hindu world nor a communist world nor an English or American world. This earth is ours, it is yours and mine to live in, a place to work and build together, and what you do in building, matters as infinitely as what I do. Can we be free of nationalistic twaddle, of racial and religious separatism, and have this spirit of cooperation in building together? This is entirely different from the so-called cooperation through any form of compulsion or fear of punishment, is it not? It really means the absence of the self, of the 'me'. And when there is this spirit of cooperation, there is at the same time an awareness of when not to cooperate, which is equally important. When a leader comes along and offers some marvelous utopian plan, a complete sociological revolution without a fundamental inner revolution, should one cooperate with such a person? And when there is a total revolution of one's whole being, is there not cooperation in which one is not out for oneself, in which one is not ambitious? Surely this is the revolution of love, which is not mere sentiment, not just a word; therefore, it is capable of cooperating, and also of not cooperating when cooperating is futile.

Questioner: You have talked about entering the house of death while living. Can one experience the feeling of dying while still alive?

KRISHNAMURTI: Most of us are interested in finding out what happens when we die, are we not? You want to know what happens after death, but I think that is a wrong question because then you are satisfied by mere explanations. The explanation of reincarnation may satisfy you more than any other, but it is still only an explanation. The mind frightened by death accepts a belief that gives it continuity. Surely, our living is a form of death because we are strangely afraid of dying, inwardly fearful of the uncertainty which lies beyond. But if we put the question differently, perhaps we can find the right answer.

Can one while living, while full of life and vigor, being alert and fully conscious, enter the house of death? Can you experience death, not at the moment of unconsciousness when the physical organism is gone, but while living, conscious, wide-awake? What is death? I am not going to give an explanation of what happens with the ending of the physical organism, whether the psychological mind, the bundle of instinctive responses, racial, inherited, and acquired, continues as memory. You can inquire into that and there will be innumerable answers which will satisfy you. But surely that is not the discovery of what death is. Can you while living—putting away all the fears, the longings, the explanations, the hope that there will be a continuity, and so on—find out what death is? The acceptance of any form of belief as to what death is, is not the solution. The mind that is satisfied, that has some kind of psychological security, is incapable of finding out the truth about death, is it not?

So, what is death? We know the obvious physical cessation. Is that all? Can you strip the mind of all the things you have learned about death, the knowledge you have acquired from books, the beliefs that have given you comfort in the hope that you will continue? Explanations have no value because they do not give you the real significance of death. Can you put them all aside and find out what death is? Can the mind be unburdened of all knowledge with regard to death? Only then is it free to find out what death is, is it not? After all, you do not know what death is, do you? And to find out what death is, must not your mind free itself of all knowledge and say, "I do not know"? In the presence of something it does not know, is it not important to find out if the mind is capable of saying, "I do not know"?

Do you understand, sirs? You have explanations of death based on your hopes, fears, and prejudices, on what other people have said or on your own desire to continue, but that is not the experiencing of what death is, is it? The fact is that you do not know, and can you really, honestly say that you do not know? When the mind can say, "I do not know," has it not already freed itself from the known, and is it not therefore capable of understanding the unknown, which is death? After all, we are afraid of death because we cling to the known. Death is the unknown, and we function only within the field of the known: "my name," "my family," "my job," "my virtue," "my temperament"—all that is in the field of the known, in which the mind functions and has its being. Now, can the mind free itself from the known, from the past, from all tradition, from all knowledge? And when it does, is not the mind in a state of not knowing? Being free from the known, is it not capable of understanding or experiencing the unknown, which is death? If we can experience the unknown immediately and directly, it will have an extraordinary significance in our relationships; then we shall create quite a different social order.

Our present society, whether communist or capitalist, is based on acquisitiveness; there may not be the acquisitiveness of property, but there is the acquisitiveness of power, position, prestige. A man who really understands this problem of death is no longer concerned with acquisition in any form; though he may hold a little property, his mind has lost its acquisitiveness. Therefore it is really very important to understand these fundamental issues, because in understanding them, we shall experience an inward revolution which will have a far-reaching effect in our social relationships. To bring about social reformation in any form without this inward revolution will not solve our problems because our problems are much deeper, they are much more psychological than economic.

Now, sirs, you have listened for nearly an hour, and what will you do about it? If you merely go back to your old routine, you will be incapable of responding to the challenge of the new. The world is in a tremendous, unprecedented crisis, and if you merely act as the collective, your response will not be new; therefore, it will not produce that creative action which the challenge demands. Your response can be new only when you are completely out of your tradition, when you are no longer a Hindu, a Christian, a Buddhist or a communist, when you no longer belong to any particular society. Only then are you capable of being free and therefore responding truly.

December 12, 1954

India, 1955

First Talk at Rajghat School, Banaras

If we can begin by considering what it is to be serious, then perhaps our investigation into the whole process of our thinking and responding to the various challenges of life will have deeper significance.

What do we mean by being serious? And are we ever really serious? Most of us think very superficially; we never sustain a particular intention and carry it through because we have so many contradictory desires, each desire pulling in a different direction. One moment we are serious about something, and the next it is forgotten, and we pursue a different object at a different level. And is it possible to maintain an integrated outlook towards life? I think this is a fairly important question to consider because I wonder how many of us are serious at all? Or are we serious only about those things which give us satisfaction and have but a temporary meaning?

So I think it would be very interesting, not merely to listen to a talk which I happen to be giving, but earnestly to try to find out together what it means to be serious. When a petty mind gives its effort to being serious, its seriousness is bound to be very shallow because it is without any understanding of the deeper significance of its own process. One may give one's energies to a particular object, spiritual or mundane, but as long as the mind remains petty, complex, without any understanding of itself, its serious activities will have very little significance. That is why it seems to me very important, especially at this time when there are so many complex problems, so many challenges, that a few of us at least should have a sustained interest in trying to find out if it is possible to be earnest or serious without being distracted by the superficial activities of the mind.

I don't know if you are interested in this problem, but it is surely quite important to find out why most people are not really serious, because it is only a serious mind that can pursue a particular activity to its end and discover its significance. If one is to be capable of action which is integral, one must understand the ways of one's own mind, and without that understanding, merely to be serious has very little meaning. I wonder if any of you are following all this, and whether I am explaining myself?

We see the disintegrating process that is going on in the world. The old social order is breaking down, the various religious organizations, the beliefs, the moral and ethical structures in which we have been brought up, are all failing. Throughout our so-called civilization, whether Indian, European, or whatever it be, there is corruption, and every form of useless activity is being carried on. So, is it possible for you and me to be aware of this whole process of disintegration and, stepping out of it as individuals, be serious in our intention to create a totally different kind of world, a different kind of culture, civilization? Do you think we could discuss this instead of my giving a talk?

The problem is this: Being caught up in this social, religious, and moral disintegration, how can we as individuals break away and create a different world, a different social order, a different way of looking at life? Is this a problem to any of you, or are you content merely to observe this disintegration and respond to it in the habitual manner? Can we this evening discuss this problem together, think it right through, and resolve it in ourselves? Do you think it would be profitable to discuss what we mean by change?

Questioner: Let us discuss seriousness.

KRISHNAMURTI: What do we mean by seriousness? To be serious, to be earnest, surely implies the capacity to find out what is true. Can I find out what is true if my mind is tethered to any particular point of view? If it is bound by knowledge, by belief, if it is caught in the conditioning influences that are constantly impinging upon it, can the mind discover anything new? Does not seriousness imply the total application of one's mind to any problem of life? Can a mind which is only partially attentive, which is contradictory within itself, however much it may attempt to be serious, ever respond adequately to the challenge of life? Is a mind that is torn by innumerable desires, each pulling in a different direction, capable of discovering what is true, however much it may try? And is it not therefore very important to have self-knowledge, to be serious in the process of understanding the self with all its contradictions? Can we discuss that?

Questioner: Would you kindly tell us if life and the problems of life are the same.

KRISHNAMURTI: Can you separate the problems of life from life itself? Is life different from the problems which life awakens in us? Let us take that one question and follow it right through.

Questioner: What about the atomic and the hydrogen bombs? Can we discuss that?

KRISHNAMURTI: That involves the whole problem of war and how to prevent war, does it not? Can we discuss that so as to clarify our own minds, pursue it seriously, earnestly, to the end and thereby know the truth of the matter completely?

What do we mean by peace? Is peace the opposite, the antithesis of war? If there were no war, would we have peace? Are we pursuing peace, or is what we call peace merely a space between two contradictory activities? Do we really want peace, not only at one level, economic or spiritual, but totally? Or is it that we are continually at war within ourselves, and therefore outwardly? If we wish to prevent war, we must obviously take certain steps, which really means having no frontiers of the mind because belief creates enmity. If you believe in communism and I believe in capitalism, or if you are a Hindu and I am a Christian, obviously there is antagonism between us. So, if you and I desire peace, must we not abolish all the frontiers of the mind? Or, do we merely want peace in terms of satisfaction, maintaining the status quo after achieving a certain result?

You see, I don't think it is possible for individuals to stop war. War is like a giant mechanism that, having been set going, has gathered great momentum, and probably it will go on and we shall be crushed, destroyed in the process. But if one wishes to step out of that mechanism, the whole machinery of war, what is one to do? That is the problem, is it not? Do we really want to stop war, inwardly as well as outwardly? After all, war is merely the dramatic outward expression of our inward struggle, is it not? And can each one of us cease to be ambitious? Because as long as we are ambitious, we are ruthless, which inevitably produces conflict between ourselves and other individuals, as well as between one group or nation and another. This means, really, that as long as you and I are seeking power in any direction, power being evil, we must produce wars. And is it possible for each one of us to investigate the process of ambition, of competition, of wanting to be somebody in the field of power, and put an end to it? It seems to me that only then can we as individuals step out of this culture, this civilization that is producing wars.

Let us discuss this. Can we as individuals put an end in ourselves to the causes of war? One of the causes is obviously belief, the division of ourselves as Hindus, Buddhists, Christians, communists, or capitalists. Can we put all that aside?

Questioner: All the problems of life are unreal, and there must be something real on which we can rely. What is that reality?

Krishnamurti: Do you think the real and the unreal can so easily be divided? Or does the real come into being only when I begin to understand what is unreal? Have you even considered what the unreal is? Is pain unreal? Is death unreal? If you lose your bank account, is that unreal? A man who says, "All this is unreal; therefore, let us find the real," is escaping from reality.

Can you and I put an end in ourselves to the factors that contribute to war within and without? Let us discuss that, not merely verbally, but really investigate it, go into it earnestly and see if we can eradicate in ourselves the cause of hate, of enmity, this sense of superiority, ambition, and all the rest of it. Can we eradicate all this? If we really want peace, it must be eradicated, must it not? If you would find out what is real, what is God, what is truth, you must have a very quiet mind, and can you have a quiet mind if you are ambitious, envious, if you are greedy for power, position, and all that? So, if you are really earnest, really serious in wanting to understand what is true, must not these things be put away? Does not earnestness, seriousness, consist in understanding the process of the mind, of the self, which creates all these problems, and dissolving it?

Questioner: How can we uncondition ourselves?

Krishnamurti: But I am showing you! What is conditioning? It is the tradition that has been imposed upon you from childhood, or the beliefs, the experiences, the knowledge that one has accumulated for oneself. They are all conditioning the mind.

Now, before we go into the more complex aspects of the question, can you cease to be a Hindu, with all its implications, so that your mind is capable of thinking, responding, not according to a modified Hinduism, but completely anew? Can there be in you a total revolution so that the mind is fresh, clear, and therefore capable of investigation? That is a very simple question. I can give a talk about it, but it will have no meaning if you merely listen and then go away agreeing or disagreeing. Whereas, if you and I can discuss this problem and go through it together to the very end, then perhaps our talking will be worthwhile.

So, can you and I who wish to have peace, or who talk about peace, eradicate in ourselves the causes of antagonism, of war? Shall we discuss that?

Questioner: Are individuals impotent against the atomic and hydrogen bombs?

KRISHNAMURTI: They are going on experimenting with these bombs in America, in Russia, and elsewhere, and what can you and I do about it? So what is the point of discussing this matter? You may try to create public opinion by writing to the papers about how terrible it is, but will that stop the governments from investigating and creating the H-bomb? Are they not going to go on with it anyhow? They may use atomic energy for peaceful as well as destructive purposes, and probably within five or ten years they will have factories running on atomic energy, but they will also be preparing for war. They may limit the use of atomic weapons, but the momentum of war is there, and what can we do? Historical events are in movement, and I don't think you and I living here in Banaras can stop that movement. Who is going to care? But what we can do is something completely different. We can step out of the present machinery of society which is constantly preparing for war, and perhaps by our own total inward revolution, we shall be able to contribute to the building of a civilization which is altogether new.

After all, what is civilization? What is the Indian or the European civilization? It is an expression of the collective will, is it not? The will of the many has created this present civilization in India, and cannot you and I break away from it and think entirely differently about these matters? Is it not the responsibility of serious people to do this? Must there not be serious people who see this process of destruction going on in the world, who investigate it, and who step out of it in the sense of not being ambitious and all the rest of it? What else can we do? But you see, we are not willing to be serious, that is the difficulty. We don't want to tackle ourselves, we want to discuss something outside, far away.

Questioner: There must be some people who are very serious, and have they solved their problems or the problems of the world?

KRISHNAMURTI: That is not a serious question, is it? It is like my saying that others have eaten when I myself am hungry. If I am hungry, I will inquire where food is to be had, and to say that others are well fed is irrelevant, it indicates that I am not really hungry. Whether there are serious people who have solved their problems is not important. Have you and I solved our problems? That is much more important, is it not? Can a few of us discuss this matter very seriously, earnestly pursue it and see what we can do, not merely intellectually, verbally, but actually?

Questioner: Is it really possible for us to escape the impact of modern civilization?

KRISHNAMURTI: What is modem civilization? Here in India it is an ancient culture on which have been superimposed certain layers of Western culture like nationalism, science, parliamentarianism, militarism, and so on. Now, either we shall be absorbed by this civilization, or we must break away and create a different civilization altogether.

It is an unfortunate thing that we are so eager merely to listen because we listen in the most superficial manner, and that seems to be sufficient for most of us. Why does it seem so extraordinarily difficult for us seriously to discuss and to eradicate in ourselves the things that are causing antagonism and war?

Questioner: We have to consider the immediate problem.

Krishnamurti: But in considering the immediate problem, you will find that it has deep roots, it is the result of causes which lie within ourselves. So, to resolve the immediate problem, should you not investigate the deeper problems?

Questioner: There is only one problem, and that is to find out what is the end of life.

Krishnamurti: Can we discuss that really seriously, go into it completely, so that we know for ourselves what is the end of life? What is life all about, where is it leading? That is the question, not what is the purpose of life. If we merely seek a definition of the purpose of life, you will define it in one way and I in another, and we shall wrangle and choose which is the better definition according to our idiosyncrasies. Surely, that is not what the questioner means. He wants to know what is the end of all this struggle, this search, this constant battle, this coming together and parting, birth and death. What is the whole of existence leading to? What does it mean?

Now, what is this thing which we call life? We know life only through self-consciousness, do we not? I know I am alive because I speak, I think, I eat, I have various contradictory desires, conscious and unconscious, various compulsions, ambitions, and so on. It is only when I am conscious of these, that is, as long as I am self-conscious, that I know I am alive. And what do we mean by being self-conscious? Surely, I am self-conscious only when there is some kind of conflict; otherwise, I am unconscious of myself. When I am thinking, making effort, arguing, discussing, putting it this way or that, I am self-conscious. The very nature of self-consciousness is contradiction.

Consciousness is a total process, it is the hidden as well as the active, the open. Now, what does this process of consciousness mean, and where is it leading? We know birth and death, belief, struggle, pain, hope, ceaseless conflict. What is the significance of it all? To find out its true significance is what we are trying to do. And one can find out its true significance only when the mind is capable of investigation, that is, when it is not anchored to any conclusion. Is that not so?

Questioner: Is it investigation, or reinvestigation?

Krishnamurti: There is reinvestigation only when the mind is tethered, repetitive, and therefore constantly reinvestigating itself. But to be free to investigate, to find out what is true, surely that requires a mind that is not held in the bondage of any conclusion.

Now, can you and I find out what is the significance of this whole struggle with all its ramifications? If that is one's intention and one is serious, earnest, can one's mind have any conclusion about it? Must one not be open to this confusion? Must one not investigate it with a free mind to find out what is true? So, what is important is not the problem but to see if it is possible for the mind to be free to investigate and find out the truth of it.

Can the mind be free from all conclusions? A conclusion is merely the response of a particular conditioning, is it not? Take the conclusion of reincarnation. Whether reincarnation is factual or not is irrelevant. Why do you have that conclusion? Is it because the mind is afraid of death? Such a mind, believing in a certain conclusion which is the result of fear, hope, longing, is obviously incapable of discovering what is true with regard to death. So, if we are at all serious, our first problem, even before we ask what this whole process of life means, is to find out whether the mind can be free from all conclusions.

Questioner: Do you mean that for serious thinking the mind must be completely empty?

KRISHNAMURTI: What do we mean by freedom? What does it mean to be free? You assume that if the mind is free, not tethered to any conclusion, it is in a state of vacuum. But is it? We are trying to find out the truth of what is a free mind. Is a mind free that has concluded? If I read Shankara, Buddha, Einstein, Marx, it does not matter who it is, and reach a conclusion or believe in a certain system of thought, is my mind free to investigate?

Questioner: Has comparison no place in the process of investigation?

KRISHNAMURTI: Comparing what? Comparing one conclusion with another, one belief with another? I want to find out the significance of this whole process of life with its struggle, its pain, its misery, its wars, its appalling poverty, cruelty, enmity; I want to find out the truth of all that. To do so must I not have a mind that is capable of investigation? And can the mind investigate if it has a conclusion, or compares one conclusion with another?

Questioner: Can a mind be called free if it has only a tentative conclusion?

KRISHNAMURTI: Tentative or permanent, a conclusion is already a bondage, is it not? Do please think with me a little. If one wants to find out whether there is such a thing as God, what generally happens? By reading certain books or listening to the arguments of some learned person, one is persuaded that there is God, or one becomes a communist and is persuaded that there isn't. But if one wants to find out the truth of the matter, can one belong to either side? Must not one's mind be free from all speculation, from all knowledge, all belief?

Now, how is the mind to be free? Will the mind ever be free if it follows a method to be free? Can any method, any practice, any system, however noble, however new or tried out for centuries, make the mind free? Or does the method merely condition the mind in a particular way, which we then call freedom? The method will produce its own results, will it not? And when the mind seeks a result through a method, the result being freedom, will such a mind be free?

Look, suppose one has a particular belief, a belief in God, or what you will. Must one not find out how that belief has come into being? This does not mean that you must not believe—but why do you believe? Why does the mind say, "This is so"? And can the mind discover how beliefs come into being?

You see insecurity in everything about you, and you believe in a Master, in reincarnation, because that belief gives you hope, a sense of security, does it not? And can a mind that is seeking security ever be free? Do you follow? The mind is seeking security, permanency, it is moved by a desire to be safe, and can such a mind be free to find out what is true? To find out what is true, must not the mind let go of its beliefs, put away its desire to be secure? And is there a method by which to let go of the beliefs which give you hope, a sense of security? You see, this is what I mean by being serious.

Questioner: Are there periods of freedom in the conditioned mind?

KRISHNAMURTI: Are there periods or gaps of freedom in the conditioned mind? Which is it that you are aware of, the freedom or the conditioned mind? Please take this question seriously. Our minds are conditioned, that is obvious. One's mind is conditioned as a Hindu, as a communist, this or that. Now, can the conditioned mind ever know freedom, or only what it imagines to be freedom? And can you be aware of how your mind is conditioned? Surely, that is our problem, not what freedom is. Can you just be aware of your conditioning, which is to see that your mind functions in a particular manner? We are not talking of how to alter it, how to bring about a change; that is not the question. Your mind functions as a Hindu or a modified Hindu, as a Christian or a communist; it believes in something. Are you aware of that?

Questioner: Freedom is not an acquisition but a gift.

KRISHNAMURTI: That is a supposition. If freedom were a gift, it would only be for the chosen few, and that would be intolerable. Do you mean to say that you and I cannot think it out and be free? You see, sir, that is what I am saying: we are not serious. To know how one is conditioned is the first step towards freedom. But do we know how we are conditioned? When you make a red mark on your forehead, when you put on the sacred thread, do puja, or follow some leader, are not those the activities of a conditioned mind? And can you drop all that so that in dropping it you will find out what is true? That is why it is only to the serious that truth is shown, not to those who are merely seeking security and are caught in some form of conclusion. I am just saying that when the mind is tethered to any particular conclusion, whether temporary or permanent, it is incapable of discovering something new.

Questioner: A scientist has data. Is he prepared to give up that data?

KRISHNAMURTI: Are you talking as a scientist or as a human being? Even the poor scientist, if he wants to discover anything, has to put aside his knowledge and conclusions, because they will color any discovery. Sir, to find out we must die to the things we know.

Questioner: Can the unconditioning of the mind be done at the conscious or unconscious level, or both?

KRISHNAMURTI: Sir, what is the mind? There is the conscious mind and the unconscious mind. The conscious mind is occupied with the everyday duties—it observes, thinks, argues, attends to a job, and so on. But are we aware of the unconscious mind? The unconscious mind is the repository of racial instinct, it is the residue of this civilization, of this culture, in which there are certain urges, various forms of compulsion. And can this whole mind, the unconscious as well as the conscious, uncondition itself?

Now, why do we divide the mind as the conscious and the unconscious? Is there such a definite barrier between the conscious and the unconscious mind? Or are we so taken up with the conscious mind that we have never considered or been open to the unconscious? And can the conscious mind investigate, probe into the unconscious, or is it only when the conscious mind is quiet that the unconscious promptings, hints, urges, compulsions come into being? So, the unconditioning of the mind is not a process of the conscious or of the unconscious; it is a total process which comes about with the earnest intention to find out if your mind is conditioned.

Please look at this and experiment with it. What is important is the total, earnest intention to find out if your mind is conditioned so that you discover your conditioning, and do not just say that your mind is or is not conditioned. When you look into a mirror you see your face as it is; you may wish that some parts of it were different, but the actual fact is shown in the mirror. Now, can you look at your conditioning in a similar way? Can you be totally aware of your conditioning without the desire to alter it? You are not aware of it totally when you wish to change it, when you condemn it or compare it with something else. But when you can look at the fact of your conditioning without comparison, without judgment, then you are seeing it as a total thing, and only then is there a possibility of freeing the mind from that conditioning.

You see, when the mind is totally aware of its conditioning, there is only the mind there is no 'you' separate from the mind. But when the mind is only partially aware of its conditioning, it divides itself, it dislikes its conditioning or says it is a good thing; and as long as there is condemnation, judgment or comparison, there is incomplete understanding of conditioning, and therefore the perpetuation of that conditioning. Whereas, if the mind is aware of its conditioning without condemning or judging, but merely watching it, then there is a total perception, and you will find, if you so perceive it, that the mind frees itself from that conditioning.

This is what I mean by being serious. Experiment with this, not just casually, but seriously watch your mind in action all the time—when you are at the dinner table, when you are talking, when you are walking—so that your mind becomes entirely aware of all its activities. Then only can there be freedom from conditioning, and therefore the total stillness of the mind in which alone it is possible to find out what is truth. If there is not that stillness which is the outcome of a total understanding of conditioning, your search for truth has no meaning at all, it is merely a trap to fall into.

January 9, 1955

Second Talk at Rajghat School, Banaras

If we could pursue earnestly and deeply the question of self-contradiction, perhaps it might have great significance in our daily existence.

Why is it that human beings are torn by self-contradiction? Why is there in most of us such compulsion, resistance, and this constant demand to adjust oneself to a particular pattern? I don't know if any of us are at all aware of this contradiction within ourselves, but I think it would be very profitable and worthwhile if we could seriously go into the matter because this may be the clue to the integrated action which is so obviously essential to a creative, a completely good life. Unless one is deeply aware of this contradiction within oneself, sees from where it springs and finds out whether one can really efface it, mere patchwork reform, either political, religious, or any other, can only lead to further mischief. I think it is very important for us to understand this because our understanding of it may be the solution to all the ills that surround us—which are the result of our own self-contradictory nature, are they not?

Most of us are driven by various compulsions, various desires which are contradictory, and even if we are aware of this contradiction in ourselves, we never seem able fundamentally, deeply, to trace and eradicate the cause of it. And it seems to me that if we can understand what it is to have an integrated life, a completely good life, a life in which there is no contradiction, no compulsion of any kind, no resistance, no form of adjustment to a pattern, then perhaps we shall be able to create a new culture, a new civilization, which is after all what the world in its present state of conflict is demanding.

To respond adequately to the challenge of life, one must be entirely integrated. How is this integration to be brought about? And why are we torn by self-contradiction? Most of us are not aware of this contradiction. We blindly force ourselves into a particular pattern of action, or we follow an ideal; we are full of tensions, of conflicting desires, wanting to do one thing and doing the opposite, thinking along one line and acting in a totally different manner, and we are unconscious of this self-contradiction. We either justify or condemn what we do, and that very judgment is another contradiction in ourselves.

Now, if one can listen to what is being said, not analytically or to achieve an integrated state, but listen without any opinion, without the accumulation of previous conclusions, that is, if one can listen innocently, with a fresh mind, then perhaps what is being said will have significance. Otherwise it will become another opinion, another theory, something to be carried out, and in the very carrying out of an idea, one has already created a contradiction in oneself. The mere acceptance of a new idea is a contradiction of what has already been established, and it only further increases the struggle, but if we can totally understand what is contradiction and how it comes about, then in the very act of listening, integration will take place without any struggle.

I think it is very important to understand that merely to accept a new idea, a new philosophy, a new teaching, only creates a contradiction with what already exists, and then the problem arises of how to bridge the old with the new, or how to interpret the new in terms of the old. So, is it possible to listen without creating this contradiction between the new and the old? Can one discover for oneself how contradiction arises, and merely see the fact without making the fact into an idea, an opinion, thereby creating another contradiction? That is the problem: Can you listen to what is being said and perceive the new fact without making it into an idea or a conclusion as opposed to the old, thereby creating a further contradiction within yourself?

Surely, this is sufficiently important to discuss a little: How the mind, being conditioned, never looks at a new fact without either interpreting, judging, or having a conclusion about it. And can the mind look at the new fact without a conclusion? Which means, really, can the mind be free of conditioning, cease to think in terms of a Hindu, a Buddhist, or a Christian, and look at the new fact without interpretation? If it can, then perhaps there will be an action which is not contradictory.

Now, how does this contradiction arise in each one of us? Does it not arise when the mind is incapable of a fresh response to the new, that is, when the mind is conditioned? Our minds are conditioned by the Hindu culture or the Western culture, by religion, by certain patterns of thought, by the weight of knowledge acquired through education or experience, that very experience being the response of a particular conditioning. Such a mind obviously cannot adequately respond to the new, and hence the contradiction. Life is a process of the new all the time, continuously. It is like a flowing river. The waters of the river may look the same, but there is a continuous flow, a constant change; and if the mind is incapable of responding fully to the flow of life, or if it responds to this ceaseless movement in terms of its conditioning, then there must be contradiction, not only in the superficial mind, but also in the deeper layers of consciousness. So our problem is not how to be integrated but rather to find out if the conditioned mind can uncondition itself.

Can the Hindu mind, if there is such a thing, with its religiosity, its superstitions, its patterns of thought, its social impacts, unburden itself of all this conditioning? Only then, surely, can it fully respond to the new and thereby free itself from self-contradiction.

But most of us are concerned not with unconditioning the mind but rather with a better, a wider, a nobler conditioning. The Christian wants the mind to be conditioned in a certain pattern, and so does the communist, the Hindu, the Buddhist, and so on. They are all concerned with bettering the mind's conditioning, decorating the interior of the prison, and not with breaking away from the prison totally. And is it possible to break away totally from one's conditioning? The question is not put for you to say yes or no, because such an answer has no meaning. But if each one of us really desires to find out whether the mind can be free from the past, which is to understand the whole content of the mind, then I think it may be possible to bring about a state of mind in which there is no contradiction.

So it is really essential, if one is to respond anew to the challenge of life, to respond to it totally. When there is only a partial response, any civilization or culture must inevitably disintegrate, which is obviously what is happening in this country and elsewhere. So, can we be aware of our conditioning, which is preventing a total response to the challenge of life? By being aware, I mean just seeing the fact of one's conditioning as a Hindu, a Muslim, or what you will, without condemning or trying to bring about a change in that conditioning, because the moment we desire to bring about a change in our conditioning, we have already created a contradiction. Please, if we can really see this very simple fact, then our whole understanding of conditioning will have an altogether different meaning.

Life, which is the everyday existence of relationship, of occupation and all the things that we do, is a constant challenge; in its response to that challenge the conditioned mind brings about self-contradiction, and a self-contradictory mind, however noble, however reformatory or idealistic its activities may be, is bound to create mischief, not only at the political or social level, but also psychologically and religiously, at the deeper levels of existence. Whereas, the person who breaks away from the collective, which is the prison of conditioning, is truly individual, creative, and only such a person can help to bring into being a different kind of civilization, a new culture, because in himself there is no contradiction. His action is entire, whole, he is not torn apart by ideas, there is no gulf between action and thought, no division of mentation and the carrying out of a certain idea. Only such a person is integrated and can understand this whole process of contradiction, not he who is trying to be integrated because the very effort to be integrated is a contradiction.

The man who sees the prison of his own conditioning and revolts, not within the prison, but totally, so that his very revolt pushes him out of the prison—it is he who is really a revolutionary, and I think this is very important to understand. But only the serious will understand it, not those who are trying to interpret what is being said to suit some philosophy or belief. If you actually perceive your own conditioning as factual without either accepting or trying to adjust that conditioning to a new pattern, you thereby become a revolutionary in the deepest sense of the word, and it is only such individuals who can bring about an altogether different culture, a new civilization in this suffering world.

Questioner: Our minds are the result of the past, they are shaped by the tradition of Shankara and Buddha. Will mere self-awareness help us to free ourselves from this conditioning?

KRISHNAMURTI: If you had listened your question would have been answered by my introductory talk. Sir, is it possible to start on the journey of exploration without previous knowledge, without any book, without quoting philosophers, scientists, or psychologists? Do you understand the question? After all, to find out what is truth, what is God, or what name you will, the mind must be completely alone, uncontaminated by the past, must it not? So, don't translate what I am saying in terms of what you have already read.

The mind, your mind, is the result of time, of many yesterdays; it has this extraordinary burden of knowledge, of experience within the field of time. And can one put all that aside and say, "I know nothing"? Though one has read, though one has experienced, is it possible to put all that totally aside because one sees that knowledge is an impediment to exploration and the discovery of truth? This demands a mind that is astonishingly unafraid, that has no end in view, that does not want to achieve a result; which means, really, a mind capable of unconditioning itself, of being free from its past because it sees that any conditioning is a hindrance, a source of contradiction.

You see, sir, the difficulty for most people, and probably for all of us here, is that we have read too much, and what we read we translate in terms of our conditioning; therefore, knowledge or experience becomes a further hindrance. And what I am asking is, can you put aside everything of the past, all the things that you have learned, and look at life anew? I am not talking about putting aside knowledge of the mechanical world, but the knowledge which has for the mind a psychological significance, so that you are your own teacher. Then there is no longer a guru and a disciple because you are finding out all the time, and when there is that kind of learning there is no need for a teacher.

Questioner: But the mind is burdened by the past, and how is one to shake it off? What is the method?

KRISHNAMURTI: You want a method because you desire to achieve a result, you want to get somewhere, and that is all you are concerned with. It is like the bank clerk wanting to become the executive. Your mind is climbing the ladder of success, worldly or so-called spiritual, and such a mind will not understand because it is only concerned with attaining an end. What is important, surely, is to find out why your mind desires to achieve a result, why it wants to be free of the past. Why do you want to be free of the past? And can the mind, being itself the result of time, make an effort to be free of time? If it does, it is still within the field of time, obviously; by making an effort to be free, to arrive somewhere, it has created a contradiction in itself. The mind is the result of time, and whatever movement it makes to free itself is still within the field of time. If one sees that simply and clearly, only then is it possible for the mind to be completely still. The very perception of that fact makes the mind quiet; it does not have to make an effort to be quiet. When the mind makes an effort to be quiet, its meditation is really a bargaining, a thing of the marketplace.

Questioner: An ancient civilization like that of India has left a deep impression upon our patterns of social behavior, which are now in a process of decay. How can we retain the best features of our culture and revive the ancient spirit?

KRISHNAMURTI: Sir, a dead thing must be buried, you can't revive it, you can't go back to it, but that is what you are trying to do. Because in yourselves you are confused, you say, "Let us go back to the rishis, let us revive the ancient spirit, the dances, the rituals," all the things that are dead and gone. There is a challenge directly in front of you, and you say, "Let us go back." If you do go back, if you respond by turning your back on the new, your civilization is going to decay—which is exactly what is happening. You may go back to your temples, to Shankara, to the sacred books, to the priests, to images carved by the hand, and all the rest of it, but they are dead things and will have no meaning.

So you cannot go back. You can only respond anew to the new, and you cannot respond anew if you keep some of the old. You must let go of the old completely and respond fully to the new. If you respond partially, keeping the good things of the Indian culture and making a mixture of the old and new, then you are obviously creating mischief. A new civilization can be brought into being only by people who are capable of responding totally to the new, and you cannot respond totally to the new if you cling to the ancient culture or to some of its good things. Surely, sirs, to respond fully to the new, the mind must be free of the prison of the old; its freedom cannot be in terms of the prison. You may revolt within the prison by demanding certain intramural reforms and adjustments, but in the process of understanding the whole prison of conditioning, there comes a total revolution which is neither Indian nor Western—it is something totally new, and therefore a movement of the real. It is the movement of the real, not the revival of the old, that creates the new civilization. Sirs, the revival of the old is merely a modified continuity of the present, and this response of the old is not freedom. Freedom comes into being not through the pursuit of freedom but when each one understands the total conditioning of his own mind.

Questioner: But conditioned as we are, it is not possible to listen without contradiction.

Krishnamurti: I am afraid, sir, you have not followed what I have said. I have said, do not listen with opinions, with conclusions, which only creates opposition, but listen to find out what is the actual process of the mind, listen to understand the process of your own conditioning. Do not ask how to be free of your conditioning, but be aware of your conditioning without judgment.

Please, what I am saying is very simple, and it is this: The mind is made up of the past, it is the result of the past, and we don't have to explore that fact because it is obvious. The mind is made up of thousands of yesterdays, innumerable experiences; when it makes an effort to free itself from this conditioning, there is inevitably a contradiction. But if the mind is aware of its conditioning without any judgment, if it merely perceives that it is conditioned without wishing to change or be free of that conditioning, then the very perception of that fact in itself brings about a total revolution.

Experiment with this and you will see how extraordinarily difficult it is just to be aware of your conditioning without wishing to change or be free of it. Your mind is made up of contradictions, you are educated to compare, to condemn, to evaluate; therefore, you have already formed an opinion about your conditioning. You say that you must not be conditioned, or that an unconditioned state can never exist, which is what the communists will say, so you have already concluded. But to be aware of one's conditioning without any conclusion is in itself the revolution.

Questioner: The factor that stifles all attempts at creative expression is mediocrity. Drabness and mediocrity appear to be the inescapable curse of a classless society. Is there a way to establish equality and yet keep alive the creative fire?

Krishnamurti: Sir, what do we mean by a classless society? As long as status goes with function, it is bound to create a society of class distinctions. As long as the principal of a school has status, with all its implications, and does not keep his job merely functional, it inevitably brings about a class-conscious society. And it is very difficult for the mind not to bring in status when it is functioning, because the moment you set out to create a classless society, the commissar becomes important, and with his job goes status, which means privileges, position, authority.

"Is there a way to establish equality and yet keep alive the creative fire?" What do we mean by equality? I know we all say there must be equality, but can there ever be equality? Is there equality of function? I may be a cook, and you may be a governor. If the governor despises the cook, which he generally does because he feels himself to be much more important than the cook, then to him it is status that matters and not function, so how can there be equality? You have, by chance, a better brain than I have, you meet more people than I do, you have greater capacity, you paint, you write poems, you are an artist or a scientist, while I am merely a coolie or a clerk. How can there be equality?

Or perhaps we are not looking at this problem at all rightly. Will inequality matter very much if each one of us is doing something which he really likes, something which he loves to do with his whole being? Do you understand, sir? If I love what I am doing, in that action there is no contradiction, no ambition. I am not seeking approbation, applause, titles, and all the rest of the nonsense. I am really in love with what I am doing; therefore, the whole problem of competition, of ambition, and this antagonism which arises from comparing one craft or function with another, will cease to exist.

Surely, the creative fire is lost when status becomes important, or when there is the imposition of the pattern of equality, which is merely a theory. But if we can educate the student from childhood to love what he is doing, whatever it is, with his whole being, then perhaps there will be no contradiction and therefore antisocial activities will cease.

Sir, I think equality comes into being when there is love in our hearts, when the heart is empty of the things of the mind. When there is love, there is no sense of the great and the small; you don't touch the feet of the governor or bow more deeply to him than you do to the cook. It is because we do not love that we have lost the whole significance of equality. But love is not a thing to be made to order by Marx, it is not to be found in communist theory nor in the pattern of a new culture. It comes into being when we understand the ways of the mind. With self-knowledge comes love, not love as the sensuous or the divine, but just that feeling of loving in which there is goodness, respect, and in which there is no fear.

You hear all this, but when you go away, you will salute the governor very humbly and kick your servants, so the very listening to this becomes a contradiction. Whereas, if you listen not to achieve a result but to understand the whole significance of what is being said, which is to understand the ways of your own mind, then you will know the beauty of that extraordinary thing called love.

January 16, 1955

Third Talk at Rajghat School, Banaras

I think it would be worthwhile if we could go into the question of what it is to be really creative because it seems to me that this is the major problem in the world at the present time. Merely to be gifted, or to have talent in any one particular direction, is obviously not creativeness. I think creativeness comes about through the capacity to see life as a totality, not in fragments, to think and feel as a completely integrated human being. It may be that this sense of completeness, in which there is no contradiction, is the experiencing of reality, God, or what you will, and I think one would understand this state if one could distinguish myth from fact.

May I suggest that you kindly do not take notes. If you take notes, you are only partially listening, and I think it is much more important to experience now what we are discussing than to take notes and remember it at a future time. If we can be fully aware of and directly experience what one is talking about, it will surely have much greater significance than if we merely remember certain phrases and then try to relate them to the ordinary events of daily life.

It seems to me that what is important is to understand the everyday facts of our life, and to do this, we must obviously distinguish them from the mythology that we create about the facts. If we could distinguish fact from myth, then perhaps the major problem of life would be solved, which is this constant effort, the struggle to become, and which is really destroying a complete understanding of what life is.

If we are at all conscious of the ways of the mind, we know that there is always a contradiction in our thinking and effort to patch up or bridge over the gap between *what is* and 'what should be'. This constant struggle to become is what we know, and if we could really understand and dissolve it, then perhaps there would be a state of integration, a life of 'being' and not of 'becoming'.

After all, do we understand anything through effort? To understand, surely the mind must be quiet, and it cannot be quiet when it is in a state of effort. If you look at the fact through the screen of your opinions, biases, or knowledge and are torn between the fact and what you yourself think is true, this contradiction between the fact and the myth brings about a continuous effort on your part which is destructive. The fact is one thing, and the myth about the fact is another, and effort comes into being when there is this myth apart from the fact. If we can once really grasp that all such effort is destructive and can remove the screen of the myth from between ourselves and the fact, then our minds will be given wholly to understanding the fact.

When we are confronted with a fact, we all have different opinions about the fact, different ways of looking at it, and this breeds contention, antagonism between us. Whereas, if I can look at the fact without any opinion, without the myth, then the fact itself will have its own effect without my making an effort to comply with or adjust my mind to the fact.

So, can the mind look at the fact without having an opinion, an idea, a judgment about it, without bringing in its knowledge and previous experience? Because life is one thing, and what we think life is, is another. Life is obviously impermanent, not static; it is always in movement, in flux, but we want to make that transient thing permanent, we want to make that constant movement gratifying to ourselves. So the fact is one thing, and the myth is another, and can we free the mind from the myth of what we would like the fact to be? Can we be free of all the philosophies which people who cannot look at the fact have created and which have conditioned the mind? If we can, then there is no conflict. I think that is the real crux of the whole matter. It is very interesting to watch how the mind operates, to see how difficult it is for the mind to put away the myth, the opinions, the various philosophies, and merely observe the fact, but if we can really do this, I think it will bring about a total revolution in our thinking because it will remove the whole process of mentation which is building the myth, the self, the 'me'.

After all, the 'me' is totally impermanent, is it not? What is the 'me'? It is a series of memories, experiences, a process of conditioned thinking apart from the fact, and it is this separation of the mind from the fact through various forms of conditioning that breeds the effort which destroys creativeness. I do not think this is an oversimplification, and if we can really grasp it, we shall find that the mind then becomes merely an observer of the fact, and that the observer is not something separate from the fact.

What is the mind? It is the constant movement of thought, is it not? It is the movement of thought which is the outcome of a particular conditioning, either as a communist, as a Christian, or what not, and the accumulated experiences based on that conditioning. All that is the mind. That mind cannot look at a fact directly because it is shaped by various forms of knowledge, by personal satisfactions, by opinions, judgments, all of which prevent it from looking directly at the fact. If one really understands this, I think it will have a tremendous sociological effect. The mind is constantly seeking some form of security, some form of permanency, but there is no permanency at all. Psychologically the mind is ambitious, acquisitive, and so it creates a society which is based on acquisitiveness, society being the collective will. The fact is that there is no permanency, but the mind is seeking it, which creates the myth away from the fact; hence there is a contradiction, and so an everlasting effort by the mind to adjust the myth to the fact, and in this conflict we are caught.

So, our problem is: Can the mind be free from all forms of opinion, conclusion, judgment, hope, and look directly at the fact? And if the mind is thus free, then is there any fact except the freedom of the mind? Let us go into that a little bit.

You see, the mind is the result of time, of many yesterdays, and the thinking process is the outcome of a certain conditioning. This conditioned mind is everlastingly seeking some form of consolation, some form of permanency. That is the state of the mind of almost everybody. But the fact is that life is not permanent, life is not secure; it is a rich, timeless movement. Now, when the mind is free from its own conditioning, from its judgments, opinions, from all the things that society has imposed upon it, is the mind then different from the fact of life? Then life is the mind; then there is no separation between the fact and the mind. This is really a tremendous experience if one can do it, and such a mind, being in a state of revolution, can bring about a different culture altogether. I don't know if you see the significance of this.

You see, the mind is seeking truth, God, as something apart, seeking implies a separation, a direction, even semantically. The mind wants God to be permanent, static, and therefore its God is self-created, but the truth of God may be entirely different; it may be something which is not the product of the mind at all. So the fact may be one thing, and that for which the mind is seeking may be another. The search may lead you not towards the fact but away from the fact—which means, really, that the mind must cease to search. It searches because it is seeking comfort, security, permanency, and all the rest of it; therefore, it is moving in a direction totally apart from the reality which may never be still, the reality which the mind may have to discover every minute, every second. When the mind realizes that its search is the outcome of a particular conditioning, of a desire for security, permanency, and so on, then without any enforcement or compulsion there is a natural cessation of the movement of search, of going towards an end to be gained. Then is not the mind itself the movement of the fact, and not the movement of a desire or a hope about the fact? It is then really the movement of truth, of creativeness, because there is no contradiction; the mind is whole, completely integrated; there is no effort to be, to become.

This is really very important to understand. Perhaps we can discuss it.

Questioner: Is there anything permanent in us?

KRISHNAMURTI: If I may say so, you have not listened to what I have been saying. The fact is that everything is impermanent, whether you like it or not, but it is not a matter of acceptance. You see, that opens up an enormous question. What is acceptance? Acceptance implies that there has been disagreement between us. What have we disagreed about? Obviously, about opinions. Opinions can be accepted or rejected. But are you "accepting" the truth that life is impermanent or merely seeing the fact that it is impermanent, which has nothing to do with acceptance? You don't have to "accept" the depth of the sea—it is deep. Nobody has to convince you of the fact that a bullet is very dangerous. We "accept" when we have not really seen the fact. There is no question at all of accepting what I am saying. I am just describing the actual process of our thinking, which is that in everything we want a state of permanency, in the family, in property, in position. But life is not permanent. That is so obvious, it does not need acceptance. The fact is that life is impermanent. Now, can the mind put away all the philosophies, the practices, the systems of discipline which it follows, hoping thereby to arrive at a permanent state? Can the man be free of all that and see what the fact is? And if the mind is free to see the fact, is the fact then separate from the mind? Is not the mind itself the movement of the fact?

You see, sir, the difficulty is that we don't listen to what is being said, and we don't listen to it because we are listening to the opinions, the judgments which we have and with which we are going to contradict or accept what is being said. Just to listen to what is being said is one of the most difficult things to do. Have you ever tried really listening to somebody? Experiment with it, try actually listening to somebody as you would listen to a song or to something with which you neither agree nor disagree, and you will see how extraordinarily difficult it is because just to listen to somebody, the mind must be very quiet. To find out if what is being said is true or false, you must have a very silent mind and not interpose between the mind and what is being said your own judgments about it.

The questioner wants to know if there is anything permanent in us. How will he find out? He can find out only through a direct experience. To say that there is or is not a permanent state merely creates contradiction because it conditions the mind to think in a certain way. If the mind wishes to find out what is true, it must be free from all previous knowledge, experience, and tradition. That is an obvious fact.

Questioner: In giving talks, your ideas are born of your thinking. As you say that all thinking is conditioned are not your ideas also conditioned?

KRISHNAMURTI: Obviously, thinking is conditioned. Thinking is the response of memory, and memory is the result of previous knowledge and experience, which is conditioning. So all thinking is conditioned. And the questioner asks, "Since all thinking is conditioned, is not what you are saying also conditioned?" It is really quite an interesting question, is it not?

To speak certain words, there must be memory, obviously. To communicate, you and I must know English, Hindi, or some other language. The knowing of a language is memory. That is one thing. Now, is the mind of the speaker, myself, merely using words to communicate, or is the mind in a movement of recollection? Is there memory not merely of words but also of some other process, and is the mind using words to communicate that other process? Is this too complicated? It is really a very interesting problem if you actually follow it through.

You see, the lecturer has his store of information, of knowledge, and he deals it out; that is, he remembers. He has accumulated, read, gathered; he has formed certain opinions according to his conditioning, his prejudices, and he then uses language to communicate. We all know this ordinary process. Now, is that taking place here? That is what the questioner wants to know. The questioner says, in effect, "If you are merely remembering your experiences, your states, and communicating that memory, then what you say is conditioned"—which is true.

Please, this is very interesting because it is a revelation of the process of the mind. If you observe your own mind, you will see what I am talking about. Mind is the residue of memory, of experience, of knowledge, and from that residue it speaks; there is the background, and from that background it communicates. The questioner wants to know whether the speaker has that background and is therefore merely repeating, or whether he is speaking without the memory of the previous experience and is therefore experiencing as he is talking. You see, you are not all observing your own minds. Sirs, to investigate the process of thought is a delicate matter, it is like watching a living thing under a microscope. If you are not all watching your own minds, you are like outside observers watching some players in the field. But if we are all watching our own minds, then it will have tremendous significance.

If the mind is communicating through words a remembered experience, then such remembered experience is conditioned, obviously; it is not a living, moving thing. Being remembered, it is of the past. All knowledge is of the past, is it not? Knowledge can never be of the now, it is always receding into the past. Now, the questioner wants to know if the speaker is merely drawing from the well of knowledge and dealing it out. If he is, then what he communicates is conditioned because all knowledge is of the past. Knowledge is static; you may add more to it, but it is a dead thing.

So, instead of communicating the past, is it possible to communicate experiencing, living? Do you follow? Surely, it is possible to be in a state of direct experiencing without a conditioned reaction to the experiencing, and to use words to communicate not the past but the living thing which is being directly experienced. I don't know if this has at all communicated to the questioner what he wanted to know.

When you say to somebody, "I love you," are you communicating a remembered experience? You have used the accustomed words, "I love you," but is the communication a thing you have remembered, or is it something real which you immediately communicate? Which means, really, can the mind cease to be the mechanism of accumulation, storing up and therefore repeating what it has learned?

Questioner: Is total forgetfulness possible?

Krishnamurti: We are not talking about total forgetfulness. That is amnesia. I know the way to the station. I can recognize various people.

Questioner: The moment the thought process is active, it is conditioned.

KRISHNAMURTI: But is it active apart from the use of words as a means of communicating what is true?

Questioner: Does one not choose expressions while communicating what is true?

KRISHNAMURTI: But the thought process is active only in the verbal sense. After all, if I know French, Spanish, or whatever language it be, I can use it to convey what is true, and then it is just a means of communication, like the telephone, is it not? But here we must be very careful not to deceive ourselves because self-deception is now tremendously easy if we are not very alert.

If you tell me something and your telling is the result of an experience which is over, then your description, your thought is from the past, is it not? Therefore thought is conditioned. But is there thinking when you are experiencing and communicating? If you are experiencing and communicating the state of love, is there thinking then in the sense which we have understood?

Questioner: I find that when the experiencing process is going on, communication totally stops.

KRISHNAMURTI: Does it stop? When you love your son, your wife, a dog, a flower, does communication stop in that moment of experiencing? You ask me a question and I reply. There is experiencing, but communication has not stopped. This is really very complex, so please pay attention. It is not a matter of opinion, you have to find out.

All book knowledge, and the communication of that knowledge, is conditioned. That is simple, is it not? Then why are you collecting knowledge? You have to read certain books in preparing to earn a livelihood, but why do you read the Vedas, the Upanishads? Why do you accumulate knowledge about God, reincarnation, philosophies, and all that?

Questioner: When you are talking, who is speaking? Are you not conscious that you are speaking?

KRISHNAMURTI: I am not at all sure that I am conscious that I am speaking. Something is being said. But we are going off on a tangent.

All accumulated knowledge, whether about machinery, jet planes, or about philosophy, is conditioned, which is obvious, and you want to know if I am speaking from knowledge. If I am speaking from knowledge, then what is communicated is conditioned, and if I am not speaking from knowledge, then you ask, "From what are you speaking?" What is happening inwardly, inside the skull? Psychologically, what is taking place? Let us go slowly into this and try to find out.

Now, is it possible not to have the burden of accumulated knowledge? If that is possible, then communication at a different level is also possible, surely. If you say that it is not possible to free the mind from all knowledge, knowledge being accumulation, then thinking and communication are conditioned. But if it is possible for the mind to be free of all accumulation, which means dying each day, each minute to the previous experience, then, though the words may have a binding or conditioning quality, what is being said is not conditioned. I think that is the fact; it is not just a clever, logical conclusion.

Questioner: I am terrified of death. Can I be unafraid of inevitable annihilation?

KRISHNAMURTI: Sir, why do you take it for granted that death is either annihilation or continuity? Either conclusion is the outcome of a conditioned desire, is it not? A man who is miserable, unhappy, frustrated, will say, "Thank God, it is soon going to be all over, I won't have to worry anymore." He hopes for total annihilation. But the man who says, "I have not quite finished, I want more," will hope for continuity.

Now, why does the mind assume anything with regard to death? We shall presently go into the question of why the mind is afraid of death, but first let us free the mind of any conclusion about death because only then can you understand what death is, obviously. If you believe in reincarnation, which is a hope, a form of continuity, then you will never understand what death is, any more than you will if you are a materialist, a communist, this or that, and believe in total annihilation. To understand what death is, the mind must be free of both the belief in continuity and the belief in annihilation. This is not a trick answer. If you want to understand something, you must not come to it having already made up your mind. If you want to know what God is, you must not have a belief about God, you must push all that away and look. If one wants to know what death is, the mind must be free of all conclusions for or against. So, can your mind be free of conclusions? And if your mind is free of conclusions, is there fear? Surely, it is the conclusions that are making you afraid, and therefore there is the inventing of philosophies. I don't know if you are following this.

I would like to have a few more lives to finish my work, to make myself perfect, and therefore I take hope in the philosophy of reincarnation, I say, "Yes, I shall be reborn, I shall have another opportunity," and so on. So, in my desire for continuity I create a philosophy or accept a belief which becomes the system in which the mind is caught. And if I don't want to continue because life for me is too painful, then I look to a philosophy that assures me of annihilation. This is a simple, obvious fact.

Now, if the mind is free of both, then what is the state of the mind with regard to the fact which we call death? Do you understand, sirs? If the mind has no conclusions, is there death? We know that machinery wears out in use. The organism of X may last a hundred years, but it wears out. That is not what we are concerned with. But inwardly, psychologically, we want the 'I' to continue, and the 'I' is made up of conclusions, is it not? The mind has got a series of hopes, determinations, wishes, conclusions—"I have arrived," "I want to go on writing," "I want to find happiness"—and it wants these conclusions to continue; therefore, it is afraid of their coming to an end. But if the mind has no conclusions, if it does not say, "I am somebody," "I want my name and my property to continue," "I want to fulfill myself through my son," and so on, which are all desires, conclusions, then is not the mind itself in a state of constant dying? And to such a mind, is there death?

Don't agree. This is not a matter of agreement, nor is it mere logic. It is an actual experience. When your wife, your husband, your sister dies, or when you lose property, you will soon find out how you are clinging to the known. But when the mind is free of the known, then is not the mind itself the unknown? After all, what we are afraid of is leaving the known, the known being the things that we have concluded, judged, compared, accumulated. I know my wife, my house, my family, my name, I have cultivated certain thoughts, experiences, virtues, and I am afraid to let all that go. So, as long as the mind has any form of conclusion, as long as it is caught in a system, a concept, a formula, it can never know what is true. A believing mind is a conditioned mind, and whether it believes in continuity or annihilation, it can never find out what death is. And it is only now, while you are living, not when you are unconscious, dying, that you can find out the truth of that extraordinary thing called death.

January 23, 1955

Talk to Parents at Rajghat School, Banaras

What is the responsibility of a parent? Perhaps it might be of interest to discuss that, even though there are very few parents here. Why do we, as parents, want to educate our children at all? It is generally understood that parents desire their children to be educated to fit into society, to adjust themselves and adapt their thoughts to society, which really means helping them to prepare for a profession of some kind so that they can earn a livelihood. They want their children to be educated to pass examinations, to take a degree at some university, and then to have a fairly good job, a secure position in society. That is all most parents are concerned with. To put their children through college they pay so much money—easily if they are wealthy, with great difficulty if they are not—and to them, education is a matter of adding a few letters after the student's name, which they hope will make him a so-called good citizen, a respectable member of society. What parents are primarily interested in, especially in a country like this where there is overpopulation and a heavy burden of tradition, is to help the student have a job so that he won't starve. I am not criticizing, but merely stating a fact. Here, fortunately, the problem of war is not imminent, whereas in Europe and America conscription in various forms has been introduced and the boys have to go through the military system; they are trained in a particular military unit to fight, to destroy, and are released only after three or four years to enter a civilian occupation and carry on their life. In India this is not insisted upon.

So, what is the responsibility of parents? Does their responsibility end the moment the boy or the girl has taken a degree and is married off? What do we mean by responsibility? To what are we responsible? Is it our responsibility to see that the young people fit into a particular society irrespective of whether that society is good or bad, revolutionary or corrupt? Is it our responsibility to make the boy or the girl conform, regardless of what he or she wants to do and is capable of? Is that what we mean by responsibility?

Questioner: Whether he lives in America, in Russia, or in India, a parent who really loves his child will be deeply concerned to insure that he has an ingrained sense of social obligation which will be natural to him and which, as he grows up, he will express in a certain way according to his capacities.

Krishnamurti: The parent spends so much money on the education of his child, which means putting him through the university and all that. Such education may enable the student to fit into society, but will it help him to be creative?

Questioner: The parent will judge education on the basis of whether or not it makes his child an asset from the social point of view.

Krishnamurti: That brings up the complex question of what is the cultural or social background of the parent and the educator, does it not? It means, really, investigating to find out what society is, and whether education is merely a matter of conditioning the child to serve society according to the established pattern. On the other hand, when he grows up and leaves the university, should the student be in opposition to society? Or should he be capable of creating a new kind of society altogether? As parents, what is it that we want?

Questioner: There is one thing we don't want—that a young man who has had a good education in an expensive school should just demand comforts from society. Such people give nothing in return, and they are impoverishing the country.

KRISHNAMURTI: That is, how can education help the student, from childhood right through adolescence to maturity, not to be antisocial? Now, what do we mean by being antisocial? If a boy is educated not to be antisocial in Russia, it means conditioning him to fit into the communist society. Here, when we talk of educating him not to be antisocial, we also mean conditioning him not to break out of the established pattern. As long as he conforms and stays within the pattern of a particular society, we call him a social asset, but the moment he breaks away from the pattern we say he is antisocial.

So, is it the function of education merely to mold the student to fit into a particular society? Or should education help him to understand what society is, with its corrupting, destructive, disintegrating factors, so that he comprehends the whole process and steps out of it? The stepping out of it is not antisocial. On the contrary, not to conform to any given society is true social action.

Questioner: If education makes the students so self-centered that when he leaves college he has a complete disregard of poverty and no feeling for the poor, then surely that education is wrong, and a thoughtful parent will be concerned to see that such a thing does not happen.

KRISHNAMURTI: Then how can education help the student not to become mediocre, not to fall into the mediocrity of the rich, of the poor, or of the middle class? What kind of education should there be in order to break up the mediocrity of the mind, if we can put it that way? Not to be mediocre, surely, the boy must be able to do things with his hands as well as with his mind, he must not say, "This is good," "That is bad," he must be neither Brahmanical nor anti-Brahmanical, neither pro-this nor contra-that—which means, really, that there must be an environment in which the student is stimulated all around and not merely on the intellectual side.

Questioner: As a father, what can I do at home to prevent mediocrity in the child?

KRISHNAMURTI: If the father is mediocre, that is, if his tastes are conventional, if he is traditional in his outlook, if he is afraid of his neighbors, of his wife, or losing his position, then how can he help to prevent mediocrity in the child?

Questioner: Granting that the parent is mediocre, how is he to approach the problem of his relationship with his child?

KRISHNAMURTI: Education, surely, is the understanding of the relationship between oneself and the child, between oneself and society. The understanding of relationship is education. But is it possible to understand relationship if the mind has a fixed point?

Questioner: What do you mean by having a fixed point?

KRISHNAMURTI: Having a belief in something, a religious opinion, a dogmatic conclusion, a narrow attitude to life. And will such a parent be able to understand the relationship between himself and his neighbor or his child? Obviously not, because he starts from a fixed opinion, his thought is already formed. After all, relationship is a living thing, whether it be one's relationship with people, with property, or with ideas, and if one starts with a preformed attitude towards people, property, or ideas, then there is no understanding of relationship.

Now, what is our relationship with people? If I am a parent, what is my relationship with my child? First of all, have I any relationship at all? The child happens to be my son or my daughter, but is there actually any relationship, any contact, companionship, communion between myself and my child, or am I too busy earning money, or whatever it is, and therefore pack him off to school? So I really have no contact or communion at all with the boy or the girl, have I? If I am a busy parent, as parents generally are, and I merely want my son to be something, a lawyer, a doctor, or an engineer, have I any relationship with him even though I have produced him?

Questioner: I feel I ought to have a relationship with my child, and I am hoping to establish one on which he can depend. How am I to proceed?

KRISHNAMURTI: We are discussing the relationship of the parent with his child, and we are asking ourselves if there is any relationship at all, though we say there is. What is that relationship? You have produced the child and you want him to pass through college, but have you actually any other relationship with him? The very rich man has his amusements, his worries, and he has no time for the child, so he sees him occasionally, and when the child is eight or ten years old, he packs him off to school, and that is the end of it. The middle class are also much too busy to have any relationship with the child, they have to go to the office every day, and the poor man's relationship with the child is work, for the child must also work.

So, let us establish what the word *relationship* means in our life. What is the relationship between myself and society? After all, society is relationship, is it not? And if I really had a feeling of deep love for my child, that very love would create quite a revolution because I would not want my child to fit into society and have all his initiative destroyed, I would not want him to be weighed down by tradition, by fear and corruption, bowing to the highly-placed and kicking the lowly. I would see to it that this decaying society ceased to exist, that wars and every form of violence came to an end. Surely, if we love our children, it means that we must find a way of educating them so that they do not merely fit into society.

Questioner: How best can we equip the child to meet the present society?

KRISHNAMURTI: We know what society is, with its corruption and all the rest of it. Is it the function of education to help the child to fit into any particular society, whether communist, socialist, or capitalist? When he does fit into society, he is in constant rebellion there, is he not? Are we not at each other's throats in society, actually or psychologically?

Questioner: How can we help the child not merely to rebel within society, but to break away front this society altogether?

KRISHNAMURTI: That is just the point. Do you as a parent want your child to rebel in the deepest sense of that word? Do you want to help him to free himself from this society and create, not a society which is communistic, this or that, but an altogether different kind of society, a new culture?

Questioner: We can help him with our limitations.

Krishnamurti: Then we shall limit the child also. Is it possible to educate the child not to conform to your limitations or my limitations but to understand himself and create his own society? Is it possible for us all, both inside and outside the school, to help the student to bring about an atmosphere of freedom in which there is no fear so that he understands the whole social structure and says, "This is not a true society, I shall step out of it and help to build a society which is totally new"? Otherwise, he merely falls in line.

So, what is the function of education? Is it not to help the student to understand his own compulsions, motives, urges, which create the pattern of a destructive society? Is it not to help him to understand and break through his own conditionings, his own limitations?

Questioner: I think it is first necessary for the child to understand the society in which he is; otherwise, he cannot break away from it.

Krishnamurti: He is part of society, he is in contact with it every day and sees its corruption. Now, how are you going to help him, through education, to understand the implications of this society and be free of it so that he can create a different kind of social order?

Questioner: A common child inevitably conforms to the pattern of society.

Krishnamurti: There is no such thing as a common child, but there may be a common teacher who is scared stiff. That is why the educator needs educating. He also must change and not merely conform to society.

Questioner: Since we have our own limitations, should we impose them on the child?

Questioner: It is not imposition, it is helplessness.

Krishnamurti: So, being aware of our limitations and our helplessness, how shall we bring about the right kind of education?

Questioner: We want to hear that from you, that is why we are here.

Krishnamurti: Unless the educator himself is educated, it is not possible to help the student to break down his limitations, is it? The education of the educator is the one essential factor. Now, is the educator willing to educate himself? That means, really, is he willing to understand his own status, to be aware of his limitations and break through them as much as he can, thereby helping the boy or the girl to break through?

Questioner: One can try.

Krishnamurti: If the educator himself does not see the necessity of breaking down his own limitations as much as he can, he will obviously impose those limitations on the child.

Questioner: He sees the necessity of breaking down his own limitations, but however much he may try, he is still limited.

Krishnamurti: So, what do we propose to do? Are we prepared as grown-up men and women, so-called mature human beings, to understand our limitations and break them down? Otherwise, through our influence, we are bound to impose these limitations on the children. First of all, as parents and educators, are we aware of our limitations?

Questioner: I am aware that the limitations are there, but I don't know how to get out of them.

KRISHNAMURTI: Do we know what the word *limitation* implies? Is it a limitation to call ourselves Hindus?

Questioner: That cannot be a limitation.

KRISHNAMURTI: But it is because it divides people. Are we prepared to break through all that and cease to be Hindus or Muslims?

Questioner: I think one is prepared to go that far.

KRISHNAMURTI: If the teachers, the educators, are prepared to do that, then the implications are tremendous. After all, when you call yourself a Hindu, what does it mean? There is not only the geographical division but also the division that is created by belief in certain forms of religion, in certain traditions, in a certain kind of social order. Are we as educators prepared to drop these beliefs, which means going against the present society? Are we prepared to go that far? Unless the educator dedicates himself to education, and particularly if he has daughters to be married off, as he generally has, he will merely conform. Should not the educator dedicate himself to education in the right sense of the word? And will the parent help the teacher to dedicate himself to right education?

I think most people throughout the world recognize that the present system of education has failed because it has produced wars, moral decay, and all the rest of it; and also, except among a very few people, all creative thinking has ceased. So, what is the right kind of education, and how are we to bring it about? It obviously cannot be brought about through somebody saying, "This is right education," and all of us merely agreeing and following the pattern, but rather the teacher and the parent, the whole lot of us, must sit down together and find out what right education is, which means that the parent and the teacher have to be educated as well as the student.

It seems to me that right education is to help the student to be free because it is only in freedom that one can be creative. Freedom implies not courage but having no fear, which is entirely different. To have no fear is a state in which there is no conformity, no imitation, and therefore no following of any authority. All that is implied in freedom. To find out what it means to have no authority in education, one has to go into the implications of it. Having no authority does not mean that the boy does exactly what he likes, but the moment the boy knows there is authority, he is afraid; therefore, we have already introduced the imitative process.

Now, are we as parents prepared to relinquish our authority so that the boy is really free, not just to pursue superficial distractions, but free to find out what is true, to question all tradition, to question the very authority of the parents? If we really mean that the boy should be free, all that must follow.

Questioner: Unless we are free, we cannot give freedom to the child.

KRISHNAMURTI: That means you will have to wait for centuries. Is what you say an actual fact or merely a speculative idea? All initiative and creative thinking are obviously destroyed if there is no freedom for the child—which does not mean allowing the boy to do whatever he likes. But is the parent willing to let go of his authority, with all its implications, so that the child finds out what is true? Are the parents willing to educate themselves to that extent?

You see, the parent must feel the necessity of this as strongly as he feels the necessity of his next meal. Freedom implies self-knowledge. To understand oneself is the first step towards freedom. And are we prepared to say, "I want to understand myself so that the child will understand himself and create a new society"? Or are we only concerned with helping the child to conform? Will the parents help to create an educational center where there is no fear? Superficially, that means no examinations because examinations do bring about a state of fear, a sense of competition. Are the parents prepared to create an educational center where the boy is not taught to surpass some other boy, where the students are not given marks and divided as the stupid and the clever, but where each boy and each girl is an individual to be helped to find his or her vocation? If the parents are not prepared to create educational centers of this kind, then how do you expect them to come into being?

That is why, sirs, I raised the question of whether parents have any relationship with their children. If the parent loves the child, this will be the consequence. He will want the child to be free in the deep sense of the word, not merely to do amusing and sensational things which are destructive. As parents, are we prepared for all this? It is because the parents do not demand it that educational centers of this kind do not exist, but the parents do demand that the children pass examinations, and so you have the thing you demand.

January 27, 1955

Fourth Talk at Rajghat School, Banaras

If each one of us could really solve any given human problem, I think a great deal of our misery and incapacity to meet life would come to an end. Is it that we don't know how to go about solving a problem and must therefore depend on others to solve our problems, or is it that we are not really aware of the problems that we have? I think it would be worthwhile if we could at this meeting find out if there is an actual problem which all of us have, a problem which is significant, and then see if together we cannot resolve it, because if we can once resolve for ourselves any human problem, then we shall have the capacity to resolve all future problems as they arise. As long as we are not capable of resolving a problem, we neglect, suppress, or escape from it, thereby giving root to a multiplicity of other problems. When we don't know how to tackle a problem and merely escape from it, that very escape becomes another problem, so one problem breeds several more; whereas, if we could attack and understand any given problem, then perhaps we should be able to bring about a mind which is not burdened with problems but is capable of meeting each human problem as it arises. Such a mind, being silent, always gives the true response, and it is because we cannot give the true response to every challenge that our problems increase.

After all, a problem which all of us have, if we are conscious of it, is the inadequacy of our response to any challenge. Not being capable of responding adequately to challenge, we give rise to a problem, and having a problem, we escape from it or try to find an immediate or convenient solution, which again becomes another problem. So one problem always breeds several other problems, which is what is happening, not only in the life of the individual, but also in the collective life of the group, of the nation. This is obvious, is it not? We go after peace, individually or collectively, and in the very search for peace we are introducing various elements which produce conflict, misery, strife.

Now, can we understand how to meet any human problem? If we are at all aware of a problem, how do we actually meet it? Could we dwell on that for the moment? Because I think the really important thing is not what the problem is, but how we approach it. Surely, the problem is one thing, and our approach to the problem is another. Can one be conscious of one's approach to any problem, actually and not theoretically? What is one's process of thinking when one is confronted with a problem? Please don't merely listen to me, but watch your own mind and see how you approach your own problems. Don't you always approach any problem with a conclusion, that is, with your mind already made up about the problem? In other words, you have various theories, opinions, formulas with regard to the problem, and with that mentality you approach the problem or seek an answer. Either the mind is approaching the problem with a conclusion, with a formula, with a belief, or it is seeking an answer, so its approach is essentially an evasion of the problem, is it not? If you watch your own mind, you will see this process in operation.

What is the state of a mind that is seeking an answer, a solution? Obviously, it is seeking in terms of its own gratification. Please watch your own mind because I am only describing what is actually taking place. If you are merely listening to me, what I am saying will be utterly superficial, but if you are following the description of your own mind, which means being aware of your own mental processes, then what is being said will have significance.

When the mind seeks a solution to a problem, its approach is invariably a process of choice, its choice being based on its own gratification; it wants an easy solution, an answer in which no effort will be needed. In its search for a solution to the problem, the mind is looking through the various memories it has collected, the experiences it has gathered, and it chooses from among those experiences the answer most suitable to the problem. So your approach to the problem is that of choosing the most gratifying solution, is it not? Please watch, investigate your own mental processes, and you will see that your mind approaches any problem with opinions, conclusions, or it seeks an answer, or it tries to find ways and means of avoiding the issue. That is our general approach to every problem, which means that the mind is not tackling the problem directly but is translating the problem in terms of its old memories, its conclusions, concepts, formulas. So the problem remains and takes root in the soil of the mind because the mind is not fresh in its approach. If the mind could be made fresh, then its response to the problem would be entirely different.

Now, can we proceed from there? The question is not how to resolve the problem but whether the mind can be fresh in its approach, for the problem exists only because of the inadequacy of the mind's response to the challenge. However much the mind may wish to solve the problem, as long as its response is inadequate, there will be a problem. It is because the mind is inadequate, not fresh in its response, that it is incapable of dealing with the problem in its totality, and hence there must be a further multiplication of problems, which means an increase of pain, misery, and suffering. Psychologically, this is what is actually taking place, is it not? To see it does not require much thought, and there need not be a great ado about it.

So, is it possible to approach any problem afresh, with a mind that is not burdened with conclusions, that is not seeking an answer or a means of evasion? Can the mind make itself fresh, innocent, so that it is capable of meeting the problem anew? Innocence is not the cutting off of experience because you cannot cut off experience. But the mind is the result of experience, of the process of time, and how can the mind, being the result of time and therefore of experience and knowledge, make itself new, fresh, innocent, to understand the problem? If the approach is innocent, the problem will be tackled with wisdom, with understanding, but as long as the mind comes to the problem with previous knowledge, the problem multiplies. I don't know if you have ever watched this process in your approach to a human problem. Even in mathematical problems it works, I believe.

You have a problem. If the mind approaches the problem as though it had never thought about it before, if it comes upon the problem being fully aware of its own bondages and hindrances so that it is free of them, then is there a problem? I hope I am making myself clear. We say that we must understand the problem, we must find an answer to it, we must search out the cause and resolve it, but the very instrument that is seeking the cause and is trying to find an answer is itself the problem; the problem is not outside of itself. So, how does the mind of each one of us approach a problem? Go very slowly and investigate how your own mind approaches any problem. Be aware of the process.

Now, can the mind ever confront a problem without seeking a solution, without having any conclusions about it, and without running away? That is, can the mind face the problem and not look back upon its own experiences, not delve into the pigeonholes of memory in order to choose the answer most suitable to the problem? Can the mind ever say, "I don't know how to tackle the problem"? Do you understand, sirs? Because it is very important actually to feel, and not just to say, that in front of any given human problem, the mind, which is the result of the past, is confronted with something new and therefore cannot answer with the memories of the old.

So, can the mind be in a state of not-knowing? And should not the mind always be in that state? Surely, the man who says, "I know," does not know. He knows only the things that have occurred and are over, and therefore he is burdened with memory. But the man who says, "I do not know" is in a process of investigation, of constant inquiry; therefore, his mind never accumulates and then responds from the accumulation. Being actually and not theoretically in the state of not-knowing, is not his mind really experiencing out of silence? And to such a mind, is there a problem to be solved? Such a mind is not in a condition of lethargy, it is completely alive; therefore, it neither has a problem nor is it creating a problem. Then begins, I think, an extraordinary thing, which is the whole sense of what is holy, what is sacred.

You see, further inquiry in this direction will only be a description, therefore a speculation, unless you are actually experiencing as we go along. One may have an occasional comprehension of what is holy, of what is true, but a second later it becomes memory, and therefore it has already turned to ashes, and I think one is inevitably caught in sorrow, in misery, as long as one does not understand this whole problem. Therefore it is essential that the mind should know itself and its workings, which is self-knowledge. Without self-knowledge, any verbal statement, any belief or nonbelief really has no value at all. The mind must start, not with 'what should be', but with *what is*, it must begin by watching itself from moment to moment, seeing its actual responses and not getting lost in speculative hopes and fears. Actually moving with each response as it takes place brings about an astonishing awareness of the mind in which every thought, because it moves slowly, can be completely understood, all the details being immediately perceived. Without such a mind, all searching for reality, going to priests, doing puja, is really rubbish; it has no meaning, but for most of us the rubbish has become extraordinarily significant. To put away all that rubbish is to understand the ways of the mind and how it operates in relation to that rubbish. Then the mind can go extraordinarily far; then the mind itself becomes a limitless, timeless thing.

Questioner: Throughout my working day the mind masks its mediocrity behind socially useful ends, but during the time of meditation it is faced with its mediocrity, it is in torture and despair. What am I to do about it?

KRISHNAMURTI: Sir, what do you mean by meditation? And to what are you giving importance? To everyday work, with its social responsibilities and so on, or to meditation? I am not putting meditation in opposition to the operation of the mediocre mind while it is working or helping to bring about various social reforms. I am asking why the mind separates the two and gives greater significance to one than to the other.

Questioner: In the ordinary working day one is conscious of the usefulness of the social ends to which the mind is directed, therefore, the attention is not on mediocrity, but when one sits quietly for awhile, the mask is down, so one is conscious of mediocrity and nothing else.

KRISHNAMURTI: You are saying that when it is not occupied, the mind is aware of its mediocrity; all the masks having fallen away, the mind is confronted and tortured by its own pettiness, so what is one to do? As long as the mind is occupied with social and other activities, it is unaware of itself, but the moment it stops being occupied, the whole content of the mind is revealed to itself.

Questioner: Not necessarily.

KRISHNAMURTI: The moment the noise stops, one is aware of the mediocrity of the mind, and you are asking what one is to do about it.

Now, is not an occupied mind mediocre? Surely, an occupied mind is petty, whether it is occupied with business, with physics, with the kitchen, or with the sacred books and the pursuit of God. Please go slowly with me, sirs, let us go into it together. The mind of the housewife, that is, of a lady who is concerned with the kitchen, with food, with children, with keeping the household clean, and so on, you would consider very trivial, whereas the man who is seeking God, who does puja and all the rest of it, is looked upon as being very noble, but his mind also is occupied, is it not? Only the occupation is different, that is all. The object of occupation is at a different level, but the mind is still occupied. And is not the mind that is everlastingly occupied, with itself or with anything else, mediocre? What does mediocrity mean? Average, ordinary—which is what our minds are, is it not? Our minds are constantly occupied, the student with his examination, the father with his job, and so on.

Now, can the mind be free from occupation? Can it do the kitchen work, study physics, or what you will, and still not be occupied so that the mind has space and is not filled with occupation? Can the mind ever stop producing thoughts—which is occupation, is it not? When the mind is occupied with the kitchen, with God, with sex, with this or that, it is obviously producing thoughts, thinking. And is not thinking itself mediocre? Because after all, what is thinking? It is the response of the background, the response of memory, of experience; and is not the investigation of that process, which is what we have done just now, real meditation? To meditate is to find out whether the mind can really stop producing thoughts one after another, which means being aware of and observing the processes of one's own thinking so that the mind sees and understands the fact that its thinking is conditioned, and therefore thought comes to an end. Only then is there not a state of mediocrity. Then the mind can act totally differently for any social end.

Sir, after all, there is space, there is silence between two words, between two notes, but to most of us the word or the note is important, not the silence. If there were no silence, there would be one continuous noise, and that is the state of the mind which is ceaselessly occupied; like a machine that is kept in constant operation, it wears itself out. But the mind that has space, that has wide gaps of silence, renews itself in that very silence, and therefore its action in any direction has quite a different significance.

Questioner: Can the mind work and at the same time not be occupied?

KRISHNAMURTI: Try it, sir. For most of us, work is occupation. The moment the mind "works," as one calls it, it is thinking, and therefore it is occupied.

Sir, the difficulty in answering these questions is that in your listening you are not aware of what is actually taking place, you do not see the process of your own mind in operation. You are listening to me, that is all, and saying that it does not work; you are just sitting there while somebody else is speaking, and therefore it has no meaning. When you go to a football match in which you are not participating, you sit on the seats and criticize the players. Similarly, you are here merely as spectators at a game which is called a lecture or a talk. Whereas, if you were not mere spectators but through the description of the speaker you were actually watching your own minds in operation, then you would find an extraordinary thing happening to you, the coming into being of a state in which there is neither the spectator nor the player. You see, that is why it is very important to have self-knowledge. Have I answered your question?

Questioner: You said the teacher should have the intention not to influence the child. Is it possible to avoid influence altogether?

KRISHNAMURTI: What do you think, sirs? Are you waiting for me? Again you are assuming the role of the spectators.

What is influence? Don't you know what influence is? Are you not influencing your children? The teacher, the parents, the government, the Bible, the Upanishads, the sun, the food we eat, the words we use—everything is influencing us, is it not? Take the word *love.* What an extraordinary neurological influence merely the word itself has on us. So everything is influencing us, and we in turn are influencing others. When we read a newspaper, we are being influenced by the proprietors, by the columnist, by the pictures; we are influenced by propaganda, by the so-called spiritual magazines, by books, by lectures, by the way we dress, the way we sit. Everything is influencing us, and the questioner wants to know whether there can ever be the cessation of influence, even when one has the intention not to influence the child. This is really a complex question, so let us take time to go into it.

We see that everything, physical and mental, influences us. Where is one to draw the line? I may not want to influence my child, but influence is going on, conditioning his mind; the magazines he reads, his friends at school, his teachers, everything around him is influencing him. Consciously or unconsciously I am myself influencing the child, and the whole culture or civilization in which we live is conditioning his mind to be a communist or a capitalist, a Hindu or a Christian, and so on. So the question is not whether it is possible to stop all influence but whether one can help the child to understand and be free of the influences which are conditioning him. Is it possible for education to help the student to be so intelligent that he will see and understand for himself those influences which are conditioning his mind, and put them away? Surely, that is our inquiry, not how to stop influence, or what kinds of influence the child should have.

Now, what is it that conditions the mind? If the mind were completely secure, it would have no fear, would it? And when the mind has nothing to lose, it is completely secure, is it not? Which means that in its own insecurity there is security. As long as the mind demands to be secure, as long as it is seeking permanency in any form, it creates influences which will condition it. But cannot the mind be aware of total insecurity, of being completely insecure—which in fact it is? Life is insecure, impermanent. The resistance, the denial of the fact that life is completely insecure produces opposition between the desire to be secure and the fact, thereby creating fear, and it is this fear that conditions the mind, the fear that comes into being when you do not accept the fact. This fear may be described in different terms as the fear a boy has towards his parents, or the fear of not passing an examination, or the fear of being scolded, or the fear which arises when the mind wants to fulfill and is denied. The mind which is ambitious at any level has always with it the shadow of fear because however much its ambition is being fulfilled, it may at any moment be thwarted.

So, can the student be given an environment of complete security?—which means, really, an environment in which he is not compared with the less clever or the more clever, in which there is no sense of condemnation, so that he feels completely at home. He generally does not feel at home with his parents because they do not know what it means to give the child that feeling of complete security. The parents want the boy to be something, they say, "You are not studying as well as your brother, who is so clever," and so they destroy the poor boy by instilling fear. When the mind of the student feels completely secure, he can study more easily, but that means the educator must be totally free of his own demand to be secure because the moment he demands security, he instills fear. That is why teaching is a dedication, not a job.

Questioner: I am an engineer by profession, and I think it is obvious that your idea of truth goes far beyond the standard or commonplace meaning of that word. Could you kindly explain further.

KRISHNAMURTI: Sir, an engineer is surely concerned with facts, not with speculations. If he has to build a bridge, he must examine the proposed site and not imagine what the site should be. He may be aware of the aesthetic value of a certain line in building a bridge, which may be entirely different from what is called for by the actual facts he discovers at the site. With ourselves it is not like that. We think we are something, the atma, the paramatma, we have theories, speculations about the permanent and the impermanent, a vast number of beliefs, and so we are a mass of unreality which we are unwilling to face and look at. The fact is one thing, and our thoughts or opinions about the fact are entirely different. Only the mind that is capable of looking at the fact finds out what is true. The fact is that there is no such thing as permanency, and if the mind makes permanency into a fact, then that permanency is an opinion, it is what the mind would like the fact to be. It is as simple as that. If we can look at the fact without the myth of opinion, of knowledge, of judgment and evaluation, then the truth of the fact will have its own evaluation and produce its own action. To approach the fact with evaluation, with judgment, is entirely different from approaching it without judgment, without evaluation, and therefore understanding the fact.

Now, can one look at the fact that one is greedy, that one is a liar, that one is ambitious, without evaluating it, without condemning or saying it is all right? If the mind can just see the fact, then the truth of the fact operates on the mind in the most unexpected manner, and that operation is its own evaluation, not the mind's evaluation. But a mind which has gathered the truth of the fact and acts from what it has gathered is surely incapable of looking at the fact because it is looking through the screen of memory, of knowledge, of experience, of evaluation. That is why the mind must die each day to itself, to every experience, to all the knowledge it has gathered. The mind objects to that death because experience and knowledge are a means of its own security, permanency; and a mind that has permanency, a sense of security, is never creative. It is only for the mind which is totally insecure and is therefore not seeking, not wanting a state of security, that reality comes into being.

January 30, 1955

Fifth Talk at Rajghat School, Banaras

Perhaps it might be worthwhile to find out what is the function of our thinking, because without understanding the whole process of our thought, conscious as well as unconscious, the mind cannot be free to discover what is true. We may search for truth, but our search will be in vain if we do not understand the content or the background of the reaction which we call our thinking. Our thinking is obviously supposed to guide our action, but our action is now so automatic that there is hardly any thinking at all. Besides, through various forms of education, the education that we receive at school and college, as well as the whole education imposed by society, our minds are conditioned to adjust or submit to the demands of a particular culture. We accept certain things as inevitable, depending on our sociological, religious, or economic background, and having accepted, we act; hence our action becomes almost automatic. Thinking is hardly necessary any more, and it seems to me very important to reexamine the whole process of our thinking and see if we cannot totally break away from the background in which we have been brought up, thereby bringing about a revolution in our lives which will in turn create a different kind of culture altogether. Real revolution is not communist, socialist, capitalist, or anything of that kind because it can only be based on the search for reality, for God, or what you will. That search is in itself the revolution, but such revolution cannot take place as long as our thinking is merely the repetitive reaction of a certain form of conditioning.

So, it is obviously very important for all of us to find out how our minds operate, which is to have self-knowledge. If we don't know the ways of our own thinking, if we are unaware of our reactions and of how our thought is conditioned by the culture in which we have been brought up, if the mind does not penetrate deeply into the whole problem of its own background, which is really the 'me', the self—then surely all knowledge, except perhaps mechanical knowledge, becomes detrimental and mischievous. Is it not possible then to investigate the process of our thinking, not according to any formula, guide, or guru, but for ourselves, and thereby find out how the mind works?

Now, what is thinking? Can thinking ever be original, or is it always a repetitive process, the reaction of a background? Can thought lead us to reality, to God, to that extraordinary something which is beyond the process of the mind and which we call the ultimate, the absolute, or is thought a hindrance to the discovery of that reality?

Please, may I suggest that you are not merely listening to a talk. You cannot help listening because you are here and I am talking, but if in the very process of listening you observe how your own mind works, then these talks will have significance. What I am saying is nothing extraordinary, it is merely a description of the ways of the mind so that as we are listening, each one of us can be aware of the process of his own thinking. If one merely listens to a set of words and phrases and tries to catch their meaning, a talk of this kind will have no great depth, but if in the process of listening one can pursue one's own thinking and discover from what source it springs, then listening will be a self-revealing process, not just an acceptance or denial of what is being said.

Can thinking ever be the means to find out what is true, what is God? Surely, if we do not find out for ourselves what that reality is, mere reform or amelioration within the social structure can only lead to further misery. After all, man exists to find that supreme thing which is the foundation of all foundations; and without search, inquiry, without the constant watchfulness of our reactions, our thoughts and feelings, to see if they lead to that ultimate reality, to that something beyond the mundane, all our beliefs and religious activities become utter nonsense, mere superstitions leading to further mischief.

Does thought lead to reality, that reality which is never constant, which cannot be qualified in terms of time but must be discovered from moment to moment? To seek that reality, the mind must also be of that quality; otherwise, it cannot have the comprehension or the feeling of what is true. So, can thinking help to discover that reality? And can thinking be original, or is all thinking imitative? If thinking is imitative, then obviously thinking cannot lead to that reality, it is not the way out, it is not a process by which to uncover what is true. And yet our whole process of search is the cultivation of thinking, of various practices, disciplines, which are all based on thought. If thought can open the door to reality, then it has significance, but thought may be a barrier to reality, so one must find out the truth of the matter for oneself, and not merely accept or reject.

Surely, what we call thinking is the response of memory. That is fairly obvious. You have been brought up in a certain tradition; as a Hindu, a Christian, a Buddhist, a communist, or whatever it be; you have various associations, memories, beliefs, and that background responds to any challenge, which is called thinking. So the background is not different from thinking; thinking is the background. When you are asked a question about your religion, what you believe in, immediately your mind responds according to your conditioning, in terms of the various traditions, experiences, and beliefs that you have. You respond according to your particular background, as a Christian or a communist also does. So thinking is an impediment in the sense that it is merely the response of the background, of a particular conditioning. Surely, that again is obvious. Such a response, which we call thinking, definitely cannot open the door to reality. To find out what reality is, one must totally cease to be a Hindu, a Christian, a communist, this or that, so that the mind is no longer conditioned and is therefore free to discover what is true.

Is it possible for the mind to be free from its whole conditioning as a Hindu, a Muslim, a Christian, or whatever it be? And who is the entity that is going to free the mind from its background? Do you understand the question? When you say, "I must be free from my conditioning as a Hindu," who is the entity that is going to bring about this freedom? Who is the analyzer of the background? Can the analyzer break up the background? Am I making myself clear?

As a Hindu I have certain formulas, concepts, beliefs, traditions, and I see the necessity of being free from them all, for if I am not, it is obviously impossible to find out what reality is. If I am conditioned as a communist, or if my mind is molded according to any other belief, how can I ever find out what is real? Such a mind can only experience that to which it has been conditioned. Unless the mind is free from all conditioning, its search is merely a sociological reaction and it will find only what it has been conditioned to. Then how am I to free myself from all conditioning? Is there an entity who is going to help me to free myself from conditioning? That is, is there in me a thinker, an analyzer, an observer, who is not contaminated by my conditioning?

You see, so far we have assumed that there is a thinker apart from thought, have we not? We are used to the idea that there are two separate processes, one being a permanent state as the thinker, the analyzer, the observer, and the other being the movement of thought. We have always believed that there is the paramatma, a permanent spiritual entity who by analyzing the process of thinking is going to reject whatever is false and keep only what is true. Now, is there such a permanent entity apart from impermanent thought? Or is there only thinking, which is entirely impermanent and therefore creates the thinker in order to make itself permanent? Surely, thinking creates the thinker, it is not the thinker who creates the thought. This is really very important to understand for oneself, it is not a thing to accept or reject. Has not thinking created the thinker, and not the other way round?

After all, if there were no thinking, would there be a thinker? It is thinking that gives rise to the thinker, and the thinker then becomes the permanent analyzer, the observer who is untouched by time, but that entity has been created by thought, surely. It is like a diamond. The qualities of the diamond make the diamond. Remove the qualities of the diamond, and there is no diamond at all. Similarly, various desires, urges, compulsions create in their movement the entity which becomes the actor, the embodiment of will, which is the 'I' of assertive action, of assertive thought. But that will is made up of many desires. If there were no desires, there would be no will, no 'I'.

So, if there is only thinking and not the thinker, then the thinker who says, "I will free myself from my conditioning"—is himself the outcome of conditioned thought; therefore, the thinker, the observer, the analyzer, the experiencer, cannot free the mind from its conditioning. The mind may separate itself as the thinker and the thought, as will and desire, as the good and the bad, as the higher self and the lower self, but that whole process is still within the field of thought; it is only a self-deception leading to a great deal of mischievous action. The question then is: Can the mind free itself from its own conditioning when there is no censor, no analyzer, no superior self who is going to cleanse the mind?

Are you following this? Please, if this much is not clear, to go further will have no meaning. It is essential to understand this; otherwise, you will cling to the idea of a higher self, a spiritual something which is God-given, timeless, but encased in ignorance, and which is always pushing away the ignorance that is coming upon it—which is all absurd. And if there is no permanent self at all but only thinking, which creates the permanent self in different forms, then can thinking free the mind to find out what is true?

As long as we have not found out what is true, what is God, what is that extraordinary something which fills life with greatness, goodness, and beauty, all our activities at whatever level can have only a superficial meaning. Unless we are directly experiencing that which is true from moment to moment, our culture becomes mechanical and therefore destructive. Surely, man exists to find God, not merely to earn a livelihood and adjust himself to a particular pattern of society. Society does not help man to find truth. On the contrary, society prevents man from discovering what is true because society is based on the desire to be secure, to have permanency, and a mind that is secure, safe, that is seeking permanency, can never find reality. But the man who understands what is true, who is experiencing reality from moment to moment, helps to bring about a totally new society. Reformation, adjustment, or any form of revolution within the framework of society can only lead to further misery and destruction as is shown in the world at the present time, where every effort to solve one problem leads to a hundred more. Whereas, if the mind can understand what is true, experience it directly, then that very understanding creates its own action which brings about a new culture.

Our question then is: Can the mind free itself from its own conditioning? If there is no 'I', no self, no atma to free it, then what is it to do? Do you follow the problem? We have invented the 'I' which is going to free the mind from conditioning. But as we investigate the process of the 'I', we discover that the 'I' has no reality, it is merely a product of thought, which is a reaction of the background. So there is only thinking, thinking according to the background. Thinking is the response of the background, which is the mind's conditioning as a Christian, a Buddhist, a Hindu, and so on. If thought is the response of the background, and all background is conditioning, then thought cannot lead to freedom, and it is only in freedom that you can find out what is true.

So, to find what is God, what is true, thought must come to an end. Please, this is not only logical, it is factual. Thought must come to an end. But the moment you ask, "How am I to end thought?" there is an entity who operates, who practices the "how" in order to put an end to thinking. So there is no "how" at all, and this is very important to understand because for all of us the "how" is the most important thing. We say, "How am I to do this, what is the discipline I must practice?" and all that business, which we now see has no meaning. So at one sweep we get rid of this whole problem of the "how."

This may sound too facile, but it is not facile, it is not easy; on the contrary, it demands a great deal of attention, not concentration, but attention. Concentration is exclusive because it implies a motive, an incentive, whereas attention has no motive and is therefore not exclusive. In the mind's observation of itself, there comes self-knowledge, which is not the knowledge of the higher self. The higher self is an invention of the mind that wants to escape from the actuality of thought in relationship to people, to things, and to ideas. When it wants to escape from *what is,* the mind goes off into all kinds of absurdities. But when the mind begins to inquire into the process of its own being, when it sees the implications of thought and how thought comes into being, then that very perception puts an end to thought. There is no thinker who puts an end to thought; therefore, no effort is involved. Effort arises only when there is an incentive to gain something. If the mind has as an incentive the desire to break away from its conditioning, then that incentive is the reaction of its conditioning in a different direction.

So, it is very important to understand the whole process of our thinking, and the understanding of that process does not come through isolation. There is no such thing as living in isolation. The understanding of the process of our thinking comes when we observe ourselves in daily relationship, our attitudes, our beliefs, the way we talk, the way we regard people, the way we treat our husbands, our wives, our children. Relationship is the mirror in which the ways of our thinking are revealed. In the facts of relationship lies truth, not away from relationship. There is obviously no such thing as living in isolation. We may carefully cut off various forms of physical relationship, but the mind is still related. The very existence of the mind implies relationship, and self-knowledge lies through seeing the facts of relationship as they are without inventing, condemning, or justifying. In relationship the mind has certain evaluations, judgments, comparisons, it reacts to challenge according to various forms of memory, and this reaction is called thinking. If the mind can just be aware of this whole process, you will find that thought comes to a standstill. Then the mind is very quiet, very still, without incentive, without movement in any direction, and in that stillness, reality comes into being.

Questioner: It is difficult to follow you, and I find it much easier to follow people who have understood your teaching and can explain them to us. Don't you think there is need for such people to spread your teachings? It was recently pointed out in a newspaper article that you are intolerant of all beliefs and guides which help us.

KRISHNAMURTI: As long as one wants to follow, there will be a guide, and following destroys the possibility of finding out what is true. If the mind follows anybody, it is following its own interest, which is not to understand what is true. You are surely not following me because I am only trying to point out the operations of your own mind. If you follow somebody, you are not inquiring into the ways of your own mind, and without understanding the ways of your own mind, to follow another can only lead you to more misery. To follow another is evil, it does not matter who it is, whether it be Christ, Buddha, myself, or anybody else. Following is destructive, for imitation breeds fear. It is fear that makes you follow, not the search for truth. We don't understand the miseries of life, the transient happiness, the mystery of death, the extraordinary complexities of relationship, and we hope that by following somebody all this will somehow be explained and disappear. But to understand all these complexities is not to follow anybody. This mass of complexities has been created by each one of us, and we have to understand the cause of it, which is our own thinking.

The questioner says, "I find it much easier to follow people who have understood your teachings and can explain them to us," which is to have interpreters. For God's sake, sirs, keep away from interpreters because the interpreter is bound to interpret according to his conditioning and his vested interest. This again is so obvious, it does not need much thinking. But you see, you want somebody to help you, and the moment you demand help, you have brought into being the whole process of corruption, which really indicates that you have no confidence in being able to go to the source of things for yourself. The source is not me, but you, the way you think. The source is yourself, and why should you follow anybody or listen to interpreters to understand yourself? What is it the interpreters understand which you don't understand? They may have a better command of words than you or I, but keep away from interpreters; do not become a follower because the source of mischief is in yourself, in the ways of your own thinking, and as long as you are imitating, following someone who is interpreting, you are escaping from yourself. The escape may be pleasant, it may temporarily give you gratification, but there is always in that escape the sting of sorrow.

And you don't have to spread my teachings because if you don't understand yourself, you cannot spread them. You may be able to buy and distribute a few books, but surely that is not at all so essential as to understand yourself. When you understand yourself, then you will spread understanding in the world, you will bring greater happiness to man. But if you are spreading somebody else's teachings, you are creating more mischief, for then you are merely propagandists, and propaganda is not truth.

"It was recently pointed out in a newspaper article that you are intolerant of all beliefs and guides which help us." Sirs, what is tolerance? Why should you be tolerant or intolerant? Facts don't demand either tolerance or intolerance. Facts are there for us to take them or leave them. Why do we beat this drum of tolerance? All beliefs, the Christian, the Hindu, the Muslim, are a source of enmity between people. Is it being intolerant to point out that obvious fact? But if you cling to your belief, you will say I am intolerant because you are unwilling to look at the fact. The fact is so patent that as long as we are divided as Muslims, Hindus, Christians, it is bound to create antagonism. We are human beings, not a mass of conflicting beliefs. But you see, we have a vested interest in our belief. Belief is profitable. Societies are founded on it, religions with their priests thrive on it, and to them any questioning of belief is intolerance. But the man who faces facts as they are is surely not concerned with either tolerance or intolerance.

Belief is not reality. You may believe in God, but your belief has no more reality than that of the man who does not believe in God. Your belief is the result of your background, of your religion, of your fears, and the nonbelief of the communist and others is equally the result of their conditioning. To find out what is true, the mind must be free from belief and nonbelief. I know you smile and agree, but you will still go on believing because it is so much more convenient, so much more respectable and safe. If you did not believe, you might lose your job, you might suddenly find that you are nobody. It is being free of belief that matters, not your smiling and agreeing in this room.

With regard to guides, gurus, and all the rest of it, you follow because you have a motive, an incentive, which is that you want to be happy, to find God. So you are always seeking, and the guru is supposed to help you to find. But can a guru help you to find what is real? Reality must be outside the field of time, it must be something totally new, uncontaminated by the past or the future. If it is outside the field of time, then the mind, which is the result of time, can never find it. As long as you are following somebody in order to find reality, God, you are merely following the desires of your own mind. You are following because it gratifies you; therefore, it is not leading you to truth. That is why it is important not to follow, not to have gurus. When you seek, your search is the outcome of your desire, and your desire projects that which you are seeking. It is only when the mind is not seeking, when it is really quiet, completely still, without any form of incentive, that there is the coming into being of that thing which is not caught by the mind, which is not found in books, and of which no guru knows because to know is not to know.

Questioner: When you say that discipline is destructive, how can you obviate the danger of producing an army of sanctimonious nincompoops?

Krishnamurti: I don't know what the questioner means, but we can see for ourselves the effects of so-called discipline. Now, what do we mean by discipline, and why should there be discipline? We have accepted discipline as necessary in schools, in daily life, in the political party, we discipline ourselves to find reality, and so on. There are various forms of discipline at different levels of our conscious and unconscious activities. Discipline is a process of resistance, of submission or adaptation, is it not? You adapt yourself to society's demands because if you don't, you will be destroyed; you suppress yourself and submit to society in order to be a good or moral citizen, and so on. Surely, discipline implies shaping the mind to a certain formula, either externally imposed or imposed by yourself. Through tradition, the evaluations of religion, culture, and all the rest of it, society imposes a certain discipline on the mind. It says, "Keep within limits; otherwise, you will not be respectable, you will become dangerous," and so on, which one can understand. But the idea of imposing a discipline on oneself seems wholly absurd because who is the entity that disciplines? The mind has divided itself as the one who disciplines and the part which is to be disciplined, but it is all the same mind playing a trick on itself. Surely, that is obvious. For its own convenience the mind has divided itself as the one who disciplines and the part that has to be disciplined, and we play this game with ourselves, which is absurd because it has no reality at all. It is a convenient form of self-deception.

Now, can a mind which is so disciplined, which is controlled, shaped through tradition, through certain evaluations which society calls moral—we are not now questioning whether they are moral or immoral—can such a mind ever find out what is true? Or does the mind, in seeking what is true, create its own way of life which is disciplinary? Obviously, the man who is seeking truth must be virtuous, but virtue is not an end in itself. Virtue is to bring order, it has no validity in itself. If virtue has validity in itself, it leads to respectability, which society loves. But the mind that is understanding itself creates its own order, which is not an imposition, not an adjustment to any form of compulsion. The mind that is aware is all the time bringing order within itself, which is not the order imposed by society or religious sanctions though outwardly they may seem to correspond. But a mind that is merely controlled through fear of going wrong, through fear of what people will say, that is imitating, trying to live according to what Shankara or anyone else has said—such a mind can never find out what is real. It is only the free mind that can discover the real, and to be free the mind has to understand itself. But merely to state that the mind is free has no meaning. It is like the schoolboy wanting to do exactly what he likes, which he calls freedom. That is obviously not freedom. Whereas, if the mind is aware of its own ways in relationship, if it is capable of watching its own movements without condemnation or evaluation, then it will understand what it is to be free, and only such a mind can discover that which is eternal.

February 6, 1955

First Talk in Bombay

I think that one of the greatest problems confronting man at this present time is the question of creativeness, how to bring about the creative release of the individual, and if we can consider the question, not merely verbally, but go into it very deeply, perhaps we shall be able to discover the full significance of that word *creativeness*. It seems to me that this is the real issue, not what kind of political reform to work for, or what kind of religion to follow. How is it possible to bring about the creative release of the individual, not only at the beginning of his existence, but throughout life? That is, how is the individual to have abundant energy rightly directed so that his life will have expansive and profound significance? If this evening we can really go into this matter, I think we shall be better able to understand the subsequent talks.

I feel that revolution is necessary at the most profound level, not fragmentary revolution, but integrated revolution, a total revolution starting not from the outside but from within, and to bring about that total revolution, surely we must understand the ways of our own thought, the whole process of our thinking, which is self-knowledge. Without the foundation of self-knowledge, what we think has very little meaning. So it is important, is it not, that from the very beginning we should understand the process of our thinking, the ways of our mind; and the revolution must take place, not in any given department of thought, but in the totality of the mind itself. But before we go into that, I think it is essential to find out what it means to listen.

Very few of us listen directly to what is being said, we always translate or interpret it according to a particular point of view, whether Hindu, Muslim, or communist. We have formulations, opinions, judgments, beliefs through which we listen, so we are actually never listening at all; we are only listening in terms of our own particular prejudices, conclusions, or experiences. We are always interpreting what we hear, and obviously that does not bring about understanding. What brings about understanding, surely, is to listen without any anchorage, without any definite conclusion, so that you and I can think out the problem together, whatever the problem may be. If you know the art of listening, you will not only find out what is true in what is being said but you will also see the false as false and the truth in the false; but if you listen argumentatively, then it is fairly clear that there can be no understanding because argument is merely your opinion against another opinion, or your judgment against another, and that actually prevents the understanding or discovery of the truth in what is being said.

So, is it possible to listen without any prejudice, without any conclusion, without interpretation? Because, it is fairly obvious that our thinking is conditioned, is it not? We are conditioned as Hindus, or communists, or Christians, and whatever we listen to, whether it is new or old, is always apprehended through the screen of this conditioning; therefore, we can never approach any problem with a fresh mind. That is why it is very important to know how to listen, not only to what is being stated, but to everything. It is clearly necessary that a total revolution should take place in the individual, but such a revolution cannot take place unless there is effortless comprehension of what is truth. Effort at any level is obviously a form of destruction, and it is only when the mind is very quiet, not making an effort, that understanding takes place. But with most of us, effort is the primary thing; we think effort is essential, and that very effort to listen, to understand, prevents comprehension, the immediate perception of what is true and what is false.

Now, being aware of your conditioning, and yet being free of it, can you listen so as to comprehend what is being said? Can you listen without making an effort, without interpreting, which is to give total attention? For most of us, attention is merely a process of concentration, which is a form of exclusiveness, and as long as there is the resistance of exclusive thinking, a total revolution obviously cannot take place, and it is imperative, I feel, that such a revolution should take place in the individual, for only in that revolution is there creative release.

So, the mind is conditioned by modern education, by society, by religion, and by the knowledge and the innumerable experiences which we have gathered; it is shaped, put into a mold, not only by our environment, but also by our own reactions to that environment and to various forms of relationship.

Please bear in mind that you are not merely listening to me, but are actually observing the process of your own thinking. What I am saying is only a description of what is taking place in your own mind. If one is at all aware of one's own thinking, one will see that a mind that is conditioned, however much it may try to change, can only change within the prison of its own conditioning, and such a change is obviously not revolution. I think that is the first thing to understand—that as long as our minds are conditioned as Hindus, Muslims, or whatnot, any revolution is within the pattern of that conditioning and is therefore not a fundamental revolution at all. Every challenge must always be new, and as long as the mind is conditioned, it responds to challenge according to its conditioning; therefore, there is never an adequate response.

Now, we all know that there is a great crisis in the world at the present time; there is enormous poverty and the constant threat of war. That is the challenge, and our problem is to respond adequately, completely, totally to this challenge, which is impossible if we do not understand the process of our own thinking. Our thinking is obviously conditioned; we always respond to any challenge as Hindus, Muslims, communists, Socialists, Christians, and so on, and that response is fundamentally inadequate; hence the conflict, the struggle, not only in the individual, but between groups, races, and nations. We can respond totally, adequately, fully, only when we understand the process of our thinking and are free from our conditioning, that is, when we are no longer reacting as Hindus, communists, or what you will, which means that our response to challenge is no longer based on our previous conditioning. When we have ceased to belong to any particular race or religion, when each one of us understands his background, frees himself from it and pursues what is true, then it is possible to respond fully, and that response is a revolution.

It is only the religious man that can bring about a fundamental revolution, but the man who has a belief, a dogma, who belongs to any particular religion, is not a religious man. The religious man is he who understands the whole process of so-called religion, the various forms of dogma, the desire to be secure through certain formulas of ritual and belief. Such an individual breaks away from the framework of organized religion, from all dogma and belief, and seeks the highest; and it is he who is truly revolutionary because every other form of revolution is fragmentary and therefore inevitably brings about further problems. But the man who is seeking to find out what is truth, what is God, is the real revolutionary because the discovery of what is truth is an integrated response and not a fragmentary response.

Is it possible, then, for the mind to be aware of its own conditioning and thereby bring about freedom from its conditioning? The mind's conditioning is imposed by society, by the various forms of culture, religion, and education, and also by the whole process of ambition, the effort to become something, which is itself a pattern imposed on each one of us by society, and there is also the pattern which the individual creates for himself in his response to society.

Now, can we as individuals be aware of our conditioning, and is it possible for the mind to break down all this limitation so that it is free to discover what is truth? Because it seems to me that unless we do free the mind from its conditioning, all our social problems, our conflicts in relationship, our wars and other miseries, are bound to increase and multiply—which is exactly what is happening in the world, not only in our private lives, but in the relationship between individuals and groups of individuals which we call society.

Taking that whole picture into consideration and knowing all the significance of it, is it possible for the mind to be aware of its conditioning and liberate itself? Because it is only in freedom that there can be creativeness, but freedom is not a reaction to something. Freedom is not a reaction to the prison in which the mind is caught, it is not the opposite of slavery. Freedom is not a motive. Surely, the mind that is seeking truth, God, or whatever name you like to give it, has no motive in itself. Most of us have a motive because all our life, in our education and in everything that we do, our action is based on a motive, the motive either of self-expansion or self-destruction. And can the mind be aware of and liberate itself from all those bondages which it has imposed upon itself in order to be secure, to be satisfied, in order to achieve a personal or a national result?

I think the revolution of which I am talking is possible only when the mind is very quiet, very still. But that quietness of the mind does not come through any effort—it comes naturally, easily, when the mind understands its own process of action, which is to understand the whole significance of thinking. So the beginning of freedom is self-knowledge, and self-knowledge is not in the withdrawal from life but is to be discovered in the relationships of our everyday existence. Relationship is the mirror in which we can see ourselves factually, without any distortion, and it is only through self-knowledge, seeing ourselves exactly as we actually are, undistorted by any interpretation or judgment, that the mind becomes quiet, still. But that stillness of mind cannot be sought after, it cannot be pursued; if you pursue and bring about stillness of mind, it has a motive, and such stillness is never still because it is always a movement towards something and away from something.

So there is freedom only through self-knowledge, which is to understand the total process of thinking. Our thinking at present is merely a reaction, the response of a conditioned mind, and any action based on such thinking is bound to result in catastrophe. To discover what is truth, what is God, there must be a mind that has understood itself, which means going into the whole problem of self-knowledge. Only then is there the total revolution which alone brings about a creative release, and that creative release is the perception of what is truth, what is God.

I think it is always important to ask fundamental questions, but when we do ask a fundamental question, most of us are seeking an answer, and then the answer is invariably superficial because there is no yes or no answer to life. Life is a movement, an endless movement, and to inquire into this extraordinary thing called life, with all its innumerable aspects, one must ask fundamental questions and never be satisfied with answers, however satisfactory they may be, because the moment you have an answer, the mind has concluded, and conclusion is not life—it is merely a static state. So what is important is to ask the right question and never be satisfied with the answer, however clever, however logical, because the truth of the question lies beyond the conclusion, beyond the answer, beyond the verbal expression. The mind that asks a question and is merely satisfied with an explanation, a verbal statement, remains superficial. It is only the mind that asks a fundamental question and is capable of pursuing that question to the end—it is only such a mind that can find out what is truth.

Questioner: In India today we see a growing disregard of all sensitive feeling and expression. Culturally we are a feeble, imitative country; our thinking is smug and superficial. Is there a way to break through and contact the source of creativity? Can we create a new culture?

KRISHNAMURTI: Sir, this is not only a question for Indians, it is a human question, it is asked in America, in England, and elsewhere. How to bring about a new culture, a creativity that is explosive, abundant, so that the mind is not imitative? A poet, a painter longs for that, so let us inquire into it. Naturally I cannot discuss this question with so many, but we are going to inquire into it, so please listen.

What is civilization, what is culture as we know it now? It is the result of the collective will, is it not? The culture we know is the expression of many desires unified through religion, through a traditional moral code, through various forms of sanction. The civilization in which we live is the result of the collective will, of many acquisitive desires, and therefore we have a culture, a civilization which is also acquisitive. That is fairly clear.

Now, within this acquisitive society, which is the result of the collective will, we can have many reformations, and we do occasionally bring about a bloody revolution, but it is always within the pattern because our response to any challenge, which is always new, is limited by the culture in which we have been brought up. The culture of India is obviously imitative, traditional; it is made up of innumerable superstitions, of belief and dogma, the repetition of words, the worship of images made by the hand and by the mind. That is our culture, that is our society, broken up into various classes, all based on acquisitiveness; and if we do become nonacquisitive in this world, we are acquisitive in some other world, we want to acquire God, and so on. So our culture is essentially based on acquisitiveness, worldly and spiritual; and when occasionally there is an individual who breaks away from all acquisitiveness and knows what it is to be creative, we immediately idolize him, make him into our spiritual leader or teacher, thereby stifling ourselves.

As long as we belong to the collective culture, collective civilization, there can be no creativeness. It is the man who understands this whole process of the collective, with all its sanctions and beliefs, and who ceases to be either positively or negatively acquisitive—it is only such a man who knows the meaning of creativeness, not the sannyasi who renounces the world and pursues God, which is merely his particular form of acquisitiveness. The man who realizes the whole significance of the collective and who breaks away from it because he knows what is true religion, is a creative individual, and it is such action that brings about a new culture. Surely, that is always the way it happens, is it not?

The truly religious man is not the one who practices so-called religion, who holds to certain dogmas and beliefs, who performs certain rituals or pursues knowledge, for he is merely seeking another form of gratification. The man who is truly religious is completely free from society, he has no responsibility towards society; he may establish a relationship with society, but society has no relationship with him. Society is organized religion, the economic and social structure, the whole environment in which we have been brought up, and does that society help man to find God, truth—it matters little what name you give it—or does the individual who is seeking God create a new society? That is, must not the individual break away from the existing society, culture, or civilization? Surely, in the very breaking away he discovers what is truth, and it is that truth which creates the new society, the new culture.

I think this is an important question to ponder over. Can the man who belongs to society—it does not matter what society—ever find truth, God? Can society help the individual in that discovery, or must the individual, you and I, break away from society? Surely, it is in the very process of breaking away from society that there is the understanding of what is truth, and that truth then creates the ripples which become a new society, a new culture. The sannyasi, the monk, the hermit renounces the world, renounces society, but his whole pattern of thinking is still conditioned by society; he is still a Christian or a Hindu, pursuing the ideal of Christianity or of Hinduism. His meditations, his sacrifices, his practices are all essentially conditioned, and therefore what he discovers as truth, as God, as the absolute, is really his own conditioned reaction. Hence society cannot help man to find out what is truth. Society's function is to limit the individual, to hold him within the boundary of respectability. Only the man who understands this whole process, whose action is not a reaction, can find out what is truth, and it is the truth that creates a new culture, not the man who pursues truth.

I think this is fairly clear and simple; it sounds complicated, but it is not. Truth brings about its own action. But the man who is seeking truth and acting, however worthy and noble he may be, only creates further confusion and misery. He is like the reformer who is merely concerned with decorating the prison walls, with bringing more light, more lavatories, or what you will, into the prison. Whereas, if you understand this whole problem of how the mind is conditioned by society, if you allow truth to act and do not act according to what you think is truth, then you will find that such action brings about its own culture, its own civilization, a new world which is not based on acquisitiveness, on sorrow, on strife, on belief.

It is the truth that will bring about a new society, not the communists, the Christians, the Hindus, the Buddhists, or the Muslims. To respond to any challenge according to one's conditioning is merely to expand the prison or to decorate its bars. It is only when the mind understands and is free from the conditioning influences which have been imposed upon it, or which it has created for itself, that there is the perception of truth, and it is the action of that truth which brings into being a new society, a new culture.

That is why it is very important for a country like this not to impose upon itself the superficial culture of the West nor, because it is confused, to return to the old, to the Puranas, to the Vedas. It is only a confused mind that wants to return to something dead, and the important thing is to understand why there is confusion. There is confusion, obviously, when the mind does not understand, when it does not respond totally, integrally to something new, to any given fact.

Take the fact of war, for example. If you respond to it as a Hindu who believes in ahimsa, you say, "I must practice nonviolence," and if you happen to be a nationalist, your response is nationalistic. Whereas, the man who sees the truth of war, which is the fact that war is destructive in itself, and who lets that truth act, does not respond in terms of any society, in terms of any theory or reform. Truth is neither yours nor mine, and as long as the mind interprets or translates that truth, we create confusion. That is what the reformers do, what all the saints have done who have tried to bring about a reformation in a certain social order. Because they translate truth to bring about a given reform, that reform breeds more misery and hence needs further reform.

To perceive what is truth, there must be a total freedom from society, which means a complete cessation of acquisitiveness, of ambition, of envy, of this whole process of becoming. After all, our culture is based on becoming somebody, it is built on the hierarchical principle—the one who knows and the one who does not know, the one who has and the one who has not. The one who has not is everlastingly struggling to have, and the one who does not know is forever pushing to acquire more knowledge. Whereas, the man who does not belong to either, his mind is very quiet, completely still, and it is only such a mind that can perceive what is truth and allow that truth to act in its own way. Such a mind does not act according to a conditioned response, it does not say, "I must reform society." The truly religious man is not concerned with social reform, he is not concerned with improving the old, rotting society because it is truth and not reform that is going to create the new order. I think if one sees this very simply and very clearly, the revolution itself will take place.

The difficulty is that we do not see, we do not listen, we do not perceive things directly and simply as they are. After all, it is the innocent mind—innocent though it may have lived a thousand years and had a multitude of experiences—that is creative, not the cunning mind, not the mind that is full of knowledge and technique. When the mind sees the truth of any fact and lets that truth act, that truth creates its own technique. Revolution is not within society but outside of it.

Questioner: The fundamental problem that faces every individual is the psychological pain which corrodes all thinking and feeling. Unless you have an answer and can teach the ending of pain, all your words have little meaning.

KRISHNAMURTI: Sir, what is teaching? Is teaching merely communication, words? Why do you want to be taught? And can another teach you how to end pain? If you could be taught how to end pain, would pain cease?

You may learn a technique for ending pain, physical or psychological, but in the very process of ending one particular pain, a new pain comes into being.

So what is the problem, sirs? Surely, the problem is not how to end pain. I can tell you not to be greedy, not to be ambitious, not to have beliefs, to free the mind from all desire for security, to live in complete uncertainty, and so on, but those are mere words. The problem is to experience directly the state of complete uncertainty, to be without any feeling of security, and that is possible only if you understand the total process of your own thinking, or if you can listen with your whole being, be completely attentive without resistance. To end sorrow, pain, either one must understand the ways of the mind, of desire, will, choice, going into that completely, or else listen to find the truth. The truth is that as long as there is a point in the mind which is moving towards another point, that is, as long as the mind is seeking security in any form, it will never be free from pain. Security is dependency, and a mind that depends has no love. Without going through all the process of examination, observation, and awareness, just listen to the fact, let the truth of the fact operate, and then you will see that the mind is free from pain. But we do neither; we neither see, observe to find out what is truth, nor do we listen to the fact with our whole being, without translating, twisting, interpreting it. That is, we neither pursue self-knowledge, which also brings an end to pain, nor do we merely observe the fact without distortion, as we look at our face in the mirror. All that we want is to know how to end pain, we want a ready-made formula by which to end it, which means, really, that we are lazy, there is not that extraordinary energy which is necessary to pursue the understanding of the self. It is only when we understand the self—not according to Shankara, Buddha, or Christ, but as it actually is in each one of us in relation to people, to ideas, and to things—that there is the cessation of pain.

February 16, 1955

Second Talk in Bombay

One of our greatest difficulties is the understanding of the whole significance of desire. For most of us, desire has become an urge which must be controlled, guided, shaped, and given impetus in a certain direction, but I would like to talk about it this evening from a different point of view altogether, which to me is the truth. If we can understand desire, which is really very complex, then perhaps we shall be able to bring about quite a different action in our daily life. If instead of trying to control, sublimate, or transcend desire, we can be confronted with the fact of desire and begin to understand its ways, then I think there will come about a totally different kind of attention. But the difficulty is going to be that most of us have opinions about desire; we want to suppress it in order to achieve a state of desirelessness, or we are caught up in it so vehemently and persistently that the mind becomes a confusing field of contradictory thoughts.

Now, I am not going to indulge in any theory, in any speculation, I am going to deal only with the fact and not with anything else. So, if I may suggest, please just listen to what is being said here without relating it to your previous conclusions; just let your mind follow it without interfering, and I think you will find that an extraordinary thing takes place in spite of yourself. If you can listen in that manner so that you are confronted with the fact and do not translate what you hear in terms of what you know or in terms of what has been said by Shankara, Buddha, or anyone else with regard to desire, then you will find that a peculiar thing happens—the very fact itself brings about an action. The mind may give opinions or ideas about the fact, but it cannot deal with the fact. All it can do is to look at the fact, and in the very process of observation, in the very awareness of the fact, there begins a radical transformation. It is the fact itself that alters the way of thinking and not the multiplication of opinions or conclusions about the fact.

So, let us quietly talk over together this whole problem of desire. After all, desire is energy—energy which is outward going—and because it is assertive, dominating, powerful, society tries to control and shape it. Society is the product of that desire, which seeks to shape itself in order to be more efficient and to function within the limits of social morality. Again, that is a simple fact. This outward-going desire, which is energy, must be controlled, shaped, guided, disciplined—at least, that is what society, what religions and our own compulsive urges demand. But in the very process of disciplining desire, there is frustration because anything that is blocked must find a way out.

Surely, sirs, everywhere there are blockages of desire established by society: Thou shalt do this and not that, this is right and that is wrong, and so on. All the religious books, all the teachers, and our own pain and pleasure indicate that desire must be shaped, controlled, disciplined, and in that very process there is frustration, there is conflict, not only at the superficial level, but also at the deeper levels of our consciousness. If there were no blockages, if this outward-going desire, this outward-going energy were given freedom, there would be no frustration, but society, conventional morality, our whole education, and our own fears all shape, control, and block it, and that very blocking is frustration. This is a very simple psychological fact in our everyday life, it is not a philosophical speculation.

So this outward-going energy meets a wall of social morality, of so-called religion, and all the rest of it, and then it begins to recoil inwardly. This inward recoil is not a free movement, it is merely a reaction. That is, outward-going energy has met a blockage in its forward movement, so it reacts inwardly and says, "I must be noble, I must be good, I must be unselfish, I must find God." Whether this inward movement is superficial or deep, it is still only a recoil, and this whole process of outward-going and inward-going energy is the movement of the self, the 'me'. Again, this is an observable, experienceable fact, it is not a theory, an opinion. This outward and inward movement of desire creates a society, a culture, a religion, and a relationship based on the 'I', the self, and in this movement, energy becomes less and less because it is a process of self-enclosure. When desire is controlled, disciplined, it may act efficiently, but it loses its tremendous vitality.

Please just listen to what I am saying, don't translate it in terms of what you have learned. Our problem is this: In the process of its outward and inward movement, this extraordinary energy, desire, gets throttled because through pain and pleasure, the 'I' learns to control, to shape, to guide desire—that is, by its own activity, energy is conditioning itself. Watch this process actually taking place in yourself, and you will quickly see what it means. The moment thought says, "I must suppress, shape, discipline desire, I must canalize energy to make it efficient, moral, socially respectable," and all the rest of it, in that very process energy is decreased, destroyed; and one needs tremendous free energy, not disciplined energy, to find out what is truth or God. So it is not a matter of suppressing, sublimating, controlling desire, but what matters is for this outward and inward movement of desire to come to an end.

Is this all too difficult, sirs? I do not think so. You see, our minds want examples, details, practical applications, but that is not the first question. The first question is to understand the whole process, and then we can work out the details. So let us look at this whole thing and not ask how it is to be made practical. Once you understand the full significance of this extraordinary phenomenon of the outward and inward movement of desire, which is energy, you will find that that very understanding brings about its own action which is much more practical than the "practicality" we practice now.

What is it that we are doing now? There is outward-going energy, which is desire, which is thought, and in its outward movement this energy is blocked, so there is frustration, there is pain, suffering. Therefore desire withdraws and seeks inwardly for a state in which there will be no pain, a permanent state of peace. This turning inward of the mind in search of a state in which it will not be disturbed, in which it will have a sense of peace, security, is merely a reaction, so the opposites are created. Meeting frustration in its outward movement, desire turns inward, and this very turning inward sets going the dual process of the outer and the inner, the whole conflict of duality.

Now, must not this outward and inward movement of desire cease in order that energy shall be released in a totally different direction? Do you understand the question, sirs? I have a desire, and that desire is frustrated by society, and by my own moral sanctions; being frustrated, there is fear, pain, suffering, and then desire seeks inwardly for a state in which there will be no suffering, in which there will be peace, a permanent tranquillity, and so on. Once it went outward, and now it is recoiling within, but it is still the same movement of desire. This movement is the self, the 'me', it is self-enclosing, and therefore energy is becoming less and less. Desire—instead of releasing energy like a river, instead of creating tremendous vitality, complete abandonment—through the very disciplining of itself, destroys energy, and that is what is happening to most of the people in the world. But you must have complete abandonment, tremendous attentive energy to find out what is truth, God.

Our problem, then, is not how to be without desire, or how to suppress or sublimate it, but to understand this outward and inward movement of desire, which creates its own narrowing discipline in the shape of individual and social sanctions, thereby gradually destroying this extraordinary energy. That is what is happening in our daily life, is it not? I put out my hand in friendship to somebody, and he hits it, but I have ideals, and instead of attacking the man I withdraw my hand and begin to cultivate compassion, goodness, kindness. Therefore that energy is not set free, but is being dissipated through inner conflict.

So our problem is how to bring about a state of energy which is completely still so that that energy can be used by reality in any direction it wishes. At present, we only know this outward and inward movement of desire which has produced all kinds of misery, mischief, passing joys, and a culture based on the search for security, and whether that desire is seeking within or without, it is essentially the same movement. Now, can that outward and inward movement come to an end? Please listen. The mind cannot make it come to an end because any effort on the part of the mind to bring that movement to an end is still the same desire moving in another direction, and therefore a dissipation of energy. So the mind has got into a vicious circle. But if this energy, which is everlastingly going outward or recoiling within, can become still without any form of compulsion, if it can be quiet, free from all outward and inward movement, then you will find that, like a river, this energy creates its own right action because it is free from the self. Being still, energy perceives what is truth; then energy itself is truth, and that truth creates its own movement, which is not the movement of going out or recoiling within.

If one has understood all this, then discipline will have quite a different meaning, but at present discipline is merely conflict, conformity, and is therefore destroying energy. Look at what has happened to almost all of us. We have conformed to such an extent that we no longer have any creative energy; there is no initiative left in us, and it is only the man who has this creative energy, this enormous initiative, that finds out what is truth, not the man who conforms, who disciplines, shapes his desires.

What I am describing is a fact, not a theory or a mere idea, and if you listen to the fact, perceive it as it actually is without any judgment or conclusion, without any sense of resistance, then the fact itself will operate, and that is true revolution. The revolution brought about by a cunning mind, whether it be the mind of a Marx, a Shankara, or a Buddha, is no revolution at all. There is revolution only when this outward and inward movement of desire comes to an end without compulsion. Any form of compulsion, any effort of the mind to shape desire in a particular direction, is still part of the same movement. It is only when this movement stops that there is a quietness which is rich, full, vital, and in that quietness there is abundance of energy and not the diminution of energy. Then that which is quiet is the real, and the real produces its own action, its own activity.

So, it is not a matter of suppressing desire, but don't immediately ask, "Then can I do what I like?" You try doing what you like and you will see how difficult it is. Your parents, your grandmother, your neighbors, your religion and society, everything about you says, "do" and "don't," so your mind is already conditioned, and any movement of a conditioned mind, whether outward or inward, is still part of its conditioning. Only when that movement ceases—but not in terms of discipline or the edicts of society—is there freedom. Freedom is not a reaction, it is not freedom from something; it is a state of being, and it is only in that state that energy is free to create.

This is very simple to understand, it does not need a great deal of mental training or the reading of books on philosophy, and if you really grasp it, you will see that there is a totally different kind of action taking place in your life. Then there is no conflict, and where there is no conflict there is more energy, greater vitality. In the mind that is free from this outward and inward movement, there is immense attention, not fixed at any point. Attention which is directed is not attention at all, it is concentration, but attention without a fixed point is total awareness, and in that state the mind is creative, awake. And to find what is real, the mind must have this extraordinary energy, which is really the capacity to give complete attention without having any incentive. Our attention now is always with an incentive, a motive, and in that there is fear, conflict, strain, and the dissipation of energy.

Questioner: Please tell us plainly who you are and by what authority you speak. Your presence and your words intoxicate me. Is not intoxication bad in any form?

Krishnamurti: Surely, sir, who the speaker is or by what authority he speaks is not very important. There is no authority, he is only explaining what is the fact. He is not giving any system of philosophy, any method of meditation, or panacea, but is merely describing the fact because the fact is the truth. Our minds are generally incapable of looking at facts without distorting them, but the mind that can look at a fact without opinion, without judgment, without a conclusion, such a mind is free, and a free mind brings its own authority. Not that you must obey, follow it, or be intoxicated by it; on the contrary, you must not follow, nor must you be intoxicated, for then you might as well take a drink. It is the lazy mind that so easily gets intoxicated, whether by a ritual, by a speech, or by some person in authority.

"Is not intoxication bad in any form?" Surely. But why do we look at everything in terms of good and bad, sirs? What is important is to see that intoxication in any form distorts one's own thinking, whether it be the intoxication of a Hitler or of any other person, the intoxication of a utopia according to the communists, or the intoxication of drink. And if you listen to the truth but do not let it operate, it poisons you. Please follow this. If you listen and see the truth for yourself, yet do not give it freedom to operate, then that very perception breeds the poison of conflict which is going to destroy you. That is, if you see what is true and do something else, the contradiction is a poison which destroys all your energy. That is why it is much better not to come to these meetings, sirs, if you want to remain as you are. It is good to be without the affliction of conflict, contradiction, pain, suffering, but to have that goodness, that tranquillity in which there is no conflict, you must allow the truth to operate, it must not be you who operates on the truth. To follow another, to be mesmerized by words, by books, by a strong personality, creates conflict and dissipates that extraordinary energy which is necessary to find out what is truth. What is important is to find out what is truth and let that truth bring about its own action.

Questioner: What is this self-knowledge of which you speak, and how can I acquire it? What is the starting point?

Krishnamurti: Now again, please listen carefully because you have extraordinary ideas about self-knowledge—that to have self-knowledge you must practice, you must meditate, you must do all kinds of things. It is very simple, sir. The first step is the last step in self-knowledge, the beginning is the end. The first step is what matters because self-knowledge is not something you can learn from another. No one can teach you self-knowledge, you have to find out for yourself; it must be your own discovery, and that discovery is not something tremendous, fantastic, it is very simple. After all, to know yourself is to watch your behavior, your words, what you do in your everyday relationships, that is all. Begin with that and you will see how extraordinarily difficult it is to be aware, just to watch the manner of your behavior, the words you use to your servant, to your boss, the attitude you have with regard to people, to ideas, and to things. Just watch your thoughts, your motives, in the mirror of relationship, and you will see that the moment you watch, you want to correct, you say, "This is good, that is bad, I must do this and not that." When you see yourself in the mirror of relationship, your approach is one of condemnation or justification, therefore you distort what you see. Whereas, if you simply observe in that mirror your attitude with regard to people, to ideas, and to things, if you just see the fact without judgment, without condemnation or acceptance, then you will find that that very perception has its own action. That is the beginning of self-knowledge.

To watch yourself, to observe what you do, what you think, what your motives and incentives are, and yet not condemn or justify, is an extraordinarily difficult thing to do because your whole culture is based on condemnation, judgment, and evaluation; you have been brought up on, "Do this and not that." But if you can look in the mirror of relationship without creating the opposite, then you will find that there is no end to self-knowledge.

You see, the inquiry into self-knowledge is an outward movement which later turns inward; first we look at the stars, and then we look within ourselves. In the same way, we look for reality, for God, for security, happiness, in the objective world, and when it is not found there, we turn inward. This search for the inner God, the higher self, or what you will, completely ceases through self-knowledge, and then the mind becomes very quiet, not through discipline, but just through understanding, through watching, through being aware of itself every minute without choice. Don't say, "I must be aware every minute," because that is just another manifestation of our foolishness when we want to get somewhere, when we want to arrive at a particular state. What matters is to be aware of yourself and to keep on being aware without accumulating because the moment you accumulate, from that center you judge. Self-knowledge is not a process of accumulation, it is a process of discovery from moment to moment in relationship.

Questioner: I am old and I can no longer escape from the imminent approach of death. How can I face it unafraid?

KRISHNAMURTI: I do not think this is a problem only for the old, it is a problem for all of us. Now, what is death, and why is there fear of death? Either that fear exists because of the unknown tomorrow or because death means letting go of the known. Do you understand? Either we are afraid of the unknown future, of what lies beyond, or of losing the known, the known being "my family," "my virtue," "my bank account," "my friends," all the things which we have gathered and which we cherish, the things we cling to. All that is the known, and we are afraid to let go of that, or we are afraid of the unknown something which lies beyond. That is the fact.

Now, we always want to know what happens beyond death, whether there is survival or annihilation. I think that is a wrong question, sirs. The right question is whether it is possible to know death while living, to enter the house of death consciously while you are vital, full of health, not when you are drugged by disease, or when you are losing your consciousness through the inevitable process of old age. Can you know what death is now, while you are living, conscious, while you have vitality, energy, while you have no overwhelming disease? That is the question, sirs, because when you know what death is, then there is no fear of death, then all the theories, the beliefs, the hopes and fears are gone.

So let us go into this question together, you and I. The question is not what life will be like in the unknown future, or whether you will continue beyond death, or how to let go of the known, but whether it is possible to know death while living, to enter the house of death while fully conscious, with complete awareness. That is the question, and it is an extraordinarily vital one, is it not?

The old man full of years and the young man who is going to be full of years will both have the same end, and can they both know now what death means? You put yourself that question, sirs. I am putting it for you, but you put it to yourself, and if you put it to yourself with vigor, with attention, with earnestness, you will find the answer.

What does death mean? Please listen. What does death mean? Not the unknown, but letting the known go completely, the known being the thousand yesterdays with all their memories, experiences, knowledge, joys, and pains. To let all that go is to be completely alone, which is not loneliness, with its fear and ugliness, but a state of complete dissociation from the past. That state of aloneness is the death which we fear. We are afraid to be cut off from the known, cut off from our families, our friends, cut off from all the things which we want. But aloneness is not mere isolation, it is an extraordinarily rich state, a state of incorruption, because aloneness implies the cutting away of all knowledge, all experience—experience being a form of continuity through memory.

Do listen, sirs, and don't say, "I must be alone, and how am I to be in that state?" It is the foolish mind, the lazy mind that asks how. But a mind that is really attentive to what is being said, that is not mesmerized by words, will be in that state in which the mind is no longer contaminated by the past or by the edicts and compulsions of society. Then the mind is totally innocent, it is a fresh mind, a new mind, and such a mind alone has no fear of death.

If you have really listened to this you will find that, simply and without any kind of problem, an awakening comes, and then you will observe that your mind is cleansed by the very strange miracle of listening to what is a fact. When you listen to the fact without resistance, you have a fresh mind, a mind no longer caught by the conclusions of the past, and only such a mind is without fear. Because it is alone, such a mind is the eternal, the real, for truth is alone from moment to moment. Truth is not continuous. The moment you think in terms of continuity, you have already accumulated a fact of yesterday. Only the mind which is fresh, innocent, alone, can see the truth, and such a mind is in a state of constantly renewed discovery of what is truth.

February 20, 1955

Third Talk in Bombay

One of the fundamental issues that we are all faced with is the choice between good and bad. Choice implies conflict, and conflict, surely, is a destructive element, a waste of energy. We know this conflict in our daily existence, the everlasting struggle to maintain the good and to avoid evil; and it seems to me not only that this conflict is a dissipation of energy, but that the very struggle to choose and maintain the good destroys creative release. And is it possible not to choose, and thereby have no conflict, but always to maintain that which is good?

I do not know if you have thought about this problem at all. Most of us are caught in the conflict created by the choice between good and bad, but if one is at all alert and awake to the issue, one observes that this conflict is a continual waste of energy, and surely one needs a great deal of energy to find out what is truth. The attempt to maintain the good through effort, through struggle, through choice invariably dissipates energy, and the good then becomes merely a noncreative action, a reaction to the bad, which is a form of frustration.

So, the conflict between good and bad is destructive, degenerative, as all conflicts are, and is it possible not to have conflict between good and bad but always to maintain that which is good without introducing the element of choice? This is really a very important question because it is this maintenance of the good without choice that brings about the fullness of energy, and only then is it possible for the mind to be still. That is, to have a quiet mind, a still mind, one needs a great deal of energy, and that immense energy cannot come into being as long as energy is dissipated through conflict of any kind. Any form of choice is conflict, and is it possible to lead a life in which there is no choice at all?

Now, how is one to maintain the good without conflict? Perhaps you have never put this question to yourself because you are used to the everlasting struggle between that which is evil and that which is good. Your whole outlook, your way of life, your social and religious structure, all condition the mind to choose between good and evil; and is it possible not to have this struggle at all, but at the same time to maintain that which is good?

Do you understand the question? Most of us are used to conflicts, and all conflict is obviously a waste of energy. One needs tremendous energy for the mind to be still, and only a still mind can find that which is the truth, the eternal, the highest. Stillness of mind is not the outcome of practice, of choice, of the struggle to achieve a result, but our whole life, from childhood until we die, is a constant battle between that which is good and that which is evil, between *what is* and 'what should be'. Our life is a ceaseless effort to become something, and is it possible for the mind to be without this conflict?

I think this is an important question to ask ourselves—not how to achieve and maintain goodness, but whether it is at all possible to maintain goodness and yet not be caught in the conflict of the opposites? It is possible only when we realize what an extraordinarily destructive thing conflict is, not only within ourselves, but outwardly. After all, the conflict without is a projection of the conflict within. But we do not see the falseness of conflict. We accept conflict as part of life, and we think it is necessary for various reasons, for progress, for inquiry, for every form of achievement; we are used to it, we are conditioned to think in that way.

Now, is action without conflict at all possible? Surely it is possible only when we love what we are doing, but in our hearts we love nothing, and so action is this process of conflict which is continually going on. I do not know if you have noticed that when you love to do something, there is no conflict in it at all, action is entirely stripped of conflicting elements; there may be various forms of obstruction, but that very action is the overcoming of the obstruction.

So, is it possible to love the good, and not have this endless conflict between the good and the bad? Please, there is no method. The moment you have a method, that very method is a process of struggle to achieve a result. What matters is for the mind to be fairly quiet so that it is capable of receiving that which is true. Now, I am saying that every form of struggle is destructive, that in conflict there is no love, and that when you love something completely, all conflict ceases. Just listen to this, see the fact as it is, neither accepting nor rejecting it; let your mind inquire, go into it, see the truth of it without effort, without resistance. Then you will find that the maintenance of the good is not such an extraordinary thing, that it is possible to love and to maintain the good without conflict, and this implies attention. When you love something or some person, you are full of attention, and it is that attention which has the quality of goodness.

Desire is energy, and when we treat it as something evil, to be suppressed, controlled, shaped according to the sanctions of religion and society, desire becomes destructive, which does not mean that we must yield to every form of desire. Mere control of desire, without understanding the whole process of desire, destroys that extraordinary energy which is required to find the eternal. In creative energy lies a life of goodness, a life in which the eternal is not absent, but such a life is possible only when we understand the whole process of conflict.

Conflict exists as long as there is the outward movement of desire, which meets with frustration and then recoils. This movement, with its frustration and recoil, sets going the conflict between good and bad, and as long as there is this movement, there can be no goodness. Goodness can come into being only when the mind is really very still, and that stillness arises only when there is abundance of energy. That is why the question of discipline is very important.

We use discipline to achieve a result. Psychologically, inwardly, we discipline ourselves in order to maintain the good, and the discipline itself is a process of conflict. It is a conflict between one desire as opposed to another, and this conflict of desires is a dissipation of energy.

So, is it possible for the mind to inquire, to go into and see the truth of all this, and then to let that truth operate without pursuing or operating upon the truth? This whole process is true meditation.

Sirs, why do we ask questions? Is it to find an answer, a solution to a problem, or is it to explore the problem? If the mind is merely concerned with the solution, with seeking an answer to the problem, it is restricted and therefore incapable of exploring the problem. In considering these questions we are concerned, surely, with the exploration of the problem, and that very exploration of the problem is its own answer. It is not necessary to seek a solution to the problem, for in the very process of exploring the problem, you will find the solution. And that is what we are going to do—to explore, to investigate the problem together. But to be capable of exploring any problem, the mind must be free of conclusions, it must not be tethered to any form of experience or belief. And when the mind is free of conclusions, of experiences, when it is no longer tethered to a belief, then has it any problem? It is only the mind that clings to a belief, that has a conclusion, that approaches life through a series of experiences which are the reactions of a particular conditioning—it is only such a mind that creates problems. But if the mind is aware of how problems are created and is capable of exploring, of inquiring into a problem without a conclusion and without seeking a solution, then surely the problem ceases.

Questioner: You say that to be creative there must be complete abandonment, and yet there must also be austerity. Can the two exist together?

KRISHNAMURTI: Sir, what is beauty, and how does the state of creative beauty come into being? Obviously, there must be love. And love means total abandonment, does it not? Not abandonment through desire, but the abandonment in which there is no sense of restriction, no hope of achieving a result, and therefore no fear. There can be complete abandonment only when there is no self, no 'me', and when there is no self, in that abandonment is there not austerity, simplicity?

To most people austerity means the destruction of beauty about them. Outwardly they deny all worldliness and have only a few things, but inwardly they are not at all simple; on the contrary, they are extraordinarily complex, full of burning desires, longing to achieve a certain result. Surely, that is not austerity. But to be austere does not mean the denial of desire. Please listen. Abandonment comes only when the self is not, but the self cannot be destroyed by merely suppressing desire. After all, desire is energy, and if you destroy energy, nothing is possible. You need tremendous energy for the mind to be still, to find out what is God, what is truth, and if that energy is controlled, shaped through fear, through every form of conditioning, then it cannot flow with abandon, it cannot be free, and yet when that energy is free, it will create its own austerity.

It is this abandonment with austerity that makes for beauty, and then it is love. If one has no love, how can one appreciate beauty or create that which is beautiful? But there is no love as long as there is no abandonment, and that abandonment will come into being only when there is no 'me', no self. So this creative state can arise only when there is love, abandonment, and austerity; but mere austerity without abandonment, without love, has no meaning at all.

The problem, then, is not how to be austere, not how to abandon or put away the self, but to inquire into what we mean by love. You see, we have divided love as the divine and the earthly, and so we have created a battle between the urge of the flesh and the urge to seek the divine, between the noble love and the physical love. And is it possible to love, not divinely or physically, but just to have the goodness and the perfume of love in one's heart with all the things of the mind removed from it? Surely, that is possible only when we give our hearts to something completely; then there is no conflict, then there is abandonment, and that very abandonment creates its own austerity, as a river creates the banks which hold it.

But the respectability of society has no place in this austere abandonment. What society demands is respectability, control, mediocrity, but a mediocre mind cannot abandon itself; it is neither hot nor cold, it is full of fears, apprehensions, and such a mind cannot possibly know what love is. Most of us are merely controlled by the sanctions of society, by the social morality which says, "This is good and that is bad"; we are caught in the conflict between *what is* and 'what should be', and that is why we have ceased to love. We are merely imitative machines, so we never know that state of abandonment in which there is austerity and which is the only creative state. You cannot find God, that which is truth, without total abandonment, without being free of all belief, all dogma, all fear, which means opening your heart completely and not filling it with the things of the mind. There can be goodness, generosity, only when the mind is quiet; beauty, that something which is really God, which is love, which is truth, comes into being only when there is complete abandonment of the self. And the self cannot be abandoned by any regulation, by any practice, by any meditation. The self must cease through awareness of its own limitation, the falseness of its own existence. However deep, wide, and extensive it may become, the self is always limited, and until it is abandoned, the mind can never be free. The mere perception of that fact is the ending of the self, and only then is it possible for that which is the real to come into being.

Questioner: You spoke the other day of the urgency of total attention. Please explain what you mean by total attention.

KRISHNAMURTI: It is not a question of what I mean by total attention, but let us inquire into it together, and then perhaps we shall be able to find out what total attention is.

What do we mean by attention? You are listening to what is being said, and you have other thoughts—your mind goes wandering off, and you pull it back in order to listen. Is that attention? You want to look out of the window because you are bored with what is taking place in the room, but politeness and courtesy demand that you listen, so you pull your thought back from the sea and listen. Is that attention? Is there attention when you make an effort to listen, when you try to concentrate in order to understand, in order to find out? That is what you do, is it not? You make an effort to listen, and that process of concentration is really exclusion; you want to think of other things, but you force your mind to come back because you want to get somewhere or achieve a result.

Is there attention as long as there is incentive? A schoolboy pays attention when the teacher tells him to because he has the incentive of passing an examination. Such attention is effort, concentration, which is the exclusion of every other thought and putting your mind on a particular thought in order to achieve a result. So there is an incentive, a motive, and as long as there is this motive to achieve something, is there attention? That is the concentration which we all know and in which there is obviously exclusion, the shutting out of everything else in order to concentrate on a particular subject. Surely, that is not attention, is it? If there is effort, is there attention? And there must be effort as long as there is incentive.

Now, is attention possible without incentive, without motive? We know attention or concentration through motive; I want to meditate, or I want to pass an examination, or I want to achieve a certain position, so I exclude everything else and concentrate. If I do not exclude, I dissipate, so in order not to dissipate I force myself to concentrate, which is a process of exclusion. This involves a constant strain, a constant waste of energy, because there is effort, resistance; and where there is resistance, is there attention? Attention, surely, means a state of mind in which there is no resistance. The moment you create resistance, you are merely concentrating, which is entirely different from attention.

Now, if you are listening to what is being said, not in order to find God, or to get somewhere, or to achieve a result, but without any incentive so that there is no strain of any kind, then you will discover that your mind is so extensively aware that you are also listening to the crows, to the train, to the noise of buses, to all the various sounds; and when there is this attention without motive, without incentive, it can turn to concentration without exclusion, it can look, observe, watch, without resistance.

You try and you will find out for yourself that as long as there is mere concentration, there must be effort—even though you are so interested in what you are doing that you are absorbed in it—such concentration is a process of exclusion, and therefore there is resistance. Absorption is not attention because in absorption there is exclusion. Concentration is not attention because in it there is incentive, motive; and where there is incentive, motive, there must be resistance. Whereas, if you listen to this, which is an obvious fact, and understand the truth of it, then you will see that there is attention without incentive, attention without any fixed point; the mind is not resisting, it is completely open, and such a mind, being full of attention, can turn and concentrate without resistance.

Sirs, when there is a moment of creativeness, of great joy, there is no resistance. In that moment of creative reality, the mind is completely quiet and attentive, it has no motive. The translation of what it has seen into words, into a poem, into some form of communication, may require concentration, a focusing—let us leave out the word concentration—but that focusing is not resistance. All that we know is resistance, which means really that we are doing things which we do not love; our hearts are not in what we do, and so the mind has to invent motives or incentives in order to achieve. But if you understand the whole process of incentive, concentration, effort, see the actual fact of it, how your mind operates, then you will also see what an extraordinary thing it is to have attention without motive, a mind that is completely alert, fully aware, sensitive. Only such a mind can focus without resistance.

Questioner: What do you mean by aloneness?

Krishnamurti: Sir, let us find out. Now, to find out, please give attention, if I may use that word attention, not merely to what I am saying, but to the working of your own mind. Be aware of your own mind, not in order to alter it, not in order to make it more beautiful, more this and less that, but just be aware, attentive, and we shall find out together what it means to be alone.

I think most of us know what it means to be lonely, we are familiar with that extraordinary fear, anxiety, which comes from the self-enclosing process of the mind, and which we call loneliness. Have you not felt, at one time or another in your life, a sense of complete isolation? There comes a certain barrier, a sense of destruction, of frustration, or the cessation of all relationships. Surely we have all felt this, and having felt it we are afraid of it, we run away from it, so we turn to religions. Please watch your own mind, you are not merely listening to me. This is actually what is happening to all of us, to human beings everywhere. Because we are lonely, we want to be loved; because we are lonely, we turn on the radio, go to the cinema, and seek every other form of distraction, noble and ignoble, religious and nonreligious. This is our life. We do not want to face the state of loneliness, which is extraordinarily fearful—at least we think it is fearful—so we run away, we escape, we take flight from that loneliness. We seek companionship, love, we have a wife or a husband, we worship an authority, and so on, always depending on another through some form of attachment because then we do not have to face in ourselves that which is lonely, which is empty, which is so completely self-enclosing. Whether you accept it or not, that is the actual fact, it is what is happening psychologically to most people.

Now, if you can look at the emptiness, that sense of being cut off from all relationships, without escape, if you can be with it without fear, without trying to fill it or alter it in any way, then you will find that it is really the complete abandonment of society, an aloneness which is not an escape, but which has no recognition by society. Do you understand what that means? Society is a process of recognition—one is recognized as a saint, as a writer, as a good man, as a bad man, as a capitalist, a communist, or whatever you like. In breaking away from all that, the mind is completely alone—not lonely, but alone. It is no longer influenced by society, it is completely dissociated from all recognition; therefore, it is capable of being alone. Surely, there must be such aloneness for reality to be. Only the mind that is alone, incorrupt, innocent, though it may have thousands of years of experience—only such a mind is capable of perceiving that which is God, truth. And that is possible only when we face loneliness, this loneliness in our hearts which we try to cover up by every means—by so-called love, by distraction, through worship, through amusements, through knowledge. When the mind sees the futility of all that and remains with that which is completely self-enclosing, limiting, empty, then in that emptiness there comes aloneness. Then the mind is fresh, alone, innocent, and it is only such a mind that receives the eternal.

February 23, 1955

Fourth Talk in Bombay

I think most of us must be greatly concerned with the problem of action. When we are confronted with so many issues—poverty, overpopulation, the extraordinary development of machinery, industrialization, the sense of deterioration inwardly and outwardly—what is one to do? What is the duty or the responsibility of an individual in his relation to society? This must be a problem to all thoughtful people, and the more intelligent, the more active one is, the more one wants to throw oneself into social reform of some kind or other. So what is one's real responsibility? I think this question can be answered fully and with vital significance only if we understand the whole purpose of civilization, of culture.

After all, we have built the present society; it is the outcome of our individual relationships, and does this society fundamentally help man to find reality, God, or what name you will? Or is it merely a pattern which determines our response to the issue as to what kind of action we should take in our relationship to society? If the present culture, civilization, does not help man to find God, truth, it is a hindrance; and if it is a hindrance, then every reform, every activity for its amelioration is a further deterioration, a further hindrance to the discovery of reality, which alone can bring about true action.

I think it is very important to understand this and not merely be concerned with what kind of social reform or activity one should identify oneself with. Surely, that is not the problem. The problem is obviously much deeper. One may very easily get lost in some kind of activity or social reform, and then it is a means of escape, a means of forgetting or sacrificing oneself through action, but I do not think that will solve our many problems. Our problems are much more profound, and we need a profound answer, which I think we shall find if we can go into this question as to whether the culture we have at present—culture implying religion, the whole social and moral framework—helps man to find reality. If it does not, then the mere reformation of such a culture or civilization is a waste of time, but if it is helpful to man in the true sense, then all of us must give our hearts completely to its reformation. On that, I think, the issue depends.

By culture we mean the whole problem of thought, do we not? With most of us, thought is the outcome of various forms of conditioning, of education, of conformity, of the pressures and influences to which it is subjected within the framework of a particular civilization. At present our thought is shaped by society, and unless there is a revolution in our thinking, the mere reformation of a superficial culture or society seems to me a distraction, a factor which will ultimately bring about greater misery.

After all, what we call civilization is a process of educating thought in the Hindu mold, in the Christian or the communist mold, and so on; and can thinking so educated ever create a fundamental revolution? Will any pressure, any shaping of thought, bring about the discovery or the understanding of what is truth? Surely, thought must free itself from all pressure, which means really from society, from all forms of influence, and thereby find out what is truth; then that very truth has an action of its own which will bring about an altogether different culture.

That is, does society exist for the unfolding of reality, or must one be free of society to find reality? If society helps man to find reality, then every kind of reformation within society is essential, but if it is a hindrance to that discovery, should not the individual break away from society and seek what is truth? It is only such a person who is truly religious, not the man who performs various rituals or who approaches life through theological patterns, and when the individual frees himself from society and seeks reality, does he not bring about in his very search a different culture?

I think this is an important issue because most of us are merely concerned with reformation. We see poverty, overpopulation, every form of disintegration, division, and conflict; and seeing all that, what is one to do? Should one start by joining a particular group or by working for some ideology? Is that the function of a religious man? The religious man, surely, is he who seeks reality, and not the man who reads and quotes the Gita, or who goes to the temple every day. That is obviously not religion, it is merely the compulsion, the conditioning of thought by society. So what is the earnest man to do, the man who sees the necessity for and desires to bring about an immediate revolution? Shall he work for reformation within the framework of society? Society is a prison, and shall he merely reform the prison, decorating its bars and getting things done more beautifully within its walls? Surely, the man who is very much in earnest, who is really religious, is the only revolutionary, there is no other, and such a man is he who is seeking reality, who is trying to find out what is God or truth.

Now, what is to be the action of such a man? What shall he do? Shall he work within the present society, or shall he break away from it and not be concerned with society at all? The breaking away does not mean becoming a sannyasi, a hermit, isolating himself with peculiar hypnotic suggestions, and yet he cannot be a reformer because it is a waste of energy, of thought, of creativity for the earnest man to indulge in mere reformations. Then what shall the earnest man do? If he does not want to decorate the prison walls, remove a few bars, introduce a little more light, if he is not concerned with all that, and if he also sees the importance of bringing about a fundamental revolution, a radical change in the relationship between man and man—the relationship which has created this appalling society in which there are immensely rich people, and those who have absolutely nothing, both inwardly and outwardly—then what is he to do? I think it is important to put this question to oneself.

After all, does culture come into being through the action of truth, or is culture manmade? If it is man-made, it will obviously not lead you to truth. And our culture is man-made because it is based on various forms of acquisitiveness, not only in worldly things, but also in the so-called spiritual things; it is the outcome of the desire for position in every form, self-aggrandizement, and so on. Such a culture obviously cannot lead man to the realization of that which is the supreme, and if I see that, what shall I then do? What will you do, sirs, if you actually realize that society is an impediment? Society is not merely one or two activities, it is the whole structure of human relationship in which all creativeness has ceased, in which there is constant imitation; it is a framework of fear where education is mere conformity and in which there is no love at all, but merely action according to a pattern described as love. In this society the principal factors are recognition and respectability because that is what we are all striving for—to be recognized. Our capacities, our knowledge must be recognized by society so that we shall be somebodies. When he realizes all this and sees the poverty, the starvation, the fragmentation of the mind into various forms of belief, what is the earnest man to do?

Now, if we really listen to what is being said—listen in the sense of wanting to find out what is truth so that there is not the conflict of your opinion opposed to my opinion, or your temperament opposed to mine—if we can set all that aside and try to find out what is truth, which requires love, then I think in that very love, in that sense of goodness, we shall find the truth which creates a new culture. Then one is free of society, one is not concerned with the reformation of society. But to find out what is truth requires love, and our hearts are empty, for they are filled with the things of society. Being filled, we try to reform, and our reformation is without the perfume of love.

So what is a man to do who is earnest? Shall he seek truth, God, or what name you will, or shall he give his heart and mind to the improvement of society, which is really the improvement of himself? Do you understand, sirs? Shall he inquire into what is truth, or shall he improve the conditions of society, which is his own improvement? Shall he improve himself in the name of society, or shall he seek truth, in which there is no improvement at all? Improvement implies time, time to become, whereas truth has nothing to do with time, it is to be perceived immediately.

So the problem is extraordinarily significant, is it not? We may talk about the reformation of society, but it is still the reformation of oneself. And for the man who is seeking what is real, what is truth, there is no reformation of the self, on the contrary, there is the total cessation of the self, which is society, therefore he is not concerned with the reformation of society.

The whole structure of society is based on a process of recognition and respectability; and surely, sirs, an earnest man cannot seek the reformation of society, which is the improvement of himself. In reforming society, in identifying himself with something good, he may think he is sacrificing himself, but it is still self-improvement. Whereas, for the man who is seeking that which is the supreme, the highest, there is no self-improvement; in that direction there is no improvement of the 'me', there is no 'becoming', there is no practice, no thought of 'I shall be'. This means really the cessation of all pressure on thought, and when there is no pressure on thought, is there thinking? The very pressure on thought is the process of thinking, thinking in terms of a particular society or in terms of a reaction to that society, and if there is no pressure, is there thinking? It is only the mind that has not this movement of thought which is the pressure of society—it is only such a mind that can find reality, and in seeking that which is the supreme, such a mind creates the new culture. That is what is necessary—to bring about a totally different kind of culture, not to reform the present society. And such a culture cannot arise unless the earnest man pursues completely, with total energy, with love, that which is real. The real is not to be found in any book, through any leader; it comes into being when thought is still, and that stillness cannot be bought by any discipline. Stillness comes when there is love.

In considering some of these questions, I think it is important that we should directly experience what is being said, and you cannot do that if you are merely concerned with an answer to the question. If we are to go into the problem together, we cannot have opinions about it, my theory against your theory, because theories and speculations are a hindrance to the understanding of a problem. But if you and I can quietly, hesitantly penetrate deeply into the problem, then perhaps we shall be able to understand it. Actually there is no problem, it is the mind that creates the problem. In understanding the problem one is understanding oneself, the operations of one's own mind. After all, a problem exists only when any issue or disturbance has taken root in the soil of the mind. And is not the mind capable of looking at an issue, of being awake to any disturbance, without letting that disturbance take root in the mind? The mind is like a sensitive film, it perceives, it feels various forms of reaction, but is it not possible to perceive, to feel, to react with love, so that the mind itself does not become the soil in which the reaction takes root and becomes a problem?

Questioner: You have said that total attention is good; what then is evil?

KRISHNAMURTI: I wonder if there is such a thing as evil? Please give your attention, go with me, let us inquire together. We say there is good and evil. There is envy and love, and we say that envy is evil and love is good. Why do we divide life, calling this good and that bad, thereby creating the conflict of the opposites? Not that there is not envy, hate, brutality in the human mind and heart, an absence of compassion, love, but why do we divide life into the thing called good and the thing called evil? Is there not actually only one thing, which is a mind that is inattentive? Surely, when there is complete attention, that is, when the mind is totally aware, alert, watchful, there is no such thing as evil or good; there is only an awakened state. Goodness then is not a quality, not a virtue, it is a state of love. When there is love, there is neither good nor bad, there is only love. When you really love somebody, you are not thinking of good or bad, your whole being is filled with that love. It is only when there is the cessation of complete attention, of love, that there comes the conflict between what I am and what I should be. Then that which I am is evil, and that which I should be is the so-called good.

Now, is it at all possible not to think in terms of fragmentation, not to break life up into the good and the evil, not to be caught in this conflict? The conflict of good and evil is the struggle to become something. The moment the mind desires to become something, there must be effort, the conflict between the opposites. This is not a theory. You watch your own mind and you will see that the moment the mind ceases to think in terms of becoming something, there is a cessation of action which is not stagnation; it is a state of total attention, which is goodness, but that total attention is not possible as long as the mind is caught in the effort to become something.

Please do listen, not only to what I am saying, but to the operations of your own mind, and that will reveal to you with what extraordinary persistence thought is striving to become something, everlastingly struggling to be other than it is, which we call discontent. It is this striving to become something that is "evil" because it is partial attention, it is not total attention. When there is total attention, there is no thought of becoming, there is only a state of being. But the moment you ask, "How am I to arrive at that state of being, how am I to be totally aware?" you have already entered the path of "evil" because you want to achieve. Whereas, if one merely recognizes that as long as there is becoming, striving, making an effort to be something, one is on the path of "evil," if one is able to perceive the truth of that, just see the fact as it is, then one will find that that is the state of total attention, and that state is goodness; there is no strife in it.

Questioner: Great cultures have always been based on a pattern, but you speak of a new culture which is free of pattern. Is a culture without pattern ever possible?

KRISHNAMURTI: Must not the mind be free of all patterns to find reality? And being free to find that which is real, will it not create its own pattern, which the present society may not recognize? Can the mind which is caught in a pattern, which thinks in a pattern, which is conditioned by society, find the immeasurable which has no pattern? This language which is being spoken, English, is a pattern developed through centuries. If there is the creativity which is free of patterns, then that creativity, that freedom, can employ the technique of language, but through the technique, the pattern of language, reality can never be found.

Through practice, through a particular kind of meditation, through knowledge, through any form of experience, all of which are within a pattern, the mind can never understand what is truth. To understand what is truth, the mind must free itself from patterns. Such a mind is a still mind, and then that which is creative can create its own activity. But you see, most of us are never free from patterns. There is never a moment when the mind is totally free from fear, from conformity, from this habit of becoming something, either in this world or in the psychological, spiritual world. When the process of becoming in any direction completely ceases, then that which is God, truth, comes into being and creates a new pattern, a culture of its own.

Questioner: The problem of the mind and the social problem of poverty and inequality need to be tackled and understood simultaneously. Why do you emphasize only one?

KRISHNAMURTI: Am I emphasizing only one? And is there such a thing as the social problem of poverty and inequality, of deterioration and misery, apart from the problem of the mind? Is there not only one problem, which is the mind? It is the mind that has created the social problem, and having created the problem, it tries to solve it without fundamentally altering itself. So our problem is the mind, the mind that wants to feel superior and thereby creates social inequality, that pursues acquisition in various forms because it feels secure in property, in relationship, or in ideas, which is knowledge. It is this incessant demand to be secure that creates inequality, which is a problem that can never be solved until we understand the mind that creates the difference, the mind that has no love. Legislation is not going to solve this problem, nor can it be solved by the communists or the socialists. The problem of inequality can be solved only when there is love, and love is not just a word to be thrown about. The man that loves is not concerned with who is superior and who is inferior; to him there is neither equality nor inequality; there is only a state of being which is love. But we do not know that state, we have never felt it. So, how can the mind that is wholly concerned with its own activities and occupations, that has already created such misery in the world and is going right on creating further mischief, destruction—how can such a mind bring about within itself a total revolution? Surely, that is the problem. And we cannot bring about this revolution through any social reform; but when the mind itself sees the necessity of this total redemption, then the revolution is there.

Sir, we are always talking of poverty, inequality, and reformation because our hearts are empty. When there is love we shall have no problems, but love cannot come into being through any practice; it can come into being only when you cease to be, that is, when you are no longer concerned about yourself, your position, your prestige, your ambitions and frustrations, when you stop thinking about yourself completely, not tomorrow, but now. This occupation with oneself is the same, whether it be that of the man who is pursuing what he calls God, or that of the man who is working for a social revolution; and a mind so occupied can never know what love is.

Questioner: Tell us of God.

KRISHNAMURTI: Instead of my telling you what God is, let us find out whether you can realize that extraordinary state, not tomorrow or in some distant future, but right now as we are quietly sitting here together. Surely, that is much more important.

But to find out what God is, all belief must go. The mind which would discover what is true cannot believe in truth, cannot have theories or hypotheses about God. Please listen. You have hypotheses, you have beliefs, you have dogmas, you are full of speculations; having read this or that book about what truth or God is, your mind is astonishingly restless. A mind which is full of knowledge is restless, it is not quiet, it is only burdened; and mere heaviness does not indicate a still mind. When the mind is full of belief, either believing that there is God or that there is not God, it is burdened, and a burdened mind can never find out what is true.

To find out what is true, the mind must be free, free of rituals, of beliefs, of dogmas, knowledge, and experience. It is only then that the mind can realize that which is truth because such a mind is quiet; it no longer has the movement of going out or the movement of coming in, which is the movement of desire. It has not suppressed desire, which is energy. On the contrary, for the mind to be still, there must be an abundance of energy, but there cannot be ripeness or fullness of energy if there is any form of outward movement and thereby a reaction inward. When all that has calmed down, the mind is still. I am not mesmerizing you to be still. You yourself must see the importance of relinquishing, putting away without effort, without resistance, all the accumulations of centuries, the superstitions, knowledge, beliefs; you must see the truth that any form of burden makes the mind restless, dissipates energy.

For the mind to be quiet, there must be an abundance of energy, and that energy must be still. And if you have really come to that state in which there is no effort, then you will find that energy, being still, has its own movement, which is not the outcome of society's compulsion or pressure. Because the mind has abundant energy which is still and silent, the mind itself becomes that which is sublime; there is no experiencer of the sublime, there is no entity who says, "I have experienced reality." As long as there is an experiencer, reality cannot be because the experiencer is the movement to gather experience or to liquidate experience—so there must be a total cessation of the experiencer. Just listen to this, don't make an effort, just see that the experiencer, which is the outward and inward movement of the mind, must come to an end. There must be a total cessation of all such movement, and that requires astonishing energy, not the suppression of energy. When the mind is completely still, that is, when energy is neither dissipated nor distorted through discipline, then that energy is love, then that which is real is not separate from that energy itself.

February 27, 1955

Fifth Talk in Bombay

I think it is important to consider the question of what is learning, and also to understand what is creativity because in the deepest and most profound sense, creativity and learning are closely related. To most of us that word *creativity* means very little—either painting a picture, or writing a poem, or having children, or enjoying the sunset on the river—but surely, creativity is not the mere expression of a feeling or a technique. Creativity is something entirely different. It is a state of mind in which all thought has completely ceased, and which may be called reality, God, or what you will; and I think this state of creativity comes into being when we understand what it is that we call learning. So please have the patience to go with me into the problem.

Do we learn anything? And what is it that we learn? Deeply, fundamentally, is there anything to know? Is it not important to ponder over this whole question of teaching and learning? Beyond all expression, beyond all verbal statement and explanation, beyond all the restless activity of the mind, is there anything to know, to learn? And what do we mean by learning?

Learning is the accumulation of experience, it is skill in action. One learns a language, a craft, a skill, one learns how to drive a car, how to draw, how to read, how to build a dynamo, or sail a ship. Learning is also the accumulation of knowledge, knowledge of various philosophies, of science, and so on. And is there anything more to learn? Can one learn about oneself? Or is the understanding, the knowledge of oneself only from moment to moment and not from accumulation to accumulation? Must not the mind understand this whole process of accumulating knowledge, with its imitative capacity, and go beyond it?

What do we actually know? What we call knowledge is the education imparted at different levels of our existence by society, by religion, and with its help we try to survive. In the process of survival our lives are nightmares of ambition, of corruption, of competition, of the struggle to be something; there is a constant battle, a conflict going on within ourselves and around us. Modern existence, which is based on self-survival, on greed, jealousy, violence, war, is an everlasting struggle which we all know. That is our life, and we have learned how to survive within that culture of ambition, of ruthlessness, of belief, of quarrels, of fragmentary thought; we have learned how to manipulate our way through this chaos, this mess. And what is it that we have learned? We have learned various techniques, various forms of expression. We are always gathering, and expressing what we have gathered. One learns the technique of painting or of building a bridge, and from that learning there is expression. We are constantly learning, accumulating knowledge, information. This is an obvious fact. And if we go beyond all that, what is it that we know? Do we know anything? We know the distance between the stars, how to build airplanes, how to split the atom, and so on, but apart from that, do we know anything at all? Do we know anything except technique, skills, facts? And must not the mind go beyond all knowledge, all learning?

Now, if without being mesmerized by words, we can listen to the description of what lies behind this extraordinary struggle to acquire knowledge, learning, and let that struggle come to an end, then I think a totally different state will come into being, and we shall find out what is true creativity. We have acquired many forms of technique, we are familiar with the complex machinery of living, of survival, and we may have studied various philosophies and be capable of scholarly disputations with erudite people, but as long as one merely practices a technique or lives along the lines of any particular philosophy, one is obviously living according to a pattern, and therefore there must be imitation, copy. And is it possible to experience that state in which there is no copy, no imitation? Surely, to find out if such a thing is possible, we must begin by inquiring what it is that we know.

Have you ever considered what it is that you know? You may be scholars, very clever people who have read, who have studied, and who have suffered in the battle of life, but what is it that you know? Do you actually know anything? You know how to survive, how to do a particular job, you know a certain technique and have acquired the skill which comes with experience. But beyond that, do you know anything at all? Can the mind ask that question and remain with it, without trying to justify itself or answer the question? Because the moment you have explanations, the moment you answer that question, you have already entered the field of the known. So, is it not important for the mind to inquire and remain in that state of inquiry, which is not to seek an answer but simply to see if you know anything at all beyond the knowledge which has already been accumulated? I hope I am making myself clear.

All that we learn and all that we know is accumulation. It is the accumulative memory which acts; therefore, it is imitation. And is it possible to find a state of being in which all knowledge has ceased and there is only that state of being? It seems to me very important to find this out because we approach existence not with the unknown but always with the known. We translate every experience in terms of the known, in terms of the past, and therefore living becomes a series of reactions based on the known, and as the known is mere imitation, copy, our lives become very dull, empty.

Now, is it possible for the mind to live in a state of not knowing? After all, what is it that we know? Everything that we know is based on experience, on conformity, fear; we know in order to survive, and with that same mentality we approach the unknown, which is reality, God, or what you will. And can the mind be totally free of the known?

Sirs, this is an important question to ask oneself, is it not? Because we are always content with the known, and when you scratch the surface of the known there is nothing, there is emptiness, a void. And surely it is very important for the mind to live completely in that void, in that silence, and from that void, that silence, to think, to express, to invite thought and thereby action. That is why we must understand what it means to learn. Beyond a certain point we cannot learn any more because there is nothing to learn, there is no teacher to teach, and we must come to that point—which means, really, being completely free from all sense of becoming something, from all sense of the 'more'. It is only when the mind is in that state of void in which there is no knowledge, in which there is no longer the experiencer who is learning, who is gathering, who is accumulating—it is only then that there is this creativity which can express itself through various skills and crafts without causing further misery.

What I am saying is not difficult. The difficulty is to ask the question and keep on asking it. If you are waiting for an answer to the question, you are not concerned with the question at all.

So, we must come to this point where there is nothing to learn, for then the mind is free from society, free from all impositions, from this struggle for social recognition, and so on; and it is only in that state of freedom from society that we can create a new culture, bring about a new civilization. We may learn how to reform a particular society, how to adjust ourselves to the prison of a particular culture, and that is what most of us are occupied with; therefore, our response to challenge is always limited, inadequate. Whereas, if the mind is completely free from society, from every form of social conditioning, which means that it is a truly religious mind, then it is in a state of silence in which there is no acquisition of knowledge, no experiencer; and it is the action of such a mind that produces a new culture, a new civilization.

Questioner: Can I be free from the past?

KRISHNAMURTI: Now, if we can actually listen to what is being said, listen to find the truth of the matter without verbal disputation or the complications of a cunning mind, then that very truth frees the mind from the past.

So, let us inquire. Can the mind be free from the past? To say that it can or cannot be free would have no validity because you don't know. All that you can do is to inquire. Some people will say that the mind can never be free from the past, others that it can be free ultimately, in the future, but a man who really wants to find out for himself will have an entirely different attitude, an attitude neither of acceptance nor of denial.

What is the mind? The mind is essentially the product of time, of many thousands of yesterdays; it is the result of tradition, and in its development through the desire to survive, it has created various forms of culture, it has gathered knowledge, information. Being the product of time, the mind has the possibility of growth, and it goes from one target to another, from one purpose to another, changing within the pattern of the known; it develops through desire and through changing the objects of desire. A child desires toys; later on its desires become those of a young man or woman, and later still, as the mind matures, it wants to know what is beyond mere everyday existence. This process of inquiry, of wanting more, is what we consider to be growth, progress. Being the product of time, the mind develops in moving from the known to the known.

Now, the questioner wants to know whether the mind can be free from the past. And what is the past? The past is tradition, memory, the various impositions, sanctions, compulsions of society; the past is all the accumulated knowledge of how to run a motor, how to build a railway, how to split the atom, and so on. To be creative, to bring a new thing into being, even the technician must be free from the past; otherwise, he merely remains a technician. And can the mind, which is the result of time, cease to think in terms of time? Surely, that is what it means to be free from the past. Can the mind cease to think in terms of time, time being the pursuit of the 'more', the whole process of moving from one object or conclusion to another?

Sirs, your mind, which is obviously the result of many thousands of yesterdays, can only function in the field of the known, and when such a mind says, "Can I be free from the known?" what is its response? Its response can only be, "I do not know." That is, when the mind asks itself whether it can be free from the results of all its yesterdays, from its memories, its pains, its joys, its experiences, its virtues, its money, its position, surely the only answer is that it does not know.

Now, can the mind remain in that state, actually and not theoretically, in which it says, "I do not know"? Can you actually experience the fact that you do not know? Do you understand what I am saying, sirs? Here is a question: Can the mind be free from the memories, from all the accumulations of the past? If you don't theorize, if you don't either positively or negatively assert, then you can be in only one state, which is that you do not know. Now, if the mind can remain there, not merely verbally, but if it can actually experience that state of not knowing, then is not the mind free from the past? It is very interesting to inquire into this question because if the mind is merely in the field of the known, which it is, then unless it has the experience of not knowing and profoundly feels that state, all its inquiry will be the reaction of the known and therefore a further development of the known. To put it differently, the mind must be quiet, completely still, and the moment the mind is still, it is in the state of not knowing. Any movement of the mind is a reaction of the known, and it is only when the mind is silent, without movement, that it is capable of being innocent, fresh, totally aware.

You may ask what all this has to do with our daily living, with our daily conflicts, miseries, quarrels, and ambitions. It has nothing whatsoever to do with it. You cannot use this to overcome that. To experience this there must be the total cessation of all ambition, greed, jealousy, of all the competitive pursuits of self-preservation by which we have built up this rotten society which is disintegrating and for which there can be no reformation. The truly religious man is he who is free of society and the recognition of society, who in his inquiry into whether he can be free from the past has come to that state of mind in which there is no movement. It is only such a mind that is capable of creating a new culture. To reform the old culture is merely to decorate the prison.

Questioner: What have you to say about the possibility of integrating one's personality?

Krishnamurti: I do not think what I have to say about it has much value, but if you and I together can find out what it is to be integrated, if we can actually experience the state of integration and not merely define or describe it, then it will have some significance.

Now, to experience, to know what is the state of integration, we must first see that we are disintegrating, which is a fact. We are torn apart by desires which are in conflict with each other. There is the conflict of good and bad, of distraction and attention. I am this and I want to be that, which is the everlasting struggle between what I am and what I should be, between the fact and the ideal. This torn apart entity which we call the 'me', with its different masks, its conflicting attractions and pursuits, is what we actually are, and merely to put together what is torn apart is not integration. Contradictory desires may be brought together through conformity, tied together by fear, by incentive, but that is not integration.

So, first we have to be aware of the fact that we are made up of different entities with different masks, different poses; and to be aware is not merely to say that we are aware but actually to see this extraordinarily contradictory thing which we are without trying to transform or control it. Because the moment we realize that we are in contradiction, we want to bring about a state of noncontradiction, which is another form of contradiction; it is merely to have another mask, another desire. And is it possible just to be aware that we are made up of different beings? The higher self, the lower self, the atma, the paramatma, and the ambitions, the fears, the jealousies, the envies, are all within the field of the mind, of thought. One desire is in opposition to another desire, and any effort to bring about integration within the field of contradiction is itself a contradiction. The moment the mind desires to be something, there is already a division, a process of effort, which is obviously a process of disintegration.

In this question is also involved the whole content of the unconscious, is it not? If we are at all alert, we know how extraordinarily contradictory we are on the conscious level. When we do not fulfill our desires, there is frustration, sorrow. And is the unconscious also contradictory? In the unconscious, in the many layers of the mind below the conscious level, are there hidden pursuits, incentives, urges that are opposing each other, or is there only one constant drive? The unconscious is also the result of centuries of accumulation, it too has been shaped by racial and cultural influences, by beliefs, by fears; and in that vast field of half-imagined, half-felt consciousness, is there not also contradiction? Is not the whole consciousness a field of contradictory desires? And when there is conflict, whether at the conscious level or at the deeper levels, there is no attention, is there? Attention, total attention, is the good, and there cannot be total attention as long as there are contradictory desires. If contradictory desires are brought together by an effort of will, the will itself is the result of another desire, and therefore it creates still another contradiction.

Now, can the mind see this whole process, not merely verbally, descriptively, imaginatively, but can it actually be aware of this total mass of opposing desires, of which the mind itself is the battlefield? Can it be aware and not wish to bring about a state of integration? Can it just be choicelessly aware and remain there, neither hoping nor despairing but merely observing the fact? Then, being aware of confusion, and not making effort to alter it or to bring about an integrated state, no longer wishing to produce any result, is not the mind still? And is not that stillness, that tranquillity, the quieting of all energy—energy being the contradictory desires which have been opposing each other? And is not that cessation of all movement a state of integration from which action takes place which is not contradictory, and which therefore does not dissipate energy?

But you see, ladies and gentlemen, unless you directly experience all this, unless you feel out the truth of what is being said, it will have very little significance.

Questioner: What is right meditation?

KRISHNAMURTI: I think the right question would be not "What is right meditation?" but "What is meditation?" And it is surely very important to find out what meditation is because it will bring about a definite action in our daily life.

Now, to find out what meditation is, must you not first see what you think about meditation? When you use that word *meditation,* you already have various conclusions about it, have you not? You meditate according to a pattern, according to what some book or some teacher has said. So you already know what meditation is, and if you already know what meditation is, then you are not really inquiring.

Do you understand what I am talking about, sirs? If you are inquiring into what is meditation, then the formulas, the repetitions, the *japams,* the various things that you do must be put aside, and the mind must be entirely quiet. Either what you are doing now is meditation or it is not. If it is meditation, then there is no problem. But to find out if what you are doing is meditation, you must be free to look at it, to question it; you cannot merely accept it. To inquire into what is meditation, surely that freedom is the first necessity.

So, can you be free from all your practices, from all your disciplines, from all your various conclusions and compulsions? And if you are freeing yourself from those things because you are inquiring into what is meditation, then that very inquiry is meditation, is it not?

Why do you discipline your mind, and who is it that disciplines the mind? Who is it that meditates, and what is it that he meditates upon? What is the drive, the urge, the incentive to meditate? You must inquire into all that, must you not? If you have the incentive to find God and your meditation is the result of that incentive, which is a form of compulsion, then you will never find God. The mind disciplines, controls, shapes itself because it has already conceived what God is, what truth is, and it thinks that if it treads a certain path, does certain things, it will achieve an end, and that in the achievement there will be perfect happiness. But as long as the mind is seeking to achieve a result, it will never find that which is truth, reality, God, that which is immeasurable, timeless, because the mind itself is the result of time. So meditation has quite a different significance. When the mind is no longer being driven by any incentive, when it is no longer conditioned by any discipline, when it is no longer seeking any result, then is not the mind in a state of meditation?

Is it not also important to inquire who is the meditator, and what it is that he is meditating upon? Is there such a thing as the meditator separate from meditation? When you discipline yourself, who is the entity that disciplines? You may say it is the higher self. Is it? Or is it merely the invention of thought, one thought controlling another thought? You may call that controlling thought the higher self, but it is still within the field of thinking, therefore within the field of time. So, to inquire into what is meditation, must not the mind be free of conclusions? If any conclusion, any experience already exists, it is within the field of time. For a fleeting second you may have an experience of what you think is reality, happiness, bliss, but to cling to that is to hold the mind within the field of time and therefore make it incapable of any further experiencing of what is truth.

To inquire into what is meditation, then, the mind must first find out if it is free from all the technical approaches which it has learned in order to meditate. The mind has learned certain practices because it wants to achieve a result, and that result it has already preconceived. But that which it has preconceived is not the real, and to meditate upon what it has preconceived, to control, discipline itself in order to achieve what it has imagined, which is a mere speculation or the reaction of its own past, is utterly useless and has no meaning; it is a process of self-hypnosis. But if the mind begins to inquire into its various practices by being aware of its own incentives, its own pursuits, then that very inquiry is meditation. Then you will find that the mind becomes extraordinarily full of energy because there is no dissipation of energy through effort, through control, through shaping itself towards a particular end. To find out what is true, there must be abundant energy, and that energy must not be in any movement; it must be still. That stillness comes into being when the mind is free from all effort, when it is no longer caught in the pattern of discipline, fear, and achievement. Then there is no accumulation of memory, no residue, no experiencer, there is only a state of experiencing. When the mind is still, when there is no movement of effort, no demand for more, no gathering of memory, only then is there the truth which is from moment to moment.

March 2, 1955

Sixth Talk in Bombay

Is it not important to consider the question of what it is that we are seeking, and why we seek at all? Why is there this extraordinary anxiety to seek and to find, and why do we waste so much energy in that struggle? And what is it that we are individually or collectively seeking? If we can go into this matter diligently, we may find that the whole process of seeking truth, perfection, God, and so on, is a hindrance; the search itself may be a distraction. It may be that the mind can find that which is beyond the measure of time only when it is no longer seeking—which does not mean that it must be contented, satisfied. So I think it is important to go into this question.

In its anxiety to find, in its restless activity to discover what is truth, the mind is never quiet, and is not this process of search a hindrance to that very discovery? Is it not possible for the mind to be quiet and yet full of vigor, to be intensely aware without this constant strife, this anxiety to find? And what is it that we are all so anxiously seeking? Each one may interpret differently the intention, the urge that lies behind this search, but what is it fundamentally that we all want to find, what is it that we hope to gain at the end of our search?

In the movement of this search we join a society, a religious body, hoping thereby to find some kind of release, some kind of quietness, and we are soon caught, enmeshed in the dogmas, the beliefs, the rituals, the taboos and sanctions of that particular religion. So the search has led nowhere but only to a series of inward and outward conflicts, adjustments in conformity to a pattern, and in this process of struggle and adjustment, we grow old. Or, if we already belong to a particular group or pattern, we break away from it and join something else, leaving one cage, one bondage to enter another. We continue in that way year after year, struggling, conforming, taking vows, adjusting, hoping thereby to find. The earnest read the Gita, the Bible, this or that, hoping to find, and the light-hearted, the easygoing seek on a different level; to them what is important is going to the club, listening to the radio, having a good job, a little money. We are all being relentlessly driven to seek, and what is it that we want to find? I think it is important for each one of us to find out what it is that he is seeking. I may be able to describe it in different ways, but the verbal expression is not the actuality of your own perception of what you are seeking. So, if I may suggest, listen to what is being said, not with exclusive concentration, but listen in that silence between two thoughts. When the mind is trying to listen to a particular thought, many other thoughts come in, and then you push those thoughts away and try to listen. But instead of doing that, perhaps you can listen in the gap between two thoughts, when you are just attentive and therefore able to listen without effort.

To put it differently, what is important is not merely to listen to what is being said but to be aware, to be conscious of what you are thinking while you are listening and to pursue that thought to the end. If your mind is occupied with resisting one thought by another thought, you are not listening at all. I think there is an art of listening, which is to listen completely without any motive because a motive in listening is a distraction. If you can listen with complete attention, then there is no resistance either to your own thought or to what is being said—which does not mean that you will be mesmerized by words. But it is only the very silent, quiet mind that finds out what is true, not a mind which is furiously active, thinking, resisting, putting out its own opinions and conclusions.

So, is it possible to listen with that ease of attention which is without motive? If you can listen in that way, then I think you will find out for yourself the true answer to the question: What is it you are seeking? There may be an immediate response to that question, with many words, phrases, conclusions, but the true answer lies much deeper than the immediate response. If you are able to listen silently, that is, without the intense activity of a mind which is ceaselessly projecting its own thoughts, then perhaps you will find out what it is that you are seeking.

Obviously, we all want to be happy because our lives are very disturbed, anxious, fearful. There is nothing permanent, and for most of us, life is a series of conflicts in the action of survival. The very desire to survive has its own destructive byproducts. And what is it that we want to find, each one of us? The very humble clerk who goes to an office every day, the lady who has plenty of money and who goes to the club or to the races, the woman who is married and has many children, the man who has a certain capacity to learn—what is it they are all seeking? And why do we seek? Is it because we are so disturbed, so discontented with what we are? Being ugly, we want to be beautiful; being ambitious, we want to fulfill our ambition; having capacity, we want to make that capacity more vigorous; being good, we want to be better; being mediocre, we want to shine; being intellectual, we want to give significance to life; being religious, we seek to find that which is beyond the mind—inquiring, begging, praying, sacrificing, cultivating, disciplining, and so on. This strain, this process of conformity, is our life, is it not?

Our life is an everlasting battlefield from morning until night, and not knowing what it is all about, we look to somebody else to tell us the goal, the end, the purpose of life. We turn to beliefs, to books, to leaders, and when they offer us something, though we may be momentarily satisfied, sooner or later we want something else.

So, what is it that we want? Being disturbed, we want to find peace; being in conflict, we want to end conflict. If we are very alert, watchful, we see the futility of all thinking, of all the ideological utopias, the different systems of philosophy; and yet we go on seeking, seeking to find something that is real, something that has no confusion, something that is not man-made or mind-made, something beyond our immediate anxieties, fears, and wars. We struggle to gain something, and when we have gained it, we proceed further, we want still more. Our life is a series of demands for comfort, for security, for position, for fulfillment, for happiness, for recognition, and we also have rare moments of wanting to find out what is truth, what is God. So God or truth becomes synonymous with our satisfaction. We want to be gratified; therefore, truth becomes the end of all search, of all struggle, and God becomes the ultimate resting place. We move from one pattern to another, from one cage to another, from one philosophy or society to another, hoping to find happiness, not only happiness in relationship with people, but also the happiness of a resting place where the mind will never be disturbed, where the mind will cease to be tortured by its own discontent. We may put it in different words, we may use different philosophical jargons, but that is what we all want—a place where the mind can rest, where the mind is not tortured by its own activities, where there is no sorrow. So our life is an endless search, is it not? And if we don't seek we think that we shall deteriorate, stagnate, that we shall become like animals, that we shall die.

What is the intention of your seeking? Surely, on that depends what you will find. If your intention is to find peace, you will find it, but it will not be peace because the mind will be tortured in the very process of finding and maintaining it. To have peace you must discipline, control, shape your mind according to a particular pattern—at least, that is what you have been told. Every religion, every society, every book, teacher, guru, tells you to be good, to conform, to adjust, to comply, to discipline your mind not to wander, and so there is always restriction, suppression, fear. You struggle because you have to achieve that which you want, the goal.

Now, does not this search seem utterly futile? To be caught in the cage of a particular discipline or to be driven from one cage, from one system, from one discipline to another, obviously has no meaning. So we must inquire not into what it is you are seeking but why you seek at all. Seeking may be a totally wrong process. The very search may be a waste of energy, and you need all that energy to find. So it may be that your approach is entirely wrong, and I think it is, no matter what your Gita, your guru, or anybody else says. You are disciplined, you meditate, you gather virtue as you gather grain, and yet you are not happy, you have not found, there is not this inward joy, this creative revolution. It may be that God can never be found by a mind which is seeking because its motive is to escape from the torture of daily existence. Whereas, the mind that ceases to struggle because it has understood this whole problem of seeking, that puts aside the conflict of search because it sees what extraordinary energy is required to be open to that which is timeless—it may be that only such a mind can find, can discover or receive that which is truth, God.

Is it possible, then, to have a very alert mind which at the same time is peaceful, not seeking. Surely, a mind which is seeking is not a quiet mind because its motive is to gain something. As long as there is a motive in search, it is not the search for reality, it is only a search for what you want. All our human search, all our human endeavor to find out, is based on a motive, and as long as we seek with a motive, whether good or bad, conscious or unconscious, the mind can never be free and therefore still. To seek happiness is never to find happiness because one is seeking with a motive, and therefore there can be no cessation of fear.

Now, can one perceive and understand immediately that all search is vain when there is a motive? Can you listen to what is being said and grasp it, see the significance of it at once, not at some future date? Truth is not in the future, and if in the very act of listening you discover the futility of your search, then that very act of listening is the experiencing of truth, and therefore your search will stop. Then your mind is no longer caught in motives, intentions.

So, it is not a question of how to free the mind from motive. The mind can never free itself from motive because the mind in itself is cause and effect, it is a result of time. When the mind says, "How am I to free myself from motive?" again the search with a motive begins, again you are entering the field of strain, of discipline, of control, of this endless struggle which leads nowhere. But if you can listen and see the truth that as long as there is a motive in search, such search is utterly vain, meaningless, and only leads to more misery, more sorrow—if you see that and are really comprehending it now, as you are listening, then you will find that your mind has stopped seeking because it no longer has a motive. You are not being mesmerized by words or by a person. You have perceived for yourself the futility of this everlasting search with a motive; therefore, your mind is still, quiet, there is no movement of search at all, and that total stillness of mind may be the state in which the timeless comes into being.

You see, the mind is so restless, it is afraid to be still, it is afraid not to know all the latest things, it is afraid not to be at all, to be simply nothing, but it is only out of nothingness that wisdom comes, not out of much learning. Wisdom comes only to the mind that is silent. A mind that is full of its own conflicts and its own workable knowledge can only produce its own misery.

Questioner: How can I cease to be mediocre?

Krishnamurti: You must first know what mediocrity is, must you not? What is mediocrity? The mediocre may have cars, luxurious houses, or they may live in a slum. They may be more powerful in their minds, and generally they are. So what is this mediocrity that you want to escape, to get away from? If I realize I am mediocre, stupid, dull, and I want to become less mediocre, more intelligent, more learned, is not that very demand for the 'more', and the effort to become the 'more', a mediocre state of mind? Please listen to this, don't agree or disagree.

The mind that has a motive, that is pursuing the ideal of what it thinks it should be, that is disciplining, controlling, shaping itself, struggling to be other than it is—is not such a mind mediocre? Do you understand? Seeing that it is mediocre, stupid, dull, that it is greedy, envious, ambitious, ruthless, or whatever it be, the mind says, "I must become nonmediocre," and is not that effort to become nonmediocre the very essence of mediocrity? In trying to become something, the mind escapes from the actual fact into the ideal, and that is what you have all done.

You are pursuing, worshiping, the ideal which you have projected. Therefore there is never an overflowing, there is never a creative abundance with austerity because your energy is constantly being dissipated in the struggle to fulfill, to become something.

That is our way of life, is it not? We are ambitious and we want to fulfill, and in the very pursuit of that which we desire, we are becoming mediocre. Virtue is essential, but the process of acquiring virtue is mediocre. The man who ceaselessly practices virtue, who deliberately disciplines his mind to be virtuous, merely becomes respectable, and that is what society wants. Society wants you to be respectable, to conform, not to be creatively abundant, revolutionary in the right sense of that word. Real revolution is not the communist or some other stupid revolution of economic and social upheaval; it is a revolution in thought, and that can come about only when you abandon society completely. In that freedom your mind is no longer conforming, adjusting, defending, suppressing; therefore, it is truly religious, and a truly religious man is the only revolutionary. Then truth acts, and such action is not in the pattern of any particular culture.

So, mediocrity cannot be changed into something more beautiful. If you are aware of being stupid and try to become clever, in the very process of becoming clever, there is mediocrity, so all such effort is a waste of energy. Whereas, if you can live with and understand that which you see to be stupid, go into it fully without judging or condemning it, then you will find that there comes a state which is totally different—but that requires complete attention, not the distraction of trying to become something.

Questioner: How can I understand the significance of my dreams?

Krishnamurti: The question is not how you can understand the significance of your dreams, but why do you dream at all? Surely, that is the problem, not how to translate the symbols, the visions, the images which the unconscious projects when the conscious mind is asleep. Because your conscious mind is wholly occupied during the day, you dream when you are asleep, and when you wake up you say, "How am I to translate those dreams?" There are innumerable ways of translating dreams. You can translate them according to Freudian or some other philosophy and get lost in the study of symbols, chasing from one authority to another, which is so utterly futile. But if you ask yourself why you dream at all, then I think it will have significance.

What is a dream, and why do you dream? Have you ever thought about it? Without turning to any philosophy, to any book, to any expert on dreams, let us find out together why you dream at all.

After all, your consciousness is not just the superficial mind that goes to the office every day, that has a few virtues, clothes, this and that; your consciousness is the unconscious as well. When you are sleeping the superficial mind is somewhat at rest, so the unconscious acts, and you have dreams; and when you wake up you say, "What am I to do now?" But if you ask yourself why you dream at all and whether dreaming is necessary, you will presently see that there is something more important than interpreting dreams.

During the day your conscious mind is occupied with trivialities, with the struggle to survive, to be something, to fulfill your ambitions, to be loved, and so on; there is never a moment of quietness, of observation, of awareness of things, not as you would like them to be in imagination, but as they actually are. Whereas if, during the waking hours, you can be aware of everything about you and your response to it, if you can observe your own thoughts and let your mind slow down so that easily, without friction, it is acquainted with every emotion, every reaction and the significance of it, then you will see that you no longer dream because your whole mind is occupied in understanding all the time, not just when you are asleep; therefore, symbols have no meaning. If during the daytime you are passively aware of every thought, of every feeling, of every reaction, watching it without interpreting, condemning, or judging it, so that it is understood, then the mind becomes very quiet, and when you sleep there are no dreams. In that sleep the mind can go much deeper and can experience something which the waking consciousness can never touch.

So, to experience that which is beyond the mind, the mind must be still during the day and must have understood all the conflicts of the day without suppression, sublimation, or escape; and you are bound to suppress, sublimate, escape, as long as you are condemning, judging, evaluating, translating. But if you can merely observe so that your observation flows with your thought, then you will see that life is not a tortuous process, and that out of it comes a great energy which enables you to break away from society with all its stupidities. This does not mean that you become a hermit or a sannyasi. Such a man has not broken away from society because he is still caught in his conditioned mind. But if you can break away from society in the true sense, then in the very breaking away there is understanding of that which is eternal.

Questioner: You seem to question the validity of time as a means to the attainment of perfection. What then is your way?

Krishnamurti: You see, the very idea of the attainment of perfection and the way to it implies time, and in wanting to know what my way to it is, the questioner is still thinking in terms of time. Sir, there may be no way at all. Let us go into it.

What do we mean by time? Let us think about it, not philosophically, but very simply, quietly, easily. There is obviously chronological time. I must have time to catch a train, time to go from here to where I live, time to receive a letter, time to talk, time to tell you a story, time to write a poem or carve an image out of marble. But is there any other form of time? You say there is because there is memory. If I had a certain experience yesterday which gave delight, it has left a memory, and I want more of that delight. So the 'more' is time in the psychological sense. I must have time to fulfill, to achieve, to gather, to become; I must have time to bridge the gap between myself, who am not perfect, and that which is perfect over there. The "over there" being in my mind. So there is space in my mind, a distance between *what is* and 'what should be', the perfect ideal. There is a fixed point as the 'me', and a fixed point as the 'non-me' which I call perfection, the higher self, God, or what you will, and to move from this fixed point as the 'me' to that fixed point as the 'non-me', I need time. So the mind has not only the chronological time which is necessary to catch a train or keep an appointment but also psychological time—time to fulfill, to achieve. If I am ambitious, I must have time to attain, to become famous, and so on, and in the same way we think of perfection. Having divided itself as the imperfect, the mind conceives a state of perfection and establishes the distance between itself and that state; and then it says, "How am I to get from here to there?" Do you understand, sirs?

I am miserable, and I think I must have time to become perfect, to find happiness, if not in this life, then in some future life, but the mind is still within the field of time, however much that field may be extended or narrowed down. All your sacred books, all your religions say that you need time to become perfect, and that you must take a vow of celibacy, of poverty, you must resist temptation, discipline, control yourself in order to get there. So the mind has invented time as a means to perfection, to God, to truth, and it thinks in those terms because in the meantime it can be greedy, brutal, saying that it will polish itself up and eventually become perfect. I say that way is totally wrong, it is no way at all. It is merely an escape. A mind that is caught in imperfection, in struggle, can only conceive of what perfection is, and that which it conceives out of its confusion, its misery, is not perfection, it is only a wish.

So, in its effort to be that which it thinks it should be, the mind is not approaching perfection, it is merely escaping from *what is*, from the fact that it is violent, greedy. Perfection may not be a fixed point, it may be something totally different. As long as the mind has a fixed point from which it moves, acts, it must think in terms of time, and whatever it projects, however noble, however idealistically perfect, is still within the field of time. All its speculations on what Krishna, Buddha, Shankara, or anyone else has said, all its imaginations, its desires for perfection, are still within the field of time, therefore utterly false, valueless. A mind with a fixed point can only think in terms of other fixed points, and it creates the distance between itself and the fixed point which it calls perfection. Though you may wish otherwise, there may be no fixed points at all. In actuality, there is not any fixed 'you' or fixed 'me', is there? The 'I', the self, is made up of many qualities, experiences, conditionings, desires, fears, loves, hates, various masks. There is no fixed point, but the mind abhors this fact; therefore, it moves from one fixed point to another, carrying the burden of the known to the known.

So time is an illusion when we think in terms of perfection. Desire has time, sensation has time, but love has no time. Love is a state of being. To love completely, simply, without either asking or rejecting, is not to think in terms of perfection or of becoming perfect. But we do not know such love; therefore, we say, "I must have something else, I must have time to reach perfection." We discipline ourselves, we gather virtues, and if we don't sufficiently gather in this life, there is always the next life, so this movement of backwards and forwards is set going.

When you think in terms of time, you are really pursuing the 'more', are you not? You want more love, more goodness, more pleasure, more ways of avoiding pain, more of the experience which delights, which brings a fleeting happiness; and the moment the mind demands more, it must have time, it must of necessity create time. This demand for the 'more' is an escape from the actual. When the mind says, "I must be more clever," that very assertion implies time. But if the mind can look at *what is* without condemnation, without comparison, if it can just observe the fact, then in that awareness there is no fixed point. As in the universe there is no fixed point, so in us there is no fixed point. But the mind likes to have a fixed point, so it creates a fixed point in name, in property, in money, in virtue, in relationships, in ideals, beliefs, dogmas; it becomes the embodiment of its own inventions, its own desires. The mind's idea of perfection is itself made more peaceful, made more noble, quiet. But perfection is not the opposite of *what is*. Perfection is that state of mind in which all comparison has ceased. There is no thinking in terms of the 'more', therefore no struggle. If you can just know the truth of that, if you can merely listen and find it out for yourself, then you will see that you are free from time altogether. Then creation is from moment to moment, without accumulation of the moment, because creation is truth, and truth has no continuity. You think of truth as continuous in time, but truth is not continuous, it is not a permanent thing to be known in time. It is nothing of that kind, it is something totally different, something that cannot be understood by a mind that is caught within the field of time. You must die to everything of yesterday, to all the accumulations of knowledge, experience, and only then that which is immeasurable, timeless, comes into being.

March 6, 1955

Seventh Talk in Bombay

It seems to me that most of us are bewildered and confused, not only with regard to what we should do, but primarily in the matter of what is right thinking, and we are groping to find a way out of this confusion. We want a leader, someone to help us out of our difficulties. Being confused, we are very gullible, and we are easily made to accept things that are irrational, or we turn to past teachers, the Christ or Buddha, to the Vedas , to the Bible, hoping to find an answer to our problems. But I think such a way of thinking makes confusion more confounded. Confusion comes, really, when we are incapable of looking at the fact without having an opinion about the fact. We never look at the fact directly, but always come to it with a conclusion, and the result is confusion. If we can see this one very simple thing, then I think we shall be able to understand the much more complex and comprehensive problem of what is religion, what is truth, what is God.

We are confused, and we do not know what we are confused about, or how confusion arises. Surely, confusion exists only when we are not capable of looking at the fact stripped of all evaluations, that is, when we have not the capacity to recognize the fact without opinion, without the traditional values which we give to it. It is the traditional value, the opinion, the judgment with regard to the fact, that brings about confusion. If you look into it you will find that this is so. We are never able to look at a fact as it is, but always come to it with judgments, with values, and hence the confusion.

Now, can the mind look at the fact without the evaluating factor? The fact is always new whereas the evaluating factor is always old. When the mind looks at the fact with the values, the opinions, the judgments it has acquired, which are all the outcome of the past, there is bound to be confusion.

So our problem is to look at the fact without evaluation, and that requires a great sense of humility, does it not? But none of us is humble—we all know, we all have values, we do not come to the fact without knowing. Not knowing is a state of humility, and I think this is very important to understand. Knowledge has nothing to do with wisdom. Wisdom comes into being without knowledge, that is, only when the mind has no evaluating factor, when the mind is not the entity that evaluates, that judges, that compares. Humility is necessary to understand a fact, and to have this sense of humility, there must be total freedom from all knowledge, for knowledge is the process of evaluation, and the fact being the new, when you approach it with a mind that is burdened with knowledge, out of that comes confusion.

Now, if the mind can be stripped instantaneously of all the past so that it is able to meet the present without the burden of knowledge, then there is no confusion. It is like a doctor observing the patient; he does not come to the patient with foregone conclusions, with his mind already made up as to what illness the patient has. But most of us approach the fact with conclusions. We have certain beliefs, certain dogmas, certain formulas, and our approach to the problem, how to deal with it, is already clearly laid out in our minds, so our minds are never fresh, never able to approach the problem anew.

We say that we need time to free the mind from all accumulative, self-protective knowledge, to unburden ourselves of all sorrow, misery, strife. But I do not think time is necessary at all. On the contrary, time is merely the outcome of our not meeting the fact without knowledge. For centuries the mind has been acquiring knowledge with which to meet the fact and has thereby introduced confusion. So, can the mind be free from all the values it has accumulated and meet the challenge anew, the challenge being the fact? It is because we do not meet the fact fully, without conclusions, that there is confusion, there is sorrow. To be free of sorrow we say we must have time, and therefore we have developed philosophies, disciplines, various ways and means to overcome it. But sorrow is the result of this very process of meeting the fact with a conclusion.

So, to be free from sorrow, must not the mind approach the fact without a belief, without a conclusion? That is, must there not be immediate freedom from memory as the evaluating factor? When I meet you, for example, if I already know you, I do so with certain values, opinions, judgments about you which memory has retained and which are based on my previous experiences with you. Now, can I look at you, have the memory of you, and yet be free of all judgment? Can I meet you, know who you are, and yet have no values, no opinions concerning you? Surely, it is our values, our judgments that bring confusion, sorrow; and being confused, being in sorrow, we say we must have time to overcome this sorrow. But is that so? Will time resolve our sorrow?

Do you understand, sirs, what sorrow is? Sorrow is our incapacity to meet the fact completely, without judgment, without belief. It is because we do not meet the fact afresh and move with it that there is sorrow. Being in sorrow, as most people are, we want time to be free from sorrow, and so we have various philosophies, schools of thought, disciplines, meditations, to overcome it. I do not think sorrow can be overcome through any discipline, through time, for sorrow is the result and not the cause, and as long as you are merely dealing with the symptom and not with the cause, there must be the prolongation of confusion, conflict, and sorrow.

So, can sorrow be overcome immediately? I think this is an important question to put to oneself because the man who is happy is not antisocial. It is the man who is frustrated, confused, miserable, and also the man who is seeking God, truth—it is such people who are antisocial because truth cannot be found as long as the mind is seeking. So, for the man who is seeking truth, as well as for the man who is confused, who is in sorrow, the problem is: Can the cause of sorrow be dissipated immediately? Is there an entirely different way of looking at it, thinking about it, so that it can be understood not in some distant future but now? Surely, there is the ending of sorrow only when I free my mind from all evaluation, from all comparison, from all social sanctions, strip it of all its accumulations so that it is in a state of humility, the state in which the mind is aware and knows nothing, and is therefore able to look at the fact without judgment.

After all, what do we mean by religion? Religion is not belief, it is not the capacity to quote sacred books, it is not the worship of an image or a symbol, it has nothing to do with the performance of a particular ritual. Religion is that state of mind in which there is no longer any search, in which there is no longer any movement which has a cause. And surely, being so confused, our problem is not to be resolved by going back to the past, to what Shankara, Buddha, Christ, or your own guru has said, but only by being able to meet life, with all its challenge, anew, afresh; and you cannot meet the challenge, the fact, in that way as long as the mind is burdened with any evaluation. It is meeting the fact with evaluation that creates confusion and sorrow. So, can the mind have memory and yet be still, thus meeting the fact without evaluation? Can the mind be free of all its many yesterdays?

Now, there is no way to be free, is there? There is no method because the very method imprisons the mind, and therefore the mind is no longer free. The pursuit of the method, of the "how," has a cause, and as long as there is a cause, an incentive, a motive, the mind is incapable of meeting the fact anew, and hence there is confusion and sorrow. So there is no way, no method, no system to free the mind.

Please listen to this without agreeing or disagreeing. I am not saying anything which you have to think about in a complicated manner or make a philosophy of. I am just describing to you a fact, and if you don't meet directly the fact which I am describing, you are going to be more confused. I say there is no way of freeing the mind, no method, because any method, any discipline, any practice binds the mind, conditions it further. When you suffer, all that you are concerned with is to find a way out, and the "way out" is the method, the system, the discipline, the practice with which you meet the fact; therefore, you are incapable of understanding the fact, so your confusion and sorrow increase.

What is important, then, is to see the truth in a flash, to be so sensitive that the fact instantly reveals the truth. But that requires a great deal of humility, and the man who has experienced, who has studied, the man who worships and practices, has no humility at all; therefore, his leadership, his advice, his learning, bring more sorrow, more confusion to the world.

So our question is: Can your mind now, at this minute while you are listening to me, be entirely stripped of all the evaluating factors, of all the many yesterdays, so that it can see what is truth? The perception of truth is not a state of experience because to experience there must be the experiencer, the evaluator. Please listen, it is very simple. As long as there is an experiencer who is the evaluator, there is no perception of what is truth. Truth has no continuity; it is only the evaluator, the observer, the experiencer, that has continuity—not truth. That which continues is the process of evaluation.

Now, as one is sitting here quietly of an evening, or when one is walking or taking the bus, is it possible to see all this vast confusion and sorrow in one's own heart and mind, and realizing the whole process of sorrow, not give it soil in which to take root, the soil of knowledge, evaluation, but look at the facts without judgment? Which means, really, looking at the facts in all humility. If you say, "I must be humble, I must remove the previous understanding from my mind and be free of all knowledge, evaluation," then the "how" becomes important, and you will never solve the problem. But if you see the truth now, as you are listening, that the mind is free from sorrow only when it looks at the fact without any judgment, without any evaluation, that is, when it meets the challenge completely, totally—if you see the truth of that immediately, then you will find there is the cessation of sorrow. It does not matter whether one is learned or ignorant, if one can just listen to what is being said and see the truth of it, then that very act of listening is the liberation from sorrow.

But the difficulty is for most of us that we want an experience of joy or ecstasy to continue; having seen clearly, we want to have an abiding sense of clarity, and the desire for the 'more' is the beginning of vanity. It is only in complete humility—which is a state in which you know nothing, a state in which there is no experiencer, no evaluator—that the mind can instantaneously receive the truth. There is no path to truth, no system by which you can attain it. You may read the Gita, the Bible, all the sacred books in the world, or even Marx, but none of them will lead you to truth. The mind that has achieved, that knows, that has practiced and experienced, that is full of its own knowledge—such a mind can never find truth or God—but only the very simple mind, the mind that is really humble and therefore able to meet the fact without any evaluation. What is important is to look at life, at every movement of life, without the burden of many yesterdays, thereby ceasing to create confusion and sorrow.

Questioner: How can I be free from fear?

KRISHNAMURTI: What is fear? Fear exists only in relationship to something, it does not exist by itself. Fear comes into being in relationship to an idea, to a person, with regard to the loss of property, and so on. One may be afraid of death, which is the unknown. There is fear of public opinion, of what people will say, fear of losing a job, fear of being scolded, nagged. There are various forms of fear, deep and superficial, but all fear is in relationship to something, so when we say, "Can I be free from fear?" it really means, "Can I be free from all relationship?" Do you understand? If it is relationship that is causing fear, then to ask if one can be free from fear is like asking if one can live in isolation. Obviously, no human being can live in isolation. There is no such thing as living in isolation; one can live only in relationship. So, to be free from fear one must understand relationship, the relationship of the mind to its own ideas, to certain values, the relationship between husband and wife, between man and his property, between man and society. If I can understand my relationship with you, then there is no fear because fear does not exist by itself; it is self-created in relationship. Our problem, then, is not how to overcome fear but to find out first of all what our relationship is now, and what is right relationship. We do not have to establish right relationship because in the very understanding of relationship, right relationship comes into being.

I think it is important to see that nothing can live in isolation. Even though you may become a sannyasi, put on a loincloth and seclude yourself, isolate yourself in a belief, no human being can live in isolation. But the mind is pursuing isolation in the self-enclosure of "my experience," "my belief," "my wife," "my husband," "my property," which is a process of exclusion. The mind is seeking isolation in all its relationships, and hence there is fear. So our problem is to understand relationship.

Now, what is relationship? When you say, "I am related," what does that mean? Apart from the purely physical relationship through contact, through blood, through heredity, our relationship is based on ideas, is it not? We are examining *what is,* not 'what should be'. Our relationship at present is based on ideas, on ideation as to what we think is relationship. That is, our relationship with everything is a state of dependency. I believe in a certain idea because that belief gives me comfort, security, a sense of well-being, it acts as a means of disciplining, controlling, holding my thought in line. So my relationship to that idea is based on dependence, and if you remove my belief in it, I am lost, I do not know how to think, how to evaluate. Without the belief in God, or in the idea that there is no God, I feel insecure, so I depend on that belief.

And is not our relationship with each other a state of psychological dependency? I am not talking about physiological interdependence, which is entirely different. I depend on my son because I want him to be something which I am not. He is the fulfillment of all my hopes, my desires; he is my immortality, my continuation. So my relationship with my son, with my wife, with my children, with my neighbors, is a state of psychological dependency, and I am fearful of being in a state in which there is no dependence. I do not know what that means, therefore I depend on books, on relationship, on society, I depend on property to give me security, position, prestige. And if I do not depend on any of these things, then I depend on the experiences which I have had, on my own thoughts, on the greatness of my own pursuits.

Psychologically, then, our relationships are based on dependence, and that is why there is fear. The problem is not how not to depend, but just to see the fact that we do depend. Where there is attachment there is no love. Because you do not know how to love, you depend, and hence there is fear. What is important is to see that fact, and not ask how to love, or how to be free from fear. You may momentarily forget your fear through various amusements, through listening to the radio, through reading the Gita or going to a temple, but they are all escapes. There is not much difference between the man who takes to drink and the man who takes to religious books, between those who go to the supposed house of God and those who go to the cinema because they are all escaping. Whereas, if as you are listening, you can really see the fact that where there is dependency in relationship there must be fear, there must be sorrow, that where there is attachment there can be no love—if as you are listening now you can just see that simple fact and comprehend it instantaneously, then you will find that an extraordinary thing takes place. Without refuting, accepting, or giving opinions about it, without quoting this or that, just listen to the fact that where there is attachment there is no love, and where there is dependency there is fear. I am talking of psychological dependency, not of your dependence on the milkman to bring you milk, or your dependence on the railway, or on a bridge. It is this inward psychological dependency on ideas, on people, on property, that breeds fear. So, you cannot be free from fear as long as you do not understand relationship, and relationship can be understood only when the mind watches all its relationships, which is the beginning of self-knowledge.

Now, can you listen to all this easily, without effort? Effort exists only when you are trying to get something, when you are trying to be something. But if, without trying to be free from fear, you are able to listen to the fact that attachment destroys love, then that very fact will immediately free the mind from fear. There can be no freedom from fear as long as there is no understanding of relationship, which means, really, as long as there is no self-knowledge. The self is revealed only in relationship. In observing the way I talk to my neighbor, the way I regard property, the way I cling to belief or to experience or to knowledge, that is, in discovering my own dependency, I begin to awaken to the whole process of self-knowledge.

So, how to overcome fear is not important. You can take a drink and forget it. You can go to the temple and lose yourself in prostration, in muttering words, or in devotion, but fear waits around the corner when you come out. There is the cessation of fear only when you understand your relationship to all things, and that understanding does not come into being if there is no self-knowledge. Self-knowledge is not something far away; it begins here, now, in observing how you treat your servants, your wife, your children. Relationship is the mirror in which you see yourself as you are. If you are capable of looking at yourself as you are without any evaluation, then there is the cessation of fear, and out of that comes an extraordinary sense of love. Love is something that cannot be cultivated; love is not a thing to be bought by the mind. If you say, "I am going to practice being compassionate," then compassion is a thing of the mind, and therefore not love. Love comes into being darkly, unknowingly, fully, when we understand this whole process of relationship. Then the mind is quiet, it does not fill the heart with the things of the mind, and therefore that which is love can come into being.

Questioner: You postulate an understanding that is absolute. To you there is no place for gradualists. How can we with our limited minds grasp your teachings?

KRISHNAMURTI: Sir, we have invented this process of gradualism for our convenience. When you go to a doctor to have an operation, do you say that the thing which necessitates operation will be eradicated gradually? When you have a bad tooth, do you say that it will gradually be extracted? You go to the dentist for an immediate extraction, or you go to the surgeon to be put on a table and cut open. But you see, we do not think in those terms. We want both pleasure and pain, and that is why gradualism exists. We have invented a philosophy of life, a so-called way of love, that gives us both pleasure and pain, and hence the conflict between good and evil. We say, "I am violent, and I must have time to overcome that violence"; therefore we have the ideal of nonviolence, and through a process of gradualism we hope eventually to become non-violent, which is just a lot of nonsense. Either we are or we are not violent, there is no becoming nonviolent.

Now, being violent, what is important is to have the capacity to deal with violence immediately and not give it time to take root in the mind and become a problem. Do you understand, sirs? To be free of violence one has to meet violence within oneself and understand it immediately, and that immediacy of understanding is not possible if one thinks in terms of time, which is the soil in which the problem takes root. But not having the capacity to meet our violence, our greed, we invent a way of dealing with the problem which has no reality, which is not a fact, it is just an ideation.

So, is it possible for you and me to meet anger, violence, or whatever it be without making it into a problem, that is, without giving soil in the mind for the problem to take root? The problem comes into being only when we are not capable of dealing with the fact immediately, and therefore we give soil for that issue to take root, which then becomes a problem. When this problem arises we say, "How am I to deal with it?" and so we have invented gradualism, the idea that gradually we shall get rid of it. I hope I am making myself clear.

If I am capable of dealing instantly with anger, with jealousy, with violence, if I am able to meet it immediately, factually, then there is no problem. The problem arises only when, not knowing how to meet that feeling, I give it shelter in the mind, soil in which to take root, and insist that to be free from it gradualism is necessary.

Our question is, then, can you and I deal with the fact immediately without making it into a problem? Please listen. Can I just look at the fact of anger, envy, ambition, or what you will, without any evaluation, without condemning or accepting it? That is, can I look at anger without giving it a name? There is a feeling, that feeling is immediately termed as anger, and the very word *anger* is a condemnation. So, can I look at that feeling without naming it, without condemning, judging, or comparing it, without identifying myself with it? That means, really, looking at the fact and retaining the memory of the fact without all the evaluating factors.

Let us approach the question differently. The questioner says, "You talk about an absolute understanding, but we cannot understand immediately, we need time." Let us find out if that is so. You think somewhere there is God, truth, that extraordinary thing which man seeks everlastingly, and that between that thing and the 'me' there is a gap, a thick wall of vanity, greed, ambition, fear, and so on. So you say, "I must have time to tear down the wall, to wear it out, or to make it transparent to that beauty, that goodness." But I say time will never do it. Whether you have one life or a hundred lives, as long as you are thinking in terms of time, you will never do it. All your sacred books, all your gurus have said that you must have time, but who is the entity that is taking time to polish the wall day after day, or to pull it down, who is it that says, "There is distance between me and that reality"? That very entity is the creator of time because he wants to achieve something and therefore thinks in terms of "getting there." So he has created this idea, this illusion that there is space between the 'me' and that reality, and having created this space, this gap which is time, he asks, "How am I to bridge it?"

Please see this. Any movement on the part of the mind towards that which it calls reality creates time, and therefore it can never bridge the gulf. As long as there is the entity who says, "I am going to discipline, control myself, I am going to practice virtue every day in order to break down the wall between myself and reality," that very entity is creating the wall, the distance between itself and reality. Virtue is essential, for virtue brings freedom, order, but virtue alone does not lead to reality. Virtue is recognition by society, and to live in society you must have virtue. Perhaps many of you are virtuous, good, kindly, compassionate, unassuming, and yet you have not that extraordinarily creative thing without which virtue has very little meaning, it is merely a social oil which enables society to run smoothly.

So, as long as the mind thinks in terms of becoming; as long as it says, "I am here and I must get there"; as long as it wants to be something, the governor, the big executive; as long as it says, "I am going to fulfill, reach God," it must have time. Now, if you can see and understand this fact, then at that moment you are not, you are nothing, and for you there is no time. Then there is no gap, there is no 'me' and "that reality," but only a state of being, and out of that comes an extraordinary joy. Then there is no striving, no dissipation of energy. You must have an abundance of energy, but not through control. If you say, "I am going to take the vow of celibacy, I am going to discipline myself in order to have more energy," that is merely another bargain. Those are all the ways and tricks of the mind in order to achieve something, to get somewhere. The person who has taken the vow of celibacy knows no love because he is concerned with himself and his own fruition.

So, what is important is to see all this—how the mind deceives itself, how the mind has created the distance between itself and that reality which it thinks exists. As long as there is any movement of the mind towards a goal, there must be gradualism, there must be time. Merely to listen to this fact, to meet and understand it in oneself, frees the mind from time. But you can listen to it, understand it only when there is no sense of 'becoming', when you don't want to be anything, only when your mind is stripped of all experiences—and it is as you are listening now. You are not being mesmerized by me, you are quiet because you are listening to something that is true. And if you can listen quietly even for a minute, for a second, then you will find that that very quietness, the very silence of that second has within it the whole abundance, the richness and the beauty and the goodness of truth. In that moment there is complete attention without any motive, and that complete attention does not wish to have something more, it does not wish to be better. That complete attention is the good, and therefore there is no better.

I say that the mind can be free immediately, and that there is no gradual process by which to free the mind through time. It is only the mind which is very quiet that can be free, and that quietness cannot be purchased by the accumulation of knowledge or virtue, it cannot be known through any discipline or sacrifice. It is only when you are listening to everything in life, when you are watching in the mirror of relationship the reflection of your own thoughts, wants, greeds, envies, purposes, just watching it without acceptance or condemnation—it is only then that the mind becomes really still. For the mind to be still, there must be abundant energy and therefore the cessation of conflict. It is only when conflict ceases at every level that the mind is still. When there is no dissipation of energy through conflict, through effort, through discipline, the mind becomes totally quiet, and that very quietness is the abundance of energy. Only then does that reality which cannot be put into words, which has no symbol, that something which cannot be described or speculated upon, come into being.

March 9, 1955

Eighth Talk in Bombay

Surely, the most important thing that all of us have to do is to understand our life and not escape from life, but our whole pattern of thinking, it seems to me, is a process of escaping from our daily conflicts, from our daily miseries and responsibilities, from the utter chaos we find ourselves in. We have to understand this confusion and not look for someone to help us to escape from it. The facts of our life are important, not the ideological escapes which all religions and most philosophies offer. We seem to find it extraordinarily difficult to live with deep fullness of thought, with intense, abundant love, and most of us are not concerned with that; we are concerned with trying to become something.

If you observe, all our religions, all our leaders, political and so-called spiritual, all our organizations, the worldly as well as the religious, offer ways of becoming something, either here or in the so-called world of the spirit. In striving, in struggling to become something, we have lost the beauty of living, and if we can understand the problem of effort, then perhaps we shall be able to understand our lives and live richly, worshiping the one day with abundance, with deep passion, and not looking to tomorrow. It is because we do not understand the eternal present that we try to find something beyond the present, tomorrow. And what is it that prevents us from understanding our life, which is so fraught with sorrow, with conflict, with ambition, with this extraordinary division between man and man? Why is it that we do not understand this whole process of living and are always looking somewhere else for truth, for life, for something which is immeasurable, beyond the limits of thought? What is it that blocks our understanding? Is it that we want to find an answer away from the facts of everyday living, something which will be much more satisfactory, more permanent, something that will give us a sense of well-being? What is it that each one of us wants out of life?

Can life offer anything but conflict and misery as long as we use life as a means to something else? Yet that is what we are all doing, is it not? We are using life, our daily living, which is an extraordinary thing in itself, to get somewhere, to reach heaven, to find truth, God, and the various philosophies; the religious teachers and systems offer the means of escape from our living and from the understanding of that living.

Now, it seems to me that the understanding of life is not a difficult problem at all, but what makes it difficult is the interpretation, the opinions, the values, the judgments that we have. It is this conditioning of the mind that creates wars, that makes for darkness and myths, and if we can actually wipe it away, not in the process of time, but from day to day, then I think we shall find that life is not a stepping stone to something greater. There is nothing greater. If I know how to live, then living itself is the truth. But it is not a question of how life should be lived. There is a vast difference between actual living and the 'what should be'. It is this curse of the ideal, the 'what should be', that has rotted our thinking. And is it possible to wipe away all our conditioning? I think that this is the real question, not how to improve our conditioning, or which is the better way of thinking. All thinking is a form of conditioning, whether it is communistic, socialistic, capitalistic, Catholic, Hindu, or what you will. And if it is possible to wipe away this whole evaluating process, to retain memory without the condemnatory and justificatory values, then we shall see that life has a tremendous significance.

So, is it possible to wipe away the many values, the ambitions that one has set up for oneself, and live a life without effort? Effort, which is based on the evaluations of memory, is a process of degeneration, it destroys the clarity of thinking and living. If you can listen without evaluation to what is being said here, then your problem is immediately solved because you perceive the truth, not somebody's interpretation of the truth. But you cannot possibly act to free the mind from evaluation, from condemnation, justification, comparison, from all the accumulated knowledge which makes you think this way or that, for any pressure on thought is another deviation. All of us think under pressure, do we not? Our thinking is a process of pressure because we want to become something, positively or negatively, and we thereby bring about frustration. Pressure on thought leads to frustration, to misery, to sorrow; and is it possible to live without pressure?

Surely, that is our problem, is it not? Our problem is to live richly, happily, sweetly, without all this sorrow. Our lives are full of sorrow, and what most of us are concerned with is how to escape from sorrow, and if we cannot escape from it, we use sorrow as the means to truth, saying that we must suffer in order to understand that which is joy, that which is ecstasy. But sorrow does not lead to ecstasy, sorrow does not lead to life, to beauty, to light.

We are in sorrow because we are always trying to become something. If you watch your own mind, you will see that every movement of thought is towards something or away from something, and so your life is a series of battles, conflicts, and miseries. Don't agree with me, but watch your own life and see how miserable it is, how petty, mediocre, uncreative. The mind is limited, everlastingly occupied, and with that mind we try to find something which is beyond the whole process of thought. Realizing that, we say we must silence the mind, so we begin to discipline, to control, to shape the mind, thereby dissipating the energy which is so necessary if the mind is to be still. So we have made our life into a tortuous affair, and can we sweep away the things that are making us into thoughtless, uncreative, imitative machines, all the repetitive phrases which have very little meaning? Can we wipe all that away, be simple and begin anew?

It is possible to do that only when we do not think in terms of time. We are used to thinking in terms of time, in terms of becoming something, are we not? Being confused, in sorrow, without love, being full of the bitterness of frustration in the everlasting struggle to become something, we say, "I must have time to be free from all that," and we never put to ourselves the question, "Can I be free, not in time, but immediately?" It is necessary to ask fundamental questions always and never seek answers to them, because to fundamental questions there are no answers. The question itself, with its depth and clarity, is its own answer. But we never put fundamental questions, and one of the fundamental questions is whether it is possible not to think in terms of time.

The mind is the result of time, of centuries of memory, it is the outcome of innumerable experiences and evaluations; and can that mind think, can that mind find, without becoming something? If you are good now, there is no problem, but if you are thinking in terms of becoming good, then the problem arises. If there is no love, the question is not how to love eventually, but what is love? If you are asking what love is, that is a fundamental question, and the answer is not to be sought, for it depends on the seriousness and depth of the questioner.

So, what is important in our daily living is not what to seek and what to find but to stop all search because in search there is pressure on thought. All search as we know it has a motive, and as long as there is a motive, an incentive in your search, what you are seeking is obviously the fulfillment of that motive; therefore, it is no longer search.

Now, can the mind stop seeking? Surely, any movement of the mind in any direction has an incentive, and the incentive breeds its own result; therefore, that result is not truth. Truth comes into being when the mind has no movement at all, when it is completely still.

But you see, the difficulty is that all of us have been educated wrongly, we have lost the initiative in thinking, we want to be helped, and probably most of you are here for that reason. Sirs, there is no help, and please realize this. There is no help-which does not mean that you must remain in despair. On the contrary. But the moment you begin seeking help you have lost the initiative, and initiative is the beginning of that extraordinary thing called creativity, which is truth. Remaining within the walls of your particular prison, the walls of your own thinking, your own conditioning, your own ambition and confusion, you want to be helped by an outside agency, and so you lose the initiative to jump over the wall. He who you think will give you a hand to jump over the wall you call your guru, or the one who loves you, or the truth; but if you are helped you have lost that creativity. Life is a process of discovery, and in living from day to day you have to find out for yourself its beauty, its extraordinary depth; and it is because you do not look, because you want to be helped, that you lose the confidence, the initiative which is so essential to the process of discovery. The sense of individual discovery of what is truth is destroyed, taken away from you, so you read the Gita, you turn to Shankara, Buddha, or Christ, you follow the book or the leader, and having established authorities, you are lost. That is a simple fact. You are lost because you have leaders, philosophies, disciplines. If they did not exist, you would not be lost because then you would have to find out from day to day, from moment to moment, you would have to discover for yourself.

There is a difference between self-confidence and the state of mind which is constantly inquiring without a motive. Self-confidence breeds aggression, arrogance; its action is a self-enclosing process, but for the mind that is in a state of constant inquiry, there is no accumulation of discovery, and only such a mind can find that which is truth. The mind that is led can never discover what is truth—but only the mind that is free from society, from all conditioning, and is therefore in a state of revolution. That is why only the truly religious man is a revolutionary, not the reformer.

So it seems to me that our problem is not to seek that which you call truth or God but to free the mind from all conditioning as a Hindu, a Muslim, a Christian, or whatever it be, and also from the conditioning which comes about when you are ambitious, envious—all of which is within the pattern of society. Society is based on reformation, and reformation is continuation of the past; and it is only when the mind is aware of all this and understands it that there is a possibility of the coming into being of that for which we all hunger and without which life has not much meaning, which is the real. But for the experiencing of the real, there must be no experiencer. The experiencer is the result of the past, he is made up of many accumulations, of many memories, and as long as there is the experiencer, the thinker, there cannot be that which is truth. When the mind is free from the thinker, from the experiencer, from the 'me' as accumulated memories with their evaluations-it is only then that the mind can be still.

Stillness of the mind is not to be thought of in terms of time. That stillness has no continuity, it is not a state to be achieved and continued or perpetuated. When the mind wants to continue an experience, there is the experiencer, and that experiencer is greed for the 'more'. The 'more' creates time, and as long as the mind is thinking in terms of the 'more', the real is not there.

Perhaps you have listened to all this quietly and easily. The mere hearing of the words is not the understanding of the words. But if you listen to the words without any effort to capture or experience something, if you just listen and do not grasp at it, then you will find that that very listening brings about in you an unconscious revolution. That is the only revolution because a conscious revolution of desire, of effort, is merely reformation. If you can listen quietly, easily, without interpretation, to what is being said and to everything about you, then you will find that you are listening not only to that which is very near but also to things that are very far away, to that which has no measure, no space, that which is not caught in words, in time. But to listen to that which is beyond measure, to that which is truth, the mind must be very quiet, and it cannot be quiet as long as it is seeking, because seeking is a form of agitation. When the mind is really still because it is caught up in the song of its own listening, only then the immeasurable, that which is eternal, comes into being.

Questioner: All our problems seem to be rooted in the dust of the past. Is it possible to be aware of the full content of the unconscious and die to it so that the mind is fresh, new?

KRISHNAMURTI: Sirs, it is very interesting to find out, when you ask a question, why you are asking it. What is the urge that makes one ask a question? Surely, it is not the answer to the question that is very important but to find out why one seeks an answer, what is the motive, the incentive, and who the entity is that is seeking an answer, be cause on the motive of the question depends the answer, and if you don't know the motive, any answer is valueless. And the moment you begin to discover the motive with all its extraordinary deviations, you are already in the field of self-knowledge, you are already understanding yourself in the mirror of your own thoughts, in the mirror of relationship; therefore, you have no questions at all. Every problem is an issue in which truth can be discovered, but if you merely put a question and wait for an answer, wait to be helped, then you have lost the initiative in the action of discovery.

Please listen, because this is really important. I feel that happiness lies in our own hands, and the key to that happiness is self-knowledge—not the self-knowledge of Freud, or Jung, or Shankara, or somebody else, but the self-knowledge of your own discovery in your relationship from day to day. In the mirror of relationship you can discover everything without reading a book, and then you will not want leaders, then leaders become destroyers. Through observation, through awareness without effort of the movement of your own thought from day to day, as you get into a bus, while you are riding in a car, when you are talking to your servant, to your wife, to your children, to your neighbor—through observing all that as in a mirror, you begin to discover how you talk, how you think, how you react, and you will find that in understanding yourself you have something which cannot be found in books, in philosophies, in the teachings of any guru. Then you are your own guru and your own disciple. But such observation needs attention, and there can be attention only when there is no incentive to alter that which you discover. As long as there is any intention to alter that which you discover, you are not totally aware. Total attention is the good, and there cannot be total attention if there is any sense of condemnation, comparison, or justification of that which you discover. Nobody can give you the key to the ending of sorrow, but it is in your own hands if you see yourself in the mirror of relationship without judging what you see. Then no religions, no books, no temples are necessary, for you will find that out of deep self-knowledge there comes a timeless thing, and therefore the creations of the mind have little importance. Then you will know love.

Now, the questioner says that all our problems seem to be rooted in the past, and he asks if it is possible to be fully aware of the whole content of the unconscious and die to it so that the mind can be fresh, new.

To uncover the various depths of the unconscious, there is the process of analysis and there is introspection. You can watch and evaluate everything you think and say, or you can analyze the mind, both conscious and unconscious, going step by step into all its deviations and interpreting every dream. Now, it seems to me that all this is very tedious and not a true way to go about it because, after all, in the process of introspection and in the process of analysis, there is always the analyzer, the one who introspects, evaluates, so there is always a division in the mind. There is always this duality of the one who watches and that which is watched, the part of the mind which introspects, analyzes, and the other part which is examined, analyzed; hence there is always interpretation, evaluation, conflict. And since this separation of the analyzer from the thing analyzed only leads to everlasting conflict, then what is the other way?

Perhaps it is not a way because there is no way, no path to truth, there is no system of meditation, no discipline which will bring that extraordinarily creative thing into our daily life. But there is a possibility, if you really pay attention to something, of being in a state when there is no thinker at all, but only thinking. This is not just a theory of mine, it is a fact. Thought is fleeting, transient, in constant flux, and when there is total attention, thought can never create the permanent as the thinker, as the experiencer, as the one who has accumulated experience or property; there is only thinking and not the thinker.

Please listen and you will see how to put away this whole process of analysis and transcend the unconscious, thereby bringing into the mind the freshness of youth, of innocency, because it is only the innocent, the fresh mind that can receive the new, not the mind that is tortured by analysis, that is shaped, controlled by discipline.

So, there is only thinking, and thinking is transient; therefore, all the things that are gathered by thinking, the values of achievement, of ambition, of desire, are also transient. As long as there is accumulation as experience, as knowledge, as tradition, as values, there must be the unconscious with all its intimations of fear, of hidden motives; and the moment you are aware of that fact clearly, simply, the moment you really see that thinking is transient, in flux, all accumulation ceases.

After all, the unconscious is the accumulation of yesterday and the many thousands of yesterdays; it is not only the accumulation of centuries of tradition, but also the accumulation that is going on in the movement of the present, in the mind's contact with the present. All that is the unconscious. The mind clings to its accumulation because it thinks in that there is clarity, in that there is hope, the cessation of fear, but that very accumulation is the cause of fear. In its accumulation the mind finds a sense of permanency, but the fact is that thought is transient, and whatever it accumulates is also transient. The mind may think that there is a permanent atma, a permanent soul, a permanent reality, but that very thinking of the permanent is impermanent. Thought, being transient, can only create the impermanent though it may deceive itself by believing that it has created the permanent. If you see the truth of that simply, immediately, you will free the whole content of the unconscious, and the mind will never accumulate again; and the moment the mind ceases to accumulate, ceases to continue as the accumulator, it is fresh, young, innocent, totally new.

You see, the difficulty is that we do not really want to be simple; we are lazy; therefore, we invent the process of time. But if you are not lazy, if your mind is alert, if you see very simply that all thinking is transient, that thought has no abiding place, that there is no fixed point around which you can think, that the fixed point is created by thinking and is therefore as transient as the thinking which created it—if you really see that simply and directly, then you will find that all evaluation ceases. Then there is memory uncontaminated by values, and therefore the mind is fresh though it may remember.

Questioner: Truth or reality appears to be just around the corner when one is listening to you but afterwards it is as far away and beyond reach as ever, and one feels utterly frustrated. What is one to do?

Krishnamurti: Why is it that when you are listening, as the questioner says, you seem to understand? Why is it that your mind is now very clear and simple? Is it that my voice is mesmerizing you? Or is it that both of us are earnest for an hour, earnest without any motive, not seeking, not wanting to achieve anything, but simply listening without any sense of being distant or near? Both of us are in a state of attention, are we not? Obviously, the speaker is not trying to convert you to anything, to any system, to any philosophy; he does not want you to join any organization, take up any discipline, and he is not offering you a thing. He is merely describing the fact, and the fact is much more significant than your opinion, than your interpretation or judgment of the fact. The speaker says, "Abstain from judgment, put away comparison, evaluation, and merely listen to the fact." He is presenting the fact without wanting you to do anything about the fact. Just be aware that you are ambitious, and that as long as there is ambition, there must be fear, frustration, the agony of unfulfillment. That is a fact. As long as you are ambitious in any direction, in this world or in the so-called spiritual world, as long as you are gathering virtue as a means to heaven, fear is inevitable. Virtue as a means to heaven only leads to respectability, which is an ugly thing, a thing to be put aside.

So, what is important is to be aware, just to see the fact that ambition in any form breeds envy, antagonism, and that in its fulfillment there is fear. And you are seeing that fact now, as you are listening. But what happens? You see the truth of the fact and for the moment that fact is real, and you cease to be ambitious; there is no fear, but when you go away from here you are caught again in the wheels of respectable society, so you have created a division. While listening to the fact you are free, but after going away from here there is contention, and then you say, "How am I to get back to the fact? I saw it very clearly yesterday, but now I don't see it." That very wanting to see the fact is creating the disturbance, the gap. But if you are deeply aware that you are craving to see that fact again, which is another form of ambition, then you will find that you don't have to attend a single meeting. Then you are your own teacher and your own disciple; then life is open and you will meet it every day fully, richly, happily. But that is not possible if there is any form of accumulation. Just to see the fact without evaluation brings freedom. You cannot translate the fact; it is a fact whether you like it or not, and when you are confronted with the fact, there is no problem.

Questioner: Love, death, and God are three unknowables, but life is without meaning unless the significance of the three is understood. How can the mind comprehend what it cannot know?

KRISHNAMURTI: The mind can comprehend only that which it knows; it cannot comprehend what it does not know. That is very simple. The mind can understand only that which it has gathered, that which it knows, because the mind itself is the result of the known, is it not? Your mind is now the result of the known, of many yesterdays, of many experiences of all the traditional memories, values, judgments, opinions, fears. Being the result of the known, how can such a mind know the unknown? It may invent, it may speculate, but its speculation is merely a reaction of the known; like any theory, like any utopia, like any philosophy, it is the reaction, the response of what is known.

So, the mind can never know the unknowable, but that is what each one of you is trying to do. The mind is seeking the unknown through the known, and that is why your disciplines, your meditations are such frustrations; they have no meaning because you are moving from the known to the known. You never ask the fundamental question, which is: Can the mind be free from the known and not pursue the unknown? Please listen. Can the mind, which is the result of the known, free itself from its own movement? Can the mind wipe away all its yesterdays, its yesterdays being the known? The known in contact with the present creates the future, which is also the result of the known.

So, can there be freedom from the known? That is our problem, not whether the mind can ever comprehend the unknown. Can the mind comprehend love? It can comprehend sensation, desire, how to curb a sensation, how to manipulate, torture, suppress, sublimate desire—but can the mind know love? Can the mind know that which is unknowable? Can the mind which measures time, distance, space, discover that which is immeasurable?

You want to know the unknowable, so your mind is always pursuing it; you read, you meditate, you smother yourself with ideas, with books, with leaders, and you never ask the question: Can the mind ever be free from the known? Do you understand?

The known is made up of the things that you have learned, the things that you have been taught—that you are a Brahmin or a non-Brahmin, a Hindu, a Christian, or a Muslim—it is made up of your desire to be the prime minister, to be a rich man, and so on. And can the mind, being the result of the known, do anything else but move everlastingly in the field of the known? Can this movement in the field of the known come to an end without any incentive? Because if there is an incentive, that is also the known.

Surely, as long as there is this movement of the known in the field of the known, it is impossible for the mind to know the unknown. So, can that movement of the known come to an end? That is the problem. If you really put that simple question without trying to find an answer, without wanting to get somewhere, and if you are earnest because it is a fundamental question to you, then you will find that the movement of the known comes to an end. That is all. With the cessation of the mind as the known, with its freedom from the movement of the known, there is the coming into being of the unknowable, the immeasurable, and in that there is an ecstasy, a bliss.

March 13, 1955

Questions

India, 1953

India, 1954

United States, 1954

India, 1954

India, 1955

Index

www.ingramcontent.com/pod-product-compliance
Lightning Source LLC
Chambersburg PA
CBHW080507161224
18961CB00002B/16

9 781934 989418